AMERICAN EDUCATION

Its Men

Ideas

and

Institutions

Advisory Editor

Lawrence A. Cremin
Frederick A. P. Barnard Professor of Education
Teachers College, Columbia University

The Church, The State,
and
Education in Virginia

Sadie Bell

ARNO PRESS & THE NEW YORK TIMES
*New York * 1969*

Editorial Note

AMERICAN EDUCATION: *Its Men, Institutions and Ideas* presents selected works of thought and scholarship that have long been out of print or otherwise unavailable. Inevitably, such works will include particular ideas and doctrines that have been outmoded or superseded by more recent research. Nevertheless, all retain their place in the literature, having influenced educational thought and practice in their own time and having provided the basis for subsequent scholarship.

Lawrence A. Cremin
Teachers College

The Church, The State,
and
Education in Virginia

THE CHURCH, THE STATE, AND EDUCATION IN VIRGINIA

SADIE BELL

PHILADELPHIA

1930

TO MY FATHER AND MOTHER

"What the world needs more than anything else to-day, more than new armies, new navies, new treaties, new aeroplanes or new gases, is a new mind."
—Thomas Woody.

PREFACE

This study offers an explanation of present day attitudes toward the problem of religion in education, the relation of church and state to that problem, from the point of view of historical development in a state which has been under the influence of three important political philosophies—that of union, that of separation, and that of co-operation without legal alliance between church and state.

The study had its origin in what seemed to be a heightened interest in recent years in the question of the place of religion in public education. The current impression that there had been a decline of religious influences in education, with a consequent decreasing concern on the part of the public schools with character education, it was felt, merited investigation. The determination of the proper place of religion in education, its proper spheres of control, it seemed, would be easier of solution, if the factors responsible for their present status were clearly understood.

In the investigation of this study, every attempt has been made to get at those sources which may be regarded as furnishing the most reliable basis for explanation of the particular aspect of the problem under consideration. This study has been greatly facilitated by the work of many editors and historians who have made available a large amount of documentary and primary sources in printed form. The laws and journals of the Assembly throughout Virginia history have been canvassed, as have been official school records of various kinds. The reaction of the public to the problem has been studied from many angles, as it appeared in newspapers, periodicals, biography, and correspondence. The reaction of foreign observers has also received attention. The different sources have been used not merely to determine the order of historical events, but also to give such an intimate picture as will enable the reader to sense the vitality of various aspects of the problem for the people of Virginia at different periods of their history.

Acknowledgment for much helpful assistance in forwarding the work and in enabling the writer to reconcile differences in sources, is made to a host of correspondents, particularly in Virginia. The writer is indebted to the staffs of the libraries of the University of Pennsylvania, the Historical Society of Pennsylvania, the Philadelphia Free Library, the Library of Congress, and the Virginia State Library for many courtesies and valuable assistance. The kindness of Dr. H. R. McIlwaine, in greatly facilitating the work during visits to the Virginia State Library, is highly appreciated.

The writer is grateful for the interest taken in this study by Dr. A. Duncan Yocum, Dr. Arthur J. Jones, and Dr. Thomas Woody of the University of Pennsylvania. To Dr. Woody, special thanks are due for the initial suggestion of the study, for constant kindly and helpful guidance; and particularly for the illumination which work with him has given of the significance of historical developments in education for a correct understanding of society.

The writer is under deep obligation to Mrs. Nettie B. Ohrenstein and particularly to Miss Sara Bell for services in connection with the manuscript.

SADIE BELL.

Philadelphia,
December 1, 1928.

THE CHURCH, THE STATE, AND EDUCATION IN VIRGINIA

CONTENTS

PREFACE

PART I

DURING THE INTEGRATION OF CHURCH AND STATE

ix

CONTENTS

CONTENTS

CONTENTS

THE CHURCH, THE STATE, AND EDUCATION IN VIRGINIA

PART I

DURING THE INTEGRATION OF CHURCH AND STATE

(From the Founding of the Colony to the Separation
from Great Britain)

CHAPTER I

THE FOUNDING OF THE COLONY AND RELIGION

Official Expression Of Policy

Religion stands tiptoe in our land,
Ready to pass to the American strand.[1]

Many motives send people forth to create new homes and
states. Adventure in itself is a sufficiently strong urge with
some; with others, the urge may be found in the lure of better
fortune, or in the hope of a happier political condition. Yet, it
has remained for religion to prove itself a very potent ally in
animating the nomadic spirit. Surround an economic, social, or
political cause with the halo of religion, make of it a "holy"
cause, and its success is apt to be assured. The adventurers
of Elizabeth's reign, eager to fly the English flag on land and
sea, the politicians of her court, compelled to match their wits
against those of her dangerous rival, Spain, knew well that the
way out of many difficulties for England was to make patriotism
a "holy" cause. Make duty to one's country and one's God
synonymous, and the politician can carry his country far. The
truth of this is demonstrated in the following pages.

Not merely because of her Patents to Gilbert (1578) and
Raleigh (1584), may Queen Elizabeth be regarded as the mother
of Virginia, but, in a truer sense, because of the basis she laid
for its permanent founding in the reign of James I.[2] This lay
in settling, immediately upon her accession to the throne (1558–
59), the difficult question of church and state.[3] It is to the Acts
of Supremacy and Conformity that the historian must look for
the political philosophy that controlled the destiny of Virginia for
almost two centuries. The philosophy of the Edict of Milan

---

[1] Herbert, G.: *The Church Militant*, as quoted in Anderson's *Colonial
Church*, I, 365; *cf.* Slaughter, P.: *Colonial Church*, 17.

[2] Hakluyt, R.: *Principal Navigations*, VIII, 17 *ff.*, 289–96; Stith, Wm.:
Hist. of Va., 4–6, 8.

[3] Cheyney, E. P.: *A Short Hist. of Eng.*, 331–35; Cobb, S. H.: *Rise of
Relig. Liberty*, 54; Anderson, J. S. M.: *Colonial Church*, I, 129–33.

(313 A. D.), born when Christianity was still the young bride of Paganism, had given way to the more crabbed philosophy of the Peace of Augsburg (1555 A. D.)[4] The union of church and state was consummated. It is therefore clear that the policy of union of church and state was current in English political thought long before Bacon's expression of it in *Colonies, or foreign plantations*,[5] and that an early official expression of the policy is to be found in the Gilbert and Raleigh Patents declaring,

. . . so alwayes that the sayd statutes, lawes and ordinances may be as neere as conveniently may, agreeable to the forme of the lawes & pollicy of England: and also, that they be not against the true Christian faith or religion now professed in the church of England, nor in any wise to withdraw any of the subjects or people of those lands or places from the allegiance of us, our heires or successours, as their immediate Soveraignes under God.[6]

Whatever the motives, economic, social, political, or religious, that inspired individuals and groups during the forty years following the Raleigh Patent in creating the Colony of Virginia, the form that it was to take politically and spiritually was now definitely outlined.

Literary Propaganda

In the year that Raleigh's Patent was issued, there appeared the first of that notable array of literary propaganda destined to prove even more effective in establishing the new Colony of Virginia than the gold that poured into the coffers of the Virginia Company of London.[7]   Hakluyt's *Discourse on Western Planting* made the Portugese and Spanish "vaunte" in carrying the cross to the infidels, the erection of "many bisshoprickes and colleges," a challenge to the "true and syncere relligion"— seeing that the English proposed

---

[4] Cheyney, E. P.: *European Background of Amer. Hist.*, 189; Haas, J. A. W.: *The Problem of The Christian State*, 18, 111; Cobb: *Rise of Relig. Liberty*, 49.

[5] Montagu, B.: *Bacon's Works*, II, 377, 385; Anderson: *Colonial Church*, I, 390–92; *cf.* also Montgomery, R.: *A Discourse Concerning the design'd Establishment Of a New Colony To The South of Carolina*, in Force's *Tracts*, I, 4.

[6] Hakluyt: *Principal Navigations*, VIII, 21, 294; *cf.* Stith: *Hist. of Va.*, 5.

[7] For a different form of propaganda, *cf.* Beverley, R.: *Hist. of Va.*, 10— the bringing over of Indians Wanchese and Manteo.

. . . in this action not filthie lucre nor vaine ostentation, as they in deede did, but principally the gayninge of the soules of millions of those wretched people, the reducinge of them from darkenes to lighte, from falsehoodde to truthe, from dombe idolls to the lyvinge God, from the depe pitt of hell to the highest heavens.[8]

If at the same time, the idle clergy at home who were "alwayes coyninge of new opynions," could be set to this work, there was hope they would become "lesse contentious, and be contented with the truthe in relligion alreadie established by authoritie."[9] Having thus made his libation to God in placing the emphasis first on the spiritual motive, Hakluyt proceeds to discuss "traficque," the "seconde chefe and principall ende."[10] From this time until the middle of the 17th century, when the stability of the colony was no longer doubtful and the advantages to the mother country could be enumerated in such social and economic gains as disburdening the nation of indigents, freeing the parishes from providing for destitute minors and orphans, ridding the country of the discontented, furnishing a home for retired soldiers, providing a source for securing timber, fish, grain, furs, and revenue, there still lingered as a religious halo sanctifying the whole scheme, the theme—*"the most Christian of all improvements, the converting many thousands of natives."*[11]

To appreciate the extent to which the religious motive was used in furthering the colonization of Virginia, one need only review such political papers as the various patents and charters, the deliberations of the Virginia Company, the sermons preached, and the pamphlets and broadsides issued. The religious tone given to the papers and deliberations of the Virginia Company undoubtedly finds its source in that famous indenture of 1589 by which Raleigh made "An Assignment . . . to diuers Gentlemen, and Merchants of London, for the inhabiting and planting of our People in Virginia":

---

[8] Hakluyt, R.: *A Discourse on Western Planting*, 9–10.
[9] *Ibid.*, 12.
[10] *Ibid.*, 95.
[11] W.[illiams], E.: *Virginia: More especially the South part thereof, Richly and truly valued*, in Force's *Tracts*, III, 4–7; *cf.* Jones, H.: *Present State of Va.*, 23, "some for Religion, and others because they could not well live elsewhere; and others because they dared not, or cared not to stay at home," which apparently echoes Lionel Gatford's *Public Good without Private Interest* quoted by Neill, E. D.: *Va. Carolorum*, 244, 277.

. . . And further the sayde Sir Walter Raleigh, as well for, and in especiall regard, and zeale of planting the christian Religion, in, and amongst the sayde barbarous and heathen countries, and for the aduancement and preferment of the same, . . .[12]

This event, Raleigh signalized by a gift of £100 for "planting the Christian Religion in those barbarous and heathen countries" —the first of the philanthropic stream of gold in behalf of religion and education in America.[13]

It was, however, the first charter, King James I's *Letters Patent to Sir* Thomas Gates *et al.*, April 10, 1606, which put the stamp upon the propagation of Christianity as an official motive. The phraseology as here given is echoed in the subsequent charters of 1609 and 1612, and in the literary propaganda of the following decades:

. . . WE, greatly commending, and graciously accepting of, their Desires for the Furtherance of so noble a Work, which may, by the Providence of Almighty God, hereafter tend to the Glory of his Divine Majesty, in propagating of *Christian* Religion to such People, as yet live in Darkness and miserable Ignorance of the true Knowledge and Worship of God, and may in time bring the Infidels and Savages, living in those Parts, to human Civility, and to a settled and quiet Government; DO, by these our Letters Patents, graciously accept of, and agree to, their humble and well intended Desires; . . .[14]

The royal sanction here given this motive was never lost sight of by the Company, whether in appealing to the support of municipalities,[15] or pleading their cause before Parliament in 1614,[16] or again ten years later just before their dissolution, when using this motive as a salient explanation of their reason for existence, they hoped to stay the King's *Quo Warranto*.[17]

The most effective evidence of the extent to which this motive influenced the Company appears in the efforts, to be described later, to create schools for the Indians.[18]

---

[12] Hazard, E.: *Hist. Coll.*, I, 44.

[13] Burk, J. D.: *Hist. of Va.*, I, 66; Stith: *Hist. of Va.*, 25–26.

[14] *Ibid.*, Appendix No. I, 1–2; Hening, W. W.: *Stat. at Large*, I, 58.

[15] Brown, A.: *Genesis of the U. S.*, I, 253; Neill, E. D.: *Early Settlement of Va.*, 44.

[16] Neill, E. D.: *Hist. of the Va. Co.*, 69.

[17] Kingsbury, S. M.: *Rec. of the Va. Co.*, II, 526, *cf.*, 352, 361; Burk: *Hist. of Va.*, I, 288; *cf.* Stith: *Hist. of Va.*, 324; for recognition of this motive by the colonists, see Kingsbury: *Rec. of the Va. Co.*, II, 308.

[18] See p. 16.

The royal stamp of approval having been given to the idea that American colonization was a holy cause, it remained for the sermons preached in behalf of the Virginia Company, and frequently under their auspices, to speed money into their treasurer's chests, and men, women, and children into their boats, with a blessing on the holy adventure. As interesting, dramatic, and effective as any writing in the English literature of that day, are the sermons in that cause. These sermons cover the period of 1608 to 1622—a gift of two pieces of gold of 40s. for a sermon in 1623 was not used as it was agreed "the Sermon should be respited for a time in reguard of the present troubles of the Companie."[19] Briefly, the chief point of emphasis was the necessity of spreading the Gospel as God's purpose, redounding as it would to the comfort of those who furthered the good work; as for the opposers—they were persecutors and adversaries of Christ.[20]

The reluctance to leave "sweete" England, the dangers of the voyage, the fear of papists settling "on the backe of us" are graphically portrayed.[21] William Crashaw who preached the sermon, February 21, 1609–10, on the occasion of Lord Delaware's departure, pictured the nature of the enterprise in a most stirring light. He gave as the reason for the inadequate support of the purpose of the plantation, the fact that "the greater part of men are unconverted & unsanctified" and "seeke merely the world and themselves."[22] He found in the Devil, Papists, and Players, the three enemies of the enterprise.[23] Like an echo of *Dale's Code*,[24] are his invectives against Popery and his injunctions to holy living:

. . . Remember thou art a Generall of English men, nay a Generall of Christian men; therefore principally looke to religion. You goe to commend it to the heathen, then practice it yourselves: make the name of Christ honourable, not hatefull unto them. Suffer no Papists; let them not nestle there; nay let the name of the Pope or Poperie be never heard of in Virginea. Take heed of Atheists the Divels Champions: and if thou

---

19 Kingsbury: *Rec. of the Va. Co.* II, 480–81.
20 Brown: *Genesis of the U. S.*, I, 256, 313.
21 *Ibid.*, I, 288, 290.
22 *Ibid.*, I, 361.
23 *Ibid.*, I, 336; see p. 12.
24 See p. 38.

discover any, make them exemplarie. And (if I may be so bold as to advise) make Atheisme and other blasphemie Capitall, and let that bee the first law made in Virginia. Suffer no Brownists, nor factious Separatists: let them keepe their conventicles elsewhere: let them goe and convert some other Heathen, and let us see if they can constitute such Churches really, the Idaes whereof they have fancied in their branes: and when they have given us any such example, we may then have some cause to follow them. Till then we will take our paterne from their betters. Especially suffer no sinfull, no leaud, no licentious men, none that live not under the obedience of good lawes: and let your lawes be strict, especially against swearing and other prophanenesse . . . Let the Sabboth be wholly and holily observed, and publike praiers daily frequented, idlenesse eschewed, and mutinies carefully prevented. Be well advised in making lawes: but being made, let them be obeyed, and let none stand for scarre-crowes; for that is the way to make all at last to be contemned . . . But if you should aime at nothing but your private ends, and neglect religion and God's service, looke for no blessing, nay looke for a curse, though not on the whole action, yet on our attempt; and never thinke that we shall have the honour to effect it.[25]

Two sermons of the year 1622 are of particular interest—that of Patrick Copland, whose name is so gloriously associated with the East Indie School, and that of John Donne, dean of St. Paul's.[26] Copland in his sermon *Virginia's God Be Thanked* spoke of the dangers of the enterprise, urged that ''faithful and approved'' preachers be sent, and told his hearers,

. . . let it be your greife and sorrow to be exempted from the company of so many honourable minded men, and from this noble Plantation, tending so highly to the advancement of the Gospell, and to the honouring of our drad Soueraigne, by inlarging of his kingdomes.[27]

Donne in his sermon eloquently urged a spiritual kingdom and the spread of the Gospel:

. . . if you seeke to establish a temporall kingdome there, you are not rectified, . . . O, if you could once bring a *Catechisme* to bee as good ware

[25] Brown: *Genesis of the U. S.*, I, 371–72; Neill, E. D.: *Eng. Coloniz. of Amer.*, 39–41; Anderson: *Colonial Church*, I, 232 *ff*.; Brown, A.: *First Republic in America*, 183–84, refers to answer to Crashaw's Sermon by John Floyd, Jesuit, ''The overthrow of the Protestants Pulpit-Babels, convincing their Preachers of Lying & Rayling, to make the Church of Rome seeme mysticall Babell. Particularly confuting W. Crashawes sermon at the crosse,'' etc.

[26] Neill: *Va. Carolorum*, 195; Kingsbury: *Rec. of the Va. Co.*, I, 161.

[27] Neill: *Eng. Coloniz. of Amer.*, 157, 161; Neill, E. D.: *Memoir Rev. P. Copland*, 52, 72; Kingsbury: *Rec. of the Va. Co.*, I, 628–29.

amongst them as a Bugle, as a knife, as a hatchet: O, if you would be as ready to hearken at the returne of a Ship, how many *Indians* were converted to *Christ Jesus*, as what Trees, or druggs, or Dyes that Ship had brought, then you were in your right way, and not till then; . . . furder and hasten you this blessed, this joyfull, this glorious consummation of all, and happie reunion of all bodies to their Soules, by preaching the *Gospell* to those men. Preach to them Doctrinally, preach to them Practically; Enamore them with your *Justice*, and (as farre as may consist with your security), your *Civilitie*; but inflame them with your *godlinesse*, and your *Religion*. Bring them to *love* and *Reverence* the name of that *King*, that sends men to teach them the wayes of *Civilitie* in this world, but to *feare* and *adore* the Name of that *King of Kings*, that sends men to teach them the waies of Religion, for the next world. Those amongst you, that are old now, shall passe one of this world with this great comfort, that you contributed to the beginning of that Common Wealth, and of that Church, though they live not to see the groath thereof to perfection: . . .[28]

Urging that the substance of their desire was to present the land "a pure Virgine to Christ,"[29] the preachers succeeded in obtaining for the Company subscriptions from all ranks, in inspiring their own brethren to brave the terrors of the Atlantic, and most significantly of all in having the planting of Virginia recognized as Christ's cause. Nor did the members of the Virginia Company send to Virginia ministers of whose hermeneutic ability they were ignorant, for it was their custom to require a trial sermon of each candidate.[30]

Of the many tracts and broadsides published under the auspices of the Company, one particularly stirred England's rival, Spain. Concerning the *Nova Britannia*, published in 1609, the Spanish ambassador wrote to his Majesty:

They have *printed a book* . . . in which they publish that *for the increase of their religion and that it may extend over the whole world, it is right that all should support this Colony with their person and their property.* It would be a service rendered to God, that Y. M. should cut short a swindle and a robbery like this, . . .[31]

The ambassador was referring undoubtedly to the statement:

---

28 Neill: *Hist. of the Va. Co.*, 360; Smith, L. P.: *Donne's Sermons*, 50–54; for references to gifts to Va. Co. for sermons, see Kingsbury's *Rec. of the Va. Co.*, I, 545, II, 114, 480.
29 Brown: *Genesis of the U. S.*, I, 286.
30 Kingsbury: *Rec. of the Va. Co.*, I, 635, *et passim*.
31 Brown: *Genesis of the U. S.*, I, 246.

. . . So I wish and intreat all well affected subiects, some in their persons, others in their purses, cheerefully to aduenture, and ioyntly take in hand this high and acceptable work, tending to aduance and spread the kingdome of God, and the knowledge of the truth, among so many millions of men and women, Sauage and blind, that neuer yet saw the true light shine before their eyes, to enlighten their minds and comfort their soules, as also for the honor of our King, and enlarging of his kingdome, . . . 32

Lest any may have scruples regarding the invasion of the Indians' country, the author defends the action by declaring that the Indians will be informed that the intention is to raise them from their inferior condition, assuring them both a heavenly and earthly kingdom:

. . . yet not to supplant and roote them out, but to bring them from their base condition to a farre better: First, in regard of God the Creator, and of Jesus Christ their Redeemer, if they will beleeue in him. And secondly, in respect of earthly blessings, . . . 33

It is for this great work of salvation "that God hath reserued in this last age of the world, an infinite number of those lost and scattered sheepe, to be won and recouered by our meanes."[34]

R.[obert] G.[ray]'s *A Good Speed to Virginia*, printed the same year, urged that none save his money in advancing God's kingdom, that England be spared the reproach of seeking the wealth of that country before the glory of God, and declared that those who withheld themselves from the enterprise were in "opposition against God, the King, the Church, and the Commonwealth."[35]

The publications of the year 1610 emphasize the fact that "The eyes of all Europe are looking upon our endeavors to spread the Gospel among the Heathen people of Virginia, to plant our English nation there."[36] The timorous are reassured of the lawfulness of the enterprise in respect to the law of God and the law

---

[32] [Johnson, R.]: *Nova Britannia*, in Force's *Tracts*, I, 6.

[33] *Ibid.*, 13.

[34] *Ibid.*, 14.

[35] Collier, J. P.: *Early English Popular Literature*, II, 29; Collier in his introduction seems inclined to attribute the pamphlet to Sir Walter Raleigh; Brown: *Genesis of the U. S.*, I, 293 *ff.*

[36] *Ibid.*, I, 463; Neill; *Early Settlement of Va.*, 41.

of man; much more precious than the "pearles of earth" which are bought, are the "pearles of heauen" sold to the heathen.[37]

A similar note rings throughout the publications of the Virginia Company period; the emphasis is always on the fact that,

. . . This is the worke that we first intended, and have publisht to the world to be chiefe in our thoughts to bring those infidell people from the worship of Divels to the service of God. . . .[38]

It was for this purpose they had already sent preachers, and hoped to send more.[39]

That the religious motive was used also by the court during this period to further the enterprise is evident from official papers. A letter written concerning efforts to procure Captain Gates for the enterprise, reads in part:

. . . His Majesty of Great Britain, desiring a happy issue of this enterprise, on account of the great benefits which He foresaw would spring from it, both for the Christian religion and for the increase of Commerce, believes no one to be better qualified for such employment than the aforesaid de Gates, . . . [40]

Nor did the King, in 1624, when he issued a Commission "to Examine Into the State of Virginia," fail to recall the motives which had inspired the venture in the beginning:

. . . Whereas amongst the many memorable works Undertaken since our Happy Reign over this our Realm those of the English Colonies and Plantations in Virginia and the Summer Islands are of Special Importance as being the first foreign Colonies planted by Our English Nation and tending not only to the propagation of God's Glory and the Christian Religion but also to the Enlargement of the Territories and dominions of our Crown and the Encrease of Trade and Commerce . . . that some persons of trust and Understanding be Employed to Discern discover and find out the whole state of the Premisses upon whose information we may proceed to the effecting thereof as we shall judge most requisite whereby the Work being Reestab-

---

37 Va. Co. of London: *A True Declaration Of The estate of the Colonie,* in Force's *Tracts,* III, 6.

38 [Johnson, R.]: *The New Life of Virginea,* in Force's *Tracts,* I, 18; *cf.* also, [Jourdain or Jourdan, Silvester]: *A Plaine Description Of The Barmvdas,* in Force's *Tracts,* III, 6; Brown; *Genesis of the U. S.,* II, 797–98; Va. Co. of London: *A Declaration Of The State Of The Colonie,* in Force's *Tracts,* III, 3.

39 [Johnson]: *The New Life of Virginea,* in Force's *Tracts,* I, 17–18.

40 Brown: *Genesis of the U. S.,* I, 448–49.

lished may proceed and prosper to our honour and those Religious and Publick Ends for which it was first Intended. . . .[41]

Sincerity Of Religious Motive

In view of the strong emphasis upon the religious motive, expressed throughout the early period of the creation of the colony, the question naturally arises with what degree of confidence is it to be assumed that this was a motive in good faith.   Historians, in weighing the various motives, have had some difficulty in determining the weight to be given the evidence which has here in part been cited; some like Beer[42] and Brown,[43] attaching little weight to the religious motive, come out boldly for an economic or political motive; others like Eggleston declare that ''Into the chain-threads of commercial enterprise was woven a woof of patriotic feeling and religious sentiment.''[44]   Others like Thomas list the names of church dignitaries and ministers who appear in the charters and hold that the religious motive cannot be questioned.[45]   Again one may refer to the list of the clergy sent over in this early period as concrete evidence of sincerity of purpose.[46]

It is rather difficult to gauge such an elusive quality as sincerity.   How attempt to reconcile Raleigh's gift for propagating Christianity with the tradition that he was president of an atheists' club, among whose members were Marlowe and Greene.[47] Smith, describing the voyage in 1606, speaks '' (of some few little better than Atheists, of the greatest rank amongst us)'';[48] but what weight should be attached to this term, seeing that Wingfield had to defend himself against the charge of atheism, because

---

[41] *Va. Mag. Hist.*, XVI, 113–14; *cf.* Hazard: *Hist. Coll.*, I, 183–84; *cf.* also *Ibid.*, I, 203; *Va. Mag. Hist.*, VII, 132; Anderson: *Colonial Church,* II, 84; Neill: *Va. Carolorum,* 10.

[42] Beer, G. L.: *British Colonial System,* 30; *cf.* also Wertenbaker, T. J.: *The First Americans,* ch. I.

[43] Brown, A.: *English Politics,* 180–82.

[44] Eggleston, E.: *The Beginners of a Nation,* 86.

[45] Thomas, R. S.: *Relig. Element in Jamestown.*

[46] Neill, E. D.: *Va. Colonial Clergy.*

[47] Campbell, D.: *Puritan in Holl., Eng., and America,* II, 133; Stith: *Hist. of Va.,* 20.

[48] Foote, H. W.: *Sketches of Va.,* 25–26.

his Bible had disappeared with his fruit and preserves.[49]   Contrast with this, the tradition that it was the influence of the Earl of Southampton, of the Ferrars, Hakluyt, and Sandys, members of the Virginia Company, that ''procured the insertion, in the charters and like documents, of those ''saving clauses'' which redeemed the movement from utter worldliness.''[50]   Was this a mere cloak as Smith is ready to imply, when, during a critical period of the colony's affairs, he exclaims:

. . . we did admire [wonder] how it was possible such wise men could so torment themselves and us with such strange absurdities and impossibilities: making Religion their colour, when all their aime was nothing but present profit, as most plainly appeared, by sending us so many Refiners, Goldsmiths, . . .[51]

At a later day, the cynical Byrd remarked:

. . . from Kiquotan they extended themselves as far as James-Town, where like true Englishmen, they built a Church that cost no more than Fifty Pounds, and a Tavern that cost Five hundred.[52]

Shall we conclude with the opinion of Professor Bassett that,

The London Company, which projected the settlement of Virginia, was at bottom a trading company.   Although it had certain creditable notions of serving the Fatherland and the Church of England, it never would have made the various attempts to plant and sustain the colony if there had not been behind its efforts the notion that the company would reap financial reward for its expensive outlays. . . .[53]

or are we to believe that,

> ''To glorifie the Lord 'tis done,
> And to no other end.''[54]

---

49 Wingfield, E. M.: *A Discourse of Va.*, in Archaeologia Americana, IV, 98.
50 Slaughter: *Colonel Church*, 15.
51 Arber, E.: *Travels and Works of Capt. J. Smith*, II, 928.
52 Wynne, T. H.: *Hist. of the Dividing Line*, I, 5.
53 Bassett, J. S.: The Relation Between the Va. Planter and the London Merchant, 553.
54 Brown: *Genesis of the U. S.*, I, 424; Neill: *Early Settlement of Va.*, 34; *Va. Mag. Hist.*, XXVIII, 391.

CHAPTER II

THE GOSPEL AND EDUCATION AMONG THE INDIANS

Propagation Of The Gospel During The Period Of The Virginia Company

It has been shown that one of the declared motives of the English in planting a colony in Virginia was the propagation of the Gospel among the natives. An attempt at evaluating the sincerity of this avowed purpose, on the basis of literary propaganda in furthering the colonization scheme, was found to be inconclusive. There remains, however, the possibility of reaching some conclusion on the basis of other evidence; namely, a consideration of the English attitude toward the Indians as an ethnic group and the amount of effort expended in actually bringing their declared purpose to some realization. A varied literature—histories, special pleadings, official correspondence, instructions, reports, and special legislation—supplies a basis for making a fairly adequate judgment.

A perusal of historical accounts of the first English contacts with the Indians, such as one may read in Hariot, or in *Captain Newport's Discoveries In Virginia*, indicates on the whole a favorable and hopeful attitude toward the Indian.[1] In *Captain Newport's Discoveries*, one reads:

... To conclude, they are a very witty and ingenious people, apt both to understand and speake our language. So that I hope in God, ... he will make us authors of his holy will in converting them to our true Christian faith, ...[2]

At least the evidence is clear that kindly means were first to be used in bringing the Indians to English notions of civility—the first adventurers placing the creation of friendly relations as a

---

[1] Hariot, T.: *Narrative First Eng. Plantation of Va.*; cf. Hakluyt's *Principal Navigations*, VIII, 348; Smith, J.: *True Travels*, I, 96–97, 99, Gray edition; Arber: *Travels and Works of Capt. J. Smith*, I, xl ff., 322–25; [Archer, G.]: *Captain Newport's Discoveries In Virginia*, in Archaeologia Americana, IV, 40 ff.

[2] *Ibid.*, 64.

basis for the propagation of Christianity above the extension of trade.[3]   That there was a possibility of necessarily stern measures in dealing with the Indians was acknowledged by a very interested party in the venture, Richard Hakluyt, who, in 1609, wrote to the members of the Virginia Company:

. . . To handle them gently, while gentle courses may be found to serue, it will be without comparison the best: but if gentle polishing will not serue, the one shall not want hammerours and rough masons enow, I meane our old soldiers trained up in the Netherlands, to square and prepare them to our Preachers hands.[4]

With regard to the methods of propagating the faith, the King's instructions under date of November 20, 1606, enjoined "kindly" treatment and "all just and charitable Courses" to be taken, penalties for whites to be determined by legislation.[5]   Undoubtedly, at this early date, this was interpreted as indicating no particular provision other than that of precept from common intercourse, as expressed by the authors of *A True Declaration*, in 1610:

. . . Partlie because there is no other, moderate, and mixt course, to bring them to conuersion, but by dailie conuersation, where they may see the life, and learne the language each of other.[6]

There is no provision in the elaborate *Dale Code* for the conversion of the Indians.   It contents itself merely with a question as to what well doing could be greater than the redemption of the Indians from "ignorance and infidelity.'"[7]   It is not until we come to the *New Life*, written in 1612, that a specific course of training begins to be formulated:

Take their children and traine them up with gentlenesse, teach them our English tongue, and the principles of religion; . . . In steed of Iron and steele you must have patience and humanitie to manage their crooked nature to your form of civilitie.[8]

---

[3] Smith: *True Travels*, I, 112, Gray edition; *cf* Stith: *Hist. of Va.*, 34; Anderson: *Colonial Church*, I, 206.

[4] Neill: *Hist. of the Va. Co.*, 28.

[5] Stith: *Hist. of Va.*, 40; Burk: *Hist. of Va.*, I, 91.

[6] Va. Co. of London: *A True Declaration Of The estate of the Colonie*, in Force's *Tracts*, III, 6.

[7] Strachey, Wm.: *Lavves Diuine, Morall and Martiall*, in Force's *Tracts*, III, 29.

[8] [Johnson]: *The New Life of Virginea*, in Force's *Tracts*, I, 18–19.

As far as can be gathered, nothing was done in an organized fashion for propagating Christianity during the decade immediately after the *First Charter*. However, by 1615, London was greeted with the news that "Pochuntas or Matoa," the daughter of an Indian king, had been converted and married to "an honest and discreete English Gentleman Maister Rolfe."[9]   In the following year, one of Pocahontas's mentors, Sir Thomas Dale, bettered the example of his predecessor, Lord Delaware, who had brought over one Indian, by bringing over a number of Indians of both sexes to be educated in England.[10]

It was not until 1617, that a really constructive effort was made to realize the declared purpose of bringing Christianity to the Indians.   In that year, perhaps, as some say, influenced by the charms of the Indian Princess Pocahontas,[11] James I sent his famous letter to the Archbishops calling their attention to the expense the leaders of the Plantation were under for the erection "of some Churches and Schooles for ye education of ye children of those Barbarians."   Though not doubting the willingness of his subjects to further the cause, yet he required and authorized the archbishops to write to the bishops of the provinces to give orders to the ministers and "other zealous men" by example and by exhortation to contribute as liberally as possible.   Further, he directed "that those Collections be made in all the particular parishes four seuerall tymes, wthin these two years next coming": the money to be delivered to the Treasurer of that Plantation for the "Godly purposes intended, and no other."[12]   But the enthusiasm of the subscribers and particularly of the members of the Virginia Company was so great that the idea of "schooles" for Indians rapidly expanded into a project for the first American "University."   At the close of 1618, an unsuc-

---

9 Neill: *Hist. of the Va. Co.*, 95; Stith: *Hist. of Va.*, 136.

10 Neill: *Hist. of the Va. Co.*, 96, 104–05; Kingsbury: *Rec. of the Va. Co.*, I, 427, 485, 496.

11 *Va. Mag. Hist.*, XXX, 146; Brown: *First Republic in America*, 248.

12 Anderson: *Colonial Church*, I, 314–16; Stith: *Hist. of Va.*, 162; Campbell, C.: *Hist. of Va.*, 146–47; Neill, E. D.: *Va. Vetusta*, 167; Brown: *First Republic in America*, 248.   The date is given as 1617 in Neill and Brown; Anderson, who saw the paper in the State Paper Office, states the date is obliterated.   The date 1617 would seem to be established by reference to this subject in instructions to Gov. Yeardley, Nov. 18, 1618, and the fact that Mr. Lorkin was solicited for the enterprise in 1618.

cessful effort was made to secure the services of Rev. Thomas
Lorkin to take charge of the enterprise.[13]   Definite instructions,
however, had been given Governor Yeardley on November 18,

. . . that a convenient place be chosen and set out for the planting of a
University at the said Henrico in time to come, and that in the meantime
preparation be there made for the building the said College for the Children
of the Infidels, according to such instructions as we shall deliver.[14]

An endowment of 10,000 acres, partly of lands ''impaled'' and
partly of land within the confines of Henrico, was granted.[15]

In February, 1619, the members of the Virginia Company
received in spectacular fashion a gift of £550 from an extremely
modest philanthropist, ''Dust and Ashes,''

. . . for the mayntenance of a conveyent nomber of younge Indians taken
att the age of Seauen years, or younger, and instructed in the readinge and
understandinge the principalls of Xrian Religion unto the age of 12 years,
and then as occasion serueth, to be trayned and brought upp in some lawfull
trade with all humanitie and gentleness untill the age of one and Twenty
years, and then to enioy like liberties and pryviledges with our natiue
English in that place.[16]

An effort was made at a number of subsequent meetings to
induce the representatives of the various ''hundreds'' to assume
responsibility for educating some of these children; but the
''Corporacon'' of Smith's Hundred, though accepting the task
from a spirit of good will, was willing to give £100 to be excused,
and seemingly this phase of the work was dropped for the time
being in view of a proposed treaty with Opachankano, so that
children might be obtained legally.[17]

The matter having dragged with apparently no action, the
donor, in January, 1622, wrote the Company reminding them

---

[13] Neill: *Eng. Coloniz. of Amer.*, 112; *Hist. of Educ. in Va., 17th Century*, 3; *Hist. of the Va. Co.*, 137–38.

[14] *Ibid.*, 137; Brown, S. W.; *Secularization Amer. Educ.*, 22; *Va. Mag. Hist.*, II, 159.

[15] Neill: *Hist. of the Va. Co.*, 137.

[16] *Ibid.*, 168–69, 172; Va. Co. of London: *A Declaration Of The State of the Colonie*, in Force's *Tracts*, III, 12; Stith: *Hist. of Va.*, 171–72; Kingsbury: *Rec. of the Va. Co.*, I, 310–11.

[17] *Ibid.*, I, 319.

that he had been disappointed in his hope of having seen realized by this time "the erectinge of some schoole or other waye whereby some of the Children of the Virginians might haue bin taught and brought up in Christian religion and good manners. . . ."[18] He suggested a new plan of bringing some of the male children to England to be educated. Further, he promised to add £450 to his gift, if eight or ten were brought over and placed in Christ's Hospital or in a "Virginian Schoole" of their own. If this scheme did not meet with the Company's approval, he hoped that his former gift would immediately be used for a "free schoole" in Southampton Hundred, where both English and Indians might be taught together.[19]

A consideration of this letter revealed that Southampton Hundred had used this money and some funds of their own in starting an Iron Work in Virginia, the profits of which were to accrue to this venture. Progress had been hindered by the death of the Captain in charge of this work and the failure to make the treaty with Opachankano. It was held inadvisable, in view of the experience with the Indians brought by Sir Thomas Dale, to bring any more to England. Furthermore, the enthusiastic tobacco-planting workmen of Virginia could not be induced to put up school buildings except at intolerable rates.[20] It would seem that this explanation satisfied the donor. Nothing more is heard of this fund in the Virginia Company records, but the disposition of the fund was a matter of inquiry before the General Court in Virginia in 1624.[21]

The disposition of another fund is better known. The year 1620 was notable for the bequest of £300 left by Nicholas Ferrar for bringing up Indian children at the college "in the grounds of Christian religion." Three children in the meantime were to be

---

[18] Neill: *Hist. of the Va. Co.*, 287.

[19] *Ibid.*, 288; Stith: *Hist. of Va.*, 214; the donor was Gabriel Barber, member of the Virginia Company, see *Va. Mag. Hist.*, XVII, 11; XIX, 383; Stith: *Hist. of Va.*, 216.

[20] Kingsbury: *Rec. of the Va. Co.*, I, 587–89; Neill: *Hist. of the Va. Co.*, 104–05; for change of name from Smith's Hundred to Southampton, see Stith: *Hist. of Va.*, 215.

[21] *Va. Mag. Hist.*, XIX, 383.

taken care of privately every year.[22]   According to Neill, this fund upon the revocation of the Company's charter was transferred to the Bermudas, or Somers Islands Company, and presumably furnished the financial basis for Copland's activities in the Bermudas; but that this fund was available to the General Court at James City in 1640 will be shown later.[23]

In the latter part of 1622, the modest and pious, scholarly gentleman, Mr. George Ruggle, left the Company a gift of £100 for the education of Infidels' children, but the final disposition of this fund seems to be unknown.[24]

In May, 1619, about £1500 had been collected for the Henrico project, with prospect of contributions to come in from the diocese of the Bishop of Lichfield. It was decided to postpone actual building until a revenue could be derived from having 1000 acres of land tilled by tenants who were to give half the profits to ''forward the worke, and for mayntenance of the Tuto*r*s & Schollers.''[25] Accordingly, fifty men were sent for this purpose in August, and in 1620 fifty more.[26] By May, 1620, over £2000 had been received for the college and almost £1500 expended, and arrangements had been made for Mr. George Thorpe to assume charge.[27] A gift of ''faire Plate & other rich Ornam*ts*'' for the communion table of the college chapel had also been received.[28] By November, the nucleus of a library had been created by gifts of ''a Mapp of S*r* Walter Rawlighes contayninge a Descripcon of Guiana,'' St. Augustine's ''City of God'' in English, and three great volumes of the works of Mr. Perkins.[29]

---

[22] Kingsbury: *Rec. of the Va. Co.*, I, 335; Stith: *Hist. of Va.*, 172; Va. Co. of London: *A 'Declaration Of The State of the Colonie*, in Force's *Tracts*, III, 12; Neill: *Hist. of the Va. Co.*, 182; *Va. Mag. Hist.*, XIII, 394; VII, 321; [Ellyson, James T.]: *London Co. of Va.*
[23] Neill: *Eng. Coloniz. of Amer.*, 179; see p. 25.
[24] Neill: *Hist. of the Va. Co.*, 362; Stith: *Hist. of Va.*, 216; *Va. Mag. Hist.*, XIII, 305–06; *Wm. & Mary Coll. Quart.*, V, 203–04.
[25] Kingsbury: *Rec. of the Va. Co.*, I, 220; Neill: *Hist. of the Va. Co.*, 146–48; Stith: *Hist. of Va.*, 162; Brown: *First Republic in America*, 321–22.
[26] Kingsbury: *Rec. of the Va. Co.*, I, 256; Stith: *Hist. of Va.*, 165; *Va. Mag. Hist.*, VI, 231.
[27] Kingsbury: *Rec. of the Va. Co.*, I, 332, 340, 355.
[28] Neill: *Hist. of the Va. Co.*, 152, 181; Arber: *Travels and Works of Capt. J. Smith*, II, 543; Stith: *Hist. of Va.*, 171.
[29] Neill: *Hist. of the Va. Co.*, 197; cf. Kingsbury: *Rec. of the Va. Co.*, I, 589, for a gift of books in 1622.

The further history of the Indian College is briefly told. In 1621 efforts were still being made to gather sums in the hands of various bishops.[30] The endeavors of Mr. Thorpe in Virginia were approved.[31] However, in 1622, the Company had some difficulties with one of their agents, Captain Welden, about the financial returns from the college land, and financial difficulties also with Captain Argoll.[32] It may have been as a result of these difficulties that the idea was now entertained of sending the Rev. Mr. Copland as Rector of the intended College and pastor of the College tenants.[33] But by August news had reached London of the calamitous massacre of March 22.[34]

Whereas these were the efforts of philanthropy in England, encouraged by a spirit of piety and patriotism, to provide for the training of Indian children "in true Religion moral virtue and civility and for other Godly uses," it is of interest to see what were the attitudes and efforts of the English in Virginia.[35]

Reference has already been made to the failure of the *Dale Code* to give specific directions in regard to the Indians.[36] The instructions given to Governor Yeardley, in 1618,[37] on the subject of Henrico, were brought before the first legislative assembly convened in Virginia, in 1619. A formal petition was consequently made to the Virginia Company, "that towards the erecting of the University and Colledge, they will sende, when they shall thinke most convenient, workmen of all sortes fitt for that purpose. . . ."[38]

With regard to the attitude to be assumed toward the Indians in daily contact, the Assembly took a cautious note, counselling

---

30 *Ibid.*, I, 484, 521, 560.
31 Neill: *Hist. of the Va. Co.*, 228.
32 Kingsbury: *Rec. of the Va. Co.*, I, 601–04; II, 53.
33 *Ibid.*, II, 49, 76.
34 Neill: *Hist. of the Va. Co.*, 317 *ff.*, 329; Arber: *Travels and Works of Capt. J. Smith*, II, 577; Stith: *Hist. of Va.*, 211; for a second unsuccessful educational venture, Edward Palmer's "Academia Virginiensis et Oxoniensis," see Tyler, L. G.: *Williamsburg*, 111–12; Neill: *Hist. of Educ. in Va., 17th Century*, 23; *Va. Carolorum*, 27; *Va. Vetusta*, 182; *U. S. Bur. Educ., Circ. Inf.*, 1887, No. 1, 12; 1890, No. 1, 168; Bruce, P. A.: *Inst. Hist. of Va.*, I, 372; Fuller, T.: *Worthies*, I, 566–67.
35 *Va. Mag. Hist.*, II, 158–59.
36 See p. 15.
37 See p. 17.
38 *Jour., H. Burg.*, July 31, 1619, 6–7.

"neither utterly to rejecte them, nor yet to drawe them to come in." However, mindful of their purpose to convert the Indians, they exacted that,

. . . for laying a surer foundation of the conversion of the Indians to Christian Religion, each towne, citty Borrough, & particular plantation do obtaine unto themselves by just meanes a certaine number of the natives Children to be educated by them in true Religion & civile course of life.[39]

After instruction in the first elements of literature, it was intended to send these children to the college so "that from thence they may be sent to that worke of conversion."[40]

What effort was made by the various communities to obtain children and proceed to the work of training and conversion can only be conjectured. The references already made to the implied necessity of a treaty with Opachankano[41] would seem to indicate that the Indians were not so "loving, and willing to parte w*th* their children" as they had been in Rolfe's day.[42] There is, however, a record of the baptism of one Indian child, William Crashaw, at Elizabeth City, in 1624, and there may have been more.[43]   There is evidence in the accounts of the massacre of 1622 that a contributing cause was relaxation of that caution enjoined by the Assembly, in 1619, and the consequent friendly intercourse between the two races.[44]

A review of the efforts made from the beginning of the planting of the colony in 1607 shows that, though nothing constructive was done in the first decade, the King's letter of 1617 to the Archbishops resulted in the raising of over £2000 for a University of which a college for the Indians was to be part;[45] three other funds approximating £1000, and a few minor gifts. It would seem that in these efforts, there is evidence of sincere purpose in spreading the Gospel. It is of interest to discover the effect of the massacre upon this avowed purpose. A letter of the Com-

---

[39] *Ibid.*, Aug. 2, 1619, 8–10; *Colonial Records, Sen. Doc. Ex.*, 1874, 21; *cf.* Stith: *Hist. of Va.*, 195; *cf.* Hening: *Stat. at Large*, I, 113.
[40] *Jour., H. Burg.*, Aug. 2, 1619, 8–10.
[41] See p. 17, 18.
[42] *Va. Mag. Hist.*, X, 137.
[43] Slaughter: *Colonial Church*, 23.
[44] Neill: *Hist. of the Va. Co.*, 317 *ff.*; Stith: *Hist. of Va.*, 211.
[45] Kingsbury: *Rec. of the Va. Co.*, I, 355.

pany written in August, 1622, after urging a war of extermination, qualifies it by:

> . . . Yet, remembering who we are rather than what they have been, we cannot but advise not only the sparing but the preservation of the younger people of both Sexes, whose bodies may by labor and service become profitable, and their minds not overgrowne with evill Customes, be reduced to civilitie, and afterwards to Christianitie. . . .[46]

The Virginia Company, in 1623, in issuing a defence of their work recalled the expense of the last four years in prosecuting their purpose, and declared with regard to the Henrico project that "the worke by the Assistance of god shall againe [in due time] p'ceed."[47]

In 1624 they generously assumed the cost of training, under "Rev. Mr. Copeland," an Indian boy who had been brought into the country "by one William Perry."[48] While the attitude of severity of those in London was thus tempered, we read in "A Breife Declaration of the Plantation of Virginia," issued about this time, "Our Govr, Counsell and others have used their uttermost and Christian endeavours in prosequtinge revenge against the bloody Salvadges, . . . "[49]

In reviewing the literature and activities in both England and the Colony, it is seen that the project of propagating Christianity received enthusiastic attention and support. An inquiry into the reasons for failure of these efforts, while it might suggest the alleged intractability of the Indian temperament for amenity to the English mode of civility and spirituality, or the fact that the Anglican Church had not the proselyting experience and knack of the Catholic, or that the lure of gathering tobacco was greater than the glamour of gathering Indian souls, would be futile.[50] That the sincerity and zeal of the pious in England could not be matched by energy and tact on the part of the colonists was made clear. Perhaps the real seed of failure lay

---

[46] Neill: *Hist. of the Va. Co.*, 331.

[47] Kingsbury: *Rec. of the Va. Co.*, II, 395; "in due time" inclosed in ms. by copyist.

[48] *Ibid.*, II, 532, 538.

[49] *Jour., H. Burg.*, Vol. 1619–59, 28, 37. The evidence that an Indian child had been baptized at Elizabeth City in 1624 may be indicative that this policy was not used against the young. See p. 21.

[50] See p. 18; Kingsbury: *Rec. of the Va. Co.*, I, 589.

in the too elaborate scheme of a college, with preliminary training to be left to individual endeavor. It may be that the plan of "Dust and Ashes" for immediate local free schools, might have been more effective.[51]

Reviewing the evidence before us, it is patent that whether the declared purpose of converting the Indians was sincere or not, it was effective both in bringing support to the project of colonization and in emphasizing the importance of Indian education.

Propagation Of The Gospel After The Dissolution Of The Virginia Company

Literary Propaganda

Though the impetus given to organized effort in behalf of Indian education and conversion was checked by the massacre of 1622 and the dissolution of the Virginia Company in 1624, the memory of that purpose lingered on both in England and the colony; and, while not always favored by events, found expression in literature, legislation, and action throughout the colonial period.

The first significant literary propaganda urging extension of the Gospel, which now appeared, was *A Petition of W. C. Exhibited To The High Court Of Parliament*, in 1641. Signed by over seventy ministers, and embracing all the colonies in its view, it is a sincere and eloquent plea for more vigorous prosecution of a work acknowledged to be "pious and charitable." The charity of "Apostolicall men" of the past to them must now in turn be passed on to the Indians in order to make "all nations blessed by the coming of Christ." Particularly important in effecting this purpose is a supply of "able and conscionable Ministers" for the want of which in Virginia they are "more likely to turne Heathen, then to turne others to the Christian faith."[52]

In 1651, there appeared in London a pamphlet, issued on behalf of a number of Virginia merchants, urging the conversion

---

[51] See p. 18.
[52] C.[astell], W.: *A Petition of W. C. Exhibited To The High Court Of Parliament*, in Force's *Tracts*, I, 3, 4, 5; Hazard: *Hist. Coll.*, I, 527.

of the Indians and the settling of the Virginia borders as a patriotic motive.[53]

Samuel Hartlib, Milton's friend, wrote, in 1655, a unique pamphlet which urged silk-worm culture as a medium for civilizing and converting the Indians.[54]

A keen and well studied analysis of religion and education, addressed to the Bishop of London, and published in 1662, delineated the effects of the scattered plantation system upon the religious and educational progress of the whites, and, in turn, upon the Indians. No "rationall Heathen" in the opinion of the writer would "commit their Children to the teaching and education of such Christians, whom they shall perceive to want Schooles of learning . . . for their own.''[55]

There now intervened a period in which owing to the circumstances surrounding Bacon's Rebellion, little effort was made from any point of view in behalf of the Indians. Morgan Godwyn, who had been pastor of Marston Parish near Williamsburg, some time after 1665, wrote, in 1680, *The Negro's and Indians Advocate*. He pictured the Virginian attitude toward the propagation of Christianity in these words:

. . . to propagate Christianity among the heathen,—. . . although (as must piously be supposed) it were the only end of God's discovering these countries to us, yet is that lookt upon by our new race of Christians, so idle and ridiculous, so utterly needless and unnecessary, that no man can forfeit his judgment more, than by any proposal looking or tending that way.[56]

A review of the problem of Indian education and conversion, based on extensive observation in the colony, appeared in 1724. It was written by Rev. Hugh Jones, former professor in William and Mary College, who had seen two Indian schools, those at Christ Anna and Brafferton, in operation, and had made an effort to understand the Indian character and the English attitude towards it. He was opposed to the baptism of Indians unless some training had been received or was assured. In his view,

---

[53] Alvord, C. W., & Bidgood, L.: *First explorations of the Trans-Allegheny Region*, 105 *ff.*; Salley, A. S.: *Narratives of Early Carolina*, 5 *ff.*
[54] [Hartlib, S.]:*The Reformed Virginian Silk-Worm*, in Force's *Tracts*, III; *cf.* Dircks, H.: *Biographical Memoir Samuel Hartlib*, 83–84, 73.
[55] G.[reene], R.[obert]: *Virginia's Cure*, in Force's *Tracts*, III, 6.
[56] Anderson: *Colonial Church*, II, 561.

their Christian education should consist of learning their prayers, catechism, church attendance, and accustoming themselves not to lie, swear, or steal. Except those sent to Brafferton, they should not be taught to read and write, "which as yet has been found to be dangerous upon several political Accounts, especially Self-Preservation." Of those sent to Brafferton, upon completing their instruction, instead of idling or returning to their towns —some should be sent to sea or apprenticed to trades; others, for whom financial support must be assured, should enter the mission field in the company of missionaries from the Society for Propagation of the Gospel.[57]

It is clear, that the conception of Indian education which prevailed in this period hardly went beyond that of catechetical instruction.

Legislative Attitude

With this picture before us of the Indian program as revealed in the literature of the period, it is of interest to discover the attitude of the Legislature toward this problem.

The Virginia Assembly of 1632 enacted specific legislation with regard to religious instruction of "youth and ignorant persons," but there is nothing to indicate the applicability of the law to Indians; and the fact that they were declared at this time to be "unreconcilable enemies" undoubtedly signified an intention to dispense with efforts at instruction.[58]

In 1640, however, there is a record of the further history of the Indian boy brought to England in 1624 by William Perry. After ten years in England, he had been brought to Virginia and was now presented to the General Court by his guardian, Mr. George Menifye, Esq., who hoped to obtain a provision for him from the Nicholas Ferrar fund.[59] The Court upon examination found him "to have been well instructed in the principles of religion, taught to read, instructed to writing:" and accordingly recommended an "allowance of 8 pounds *per annum*."[60] In 1642, the Court

---

[57] Jones: *Present State of Va.*, 14–19, 70–71.
[58] Hening: *Stat. at Large*, I, 157; *Va. Mag. Hist.*, VII, 338; *cf.* XXIII, 229.
[59] See p. 22, 19.
[60] *Va. Mag. Hist.*, XI, 282.

granted "permission to keep an indian boy, instructing him in christian religion."[61] How common this practise may have been is not known.

In 1641,[62] and again in 1645[63] and 1646,[64] legislation similar to that of 1632 was enacted. The year 1646, however, saw the following legislation enacted, undoubtedly a reflection of the massacre of 1644,[65] and evidence that the Indians were not included in the previous legislation:

. . . And it is further enacted & consented, That such Indian children as shall or will freely and voluntarily come in and live with the English, may remain without breach of the articles of peace, provided they be not above twelve yeares old.[66]

No further ameliorating legislation appeared until the years 1655–58,[67] when there was an effort to place the relations of the Indians and whites on a just and humane basis. Of particular interest is the attempt to place the procedure with regard to educational activities on a legal basis. Parents were at liberty to choose their children's guardians; the government undertook to see that they were not treated as slaves, that they would be brought up "in Christianity, civillity and the knowledge of necessary trades;" and upon certification by the county commissioners would allow a salary to deserving and requiring guardians.[68] Parents were permitted to give their children as servants, if certain formalities were gone through in the county court, and "Provided that due respect and care be had that they the said Indian servants be educated and brought vp in the Christian religion. . . ."[69]

In 1658, transfer of Indian children, from any person to whom assigned for whatever purpose, was declared illegal and all were

---

61 *Ibid.*, VIII, 68.
62 *Ibid.*, IX, 52.
63 Hening: *Stat. at Large*, I, 290.
64 *Ibid.*, I, 311.
65 *Va. Mag. Hist.*, VII, 338; XXIII, 229.
66 Hening: *Stat. at Large*, I, 326.
67 *Ibid.*, I, 391, 394–96, 410, 455, 481–82.
68 *Ibid.*, I, 396.
69 *Ibid.*, I, 410.

to be free and at their own disposal at the age of twenty-five years.[70]

A provision for the maintenance and education of Indian hostages, with an allowance of 1200 pounds of tobacco yearly for the maintenance and education of each when necessary, was made in 1663.[71]

It is impossible to gather from the records for this period any evidence of the extent to which Indian parents availed themselves of these provisions. The difficulties between the colonists and the Indians which culminated in Bacon's Rebellion (1676) preclude the thought that anything was extensively done in regard to Indian education.[72]

No legislation for Indian education now appears until 1705, when in the provisions for ridding the country of the Nansiattico Indians, it was decreed that all children of this tribe under twelve years were to be bound as servants to the English until they were twenty-four years of age, and that provision be made for bringing up the children, born during servitude, in the Christian faith.[73] In accordance with this legislation, four children were indentured to the governor, and nine children to various members of the Council by lot.[74]

A questionnaire relative to educational and religious conditions sent by the Commissary, Rev. James Blair, in 1724, upon instructions from London, to the ministers of the various parishes, asked the question, "Are there any Infidels, bond or free, within your Parish; and what means are used for their conversion?"[75] Only four of twenty-nine ministers answering the questionnaire as a whole make any reference to Indians. Of these, two mention that some are sent to the Boyle Indian school, one refers to the Christ Anna school, and one indicates the presence of a few Indian servants.[76]

---

[70] *Ibid.*, I, 455; 481, indicates this legislation was due to the practise of stealing Indians, "to the greate scandall of Christianitie."

[71] *Ibid.*, II, 194.

[72] *Ibid.*, II, 333, solemn fast days declared in April and May, 1676, imploring divine assistance in war against Indians.

[73] *Jour., H. Burg.*, April 27, 1705, 97–98.

[74] McIlwaine, H. R.: *Exec. Jour., Council Col. Va.*, III, 5–6.

[75] Perry, W. S.: *Amer. Col. Church*, I, 261, *cf.* 261–346.

[76] Based on writer's tabulation from Perry, as cited above, see Appendix I, p. 653.

In 1730, the Assembly decided to defer the question of provision for Indian education.[77] In fact, the Virginian historian Stith, who wrote in 1747, stated that since the dissolution of the Virginia Company in 1624, "there was no publick Attempt, nor any School or Institution, purposely designed for their Education and Conversion, before the Benefaction of the late Honourable *Robert Boyle,* Esq; . . ."[78]

Educational Efforts

The Boyle benefaction, the largest given for Indian education in the colonial period, and around which centered the most consistent effort in their behalf, had its beginnings in the efforts of the Commissary, Rev. James Blair, and some other ministers and leading men of Virginia to establish a free school and college. There is no indication in the official records of the discussion relative to the creation of the College of William and Mary that any provision was intended for Indians. However, in the subscription paper issued at the initiating of the enterprise, reference is made to the purpose in the words "and perhaps a foundation for ye Conversion of our neighboring Heathen (Indians) to the Christian Faith."[79]

In February, 1692, Commissary Blair wrote to Governor Nicholson, "Mr. Boyle died . . . & left a considerable Legacy for pious uses, which, when I understood, I made my interest with his executors . . . and I am promised £200 of it for our college."[80]

By the time the charter of the college was granted in 1693,[81] the destiny of the fund was determined and the charter recognized the purpose of the college as being in part, "that the Christian Faith may be propagated amongst the Western *Indians,* to the Glory of Almighty God."[82]

---

[77] *Jour., H. Burg.,* May 26, 1730, 62–63.

[78] Stith: *Hist. of Va.,* 217.

[79] Motley, D. E.: *Life of Blair,* 27; *cf. Jour., Va. Council,* III, Appendix, 1511, subscription paper, 1696, purpose given as "the P'pogation of the Xtian faith in the West Indies."

[80] Perry: *Amer. Col. Church,* I, 8.

[81] Motley: *Life of Blair,* 29; Tyler: *Williamsburg,* 120.

[82] Hartwell, H., Blair, J., & Chilton, E.: *Present State Va.,* 72; Parks, W.: *The Charter, and Statutes of the College of William and Mary in Vir-*

The executors of the Boyle fund invested it in property in England known as the Brafferton estate; the income of which, after setting aside "£45 for Harvard College, and £45 for the Society for the Propagation of the Gospel in New England," was to go to the college for maintaining one Indian child for every £14 received.[83] The deed of gift stipulated that the children were to be kept in "sicknesse and health in meat drink washing and lodging Cloathes Medicines books and Educacon from ye first beginning of letters till they should be ready to receave Ordrs. . . ."[84]

The income of this fund was sufficient, according to the instructions issued by Governor Nicholson to the agents negotiating some Indian treaties in 1700, to provide in this manner for nine or ten children. The children that were to be sent were to be about seven or eight years of age and have a "careful Indian man of their own country to wait upon them & to serve them & to talk continually with them in their own language" as this knowledge would be essential when they went back as teachers to their own people.[85]

This seems to have been the initial attempt to obtain children for the school; for in a letter in February, 1700, to the Archbishop of Canterbury, the Commissary speaks of hoping to have the college finished by next winter and of his efforts to have a proposition "for the encouragement of the Christian Education of our Negro & Indian children" embodied in a prospective revisal of the laws.[86] In fact, the question of the conversion of the Indians had been a subject of discussion in the Assembly during the spring of 1699, because of some "Instructions" on the subject sent from England. In reply, the committee of the House of Burgesses had declared:

---

ginia, 3, in a bound volume of pamphlets in library of Historical Society of Pennsylvania.

[83] Tyler: *Williamsburg*, 119.

[84] *Va. Mag. Hist.*, XXIV, 375; Tyler's *Williamsburg*, 119, gives the amount provided in the will as £4,000, but Bruce's *Inst. Hist. of Va.*, I, 396, gives the amount at which Brafferton was valued as £5,400. The *So. Lit. Messenger*, Oct., 1856, XXIII, 277, quotes from Duyckinck's *Cyclopaedia of American Literature*, saying there was "laid out £5,400 for the purchase. . . ."

[85] Perry: *Amer. Col. Church*, I, 121, 123–24.

[86] *Ibid.*, I, 112.

And as to the Conversion of the Indians this Com*tee* doth not doubt of the care of the Colledge therein being encouraged and obliged thereto by the Donation of a pious and noble Benefactor.[87]

The Commissary's proposition came up in October, 1699, and though a matter of frequent consideration until some time in November does not seem to have been favorably acted upon.[88] The nature of its provisions is not indicated in the Virginia records, but is perhaps identified by the following paper given without date by Meade:

A Proposition for Encouraging the Christian Education of Indian, Negro, and Mulatto Children

It being a duty of Christianity very much neglected by masters and mistresses of this country (America) to endeavour the good instruction and education of their heathen slaves in the Christian faith,—the said duty being likewise earnestly recommended by his Majesty's instructions,—for the facilitating thereof among the young slaves that are born among us; it is, therefore, humbly proposed that every Indian, negro, or mulatto child that shall be baptized and afterward brought to church and publicly catechized by the minister in church, and shall, before the fourteenth year of his or her age, give a distinct account of the Creed, the Lord's Prayer, and Ten Commandments, and whose master or mistress shall receive a certificate from the minister that he or she hath so done, such Indian, negro, or mulatto child shall be exempted from paying all levies till the age of eighteen years.[89]

No legislation for Indian education now appears until the specific legislation, in 1705, regarding the Nansiattico Indians mentioned above.

The history of the Boyle Indian school reaches its most interesting period with the coming, in 1710, of Governor Alexander Spotswood. He inaugurated a new era in the colony's relations with the Indians. On the one hand, he attempted to instil a more favorable attitude toward the Indians in the Assembly, assuring

---

[87] *Jour., H. Burg.*, May 22, 1699, 172–74.

[88] *Jour., Va. Council*, Oct. 5, 1699, III, 1523; Nov. 9, 1699, 1525.

[89] Meade, W.: *Old Churches, Ministers and Families*, I, 265, footnote: Meade says, "About this time I find the following proposition, which is preserved among the archives of Lambeth." Blair, in his letter to the Archbishop of Canterbury says: "I have enclosed copies of these propositions, & in the margin have marked the opinion of that committee about the severall articles of them." Perry: *Amer. Col. Church*, I, 344, gives this paper in material for 1724, but there is no indication in Virginia records that legislation of this kind was under discussion in 1724.

the Assembly that "the best of Securitys to our persons and Estates" lay in making them Christians; and, on the other hand, to assure the Indians, by treaties and his personal interest and activity in securing Indian children for the College, that the dawn of peace had arrived.[90]

It seems the reluctance of parents to part with their children, had resulted in their being obtained by purchase of those taken in war.[91] It appeared likely, too, that the Indian memory of a breach of compact, by a former government with regard to the education of Indian children, would prove a barrier to Spotswood's efforts to fill the Boyle school.[92] However, Spotswood's diplomacy, particularly in remitting the tribute from various Indian tribes and insistence on hostages to confirm treaties, resulted in sending enough children to make it likely that the Boyle fund would be exhausted. In May, 1712, there were fourteen children, and Spotswood, confessing his failure to obtain supplementary funds from the Assembly, wrote to the Bishop of London, hoping to secure his interest with "the Society for propagating the Gospel."[93] In July, 1712, the Bishop was informed that there were twenty children, and that "they have a Master to teach them and are decently cloathed and maintained."[94]

Spotswood's enthusiasm was now glowing indeed, and he urged the Bishop

... to move the Society for propagating the Gospel for one or two Missionarys to reside at the principal towns of the Indians and have a Church or Chappell built there, and a School-house with an allowance for a Clerk who may also serve as Usher.[95]

Although the matter was presented in a letter by the Bishop to the Society, it seems no constructive action was taken.[96]

[90] *Jour., H. Burg.*, Nov. 8, 1811, 301–02; *cf.* McIlwaine: *Exec. Jour., Council Col. Va.*, III, 287–88, 440, 442–43.
[91] Beverley: *Hist. of Va.*, 216; Spotswood, A.: *Letters*, I, 123–25.
[92] *Ibid.*; it may be that reference is here made to the transportation of the Nansiattico Indians above 12 years, see p. 27.
[93] Spotswood: *Letters*, I, 156; probably, three were the boys placed by the Queen of Pamunky—McIlwaine: *Exec. Jour., Council Col. Va.*, III, 290–91.
[94] Spotswood: *Letters*, I, 174.
[95] *Ibid.*, I, 175. A similar letter went to the Archbishop of Canterbury, *Ibid.*, I, 176.
[96] Perry: *Amer. Col. Church*, I, 192. Spotswood was elected a member of this Society—Spotswood: *Letters*, II, 255.

In 1714, Spotswood succeeded in making treaties with the Saponies, Tuscaruro and other Indians, which were featured by a provision for the Christian education of the children.[97] Inspired by the seeming good will thus created, Spotswood inaugurated an Indian Trading Company with headquarters at Christ Anna, where, in accordance with his views on the subject of Indian education, he immediately proceeded to erect a school and install a schoolmaster, Rev. Charles Griffin. The funds for the building were to come from the company, and the maintenance of the children from part of the forfeitures arising from violations of the act relative to the trading company. However, the Governor engaged to pay the teacher's salary of £50 a year personally while in office.[98]

The most significant feature of the scheme was the proposal to grant

... to those educated at the Colledge or at the School, to hold any Place of Trust or profit under this Company, which, by former Laws of the Colony, they were prohibited to do.[99]

Of all ventures in behalf of Indian education in Colonial Virginia, this seems to have been the happiest. Visitors to the school all testified to the skill and success of Mr. Griffin in teaching, and winning the devotion of parents and children. As many as seventy or more children were at times in his care.[100]

A picture of the school is seen in a letter of Mr. Griffin's, in 1716, to the Bishop of London:

The greatest number of my scholars can say the belief, the Lord's prayer, & ten Commds perfectly well, they know that there is but one God & they are able to tell me how many persons there are in the Godhead & what each of those blessed persons have done for them. They know how many sacraments Christ hath ordained in his Church & for what end he instituted them, they behave themselves reverently at our daily prayers & can make their responses, . . .[101]

---

[97] *Jour., H. Burg.*, Nov. 17, 1714, 77–80; Nov. 24, 714, 88–90; McIlwaine: *Exec. Jour., Council Col. Va.*, III, 365, 365–66.
[98] Spotswood: *Letters*, II, 90; cf. *Jour., Va. Council*, III, 1561–62.
[99] Spotswood: *Letters*, II, 89.
[100] *Ibid.*, II, 138; McIlwaine: *Exec. Jour., Council Col. Va.*, III, 397; Bell, L. C.: *The Old Free State*, I, 59–60, citing Maury, A.: *Memoirs of a Huguenot Family*, 270–71, (sic); Wynne: *Hist. of the Dividing Line*, I, 75; Jones: *Present State of Va.*, 14.
[101] Perry: *Amer. Col. Church*, I, 196.

In addition to this catechetical instruction, the children were taught to read and write.[102]

The date of discontinuance of this school is not definitely known, but has been placed by Tyler as about 1720.[103]

While this school at Christ Anna was thus flourishing, the Boyle Indian school which had twenty children in 1714, dwindled to a few in 1716;[104] but these children were not neglected, as is evident from the following requisition on June 20, 1716:

> Ordered, that the Clerk of the Colledge write to Mr. Perry to send in for the use of the Indian children such a number of Testaments, Bibles and the whole Duty of man as shall be necessary, and likewise paper Quills and Ink powder for the use of the sd children.[105]

There is no evidence that the school after this time was ever so large as it had been in 1714. In 1732, the surplus of the fund was such that permission was asked of the Bishop of London to furnish a library in the room over the Indian school.[106]

In 1752, Governor Dinwiddie had the subject of Indian education presented by his commissioners sent to negotiate a treaty with the chiefs of the Six Nations, informing them, if they were reluctant to send their children to distant Brafferton, the government was willing to send teachers to them.[107] The offer to educate children at Brafferton was likewise made in a treaty between Virginia and the Catawba and Cherokee Indians in 1756.[108] But the Cherokee boys who were sent, remained only a few months and the governor wrote the chiefs asking that boys under eight be sent.[109] In that same year, the governor wrote to the Lords

---

[102] Bell: *The Old Free State*, I, 60; Maury: *Memoirs of a Huguenot Family*, 272.

[103] Tyler: *Williamsburg*, 130–32; cf. *Va. Mag. Hist.*, XIII, 282; cf. McIlwaine: *Exec. Jour., Council Col. Va.*, III, 442–43, 479, 481; the dissolution was undoubtedly hastened by the opposition to the Indian trading company as a monopoly—see Bassett, J. S.: *The Writings of Colonel William Byrd*—Introduction lxi, and the *Va. Mag. Hist.*, XXII, 410; and the corruption of the Indians by the whites—Wynne: *Hist. of the Dividing Line*, I, 188.

[104] *Va. Mag. Hist.*, IV, 172.

[105] *Ibid.*, 173.

[106] *Wm. & Mary Coll. Quart.*, IX, 220.

[107] *Va. Mag. Hist.*, XIII, 151–52, 173.

[108] *Ibid.*, XIII, 250.

[109] Dinwiddie, R.: *Records*, II, 446.

of Trade, requesting permission to place a teacher for Indian children at each of the forts of the Western frontier, "to teach the Children Eng. and Morality, and to give them a true Notion of the Supreme God."[110]

Burnaby, who visited the school in his travels, 1759–60, notes that there are five or six children present, that the master has £60 sterling and a house, and that "his business is to instruct the Indians in reading, writing, and the principles of the Christian religion."[111]   The last notice of the school in operation as given by a traveler, occurs in 1773.[112]

In the reorganization of the college effected by Jefferson, in 1779, Brafferton was retained as the sixth school of the college, but whether any children were present, does not appear.[113]

The fund was eventually diverted after the Revolution to the conversion and religious instruction of negroes in the British West Indies.[114]   With Jefferson as a visitor of the college, it is likely that if the fund had not been thus diverted, it would have been used for creating in the college a school of Indian Anthropology.[115]

It is seen from this review of the history of the efforts to realize the declared purpose of propagating the gospel in Virginia, that the purpose was kept consistently in mind throughout the colonial period.   There was, at the same time, a great deal of difficulty in realizing this purpose because of the feeling of animosity aroused by the events of 1622, 1644, and 1676.   Spotswood inaugurated an era of better feeling, but failed to influence subsequent legislatures to follow his example in creating local free schools—a solution of the problem likewise emphasized by Governor Dinwiddie.

It must be kept in mind that during the colonial period, the Indians progressively and rapidly disappeared from Virginia.

---

[110] *Ibid.*, II, 339.

[111] Burnaby, A.: *Travels in America*, 52, 190.

[112] *Va. Hist. Register*, VI, 146, citing Smyth's *Travels in Va.*, in 1773; *cf.* Morrison, A. J.: *Travels in Va.*, Ch. I; in Morrison's *Travels in the Confederation*, II, 79, J. D. Schoepf visiting Williamsburg, 1783, notes discontinuance.

[113] *Va. Gazette*, Dec. 18, 1779.

[114] *Wm. & Mary Coll. Quart.*, III, 39; XVI, 172, Ser. 2, I, 16–23.

[115] Jefferson, T.: *Notes on Va.*, 224.

Though no reliable figures are available, it is estimated that at the time of first settlement by whites, there were 17,000 Indians between the sea and the Alleghany mountains.[116] By 1699, the number had probably dwindled to 3,000.[117] As the Indians dwindled in number, and the white population increased, it seemingly became less necessary from a politic point of view to conciliate the Indians; nevertheless as has been shown the opportunity at Brafferton was emphasized in treaties as late as 1756, and the opportunity was available to them as late as 1779.

Byrd, in his study of the Indian question, held that the English, if sincere in the matter of the conversion of the Indians, had failed to make use of what he regarded as the most effective method of conciliation, namely, intermarriage. He said:

. . . Besides, Morals and all considered, I cant think the Indians were much greater Heathens than the first Adventurers, who, had they been good Christians, would have had the Charity to take this only method of converting the Natives to Christianity. For, after all that can be said, a sprightly Lover is the most prevailing Missionary that can be sent amongst these, or any other Infidels.[118]

In 1784, when the equalitarian notions of the Revolutionary period had had time to impress some members of the Legislature, a bill was introduced "for the encouragement of marriages with the Indians." It does not seem to have survived a second reading.[119]

Comparing the high hopes in which the thought of bringing Christianity to the Indians was envisaged at the time of the founding of the Colony with the outcomes of the efforts made in their behalf, it is clear from the evidence presented, that these outcomes fell far below those sanguine expectations.

Rev. Charles Griffin was, so far as we know, the most successful Indian missionary; but he was unable to induce the Indians to follow him to the Boyle school. There was practically no con-

---

[116] *Wm. & Mary Coll. Quart.*, XIX, 74.

[117] Bruce: *Inst. Hist. of Va.*, I, 9–10; Beverley: *Hist. of Va.*, 183, writing in 1705, estimated that there were less than 500 fighting men. The Perry questionnaire, 1724, indicates two settlements and a few Indian servants, see Appendix I. No later figures seem available; *cf.* MacLeod, W. C.: *Amer. Indian Frontier*, 545–46.

[118] Bassett: *The Writings of Colonel William Byrd*, 9.

[119] *Jour., H. Del.*, Nov. 16, 1784, 35.

certed or consistent movement on the part of the clergy to handle
the problem.   The Legislature, though it did not oppose individual effort, failed to give any support which would lead to such
constructive effort as would be implied in the creation of schools.
The Virginians, however, envisaged early the necessity of an educational program and attempted to bring a realization of that
necessity home to the Indians.   Their schools for Indians ante-
date those of the Quakers in Pennsylvania.   The colonists were
unable, nevertheless, to establish that attitude of cordiality characteristic of the relations between the Quakers of Pennsylvania
and the Indians.[120]   There is no evidence that Christianity took
hold of the Indian heart and mind.

---

[120] Woody, T.: *Early Quaker Educ. in Penn'a.*, 267.

CHAPTER III

THE CIVIL GOVERNMENT AND RELIGION

The Process Of Integration Of Church And State

In an enterprise sanctified by a holy purpose, such as the founding of Virginia, it is pertinent to inquire into the nature of the government created for those who were to reveal Christianity to the heathen.

As has been indicated, the political philosophy determining the government of Virginia must be sought in the Acts of Supremacy and Conformity and in the Gilbert and Raleigh Patents.[1] The basic principle of this philosophy was that colonization was an extension of the civil and religious government of the mother country, into a new territorial sphere. Civil and religious legislation was to be in harmony with that of England.

This is specifically emphasized in the Instructions of November, 1606, accompanying the First Charter, where it was ordered that a provision should be made "that the true Word and Service of God be preached, planted, and used, . . . according to the Rites and Doctrine of the Church of *England.*"[2] The significance of this for the relation between the civil and spiritual aspects of the government is apparent upon an analysis of that relationship as it existed in England. There, practically every vital aspect of Church life—articles of faith, discipline, support, legal existence —was under the control of Parliament. Citizenship in the state and membership in the Church were synonymous, so that uniformity assumed a civil aspect, particularly in its implications with regard to law and order.[3] It is because they are indicative of a proposed policy of union of church and state, of the establishment of the Anglican Church as the church of Virginia, of the creation of a virtual theocracy, that the instructions of 1606 are significant.

---

[1] See p. 3.
[2] Stith: *Hist. of Va.*, 37; Hening: *Stat. at Large*, I, 68.
[3] Cobb: *Rise of Relig. Liberty*, 54–55; Anderson: *Colonial Church*, I, 132, 206.

The first serious attempt to create an ordered government in the colony was made upon the arrival of Sir Thomas Gates, in May, 1610, and the institution of *Dale's Code*.[4] An analysis of this code shows that not only were the duties of the clergy so closely defined as were the religious duties of the citizens, but also that the control and oversight of the religious functioning of the colony were placed not in the clerical arm, but in the military and civil arm of the government.[5]

The colony remained under this code until 1619, when the first legislative assembly met, and, duly invoking sanctification by God, proceeded to draw up laws based on instructions from England.[6] While the churchwardens now practically replaced the military in their police function, the clergy were liable to censure for neglect of duty by the Governor and Council and could not proceed to excommunication without first presenting their opinion to the Governor. If at any time, the minister was at a loss as to his proper procedure, all he need remember was that he was to exercise his ''ministerial function according to the Ecclesiasticall Lawes and orders of the church of Englande''—an instruction sufficient to indicate that a definite union existed between church and state.[7]

Among the factors contributing to place the colony on a religio-civil basis, aside from precedent in the home government and the motive of bringing Christianity to the heathen, was undoubtedly the personnel of the Virginia Company. With the Church of England so strongly represented in its membership, it was inevitable that an effort would be made to insure the orthodoxy of the clergy sent.[8] In fact, it was a doubt as to the loyalty of Sir Edwin Sandys in this respect that contributed to the dissolution of the Company. In 1623, a deposition was made in regard to a conversation between Captain Bargrave and Sir Nathaniel Rich, a member of the opposition, to the effect, that Sandys'

---

[4] Prince, W. F.: *First Criminal Code of Va.*, 311.
[5] Strachey: *Lavves Diuine, Morall and Martiall*, in Force's *Tracts*, III; for authorship, see Prince's *First Criminal Code of Va.*, 341.
[6] *Jour., H. Burg.*, July 30, 1619, 3–4; Aug. 2, 1619, 9–10; *Va. Mag. Hist.*, II, 154.
[7] *Jour., H. Burg.*, Aug. 4, 1619, 13–14.
[8] Thomas: *Relig. Element in Jamestown*, 6; *Va. Mag. Hist.*, IV, 344; Kingsbury: *Rec. of the Va. Co.*, I, 314; Anderson: *Colonial Church*, I, 322.

. . . intent was to *erect a free state in Virginia*, . . . And to that intent
(he, Capt. Bargrave, affirmed to me) Sir Edwin Sandys moved my Lord of
Canterburye to give leave to the Brownists and Separatists of England to
goe thither. For which my Lord grace of Canterburye sayed to Bargrave
that he should never like well of Sir E. Sandys, those Brownists by their
doctrine clayming a liberty & disagreeing to the government of monarchies.[9]

Every precaution was taken as far as law could effect it, in
the early decades of the colony, to insure the uniformity of the
colonists with regard to loyalty to the principles of church and
state. The Charter of 1609 was averse to the emigration of any
"suspected to effect the superstitions of the Church of *Rome*"
and enjoined the Oath of Supremacy upon all.[10] In July, 1620,
the Virginia Company set up special machinery to insure the
administration of the Oath of Allegiance.[11] Rigorous orders were
issued, in 1634 and 1637, to officers of seaports to permit none to
pass without proof of having taken the oaths "and the like Testimony from the Minister of the Parish of his Conversation, and
Conformity to the Orders of Discipline of the Church of England."[12] In 1636, a similar order was issued against "uncon-
formable" ministers and none was permitted to pass without
sanction from the Archbishop of Canterbury and the Bishop of
London.[13]

The evidence presented makes it clear that as far as the government of England was concerned, the legal sanctions surrounding
the creation and establishment of the colony rested primarily in
the principle that the colony of Virginia was merely a territorial
extension of civil and spiritual England. The nature of the
government was to all intents and purposes an Anglican theocracy, and it is important in the understanding of later Virginia
history to see what was the machinery of this organization and
how it worked in practise.

Legal Machinery Prior To The Commonwealth Era

In instituting the policy of union of church and state, England
did not leave the functioning of the ecclesiastical element to the

---

[9] Brown: *First Republic in America*, 529–30.
[10] Stith: *Hist. of Va.*, Appendix, II, 22; Hening: *Stat. at Large*, I, 97–98.
[11] Kingsbury: *Rec. of the Va. Co.*, I, 400.
[12] Hazard: *Hist. Coll.*, I, 347, 421.
[13] *Ibid.*, I, 420; Anderson: *Colonial Church*, II, 21.

control of the colonists; but sought to guide it in its general aspects, and frequently in its specific details, by definite instructions to the governors sent to rule the colony. A review of these instructions to governors preceding the Commonwealth Era, (1649–60), indicates the source of much of the ecclesiastical legislation of the period.[14] In this legislation, we read of the appointment of places "sequestreed" for divine worship,[15] of tenants for ministers' glebes,[16] of tithes[17] and tobacco and corn for ministers' salaries,[18] of reverence due ministers,[19] of the ministers' police, civic, and ecclesiastical duties, of the oversight of citizens' behavior and morality placed on a religious basis,[20] of compulsory Sabbath church attendance,[21] and compulsory catechetical instruction.[22] What touched the daily lives of the people most, however, was the enormous power given the ministers and particularly the churchwardens to prevent "all ungodly disorders" and the power of presentation by the churchwardens to the courts.[23]

Beyond the details of this legislation, there was the general direction that there be a church uniformity "as neere as may be to the canons in England; both in substance and circumstance, and that all persons yeild readie obedience unto them under paine of censure."[24] Particular care was to be taken in respect to the conformity of ministers, not only as to their proper ordination, but also as to their procedure with regard to the liturgy.[25]

That part of the religio-civil machinery which came in time to assume the greatest importance was, however, the vestry. This lay in the fact, that, in 1642, the power of imposing a minister upon a community which had at times been assumed by the Gen-

---

[14] *Va. Mag. Hist.*, II, 154, 158; Stith: *Hist. of Va.*, 194; Hening: *Stat. at Large*, I, 113 ff.; *Va. Mag. Hist.*, II, 55, 281, 393; Perry: *Amer. Col. Church*, I, 1.
[15] Hening: *Stat. at Large*, I, 122.
[16] *Jour., H. Burg.*, July 31, 1619, 7.
[17] Hening: *Stat. at Large*, I, 144, 207.
[18] *Ibid.*, I, 124, 328.
[19] *Ibid.*, I, 124.
[20] *Jour., H. Burg.*, Aug. 2–4, 1619, 9–14.
[21] Hening: *Stat. at Large*, I, 144.
[22] *Ibid.*, I, 156; *Jour., H. Burg.*, Aug. 4, 1619, 13.
[23] Hening: *Stat. at Large*, I, 156, 227, 240, 309.
[24] *Ibid.*, I, 123; *Va. Mag. Hist.*, XXV, 348.
[25] Hening: *Stat. at Large*, I, 277, 341.

eral Court[26] was now delegated to the vestry in conjunction with the commander and county commissioners resident in the parish, or, in the case of non-residence of these officials, in the vestry alone. Upon recommendation and presentation of the minister by the vestry to the governor, admission into the office was to be made by the governor. Any complaint against the minister to the vestry, and in turn by the vestry to the governor, was to receive the consideration of the governor and council and to be met by suspension or other fitting punishment if required—removal to be left to the Grand Assembly.[27]

It is clear from an analysis of the machinery of church and state thus set up before the Commonwealth Era, that no aspect of the religious organization was without civil contact. In all that the layman or minister did in accordance with the law, he was a good citizen not only of church, but also of state; in all that he did contrary, he not only sinned against the church, but also offended against the state.

Legal Machinery During and After the Commonwealth Era

Before the elaborate machinery of government thus erected could be fairly tested, it had to suspend any attempt at vigorous operation because of the new political régime in England. The evidence indicates but a meager concern of officialdom of the Commonwealth Era with religious affairs in Virginia. It satisfied itself with a recommendation that religion be ''countenanced.''[28] From legislation passed in 1658, which proceeded to ''settle'' the church government in instructions permitting vestries, churchwardens, and parishioners to treat various matters at ''their owne ordering and disposeing from time to time as they shall think fitt,'' it is clear that religious procedure was regarded as being on a tentative basis.[29]

The restoration of the monarchy was marked by the reëstablishment of church and state, undoubtedly on the basis of instruc-

---

[26] *Va. Mag. Hist.*, XXXI, 146.
[27] Hening: *Stat. at Large*, I, 240 *ff.*
[28] *Ibid.*, I, 364, 510; Jefferson: *Notes on Va.*, 166; *Jour., H. Burg.*, Dec. 31, 1653, 128; *Va. Mag. Hist.*, XVII, 363.
[29] Hening: *Stat. at Large*, I, 433.

tions from the Council for Foreign Plantations.[30]   The instructions Governor Berkeley brought with him in 1662, after enjoining recognition of and furtherance of the welfare of the Church of England, added curiously enough that,

> . . . because Wee are willing to give all possible encouragement to persons of different persuasions in matters of Religion to transport themselves thither with their stocks, You are not to suffer any man to be molested or disquieted in the exercise of his Religion, so he be content with a quiet and peaceable enjoying it, not giving therein offence or scandall to the Government: . . .[31]

The new Virginia legislation ignored the liberal attitude here indicated and proceeded to reëstablish the Church of England on a stronger basis than ever. It provided for the reintroduction into the church of all the paraphernalia of the Established Church, with provision for annexing thinly inhabited to more thickly populated parishes, and raising subscriptions in order to assure the minister his salary of an equivalent of £80 per annum, besides his perquisites and glebe.[32] Most significant of all was the insistence upon conformity in the minister, as shown by proof to the governor of ordination by an English bishop and of subscription to the orders and constitutions of the Church of England, whereupon the governor might proceed to induct into such parish as would make presentation. Nonconformity was to be punished by suspension and silence, and, if persisted in, by expulsion from the country.[33]

The duty of the churchwardens in making presentments to the courts was again emphasized, and, in addition, they were to have regard to the physical condition of the church and the collection of the ministers' salary.[34]

As for the vestry, it was their duty in addition to the presentation of ministers, to levy upon the parish for the necessary expense to run it.[35] Very important was the constitution of the

[30] Hazard: *Hist. Coll.*, II, 607; *Va. Mag. Hist.*, III, 15; XVIII, 293–94; Burk: *Hist. of Va.*, II, 124.

[31] Anderson: *Colonial Church*, II, 549.

[32] Hening: *Stat. at Large*, II, 30, 29, 37, 45.

[33] *Ibid.*, II, 46; *cf.* 47.

[34] *Ibid.*, II, 51, 52.

[35] *Ibid.*

vestry—twelve men elected by the major part of the parish, from whose number they proceeded with the minister to elect the two churchwardens of the parish. Most significantly, once the vestry was constituted in this fashion, removals by death or departure from the parish were filled by the minister and the remaining body of the vestry. The Oaths of Allegiance and Supremacy and subscription of conformity were of course required of the vestry.[36]

If any further evidence were needed of the intention to reëstablish the government upon the basis of church and state as securely as before the Cromwell Era, it is found in the legislation enacted with regard to Sabbath observance and attendance, with its specific penalties of £20 sterling directed against the Quakers for every month's non-attendance at church, and of 200 pounds of tobacco for each time they were taken in their "unlawfull assemblyes and conventicles."[37]

Indeed, the Assembly acknowledged the object of the legislation of the year 1662 in the statement:

. . . because it is impossible to honour the king as wee should unlesse we serve and feare God, as wee ought, and that they might shew their equal care *of church and state* . . . they have set downe certain rules to be observed in the government of the church, . . .[38]

The form of government thus erected remained essentially this throughout the period to the Revolutionary War; subsequent legislation varying the detail of its operation, but not its more significant characteristics. The legislation of 1662 signified the integration of church and state.

External Forces in the Process of Disintegration

The integration of church and state was accomplished in so far as legal process could do so, but the legal machinery thus set up had not only inherent defects, which were to lead to its disintegration, but was unable, as will be made clear, to withstand the

---

[36] *Ibid.*, II, 25, 44–45.
[37] *Ibid.*, II, 48; Bancroft, G.: *Hist. of U. S.*, II, 200–01; Bruce, P. A.: *Social Life of Va., 17th C.*, 32.
[38] Hening: *Stat. at Large*, II, 43.

pounding of outside forces determined to break it down. It was these outside forces, as will appear, which made evident the inherent defects of the machinery which had been set up.

The Puritans

Reference has already been made to the charge against Sir Edwin Sandys that he was favorably inclined to Brownists and Separatists.[39]   The evidence that Sandys was favorably inclined to the Leyden Puritans is quite clear, but there is nothing to indicate in a review of the Virginia Company Records that it was inclined to set up a policy in opposition to the government.[40]   In this connection, historians point out that the Puritan struggle was one within the church itself, and that it was not until 1642 and the passage of the Act of Uniformity that the implication of "dissenter" could be ascribed to the term Puritan.[41]   As far as the Company was concerned, it protected itself by setting up machinery for the administration of the Oath of Allegiance.[42] It would therefore be without significance to determine the number of Puritans who came into the colony in its early days,[43] or whether the first ministers had Puritan leanings,[44] where their first settlements were,[45] or whether the small band who came in 1619 had increased to more than a thousand in 1638,[46] if it were not for certain Virginia legislation in 1630, 1632, 1643, and 1647, enforcing conformity with the Church of England.[47]   Though it has previously been shown that legislation of this kind was in line with the basic governmental policy of the colony, it is generally held that the legislation of 1643 and 1647 was directed against the Puritans. The circumstances, to which the legislation of 1643

---

[39] See p. 38; Cheyney: *European Background of Amer. Hist.*, 222.

[40] *Va. Mag. Hist.*, XXIX, 235 *ff.*; Beard, C. A., & M. R.: *Rise Amer. Civilization*, I, 46–47; for Sandys' political and religious views, see Gayley, C. M.: *Shakespeare and Founders of Liberty in America*, 83–85.

[41] McIlwaine, H. R.: *Struggle of Prot. Dissenters*, 14–15; Bruce: *Inst. Hist. of Va.*, I, 252.

[42] See p. 39.

[43] Beverley: *Hist. of Va.*, 50.

[44] Neill: *Eng. Coloniz. of Amer.*, 278 *ff.*; Bruce: *Inst. Hist. of Va.*, I, 252; Fiske, J.: *Old Va.*, I, 301.

[45] *Ibid.*, 302.

[46] *Ibid.*, 301.

[47] Hening: *Stat. at Large*, I, 149, 155, 277, 341.

and 1647 is attributed, have appealed to the fancy of historians. A request for missionaries from Puritan New England made in 1642, was followed by a visitation interrupted by the Indian Massacre of April, 1644. This event, which was regarded by New England as retribution upon the hostile Virginia government, so wrought upon Governor Berkeley's chaplain, Rev. Thomas Harrison, that he joined the Puritans. The subsequent favor of the Cromwell government to Harrison availed him and the Puritans little against the determined resistance of the colonial government, and most of the Puritans undoubtedly followed the example of those who in 1649–51 began an exodus to Maryland.[48]

The chief significance of the history of the Puritans in Virginia lay in the determination of the government to make the boast of its conformity and its allegiance to the principles underlying the government no merely idle display of words, but a definite realization. As Bancroft indicates, the development of Puritanism in England had given it a significance hostile to English political philosophy: "to tolerate Puritanism was to nurse a republican party."[49]

The Catholics

The mighty invectives hurled against papists and popery in the sermons and literary propaganda which featured the creation of the colony, make all the more interesting a study of the extent to which Catholicism was kept from the colony.

The efforts made by the Virginia Company and the government to keep all those not loyal to English principles of church and state out of the colony have been indicated in the discussion of the Puritans. In the case of the Catholics, taking the Oath of Allegiance was contrary to papal injunction.[50] Though some Catholics may not have scrupled to take the oath and come to Vir-

---

[48] Latané, J. H.: *Early Relation Between Md. & Va.*, 31 *ff.*; *Va. Mag. Hist.*, IV, 342–48, 469 *ff.*; V, 106–08, 228–32; Randall, D. R.: *Puritan Colony in Md.*, 19–22; Claiborne, J. H.: *Wm. Claiborne of Va.*, 116; Hammond, J.: *Leah and Rachel*, in Force's *Tracts*, III, 22.

[49] Bancroft: *Hist. of U. S.*, I, 207; for a discussion of English political philosophy as represented in Arminianism and Puritanism, see Campbell: *Puritan in Holl., Eng., and America*, II, 238, 301 *ff.*

[50] Brown: *First Republic in America*, 12; *cf.* Stratemeier, G. B.: *Thomas Cornwaleys*, 23–24.

ginia, there is no official evidence of their presence. It was not until the arrival of Lord Baltimore, in 1629, that we find expression of the official attitude toward Catholicism. Lord Baltimore's refusal to take the Oaths of Allegiance and Supremacy tendered him, excluded him from Virginia. The Council justified their act of exclusion in a letter to the Lords of the Privy Council on the basis of loyalty, and declared that among all its blessings,

. . . there is none whereby it hath beene made more happy than in the freedome of our Religion which wee have enjoyed, and that noe papists have beene suffered to settle there aboard amongst us; the continuance whereof wee most humbly implore from his most sacred Majestie, . . . [51]

The most significant outcome of Lord Baltimore's visit was the grant of the Maryland Charter to the second Lord Baltimore in 1632;[52] a grant in its essence contrary to the policy which actuated the creation of Virginia.[53] This expropriation of Virginia territory served to intensify Virginian intolerance of Catholicism; and resentment against Maryland could be softened, according to Governor Harvey, neither by the obligations of Christianity nor his Majesty's commands.[54] For two decades or more the attempt to hold the trading post of Kent Island was made the basis of a religious and commercial war.[55] Furthermore, Virginia resentment in 1641 and 1643 did not content itself with general legislation regarding conformity,[56] but singled out popish recusants for special penalties.[57]

The anomaly presented in the grant to Maryland was soon to be repeated on a smaller scale within Virginia itself. About the year 1650, there came to Virginia, a Catholic family by the name of Brent who settled on the Virginia side of the Potomac. So discreet was their conduct that in 1668, Captain Giles Brent received a testimonial from the Stafford County Court that, in

---

[51] *Va. Mag. Hist.*, VII, 373–74.

[52] *Virginia and Maryland, Or, The Lord Baltamore's printed Case*, in Force's *Tracts*, II; Stratemeier: *Thomas Cornwaleys*, 7.

[53] *Cf. Ibid.*, 12–13; Anderson: *Colonial Church*, II, 117.

[54] *Va. Mag. Hist.*, VIII, 161.

[55] Latané: *Early Relations Between Md. and Va.*, 8, 11; Burk: *Hist. of Va.*, II, 113; Claiborne: *Wm. Claiborne of Va.*, 134; Stratemeier: *Thomas Cornwaleys*, 45.

[56] *Cf.* Hening: *Stat. at Large*, I, 123, 155.

[57] *Va. Mag. Hist.*, IX, 56, Hening: *Stat. at Large*, I, 268.

their twenty-one years' experience of him, he had seduced no one to the Catholic religion.[58]   Whether on this basis, or because in the course of time they had acquired an interest by purchase of a large territory in what is now Prince William County, which might serve as a defence against Indian depredations and incursions,[59] they received from King James II, in 1687, on behalf of themselves and settlers on their tract of land, the right to "the free exercise of their Religion without being prosecuted or molested upon any penall laws or other account for the same."[60] This dispensation was undoubtedly due to the Catholic sympathies of King James II, and an echo of his Declaration of Indulgence, 1687, which had been recognized in Virginia, only by a proclamation of the governor, Lord Howard of Effingham, who was a Catholic.[61]   There is no evidence that a previous instruction of the King to the governor, in 1685, directing him "to permit a liberty of conscience to all persons," received specific recognition in legislation.[62]   The action of Effingham in dispensing with the Oaths of Allegiance and Supremacy and admitting as councillors men reputed to be Catholics, caused unfavorable comment and resentment against the King and his governor.[63] The accession of William III and Queen Mary was hailed by Virginians with an address to the throne, expressive of their joy in "rescueing us our Religion, lawes and Liberties from the Dangers & feares wee were ready to Sinke under."[64]   This joy was undoubtedly due to the fact that the Act of Toleration (1689) did not extend to Catholics.[65]

---

[58] *Va. Mag. Hist.*, VIII, 239, XXX, 35; *cf.* Stratemeier: *Thomas Cornwaleys*, 24, regarding instructions to Catholics by Cecilius Calvert, to be discreet.

[59] *Va. Mag. Hist.*, II, 272–75.

[60] *Ibid.*, XVII, 308–10; *Tyler's Quart.*, V, 166, implies that the basis for this grant was the proposed settlement of French Huguenots on this tract; a letter of April 1, 1689, *Va. Mag. Hist.*, II, 272–75, indicates indifference as to whether the tract is settled by Catholics or Huguenots; *cf.* also *Ibid.*, II, 370–73.

[61] Cheyney: *A Short Hist. of Eng.*, 503; Bruce: *Inst. Hist. of Va.*, I, 244.

[62] Wertenbaker, T. J.: *Va. Under the Stuarts*, 255.

[63] *Ibid.*, 256; *cf. Va. Mag. Hist.*, VI, 389 *ff.*, 394; XX, 3 *ff.*; Burk: *Hist. of Va.*, II, 299; Wise, J. C.: *Eastern Shore*, 243; for a favorable view of Effingham, see Osgood, H. L.: *Amer. Colonies in the 17th C.*, III, 302.

[64] *Jour., H. Burg.*, May 21, 1691, 370.

[65] Cheyney: *A Short Hist. of Eng.*, 512.

The instructions to governors in the subsequent period which barred papists from any indulgence relieved Virginians somewhat from their fear of Catholicism.[66]   Events, which at times threatened a Catholic invasion of England from France and Spain, were noticed in vigorous addresses of sympathy to England, full of contempt and scorn for the "perfidious Casuistry" of popery.[67]   The attitude toward Catholicism was such that in the course of time, any papists that may have existed in Virginia excelled the Brents in discreetness;[68] for, in 1755, when a shipment of over a thousand Catholic French Acadians came to Virginia, Governor Dinwiddie declared their arrival "has occasion'd a gen'l discontent among the People, as we had no Roman Catholicks here before."[69]   The persuasions of Dinwiddie yielded them only a temporary refuge.   In the spring of 1756, the Assembly, contending that the visitors were tampering with the negroes and that they would soon find their way to the French and Indians on the frontier, declared their unwillingness to give a penny for their further support in Virginia; but any required amount to transport them elsewhere, preferably to Great Britain.   An act for this purpose was accordingly passed.[70]   The perturbation of the government further expressed itself in "An Act for disarming Papists, and reputed Papists, refusing to take the oaths to the government."[71]   In an address to the General Assembly, Governor Dinwiddie contrasted protestant and papist government and asked them to consider,

... whether these Colonies are still to remain under the happy Constitution of *Great-Britain*, or become subject to the Arbitrary Power of a despotic Prince; if under the former, you are safe in your Lives, Religion, Liberties and Estates; if to the Latter (which Heaven avert) reflect, I beseech you, on the dreadful Change, on the sad Necessity of giving up your Liberty for Slavery, the purest Religion for the grossest Idolatry and Superstition,

---

66 *Va. Mag. Hist.*, XX, 226 *ff.*; XXI, 225–29.
67 *Jour., H. Burg.*, Oct. 19, 1696, 89; Feb. 20, 1745, 153; *cf. Jour., Va. Council*, II, Sept. 5, 1744, 933–34; Feb. 21, 1745, 963–64.
68 See p. 46.
69 Dinwiddie: *Records*, II, 347.
70 *Ibid.*, II, 379, 408, 410; *Jour., H. Burg.*, Mar. 29, 1756, 342–45; April 7, 1756, 357–58; Hening: *Stat. at Large*, VII, 39; *Va. Mag. Hist.*, VI, 386 *ff.*
71 *Jour., H. Burg.*, May 1, 1756, 391; Hening: *Stat. at Large*, VII, 35–39.

the legal and mild Government of a Protestant King, for the arbitrary Exactions, and heavy Opressions of a Popish Tyrant.[72]

The fortunes of war saved Virginia from the Popish tyrant, but the scorn for papists lingered on. A writer in the *Virginia Gazette,* in 1767, in "A Comparison between the present Age and former Ages" says:

. . . To infer the truth of a religion from the number of its professors is falsely to conclude the fineness of the cloth from the largeness of the measure. How vain and ridiculous is it in the Papists, who think this argument of universality so invincible a proof of the truth of their religion? If multitude be an argument that men are in the right, in vain then hath the scripture said "Thou shalt not follow a multitude to do evil."[73]

By the close of the colonial period, popery merely served to furnish an evening's diversion for the élite. Fithian writes:

. . . So soon as we rose from supper, the Company formed into a semicircle round the fire, & Mr. Lee, by the voice of the Company was chosen *Pope,* . . . and the rest of the company were appointed Friars, in the Play call'd "break the Pope's neck"—Here we had great Diversion in the respective Judgments upon offenders. . . .[74]

In the history of church and state in Virginia, Catholicism is chiefly interesting for the apparent success of the government in practically suppressing it.[75] This was due to a number of favoring circumstances. In Maryland, Catholicism had acquired a location under congenial auspices. Events abroad, which rendered Catholicism synonymous with opposition not only to the ecclesiastical but also to the civil aspects of the established government, contributed on the one hand to the passivity of Catholicism, and, on the other, to the watchfulness of the colony. Dissent as represented in Catholicism was significant in contributing to a greater emphasis on uniformity from its legal aspects.

---

[72] *Jour., H. Burg.,* Sept. 20, 1756, 401–02; Dinwiddie: *Records,* II, 514–15.
[73] *Va. Gazette,* Dec. 3, 1767.
[74] Fithian, P. V.: *Journal & Letters,* 65.
[75] Humphrey, E. F.: *Nationalism and Religion,* 252; Humphrey quotes Rev. John Carroll, (based on Shea, J. G.: *Life and Times Rev. John Carroll,* II, 257) that there were 15,800 Catholics in Maryland, and 200 in Virginia, in 1785.

The Huguenots

The need for populating the forests and hills of Virginia as a barrier against the French and Indians, the desire to open up Virginia territory from an economic standpoint, urged as early as 1651 by Virginia merchants,[76] influenced the attitude of the leading men of the colony and so the policy of the government into admitting dissenters.   The failure of the Earl of Arlington and Lord Culpepper to hold the extensive grant made to them in 1673,[77] threw upon the market, in 1684, a large territory for speculation.[78]

William Fitzhugh, who was interested in developing the tract of 30,000 acres acquired by George Brent and his partners, made a serious effort to obtain as settlers the French Protestants whom the revocation of the Edict of Nantes, in 1685, had thrown on the charity of England.[79]   The Huguenots, overwhelmed by the official and personal acts of courtesy and kindness of Protestant England, made an effort to overlook certain differences in ritual and liturgy.[80]   There was undoubtedly an effort, too, on the part of the English to persuade the visitors to overlook these differences and to conform to the church of England.[81]   By 1699, the King was

> . . . pleased to order that as a Charitable assistance to the Petitioners in their undertaking, allowances be made . . . for their transportation, & for the building a Church & for a competent number of Bibles, common Prayer books, & other books of devotion, as also for the necessary accomodation for lodging of 2 Ministers who are to accompany them, . . .[82]

In the years 1699 and 1700, about eight hundred of them arrived in Virginia and were welcomed with substantial evidences of official favor.[83]   Governor Nicholson called upon all Christian people to further by ''Charitable and Christianlike acts'' the

---

[76] See p. 23.
[77] Hening: *Stat. at Large*, II, 569 *ff*.
[78] *Va. Mag. Hist.*, XXXII, 192 *ff*.
[79] *Tyler's Quart.*, V, 164; *Va. Mag. Hist.*, I, 408.
[80] Baird, C. W.: *Huguenot Emigration*, II, 156 *ff*., 161.
[81] *Ibid.*, II, 162.
[82] Perry: *Amer. Col. Church*, I, 114.
[83] Beverley: *Hist. of Va.*, 228.

"Pious Charity of his most Sacred Maj'tie."[84]   Their principal settlement was at Manakin Town, 20 miles above Richmond, where a tract of 10,000 acres was given them.[85]   The Assembly passed an act granting immediate citizenship, the right to conduct worship under their French ministers, and exemption from the payment of public and county levies for seven years, a privilege extended in 1706 to December, 1708.[86]   They immediately constituted themselves a parish and proceeded to set up the machinery of the Established Church, though retaining the French language.[87]   There were, however, rumors in 1702, that the French were not conforming to the liturgy of the Anglican Church, so that the Governor felt impelled to recommend to Commissary Blair, that he "take care that the French Ministers at Manican Town conforme themselves to the Liturgy of the Church of England."[88]

Although the Huguenots conformed themselves to the extent of setting up the machinery of the Established Church, and later showed a predisposition to favor the use of the English language and the Anglican liturgy,[89] it must be remembered that in their origin they represented a form of Protestantism not in conformity with that church, and, in that sense they were dissenters. The success of the government in settling them at a strategic point for extending the lines of population, set, as will appear, a precedent in the government's policy toward dissenters.[90]

The German Protestants

The anxiety to populate the country to serve as an Indian barrier and stimulus to economic prosperity, evident in the admission of the Huguenots was destined, as will be made clear, to have serious consequences for the policy of union of church and state.

[84] Brock, R. A.: *Huguenot Emigration*, 61; McIlwaine: *Exec. Jour., Council Col. Va.*, II, 123, 127–28.
[85] *Ibid.*, II, 101, 116, 369, 400.
[86] Hening: *Stat. at Large*, III, 201; *Jour., Va. Council*, I, 464; *Va. Mag. Hist.*, XI, 289 *ff.*; Brock, *Huguenot Emigration*, ix.
[87] *Ibid.*, 69.
[88] McIlwaine: *Exec. Jour., Council Col. Va.*, II, 261.
[89] Brock: *Huguenot Emigration*, 112.
[90] McIlwaine: *Struggle of Protestant Dissenters*, 39.

The precedent set in the case of the Huguenots was followed by an invitation to the Protestant Germans driven from the Palatinate. In the absence of their leader, they were settled by order of the Virginia Executive Council, in April, 1714, in territory above the falls of the Rappahannock River, near Fredericksburg, forming a northern German frontier to the Huguenot southern.[91]

At the subsequent session of the Assembly, an address of the House of Burgesses to Governor Spotswood indicated that the Germans were "heartily" welcome; and as an evidence of official favor they were granted a seven years' exemption from levies.[92] The sincerity of Governor Spotswood in securing the frontiers at Germanna and the Indian trading-post, Christ Anna, as Indian barriers,[93] began to be questioned in view of his zeal for associating his own commercial ventures with the territory opened.[94] Whether because developing the governor's iron mines did not appeal to the Germans as a means of livelihood,[95] or because of difficulties regarding adjustment of their transporation expenses,[96] or because the governor refused them titles to their land,[97] an exodus from Germanna soon began, resulting in its abandonment.

What is of special interest in this settlement, is the question of the religious faith of these Germans. John Fontaine who visited them in 1715 noted in his diary:

. . . They go to prayer constantly once a day, and have two sermons on Sunday. We went to hear them perform their service, which was done in their own language, which we did not understand: but they seemed to be very devout and sang the psalms well.[98]

91 McIlwaine: *Exec. Jour., Council Col. Va.*, III, 371–72; *Va. Mag. Hist.*, XIII, 362; McIlwaine: *Struggle of Prot. Dissenters*, 37; Brumbaugh, G. M.: *Genealogy Of The Brumbach Families*, 245–51.
92 *Jour., H. Burg.*, Nov. 24, 1714, 90; Dec. 10, 1714, 101; Dec. 18, 1714, 110; cf. McIlwaine: *Exec. Jour., Council Col. Va.*, III, 372.
93 *Va. Mag. Hist.*, XIII, 362.
94 At Germanna, where the Germans were settled, the governor sought to use them in the development of his iron mines; "Animadversions on a Paper Entituled Virginia Addresses, Printed in Philadelphia," *Va. Mag. Hist.*, XXII, 410 *ff.*, XXIII, 66 *ff.*; cf. Jones: *Present State of Va.*, 58–59.
95 *Va. Mag. Hist.*, III, 190.
96 *Ibid.*, XII, 350.
97 *South Atlant. Quart.*, IX, 149.
98 Groome, H. C.: *Fauquier During the Proprietorship*, 120–21.

By 1719, there is evidence that they were not quite happy in their relationship to the governor. They are planning to send a mission abroad to obtain a minister and "do humbly ask if it is proper to desire the governor to give us an attestation & passport to witness that we are inhabitants here."[99] This mission brought a memorial to the Society for propagating the Gospel in which they refer to their wish to obtain a young German minister to assist their present minister, Mr. Haeger, now about seventy-five years old. This minister they wish ordained by the Bishop of London, and that he bring over the Liturgy of the Church of England, translated into High Dutch. They hope for the countenance and assistance of the English Bishops and the "venerable society" in granting "their usual allowance for the support of a Minister, and if it may be so, contribute something towards the building of their church."[100] The Society's policy limited its activities in Virginia, and the only fruit of this memorial was the receipt of "twenty-five copies of the book of common prayer, printed in German."[101]

This attempt at conformity with the Established Church seems to have resulted in failure. By 1721, the Germans began to divide themselves into a settlement of Reformed Lutherans at Germantown near the Little Fork of the Rapahannock and of Lutherans who moved into the present Madison County.[102] In 1730, the community at Germantown petitioned the Assembly, setting forth that

... they have for several Years maintain'd a Minister of their own Nation and yet have lately been taxed for the paying the Salary of the Parson of the Parish in which the said Town lies, And praying to be Exempted from that Tax during the life of Mr. Hæger their said Minister.[103]

---

[99] *Va. Mag. Hist.*, VI, 385–86.

[100] Perry: *Amer. Col. Church*, I, 247–48—Perry gives minister's name as Hœger; Slaughter, P.: *Geneal. and Hist. Notes on Culpeper County*, 44–45.

[101] Groome: *Fauquier During the Proprietorship*, 125; cf. *Va. Mag. Hist.*, XXII, 250–51.

[102] *South. Atlant. Quart.*, IX, 149; Wm. J. Hinke in *Va. Mag. Hist.*, XIV, 136, declares that the 1714 settlement consisted of 12 German Reformed families—followed in 1717 by 20 German Lutheran families and in 1719 by 40 German families—denomination not indicated; McIlwaine: *Exec. Jour., Council Col. Va.*, III, 371, gives the number coming in 1714, as 42 men, women, and children.

[103] *Jour., H. Burg.*, May 26, 1730, 62–63.

This petition after due consideration was granted and a law passed exempting them from the payment of parish levies.[104] If the Mr. Haeger of 1730 was the Mr. Haeger of 1719, and in his late 80's, it is very likely that the old modes of religious faith persisted. Yet the Assembly granted an exemption from parish levies to what would seem to have been, undoubtedly, a dissenting congregation. Perhaps their former expression of willingness to conform, and the use of their native language protected the Germans from any rigorous demands of conformity.

The Lutherans who moved from the Germanna settlement went west and in the Robinson River Valley of Madison County established themselves as the Hebron Lutheran Congregation.[105] By 1730, some had continued westward into the Shenandoah Valley.[106] A report of their pastor, Rev. John Caspar Stoever, Sr., 1737, issued as a plea to their Christian friends in Europe for assistance in continuing their worship, and for building a church and school, and support of their ministers, presupposes a continuation of their inherited faith.[107] The evidence indicates, however, that as far as official Virginia was concerned, there was no molestation of the worship of these formerly so heartily welcomed Germans. Indeed, to them the government was obligated for assistance in opening up mountainous western Virginia and in holding it against the Indians and French.

It would seem, that it was not until the Moravian missionaries from Pennsylvania came through in the forties, that the meaning of dissent from the Established Church came home to the Germans. Perhaps emboldened by the plea in Colonel Wm. Byrd's *Neu-gefundenes Eden* (1737), for the Germans and Swiss to settle in Virginia, the Moravians came into the country and established contact with those who spoke a similar language.[108] The movements of those who came in 1743 and 1744 seem to have been without incident.[109] In 1747, they found that preachers travel-

---

104 *Ibid.*, July 9, 1730, 10–11; *Jour., Va. Council*, II, June 19, 1730, 765; Hening: *Stat. at Large*, IV, 306.
105 *Va. Mag. Hist.* XIV, 136–37; Yowell, C. L.: *Hist. Madison Co.*, 105.
106 *Va. Mag. Hist.*, XIII, 120–23; XIV, 147 *ff*.
107 *Ibid.*
108 Byrd, Wm.: *Neu-gefundenes Eden*; *Va. Mag. Hist.*, XI, 381.
109 *Ibid.*, 370 *ff*.

ing without a passport from England were liable to arrest.[110]
In 1748, they were informed of Governor Gooch's proclamation
of 1747, which strictly required

. . . all Magistrates and Officers to discourage and prohibit as far as legally
they can all Itinerant Preachers, whether New Lights, Moravians, or Methodists, from teaching, preaching, or holding any meetings in this Colony.[111]

The missionaries attempted to counter with the Act of Parliament passed in their favor.[112]

It would seem that as long as the Germans lived quietly in
their settlements, establishing homes and contributing to the
wealth of the colony, they were not molested. This is confirmed
in a study of the history of the Mennonite group in Virginia.
Though they appear to have come into Page County in the early
thirties of the 18th century,[113] there is no notice of them in the
Assembly records until 1769 when a petition is received praying
exemption from penalties for declining military duty.[114] In
1775, they petitioned that they might receive the indulgence of
"affirming," already granted the Quakers.[115]

The history of the Germans shows that while they may have
been grieved in spirit and pocket because of matters of conscience, that, on the whole, they submitted passively enough, living their lives quietly and arousing but little attention of the
government.

The Quakers

The closing years of the Commonwealth Era saw the arrival in
Virginia of the first Quaker missionaries. Their presence in
Northampton County (1657–60) attracted sufficient attention to
incur various forms of prosecution, probably on the principle

---

110 *Ibid.*, XII, 60.
111 *Ibid.*, XI, 228; *cf.* also *Jour., Va. Council*, II, Mar. 31, 1747, 995–96—
Governor Gooch's remarks regarding burning of the Capitol: "It is with
Hearts full of the most unfeigned Concern, that we observe a Spirit of
Enthusiasm introduced among the People by Itinerant Preachers; A Spirit,
more dangerous to the Common Welfare, than the furious Element, which
laid the Royal Edifice in Ashes."
112 *Va. Mag. Hist.*, XII, 64, *cf.* 67.
113 *History of the Mennonite Conference of Va.*, 12.
114 *Jour., H. Burg.*, Nov. 14, 1769, 256.
115 *Ibid.*, June 12, 1775, 217.

enunciated by a court of a little later period, that "There is no toleration for wicked consciences."[116]   In 1660, an act was passed for their complete suppression on the basis that their views were inimical to religion, law, and "all bonds of civil societie."[117]   This act was followed, in 1662, by the enactment of a statute of Elizabeth's reign which imposed a fine for every month's absence from Sabbath church attendance of £20 sterling, and of 200 pounds of tobacco for each time they were taken "in unlawfull assemblyes and conventicles," insolvency in any individual case to be borne by the rest.[118]   The next year, an act for "prohibiting the unlawfull assembling of Quakers" was directed against the assembling of five or more persons, of the age of sixteen or above, for the purpose of religious worship not authorized by law; a third conviction of the offence to result in banishment.[119]   In addition, penalties were imposed on masters of ships bringing them in, and upon residents who should venture to entertain Quakers to teach or preach.   Half of the fine was to go to the informer and half to the parish in which the offence took place.

A particular effort was made in accordance with this legislation to suppress the Quakers in that part of Accomac County which has since become part of Maryland; an attempt made difficult according to charges made to England by the toleration of that Colony.[120]   Care, too, seems to have been taken in maintaining the religious purity of the Assembly.   The charge that Mr. John Porter, burgess for Lower Norfolk was "well affected" to the Quakers was put to the touchstone of the Oaths of Allegiance and

[116] Bancroft: *Hist. of U. S.*, II, 201; Weeks, S. B.: *Southern Quakers and Slavery*, 13 *ff.*; Bruce: *Inst. Hist. of Va.*, I, 222; Wise: *Eastern Shore*, 155 *ff.*; *Va. Mag. Hist.*, V. 41; VIII, 166; Meade: *Old Churches, Ministers and Families*, I, 427; Stillé, C. J.: *Life and Times of John Dickinson*, 12, Dickinson family, Quakers, came to Virginia, 1654; Bell, J. P. P.: *Our Quaker Friends*, 176.
[117] Hening: *Stat. at Large*, I, 532.
[118] *Ibid.*, II, 48.
[119] *Ibid.*, 180–83.
[120] Neill: *Va. Carolorum*, 311; *Va. Mag. Hist.*, XIX, 173 *ff.*; Weeks: *Southern Quakers and Slavery*, 29.

Supremacy, and upon his refusal to take them, the charge was held sustained and he was dismissed.[121]

Neither prosecution nor persecution diminished the missionary zeal of the Quakers; and, in 1672, George Fox, the founder, and William Edmundson, their famous preacher, visited Virginia.[122] The peevishness and brittle temper of the governor did not interfere with their proselyting success.[123]   Prosecution, however, continued and we read of a long array of charges in 1682 against "John Pleasants and Jane Tucker als Larcome als Pleasants (quakers)."[124]

From a legal standpoint, the Declaration of Indulgence, 1687, should have brought some amelioration, and the fact that "A Bill for repealing the act prohibiting the vnlawful assembling of *Quakers*," appeared in the House of Burgesses, may have inspired for a short time such hope.[125]   This bill seems to have failed in Council.[126]   The Quakers, with other dissenters, came under the Toleration Act passed by Parliament in 1689.   Upon taking the Oaths of Allegiance and Supremacy with a declaration against transubstantiation, permission was given to worship in meeting houses of their own, if legally registered.   Their ministers were to be licensed to preach under certain regulations. Quakers upon making a declaration of fidelity to the government and subscribing a certain declaration of faith need not take the regular oaths.[127]   There was, however, no immediate recognition of the Toleration Act in Virginia law.   In February, 1691, a critical situation, from the Virginia standpoint, arose in the attitude of the inhabitants of Pennsylvania, who declared they would have no quarrel with the French and Indians.   The Virginia

---

[121] *Ibid.*, 23; Burk: *Hist. of Va.*, II, 131–32; Hening: *Stat. at Large*, II, 198.

[122] Weeks: *Southern Quakers and Slavery*, 29–30; Fiske: *Old Va.*, II, 57.

[123] *Ibid.*; Neill: *Va. Carolorum*, 339–41; Weeks: *Southern Quakers and Slavery*, 30.

[124] *Va. Mag. Hist.*, XVI, 218; *Edward Pleasants Valentine Papers*, II, 1068.

[125] *Jour., H. Burg.*, May 7, 1688, 308; May 8, 1688, 310; May 10, 1688, 318.

[126] *Cf. Tyler's Quart.*, II, 271.

[127] Gee, H., & Hardy, W. J.: *Documents Eng. Church Hist.*, 654–64; McIlwaine: *Struggle of Prot. Dissenters*, 28–29.

Council decided then to order the justices of the peace, sheriffs, and other officers of the colony to see to it:

> . . . that none of the persons usually Called Quakers doe presume to meete at any place whatsoever without doeing and performing what by the before recited Act of Parliament is required and Comanded, upon penalty of being prosecuted, and suffering such paines and penalties as by the said Act are to be Inflicted on those who doe not Comply there with.[128]

This recognition of the Toleration Act, the first so far as known, is of interest because of the manner in which it was used, in the frank recognition that the order was one for "restraining the Meeting of the Quakers."[129]   The Quakers seem to have taken steps almost immediately to comply with this order, for under date of April 1, 1692, there is a record that "Several Quakers petition for Places to be appointed for their meeting."[130]

The Quakers, having become strong in Henrico County, returned John Pleasants as a member of the House of Burgesses, but he was tendered "ye oath prescribed by act of Parliament instead of the Oathes of Allegiance, & supremacy" and also the oath of Burgess, and his religious scruples forbidding, his place was declared vacant.[131]   It would appear that the Act of Toleration was favored as an instrument of restraint rather than as one of privilege; for apparently neither the right of declaration permitted by that Act, nor the right of affirmation permitted by an act of Parliament in 1696, was specifically recognized in law in Virginia as far as present evidence would indicate, until 1705.[132]

Bruton parish in 1694 ordered its churchwardens to demand and receive from Quakers the parish dues in arrears.[133]   In 1696,

128 McIlwaine: *Exec. Jour., Council Col. Va.*, I, 161; the act referred to is the Toleration Act; *cf. Ibid.*, 167, for the order as approved.

129 *Ibid.*, 167; the publication of this information in *Exec. Jour., Council Col. Va.*, throws a new light upon the reference to the act in Hening: *Stat. at Large*, III, 171; this recognition did not amount to law, as the order was passed by the Executive Council, Feb. 20, 1691, while the Assembly was not in session from May, 1688, to April 16, 1691, see *Jour., Va. Council*, I, vii; Campbell: *Hist. of Va.*, 346.

130 McIlwaine: *Exec. Jour., Council Col. Va.*, I, 527; *Va. Mag. Hist.*, XX, 118; *cf. Edward Pleasants Valentine Papers*, II, 1071.

131 *Jour., H. Burg.*, 412–13, Mar. 3, 1693; *Wm. & Mary Coll. Quart.*, XXIV, 265, V, 138.

132 See p. 65; Hening: *Stat. at Large*, III, 298; McIlwaine: *Struggle of Prot. Dissenters*, 29–30; *Stat. of the Realm*, VII, 152.

133 Goodwin, W. A. R.: *Hist. Sketch Bruton Church*, 19.

Quakers began the long array of petitions against fines for failing to appear at military musters.[134]   Three years later, there is a note in the *Executive Journals of the Virginia Council*, that "divers Complaints have been made of the evill and Seditious practices used in Severall parts of the Country, by the people, called Quakers," and Commissary Blair is requested to consider "the most proper methods for preventing the like for the future."[135]

It was not until 1699, that the Act of Toleration was recognized, rather *sub rosa*, by the Virginia Assembly in its applicability to all dissenters and attendance at their own services legalized for all dissenters.[136]   The chief amelioration for the Quakers in the Act of Toleration lay in the permission to build meeting houses and hold meetings and in their license to preach; they had no military exemption and were compelled to pay their share of parish dues, upon pain of fine or imprisonment.[137]   Their petitions for redress in these points were futile, and it was practically on this basis of a limited toleration that the Quakers remained until the Revolutionary War.[138]

In the 1720's and 1730's, Quakers were quite strong in the territory south of the James River, particularly in Nansemond County, a county whose poor tobacco made it little pleasing to the clergymen of the Establishment.[139]

---

[134] *Jour., H. Burg.*, Oct. 7, 1696, 76–78; it may be that Quaker petitions referred to in *Ibid.*, April 24, 1691, 342, Mar. 20, 1693, 433, refer to the same subject.

[135] McIlwaine: *Exec. Jour., Council Col. Va.*, I, 441.

[136] See p. 65; Hening: *Stat. at Large*, III, 170–71; McIlwaine: *Struggle of Prot. Dissenters*, 29; This recognition did not extend to the "affirmation" aspect of the Act of Toleration. Note, however, a proclamation of Gov. Spotswood, dated as late as May 14, 1718, annulling the act of 1663 prohibiting the unlawful assembling of Quakers; given from York County Records, *Tyler's Quart.*, II, 271; McIlwaine: *Exec. Jour., Council Col. Va.*, III, 469, 611; for prosecution of a Quaker, in 1712, for reflecting on the Church of England, see *Ibid.*, 299; *cf. Wm. & Mary Coll. Quart.*, V, 159.

[137] *Cf.* Goodwin: *Hist. Sketch Bruton Church*, 20; McIlwaine: *Struggle of Prot. Dissenters*, 34; payment of tithes was confirmed as compulsory by *Stat. of the Realm*, VII, 152, which confirmed affirmation, see p. 58.

[138] *Jour., H. Burg.*, Feb. 5, 1727, 8; Feb. 6, 1727, 9; Nov. 15, 1738, 341; Appendix, Nov. 14, 1738, 445; *Va. Mag. Hist.*, XXXII, 244; *cf. Edward Pleasants Valentine Papers* II, 1196.

[139] Jones: *Present State Va.*, 23–24; *cf.* McIlwaine: *Struggle of Prot. Dissenters*, 28; Wynne: *Hist. of the Dividing Line*, I, 42.

The Quakers were not content to confine themselves to this territory alone. With the Act of Toleration, conditions had somewhat changed and a boon they could not have obtained before it, was now freely granted; perhaps all the more so, in that it concerned the populating of the then western frontier and what is now northwestern Virginia. In 1732, Alexander Ross and others obtained from the Governor and Council, a grant of 100,000 acres in the neighborhood of Opequon Creek, a branch of the Potomac, in what is now Frederick County.[140] Thus began the filtering in of Quakers into the Upper Shenandoah Valley.[141] In 1733, Quakers crossed the Potomac into what are now Loudoun and Fairfax Counties.[142]

As the Quakers began to come in larger numbers, they secured, at times, exemption from personal appearance at military muster "by sending a Man in their stead."[143] No modification with respect to parish levy was obtained; particularly interesting is the petition of 1738 for parish levy exemption which is based on the similar favor to German Protestants[144] and the fact that they are not numerous.[145] Taking up the implication that "hypocritical Pretenders" to Quakerism would attempt to escape the levy, they say,

. . . we shall hold ourselves under Obligation, to detect them; so as the Government shall not be imposed on, nor Your Favor any ways abused: And further be pleased to know, it is for Tender Conscience Sake, and not wilfully or obstinately we have hitherto suffered, having sustained more than Treble Damages, for our Conscientious Refusal: . . .[146]

This petition received publicity in the *Virginia Gazette* of November 10–17, 1738; a favor which moved a writer, the following week, to ask the editor to print his "Instructions how to make a perfect Quaker," a composition which if indicative of the attitude of very many Virginians would explain the failure

---

140 *W. Va. Hist. Mag. Quart.*, III, 55; Bell: *Our Quaker Friends*, 193.
141 *Ibid.*; Cartmell, T. K.: *Shenandoah Valley Pioneers*, 211 *ff.*; *Va. Mag. Hist.*, XIII, 127.
142 *Ibid.*, 289.
143 *Cf. Jour.*, H. Burg., Sept. 3, 1734, 186–87; Aug. 16 & 23, 1736, 256, 268.
144 See p. 52, 54.
145 *Jour.*, H. Burg., Vol. 1727–40, xi, 445.
146 *Ibid.*; *Wm. & Mary Coll. Quart.*, XIV, 23–24.

of the petition.[147] There is evidence, however, that Quakers, if not favored to the extent of receiving a tender regard for their pockets, were nevertheless countenanced by high minded men presumably in high places. Rev. Anthony Gavin, of St. James parish, Goochland County, writes the Bishop of London, in 1738, that he has baptized fifteen Quakers; however, he struggles "with many difficulties from Quakers who are countenanced by high minded men, but I wrestle with wickedness in high places."[148]

The history of the Quakers until the Revolutionary War is the history of their petitions for exemptions from penalties suffered for conscience. In 1757, they petitioned to "be exempt from appearing as Musters, and from all other military Service whatsoever."[149] An act of 1748 had continued all the elaborate machinery of provision for the clergy of the Established Church and particularly insisted on the levy of all tithables in the parish for the support of the parish organization and the established clergy.[150] There was no acknowledgment of dissenters; to all intents and purposes the union of church and state still existed. It required more than the petitions of the Quakers to compel recognition of the dissatisfaction of dissenters.

The significance of the Quakers in the history of the dissenter movement is the evident intention of the government to suppress dissent in the thickly populated sections of the colony, as in the southeastern section, where the Established Church had its prior historical foothold. The Quakers of 1732, intending to settle on the frontier, like the Germans or the earlier Huguenots were received more kindly. It was in the Quakers that other dissenting groups found a precedent to discard the role of passivity and make a determined effort to break down the wall of church and state which hemmed in their free exercise of conscience.

The Baptists

It has been shown with what hostility the colonial government looked upon such religious groups as the Puritans, whose prin-

---

[147] *Va. Gazette*, Nov. 17–24, 1738.
[148] Perry: *Amer. Col. Church*, I, 360; Campbell: *Hist. of Va.*, 433.
[149] *Jour., H. Burg.*, April 26, 1757, 435–36; Mar. 28, 1767, 100–01.
[150] Hening: *Stat. at Large*, VI, 88.

ciples they regarded as subversive of union of church and state, or the Quakers whose principles they regarded as subversive of all law and order.

There were, however, other religious groups in the 17th century whose attitude toward the question of church and state was just as clearly defined. In 1611, the English Baptists meeting at Amsterdam made a declaration of momentous consequences in the development of political philosophy; their statement was that

> . . . The magistrate is not to meddle with religion or matters of conscience, nor compel men to this or that form of religion; because Christ is the King and Lawgiver of the Church and conscience.[151]

They probably found little encouragement in the Virginian attitude toward the Quakers, in the 17th century, to attempt their way thither.[152]   The first Baptist Association in America formed at Philadelphia, in 1707, was followed soon by the presence of Baptists in Maryland and Virginia.[153]   They seem to have appeared first in Virginia in the southeastern section, pushing out from the territory around Norfolk.[154]   A second group, members of a Maryland congregation, came in 1743 and settled in present Berkeley County in the neighborhood of the Quakers who came in 1732.   These were known as Regular Baptists.[155] A third group known as Separatists, an outcome of the Whitefield revival in New England, came in 1754, established contact with the group in Berkeley County, then went on into North Carolina, but returning, established in 1760 the first Separate Baptist Church in Virginia.[156]

The Regular Baptists by conforming to the Act of Toleration and applying for and obtaining licenses seem to have attracted less attention than the Separatists.[157]   Probably, too, their position on the northwestern frontier contributed to their protection.

---

[151] Cobb: *Rise of Relig. Liberty*, 64.

[152] *Cf.* Keen, W. W.: *Bi-Centennial First Baptist Church*, 13.

[153] *Ibid.*, 33; Osgood, H. L.: *Amer. Colonies in the 18th C.*, III, 83.

[154] Cobb: *Rise of Relig. Liberty*, 111; Campbell: *Hist. of Va.*, 553; *Southern Review*, XIII, 140–41.

[155] Semple, R. B.: *Hist. of Baptists*, 1, 288.

[156] *Ibid.*, 5; *cf.* Taylor, J. B.: *Va. Baptist Ministers*, 29, date given as 1764.

[157] Semple: *Hist. of Baptists*, 294.

The Separatists began extending their activities shortly after 1760 in the more thickly populated eastern and central part of the state. In 1768, at least three of their ministers who had failed to comply with the Act of Toleration were thrown into prison.[158] Though the Deputy-governor, John Blair, seemed to favor mild treatment for these people,[159] these arrests appear to have set a precedent which was followed until almost the eve of the Revolution.[160] While their preachers were being thrown into prison, the Baptists began like the Quakers to send petitions which in their hands became salient instruments of publicity for their principles.

Dissenting groups by this time had come to be too large and important an element in the social, economic, and political life of Virginia to be effectually suppressed by mulcting of money or confinement in jail. There was probably, too, an element in Virginia, which though loyal enough to the established church, looked with abhorrence upon the procedure necessary to adequately suppress dissent.[161]

As long ago, as 1752, the Commissary had brought in a bill entitled *"An Act for allowing his Majesty's Protestant Subjects dissenting from the Church of* England *the Exercise of their Religion."*[162] It seems to have received no further action than a second reading. The determined resistance of the Baptists now gave a publicity to dissent which could no longer be safely ignored. Events began to demand action to allay the irritation of society in general.[163] Accordingly, an instruction was given the committee for religion to bring in "a Bill for exempting his Majesty's Protestant Dissenters from the Penalties of certain Laws."[164] The subject was taken up in November, 1769, and in June, 1770, but did not proceed beyond a reading.[165]

---

[158] *Ibid.*, 14–15.

[159] *Ibid.*, 15–16.

[160] *Va. Mag. Hist.*, XI, 415–17; XIX, 438; XX, 319; Taylor: *Va. Baptist Ministers, passim*; Cobb: *Rise of Relig. Liberty*, 113.

[161] Hunt, G.: *Writings James Madison*, I, 22–23; *cf.* Henley, S.: *The Distinct Claims of Government and Religion.*

[162] *Jour., Va. Council*, April 11, 1752, II, 1078.

[163] Eckenrode, H. J.: *Sep. Church and State*, 38.

[164] *Jour., H. Burg.*, May 11, 1769, 205; Eckenrode: *Sep. Church and State*, 38, "The movement for a new toleration law began as early as 1769" overlooks the 1752 effort.

[165] *Jour., H. Burg.*, June 18, 1770, 78–79.

The Baptists now, in 1770, petitioned against the inconvenience
of compelling their licensed preachers to comply with the military laws and called attention to the hardships they suffered from
their ministers not being permitted to preach except in designated meeting houses.[166]   In 1772, the House of Burgesses was
overwhelmed with petitions from the counties of Mecklenburg,
Amelia, Sussex, Lunenburg and Caroline, protesting against the
imprisonment of their preachers and the denial of the benefits
of the Toleration Act.   They resented particularly the necessity
of applying to the General Court which sat only twice a year
and then admitted only a single meeting house in each county.[167]
The answer of the House to these petitions consisted in again
taking up the bill in behalf of the Protestant dissenters, which it
ordered printed.[168]   The publication of this bill was followed in
May, 1774, by a petition from Baptist ministers praying that
they and other Protestant dissenting ministers be given ''liberty
to preach in all proper places, and at all Seasons, without restraint.''[169]   The meaning of this objection is made clearer in
the petition from Baptists and other Protestant dissenters, the
following year, when they state the provision of the bill,

. . . not admitting public Worship, except in the day time, is inconsistent
with the laws of *England,* as well as with the practice and usage of the
primitive Churches, and even of the english Church itself.[170]

The battle for toleration was gradually assuming a different
angle, plea for privilege was giving way to a plea for equality.[171]
The Baptist conception of political philosophy enunciated in 1611
was now engaged full tilt in pounding against the political philosophy involved in the conception of integration of church and
state.   In opposition to the philosophy enunciated in ''An Address to the Anabaptists,'' that a

. . . Legislature would meet in a new Society to very little Purpose if they
did not form a *religious* as well as a *civil* Establishment, not only because

---

[166] *Ibid.*, May 26, 1770, 19–20.
[167] *Ibid.*, Feb. 22, 1772, 182–83; Feb. 24, 1772, 185–86; Feb. 25, 1772,
188; Mar. 14, 1772, 244–45.
[168] *Ibid.*, Mar. 17, 1772, 248–49.
[169] *Ibid.*, May 16, 1774, 100–02.
[170] *Ibid.*, June 13, 1775, 221–25.
[171] *Ibid.*

their Union has ever been found necessary to support Government, but that a State could not expect to thrive which should seem to rely on her own Strength, by providing State Regulations only, without endeavoring to conciliate the Divine Favour, by establishing Modes of Piety and Devotion. . . .[172]

the Baptists were determined at an association meeting in 1775, "that the church establishment should be abolished, and religion left to stand upon its own merits."[173]

The Presbyterians

The founder of Presbyterianism in America was Francis Makemie.[174] His arrival in Accomac County occurred before 1690.[175] In April, 1699, he distinguished himself by calling the attention of the government in a petition, to the fact that the Toleration Act of 1689 had received no official recognition in Virginia. The order of the Council, in 1691, making the Toleration Act applicable to Quakers had no validity in law;[176] but, Rev. Josias Mackie, in charge of the Presbyterians in Norfolk County, had availed himself, in 1692, as did the Quakers, of the opportunity to comply with the order so as to have a registered meeting house.[377] Makemie prayed that a proclamation be issued declaring freedom and liberty of conscience and that dissenters be not interfered with in the free and open exercise of religion. Called before the Governor and Council, he was advised that all dissenters would have such liberty allowed them as the law directed on condition that the peace of the government would not be disturbed.[178] It is to the eloquence and influence of Makemie that the recognition granted in 1699 is attributed.[179]

---

[172] *Va. Gazette*, Feb. 20, 1772.
[173] Semple: *Hist. of Baptists*, 62.
[174] Clayton-Torrence, W.: *Trial Bibli. Col. Va.*, 91; Wise: *Eastern Shore*, 281; Bell: *The Old Free State*, I, 367.
[175] Campbell: *Hist. of Va.*, 371.
[176] See p. 58, n. 129.
[177] See p. 58; Bruce: *Inst. Hist. of Va.*, I, 273–74; *cf.* Osgood: *Amer. Colonies in the 18th C.*, III, 469.
[178] *Wm. & Mary Coll. Quart.*, XXV, 144; Bruce: *Inst. Hist. of Va.*, I, 262.
[179] Wise: *Eastern Shore*, 281–82; *Va. Mag. Hist.*, IV, 253; Hening: *Stat. at Large*, III, 171; Makemie's ability is attested in *A Plain & Friendly PERSWASIVE . . . For Promoting Towns & Cohabitation*, given in *Va. Mag. Hist.*, IV, 252 *ff.*

Makemie, and likewise Mackie, applied immediately to their respective county courts, Accomac and Princess Anne, for licensing of two meeting houses each and received their certificates.[180]

After Makemie's death, in 1708,[181] Presbyterianism in southern and eastern Virginia seems to have declined in numbers and influence.[182]

It was, however, destined for a revival—for in 1727, there began a mighty immigration of Scotch-Irish Presbyterians into Philadelphia, and from there Presbyterianism in the next decade streamed into northern Virginia, particularly into the Shenandoah Valley.[183]   These Presbyterians came under the influence of the Synod of Philadelphia, which, in 1729, adopted the Westminster standards of 1647, with the express exemption of such clauses as implied "that the civil magistrate hath a controlling power over synods with respect to the exercise of their ministerial authority or power *to persecute any for their religion.*"[184]   In 1737 and 1738, they took steps to constitute themselves a congregation legally.   With the aid of the Synod of Philadelphia, they received authority from Governor Gooch, on condition of conforming to the Act of Toleration by taking the oaths and registering their meeting places and behaving peaceably to the government.[185]

Presbyterianism in Virginia was now destined to be stirred by the Tennent revival in New Jersey, begun about 1732; and by the division, in 1741, of the Synod of Philadelphia into "Old Side" and that of New York into "New Side" on the basis of attitude toward various aspects of doctrine and discipline.[186]

---

[180] Foote: *Sketches of Va.*, 44–50; *Va. Mag. Hist.*, VII, 362; Osgood: *Amer. Colonies in the 18th C.*, III, 469.

[181] Clayton-Torrence: *Trial Bibli. Col. Va.*, 91.

[182] Foote: *Sketches of Va.*, 84; Campbell: *Hist. of Va.*, 414, states that in 1727 there was one congregation; *Va. Mag. Hist.*, X, 214, gives the qualification under the Toleration Act, April 2, 1729, of Mr. William Dalglish, Presbyterian minister, Richmond County.

[183] Campbell: *Puritan in Holl., Eng., and America*, II, 484–85; Cobb: *Rise of Relig., Liberty*, 100; Osgood: *Amer. Colonies in the 18th C.*, II, 521–22.

[184] Schaff, P.: *Church and State in the U. S.*, in Am. Hist. Assoc., 1888, II, 49.

[185] Foote: *Sketches of Va.*, 103–04; Waddell, J. A.: *Annals Augusta Co.*, 17–19; Osgood: *Amer. Colonies in the 18th C.*, III, 469.

[186] Foote: *Sketches of Va.*, 116; Osgood: *Amer. Colonies in the 18th C.*, III, 470; Campbell: *Hist. of Va.*, 438.

Through the visit of William Robinson, a representative of the New Side Presbytery of Newcastle, Delaware, Virginia came essentially under the dominance of New Side Presbyterianism; a condition favored by preliminary sowing of seed by Whitefield, who preached in 1740, at Williamsburg, and whose sermons appeared in the Hanover district, in 1743.[187] The ministers, who followed Robinson into central Virginia by their proselyting activity and reputed reflections on the clergy, aroused the ire of the establishment. In 1745, Governor Gooch charged the Grand Jury "to make strict inquiry after those seducers" for presentment or indictment to the court, who, he declared, were prosecuting "not liberty of conscience, but freedom of speech."[188] The Philadelphia Synod, who felt their responsibility in having introduced Presbyterianism anew in 1738, took occasion to notice this charge at their meeting that spring, and in an address to Governor Gooch to disavow any connection with the New Lights.[189]

In the meantime, Robinson was preparing his disciple, Samuel Davies, future president of Princeton to enter the Virginia field.[190] In 1747, the year in which Gooch issued his proclamation against "Itinerant Preachers, whether New Lights, Moravians, or Methodists,"[191] Davies assumed charge of what was to be, in Presbyterian annals, the famous Hanover Presbytery. In 1748, Davies had four meeting houses licensed, but the success which followed his ministry was such that "Seven meeting houses situated in 5 counties have been licensed for Mr. Samuel Davies."[192] These prolific favors to Davies were undoubtedly the choice of the lesser of two evils upon the part of the General Court. In 1748, Davies attempted to secure the licensing of another minister, but was blocked by the Council.[193] There now

---

[187] Foote: *Sketches of Va.*, 120–23; Davies, S.: *Letters*, 3–6.

[188] Burk: *Hist. of Va.*, III, 119 *ff*.; Foote: *Sketches of Va.*, 135 *ff*.; Osgood: *Amer. Colonies in the 18th C.*, III, 471.

[189] Foote: *Sketches of Va.*, 138–39.

[190] A "Memoir of the Rev. Samuel Davies" appears in *Va. Evang. & Lit. Mag.*, Mar., 1819, II, 112 *ff*.; and *cf.* also Barnes, A.: *Sermons*, I, xi-lxviii.

[191] See p. 55; *Va. Mag. Hist.*, XI, 228; Campbell: *Hist. of Va.*, 438.

[192] Perry: *Amer. Col. Church*, I, 366; Lang, J. D.: *Relig. & Educ. in Amer.*, 85.

[193] Foote: *Sketches of Va.*, 165.

began a tremendous, triangular struggle as to the interpretation to be placed on the Act of Toleration which had been incorporated into Virginia law by such casual reference in 1699. The General Court was determined to check the extension of dissenting activities by withholding the licensing privilege from preachers and limiting the number of meeting-houses.[194] The English government was inclined to insist upon Toleration as "essential to the enriching and improving of a Trading Nation,"[195] but hoped that Mr. Davies would not give "cause of complaint" to the clergy and people in general.[196] Mr. Davies and his friends held that the settling of Virginia by the Presbyterians had been beneficial to Virginia, that the movement would not have been initiated if they had suspected any restraint upon conscience would be imposed, and they were merely asking for their legal rights under the Act of Toleration.[197]

The eloquence and cogency of Davies as a letter writer secured for him in England an opinion from the Attorney General, Sir D. Ryder, confirming the opinion that such procedure as was common under the Act of Toleration in England was legal in Virginia.[198] There was no official recognition of this opinion in Virginia, and Davies on a visit to England in 1753–54 spent considerable time in finding a solution for the various Presbyterian difficulties, particularly, in having the problem of licensing meeting houses cleared up. In 1755, he was advised by letter to apply first to the county court, then, if necessary, to the Governor and Council, then to the Governor—and on his refusal, to proceed to "use such house or place for religious worship, as if it had been licensed, . . ."[199]

The struggles of the French and Indian War were now favorable to the procedure last advised.[200] The government at Williamsburg could not look too closely upon the conduct of a group of people whose leader was so eloquently endeavoring to persuade

---

194 *Ibid.*, 170.
195 Perry: *Amer. Col. Church*, I, 379–80.
196 *Ibid.*
197 Foote: *Sketches of Va.*, 182, 186.
198 *Ibid.*, 213.
199 *Ibid.*, 296–97.
200 *Ibid.*, 307.

the people in general to remove "The Curse of Cowardice" in the prosecution of that war.[201] A papist was always more to be feared than a Protestant dissenter.[202] Then, too, the Establishment found itself at that time with a case of its own versus the people, and in trying to take care of the disintegrating forces within, found itself unable to cope effectively against the forces hammering upon it from without.

When Davies went to Princeton, in 1759,[203] he left a strongly established church; one that seemingly was reconciled to existence under the limitations imposed upon it. But, not even the fact that they suffered comparatively no molestation in the exercise of their religion was sufficient to keep the Presbyterians permanently quiescent, particularly in view of the activity of the Baptists.[204] Upon consideration of the Assembly's Toleration Bill, printed in 1772,[205] they, like the Baptists, protested against it by sending, in 1775, a petition of objections on the basis that their ministers could not limit themselves to designated meeting-houses if they were to follow the example of Christ and his disciples; nor were they able to prognosticate what would be the most desirable places to designate as meeting-places; nor could they yield the privilege of night meetings, a practise sanctioned by the Apostles, particularly St. Paul. They disdained the stigma of disloyalty implied in the requirement to keep their doors open in time of divine service; as for baptizing or receiving servants, they felt bound to the injunction to "teach all nations." Furthermore, they proposed "that freedom in speaking and writing upon religious subjects," be granted, and also the right to property for religious and educational purposes. Above all, they prayed for "an unlimited impartial Toleration."[206] They recalled the assurance under which Presbyterians had entered Virginia in 1738; prayed that no bill would pass, "but such as

---

[201] Davies, S.: *The Curse of Cowardice.*
[202] McIlwaine: *Struggle of Prot. Dissenters,* 64.
[203] Eckenrode: *Sep. Church and State,* 34.
[204] *Jour., Va. Council,* III, 1583–84, appendix; *Jour., H. Burg.,* May 17, 1774, 102–03.
[205] See p. 64.
[206] *Jour., Va. Council,* Nov. 11, 1774, III, 1590–93, Appendix; James, C. F.: *Struggle for Relig. Liberty,* 42–47.

will secure to the Petitioners equal liberties and advantages with their fellow Subjects.''[207]

Presbyterianism was advancing from the strictly legal position held in Davies' time to the bolder Baptist position of religious liberty as a natural right.[208] Integration of church and state was thus forced to meet the greatly increased strength of the principle of separation of church and state.

The Methodists

Methodism in Virginia came at a time when the government was too spent, apparently, by its attempt to handle the more important problems of toleration of such groups as the Baptists and Presbyterians to take official notice of a group who still nominally declared their allegiance to the Anglican Church.[209]

The visits of Whitefield, in 1740, at Williamsburg, and some years later at Hanover,[210] while contributing to the spirit of dissent in Virginia, did not further the extension of Methodism which had its origin, in the immediately preceding years, in England.[211]   In 1763, Rev. Devereaux Jarratt, a regularly ordained minister of the establishment received a charge in Dinwiddie County.   His work was marked by a revival which had many features in common with Methodism, and when Methodism, which was introduced into Virginia by Robert Williams at Norfolk, in 1772, spread into Sussex and Brunswick counties, Jarratt co-operated sympathetically with its leaders and was in consequence looked upon askance by the established clergy.[212]

While Methodism came too late to receive attention from the official government before the Revolution, it was not without its

---

[207] *Jour., H. Burg.*, June 5, 1775, 186–89; James: *Struggle for Relig. Liberty*, 40–41; Eckenrode: *Sep. Church & State*, 40; at least one member of the Established clergy came out strongly for recognition of the dissenters' position, cf. Henley: *The Distinct Claims of Government and Religion.*

[208] Osgood: *Amer. Colonies in the 18th C.*, III, 474–75.

[209] Hawks, F. L.: *Contrib. Ecc. Hist.*, I, 148, 166; see, however, p. 55 for Governor Gooch's precautionary warning against Methodists in 1747.

[210] Bennett, W. W.: *Memorials of Methodism*, 35.

[211] Peyton, J. L.: *Hist. Augusta Co.*, 86; Buckley, J. M.: *Hist. of Methodists*, 85.

[212] *A Brief Narrative of the Revival of Religion in Virginia*; Bennett: *Memorials of Methodism*, 51, 62–63; Buckley: *Hist. of Methodists*, 134, cf. statement by Gooch, see p. 55; Branch: *Hist. Papers*, June, 1901, I, 3–21.

publicity. On January 1, 1767, the *Virginia Gazette* published a poem entitled "Methodist," which had appeared in England. This was followed during the month by a half dozen other references to Methodism. One of the writers was moved to reflect in verse on the ridicule poured upon religion and the professors of it:

> See human nature sunk in shame!
> See scandals pour'd on Jesus' name![213]

In July, 1772, the *Gazette* published "*The* Origin *of a* Methodist, *A new Song, set to a very melancholy Air*," reminiscent of the "Intructions how to make a perfect Quaker" published many years before.[214] But scorn and ridicule did not stop the Methodists; their minister, Rev. Joseph Pillmoor, preached in July, 1772, to almost 3,000 people in the fields. "They flock to him from all Quarters, and invite him to preach in every Neighborhood. The Women call him *The dear divine man*."[215]

A Methodist petition, in 1776, to the Assembly, repudiating the thought of an alignment with dissenters, declared they were "a Religious Society in Communion with the Church of England," doing all in their "power to strengthen and support the said Church."[216]

This did not alter the fact that their proselyting activity resulted in weakening the church and that essentially they were dissenters, as was fully recognized by their organization into an independent church in 1784.[217]

Dissent And Disintegration

The history of dissent in Virginia, as has been shown, was that of an external force battling against the rampart of integration of church and state. Only the necessity of protecting the frontiers and spurring economic development modified, on the part of the government, the policy of integration.[218] As the dissenters

---

[213] *Va. Gazette*, Jan. 22, 1767.
[214] See p. 60.
[215] *Va. Gazette*, July 30, 1772; Bennett: *Memorials of Methodism*, 53–54.
[216] *Va. Mag. Hist.*, XVIII, 143–44.
[217] Humphrey: *Nationalism and Religion*, 167–69; *cf.* Niles: *Register*, XXI, 148.
[218] *Cf.* Campbell: *Hist. of Va.*, 453–54.

drove into the colony from the north-west and north, from the southeast and south, they attracted too much publicity to make homogeneity any longer possible. All the dissenters suffered, at one time or another, from the obstacles in the way of setting up their own churches; and, throughout the period, from the financial difficulty of taking care of their own religious organization as well as that of the Established Church. Aside from resentment aroused among the dissenters by these difficulties, there were certain phases of the discipline of the Anglican Church which found as little favor among its own members. Presentments for Sabbath breaking are recorded in the very early days of the colony and continue fairly consistently to the close of the colonial period.[219] It is true that as dissenters increased, presentments were directed largely against them; but there is evidence enough that these presentments were often made of members of the church, who found greater attraction in other business and the lure of the Virginia hills.[220]

In the close alliance between church and state, there was indeed little that touched the lives of the people which escaped oversight by the establishment. Performing marriage rites was the legal prerogative of the established clergy.[221] Dissenters married by their own ministers were considered illegally married; and, besides subjecting their children to the brand of illegitimacy, subjected the officiating minister to a fine.[222]

Another problem which came close to the dissenters was that of baptism, which as part of the discipline of the Established Church was a compulsory initiation into citizenship, of every child born in Virginia. In 1662, an act was passed imposing on parents of "scismaticall" notions, who "out of the new fangled conceits of their owne hereticll inventions" refused to have their children baptized, a fine of 2000 pounds of tobacco.[223] There is

---

219 *Va. Mag. Hist.*, XXI, 57; *Wm. & Mary Coll. Quart.*, VII, 271.

220 *Ibid.*; *Va. Mag. Hist.*, XXI, 57; XXVI, 4; Waddell: *Annals Augusta County*, 42; Peyton: *Hist. Augusta County*, 57; Bruce: *Inst. Hist. of Va.*, I, 30–37; Goodwin: *Hist. Sketch Bruton Church*, 41.

221 Hening: *Stat. at Large*, I, 332; II, 50–51; III, 149, 441; VI, 81.

222 *Va. Mag. Hist.*, XVI, 218; XXVIII, 364; Waddell: *Annals Augusta Co.*, 85; *cf.* 175; Eckenrode: *Sep. Church and State*, 66; *cf.* Hening: *Stat. at Large*, X, 361.

223 Hening: *Stat. at Large*, II, 165–66.

proof of indictments under this law in the 17th century; but, by the middle of the 18th century, dereliction of this kind, in view of the increasing number of dissenters, was probably overlooked.[224]

There was, however, dissent of a different kind, not that indeed of organized groups, but that of individuals against whom such charges as blasphemy, atheism, free-thinking, and deism could be hurled—a kind of dissent more subtle but no less effective than organized dissent in undermining the wall of union of church and state.

The catalogue of individual dissent begins early. In 1634, a sentence of excommunication for forty days was passed for scornful speeches and putting on a hat in church.[225] An unproved charge of atheism and blasphemy, in 1654, resulted in an apology upon his knees, in addition to a fine, for the accuser.[226] In 1683, a resident of Lower Norfolk ventured to assert that "a great part of the Bible was false."[227] Drastic legislation was passed in 1699, and reënacted in 1705, against those avowing "Atheisticall principles"—which were defined as denying "the being of a God or the holy Trinity," or asserting or maintaining "there are more Gods than one," or denying the truth of the Christian religion or the divine authority of the Old and New Testaments.[228] The most significant of the disabilities imposed by this act was the deprivation of the right of guardianship of children; no atheist father was to lead his child astray.[229] Among the vices of the age, for the combating of which a pious Anglican left, in 1710, the interest of £100 sterling, were those of "atheism and irreligion."[230] In 1736, Commissary Dawson asked the Bishop of London for an "antidote" against the heretical book called *The Plain Account.* The next year, this appeared in an article in

---

[224] Bruce: *Inst. Hist. of Va.*, I, 220–21; *Jour., H. Burg.*, Nov. 8, 1748, 275–77; Jefferson: *Notes on Va.*, 232; *Edward Pleasants Valentine Papers*, II, 1069.

[225] Hening: *Stat. at Large*, I, 223.

[226] *Ibid.*, I, 387; *Va. Mag. Hist.*, V, 98.

[227] Bruce: *Inst. Hist. of Va.*, I, 277.

[228] Hening: *Stat. at Large*, III, 168, 358; *cf.* also, II, 333; IV, 244–45.

[229] Jefferson: *Notes on Va.*, 235.

[230] *Wm. & Mary Coll. Quart.*, VII, 187; Meade: *Old Churches, Ministers, and Families*, I, 361.

the *Virginia Gazette* calling attention to the Rev. Mr. Law's book, *"A Demonstration of the gross and Fundamental Errors of a late Book,* called, *A Plain Account."*[231]

Whether or not Sir John Randolph, burgess for the college of William and Mary, was one of those "well meaning people" referred to by the Commissary as being endangered by *The Plain Account,* he apparently felt it incumbent in his will to justify his attitude toward religion and vindicate his memory from such charges as "Deist, Heretic, and Schismatic."[232] In the opinion of Governor Gooch, in 1753, orthodoxy was yielding before free thinking. He wrote to the Bishop of London, "ffree thinkers multiply very fast having an eminent Layman for their Leader, and the current runs in some places almost w*t*hout opposition."[233]

The *Virginia Gazette,* the forum of Virginia, opened its pages freely to the religious opinion of the day; nor did it attempt on the one hand to hide the prevalence of dissent, nor on the other, the scorn of the orthodox for heretical opinion.[234] In a picture of "The Present Age," we read:

> For, of all ages ever known,
> The present is the oddest;
>
> .   .   .   .   .   .
>
> No Lawyers now are fond of fees,
> Nor Clergy of their dues;
> Few people at the play one sees,
> At church what crowded pews!
>
> .   .   .   .   .   .
>
> No pleasure-chaises fill the streets,
> Or crowd the roads on Sunday;
>
> .   .   .   .   .   .
>
> Just turn the picture upside down,
> I fear you'll see the right on 't.[235]

---

[231] Perry: *Amer. Col. Church,* I, 359; *Va. Gazette,* Feb. 10–17, 1737; Palmer, W. S., & Du Bose, W. P.: *Liberal and mystical writings of William Law;* Fiske: *Old Va.,* II, 264; Meade: *Old Churches, Ministers, and Families,* I, 361; *cf.* II, 292.

[232] *Va. Gazette,* April 29–May 6, 1737; *Va. Mag. Hist.,* III, 265; *Wm. & Mary Coll. Quart.,* Ser. 2, IV, 286.

[233] *Va. Mag. Hist.,* XXXII, 332, 209 *ff.*; *cf.* Chalkley, L.: *Chronicles Scotch-Irish Va.,* I, 71; *cf.* Waddell: *Annals Augusta Co.,* 85.

[234] *Cf. Sewanee Review,* XX, 213 *ff.*

[235] *Va. Gazette,* Nov. 26, 1767.

A literary prelude to the Dayton trial may be found in

The FREETHINKERS FAITH

AN Esquire born, a Templar bred;
The Bible I have never read;
Your Bishops, down from Paul to Grindal,
Are Asses all to Hobbes and Tindal;

.   .   .   .   .   .

The law which most my Temper suits,
I claim in common with the Brutes;

.   .   .   .   .   .

For, though the Clergy would Corrupt us,
Post Mortem nulla est Voluptas.
And with this Thought my Heart I cherish,
Proud Man is like the Beasts that perish.[236]

The intense interest which every phase of religion had for Virginians is illustrated in perhaps no better way than the lively discussion aroused by the promulgation of a fast day upon the news of the Boston Tea Party.[237]   The legislative predilection for the proclamation of Fast Days appealed to the light pen of the author of *Considerations On The Present State of Virginia,* attributed to John Randolph.   Referring to the dissolution of the Assembly on that occasion, he says:

. . . Our late Dissolution, though it was no Surprise to the Members, yet astonished many, when they were informed of the Occasion of it.   Fasting, when observed and repeated in a proper Manner, may be very salutary to the natural Body; but how the political Body can be benefited by changing the Hour of Dining, and making the Repast in the Evening, instead of the afternoon . . . is what, I confess, cannot be accounted for by me.[238]

To which Robert Carter Nicholas replied:

. . . Not only Individuals, but, in a more especial Manner, *Nations* and *Countries,* as having their existence *solely,* in this Life, have been considered by all Ages, and particularly by all good Christians, as under the Guidance of Heaven.   In Cases of general Calamity, either already felt or apprehended, what can be more decent and proper than to look up to that Provi-

---

[236] *Ibid.,* Sept. 15, 1774.
[237] *Jour., H. Burg.,* May 24, 1774, 124.
[238] Swem, E. G.: *Considerations on the Pres. State Va.,* 29; in 1729, a fast day was proclaimed because of a threatened invasion of caterpillars. *Va. Mag. Hist.,* XXXIV, 98.

dence, . . . Can any Means be better adapted to this End, than withdrawing our Attention, for a Season, from the Business and Cares of the World, and mortifying all our *Corrupt Affections* by FASTING and PRAYER?[239]

Upon consideration, it is evident that it was not so much the number of the dissenters as it was the variety of dissent and the publicity given to it by prosecution, by the deliberations of the Assembly, and by discussion in the press, which made it effective in breaking down the integration of church and state.

Internal Forces In The Process Of Disintegration

The effectiveness of dissent in contributing to the disintegration of church and state was materially increased by inherent defects in the machinery of the integration of church and state.

The Vestries

In the organization of church and state set up in 1662, the pivotal center was found in the closed vestry. By the time of Bacon's Rebellion, the self-perpetuating vestry had become an issue of sufficient importance to receive special action in the remedial legislation which was rushed through in 1676.[240] The desired reform was indicated in the legislation which proposed triennial election,[241] a reform that was emphasized in the various county grievances to the English Commission in 1677.[242] Necessity for reform in the vestry was acknowledged by the Bishop of London that same year.[243]

The powers of the closed vestry became irksome not only to the people; the ministers also soon found that they were at the mercy of the "Plebian Juntos" as Godwyn in his *Negro's and Indians Advocate* called them.[244]

The right of presentation of the minister by the vestry preceding induction had been reënacted in law in 1662.[245] Undoubtedly, there had crept into the system a number of abuses,

[239] Swem: *Considerations on the Pres. State Va.*, 79–80.
[240] Wertenbaker: *Va. Under the Stuarts*, 169; Fiske: *Old Va.*, II, 71.
[241] Hening: *Stat. at Large*, II, 356.
[242] *Va. Mag. Hist.*, II, 172, 289, 388.
[243] *Ibid.*, XXII, 146–47.
[244] Neill: *Va. Carolorum*, 343.
[245] Hening: *Stat. at Large*, II, 46.

sometimes from a spirit of economy with regard to taxes, again from a wish to have adequate trial of a minister before presentation. To have no minister at all was an easy solution of the levy problem. In 1681, Lord Culpeper wrote:

. . . And the parishes paying the ministers themselves, have used to claim the right of presentation, (or rather of not paying) whether the governor will or not, which must not be allowed, and yet must be managed with great caution.[246]

In 1682, Lord Culpeper was given power to collate when places were void.[247] This power to collate was repeated in instructions to later governors, usually in general terms such as so ''often as any of them shall happen to be void.''[248]

In 1689, Rev. James Blair was appointed Commissary of the Bishop of London; and, as events proved, a most important step had been taken in the direction of withdrawing ecclesiastical affairs from the hands of the governor into the hands of the church and the people. A contest now arose as to the powers which inhered in the offices of commissary and governor in regard to ecclesiastical authority as representatives of the Bishop of London and the Crown. The contest centered in the question as to how much time the vestry should be allowed in which to present a minister before the governor should proceed to induction. It was possible in this matter for a governor to play both fast and loose. In 1696–97, the Commissary presented a memorial against Governor Andros charging him with playing too loose. He said:

. . . And the vestries of vacant Parishes finding a double advantage by keeping no minister, viz.: both saving the money of his Salary in their own pockets, and pleasing (as they think), the Govr who neither urges them to provide ministers, nor goes about to provide them for them (as he might safely do by the Ordinary's Power in that matter invested in him by the King's Instructions), it is an easy thing to foresee what will become of that poor Church in a little time.[249]

---

[246] Campbell: *Hist. of Va.*, 331.
[247] *Va. Mag. Hist.*, XIX, 244.
[248] *Ibid.*, XX, 230, 343.
[249] Perry: *Amer. Col. Church*, I, 11.

Blair further charged that the vestries were beginning to withhold glebes, maintaining that they were due to none but inducted
ministers.[250]

In Governor Nicholson's time, the difficulty was referred to
the Attorney General of England.[251]   Lord Northey's opinion
was that upon the vestry's failure to present within six months
after a place was void, their privilege lapsed, and the Governor
had the right of collation.[252]   Governor Nicholson's threat to use
the benefit of the lapse resulted in some inductions.[253]   In 1706,
when the bill entitled "An Act concerning ye Church Clergy and
other parochial affairs" came up for discussion, the arguments
in the Council against a provision for new and sexennial vestries
were that it would occasion parties and factions, that broils
would be renewed every six years, that the elections being made
by freeholders and housekeepers promiscuously, the greater part
being "mean" people, would be likely to carry the election in
their favor, and finally that the change proposed would extend
to an innovation in the Constitution.[254]

In the early years of his governorship, Spotswood apparently
permitted the procedure established in 1703 to continue, though
he objected privately to England about the failure of induction.[255]   By 1719, he made it very clear that in his opinion the
right of the governor to collate was in no way dependent upon
the six months' lapse.[256]   To this the Commissary objected as
contrary to the precedent established.

In 1718, the House of Burgesses attempted to include among
instructions for charges to be presented in England against the
governor:

. . . That he insists upon his having a Right of Patronage and hath presented and Inducted Ministers contrary to our law, and contrary to Sr
Edward Northeys opinion upon our laws.[257]

---

[250] *Ibid.*, 13.

[251] *Ibid.*, 226.

[252] Barton, R. T.: *Reports Randolph & Barradall*, II, B 2–3; Goodwin: *Hist. Sketch Bruton Church*, 76–77.

[253] Perry: *Amer. Col. Church*, I, 226–27.

[254] *Jour., Va. Council*, I, June 5, 1706, 467–68.

[255] Spotswood: *Letters*, I, 66.

[256] Perry: *Amer. Col. Church*, I, 202, 321; Spotswood: *Letters*, II, 292; McIlwaine: *Struggle of Prot. Dissenters*, 9 *ff*.

[257] *Jour., H. Burg.*, Nov. 21, 1718, 229–30.

At the same time, there was secured an opinion of Attorney General Raymond favorable to the established precedent.[258]   Yet, there was not wanting legal opinion in England confirming Spotswood's view that the right of collation was the King's prerogative, and that the governor by the authority transferred to him might exercise it.[259]   Diplomacy in England, however, was more powerful than any interpretation of law.   The vestries, as collectors of the taxes with which the ministers' salaries were paid, became by that fact the patron of the livings and against that elemental fact as Blair foresaw and Spotswood himself finally admitted, the civil government was helpless.[260]   It could resort only to a *laissez faire* policy; the Bishop of London's suggestion was that a lapse of eighteen months be allowed.[261]   Governor Spotswood was recalled.   In 1724, the commissary knew of only four ministers as being inducted.[262]   The issue was finally settled in 1748, by enacting:

. . . That the sole right of presentation shall be, and remain, in the several vestries, for and during the term of twelve months next after a vacancy shall happen in their respective parishes.[263]

The power of the vestry in this respect became such that, in 1752, Rev. John Camm wrote to the Bishop of London:

. . . It is ordinary to have three or four Clergymen preaching in a vacant parish by turns as so many Rivals for the favor of the Vestry which they may some times be tempted to court by not the most decent methods, such as canvassing votes, treating not excepted, like electioneering Candidates, and running down and depreciating the abilities and reputation of each other, bringing hereby scandal upon the function. . . .[264]

The difficulties of the people with the closed vestries became more acute after the beginning of the 18th century; time allowed the entrance of various abuses, and the increase of population meant the adjustment of parochial affairs in a way that some-

---

[258] Perry: *Amer. Col. Church*, I, 197–98.
[259] *Ibid.*, I, 244, 245.
[260] McIlwaine: *Struggle of Prot. Dissenters*, 11; Osgood: *Amer. Colonies in the 18th C.*, III, 98; Perry: *Amer. Col. Church*, I, 226 *ff.*
[261] *Ibid.*, I, 345.
[262] *Ibid.*, I, 259.
[263] Hening: *Stat. at Large*, VI, 90.
[264] Perry: *Amer. Col. Church*, I, 388.

times proved unsatisfactory to the old, and then again to new communities in the county. Frequently these complaints to the House of Burgesses ended in a request for permission to choose a new vestry.[265] Again, these complaints concerned the tearing down of old chapels and the erection of new chapels in inconveniently situated places.[266] At times, the House enjoined a vestry to build a chapel to suit the needs of a certain portion of the church.[267] Disputes of inhabitants with the vestry had a way of coming to the Assembly for settlement,[268] and when such settlement was unsatisfactory to some of the vestry, they did not hesitate to use obstructive tactics, as was the case when two vestrymen of Suffolk Parish, Nansemond County, refused to cooperate in building a new church.[269] In the early months of 1767, the readers of the *Virginia Gazette* were regaled with a number of effusions concerning the vestry of Portsmouth parish, who had received from the builder, a church "although split from top to bottom."[270]

The only redress the people had against what they sometimes called the "divers arbitrary and illegal proceedings" of the vestry lay in petition to the Assembly. The parish of Elizabeth City, in 1695, petitioned for the election of a new vestry, a petition which was granted them in 1727.[271] After 1750, dissolutions of vestries were granted more readily. In 1759, the vestries of six parishes were dissolved at one time because of "arbitrary and illegal practices."[272] In 1769, the vestry of Augusta parish, Augusta County, was dissolved because a majority of the vestry were dissenters; at the same time, two others were dissolved for "unwarrantable proceedings" and neglect and mismanagement of business.[273] Such dissolutions of vestries usually involved the

265 *Jour., H. Burg.*, Aug. 30, 1701, 275.
266 *Ibid.*, April 10, 1703, 34.
267 *Ibid.*, Aug. 29, 1715, 154–55; Nov. 24, 1720, 277–79.
268 *Va. Mag. Hist.*, XXXII, 246.
269 *Ibid.*, XIV, 18.
270 *Va. Gazette*, Jan. 8, 1767; Feb. 19, 1767; two articles by "Timothy Trimsharp" and "A Honest Man."
271 *Jour., H. Burg.*, April 24, 1695, 9–10; Mar. 30, 1727, 51–52; Hening: *Stat. at Large*, IV, 240.
272 *Ibid.*, VII, 301–03.
273 *Ibid.*, VIII, 432; *Wash. & Lee Hist. Papers*, No. 3, 1892, (Paper 1), 15.

taking of much evidence and many hours' time of the members of the committee in charge. An interesting case of this kind occurs in the dissolution of St. John's Vestry, King William County, in 1772; the lengthy report of the committee appears in full in the *Journals* of the House.[274]

The effort to remedy the vestry situation is reflected in the attempts to pass blanket bills for dissolution of the vestries and the election of new ones. Bills for this purpose appeared in the House in 1740, 1742, 1744, 1748.[275] Nothing was accomplished. In 1757, an act was passed to interpret the ancient act "Vestries appointed,"[276] so as to permit the resignation of a vestryman; but there was no change in the feature making it a closed vestry.[277] In 1770 and 1772, "An Act for better regulating the election of Vestries" was under consideration, but rejected.[278] As late as 1774, there appeared in the *Virginia Gazette* for the consideration of the House of Burgesses, a proposal:

THAT it be enacted that the Vestries of every Parish be elected by their Parishioners respectively, every ten, twelve, or fourteen Years; which will effectually remedy the many and various Impositions, and illegal and arbitrary Measures, that are so frequently and justly complained of. It will quiet and ease the Minds of Numbers of Parishioners, will prevent the frequent Applications to the Assembly for Redress, and will thereby save a great Deal of Time and Expense.[279]

The numerous powers of the vestry—election of ministers and churchwardens, their powers with regard to taxation, processioning lands, care of the poor, determination of parish expenses—made them the center around which church and state functioned.[280]

---

[274] *Jour., H. Burg.*, Mar. 10, 1772, 225–32.

[275] *Ibid.*, June 5, 1740, 417–18; May 19, 1742, 27–28; Oct. 1, 1744, 112–13; *Jour., Va. Council*, Oct. 12, 1744, II, 947; *Jour., H. Burg.*, Mar. 10, 1748, 334.

[276] Hening: *Stat. at Large*, II, 44.

[277] *Ibid.*, VII, 132.

[278] *Jour., H. Burg.*, June 18, 1770, 78–79; *Jour., Va. Council*, Mar. 18, 1772, III, 1458.

[279] *Va. Gazette*, May 12, 1774.

[280] Beverley: *Hist. of Va.*, 204; Fiske: *Old Va.*, II, 98–99; Flippin, P. S.: *Financial Admin. Va.*, 20.

The failure of the vestries to function without considerable vexation to the governor, the clergy, and the people, was one of the factors within the organization of church and state that contributed to its disintegration.[281]

The Clergy And Their Salaries

The intention of the Virginia Company with regard to the salaries of ministers was to have them approximate the value of £200 per annum. An important element in the raising of this sum was to be the minister's glebe.[282]

As far as can be gathered, the early colonial provision for ministers was based, in addition to the glebe, on tithes of tobacco and corn, assessed upon the individuals of the parish; against them, in case of non-payment, the minister had direct redress to the General Court.[283] The assessment in favor of Rev. Francis Bolton in Accomack was ten pounds of tobacco and one bushel of corn for every tithable.[284] This, from an act of 1632, seems to have been the regular allowance.[285] This act also decreed the 20th calf, kid, and pig for the minister, a provision which was repealed the following year.[286] There were a number of law suits by ministers regarding their tithes in this early period; but that of Rev. Mr. William Cotton resulted in the delinquent tithe payer's being compelled to "buyld a pare of stocks, & sitt in them three seuerall Sabouth days in the time of Dyvine Servis, and there ask Mr. Cotton forgiueness."[287] Thus inauspiciously, opened the history of the clergy's salaries in Virginia.

The legislation of 1643 continued the tobacco and corn arrangement.[288] In 1649, the author of *A Perfect Description of Virginia* estimated the minister's living as worth £100.[289] An exemption from public levies was granted the minister and six of

---

281 Cobb: *Rise of Relig. Liberty*, 87.
282 *Jour., H. Burg.*, July 31, 1619, 7; *Va. Mag. Hist.*, II, 154, 158.
283 Hening: *Stat. at Large*, I, 124; *Va. Mag. Hist.*, XXV, 230–31; XXX, 360; XXXI, 214.
284 *Ibid.*, V, 130.
285 Hening: *Stat. at Large*, I, 159.
286 *Ibid.*, I, 220; *Va. Mag. Hist.*, XXV, 349.
287 *Ibid.*, V, 129, *cf.* 363; Wise: *Eastern Shore*, 45.
288 Hening: *Stat. at Large*, I, 242.
289 *A Perfect Description of Virginia*, in Force's *Tracts*, II, 8.

his servants in 1656.[290]   In 1662, the first definite salary arrangement was ordered in the statement that "provision be made for his maintenance in the valuable and current comodityes of the country as may be really worth *at least* ffouerscoure pounds per ann. besides his *perquisites* and glebe.[291]   Fluctuations in the value of tobacco were such, however, that Lord Culpeper, in 1683, and Commissary Blair, in 1697, called the attention of the government to the fact that this level was not as a rule reached.[292]

An attempt, in 1691, to create a scheme for establishing ports and imposing export duties, one third of the profit of which was to increase ministers' salaries, was disapproved in England.[293] Commissary Blair petitioned that same year in behalf of the better payment of the clergy's salaries.[294]   The salary question was also taken up in 1693; and, upon a letter from the King, in 1695.[295]   The discussion at this time indicated a desire on the part of some to keep the amount of tobacco at 13,333 lbs.[296]   The practise had arisen in some places, owing to the variable quality and value of tobacco and the endeavor to have it approximate £80 in value, to allow from 16,000 to 20,000 lbs.   When the matter came up the following year, there were many vehement addresses and conferences; the pressure was such that the quantity of tobacco rose from 14,000 to 16,000 lbs.[297]   The minister was also to have a glebe and convenient dwelling house.[298]   At the same time, it was decreed that fines for various moral offences were to be used by the parish to "ease" the maintenance of the minister.[299]

In the period to 1727, when the next important legislation was passed, there were evidences of dissatisfaction with the situation,

---

[290] Hening: *Stat. at Large*, I, 424; Neill: *Va. Carolorum*, 244.
[291] Hening: *Stat. at Large*, II, 45.
[292] Bruce: *Inst. Hist. of Va.*, I, 153; Perry: *Amer. Col. Church*, I, 11 *ff.*
[293] Hening: *Stat. at Large*, III, 67; Osgood: *Amer. Colonies in the 18th C.*, I, 163; Bruce: *Inst. Hist. of Va.*, I, 156.
[294] *Jour., H. Burg.*, April 27, 1691, 344.
[295] *Jour., Va. Council*, Nov. 5, 1693, I, 200; April 23, 1695, I, 214; *Jour., H. Burg.*, April 20, 1695, 4–5; April 23, 1695, 8–9.
[296] *Ibid.*, May 16, 1695, 36–37.
[297] *Ibid.*, Oct. 16 to 31, 1696, 86–102; *Jour., Va. Council*, Oct 17, 1696, I, 240; Oct. 30, 1696, 243; Conway, M. D.: *Barons of the Potomac and Rappahannock*, 4–5, 11 *ff*; Hening: *Stat. at Large*, III, 151.
[298] *Ibid.*, III, 152.
[299] *Ibid.*, III, 140.

in elaborate discussions of the problem in the Assembly in 1705 and 1706;[300] in efforts to increase the salary or to hold it to the level imposed;[301] and in attempts to remedy the handling of the tobacco in a manner favorable to the clergy.[302]

The legislation of 1727 repealed that of 1696, and while it held the salary to the same level, it made such provisions for its handling, that this amount was net to the minister and the handling was done by designated authorities. Glebes were to contain at least two hundred acres, and buildings in good condition.[303]

No startling developments in the salary situation occurred until 1748, when a sermon on pride preached by Rev. William Kay, of Lunenburg parish, offended the sensibilities of his most powerful vestryman who had him ousted from one of the parish churches. Mr. Kay took the matter to court and was awarded £30 damages, which was sustained on appeal to England; in 1753, he received £200 from the Virginia General Court in lieu of salary. The most significant phase of the matter for the clergy was the right thus established to sue for trespass; for the people, notification that the clergy were ready to defend their position by appeal to law.[304] The right, thus confirmed, had been anticipated in an act of 1748, in which their salary was determined at "sixteen thousand pounds of tobacco, and cask, with an allowance of four *per* cent, for shrinkage."[305] Tobacco as a medium of currency was, however, still a fluctuating one. In 1753, an effort was made to stabilize the ministers' salaries in the counties of Frederick, Augusta, and Hampshire by fixing them at

---

300 *Jour., H. Burg.*, Oct. 27, 1705, 137 *ff.*; May 30, 1706, 208 *ff.*; *Jour., Va. Council*, May 30, 1706, I, 463.

301 *Va. Mag. Hist.*, XII, 287; *Jour., Va. Council*, May 10, 1722, II, 665; May 18, 1722, 668; *cf.* Chamberlayne, C. G.: *Vestry Book Christ Church Parish*, 177, 180–81; *Jour., Va. Council*, III, 1534; *Jour., H. Burg.*, May 19, 1722, 332–33; Nov. 14, 1720, 265–66.

302 *Va. Mag. Hist.*, XXV, 384 *ff.*; *Jour., Va. Council*, Dec. 3, 1714, I, 579; *Jour., H. Burg.*, Sept. 7, 1715, 163, 165 *ff.*; June 12, 1723, 387–89; Jones: *Pres. State Va.*, 71.

303 Hening: *Stat. at Large*, IV, 206; *Jour., H. Burg.*, Feb. 28, 1727, 28; *Jour., Va. Council*, Feb. 21, 1727, II, 730.

304 Perry: *Amer. Col. Church*, I, 389; Osgood: *Amer. Colonies in the 18th C.*, III, 475; Eckenrode: *Sep. Church and State*, 21.

305 Hening: *Stat. at Large*, VI, 88; usually referred to as the act of 1748, it was actually signed May 11, 1749, *Jour., H. Burg.*, May 11, 1749, 401–04.

£100 in currency.[306] This principle was extended, in 1755, for the whole colony so that all debts including taxes could be discharged in money at the rate of two pence per pound of tobacco; for which reason the act was usually referred to as the Two Penny Act.[307] This law was to be effective immediately for ten months only, and did not have the usual clause suspending its operation until royal sanction was obtained.[308] A petition of the Clergy presented in May of this year, asking for an increase of salary was rejected.[309] An upward trend in the tobacco market, at this time, made it more desirable to be paid in tobacco than money, and the clergy determined to insist on tobacco payments.[310] They presented their case to the Bishop of London.[311] In 1758, an act similar to that of 1755 was passed.[312] The failure again to enact the suspending clause, which, in the law of 1755 and in this law, was technically required in view of the royal sanction of the law of 1696, rendered it, in the opinion of the clergy, null and void and constituted an attempt to abrogate the royal authority in the colony; and, in this light of "Treason," it was regarded by the Bishop of London in a letter to the Lords of Trade and Plantations.[313] In 1759, the Clergy, without seeking redress from the Assembly, had Rev. John Camm take the matter to England; and he, upon receiving an order of the Privy Council declaring the Act of 1758 illegal, proceeded on his return to file suit—a case which dragged through the colonial and English courts until dismissed in 1767 on a technicality.[314]

A number of other cases came up;[315] but the case, which indicated in the clearest manner how far the temper of the colony had traveled from that solidarity of church and state created in 1662, appeared in the lawsuit of Rev. Thomas Maury, brought, in 1763, against the vestry of Hanover County. The scintillating

---

[306] Hening: *Stat. at Large*, VI, 369.
[307] *Jour., H. Burg.*, 1761–65, xxxviii *ff.*
[308] Hening: *Stat. at Large*, VI, 568.
[309] *Jour., H. Burg.*, May 15, 1755, 255–57.
[310] *Ibid.*, 1761–65, xxxviii *ff.*
[311] Perry: *Amer. Col. Church*, I, 440.
[312] Hening: *Stat. at Large*. VII, 240.
[313] Perry: *Amer. Col. Church*, I, 461.
[314] Burnaby: *Travels in America*, 49 *ff.*; Eckenrode: *Sep. Church and State*, 25, 27; *Va. Mag. Hist.*, X, 354, 355; Bancroft: *Hist. of U. S.*, V, 172.
[315] Cobb: *Rise of Relig. Liberty*, 109.

forensic ability of Patrick Henry impressed the jury with the thought that the use of the royal prerogative in opposition to salutary legislation for the people was tyranny; that the clergy in their failure to acquiesce in the law had not shown themselves to be "useful members of the state"; and that they (the jury) should take heed not "to rivet the chains of bondage on their own necks."[316]

The whole Parsons' Cause, as the issue of the clergy's salary was called, had had ample publicity in the pamphlet campaign initiated by Colonel Landon Carter, the opponent of Rev. William Kay, and in that of Rev. John Camm, as well as in the writings of Richard Bland who espoused the people's side.[317] Patrick Henry accentuated the fact that the disintegration of the union of church and state had begun.

In 1769, the matter of paying the salary in tobacco or money was left optional to agreement by the vestry and minister.[318] In January, 1771, "Philo-Dicaios," having recently come across this act, wrote a letter to the Clergy and Commissary through the *Virginia Gazette,* in which he objected that it was impossible in October to divine the price of tobacco in June.[319] In an April letter, he objected to the alternative possibility presented to him that the vestry might pay at the highest prices; he would have no such power levied in the vestries, "even to do their Ministers a Favour." Any discretionary powers left in the vestry only served to make the minister more dependent.[320]

Aside from consideration given to cases of individual adjustment of salary,[321] and an act passed in 1775 regarding the handling of tobacco for those ministers who received their salary thus instead of money,[322] no further action was taken before the Revolution in this matter.

---

316 *Jour., H. Burg.,* 1761–65, lii.
317 Clayton-Torrence, *Trial Bibli. Col. Va., 1754–1776,* 19–20, 24–25, 36–38; *Jour., H. Burg.,* 1761–65, xxxviii *ff.*
318 Hening: *Stat. at Large,* VIII, 384.
319 *Va. Gazette,* Jan. 31, 1771.
320 *Ibid.,* April 25, 1771.
321 *Jour., H. Burg.,* July 17, 1771, 129–30; Mar. 24, 1772, 267–69; *Jour.. Va. Council,* III, 1759, Appendix; *Jour., H. Burg.,* June 3, 1775, 184; June 6, 1775, 192–96.
322 *Cf. Ibid.,* June 22, 1775, 275–76; Hening: *Stat. at Large,* IX, 97.

With this negative attitude toward wishes of the clerical group as a whole, symbolic of the complete disintegration of union between church and state which was soon to take place, the history of the clergy's salaries closes.

The Episcopate

Hardly had the ruffled feelings of the people and the clergy occasioned by the law suits involving the clergy's salary question had an opportunity to be soothed, before, like piling "Ossa upon Pelion," there occurred a tremendous agitation concerning the question of creating a Virginia Bishop and establishing all the panoply of an American Episcopate.

A bishop had been recommended in 1661 by the writer of *Virginia's Cure.*[323] The Commissary had been created in 1689 as a substitute; for, already at that early date, the aversion to "spiritual courts" noted by Rev. Hugh Jones, in 1724, was seemingly familiar to the Bishop of London.[324] Though some attempts were made, nevertheless, looking to the creation of bishops,[325] it was not until the Society for the Propagation of the Gospel had grown strong in some of the other colonies and a fund had been accumulated for that purpose in England, that agitation for the creation of an American Episcopate, to include Virginia, began in earnest.[326] The missionary zeal of "The United Convention of New York and New Jersey"[327] resulted in the Commissary Rev. James Horrocks' calling a convention of the clergy.[328] The meeting on June 4, 1771, attended by twelve, out of approximately one hundred clergymen in Virginia, resolved, with four ministers dissenting, to proceed further in the matter of the Episcopate.[329] The mere announcement of the subject of the convention had already precipitated in the *Virginia Gazette,* a discussion of the merits of

---

[323] G.[reene]: *Virginia's Cure,* in Force's *Tracts,* III, 18.
[324] Cross, A. L.: *Anglican Episcopate,* 33–34, 43–45; Jones: *Present State of Va.,* 97, 110.
[325] Cobb: *Rise of Relig. Liberty,* 458, *ff.*; Cross: *Anglican Episcopate,* 90–91; Slaughter: *Colonial Church,* 30, 35.
[326] *Va. Gazette,* June 27, 1771; *cf.* Foote: *Sketches of Va.,* 198.
[327] Hawks: *Contrib. Ecc. Hist.,* I, 126.
[328] Cross: *Anglican Episcopate,* 231; *Va. Gazette,* May 9, 1771.
[329] *Cf. Wm. & Mary Coll. Quart.,* V, 152–54.

the proposed action.[330]   A protest against the proceedings of the
Convention signed by two participants, Samuel Henley, Professor
of Moral Philosophy, and Thomas Gwatkin, Professor of Mathematics and Natural Philosophy in William and Mary College,
appeared in the June 6 number of the *Gazette.*   The chief objections noted were that the consideration of an *American Episcopate,* affecting as it did the "natural rights and fundamental
laws" of other colonies, was outside the province of Virginia
clergy; further, that an *American Episcopate* would greatly
weaken the connection between England and the colonies; that
such an application on the part of the clergy without concurrence
of the Assembly was "an usurpation directly repugnant To the
Rights of Mankind."   This protest was immediately answered by
Rev. John Camm and was followed by letters pro and con of the
advocates of either side.   As far as official cognizance of the dispute was concerned, it was ended by a vote of thanks to the four
dissenters by the House of Burgesses on July 12, in which they
referred to the movement as a "pernicious Project . . . by which
much Disturbance, great Anxiety, and Apprehension, would certainly take Place among his Majesty's faithful *American* Subjects."[331]   No attempt on the part of the proponents of the plan
to make clear that what was intended was to invest the bishop
with "no Authority but purely of a spiritual and ecclesiastical
Nature";[332] the necessity of a bishop to act as "Head" in maintaining discipline among the clergy,[333] that to grant this to the
General Court was a usurpation of ecclesiastical authority by laymen;[334] the necessity of a bishop in order to dispense with ordi-
nations abroad, so inimical to the creation of a native clergy;[335]
and finally that in view of her purely Episcopal form of government, to dispense with a bishop was "unchurching" her altogether,[336] had weight in the view of the opponents who regarded

---

[330] *Va. Gazette*, May 30, 1771.
[331] *Jour., H. Burg.*, July 12, 1771, 121–22.
[332] *Va. Gazette*, June 6, 1771.
[333] *Ibid.*, June 11, 1771.
[334] *Ibid.*, June 13, 1771; Aug. 15, 1771; Eckenrode: *Sep. Church and State*, 30.
[335] *Va. Gazette*, June 27, 1771.
[336] *Ibid.*, Oct. 10, 1771.

the scheme as subversive of "religious Freedom";[337] as introducing a "*new* Jurisdiction" into the Colonies; as having a very likely tendency to draw "civil causes" into spiritual Courts; as a scheme tending to "enslave the Colonies" and to introduce tyranny.[338] The argument soon resolved itself into a question whether the deprivation of the essential right of the Church to a bishop was not equivalent to denying her "Toleration."[339]

The whole issue might soon have been dropped in view of the emphatic position taken by the House, were it not that Rev. Henley's stand on the Episcopate had aroused Robert Carter Nicholas, vestryman of Bruton parish, against him.[340] The influence of Nicholas defeated Henley in an election to that parish. Charges concerning Henley's orthodoxy, extending finally to charges of Socinianism enlivened the *Virginia Gazette* until practically the eve of the Revolution.[341]

Brilliant as were at times the arguments on either side, it did not seem possible for them to be maintained always with requisite dignity. The whole episode was far from being conducive to the rehabilitation of the prestige of the Established Church in the eyes of the people. It was one more symbol of the disintegration of church and state from within.

The Culmination of the Movement Toward Disintegration

The way for separation of Virginia from Great Britain was paved by Governor Dunmore's dissolution of the General Assembly, May 25, 1774. A General Convention of representatives of the colony held at Williamsburg, on May 6, 1776, proceeded to draw up a *Declaration of Rights* and frame a Constitution. The *Declaration of Rights* unanimously adopted June 12, 1776,[342] contained a particular expression of the attitude of the Assembly toward the question of religion; namely,

---

[337] *Ibid.*, July 18, 1771.
[338] *Ibid.*, June 20, 1771.
[339] *Ibid.*, Oct. 10, 1771; Jan. 9, 1772; Jan. 16, 1772.
[340] See p. 75.
[341] *Va. Gazette*, May 20, June 3, Dec. 16, 1773; Feb. 24, Mar. 10, May 12, 1774; Mar. 31, 1775.
[342] Hening: *Stat. at Large*, IX, 109–12.

That religion, or the duty which we owe to our CREATOR, and the manner of discharging it, can be directed only by reason and conviction, not by force or violence, and therefore all men are equally entitled to the free exercise of religion, according to the dictates of conscience; and that it is the mutual duty of all to practice Christian forbearance, love and charity towards each other.[343]

This declaration formed the basis of the subsequent legislation leading to the disestablishment of the Anglican Church and the complete separation of that union of church and state which had been the basic political philosophy of the colony under the régime of England.

The official recognition of the position of the dissenters on the question of conscience was not, according to the legal interpretation of that time, sufficient in itself to annul the legislation of the Colonial period on the union of church and state. There now began a titanic struggle between the dissenters and the members of the church—on the one hand, to tear down every trace of the establishment, and on the other, to save as much of it as was possible. Every step in the process meant a flood of petitions pro and con flooding the Assembly and the *Virginia Gazette.*

The position taken in the petitions of the dissenters was that taxation for parochial charges, where no equivalent was received, was unjust; that an establishment in the interests of a single denomination was discrimination. They demanded that marriage and burial be by their own ministers; that all taxes on conscience be abolished; that every denomination be placed on an equal footing; that every vestige of British tyranny and bondage be blotted out.[344]

The plea of those in sympathy with the establishment was that the activities of the dissenters were opposed to the principles of true Christianity; subversive of morals, destructive of family

---

[343] *Ibid.*, 111–12; *Cf.* Henley; *The Distinct Claims of Government and Religion*, 10–11—'' The rights of conscience are unlike the claims of Society, and cannot therefore be submitted to its direction.''

[344] *Va. Gazette*, April 26, 1776; Nov. 8, 1776; *Va. Mag. Hist.*, XVIII, 270, 265, 40–42; *Jour., H. Del.*, Oct. 16, 1776, 15; Oct. 11, 1776, 7; *Va. Mag. Hist.*, XVIII, 255; *Jour., H. Del.*, Oct. 22, 1776, 21; *Va. Mag. Hist.*, XVIII, 140; *Jour., H. Del.*, Nov. 1, 1776, 35; Force, P.: *Archives*, Ser. 5, Vol. II, 815; *Jour., H. Del.*, Oct. 25, 1776, 26; *Va. Mag. Hist.*, XVIII, 148; *Jour., H. Del.*, Nov. 9, 1776, 48.

peace, tended to the alienation of slaves; that the establishment had a presumptive right of tenure, that it was conducive to the peace and happiness of the state; that the doctrines of Christianity were synonymous with the inculcation of virtue, and that from that point of view any hardships of an establishment ought to be considered lightly; and that it was difficult to conceive of all denominations on a level without some attempting at preëminence.[345]

A number of resolutions, taking into cognizance these points of view,[346] led to an act in December, 1776, annulling all previous legislation rendering "criminal the maintaining any opinions in matters of religion, forbearing to repair to church, or the exercising any mode of worship whatsoever," freeing dissenters from all taxation for the established church. The property of the church was however reserved to its use and the question of a general assessment, or the propriety of leaving each religious society to voluntary contribution for support, was left to future consideration. For the present, the support of the established church was left to voluntary contribution and the salaries of the clergy suspended until the end of the next Assembly.[347]

The suspension of salaries resulted in virtually breaking the union of church and state; not only in that the precedent once established, it was easy to renew the suspension annually until 1779, when all previous legislation for the support of the clergy was repealed,[348] but also, in that it gave those in favor of complete separation added encouragement in their battle to eliminate every trace of the previous establishment.

Of the issues left undecided in 1776, that of the question of a general assessment revived a flood of petitions pro and con; the one party holding to the principle of civil non-interference, the other to the principle that religion as conducive to the good order and prosperity of the state ought to receive a regulated, not a pre-

---

[345] *Wm. & Mary Coll. Quart.*, XVII, 211–12; *Va. Mag. Hist.*, XVIII, 146; *Jour., H. Del.*, Nov. 8, 1776, 47; May 22, 1777, 27; May 29, 1777, 36; Dec. 11, 1777, 75; *Va. Mag. Hist.*, XVIII, 143.

[346] *Jour., H. Del.*, Nov. 19, 1776, 63; James: *Struggle for Relig. Liberty*, 78 ff.

[347] Hening: *Stat. at Large*, IX, 164 ff.; X, 198, indicates actual suspension ᴠas as of Jan. 1, 1777; Eckenrode: *Sep. Church and State*, 52.

[348] Hening: *Stat. at Large*, X, 111, 197.

carious support.[349]   It was the brilliantly facile pen of James
Madison which wrote the memorial finally defeating the assessment bill.   It never came out of the committee where it was
buried in 1785 by a flood of petitions paraphrasing Madison's
memorial.[350]   Madison's argument was that religion by its inherent nature was wholly exempt from cognizance by the civil
aspects of society.

In the meantime, the members of the Anglican Church, seeing
the necessity of some definition of their legal status, appealed, in
1784, for an Act of Incorporation.[351]   This was granted and reserved to them the property they had acquired under the old
régime; but, its various provisions went farther and amounted to
a regulation of the discipline of the church.[352]   The passing of
this Act showed clearly the difficulty of any legislative action
with reference to religion which should be free of the interpretation, on the part of some, as an attempt at civil interference with
religion.   It was attacked immediately on that basis and because
some of its provisions were objectionable to Episcopalians themselves; it was repealed in January, 1787.[353]

The inconsistency of legislation of this kind with the spirit of
the *Declaration of Rights* was made clearer by the passing in 1786
of Jefferson's ''Act for establishing religious freedom'' which had
been in abeyance since 1779.[354]   Holding boldly in its preamble
''that the opinions of men are not the object of civil government,'' it declared:

---

[349] *Jour., H. Del.*, June 3, 1777, 54; Dec. 5, 1777, 57; *Va. Gazette*, Mar.
28, 1777; *Jour., H. Del.*, Nov. 27, 1738, 36; May 15, 1784, 8; Nov. 4, 1784,
11; June 4, 1784, 36; Nov. 11, 1784, 19; Nov. 20, 1784, 32; Oct. 26, 1785,
6; Oct. 27, 1785, 8.

[350] Eckenrode: *Sep. Church and State*, 74 *ff.*, 113; James: *Struggle for
Relig. Liberty*, 134 *ff.*, Appendix G.; Niles: *Register*, July 5, 1817, 295–97;
Jour., H. Del., 1785 *passim;* Leland, J. *Hornworm and Pismire; Edward
Pleasants Valentine Papers*, II, 1237.

[351] Eckenrode: *Sep. Church and State*, 79–80.

[352] Hening: *Stat. at Large*, XI, 532–37.

[353] Eckenrode: *Sep. Church and State*, 81, 101, 129; Hening: *Stat. at
Large*, XII, 266; *Jour., Senate*, Jan. 10, 1787, 101.

[354] Eckenrode: *Sep. Church and State*, 113; Hening: *Stat. at Large*, XII,
84; Pollock, J. K.: *Amer. Gov't*, 45; James: *Struggle for Relig. Liberty*,
263; for its unfavorable reception ''By A Citizen Of Philadelphia,'' see
*Considerations On . . . An Act For The Establishment Of Religious Free-
dom.*

. . . That no man shall be compelled to frequent or support any religious worship, place or ministry whatsoever; nor shall be enforced, restrained, molested or burthened in his body or goods, nor shall otherwise suffer on account of his religious opinions or belief; but that all men shall be free to profess and by argument to maintain their opinions in matters of religion, and that the same shall in no wise diminish, enlarge or affect their civil capacities.[355]

But while, as we have seen, the Virginia legislature was ready to enunciate these bold principles of a new political philosophy, it moved more slowly in enacting the supplementary legislation which would make this philosophy a guide in practise—waiting first until the people made their attitude clear by petition.[356] There now began a drive to remove the *final vestiges* of Episcopalian power. Rumors of concerted action to deprive them of their glebes, led to a statement by the Convention of the Protestant Episcopal Church, in 1786, that any such measure was "unworthy the justice and wisdom of the General Assembly."[357] The drive of the Baptists and Presbyterians, however, was relentless. Though from the history of the origin of dissenters in Virginia, it is evident that except for the Quakers, their financial contribution, particularly that of the Baptists and Presbyterians, does not fall until after the second decade of the 18th century, dissenters maintained that the property of the Protestant Episcopal Church had been public property contributed by the general public and should revert to it; that retention was contrary to the *Declaration of Rights* and the Constitution.[358] The issue was contested until 1802 when the Assembly ordered the glebes sold, the proceeds to be appropriated to the poor or such objects as the majority of the voters in the county should designate.[359] An appeal to the courts to declare the Act of 1802 unconstitu-

---

[355] James: *Struggle for Relig. Liberty*, 263; cf. Hening: *Stat. at Large*, XII, 86; *Acts of Assembly*, 1830-31, 10.

[356] Cf. Lipscomb, A.: *Writings T. Jefferson*, XVII, 461.

[357] *Jour., H. Del.*, Dec. 5, 1786, 87.

[358] Eckenrode: *Sep. Church and State*, 131; *Jour., H. Del.*, Oct. 30, 1790, 26; Nov. 17, 1790, 37; Nov. 18, 1790, 73; Nov. 8, 1791, 43; Nov. 25, 1794, 39; Nov. 17, 1795, 21; Dec. 14, 1796, 167.

[359] *Acts of Assembly, Code*, 1803, 421-22; Eckenrode: *Sep. Church and State*, 147.

tional failed.[360]   With the deprivation of the glebes, all vestige of the union of church and state technically disappeared.[361]

The Significance of Disintegration

The quarter of century after the *Declaration of Rights* was for Virginia essentially one of readjustment to a new political philosophy.   It has been shown with what intense interest every phase of the religio-civil philosophy of integration was canvassed by the opinion of the eighteenth century; and with what effects upon the sensibilities of both parties to the question.   That it rendered the adherents of both schools of thought in the later history of Virginia sensitive to the effects of these philosophies upon the problem of the education of the youth of the state will be shown. The extent to which the controversies leading to the separation of church and state had rendered those opposed to union watchful, is reflected in the proud boast of Virginians that ''The fact remains that no taxes for religious purposes were ever paid in Virginia after January 1, 1777.''[362]   The significance of the attitude here implied and the validity of this boast are matters of future consideration.

---

[360] *Ibid.*, 148 *ff.*
[361] *Cf.* Humphrey: *Nationalism and Religion*, 489–90.
[362] Eckenrode: *Sep. Church and State*, 53.

CHAPTER IV

EDUCATION AS AFFECTED BY THE INTEGRATION OF CHURCH AND STATE
(1607–1776)

Initial Educational Efforts

The motive of bringing Christianity to the Indians had a very definite influence, as has been seen, in the plans for the first Indian schools. It will be recalled with what enthusiasm the idea of schools for Indian children, advanced in the letter of King James I, was expanded into a scheme for a University.[1] The transition in plan can be ascribed to no specific royal authority. None of the previous royal documents in behalf of the Company, such as the charters of 1606, 1609, or 1612 had indicated any concern for education beyond the implications to be found in propagating the gospel and continuing the "true Worship of Almighty God."[2] The absence of any policy in the founding of Virginia, with regard to the education of the colonists' children, received the following caustic comment from an Englishman who traveled through the colony in the early years of the nineteenth century:

James I. in enrolling the Established Church among the provisions of the Virginia Charter, with so marked a silence on the subject of established education, was but extending the intolerance he was so liberally dealing out at home. Pedantic and shallow as he was, it cannot be conceived he was ignorant of the necessity for education in a wild, warm, and luxurious country, which offered every temptation to disorder and immorality. We must suppose that he held the church to be in itself a sufficient means of instruction, or the best organizer of any supplementary one. But a school is as important to a country as a church. Upon points of doctrine sects will differ, but there can be no dispute with regard to practical morals, and to expect that grown people who have never been instructed in these when young, will either obey the laws or attend places of worship, is as reasonable as to suppose that a human being will walk because he has attained the age of twenty-one, if his legs have been kept manacled from childhood. . . .[3]

---

[1] See p. 16.
[2] Stith: *Hist. of Va.*, Appendix, 1–32, 20.
[3] Bernard, J.: *Retrospections of America*, 3.

The manner in which the Virginia Company obtained authority to concern itself with education is indicated by Captain John
Smith as follows:

> At last [they] got a Commission in their owne names, . . . also privileges
> for Cities; Charters for Corporations, Universities, Free-scholes, and Glebe-
> land; putting all those in practice before there was either people, students,
> or schollers to build or use them, or provision or victuall to feed them [that]
> were then there: . . .[4]

It is in this statement, too, that we come to the nearest hint of an
educational policy on the part of the Company. A review of
their records indicates that this was not so much a comprehensive
policy on the subject, as a favorable attitude towards it. The
custom of resorting to voluntary contribution, which had its impetus in the king's letter,[5] was evidently the one relied on by the
Company to initiate and further education for the children of
the colonists.

It was on the basis of voluntary subscription that the first
"publique free schoole," the East India school, was planned. The
history of this school does not begin until 1621. Before this, the
Assembly of 1619 had met, and, if one were to judge wholly from
the fact that no provision beyond that of catechetical instruction
for those "not yet ripe to come to the Coῆunion" was made, it
would seem, that either there was little need of educational provision, or that there was little interest in it.[6] The discussion regarding the East India school points to a different conclusion;
both the purpose and necessity of establishing a school in Virginia are revealed in the following statement:

> . . . they therefore conceaued it most fitt to resolue for the erectinge of a
> publique free schoole wch beinge for the educa͡on of Children and ground-
> inge of them in the principles of religion Ciuility of life and humane learn-
> inge serued to carry with it the greatest waight and highest consequence
> vnto the Planta͡cons as that whereof both Church and com͠onwealth take
> their originall founda͡con and happie estate, this beinge also like to proue a
> worke most acceptable vnto the Planters, through want whereof they haue

---

[4] Arber: *Travels and Works of Capt. J. Smith*, II, 929.
[5] See p. 16.
[6] *Jour., H. Burg.*, Aug. 4, 1619, 13.

bin hitherto constrained to their great coste to send their Children from thence hither to be taught.[7]

This school, planned on a broad basis, in consonance with the theory of integration of church and state, was to be a "Collegiate or free schoole" and "haue dependance vpon the Colledge in Virginia w*ch* should be made capable to receaue Schollers from the Shoole."[8] As the initiator of the enterprise, the Rev. Mr. Copland suggested the usher for the school and was one of the committee appointed to "conferr with him about the methode of teachinge and the booke he intends to instruct Children by,"— clearly with the intention of assuring the orthodoxy of the instruction.[9] Mr. Copland's usher decided to remain in England;[10] the Indian massacre of 1622 intervened, and it was not until 1625 that we read of the "unseasonable arrival" of Mr. Caroloff whose acts in the opinion of the Governor and Council "will overbalance all his other sufficiency though exceeding good."[11] If the records of the minutes before the General Court are any indication, this school never went into operation.[12]

The only other proposal for education during the period of the Virginia Company was that in connection with the gift of "Dust and Ashes."[13] Concerning the master for the proposed school, the donor humbly craved that he "may not be allowed to goe ouer except he first bringe in to the Companie sound testimony of his sufficiency in learninge and sincerity of life."[14]

Further indication that education in the colony was to be "without any difference at all from our courses receiued here at home" is found in John Brinsley's *A Consolation For Ovr Grammar Schooles*, dedicated among others, to the Virginia Company.[15] The aims of education, which are seen to be in

---

[7] Kingsbury: *Rec. of the Va. Co.*, I, 539; Neill: *Hist. of the Va. Co.*, 254.
[8] Kingsbury: *Rec. of the Va. Co.*, I, 540.
[9] *Ibid.*, I, 607.
[10] *Ibid.*, I, 629.
[11] Neill: *Hist. of the Va. Co.*, 257; *Memoir of Rev. P. Copeland*, 83–84; *Eng. Coloniz. of Amer.*, 171.
[12] *Va. Mag. Hist.*, XXIII, 131, 274; Bruce: *Inst. Hist. of Va.*, I, 349—for a different point of view, see *Va. Educ. Jour.*, XVI, 408.
[13] See p. 17.
[14] Neill: *Hist. of the Va. Co.*, 288.
[15] Brinsley, J.: *A Consolation For Ovr Grammar Schooles.*

accordance with the policy of integration, are thus given by Brinsley:

> . . . The first and chiefe whereof (as I conceiue) is this, That his pure relig-
> ion, honour, and true worship, may be set vp, and aduanced in them; the
> next, that the wealth and sauing of all his poore people in those places, both
> of their soules and bodies, may be by you procured, so farre as in your power
> shall lie. And these things to be effected principally, by a learned, holie,
> and faithfull Ministerie, protected and assisted by a godlie Magistracie, and
> by propagating and spreading all good learning and knowledge amongst
> them. To this purpose God hauing ordained Schooles of learning to be a
> principal meanes . . . for the breeding and nourishing of such a holie Min-
> isterie, with a wise and godlie Magistracie, and people to be perpetuallie pre-
> serued; your care as I take it, in the next place (that I may speak with all
> reuerence and submission) ought to be for prouision of meete Schooles and
> Seminaries for them, according to the natures and conditions of the places,
> and as God shall raise vp meanes thereto. . . .[16]

One object according to Brinsley in having education in the colony in harmony with that of England was "that so from vs may be sent continuall supplies of teachers."[17]

The type of education to be given in the "free schools" and furthered by Brinsley's pamphlet was clearly that of our secondary education looking to the ministry, the professions, and politics; but it was to be in harmony with the thought of education functioning under the control of the church supported by the state. The activities of the Virginia Company, however, compelled consideration of another type of education, that of apprenticeship for the hundreds of poor and orphaned children gathered from overburdened parishes and London and sent to Virginia.[18] The emphasis here was purely that of economic necessity, and while nothing was said of spiritual instruction, that had already been taken care of as seen in the catechetical legislation of 1619.[19]

The direction given to education by the close of the Virginia Company period was clearly one in harmony with the essential spirit of integration of church and state; what we get is an indication of intention—it remained for the legislation of the subse-

---

[16] *Ibid., Epistle Dedicatorie.*
[17] *Ibid.*
[18] Kingsbury: *Rec. of the Va. Co.,* I, 287, 555.
[19] *Ibid.,* 305–06; see p. 96.

quent period to institute, as will be seen, the machinery looking to effective control in that direction.

Catechetical Instruction

The principal legislative interest in education from 1624 to 1660 was in the spiritual instruction, not only of such groups as the poor, orphans, apprentices and servants, but of all, of whatever social or economic status. The law of 1632 was very explicit in the requirement that the minister, every Sunday, give the necessary religious instruction consisting of the Ten Commandments, the articles of the belief, the Lord's prayer, and the catechism, as given in the book of common prayer; and that it was the duty of parents, masters and mistresses to send their children, servants, or apprentices at the appointed time. Refusal to send or to learn was upon pain of censure by the county court, with the burden of presentation placed upon churchwardens.[20] In 1641, the Assembly limited the catechetical instruction to the period from the first Sabbath in March till the last in November.[21] The Assembly at this time, and again in 1645, imposed a fine of 500 pounds of tobacco on the minister for failure to give this instruction.[22] A similar penalty was placed in 1646 upon masters of families for failure to send their children or servants.[23]

The stringency of the legislation at this time is undoubtedly to be associated with the movement to eliminate Puritanism from the colony. In 1645, Governor Berkeley's former chaplain, Rev. Thomas Harrison, was presented to the General Court, by the churchwardens of Elizabeth River parish, for failure to catechize ''on Sunnedayes in the afternoone.''[24]

Catechetical instruction would seem to have been wholly in the hands of the ministers until 1661, when to meet the situation of those parishes which were without ministers, the Assembly revived the ancient practise of Queen Elizabeth's day of permitting the appointment of readers ''of sufficient abilities to read the prayers and homilies of the church (where they can be procured)

---

[20] Hening: *Stat. at Large*, I, 156, 157.
[21] *Va. Mag. Hist.*, IX, 52.
[22] Hening: *Stat. at Large*, I, 290.
[23] *Ibid.*, I, 311–12.
[24] James, E. W.: *Lower Norfolk Co., Va. Antiquary*, II, 12.

and to catechise children and servants.''[25] These readers were to be approved by the next adjacent ministers.[26] In 1662, it was ordered that neither minister nor reader teach any other catechism than that in the book of common prayer; the minister was to expound no other, and the reader was to expound neither the catechism nor the scriptures.[27] It is thus every precaution was taken to insure orthodoxy, and it is hardly likely that children were encouraged to make more than a mere memoriter study of the catechism.

An example of vestry action regarding catechetical instruction is found in the following record of action taken at a vestry meeting in Christ Church parish, Middlesex County, in 1689:

> It is also Ordered That for the Future the Prish be Served by Thre Clerks, Each Church haveing one Distinct, Who shall Duely on ye Lords Day Read Divine Service, and a Homily and also hear ye Children The Catechisme of the Church of England, Moreover Each Clerk shalbe a Man of good Sober life and Conversation, . . .[28]

In 1691, Governor Nicholson used his influence with the General Court to sanction a scheme for the use of readers in the outlying parishes of the southeastern counties, Isle of Wight, Nansemond, Norfolk, and Princess Anne. For their encouragement, he urged that the privilege to teach schools be granted them, on condition that the county courts were to see that the readers appointed were in conformity with the church.[29] Such readers would, of course, have had authority to give catechetical instruction. It appears from a memorandum given this year by Nicholson to Commissary Blair to be presented to the Bishop of London, that it was his wish, if a scheme for towns were advanced, that approval should be given for maintaining a schoolmaster for at least English and writing in every town, and it was his opinion that ''A small encouragm't to the Parish Clerk or reader may perhaps enable him to keep such a school.''[30] As Nicholson

25 Hening: *Stat. at Large*, II, 29.
26 *Ibid.*
27 *Ibid.*, II, 47.
28 Chamberlayne: *Vestry Book Christ Church Parish*, 61.
29 James: *Lower Norfolk Co., Va. Antiquary*, I, 65–66; Bruce: *Inst. Hist. of Va.*, I, 333; *cf.* Wells, G. F.: *Parish Educ. Va.*, 20–22.
30 *Va. Mag. Hist.*, VII, 157.

complains in this memorandum of the great scarcity of school-masters and ministers, and of the failure of ministers to catechise, it seems that he hoped to find in the use of readers a solution of the problem of Christian education of children.[31] There is no evidence of the extent to which the Governor's inclination to favor readers resulted in their use as teachers;[32] however, it would appear that either readers did begin to act as schoolmasters or that schoolmasters saw a means of adding to their incomes by acting as readers—for, in 1700, a petition was presented to the House of Burgesses asking "that Schoolmasters may have the Preference to Clerks or Readers places in the Church."[33] This petition was rejected.[34]

Seemingly, the provision already made for Christian education did not satisfy the people of Gloucester and Lancaster counties, for, in 1699, they sent a petition that "Care" be taken for the education of youth in the Christian religion. This was rejected on the basis of being already sufficiently provided for by law.[35]

The extent to which catechetical instruction was given in the second decade of the eighteenth century can be gathered from a summary of the 1724 questionnaire to the clergy. From 29 replies to the question, "At what time do you Catechise the Youth of your Parish?"—one finds that 14 confined this activity to the Sundays in Lent, 9 either extended the period of instruction beyond Lent or gave it at some time from spring to fall, 1 gave it when permitted, 4 gave no instruction, and in 1 parish, it was taken care of by the schoolmasters.[36] It is clear that in the course of the more than eighty years since the Legislature had specified the season from the first Sabbath in March till the last in November for catechetical instruction, there had arisen a great variety of procedure in this respect.

The evidence of the extent to which catechetical instruction was kept in the hands of the ministry is particularly interesting, the only exception being in Henrico parish, whose minister ex-

---

[31] *Ibid.*, 156–57.
[32] *Cf.* Wells: *Parish Educ. Va.*, 20–22.
[33] *Jour. H. Burg.*, Dec. 14, 1700, 216–17.
[34] *Ibid.*, Dec. 19, 1700, 223–25.
[35] *Ibid.*, May 10, 1699, 151–57.
[36] Perry: *Amer. Col. Church*, I, 257–348; see p. 653, Appendix I.

plained it as due to the fact that the great distance of families from the church made it difficult to bring the children when small, so "that office is done by the Schoolmasters or parents and when they grow to any bigness they care not to abide the public Catechising of a Minister."[37]   There is no evidence in the answers to the questionnaire that readers did any catechising, but this may be due to the fact that it was addressed to parishes having ministers.

In 1730, the House decided to defer the question before it, of "providing proper methods for Erecting and maintaining Schools in order to the training up of Youths to Reading and to a necessary knowledge of the Principles of Religion."[38]

With the increase of dissent, the necessity for extending the opportunities for "Christian," that is, orthodox instruction, became a serious one.   In 1754, Commissary Dawson addressing a convention of the clergy urged that:

. . . Another way of doing honor to God, credit to ourselves & advancing the interest of religion, is to procure schools to be erected in our several parishes, that the youth may have an early knowledge & love of Piety.   Impressions made upon young minds, commonly strike the deepest, & last the longest.   Schools therefore are of great importance, where the youth may have an opportunity of being taught what is proper, of reading their Bibles, of learning their Prayers & Catechism, where, in short, they may by due management, be insensibly led to think, to talk & act as become Christians.[39]

This statement is of particular interest in showing that well into the period before the Revolution, schools were regarded as the proper place for giving religious instruction.

Though from a legal point of view, the minister was the final authority as to the catechetical knowledge of his parishioners, it would seem that there gradually grew up the practise of leaving much of this instruction in the hands of schoolmasters; a custom probably favored by the fact that candidates for the ministry were frequently schoolmasters or that schoolmasters were themselves ministers.   Thus, in 1727, Governor Gooch wrote to the Bishop of London that he hoped to take care of Rev. Joseph

---

[37] Perry: *Amer. Col. Church*, I, 304–05.
[38] *Jour., H. Burg.*, May 26, 1730, 62–63.
[39] Perry: *Amer. Col. Church*, I, 417.

Smith by obtaining a school for him; and a year later, recommends three candidates for ordination, two of whom had acted as tutors in private families and the other as a schoolmaster in one of the towns.[40] One comes across similar cases throughout the colonial period.[41]

There exist two diaries of tutors at the close of the colonial period—that of Philip V. Fithian, a Princeton student and candidate for the Presbyterian ministry, tutor in the home of the liberal and religiously erratic Robert Carter, and that of John Harrower, Scotch indentured servant, tutor in the home of Coleral and religiously erratic Robert Carter, and that of John Harrower during 1773–76. Fithian usually notes his Saturday mornings as devoted to hearing the children repeat their catechism; Harrower does not seem to have been so methodic, but he noted the occasions when the children finished reading through the Bible or the Bible and New Testament, also that "the Eldest is now reading very distinctly in the Psalter according to the Church of England and the other two boys ready to enter into it."[43]

A minister as schoolmaster is noted as early as 1658,[44] and the extent to which education was in the hands of the ministry, due to the licensing law, the creation of the College of William and Mary, and the encouragement given by Commissary Dawson will appear in the discussion of Parsons' Schools.[45] It is evident that the care exercised in catechetical instruction was a direct outcome of the policy of integration of church and state.

Education of Orphans, Poor, and Apprentices

The sincerity of the government in its intention to assure religious education for all, is evident in the care it exercised that orphans, poor children, and apprentices should not be overlooked in this matter; and though the general provisions for catechetical instruction of servants and apprentices would seem to have been

---

[40] *Va. Mag. Hist.*, XXXII, 221, 227.
[41] *Ibid.*, 330; Perry: *Amer. Col. Church*, I, 432–33.
[42] Fithian: *Journal & Letters*, xix; Harrower, J.: *Diary*, 65, 78; Carter was successively Anglican, Baptist, Swedenborgian, and Papist.
[43] Fithian: *Journal & Letters, passim;* Harrower; *Diary*, 88, 106.
[44] Bruce: *Inst. Hist. Va.*, I, 333.
[45] See p. 124.

comprehensive enough, a special point was frequently made, as will appear, of emphasizing Christian instruction in the legal care exercised over various social and economic groups. The government saw to it that no group was neglected in this fundamental matter of bringing the entire population under the influence of the church.

In 1643, legislation provided for the holding of an annual orphans' Court in each county, before which overseers and guardians had to submit an account of their stewardship. It was specifically enacted that

> . . . all overseers and guardians of such orphants are injoyned by the authoritie aforesaid to educate and instruct them according to their best endeavours in Christian religion and in rudiments of learning. . . .[46]

In case of delinquency, the courts could assume charge and provide for the orphans "according to their estates and qualities."[47] The seeming limitation upon a liberal education was removed in 1656, when the law ordered that the orphan be bound to some manual trade only when the estate was so inconsiderate as not to "reach to a free education" or where there were no friends or relations willing to keep the orphan on the interest of the limited estate.[48]

The master of any orphaned apprentice was required, in 1705, "to teach him to read and write"—the necessary basis of religious instruction.[49]

It had been the custom, seemingly, from the very beginning of Virginia history, for fathers or widows to indicate in their wills the disposition they wished made of the education of their children, and this often included a statement with regard to their religious training.[50] With the coming of dissenters, and the falling from episcopal grace of one or the other parent, a serious question arose as to who was to have the disposition of the religious training of the children.[51] It was, undoubtedly, to settle this

---

[46] Hening: *Stat. at Large*, I, 260–61; Chitwood, O. P.: *Justice Col. Va.*, 80; Beverley: *Hist. of Va.*, 209.
[47] Hening: *Stat. at Large*, I, 260–61.
[48] *Ibid.*, I, 416; *cf.* also *Jour., H. Burg.*, Oct. 16, 1693, 453–54.
[49] Hening: *Stat. at Large*, III, 375.
[50] *Va. Mag. Hist.* VI, 115; Wise: *Eastern Shore*, 271.
[51] *Wm. & Mary Coll. Quart.*, IX, 127.

issue, that a bill which had been in abeyance in the Assembly since 1727, was passed in 1730, empowering the father in his will to dispose, as he saw fit, of the "custody and tuition" of his children until the age of 21, provided that custody was not entrusted to popish recusants, and further, that apprenticeship indentures already made and the rights of the courts to protect orphans were not infringed.[52] This remained the essential law concerning orphans until the close of the colonial period; the law of 1748 on the subject being merely a more detailed explanation of the salient features of other laws on the subject.[53] But, whether or not his religious training was indicated in the father's will, the orphan's religious instruction was already provided for by the law of 1643.[54]

The responsibility of apprenticing boys and girls, whose parents did not or were unable to make proper provision for their training, was placed, in 1672, upon the churchwardens who were to give an account of all such children annually to the orphans' courts.[55] In 1727, an act which was an extension of a law of 1693 on the subject, provided that where parents because of their disorderly course of life, or neglect, failed to provide for the care and education of their children "in christian principles," that the churchwardens, upon certificate from the court, were to bind out or apprentice such children—clear evidence that in Virginia law and custom, apprenticeship was regarded as including provision for religious training.[56] To all intents and purposes, neglected children were looked upon by the law as orphans, and the law assumed a similar authority over them; a point of view indicated in the law of 1748, which again emphasized the principles of the law of 1727.[57] The number of poor people had so increased by 1755, that the Assembly was constrained to order the vestries to erect poor houses; and they were ordered "to levy a reasonable allowance in their parish levies, for the education of such poor

---

52 *Jour., H. Burg.*, Feb. 22, 1727, 24–25 *ff.*; June 25, 1730, 88 *ff.*; Hening: *Stat. at Large*, IV, 285.
53 *Ibid.*, V, 449.
54 *Ibid.*, I, 260–61.
55 *Ibid.*, II, 298
56 *Jour., H. Burg.*, Oct. 26, 1693, 465–67; Nov. 10, 1693, 485; *Jour., Va. Council*, Oct. 26, 1693, I, 196; Hening: *Stat. at Large*, IV, 212.
57 *Ibid.*, VI, 32.

children as shall be placed in the said house, or houses, until they shall be bound out according to law.''[58] Provision for apprenticeship, to include learning to read and write, was extended to illegitimate children in 1769. This provision was under the control of the churchwardens, but the hearing and adjusting of complaints were reserved to the county courts.[59]

Provision for education at William and Mary College for a limited number of poor children was made in 1718 by the creation of a scholarship fund for this purpose. As late as June 21, 1776, an advertisement in the *Virginia Gazette* refers to the foundationers of the college.[60]

It is evident from this account of the legal provision for the education and Christian training of orphans, poor children, and apprentices, that the machinery of church and state as represented in churchwardens, vestries, and county courts, was invoked to take the place of adequate parental care of children more happily favored. The religious training of all children was, as seen in the discussion of catechetical instruction, subject to the approval of the clergy. Judging from the attitude assumed toward religious instruction and the provision made for it, it is clear that the Assembly recognized its significance in the broader policy of the integration of church and state.

Licensing of Teachers

A most important development in the educational history of Virginia between 1661 and 1690 was that of placing schoolmasters definitely under the control of church and state. The Act of Uniformity passed by Charles II, in 1662, had prescribed, upon pain of certain penalties, a declaration of conformity upon all officers of instruction, from deans to tutors, in every type of institution, from the university to the home.[61] No particular notice

---

[58] *Ibid.*, VI, 476; this was the first legal authorization, except for the financial provisions made for the College of William and Mary, for taxation to provide for education; it is true, for a limited group, and for a limited time. It is interesting, too, as providing for local taxation for local educational needs.

[59] *Ibid.*, VIII, 376–77.

[60] *Jour., H. Burg.*, May 20, 1718, 199; May 29, 1718, 213–14; Hening: *Stat. at Large*, IV, 74; *cf. Wm. & Mary Coll. Quart.* III, 107.

[61] Gee & Hardy: *Documents Eng. Church Hist.*, 606–09.

of this phase of the Act seems to have been taken in Virginia until, in 1683, the King's instructions to Lord Howard of Effingham provided:

And we do further direct that no school-master be hence forward permitted to come from England and to keep school within our Colony of Virginia without the License of the said Bishop.

And that no other person now there or that shall come from other parts be admitted to keep school without the License first had.[62]

Instructions in similar form were given to later governors.[63]

Lord Howard's Catholic faith was undoubtedly the reason that his memory on the subject had to be refreshed by the Bishop of London, before he issued a proclamation in July, 1686, calling attention to the fact that the Bishop of London "forbids any person to Officiate as a School-Master without his License to be obtained by Testimonials of his Character and Conformity from some understanding persons, of the Parish."[64] The real sting in the proclamation came, however, in the requirement "that no School Master be permitted or allowed or any other person or persons instructing or Teaching Youth as a School Master so to practice before license obtained from me."[65]

The effect of this was naturally to keep all instruction in agreement with the tenets of the Anglican Church and in the hands of schoolmasters subservient to the ministers of the church; or, taking the next logical step, to surrender education to the ministers themselves. The matter did not pass without protest from the Burgesses who informed the Governor, that reports from their respective counties indicated that a number of "knowing skillfull Schoolmasters" had left because their allowance would not suffice to cover the expense involved in procuring a license by personal appearance at Jamestown. The House in its own name, and that of all the inhabitants of the country, asked the governor to appoint one or more persons in each county to take care of the

---

62 McIlwaine: *Exec. Jour., Council Col. Va.,* I, 515; *Va. Mag. Hist.,* XIX, 342.

63 *Ibid.,* XXI, 350; *cf.* Osgood: *Amer. Colonies in the 18th C.,* II, 10–11.

64 McIlwaine: *Exec. Jour., Council Col. Va.,* I, 508.

65 *Ibid.; Va. Mag. Hist.,* XIX, 7–8; Beverley: *Hist. of Va.,* 77; Bruce: *Inst. Hist. Va.,* I, 334.

matter upon a moderate and reasonable fee.[66]   To this the governor yielded only to the extent that the examination should be "by the next of his Majesties Councell of this Colonie" with whom licenses were to be left, a small fee to go to the Governor's clerk for writing the same.[67]

The Declaration of Indulgence, 1687, by James II, abrogated the Act of Uniformity.   The Toleration Act of William and Mary, 1689, made no specific reference to secular teachers.[68]   It has been seen, however, in the discussion of the policy of integration of church and state, how the Virginian attitude harked back to the spirit embodied in the Act of Uniformity rather than to that in the Act of Toleration.[69]   It would seem that to all intents and purposes, Lord Howard's proclamation of 1686 remained in force, as will appear in a consideration of the license requirement for teachers in certain of the free schools, whose organization came under the direction of the Assembly.[70]   That the effect of the licensing requirement was to bring about a complete conformity of education with the Anglican Church is clear from the fact that, when, in 1693, an attempt was made on the part of some to further strengthen conformity by providing that none might undertake the education of youth except professed members of the Church of England who had subscribed to the canons, the House declared that this was already sufficiently provided for in the laws.[71]

The next important development in the licensing of school teachers occurred in 1699 during the régime of Governor Nicholson, who had received instructions similar to those of Lord Howard of Effingham.   The County Courts were ordered to return to the Council

. . . a particular account, what schooles are in their Respective Counties & whither *ye* Masters thereof are Lycensed according to *ye Sd* Instructions; and to recommend such as are fitt & Capable for *yt* Imploym*t yt* they may

---

[66] *Jour., H. Burg.,* Nov. 2, 1686, 269–70.

[67] *Ibid.,* Nov. 8, 1686, 274; Beverley: *Hist. of Va.,* 77, states the fee was 20 shillings.

[68] Gee & Hardy: *Documents Eng. Church Hist.,* 641, 654.

[69] See p. 58.

[70] See p. 110, 123.

[71] *Jour., H. Burg.,* Oct. 16, 1693, 453–55.

be lycensed accordingly; which lycenses are to be granted them without any fee or other charge.[72]

There is no evidence that the essential features of the licensing procedure established at this time received any modification during the remaining colonial period. Schoolmasters thus came under the control not only of the Church which certified to their orthodoxy, but also of the county court which had the power of recommendation. It would appear from county court records that their certification referred particularly to the competency of the teacher to teach the various subjects.[73]

The extent to which licensing was evaded probably increased with the wider coming of dissenters after the first decade of the 18th century, and this was probably frequently the case in the petty schools whose curriculum consisted of English and writing. Of these schools, Hugh Jones said in 1724:

> . . . to prevent the sowing the seeds of Dissention and Faction, it is to be wished that the *Masters* or *Mistresses* should be such as are approved or licensed by the Minister, and vestry of the Parish, or Justices of the County; the Clerks of the Parishes being generally most proper for this Purpose; . . .[74]

Elsewhere, Jones makes the statement, ''Let none be permitted to teach School in any Parish, but such as shall be nominated by the Minister and Vestry, and licensed by the President of the College.''[75]

Upon which pious wish, Oldmixon who wrote on American history not many years later, commented as follows:

> . . . I cannot help objecting to that Divine's laudable Zeal against Protestant Dissenters; he should not, methinks, have pressed to the Legislature the worst Part of the *Schism Bill*, by taking away the Liberty of teaching Children to read without Licence from the Parson of the Parish, or President of the College, who, on the present Footing, will never grant it to any one in Communion with the Churc   New-England, or of their Religion in any Part of the World.[76]

---

[72] McIlwaine: *Exec. Jour., Council Col. Va.,* I, 456.
[73] Bruce: *Inst. Hist. of Va.,* I, 337; *cf.* Stanard, M. N.; *Colonial Va.,* 272.
[74] Jones: *Present State of Va.,* 70.
[75] *Ibid.,* 84.
[76] Oldmixon, J.: *Brit. Empire in America,* I, 436.

That there was some dissatisfaction, at this time, on the part of the clergy with regard to licensing is evident from a proposition of Rev. Mr. Alexander Forbes to the House of Burgesses, requesting "That fit perfons only be Allowed to teach in private Schools and that a Method may be prescribed for Examining Licencing and Overseeing private School Masters."[77]   This proposition was rejected.   Mr. Forbes in answering the questionnaire of 1724,[78] replied that "some vagrant and loose Persons pretending to teach at a lower rate than another who would honestly mind his business can afford to do, so as to subsist by it" were the cause of the defects "of our Private schools."[79] Whether it was the dissenters or the underbidding of salaries that worried the clergy more, is not clear.

It would appear that after William and Mary College became fully organized that nearby courts would send their prospective teachers to the college to undergo their secular examination. Thus it was provided by law, in 1752, that the master of the Norfolk Academy

> . . . shall undergo an examination before the masters of the college of William and Mary, and the minister of Elizabeth parish, for the time being, and produce a certificate of his capacity, and also a license, from the governor.[80]

On January 1, 1756, Mr. Richard Collinson was examined by the President and masters of the college and was "thought capable of teaching the Grammar School at Norfolk."[81]   In that same year, in passing a law for the reorganization of the Peasley school for the benefit of the children in the parishes of Abingdon and Ware, Gloucester County, the Assembly, while not requiring the examination before the faculty of William and Mary, specified the examination before the minister of the parish and the governor's license.[82]

---

[77] *Jour., H. Burg.*, June 12, 1723, 387–89.
[78] See p. 27.
[79] Perry: *Amer. Col. Church*, I, 330–31.
[80] Hening: *Stat. at Large*, VI, 265; James: *Lower Norfolk Co., Va. Antiquary*, I, 81; Brown: *Secularization Amer. Educ.*, 35.
[81] James: *Lower Norfolk Co., Va. Antiquary*, I, 22; *Wm. & Mary Coll. Quart.*, II, 127; V, 144.
[82] Hening: *Stat. at Large*, VII, 41–43; Brown: *Secularization Amer. Educ.*, 35.

It is clear from the examples cited, that teachers, wishing to pursue their calling legally, came under the control of both church and state; and that dissenters in attempting to conduct schools were defying the government.

Higher Education and the Integration Policy

By 1661, the rapid increase in population, the coming of the first important dissenting group, the Quakers, and the civic enthusiasm created by the restoration of Charles II, compelled a more studied consideration of the problem of education.[83] In line with the renewed emphasis on the integration of church and state, the Assembly proposed to erect a college and free school for "the advancement of learning, promoteing piety & provision of an able & successive ministry."[84] But besides attempting to satisfy their immediate needs in this direction, the Assembly proposed to establish a policy looking to "the erecting of colledges and schooles in this countrye,"[85] by petitioning the king, through Governor Berkeley, for his "letters pattents to collect and gather the charity of well disposed people in England."[86] The lack of an adequate ministerial supply which was undoubtedly the primary cause of this legislation is indicated not only in the preambles to this legislation,[87] but also in the fact that the Assembly petitioned "for his majesties letters to both universities of Oxford and Cambridge to furnish the church here with ministers for the present,"[88] and in their sending the Rev. Phillip Mallory to solicit "church affaires" in England.[89] It is clear from the connection between church and education in this legislation, that the Rev. Mr. Mallory was to solicit funds to initiate the new educational policy of erecting colleges and schools which were to

---

[83] The total population in 1625 is given as 1202, as about 5,000 in 1634, as over 15,000 in 1649; Bruce: *Social Life of Va., 17th C.,* 17, 18; as above 40,000 in 1671, Hening: *Stat. at Large,* II, 515; for the agitation created by the coming of the Quakers, see p. 55 *ff.*

[84] Hening: *Stat. at Large,* II, 37, 25.

[85] *Ibid.,* II, 30.

[86] *Ibid.*

[87] *Ibid.,* 25, 37.

[88] *Ibid.,* 30–31.

[89] *Ibid.,* 34.

serve as the means for advancing religion and creating a ministerial supply.[90]

It is not without significance that in September of this year, there was presented to the Bishop of London the first important statement since the *Petition of W. C.* to Parliament, twenty years before, on the subject of religion and education in Virginia. *Virginia's Cure* indicated that "not above a fifth part" of the parishes of Virginia was supplied with ministers.[91]   The difficulty of complying with the legislation looking to orthodox instruction and the consequent opportunity for the proselyting activity of dissenters become evident at once.   The author does not fail, however, to point out that where there is a minister, attendance upon his instruction is hindered by the plantation system, and insists that the town system is the only remedy.   He declares, "Lastly, their almost general want of Schooles, for the education of their Children, is another consequent of their scattered planting, of most sad consideration, most of all bewailed of Parents there.''[92]   Among other proposals by the author is the suggestion that the king authorize collections to be made in all churches of the realm for the purpose of building towns and schools, and that Parliament designate a certain number of vacant Fellowships in both universities, as Virginia Fellowships, to be used for the education of prospective Virginia ministers, "so long as the Needs of that Church shall require it.''[93]   The advantages from the course indicated would be,

. . . they will enjoy the benefits of vertuous Examples, of publick Catechizing and Instructing their Children and Servants in the Principles and Duties of the Christian Religion, according to the Constitutions of the Church of *England;* whereby not only Children and Servants, but Parents and Masters who are ignorant, may (without being ashamed) be enlightened with true saving knowledge, and their children in Schools of Learning, may grow up to be serviceable both in Church and State.   And by good Discipline and careful tending in well order'd Societies, under faithful Teachers and Magistrates, both Parents and Children would by the grace of God grow into habits of Christian Living, . . .[94]

[90] Anderson: *Colonial Church,* II, 544–45.
[91] G.[reene]: *Virginia's Cure,* in Force's *Tracts,* III, 4.
[92] *Ibid.,* 6.
[93] *Ibid.,* 9, 10.
[94] *Ibid.,* 10–11.

The significance of the policy of integration of church and state for education is sufficiently clear in the above statements from *Virginia's Cure* which reflect so accurately the legislation of that year.

In prosecuting their purpose, the Assembly, in addition to sending Mr. Mallory to England, where he seems to have died before he was able to achieve anything substantial,[95] subscribed liberally themselves for the proposed educational scheme, obtained a subscription from the governor and ordered the commissioners of the county courts to subscribe, to receive subscriptions from persons at their courts, and to send orders to the vestries of the various parishes for the subscriptions of the inhabitants.[96]

The legislation of 1661 with regard to the erection of a college and free school was reënacted in 1662.[97]

The question now arises as to the outcome of the evident enthusiasm of the Assembly for an extensive program of educational activity; one in which they solicited the co-operation by subscription of all Virginia. There is no proof that anything was achieved beyond placing the attitude of the Assembly on record. In a true explanation of the negative result of this ample legislation, one would undoubtedly find an explanation for the fact that nothing constructive was again attempted until about thirty years later. Did the people fail to respond so decidedly as to warrant no further action on the part of the government?

[95] *Va. Mag. Hist.*, XII, 398–99; *cf.* Anderson: *Colonial Church*, II, 545.

[96] Hening: *Stat. at Large*, II, 37; the following writers, Tyler: *Williamsburg*, 112; Heatwole, C. J.: *Hist. of Educ. Va.*, 37; Maddox, W. A.: *Free Sch. Idea Va.*, 2, identify the governor giving the subscription as Governor Berkeley—Maddox has this take place in 1662. Maddox and Heatwole call attention to the implied contradiction to Berkeley's statement in 1671, "But, I thank God, *there are no free schools* nor, *printing*," Hening: *Stat. at Large*, II, 517. It is more probable that the Governor referred to here, unless we are to assume that Berkeley's subscription was given before he left the country, was the acting Governor, Col. Francis Moryson (Morrison) who was deputy-governor in Berkeley's absence, *cf.* also Hening: *Stat. at Large*, II, 149, and to whom the subscriptions referred to in Hening: *Stat. at Large*, II, 37, are directed to be sent. Hening in his comment on Berkeley's remark, II, 511, 517, says nothing of any contradiction in attitude. Furthermore, Hening, II, 17, 147, are proof that Berkeley was in England from probably the latter part of January, 1661, to the latter part of 1662, *cf.* also Anderson: *Colonial Church*, II, 543, 548, and Fox, W. F.: *Civil Gov't Va.*, 125.

[97] Hening: *Stat. at Large*, II, 56.

Anderson attributes Mallory's failure in England "to the clamour of conflicting interests which then prevailed."[98]   It must be recalled that this legislation was passed in the absence of Governor Berkeley in England. Hawks, the historian of the Protestant Episcopal Church, was of the opinion, but he cites no authority, that *Virginia's Cure* was presented to the Bishop of London at the "instigation" of Berkeley.[99]   There is evidence in the Minutes of the Council for Foreign Plantations, that Berkeley was requested on August 5, 1661, "to bring in writing such an account of Virginia and Propositions for the advantage of that Plantation as to him shall seem fit,"[100] but the definite dedication of *Virginia's Cure* to the Bishop of London, and the internal evidence of the pamphlet, point away from any such identification with the paper requested of Berkeley, and rather to the possibility that this paper was written for, or at the suggestion of, Rev. Mr. Mallory to present to his superior.[101]   To identify Berkeley with *Virginia's Cure* would imply a favorable attitude toward education which is contradicted by the fact that Berkeley made no effort in his continued long career as governor extending to 1677,[102] to realize this program in any way. Seemingly, from Berkeley's point of view, the integration of church and state was sufficiently taken care of by the insistence on uniformity, by strengthening the ecclesiastical machinery,[103] and by stringent provision for catechetical instruction.[104]   To him, the danger from learning and printing, with their propensity for creating disobedience, heresy, sects, and libels, was one too real to inspire any attitude favorable to the policy proposed by the Assembly. In fact, it will be recalled, that one of the questions asked by Bacon, in 1676, was "what arts, sciences, schools of Learning, or

---

98 Anderson: *Colonial Church*, II, 545.

99 Hawks: *Contrib. Ecc. Hist.*, I, 64.

100 Sainsbury, W. N.: *Cal. State Papers, 1661–1668*, 51.

101 Neill: *Eng. Coloniz. of Amer.*, 172, attributed *Virginia's Cure* to "a clergyman who had lived in Virginia" apparently basing it on internal evidence; Eckenrode in Wm. Clayton Torrence's *Trial Bibliography of Colonial Virginia*, 77, gives the author as Robert Greene, but states nothing further; *cf.* however, Neill: *Va. Carolorum*, 244; *Va. Mag. Hist.*, XII, 399.

102 Hening: *Stat. at Large*, II, 517.

103 See p. 42.

104 See p. 99 *ff.*

manufactorys, have bin promoted in authorety.''[105] Berkeley in
his refusal to see the connection between education and a ministerial supply, and between the need of an adequate ministerial
supply and the policy of integration, paved the way for the entrance of dissent as well as for disintegration from within.

The grant of Virginia to Lords Arlington and Culpeper, in
1673, is of interest because of the privilege given them to erect,
at their convenience, ''churches colledges chappells ffree
schools,'' with absolute authority for the appointment of all the
personnel of these institutions. No opportunity to initiate an
educational policy on the basis here indicated was given by the
Virginia Assembly, who immediately appointed a commission for
appeal to the King, looking to the restoration of their civil rights
—an appeal granted in 1684.[106]

It was not until five years later, with the appointment of Rev.
James Blair, as Commissary, that active steps were taken to
create ''a free schoole and colledge.'' The earliest extant official
notice of the project occurs in the record of a meeting of the
Council on July 25, 1690, in which the project is referred to as
''(a thing already proposed by some pious Men)'' and as ''a
designe, which by the blessing of God Almighty may be for his
Glory, the Honor of their Majesties, and the Good of this Country.''[107] In that same month, the matter was presented to a convention of the clergy, by the Commissary.[108] The proposition as
outlined to be presented to the Assembly indicated that for the
''better encouragement of learning'' there should be founded a
college ''to consist of three schools, *viz.*, Grammar, Philosophy,
and Divinity.''[109] Subscription papers indicated the object at
the time as ''The Education of our Youth, a constant supply of
our Ministry, and perhaps a foundation for ye Conversion of our

---

[105] Cotton, A.: *An Account of Our Late Troubles in Virginia,* in Force's
Tracts, I, 6.
[106] Hening: *Stat. at Large,* II, 521, 574, 518.
[107] McIlwaine: *Exec. Jour., Council Col. Va.,* I, 121–22; *Wm. & Mary
Coll. Quart.,* VII, 158–74.
[108] Tyler: *Williamsburg,* 114.
[109] Motley: *Life of Blair,* 26; Tyler: *Williamsburg,* 114; Hartwell, Blair,
& Chilton; *Pres. State Va.,* 68.

neighboring Heathen (Indians) to the Christian Faith.''[110]   A subscription paper some years later gives the purpose in part as being ''for the Pious Education of Youth in Morallity and Good Learning.''[111]

In April and May of the following year, steps were taken looking to the procuring of a royal charter. The relation of the college to church and state is indicated in the decision that a group to include the governor, four of the council, four of the clergy, and nine appointed by the House, should be named to receive the charter. Of the clergy, two were to be appointed by the Council, two by the House.[112] On May 20, the Assembly addressed the King and Queen in the following terms:

> Wee the L*t* Govern*r* Councill & Burgesses of this general Assembly . . . incited by y*e* urgent necessities of this y*o*r M*a*ties Dominion, where our youth is deprived of the benefitt of a liberal & vertuous Education, and many of our Parishes of that instruction & comfort which might be expected from a pious & learned ministry have unanimously Resolved as the best Remedy for those great evills, and as the most Suitable expression wee can make of our hearty concurrence with your M*a*ties in Supporting the Protestant Religion, & the Church of *England,* humbly to Supplicate y*o*r M*a*ties for your Royall grant & Charter to erect & endow a free Schoole & Colledge within this y*o*r M*a*ties Dominion, . . .[113]

Among the instructions given Commissary Blair who was appointed to go to England to procure the charter and solicit funds, was one to inquire whether their Majesties would bestow the patronage of some churches on the college.[114] The efforts of the Commissary in England received the support of the Archbishop of Canterbury, the Bishop of London, and other church dignitaries, due acknowledgment of which was made by the Assembly, the following year;[115] but the proposition was less favored by those who looked upon the matter from its civil aspect.[116] The

---

[110] See p. 117; Motley: *Life of Blair,* 27; *Wm. & Mary Coll. Quart.,* VII, 161.

[111] *Jour., Va. Council,* III, 1511.

[112] Jour. *H. Burg.,* May 15, 1691, 360–61; *cf. Jour., Va. Council,* May 15, 1691, I, 144.

[113] *Jour., H. Burg.,* May 20, 1691, 366–68.

[114] *Va. Mag. Hist.,* VII, 157.

[115] Tyler: *Williamsburg,* 116; *Jour., H. Burg.,* April 28, 1692, 406 *ff.*

[116] Chalmers, G.: *Polit. Annals,* 48–49; *Hist. Revolt Amer. Colonies,* I, 262; *U. S. Bur. Educ., Circ. Inf.,* 1887, No. I, 15.

matter was presented by the Commissary in an audience with the King as "an humble supplication from the Government of Virginia for your majesty's charter to erect a free school & college for the education of their youth."[117] The charter was signed on February 19, 1693,[118] and presented to the Virginia Council on September 1,[119] and to the House, on October 20, of that year.[120] The object of the charter was stated as being:

. . . to the end that the Church of *Virginia* may be furnish'd with a Seminary of the Ministers of the Gospel, and that the Youth may be piously educated in good Letters and Manners, and that the Christian Faith may be propagated amongst the Western *Indians*, to the Glory of Almighty God, to make, found, and establish a certain Place of universal Study, or perpetual College of Divinity, Philosophy, Languages, and other good Arts and Sciences, . . . We, taking the Premises seriously into our Consideration, and earnestly desiring that, as far as in us lies, true Philosophy, and other good and liberal Arts and Sciences may be promoted, and that the orthodox Christian Faith may be propagated; . . . have granted and given Leave, . . . that they, . . . for promoting the Studies of true Philosophy, Languages, and other good Arts and Sciences, and for propagating the pure Gospel of Christ, our only Mediator, to the Praise and Honour of Almighty God, may have Power to erect, found and establish a certain Place of universal Study, or perpetual College, for Divinity, Philosophy, Languages, and other good Arts and Sciences, . . .[121]

The college was to consist of one president, six masters or professors, and an hundred scholars, more or less; trustees nominated and elected by the General Assembly; an eminent and discreet person as chancellor, chosen every seven years, the first appointment, that of the Bishop of London, being that made by their Majesties; subsequent appointments resting in the Rector and visitors and governors of the College.[122] The office of rector, that of presiding officer of the board of visitors and governors, an annual appointment, was first held by Commissary Blair, who was elected President for life, by the Assembly.[123]

---

117 Perry: *Amer. Col. Church*, I, 6.
118 *Ibid.*, 546, Feb. 8, *O. S.*
119 McIlwaine: *Exec. Jour., Council Col. Va.*, I, 294.
120 *Jour., H. Burg.*, Oct. 20, 1693, 458–59.
121 Hartwell, Blair, & Chilton: *Pres. State Va.*, 72–73–74; Parks: *The Charter, and Statutes of the College of William and Mary*, 3–8.
122 Hartwell, Blair & Chilton: *Pres. State Va.*, 84.
123 Tyler: *Williamsburg*, 122.

The statutes of the college likewise stipulated that:

For avoiding the Dangers of Heresy, Schism, and Disloyalty, let the President and Masters, before they enter upon these Offices, give their Assent to the Articles of the Christian Faith, in the same Manner, and in the same Words, as the Ministers in England, by Act of Parliament are obliged to sign the Articles of the Church of England. . . .[124]

It is clear from the history of the origin of the college, that its conception was in accordance with the spirit of integration of church and state. The provision for a closed board of governors and visitors—in the power to continue themselves by election, reminiscent of the vestry organization—the precedent set in the offices of Chancellor and President, the requirement of subscription to the Anglican Church, all brought the college into conformity with that policy.[125]

At the "laying of the Foundation" of the College on August 8, 1695, the colony witnessed the actual placing in operation of the scheme proposed in 1661 to advance learning, promote piety, and provide an able and successive ministry.[126]

Education in Operation

While secular education did not come formally under the control of church and state until Lord Howard of Effingham's proclamation for licensing teachers, in 1686—to all intents and purposes, the education which was most pertinent until late in the 17th century, to the mass of the people, the ability to read and write, was really under the sway of the dominant purpose of catechetical instruction. With the establishment of the College of William and Mary, with its emphasis on philosophy, languages, arts and science, as well as divinity, the motive for extending secular education is apparent. It is true, that in the charter, secular instruction was hemmed in with every precaution to bring it under the influence of orthodoxy. It will be of some interest to examine education in operation, to glean something of the attitude towards it before and after the founding of the college.

---

[124] Parks: *Charter and Statutes of the College of Wm. & Mary,* 106–09.
[125] *Ibid., passim.*
[126] McIlwaine: *Exec. Jour., Council Col. Va.,* I, 334.

It has been shown that one of the reasons assigned for creating the East India Free School, in 1621, was that it would obviate the necessity for sending children to England for their schooling;[127] and though this practise continued throughout the colonial period,[128] provision, whether by private instruction or in schools, to take care of the necessary elementary instruction, basic to catechetical instruction, must have been made almost immediately.[129] There is no hint of any difficulty in procuring instruction with the proper tincture of Christian principles in the directions left for the bringing up of children, in wills of the 17th century. John Waltham, Accomac County, in 1640, asked his executors to confide his son at the age of six, to a "good and godlye schoolmaster."[130] Instructions for "bringing up of my sd children in the fear of God and to learn to read and write" occur in an Isle of Wight County will in 1645.[131] Similar expressions, including the explicit statement of attaining the ability to "read the Bible with facility," occur in other wills of the period.[132]

With the establishment of William and Mary College, there occur references to classical instruction, though not necessarily divorced from ecclesiastical influence. Thus, in 1716, the will of Elizabeth (Armistead) Churchill directed that her son Armistead be instructed in Latin and Greek by Rev. Bartholmew Yates, minister of Christ Church parish, and future professor of divinity in the college.[133] There were of course some parents, who, like Robert Page of Hanover County, interpreted education

---

[127] See p. 96 *ff.*

[128] *Wm. & Mary Coll. Quart.*, II, 22–24; 113–20; for contrasting views of its effects, see Bernard: *Retrospections of America*, 7–8, and *Va. Gazette,* May 31, 1776—see p. 162.

[129] For a different point of view, see Wells: *Parish Educ. Va.*, 53, 91.

[130] Wise: *Eastern Shore*, 317; Bruce: *Inst. Hist. Va.*, I, 296.

[131] *Va. Mag. Hist.*, VI, 115.

[132] *Ibid.*, V, 285; *Wm. & Mary Coll. Quart.*, VII, 248; Bruce: *Inst. Hist. Va.*, I, 303; Stanard: *Colonial Va.*, 276, *cf.* also 272 *ff.*

[133] *Ibid.*, 276; *Wm. & Mary Coll. Quart.*, VIII, 47–48; *cf.* XVII, 188; Tyler: *Williamsburg*, 41, 137; Chambersburg: *Vestry Book Christ Church Parish*, 96, 238, 342, indicate he came to the parish in 1703 and died in 1734, and that his son, same name, came as minister in the parish, in 1737; Rev. Yates, Sr., thus was one of the ministers who combined a charge with a professorship at the college.

wholly in terms of religion undefiled. In his will written in 1765, Page requested:

> . . . I desire neither of my sons may ever be allowed to go to Horse Races or Cock fights, or to any other public diversion as they are only consuming of time & that all my children may be piously brought up to that one and only thing necessary religion. . . .[134]

An advertisement, in 1772, by the minister of Charles parish in York County states that "A SOBER diligent schoolmaster capable of teaching READING, WRITING, ARITHMETICK, and the latin TONGUE" would be put into immediate possession of a school, if he came well recommended.[135]

An indication that catechetical instruction included elementary instruction is found in one of the earliest of the numerous law suits with regard to the proper execution of educational arrangements made in indentures. In 1640, a woman servant complained to the General Court, that her master had put her "to beat at the mortar for all his household," instead of living up to his covenant to "use her more like his child than his servant and that he would teach her to read and instruct her in the [principles] of religion and have a paternal care over her."[136] Elizabeth City County Court, in 1688, ordered a master, upon pain of penalty, to put his "Apprentice to Schoole & Learne him to Reade a Chapter in ye Bible."[137]

The provision for apprenticing children, whose parents failed to provide for their care and education "in christian principles," emphasized anew in law in 1727 and in 1748,[138] seems to have been applied quite rigorously in Augusta County after the latter date; the records in the vestry book or county court book indicating frequently that, in view of the parent's failure to provide for the child "in a Christianlike manner," the child was "to be

---

[134] *Va. Mag. Hist.*, XXXIV, 275–76; *cf.* Chalkley: *Chronicles Scotch-Irish Va.*, III, 108.
[135] *Va. Gazette*, Aug. 20, 1772; numerous advertisements for teachers of Latin appear in the *Virginia Gazette* from 1767 on.
[136] *Va. Mag. Hist.*, V, 234.
[137] *Wm. & Mary Coll. Quart.*, XXIV, 35.
[138] See p. 105.

bound.''[139] The law was not, however, neglected in eastern counties.[140] A summons in a Norfolk County case is here given:

Whereas Complaint was this day made to me by William Happer and John Whiddon, Church Wardens of Saint Brides Parish that Javan Armstrong is going about behaving Himself disorderly, and not bringing up [his children] in the Christian Principles, pursuent to Law, and that Hezekiah F—— hath a Son named Joshua F——, and is incapable of Supporting and bringing Him up in the Christian Principles pursuent to Law in that Case made and Provided. These are therefore in his Majestys Name to will and require You to bring the said Javan Armstrong, and Joshua F—— before the next Court to be held for this County on the Third Thursday in this Month and have then there this Warrant, herein fail not at Your Peril. Given under my Hand this Fifteenth day of July 1771.

To

Mr. John Williams   Samuel Happer[141]
          Constable

An interesting example of parish action in behalf of the education of unprovided for children, in pursuance of the law of 1755 on the subject of the poor, survives in the record of the meeting of a committee in 1757, representing the parishes of Bristol, Martins brandon, and Bath. The object of the meeting was to consider the building of a poor house at the joint expense of the three parishes. Their deliberations particularly indicated their desire ''that such poor children should be brought up in a Religious, Virtuous, & Industrious Course of Life so as to become usefull members of the Community,'' an indication of an attitude towards education wholly in consonance with a religio-civil philosophy.[142]

An interesting case of a teacher who had contracted to teach and read in church and had to sue for his money was that of Frederik Upp who taught in Augusta County for some time after

---

139 Chalkley: *Chronicles Scotch-Irish Va.*, I & II, *passim.*
140 *Wm. & Mary Coll. Quart.*, XXIV, 35; James: *Lower Norfolk Co., Va. Antiquary*, I, 36.
141 *Ibid.*; for a discussion of parish apprenticeship in general, see Wells: *Parish Educ. Va.*, 70 *ff.*
142 Chamberlayne: *Vestry Book Bristol Parish*, 165; Wells: *Parish Educ. Va.*, 64; Hening: *Stat. at Large*, VI, 476.

1760.[143]   There has also come down in the record, the articles of agreement between Joseph Goare and subscribers in which he agreed, in 1766, to teach their children "according to their capacities in reading, writing and arithmetic and all other Christian principles in my power."[144]

Evidence of the extent to which education was regarded as coming under the religio-civil organization of the parish is to be found in the history of gifts and bequests for the education of poor children and orphans and for the creation of free schools.

A summary of such evidence as has come down to us, indicates that from 1634 to the beginning of the Revolutionary War, there were at least 40 cases of provision, 31 made in wills, for the education of the poor—two specifically for orphans.[145]   Provision of this kind naturally increased with the growth in population after the beginning of the 18th century; about one third of the 40 cases occurring before that time.   In 29 cases, there is indication that the donor in each case had in mind provision for a free or public school.   With indication as to the form of control lacking in 10 cases, there is evidence of some form of parish control, such as a combination of the justices of peace, minister, and churchwardens, or the minister, churchwardens, and vestry in 21 cases. Other forms of control are the court, in 3 cases; personal direction, 1 case; justices of peace, 1 case; and trustees, in 4 cases.   As these gifts and bequests were well distributed over the colony, the preponderance of vestry control may be taken as indicative of the extent to which education was regarded as being properly under the control of church and state as represented in parish organization.   The very fact that the execution of provisions for the education of the needy was so largely intrusted to the vestry, may be taken as indicating that the donors felt confident that the religious education of the children would be taken care of without giving specific directions.[146]   In view of the fact that the aim of elementary instruction for the poorer classes was to furnish a

---

[143] Chalkley: *Chronicles Scotch-Irish Va.*, I, 449; Stanard: *Colonial Va.*, 275; Wells: *Parish Educ. Va.*, 22.

[144] Chalkley: *Chronicles Scotch-Irish Va.*, I, 465.

[145] Data tabulated from a variety of sources by writer, see p. 656, Appendix II.

[146] *Cf.* Wells: *Parish Educ. Va.*, 91, for a different point of view.

basis for the legally required catechetical instruction, it was sufficient to put the matter in the hands of the vestry.[147]   Only occasionally, did a donor take the trouble to indicate as did Rev. John Farnefold of Northumberland County, in 1702, the nature of the instruction to be given; he specified that "when they can read the Bible & write a legible hand to dismiss them & take in more."[148]   John Yeates in his will, in 1731, in providing for his free school in Nansemond County, gave £10 in cash to be used in part to procure "Testaments, Psalters, Primers."[149]

The extent to which vestries or other trustees of free schools complied after 1686 with the licensing law requiring an examination before the parish ministers, has not been determined. The Assembly, however, did not fail to stipulate that this procedure must be followed in the case of three different free schools, the Symms, Eaton, and Peasley schools, whose reorganization it effected in 1753, 1756, and 1759.[150]

The necessity for schools, as an outcome of the law of 1619 for catechetical instruction, must have been almost immediate.[151] The author of *A Perfect Description of Virginia,* in 1649, after mentioning the Symms (Symes) school, said "other petty Schools also we have."[152] The teachers, of these first schools, were undoubtedly servants or adventure schoolmasters from England. To what extent, if any, the first ministers acted as schoolmasters is not known. As far as historical evidence is concerned, it would appear that though a minister is known to have acted as schoolmaster in Elizabeth River parish in 1658,[153] and Wm. Fitzhugh, in 1690, placed his son in the home of a French minister to be educated,[154] that it was not until after the College of William and Mary was organized, that it became the vogue

---

147 An example of vestry care of a bequest for the education of poor children may be traced in the case of the bequest of William Gordon as given in Chamberlayne's *Vestry Book Christ Church Parish, passim.*
148 *Wm. & Mary Coll. Quart.,* XVII, 244–46; Maddox: *Free Sch. Idea Va.,* 8.
149 *Va. Sch. Rep't,* 1885, 231.
150 Hening: *Stat. at Large,* VI, 389; VII, 41, 317.
151 See p. 96.
152 *A Perfect Description of Virginia,* in Force's *Tracts,* II, 15.
153 Bruce: *Inst. Hist. Va.,* I, 333.
154 *Va. Mag. Hist.,* III, 9; VI, 70.

for ministers and candidates for the ministry to act as school-masters. This was undoubtedly due to the fact that they were the one group who had the knowledge necessary to teach students preparing to enter college and who could appropriately combine teaching with their profession. From 1700 to the beginning of the Revolutionary War, there is evidence that there were at least 18 ministers who acted as tutors or conducted schools, aside from members of the faculty of the grammar school and College of William and Mary who frequently had a charge in neighboring churches.[155] Teaching, as we have seen, was also a favorite occupation of candidates for the ministry.[156] To what extent the ministers concerned themselves with the spiritual welfare of their pupils is not known; but from the fact that at both the Norfolk grammar school and that of William and Mary, the school boys had a gallery of their own in church, and from the nature of the requirements for special religious instruction at the William and Mary grammar school, it is reasonable to assume that there was some preparation during the week for an understanding of the Sabbath service.[157]

The grammar school of William and Mary, because of its character as a public institution, under the supervisory control of church and state, has left the best available records as to the manner in which a school of secondary instruction was conducted. The first master of the school was Rev. Mungo Ingles who served from 1694 to 1705, and again for a few years after 1716.[158] In that year the visitors of the college resolved:

---

[155] See p. 119; *Wm. & Mary Coll. Quart.*, XIV, 74; Wells: *Parish Educ. Va.*, 23 *ff.*, lists 16 for the period, to which should be added the names of Rev. Wm. Yates—Page, T. N.: *The Old South*, 225; *Va. Hist. Register*, III, 144; and Rev. Robert Dixon or Dickson—Forest, W. S.: *Hist. Sketches Norfolk*, 461; *Va. Gazette*, Nov. 20, 1779; *Jour., H. Del.*, Dec. 6, 1788, 86–87; Appendix, II, p. 660.

[156] See p. 103; Devereaux Jarratt taught *cir.* 1751 in Albemarle County—Bennett: *Memorials of Methodism*, 60; Meade: *Old Churches, Ministers, and Families*, I, 470. Mr. Balmain, tutor in family of Richard Henry Lee went to England for orders in 1772—Ballagh, J. C.: *Letters Richard Henry Lee*, I, 70.

[157] Meade: *Old Churches, Ministers, and Families*, I, 276; Goodwin, Wm. A. R.: *Bruton Parish Church Restored*, 43–44, 55; *cf.* Lipscomb: *Writings T. Jefferson*, I, 71, for Jefferson's statement that students at William and Mary were required to learn the catechism of the Anglican Church.

[158] *Va. Mag. Hist.*, VII, 397.

. . . That it be recommended to the Ministers who preach before the Generall Court, together with such of the Governors of the Colledge as shall then be in Town, on the next Monday after such preaching Respectively to examine the Scholars, what progress they have made in their Learning pursuant to a former order of the Visitors & Governors, and that it be also recommended to such of the Clergy as are Governors at the colledge that whenever their occasions shall call them to Town, to take the trouble of examining the said scholars, and to report what they think necessary therein to the next Generall meeting.[159]

It was probably as the outcome of this inspection scheme, that, in 1719, a complaint was made that Mr. Ingles took it upon himself to make exhortations to his schoolboys, instead of confining himself to the church catechism. This was regarded by the Convention of the Clergy, then in session, as a frivolous charge, and they commended him "for giving good Instructions to his boys concerning their moralls."[160] In 1727, upon the transfer of the college from the trustees to the President and faculty, rules were drawn up for the conduct of the grammar school and a requirement was made that on Saturday and eves of holidays, a sacred lesson should be given out of either Castalio's *Dialogues,* or Buchanan's *Paraphrase of Psalms.*[161] In 1754, at a meeting of the faculty, it was resolved:

. . . Yt a person be appointed to hear such boys as shall be recommended by their parents or guardians, a chapter in the Bible every school day at 12 o'clock, and yt he have ye yearly salary of one pistole for each boy so recommended.[162]

Considerable supervision seems to have been exercised over the conduct of the masters in the grammar school. In 1710, Spotswood, after having an unpleasant experience in trying to import a schoolmaster from England, to replace the unsatisfactory one at the school, wrote to the Bishop of London, "I was not sorry for his staying behind, and I am the better pleased he did so, since I understood that the present Master of the Grammar

---

[159] *Ibid.,* IV, 161, 165; in 1704 and 1705 Ingles had some difficulty with Blair regarding his salary and a "barring out" episode in the grammar school—*Ibid.,* VII, 391; VIII, 143, 377 *ff.*; IX, 18, *ff.*, 254 *ff.*; Perry: *Amer. Col. Church,* I, 139.
[160] *Ibid.,* I, 223.
[161] Tyler: *Williamsburg,* 134.
[162] Perry: *Amer. Col. Church,* I, 552.

School is much reformed of late, and that he now gives good satisfaction in his business."[163]

Care, too, seems to have been exercised in the selection of the masters. Thus upon the resignation of the master, Mr. Blackamore, in 1716, the Board of Visitors ordered a committee to enquire if a fit person could be found in this country; otherwise they were to solicit the aid of the Bishop of London. The secretary of the Society for propagating the Gospel was also to be asked to recommend candidates to the Bishop for his approbation.[164] With all due care, however, in their selection, there was an occasional outcropping of dissatisfaction. In 1757, Governor Dinwiddie wrote to the Bishop of London stating the dissatisfaction of the visitors and the country in general with the conduct of Rev. Thomas Robinson, who had been appointed in 1742. In his fall from grace, Mr. Robinson had a companion in the Rev. Wm. Preston, professor of philosophy, in the college. The charge against them was:

. . . notoriously on Acc't of Intemperance and Irregularity laid to y'r Charge, but also because they had married, and cont'y to all Rules of Seats of Learn'g, kept their Wives, Child'n, and Serv'ts in College, w'ch must Occas'n much Confus'n and Disturbance.[165]

The visitors, upon a complaint of their very bad example to the students, ordered the President to write to the Bishop of London to recommend and send others in their places.[166]

It would seem that placing instruction under the control of the clergy was not necessarily an absolute guarantee that it would be conducted properly. Custom, or the difficulty of procuring non-clerical schoolmasters properly qualified, was such, that another minister was appointed to take the Rev. Mr. Robinson's place.[167]

In the history of the college proper, the same preference for ministers occurs; although the school of philosophy with its two departments, that of moral philosophy in which "rhetoric, logic and ethics," and that of natural philosophy and mathematics, in

---

[163] Spotswood: *Letters*, I, 4.
[164] *Va. Mag. Hist.*, IV, 169–70.
[165] Dinwiddie: *Records*, II, 697.
[166] *Ibid.*
[167] *Wm. & Mary Coll. Quart.*, II, 258–59.

which "physics, metaphysicks and mathematics" were taught, did not necessarily call for clergymen. The divinity school had one department devoted to the Hebrew tongue and the expounding of the Old and New Testaments; the other to the expounding of "the common places of divinity and the controversies with heretics."[168]

A minister, Rev. James Fontaine, was summoned in 1716 to be "the first professor of University learning there," but, he apparently never came, leaving it to his son the Rev. Francis Fontaine to represent the family name at William and Mary as professor of oriental languages in 1729.[169] He, undoubtedly, like other faculty members of the college and grammar school testified to his orthodoxy by subscribing his assent in Latin to the Articles of the Church of England, giving besides his oath to administer his duties faithfully.[170] As to the degree to which the professors succeeded in living up to the pledges thus made, there is the testimony of a witness well qualified to speak. Governor Gooch had been serving in his official capacity since 1727, and in 1745, at a time when he was quite disturbed by evidences of tendencies opposed to orthodoxy, he addressed the Assembly in the following terms:

. . . If I tell you, that there is not in any Part of the World, a College, where good Order, Decency and Discipline, are better maintain'd, where God Almighty is more constantly and devoutly worshipp'd, and where greater Care is taken to train up young Students in the Rudiments of Religion, Loyalty, Science, and good Manners, and carrying them on towards Perfection, than in This, I am sure I should speak without Artifice or Flattery, and I dare say, within the Bounds of Truth.[171]

There were, presently, signs that the "good Order, Decency, and Discipline," of the college life in the days of the pious Governor Gooch were to be seriously threatened. Times were changing; Presbyterianism was taking on new life under Davies;

---

[168] Tyler: *Williamsburg*, 137.

[169] *Wm. & Mary Coll. Quart.*, IV, 171–72; Tyler: *Williamsburg*, 130, 131, 137; Spotswood: *Letters*, II, 166–67; *Va. Mag. Hist.*, IV, 171; Cf. Jones, H. M.: *America and French Culture*, 110, who seemingly has confused the two Fontaines.

[170] *Wm. & Mary Coll. Quart.*, II, 50–51, 259.

[171] *Jour., H. Burg.*, Feb. 20, 1745, 154–55.

population was increasing; more business needed to be trans-
acted at the capital, and more people came to Williamsburg. In
1749, the Council debated the question of removing the capital
from Williamsburg:

> . . . Because the Morals of the Youth of this Colony educated at the Col-
> lege are greatly depraved by the Evil Examples they see from the Numbers
> that flock to this Place at the public Meetings, the Impressions that are
> receiv'd at those Times being too strong for all the Care of the Masters
> to overcome. And we are persuaded that while the Seat of Government is
> continued, the Evil will increase, and our Prospect from the Corruption of
> the Morals of the rising Generation is a very melancholy Consideration.[172]

In 1752, the Assembly had before it *"An act to vest the Power
of granting Licenses to Ordinary Keepers, within the City of*
Williamsburg, *and two Miles thereof, in the Visitors and Governors of the College of* William *and* Mary, *and to prevent the unlawful playing of Interludes within the same."*[173]   Three years
later, the minister, churchwardens, and vestry of Bruton parish
complained to the Assembly of the burden of providing for the
increasing number of poor, "which they conceive is owing to the
great number of idle Persons, that resort to the City of *Williamsburg* (situate in the said Parish) in publick Times, who lurk
about the Town, and Parts adjacent. . . ."[174]

While the character of the college town was changing, an
atmosphere at variance with that in the days of Gooch began to
prevail inside the college. This may be attributed in part to the
coming, in 1758, of Francis Fauquier as governor, who introduced Voltaire and the iconoclastic thought of France into the
colony; in part to the coming of professors with a new scientific
outlook.[175] The first of this new school of professors, and in view
of his profound influence upon Thomas Jefferson perhaps the
most important, was Dr. William Small, professor of Mathematics
from 1758 to 1764.[176] Jefferson in his autobiography writes:

---

[172] *Jour., Va. Council,* April 17, 1749, II, 1037–38.
[173] *Jour., H. Burg.,* April 10, 1752, 82–83.
[174] *Ibid.,* May 16, 1755, 258–60.
[175] Parton, J.: *Life Thomas Jefferson,* 27–29.
[176] *Wm. & Mary Coll. Quart.,* XIV, 75, VIII, 171 *ff.*; Beard: *Rise Amer.
Civilization,* I, 174; Burk: *Hist. of Va.,* III, 399.

. . . in the spring of 1760, went to William and Mary college, where I continued two years. It was my great good fortune, and what probably fixed
the destinies of my life, that Dr. William Small of Scotland, was then Professor of Mathematics, . . . and from his conversation I got my first views
of the expansion of science, and of the system of things in which we are
placed.[177]

That others, besides Thomas Jefferson, felt Dr. Small's influence is attested in the following tribute by Colonel John Page of
Rosewell, visitor and burgess for the college, and, in 1802, governor of Virginia:

. . . I had the benefit of a Philosophical education at College, with Mr.
Jefferson, Mr. Walker, Dabney Carr, and others, under the illustrious Professor of Mathematics, Wm. Small, Esq., afterwards well known as the
great Dr. Small, of Birmingham, the darling friend of Darwin. . . .[178]

In 1762, the Assembly voted £450 sterling out of the public
money

. . . to the Governours and Visitors of *William* and *Mary* College, to be
applied by them towards purchasing a proper Apparatus for the Instruction of the Students of the said College in Natural and Experimental
Philosophy.[179]

Five years later £69/9 was directed to be paid to make up the
deficiency of the cost of the apparatus purchased.[180]

When, in 1769, Rev. Thomas Gwatkin came to the college as
the professor of mathematics and natural philosophy, he undoubtedly found his department well equipped for work in one of the
scientific fields of the greatest American scientist of the day, Benjamin Franklin—whom the college had delighted to honor, in
1756, with the honorary degree of Master of Arts.[181] The alliance of Mr. Gwatkin and Rev. Samuel Henley, professor of moral
philosophy and divinity, in opposition to an Episcopate and the

---

[177] Lipscomb: *Writings Thomas Jefferson,* I, 3.
[178] Page: *The Old South,* 231; the Darwin referred to here is Erasmus
Darwin, grandfather of Charles Darwin; *Wm. & Mary Coll. Quart.,* XIV, 75.
[179] *Jour., H. Burg.,* Dec. 15, 1762, 150–51; *Jour., Va. Council,* Dec. 17,
1762, III, 1294.
[180] *Jour., H. Burg.,* April 2, 1767, 108.
[181] Perry: *Amer. Col. Church,* I, 552; *Wm. & Mary Coll. Quart.,* VII, 25;
VIII, 272; XXIV, 221; *Va. Gazette,* Aug. 1, 1771 contains a reference to
this apparatus by a member of the department of theology which implies
that its value was not yet recognized.

charges of heresy against the latter have already been discussed.[182]

Aside from the modernistic trend developing in the faculty, there were other factors leading to a disintegration of the discipline of both faculty and students. In 1760, a letter was written by a clergyman to one of the English bishops making serious accusations against the Commissary, who was President of the college, on the grounds of intoxication, failing to attend college prayer regularly, and playing cards in public places.[183] In 1763, the writer of this letter, Rev. Wm. Robinson, was made Commissary, but not President of the college. In a letter to the Bishop of London, he speaks of the students as being ''very disorderly in their behaviour,'' which he attributes to the fact that a student could only be disciplined for a third offence by a trial between the student and master before the visitors, which might take place anywhere between six months and two years after the offence had been committed. His suggestion was that the appointment of the President and masters be given to either the Bishop of London or the Archbishop of Canterbury.[184] The following year, Rev. James Horrocks was elected Commissary and President of the college. The visitors passed a statute asserting their prerogative to remove the President and masters at their pleasure. To this statute, the Commissary subscribed; but it was regarded by the faculty as an attempt to repeal the Royal Charter and they appealed in a memorial to the Bishop of London.[185] The visitors tried also to forbid the professors to function in neighboring churches. The bold stand of Rev. John Camm against this, in 1766, resulted in a modification of the statute to permit professors to hold livings upon obtaining the consent of the visitors.[186] This lack of discipline in the faculty was reflected in the lack of discipline among the student body; but an attempt was made this year by the faculty to establish order by requiring the ushers to attend church and chapel regularly and to visit the

---

[182] See p. 88 *ff*.
[183] Perry: *Amer. Col. Church*, I, 463–69.
[184] *Ibid.*, I, 473.
[185] *Ibid.*, I, 505, 518; Tyler: *Williamsburg*, 154–56.
[186] *Ibid.*; Perry: *Amer. Col. Church*, I, 523.

rooms of the students.[187]   It would seem that the rules of the good
old days when the college chapel was first opened, in 1732, which
required morning prayer at "six in Summer, seven in Winter,
and always five in the evening" were no longer so punctiliously
observed.[188]

The following year, Mr. Robinson again wrote his former correspondent, that

> The Visitors and Governors are perpetually clamoring for Discipline to
> preserve order and regularity among the Students, and yet for ever assum-
> ing such powers to themselves as render Discipline by the President and
> Masters impracticable.[189]

The visitors were still persistent in their right of removal and
were determined that the professors should hold no livings that
would interfere with their duties in college.[190]

These disputes and the modernistic attitude of some of the professors had far reaching effects in the attitude of the alumni of
William and Mary College toward religion and education, in the
period of adjustment to a new philosophy of church and state.
The immediate effects upon the students are somewhat more difficult to gauge.   The report of the celebration of Founders' Day,
in 1771, as given in the *Virginia Gazette,* perhaps because of the
solemnity of the occasion, indicates a well conducted and alert
student body.   The account states that after prayer and a sermon
in the chapel, "two elegant English Orations" were delivered
"with such Spirit and Propriety as to obtain the just Applause
of a numerous and attentive Audience" and that "the rest of the
Day was spent in a decent Festivity, suitable to the Occasion."[191]
Nevertheless, in 1772, Richard Henry Lee, in explaining the
reason for sending his boys to England instead of to William and
Mary College, stated, "But there, so little attention is paid either
to the learning, or the morals of boys, that I never could bring
myself to think of William & Mary."[192]   Undoubtedly, whether

---

[187] *Wm. & Mary Coll. Quart.,* IV, 131.
[188] *Ibid.,* IX, 220; Tyler: *Williamsburg,* 138.
[189] Perry: *Amer. Col. Church,* I, 524, 528.
[190] *Ibid.*
[191] *Va. Gazette,* Aug. 15, 1771.
[192] Ballagh: *Letters Richard Henry Lee,* I, 70–71.

justified or not, the impression created by the disputes of the professors was such as to cause some doubts as to the desirability of William and Mary College as a seminary of learning. "Philanthropos Americanus" wrote in the *Virginia Gazette* of February 20, 1772, in the rôle of peacemaker:

> LET Camm and Henley drop an angry Pen,
> Discord forbear,—Oh! turn out loving Men,
> Write gently, without too much Gall in Ink,
> Blessed Calvin did calmly write and think.
>
> .   .   .   .
>
> Let Christian brotherly Love abound,
> Nor talk of Pistols in that College Ground;
> In Tutors let good Example be found.

Fithian writing in his diary two years later reported thus a conversation on the subject of William and Mary with his employer, Mr. Robert Carter:

> ... He informed me that it is in such confusion at present, and so badly directed, that he cannot send his Children with propriety there for Improvement & useful Education—That he has known the Professors to play all Night at Cards in publick Houses in the City, and has often seen them drunken in the street! ... Two of the officers of the Institution, Mr. Bracken, & Mr. Henly Clergymen are at present engaged in a paper War published weekly in the Williamsburg Gazette's.[193]

Thus, in the comparatively short period of less than thirty years after Governor Gooch's highly favorable opinion of the college, as an institution wholly in accord with the spirit in which it was founded, we see that harmony shattered.

Education and the Dissenters

The extent to which the laws requiring education to be in accord with the principles of church conformity were disregarded by reason of religious dissent can only be conjectured. The chief dissenting groups, until the proclamation of Effingham relative to licensing of teachers, in 1686, were the Puritans, Catholics, and Quakers. Until that date, the chief form of legal evasion lay in finding some reason for not sending children to church for cate-

---

[193] Fithian: *Journal & Letters*, 106–07.

chetical instruction. It was probably easier for some excuse to be found in the weather or distance to keep children at home than for non-conforming ministers to escape detection in their failure to catechize. Reference has already been made to the presentation of Rev. Thomas Harrison to the General Court, in 1645, for failure to conform with the law.[194] It is probable from the zeal with which the Puritans embraced exile into Maryland, rather than remain in Virginia under unsatisfactory conditions, that they took due care to keep their children from contamination by Episcopacy. The interesting will of Ann Southey, of Northampton County, who died in 1656, entrusted her children to the guardianship of Rev. Mr. Francis Doughty. Rev. Mr. Doughty, at one time, was cited before Governor Berkeley for non-conformity, particularly in denying "the supremacy of the King, contrary to the canons of the Church of England." By 1659, Doughty had gone to Maryland. The will requested the minister

> . . . to councell my children, not only in the management of their estates, and in civill behavior in ye world, but be a means to instruct them in the feare of God & service of the Almighty and Creator, and in ye true faith in Jesus Christ, into whose hands I commit in common, all our Soules when it pleaseth him to take them from us out of this sinful life to wch I say Amen and Amen.[195]

The law of 1643 against Popish recusants, following a similar law of 1641, forbade Catholic priests to remain in the colony more than five days after notification to depart;[196] but Catholics probably found a way to instruct their children privately. From a legal point of view, Catholic education in Virginia came under the series of English laws, from 1585 to 1699, which had as their object the suppression of Catholic education, by barring the presence of priests, forbidding children to be sent abroad for education, and punishing by perpetual imprisonment the attempt to keep school or the assumption of education.[197] The law of 1730

---

[194] See p. 99.
[195] Wise: *Eastern Shore*, 271; *Va. Mag. Hist.*, V, 131.
[196] Hening: *Stat. at Large*, I, 269.
[197] Gee & Hardy: *Documents Eng. Church Hist.*, 485; Friedman, L. M.: "Parental Right to Control the Relig. Educ. of a Child," in *Harvard Law Review*, XXIX, 484; Stratemeier: *Thomas Cornwaleys*, 17–20.

which forbade the entrusting of custody of children to popish
recusants was clearly an enactment into Virginia law of what had
been Virginia practise in accordance with English law.[198] This
is indicated by a case which occurred, in 1645, in Lancaster
County, when on the ground that he was a papist, the right of
guardianship of several children entrusted to him by will was
taken away from Edwin Conway.[199] Another case, presented to
the Council, in 1691, concerning Peter Blake, ''a known Papist,''
was concluded by ordering the County Court to remove him from
his guardianship, if the charge were proved.[200] In the deprivation of the right of guardianship, Catholics were placed on the
same plane with atheists, who by the laws of 1699 and 1705 were
deprived of the same right.[201] In view of the severity of the
legislation affecting them, and the possibility of conducting education in the home by tutors, if discretion were used, it is not
surprising that formal Catholic education in schools was not ventured upon at any time during the colonial period.[202]

Only the most meager hints as to the Virginia Quaker attitude
toward education can be found in the various sources for the history of religion and education in Virginia.[203] It is very unlikely
that their attitude differed essentially from their co-religionists
in other colonies.[204] It was an essentially utilitarian education
that the colonial Quaker favored, as may be gathered from
a statement in one of the very early Quaker wills and from an

---

198 See p. 105.

199 Bruce: *Inst. Hist. Va.*, I, 266.

200 *Va. Mag. Hist.*, XX, 116.

201 Hening: *Stat. at Large*, III, 169, 359; Jefferson: *Notes on Va.*, 234–
35.

202 Guilday, P.: *Life and Times J. Carroll*, 21–22, indicates attendance of
Catholic youth during the colonial period at St. Omer's College; Burns:
Cath. Sch. System U. S., 102. Formal Catholic education in Virginia does
not appear to have come much before 1832, judging from an official account
in the *Richmond News Leader*, Dec. 31, 1925, and Burns, J. A.: *Cath. Sch.
System U. S.*, 222; see p. 579 *ff*.

203 An authoritative study of Quaker education in Virginia and Maryland,
based on original sources, is being planned under the direction of Dr.
Thomas Woody, of the University of Pennsylvania.

204 Four authoritative studies of Quaker education have been made:
Woody, T.: *Quaker Education in Pennsylvania*; *Quaker Education in New
Jersey*; Klain, Z.: *Quaker Education in North Carolina*; *Educational Activi-
ties of New England Quakers*.

account of a Quaker's attitude toward education, by a tutor in a Quaker family at the beginning of the 19th century. The will of Richard Russell of Lower Norfolk County, in 1667, provided:

. . . 'the other pte of my Estate I give & bequeath One pte of itt unto Six of the poorest mens Children in Eliz: Riv'r, to pay for their teaching to read & after these six are entred then if Six more comes I give a pte allsoe to Enter them in like manner. . . .[205]

John Davis, tutor in the family of Friend Ellicott, who lived in a settlement on the Occoquan River, wrote:

Our agreement was soon made. Quakers are men of few words. Friend *Ellicott* engaged me to educate his children for a quarter of a year. He wanted them taught reading, writing, and arithmetic. Delightful task! As to *Latin*, or *French*, he considered the study of either language an abuse of time; and very calmly desired me not to say another word about it.[206]

A picture of the religious and educational situation in a family where the mother had given up her Quaker allegiance to join the Church of England is seen in the records of a case that went, in 1708, to the General Court for adjustment. Ann Keith, daughter of George Keith, a prominent Quaker, had married George Walker when both were Quakers. When Mrs. Walker's father changed his views and became a member of the Anglican Church, she followed suit. The nature of the case and the attitude of the court can be gleaned from the following reply to Mrs. Walker's petition:

W'msBurgh Apr'll The 25th, 1708.
Ann Walker. This Day was Exhibited to us in Councell a petition which S'd petition we take to Be from yo and accordingly we have had y'r husband this Day Before us in Councell to answare the said petition upon hereing of which he only Desiers to have that athorety over his Childr. that properly Belongs to Every Christian man: that is to Bring up his Childr. in whatever Christian Religion he may Be of that is priveliged By our Christian Laws: and it Seems to be hard that any person w't ever Shall Indever or undertake to prevart or persuad any Mans Children against the Instructions and admonitions of the father: y'r husband Seems to Be very Willing to Give yo all manner of Liberty to Injoy y'r Religion provided yo Leave the Instruction of all his Children to him and that yo will Not Cause them to Read any Books Exept the Scripture but Such as he

---

[205] *Va. Mag. Hist.*, I, 326.
[206] Davis, J.: *Travels U. S.*, 253.

allows of and that yo forbare to Incense and persuad any of his Children against his Religion as Long as he professes to Be a Christian and Continews in the Exercise of it and also forbare to Interprat or Expound any part or portian of Scripture to any of his Children without his Leave or advice if he be willing to Expound Such portions as may hapen to Com in Dispute or that any of his Children may Desier to Be Informed in: We tharefore as y'r freinds Not Being Willing to Give further troble: if y'r husband will Give yo Liberty to Injoy y'r Religion without Interruption: he ought to have all the Liberty above Desiered: But if yo Can prove that he is Not a Christian and So Consequently Not within the virge of our Christian Laws then we are willing to heare yo on Wensday Morning Next but wee Shuld be Glad yo Could be Reconcilled without Such procedings.[207]

A few days later, the Council expressed the opinion that Mrs. Walker "ought to enjoy the free exercise of her Religion, and that her husband ought not to restrain her from going to Church." It did not, however, think it proper to determine anything respecting the children—"it not appearing of what age those Children are nor how far they are capable of chooseing a Religion for themselves."[208]   Aside from its interesting disposition, the case is of importance in the indication that Quaker education was not only utilitarian, but also carefully conducted from the viewpoint of religious supervision in the home.   It was undoubtedly parental religious differences of this kind, which compelled the enactment of the laws of 1727 and 1730 regarding the custody of children.[209]

To what extent the Quakers relied upon tutorial instruction in the home or upon schools may be safely inferred from detailed studies already made and cited.[210]   Unless they were in a position to give their children a "guarded" education in schools under Quaker auspices, Quakers probably preferred tutorial instruction.[211]   The licensing law of 1686 would naturally have a tendency to prevent the establishment of schools, but there is evidence that the Quakers in Frederick County had schools in their

---

207 *Va. Mag. Hist.*, XVI, 79–81; XXIII, 144–45; *cf.* also *Wm. & Mary Coll. Quart.*, IX, 127; McIlwaine: *Exec. Jour., Council Col. Va.*, III, 175.
208 Ibid., 180–81.
209 See p. 105.
210 See p. 134, n. 204.
211 *Cf.* Woody: *Quaker Educ. in New Jersey*, 10; Weeks: *Southern Quakers and Slavery*, 143–44.

territory almost immediately upon settlement.[212] Probably the fact that the Quakers in this section had received official authority to settle in this territory was taken as granting a right to conduct schools of their own.

The Huguenots in their settlement at Manakin Town adopted the English parish organization with its vestry system; a fact indicative that care for education was a matter of community concern only when children were being neglected. A review of the early records of the vestry indicates that a church was built in 1710; nothing is said of a schoolhouse.[213] Provision for education of a sort must have been available, for, in 1713, the vestry undertook the care of two girls who were being neglected by their step-father:

. . . the said Cappon taking no care as to their bringing-up nor giving them any education, it was decreed for the welfare of the said infants by the present vestry, assembled for this purpose, that the Sr Anthoine Trabue and Jeane le Villain, provide in accordance with their best judgment some good place for the abovesaid orphans, being for this purpose authorized by the present vestry to make such engagement as shall be necessary and possible for the welfare of the said children in conformity with the law of the land.[214]

Abraham Sallé, one of the vestrymen, however, found the educational opportunities unsatisfactory. In a letter to King George I, written some time after 1714, requesting permission to leave Manakin Town, he states:

. . . In the second place, our families which are pretty numerous and the place which we occupy quite limited, we find ourselves in the impossibility of procuring any situation for our children or even to have them instructed or give them any education.[215]

---

[212] See p. 60; *Wm. & Mary Coll. Quart.*, XXVI, 136; Ser., 2, VI, 39–40; Cartmell: *Shenandoah Valley Pioneers*, 215, 282, 284–85; *cf. Edward Pleasants Valentine Papers*, II, 1183–1261; III, 1569–77, 1751–60, for indication of extent of Quaker meetings; a map of Virginia Quaker Meeting places is on file in Hist. Soc. of Pennsylvania.

[213] *Va. Mag. Hist.*, XI, 300; on p. 290, in an introduction, the statement is made: "the village laid out and building commenced, the church, the parsonage and the schoolhouse first."

[214] *Ibid.*, XI, 437; Trabue and le Villain were churchwardens.

[215] *Ibid.*, XXXIV, 159–60; Sallé died at Manakin Town, 1719; the reference to limited territory is obscure in view of the grant of 10,000 acres; it may be that the dissatisfaction with educational opportunities referred particularly to a comparison with opportunities for higher education in France to which the settlers had been accustomed.

Though many of the first settlers did not acquire any considerable knowledge of English, they were ready because of the English families in their midst to favor English instruction for their children and to have the common prayers and sermons in English as well as in French.[216]   French education did not present itself as a problem for any length of time, because of the extensive intermarriage of the French and English which soon began.[217]

The German Reformed Lutherans who made up the community at Germantown, in 1721,[218] had for their reader, Jacob Holtzclaw who received his naturalization papers in 1722.[219]   Holtzclaw acted as schoolmaster for the community for many years and is referred to as such by the Moravian missionaries coming through in the forties, who apparently laboured hard to convert the schoolmaster and his children to their belief.   In 1748, Brother Gottschalk wrote in his diary:

> As Holzklo is getting old he is becoming religious. He asked his children to come into the room, and by various questions gave me an opportunity to tell them something about the Saviour.[220]

The Germans were apparently quite resolved to maintain their worship in the form they had known in the homeland, and this necessitated a training of the children in harmony with it.   It was on the basis of hopes held out to them by William Penn, that they would enjoy ''freedom in the Exercise of Religion as well as other ways,'' they declared in a petition to the Assembly, that they had come to America.[221]   That the church and the schoolhouse were in conjunction is evident from the efforts of the Lutherans in the Upper Shenandoah Valley in sending Rev. John Caspar Stoever to collect funds in Europe for a church and school; and although Rev. Mr. Stoever died at sea upon his way home, the money and books he collected came safely to hand.[222]

---

[216] Brock: *Huguenot Emigration to Va.*, 112; *cf.* Spotswood: *Letters*, II, 254; Perry: *Amer. Col. Church*, I, 256.

[217] *Va. Mag. Hist.*, XI, 289 *ff.*, 291.

[218] See p. 53.

[219] Holtzclaw's name is also spelled Holtxclow, Holtzklo, Holzkloh, and Holzklau in the various references to him.

[220] *Va. Mag. Hist.*, XII, 74; XI, 233, 376; XIII, 368; XXIX, 98.

[221] *Ibid.*, XVIII, 268.

[222] *Records of John Casper Stoever*, 4; Richards, J. W.: *Penn's Lutheran Forerunners*, 296; Bittinger, L. F.: *German Relig. Life*, 68; *cf.* Wells: *Parish Educ. Va.*, 28, for a different statement.

With the arrival of Rev. Samuel Klug, in 1738, building was begun; and when Brother Gottschalk, the Moravian missionary, came through in 1748, he noted in his diary:

> . . . Within a circle of a few miles eighty families live there together, Lutherans, mostly from Wurtemberg. They have a beautiful large church and school, also a parsonage and a glebe of several hundred acres, with seven negroes, who must cultivate the minister's land.
> The name of the minister living there is *Klug*.[223]

An interesting proof of the German practise of combining church and school is found in the agreement, in 1769, between members of the Lutheran and Reformed faiths to combine in supporting the religious and educational activities of the Peaked Mountain Church in Rockingham County. The agreement in part follows:

> . . . But since it is necessary to keep in repair the church and the school-house and support the minister and schoolmaster, therefore we have drawn up this writing that each member sign his name to the same and thereby certify that he will support the minister and schoolmaster and help to keep in repair the church and the school as far as lies in his ability. . . .[224]

When German families lived at a distance from schools, they probably resorted to family instruction; thus in his will, in 1773, George Caplener, a German settler in the Valley, requested his two oldest sons to "lorn the two youngest boys to read through the Salter."[225]

There is no hint in available records that any effort was made to make German teachers come under the licensing law. The very fact that educational activities were so closely allied with religious activities, and that the religious activities of the Germans had received a tacit sanction from the government, prob-

---

[223] *Va. Mag. Hist.*, XI, 230, XIV, 144, 147, 153, XVIII, 268; *cf.* Wayland, J. W.: *German Element Shenandoah Valley Va.*, 154; *cf.* Schuricht, H.: *German Element Va.*, I, 75, incorrect statement analogous to account in *Reminiscences of Lutheran Ministers*, 622 *ff.*

[224] *Wm. & Mary Coll. Quart.*, XIII, 247–48; this school was in use in 1785—*Ibid.*, XIV, 192; *cf. Va. Mag. Hist.*, XIII, 287; a statement that there were at least four German schools in the Valley before 1765 appears in *Ibid.*, XXX, 179.

[225] Stanard: *Colonial Va.*, 277.

ably explains why the Germans conducted their educational activities in apparent freedom.[226]

Little is known of the actual practise of Baptists during the period to 1776 in regard to the education of their children; but, undoubtedly, as ardent dissenters they endeavored to keep their children free, as much as possible, from Anglican influence. Among the Regular Baptists, the coming, in 1760, of Rev. David Thomas, whose learning had merited him the degree of Master of Arts from the then Rhode Island College, apparently had a favorable reaction upon their attitude toward learning.[227] In the Baptist scheme of life, however, in those crusading days before the Revolution, it was "regeneration" of souls, not the higher learning, that mattered. The attitude is well indicated in the statement of one of their ministers, a native of Virginia, William Fristoe, born in 1742:

> . . . Learning, . . . is highly esteemed among the Baptists, and many who have been called to and exercised public offices, have very sensibly felt the inconvenience they had to labor under for the want of it. But it is not considered essentially necessary to a gospel minister. Where the Author of nature has endued a person with a strong intellect, capable of taking in high and sublime ideas, and prying into mysterious and intricate subjects, and given him to know his dear Son, whom to know is life eternal, the ministry may be entered even without learning. For a person of this description forever to remain in silence, merely for the want of education, would be like a beautiful flower blooming in a desert, unnoticed by few, and enjoyed by none.[228]

---

[226] It would seem that the Virginia government felt no apprehension from the Germans in Virginia—the compact settlements of Germans in Pennsylvania seemed fraught with danger, according to Gov. Dinwiddie in a letter in 1754—"It was, I think, a very imprudent Step in the first Settlem't of y't Province not to mix them in their Settlem'ts with the Engl., and have English School Masters, &c."—Dinwiddie: *Records*, I, 406; there is no evidence of such a policy in Virginia, and the fact that the Germans petitioned for the laws to be printed in German indicates but little attempt to acquire an English education. *Jour., H. Del.*, Oct. 16, 1792, 53; Dec. 3, 1792, 159; Dec. 11, 1797, 19; cf. also *Ibid.*, Feb. 16, 1870, 89; Mar. 4, 1870, 162; cf. *A Memorial Of The Case Of The German Emigrants*, which seems to have been inspired with the Germans of Pennsylvania rather than Virginia in view, and apparently was one of Rev. Mr. Wm. Smith's many activities to extend education along Anglican lines.

[227] Semple: *Hist. of Baptists*, 295; Taylor: *Va. Baptist Ministers*, 43 ff.
[228] *Ibid.*, 74.

The education of John Alderson, son of a Baptist minister, and grandson of a minister in England, is given in his own statement:

. . . My father being much from home, and I being the oldest son, much dependence was placed on me, to take care of the farm: so that I had very little opportunity to learn. The chief of the books that I read, were the bible and the Baptist catechism; which last I got by heart; and not only said it over at school, but also in the public congregations, on Sundays, after sermon. By these means I was kept from all gross immoralities. . . .[229]

Presumably, most parents were satisfied with such an amount of learning as would assure a reading knowledge of the Bible and ability to transact the ordinary affairs of daily living. It was not until the Baptists had made some progress in their struggle for religious freedom, in the years immediately after 1776, that they turned their attention to the problem of education.

The interest of Virginia Presbyterians in education finds its starting point in the favorable attitude of Francis Makemie towards education. After twenty years' study and observation of religion and education in Virginia and Maryland, Makemie felt impelled to write *A Plain & Friendly Perswasive to the Inhabitants of Virginia and Maryland for Promoting Towns & Cohabitation.* Makemie's zeal for religion and education was such that he gave renewed emphasis to the plea in *Virginia's Cure* for a different social and economic order:

Cohabitation would highly advance Learning and School-Education: for this flourishes only in such places, for the smallest and meanest of schools cannot be maintained without a competent number of Scholars, which has been our great Discouragement in *Virginia* and *Maryland,* where the number to be entertained together are too few to maintain any master or mistress, who are necessitated to shift from place to place, untill they cannot live at all by that Calling: so that in many remote corners many families never had opportunities of schools, and therefore remain without all knowledge of Letters, which we have no hopes of regulating or preventing, without Towns and Cohabitation: . . .[230]

What specifically Presbyterian schools, if any, were erected by the Presbyterian communities under Makemie and Mackie, is not

---

[229] Semple: *Hist. of Baptists,* 328; Alderson was born March 5, 1738, O. S.; Taylor: *Va. Baptist Ministers,* 156–57.

[230] *Va. Mag. Hist.,* IV, 265.

known. The first settled minister among the Presbyterians who came into the Shenandoah Valley, Rev. John Craig, pastor of Augusta and Tinkling Spring Churches, in 1740, combined teaching with his ministerial duties.[231]

In the central part of the state, the numerous activities of Rev. Samuel Davies did not make it possible for him to conduct a school, but he showed his zeal in obtaining books of a religious nature for distribution not only to the negroes, in whose behalf he preached a sermon, on "The Duty of Christians to propagate their Religion among Heathens, Earnestly recommended to the Masters of Negro Slaves in Virginia," but also to the poor whites. In distributing the books, Rev. Davies requested that the recipients

. . . would not keep them by them as a private property (except the Bibles, for which they would have constant use in their families) but circulate them about among such of their neighbours, as would seriously peruse them; that they might be as extensively serviceable as possible.[232]

The necessity, from Mr. Davies' point of view, for a wider distribution of religious literature can be gleaned from his estimate of Virginia culture in a letter to "J. F.," April 1, 1755:

Though there are very few of the white People in this Colony in abject poverty, yet there are many in such low circumstances, that they cannot *spare* money to purchase good books: And there are many more, who might indeed spare so much, without injury to their temporal affairs; but as they are stupidly insensible of their *Want* of Instruction, and do not form so high an estimate of the Means of Grace, as of the Necessaries, or even Conveniences of this mortal Life; they are willing to excuse themselves from it, as a piece of *needless* expence.

On one or other of these accounts, there are few houses in *Virginia* well furnished in this important respect; and multitudes are grossly ignorant, and consequently careless, about the concerns of Immortality. To some of these I have distributed, *The Compassionate Address, Baxter's Call to the Unconverted, The Sabbath-breaker's Monitor*, &c. with the best advice I could give them, and I hope I shall be able hereafter to give you an agreeable account of the happy effects of the distribution.[233]

---

[231] *Ibid.*, XXX, 179; Peyton: *Hist. Augusta Co.*, 80; Waddell: *Annals Augusta Co.*, 21; Campbell states that the first classical school west of the Blue Ridge was that of Robert Alexander, *cf.* Campbell: *Hist. of Va.*, 429; *cf.* Morrison, A. J.: *Beginnings Pub. Educ. Va.*, 105.

[232] Davies: *Letters*, 20.

[233] *Ibid.*, 8–9.

Two years later in a letter to a correspondent, Rev. Davies mentions *The Compassionate Address,* Dodderidge's *Rise and Progress,* and Baxter's *Call* as "the most popular and useful Books among the white People in Virginia."[234]

The care of a Presbyterian father for the education of his son is indicated in the direction of Mr. Tunstall Hack, that if his son John Tunstall Hack lived, he

. . . should be placed under the care of Mr. John Wright for his instruction in learning, and the principles of religion—and when he arrived at the age of further improvement that he should be directed to the care of Mr. Samuel Davies, minister of the Gospel, or some other dissenting minister.[235]

In the activity of bringing religious literary culture to Virginia, Rev. Davies was assisted by a neighboring Presbyterian minister, Rev. John Todd, a Princeton graduate, who conducted a classical school at his home.[236]   In conducting his school, Rev. Mr. Todd was assisted by James Waddell, the famous "blind preacher" of William Wirt's *The British Spy.*[237]

The difficulties surrounding the organization of a school under Presbyterian auspices is indicated in a note under date of January 8, 1759, in the diary of Colonel James Gordon, of Lancaster County:

. . . At Court, Mr. Leland and Minis behaved like blackguards in respect to Mr. Criswell, who went to get scholars, and engaged several, though the Parsons did all they could against him, which seemed to make the people much more fond of sending their children. I think such ministers should be stripped of their gowns.[238]

Whether the opposition of the parsons was based, in part, on the authority for approval of teachers they had in the licensing law, does not appear.

Among Presbyterian ministers serving as teachers, worthy to be noted, is the name of Rev. Daniel M'Calla, or McCauley, Princeton, 1766.   Rev. M'Calla was master of Hanover Academy

---

234 *Ibid.,* 33.
235 *Tyler's Quart.,* VII, 260; *cf. Va. Mag. Hist.,* XXX, 179.
236 Davies: *Letters, passim;* McCabe, W. G.: *Va. Schools Before and After the Revolution,* 21; Morrison: *Beginnings Pub. Educ. Va.,* 117.
237 *Ibid.;* Wirt, W.: *Letters of the British Spy,* 115 *ff.*
238 *Wm. & Mary Coll. Quart.,* XI, 99.

(1776), the fore-runner of Washington Henry Academy, and author of *Hints on Education, (in Fourteen numbers)*.[239]

In the years just before the Revolution, the Presbyterians began to take that concerted action regarding the establishment of academies which was to give Virginia, two of her very important educational institutions, Hampden-Sidney College and Washington and Lee University; and start a movement in the direction of purely denominational education divorced from state control, which was to have an important influence on the future of education in Virginia.

The initiative in placing the matter of concerted action in behalf of education before the Hanover Presbytery, is attributed to Rev. Samuel Stanhope Smith.[240] The matter was taken up in successive years beginning in 1771; and, in 1774, the Presbytery appointed Mr. William Graham as tutor of the academy in Augusta, the fore-runner of Washington and Lee University.[241] It was decided at the same time that "a public school for the liberal education of youth would be of great importance on the south side of the Blue Ridge" and steps were taken for the erection of one in that neighborhood, thus laying the foundation of Hampden-Sidney.[242] Above £1300 was raised by subscription for the purpose of erecting the southern institution and £400 ordered expended for books and mathematical and philosophical apparatus, an indication of the high standard proposed. In February, 1775, the Presbytery chose Mr. Samuel Stanhope Smith as Rector of the Prince Edward Academy, later Hampden-Sidney, and entrusted to him, the Rev. Robert Smith of Pennsylvania, and William Charles Huston, professor in Princeton, the choice of an assistant. The Presbytery then decided to make a public statement of their purpose:

The Presbytery having for a long time had the liberal education of youth, in these upper parts, much at heart, and having succeeded so far in our

---

[239] M'Calla, D.: *Works Rev. D. M'Calla*, I, 15, II, 107 *ff.*; McCabe: *Va. Schools Before and After the Revolution*, 22; *Va. Educ. Jour.*, VIII, 258 *ff.*: Morrison: *Beginnings Pub. Educ. Va.*, 109.

[240] Foote: *Sketches of Va.*, 392, 393.

[241] For early history of this academy, see *Va. Mag. Hist.*, XXX, 179; Morrison: *Beginnings Pub. Educ. Va.*, 105–06.

[242] Foote: *Sketches of Va.*, 393–94.

endeavors to promote it, as to do something considerable towards erecting an academy in Prince Edward county, where we trust every necessary branch of human literature will be taught to good advantage, on the most catholic plan—and whereas some gentlemen who are unacquainted with our sentiments, may encourage this Seminary with reluctance because it is to be under the guardianship of this Presbytery, we take this opportunity to assure the publick, that though the strictest regard shall be paid to the morals of the youth, and worship carried on, evening and morning, in the Presbyterian way; yet, on the other hand, all possible care shall be taken that no undue influence be used by any member of this Presbytery, the Rector, or any assistant, to bias the judgment of any; but that all, of every denomination, shall fully enjoy his own religious sentiments, and be at liberty to attend that mode of publick worship, that either custom or conscience makes most agreeable to them, when and where they may have an opportunity of enjoying it.[243]

The substance of this statement appeared in an advertisement in the *Virginia Gazette* of October 7, 1775, giving the new name of the Academy as Hampden-Sidney. It called attention to the fact, that it was to "be subject to the Visitation of twelve Gentlemen of Character and Influence in their respective Counties; the immediate and acting Members being chiefly of the Church of England." Its curriculum, the advertisement stated, would resemble that of the College of New Jersey, except for a more particular attention to the English language.

In 1775, the Presbytery decided to equip the Augusta Academy under the direction of Rev. Wm. Graham with books, and mathematical and philosophical apparatus; for this purpose over £160 was expended. In 1776, it was decided to transfer the school to the neighborhood of the Presbyterian community of Timber Ridge, and to make Rev. Mr. Graham, Rector, and Mr. John Montgomery, his assistant.[244]

Of all the dissenting groups, the Presbyterian group was the only one, apparently, which had arrived at a conception of education beyond that of imbuing education with a strictly denominational color. It was also the first to make provision for education beyond a utilitarian type for immediate economic needs. All dissenting groups, however, in their efforts to give their children a "guarded" or separate education, divorced from the

[243] *Ibid.*, 396.
[244] *Ibid.*, 446–48.

influence of the state and state church, were laying the basis for a conception of private and denominational effort of immense consequence to educational development in Virginia; and their attitude is indicative of the effects of the disintegration of church and state control upon the conception of the relation of education to society.

Significance Of Preceding Views And Tendencies

Nothing more strikingly illustrates the extent to which the colony of Virginia had withdrawn its allegiance from the conception of the integration of church and state, than the advertisement which announced the presence of members of the Church of England and dissenters on the Board of Trustees of Hampden-Sidney.[245] The very fact that members of the Anglican Church were willing to take part in an educational enterprise in which neither the state nor the state church would have an interest, is indicative of the degree to which Anglicans themselves had become imbued with the thought that religious opinion was the affair of the individual and not of the state, and that education could be safely divorced from denominational dominance and yet come under a sufficiently adequate Christian influence.

An alliance between Anglicans and Presbyterians in educational enterprise was facilitated, too, by a like predisposition in favor of higher learning. As population increased, various sections of Virginia had probably regarded with envy, the grammar school and College of William and Mary, placed so disadvantageously from a geographic standpoint in the southeastern section of the state. Nor were counties, which were comparatively close to Williamsburg, satisfied to be dependent upon it. In 1720, New Kent County had petitioned for a free school to be maintained from the "Publick Bank," and the county of Princess Ann had petitioned for free schools to be erected and maintained in each county with a competent maintenance to be allowed for the master.[246] With only one "public" school, the grammar school of William and Mary, five "endowed schools" and a limited number of private schools, indicated as existing in

---

[245] *Va. Gazette*, Oct. 7, 1775.
[246] *Jour., H. Burg.*, Nov. 12, 1720, 264.

the 1724 questionnaire, the need for a system of education that would provide facilities for education beyond that of the petty schools was undoubtedly serious.[247]   In fact, Henry Hartwell, Commissary Blair, and Edward Chilton, in describing the condition of education in the colony in 1727, declared:

. . . on the other Hand, if we enquire for . . . well educated Children, for an industrious and thriving People, or for an happy Government in Church and State, and in short, for all the other Advantages of human Improvements, it is certainly, for all these Things, one of the poorest, miserablest, and worst Countries in all *America*, that is inhabited by Christians.[248]

What was to be in many respects, however, a most important event in Virginia colonial history, took place within the next few years with the appearance in 1730 of *TYPOGRAPHIA. AN ODE, ON PRINTING* which ushered in the establishment of the first authorized printing press in Virginia.[249]   Not quite a half century before, in 1683, John Buckner, who had printed the laws of 1680, had been compelled, with his printer, to enter into bond in £100 to discontinue printing—an event laconically noted in the *Executive Journals of the Council*, under date of February 21, 1683: "Mr. John Buckner and all others prohibited Printing."[250]   This prohibition was confirmed by the home government in instructions to Lord Howard in 1683; in 1690, his instructions extended to an interdict of all printing "without the government's especial license."   With the establishment of an authorized printing press, the appearance of a newspaper was only a matter of time.   On August 6, 1736, the first number of the *Virginia Gazette* appeared, and with it a new era in every phase of Virginia life—economics, politics, religion, education.[251]

The publicity given to the various forces leading to the disintegration of the union of church and state, created a new

---

247 Perry: *Amer. Col. Church*, I, 257–346; see p. 653, Appendix I.
248 Hartwell, Blair, and Chilton: *Present State Va.*, 2.
249 Clayton-Torrence: *Trial Bibli. Col. Va.*, 104–05.
250 McIlwaine: *Exec. Jour., Council Col. Va.*, I, 39; Hening: *Stat. at Large*, II, 517–18.
251 Clayton-Torrence: *A Trial Bibli. Col. Va.*, 113–14; *Wm. & Mary Coll. Quart.*, VII, 9–17; the only other Virginia town having a printing press before the Revolution was Norfolk, 1774—Heartman, C. F.: *Checklist Printers U. S.*, 52.

outlook upon society; it became necessary to conceive of education adjusted to a new political philosophy—that of separation of church and state. The new tendencies at William and Mary College, at Hampden-Sidney have been indicated. It was not only in the schools, but also in society at large, that the necessity for education as related not merely to spiritual needs, but also to physical, human needs became apparent. In 1773, there was organized a "Philosophical Society" numbering among its hundred members, John Clayton, member of the Royal Society and author of *Flora Virginica*, and Rev. Samuel Henley.[252] The object of the Society was "to direct the Attention of their Countrymen to the study of Nature, with a View of multiplying the Advantages that may result from this Source of Improvement."[253] The inauguration of this Society in Virginia is significant in marking the distance Virginia had traveled from a society whose chief concern in education had been the spiritual element, to one which was ready to give some place to the element of "realism," to science, in education.

The attempt to create a uniform pattern of mankind, molded in the matrix of the Anglican Church had failed. The regard for the conscience of the individual implanted in the religious conceptions of the dissenting sects had acted as a germinating seed to spring that matrix. Man came forth to demand a conception of education that would tie him to society only where he and society were mutually necessary, but would leave him free in that which concerned his conscience, in that which concerned him as an individual.

---

[252] *Va. Gazette*, May 3, 1773; *Wm. & Mary Coll. Quart.*, XXIV, 221; Beard: *Rise of American Civilization*, I, 157; Brock, R. A.: *Colonial Virginian*, 20.

[253] *Va. Gazette*, July 22, 1773.

PART II

DURING THE SEPARATION OF CHURCH AND STATE

(From the Separation From Great Britain to the Civil War)

CHAPTER V

INITIATION OF THE CIVIL STRUGGLE FOR EDUCATIONAL CONTROL

Education And The Philosophy Of Perfectibility

The disintegration of the union of church and state was brought about, as has been shown, by two forces; one burrowing from within, the other battering from without. In a sense, the dissenting forces which were opposed to the Anglican Church may be regarded as having gathered their main strength from the weakness of that church. The weakness of Anglicanism lay in its rigidity, in its endeavor to mold individuals into a uniform pattern—an aim perhaps valid enough as an object of society, on whatever basis organized—whether on a religious, civil, or a religio-civil foundation—provided the pattern appeals to the individuals concerned as one designed to meet their needs, as the most perfect attainable. The chameleon-like mind of man seems, however, never to rest satisfied with any achieved position, but always to have an urge to strive for a further perfection, a perfection to be accomplished by change, by revolution. Essentially, the response of the people of Virginia to the denominational forces which swept Virginia during the century or more from the coming of Quakerism to the spread of Methodism, may be said to be an expression of the desire to get back spiritually to the pure, unadulterated Christology of the primitive church, the perpetual human search for perfection, which finds its expression in the philosophy of the perfectibility[1] of man.

The disastrous effects, in the opinion of many, which resulted from the connection of the Anglican Church with the civil phases of the organization of society, made those who felt that they had found in one or another of the denominational societies, a

---

[1] The philosophy of perfectibility as expressed in the Physiocratic movement in France and England is discussed in Hansen, A. O.: *Liberalism and American Education*, Ch. I and II.

151

religion that was purer, holier, and better, anxious to keep that new faith from contamination with the world—the civil state.

In Virginia, the dissenting groups received their increasing numerical strength from the dominant church, from the Anglican membership. In a very true sense, it may be said that the chief denominational divisions of Virginia, at the beginning of the nineteenth century—the Presbyterians, Baptists, Methodists, and Protestant Episcopalians—were religious divisions into which the colonial Anglican Church had divided. The tradition with respect to education in the minds of the new membership of the new churches was that of the Anglican state church; and the underlying philosophy of that church had been that, in the union of church and state, it was the church, and not the state, which was to have the ascendancy in education. The state might supply the resources, but it was the church who was to carry on the actual work of education—that was to have the real direction.

Now, it appears to be one of the characteristic features of the thought of all political revolutions, that thereby a new era of progress is to begin for mankind—that a further step is being taken in pursuit of human perfection. This idea was likewise present in the thought of separation from Great Britain, in the hopes that went with transition from monarchy to republicanism. When Virginia organized itself politically as a state, it was not without giving expression to the thought that the acme of human social development lay in the protection of the natural rights of mankind. This thought was summed up in the *Declaration of Rights*.

What had really happened, then, in the disintegration of the union of church and state was a division of the civil and spiritual forces of that union into two separate forces, each seeking for that essential form of expression—for that form of life, which would lead to human betterment, to perfection.

In the attainment of that goal, mankind has generally considered education an indispensable agency. Who, now, was to direct education? What was the relation of education to these two separated forces, civil and spiritual, of society? Was there anything inherently germane to education which would confirm the principle of separation of church and state as desirable, or, on the contrary, indicate some form of integration as preferable? The attempt made to answer these questions in the decades from the separation from Great Britain to the Civil War is the concern of the following pages.

The Meaning of Separation of Church and State

To understand the reaction of the principle of separation of church and state upon education, it is necessary to gather, first of all, some impression of the meaning of separation of church and state, particularly as it was interpreted by the legislature. Fundamental to the basis of separation of church and state was the *Declaration of Rights,* unanimously adopted in 1776.

The critical reader of this *Declaration* may well wonder at the interpretation given, in the minds of those who sponsored it, to the statement that "all men are equally entitled to the free exercise of religion, according to the dictates of conscience."[2] That all the implications involved in possible interpretations by the two opposing schools of political philosophy, the integrationists and separatists, were not immediately evident has been made clear in the discussion of the legal steps taken in the culmination of the movement toward disintegration.[3] While the word "toleration" was deleted from the original draft of the bill in order to convey the broadest possible conception of religious liberty,[4] it is apparent from the fact that the Episcopalians thought it expedient and proper to ask for an act of incorporation in 1784, that the *Declaration of Rights* was not interpreted, at that time, by the integration party, as implying a complete divorce of interest in religion on the part of the civil side of the state. It was probably the enactment of this act, in 1784, that gave the alarm to the separatist party and was responsible for the reintroduction of the Jeffersonian *Bill for Religious Freedom* the next year. The significance of the more strongly worded Jeffersonian statement of the meaning of religious freedom[5]

---

[2] Hening: *Stat. at Large,* IX, 111–12.
[3] See p. 90 *ff.*
[4] Eckenrode: *Sep. Church and State,* 44–45.
[5] See p. 93.

becomes clearer upon an investigation of the practises of the General Assembly, indicative of its interpretation of the civil relation to religion.

It may readily be granted, that there is, perhaps, no way in which a government on its civil side can more effectively show a favorable inclination toward religion, and give an impressive encouragement to it, than by opening, or opening and closing, its legislative exercises with prayer or other forms of religious devotion.   The impressiveness of sanctions of this kind carries over most readily from one department of civil life to another.

That the House saw no incongruity in the spring sessions of 1777, in appointing the Rev. James Madison, a Protestant Episcopalian, as chaplain, to read prayers "at 8 o'clock, every morning," and in requesting him to preach for them on a certain Sunday,[6] is clearly indicative that the majority in the House did not regard the appointment as infringing upon the equal rights of the minority "to the free exercise of religion, according to the dictates of conscience."   It may, perhaps, be that they regarded it as the duty of the minority to practice "Christian forbearance, love and charity" in respect to the wishes of the majority, rather than their duty to dispense with religious observance altogether as their part in the "mutual duty" which the *Declaration of Rights* enjoined.   Rev. Mr. Madison officiated as chaplain through 1779, and for his services was given at various times £48, £35, £125.[7]   The principle of payment for services was retained in the case of subsequent chaplains.   There is no hint, in the official records, that the propriety of having a chaplain was in question at any time before the enactment of the *Bill for Religious Freedom*.   In 1783, the House made a standing order,

That the chaplain do compose a form of prayer, to be approved by the committee for Religion, fit and proper to be used in this House; and that it be a standing order, that divine service be performed every day, by using the said form or any other as the House may from time to time direct; and that service begin in the House immediately after the bell shall be rung for calling the House.[8]

[6] *Jour., H. Del.*, May 9, 1777, 5; May 14, 1777, 9.

[7] *Ibid.*, June 28, 1777, 109; May 30, 1778, 30; Dec. 19, 1778, 128; sums due to war depreciation of values.

[8] *Ibid.*, May 15, 1783, 7.

The *Bill for Religious Freedom,* did not immediately bring about a suspension of the custom of having a chaplain. In 1787, the chaplain was paid £8 per week for his services. In 1789, there was a complaint in the *Fredericksburg Virginia Gazette* with regard to the action of the House concerning a chaplain.[9] Though it was the manifest purpose of the *Bill for Religious Freedom* to eliminate compulsory attendance at religious assemblies, and the members of the House could probably have refrained legally from attendance, the minority probably felt an implied, and therefore distasteful compulsion, usual in cases where the majority of a group establish a certain procedure with respect to that most sensitive of human rights, the rights of conscience.[10] Furthermore, that the payment of a chaplain was a direct violation of the provision of the Bill that no one was to be "burthened" in his goods, that is, taxed for religious purposes, could not have been unknown to the Assembly. In 1796, the question of rescinding the standing order of 1783 came up and was defeated, ayes 41, noes 57.[11] In 1797, it was resolved to rescind the use of a particular form of prayer, and to give the chaplain leave to use such form as he should think proper.[12] The following year, it was voted to maintain the chaplain's salary at $20 per week.[13] In December of that year, the question of the legality of paying the chaplain from public taxes was given serious consideration, and the motion put to the members that they individually pay the Chaplain the sum of $1 each, for his services, was defeated, ayes 59, noes 70; it was voted, however, to retain the chaplain by a vote of 74 to 65; the names of the ayes and noes on both questions were inserted in the *Journal.*[14] The following January, the Assembly passed an act declaring the Jeffersonian act for establishing religious freedom was "a

[9] *Va. Mag. Hist.,* XIII, 427, citing under date of Dec. 24, 1789; *cf. Edward Pleasants Valentine Papers,* II, 1238.

[10] *Cf.* Ruling by Attorney General W. W. Potter, of Michigan, as quoted in the Philadelphia *Evening Bulletin,* Feb. 10, 1928, in which he decided that Bible reading before classes by teachers is a compulsion contrary to the principles of separation of church and state, and "as much an infringement of the right to religious freedom as is instruction."

[11] *Jour., H. Del.,* Dec. 24, 1796, 213.

[12] *Ibid.,* Dec. 5, 1797, 5.

[13] *Ibid.,* Jan. 23, 1798, 99.

[14] *Ibid.,* Dec. 5, 1798, 7-8.

true exposition of the principles of the bill of rights and constitution,"[15] but they continued to retain their chaplain.   In 1805, the vote for appointment of a chaplain stood 77 to 75.[16] A year later, the proposition to appoint a chaplain was finally defeated by a vote of 76 in favor, and 80 opposed, and the names inserted in the *Journal*.[17]   In 1809, a resolution in favor of a chaplain was again defeated.[18]   The length of time, that it took to reach the point of dispensing with a chaplain, is significant of the very gradual evolution in reaching the logical conclusion of the position implied in the *Declaration of Rights*.   It is clear that in the first decade after that *Declaration*, separation of church and state implied no animosity to religion as such, but rather hostility to the idea of union of church and state.   It was only gradually that the state sloughed off the memories and practises of that union.   It continued to proclaim Fast and Thanksgiving Days and pay for special sermons.[19]

The favorable attitude of the state toward religion may be seen in its action, in 1777, in exempting not only educational institutions but also religious societies, including their property in slaves, from taxation.[20]   "An Act for punishing disturbers of Religious Worship and Sabbath breakers" was passed in 1786, probably due to disturbances created by the excitement of the religious revivals which began in 1783.[21]   The act extended the protection of the state to ministers in the performance of their duties, conditioned upon their taking the oath or affirming their fidelity to the commonwealth.   Protection was likewise given to religious assemblies.   All labor by one's self, servant, or slave, on Sunday, except in the case of household duties or work of necessity or charity, was forbidden on penalty of 10 shillings for every offence.[22]   Apparently, the law was not rigorously enforced, for in 1789, a petition from the county of Botetourt set forth

---

[15] *Acts of Assembly*, Jan. 24, 1799, 9.
[16] *Jour., H. Del.*, Dec. 3, 1805, 6.
[17] *Ibid.*, Dec. 2, 1806, 6.
[18] *Ibid.*, Dec. 5, 1809, 10.
[19] *Va. Gazette*, April 9, 1779; *Jour., H. Del.*, Dec. 4, 1779, 79; Nov. 29, 1782, 42; Nov. 19, 1789, 70; Dec. 27, 1799, 43.
[20] Hening: *Stat. at Large*, IX, 351; *Jour., H. Del.*, Dec. 13, 1777, 77.
[21] Cleveland, C. C.: *Great Revival*, 30, 108.
[22] Hening: *Stat. at Large*, XII, 336–37; *Jour., H. Del.*, Dec. 28, 1786, 126.

. . . that they have observed with concern the decrease of the influence of religion on the manners and morals of the present generation; and praying that an act may pass requiring the magistrates to take cognizance of the crimes of profane swearing, drunkenness and Sabbath breaking, when committed in their presence, and to punish the offenders by compelling them to pay certain fines therefor.[23]

A somewhat similar law was passed in 1792.[24] Any transaction with a slave on the Sabbath, without the written consent of his master or overseer, was subject according to a law of 1802 to a fine of $10 in addition to the usual penalties for Sabbath breaking.[25]

During this period, too, though the Assembly did not grant all requests for lotteries for the building of churches, it granted quite a number, and apparently without discrimination as to denomination.[26]

As far as the General Assembly was concerned, it is evident that they regarded the separation of church and state as implying no hostility to religion as such; they therefore showed a predisposition favorable to religion in such points as they assumed, they safely might. From the ancient point of view of law and order, they readily yielded the utmost protection to ministers, to religious assemblies, and to Christian Sabbath observance. Religion was permitted to exist, to function. With this as an indication of their interpretation of the meaning of separation of church and state in its application to religion as such, it will be of some interest to discover the attitude of the Assembly toward religion in education.

Civil Control of the Education of Orphans, Poor, and Apprentices

That it was one thing to enunciate a philosophy of separation of church and state, and quite another to create the ''new mind'' in the people as a whole, necessary to give effective realization to this point of view by adequate legislation, has been

---

[23] *Ibid.*, Nov. 14, 1789, 58.
[24] *Acts of Assembly, Code*, 1803, I, 276.
[25] *Ibid.*, 432; Lewis, A. H.: *Sunday Legislation*, 205–06.
[26] Hening: *Stat. at Large*, XII, 228; XIII, 173–74, 314; *Acts of Assembly*, Dec. 10, 1796, 40.

shown.[27]   Similarly, it took time to educate the people, and the representatives of the people in the Legislature, to the implications bound up in the new political ideal not only for the ancient sanctions for the customs of daily life, but also for education. It was, of course, impossible to root out, at once, all the old forms of education which had received a sacred halo by custom and legislation.   Certain social and economic groups like the poor, orphans, and apprentices had to have immediate attention; the obligations that had been assumed in their behalf could not be suddenly dropped.   For many years after 1776, the practise of binding out children, whose parents were "not capable of bringing them up in a Christian-like manner," so that they might acquire some trade and learn how to write and cypher and read the Bible continued.[28]

Owing to the separation from Great Britain, there had developed a situation thus described by Richard Henry Lee in a letter to Thomas Jefferson in November, 1776:

> Among the various difficulties that press our Country, I know of none greater than the want of Ships and Seamen—Perhaps a good basis for remedying the latter might be an alteration of the Act of Assembly for binding our Orphan & Poor Children, and direct that, for some time at least, the whole of such children should be bound to the Sea. . . .[29]

The special character of the proposed legislation probably did not interest Jefferson who was seriously engaged in a consideration of a comprehensive educational system.[30]   Nothing was done in the direction of the Lee suggestion until 1780, when, in "An act for the defence of the eastern frontier of this commonwealth," the military and economic situations were both taken care of by modifying the law of 1748 with regard to orphans, by enacting that

> . . . the said county courts, instead of binding out all such orphans as shall come within the description in the said act contained, they shall and are hereby empowered and required to cause one half of such male orphans at least, who may live below the falls of the respective rivers in the eastern

---

[27] See p. 93, 156.
[28] For examples from 1777 to 1788 see Chalkley: *Chronicles Scotch-Irish Va.*, I, 205, 210, 212, 216, 237, 256; *Wm. & Mary Coll. Quart.*, XIII, 31.
[29] Ballagh: *Letters Richard Henry Lee*, I, 223.
[30] See p. 162 *ff*.

parts of this commonwealth, to be bound to the sea, under the most prudent captains that can be procured to take them.[31]

In 1785, apprenticeship, until the age of 21, to owners or masters of sea vessels was made applicable to boys of ten years or upwards throughout the state, who should beg for alms, or who, or whose parents, were chargeable to any county. Nothing was said of their education except that they were to be deemed registered seamen at the age of 18.[32]

In January, 1786, the authority of the father to devise the custody and tuition of his child was again confirmed.[33] At the same time, it was decreed that orphans, the profits of whose estates were insufficient for their maintenance, should, if a boy be apprenticed until the age of 21, if a girl, to the age of 18. They were to be taught an art, trade, or business specified in the indenture, also reading and writing, and if a boy, common arithmetic. Boys bound out as apprentices by their fathers might agree after the age of sixteen to serve until 24 years of age or any shorter time.[34]

By legislation in 1785 and 1786, the authority of the church-wardens with regard to the poor was vested in a board of three overseers triennially elected in districts designated by the county court in each county. The overseers were to levy the assessment for the poor, and to make monthly returns to the county courts of poor orphans and children whose parents were unable to support and bring them up "in honest courses." They were also to have charge of apprenticing orphans and poor children in the manner already indicated.[35] In 1788, it was necessary to amend the laws to provide severe penalties for failure to execute the laws with regard to the election of overseers and the collection of the levy.[36]

The Assembly, in 1792, passed "An Act to reduce into one, the several Acts concerning Guardians, Orphans, Committees,

---

[31] Hening: *Stat. at Large*, X, 385; *Jour., H. Del.*, Dec. 9, 1780, 44.
[32] Hening: *Stat. at Large*, XII, 133–34.
[33] See p. 105.
[34] Hening: *Stat. at Large*, XII, 194–98; *Jour., H. Del.*, Jan. 7, 1786, 132.
[35] Hening: *Stat. at Large*, II, 27 *ff.*, 272 *ff.*
[36] *Ibid.*, XII, 712–13; *cf. Acts of Assembly*, Code, 1803, I, 377–78.

Infants, Masters, and Apprentices.''[37]   Nothing new with respect
to the purely educational aspects of their treatment was introduced, either in this act or in an amendment to it passed in 1794.[38]
The same thing may be said of ''An Act providing for the Poor''
passed in 1792.[39]

The year 1796 is notable in the educational history of Virginia
as the date of the first law providing for an elementary school
system applicable to the whole state.   This three year free elementary school law which included all the children of every
economic status in its scope, because of its wide applicability
does not come into our present discussion.[40]

It was through the ''Act concerning the Glebe Lands,'' passed
in 1802,[41] that action was taken which, indirectly, by the creation
of special school systems, usually with reference to the poor,
opened the way to the creation of a general school system.   This
act had been preceded in 1793, by an act granting the proceeds
of the sale of the glebe land of Botetourt parish, after certain
claims were paid, to Liberty Hall, Botetourt Seminary, and
Wythe Academy.[42]   But the possibility of using the glebes as
a source for educational purposes for the poor children in a
county, as a whole, was indicated in a petition from Antrim
parish, Halifax County, in 1799.   The resolution of the House
in answer was:

. . . that the petition of sundry inhabitants of the county of Halifax, praying that the tract of land and appurtenances appropriated as a glebe for the
parish of Antrim, may be sold, and the money arising from the sale thereof,
applied to the education of poor children in the said county, or that the said
glebe may be appropriated to such pious purpose as to the Legislature may
seem best, is reasonable; and that the same ought to be vested in trustees,
and the profits thereof applied by them annually hereafter, to the support
and education of one or more poor orphan children within the said county,
to be selected by the overseers of the poor thereof; . . .[43]

The act of 1802 gave the overseers of the poor authority to sell
the glebes and appurtenances, but vested in the people the right

[37] *Ibid.*, 172–74; *Jour., H. Del.*, Dec. 27, 1792, 223.
[38] *Acts of Assembly*, Code, 1803, I, 321–22.
[39] *Ibid.*, 180 *ff.*
[40] See p. 167 for a further discussion of this act.
[41] See p. 93.
[42] *Acts of Assembly*, Nov. 23, 1793, 47.
[43] *Jour., H. Del.*, Jan. 15, 1800, 89.

to indicate for what purpose the funds thus derived were to be used.[44]   While the authority thus given the overseers was abused in a number of instances,[45] there resulted nevertheless a considerable number of cases in which the funds were applied to the creation of particular schools or for the education of poor children, specifically, or of all the children in general of the county.[46] Though the local public school under civil control as represented in municipal authority of mayor, recorder, and alderman was known to Virginia ever since the law of 1752 making provision for a school of this type in the town of Norfolk,[47] "An Act incorporating the Trustees of a Free School or Schools in King George County" passed, January 1, 1808, which created a free school system in Hanover parish, in that county, with the funds derived from the sale of the glebe land of the parish, may be regarded as the legislation which set in its typical features the precedent for civil control of local free school systems throughout the state.[48]   Wide powers were given the seven trustees, elected by the people or appointed by the court, in their authority to employ tutors, to examine into their conduct and to remove them; to make necessary rules and regulations; and in the power to fix the number and description of the scholars and to examine their progress.   No tutor was to be employed without satisfactory evidence of his qualification and morality.[49]

[No longer did the state concern itself with the religious character of the instructors of youth; contenting itself with giving an ethical tone to education.   A perfect civil society could not tolerate an uneducated poor class, because, as citizens, they were likely to be dangerous to the economic and political welfare of the state; hence the state did not hesitate to direct education into channels which would serve its welfare.   The principle of taking care of the education of orphans and poor children and of pro-

---

[44] *Acts of Assembly*, Code, 1803, I, 422.
[45] Eckenrode: *Sep. Church and State*, 152 *ff*.
[46] *Ibid.*, 153; *cf. Jour., H. Del.*, Dec. 2, 1806, 7; Jan. 17, 1807, 99; Dec. 8, 1808, 8; Dec. 11, 1810, 18; Feb. 9, 1810, 110; *Acts of Assembly*, Jan. 1, 1808, 41; Feb. 4, 1808, 76; *Va. Sch. Rep't*, 1885, Part III, 93; Maddox: *Free Sch. Idea Va.*, 42–45; *Jour., Senate*, Dec. 13, 1870, 39.
[47] Hening: *Stat. at Large*, VI, 261 *ff.*; VII, 510 *ff*.
[48] *Acts of Assembly*, Jan. 1, 1808, 41 *ff*.
[49] *Ibid.*

vision for apprenticeship as an ameliorating force in society was not new; the elimination of the church in the handling of this problem, and the transfer of concern for the problem wholly to the state, and its solution in the interests of the civil state were new.   The development of a conception of education as subservient to the civil welfare of the state becomes clearer in a consideration of the attitude toward education which finally led to the creation of the Literary Fund in 1810.   To trace that development, one must give consideration to that educational opinion which concerned itself not with educational provision for limited social and economic groups, but with educational provision for the citizens of the state as a whole.

Efforts Towards a State Educational System

On May 31, 1776, ''Academicus'' making a plea for the College of William and Mary in the *Virginia Gazette,* addressed the Convention of Virginia as follows:

. . . Whilst your minds are nobly engaged in forming such a plan of government as will be most favourable to our liberties, most likely to promote our welfare, and least liable to the attacks of corruption, it may escape your reflection, amidst this immensity of business, that it is LEARNING alone which can give any lasting stability to your structure; for will a soul, grovelling in ignorance, perceive the value of that constitution which you now design to frame?   And the moment it ceases to be valued, though reared with the utmost skill and care, it will fall to ruin. . . . It is owing also, in a great measure, to our own literary institutions that learning has been thus advantageous to us; for, from woful experience, we have found, that many of those who were educated in Britain, together with the streams of knowledge, drank deep of the fountain of corruption.   But, had it not been the case, all intercourse of that kind must henceforth be at end.   We must nourish, in our own bosoms, the future supporters of our religion and country. . . . When, hereafter, it shall be mentioned that to your virtue was owing the establishment of liberty and peace, let it also be told, that you too occasioned fair science to blossom. . . .[50]

The appeal of ''Academicus'' on behalf of enlightenment for ''the future supporters of our religion and country'' was destined for the time being to remain unheeded.   In the October session of the Assembly, however, Thomas Jefferson moved for a revisal of the laws, and in November, he, among others, was ap-

---

[50] *Va. Gazette,* May 31, 1776; see p. 119, n. 128.

pointed to a committee for this purpose.⁵¹   The work of submitting a plan for the reorganization of education was undertaken by Jefferson.⁵²   There was nothing in the fundamental law
of the state, adopted at the separation from Great Britain, per-
taining specifically to education.   The implications in the separation of church and state as affecting education were all to be
worked out.   The Committee did not submit its final report to
the Assembly until June 18, 1779, and, after Jefferson's appointment as governor; but in the meantime, in December of the previous year, the House had given leave to bring in a bill ''for the
more general diffusion of knowledge.''   This bill upon presentation was read and ordered printed, and four copies sent to each
county; the bill thus presented, was undoubtedly, Jefferson's.⁵³

The nature of the proposed bill may be gathered from the
preamble:

WHEREAS it appeareth, that however certain forms of government are
better calculated than others to protect individuals in the free exercise of
their natural rights, and are at the same time themselves better guarded
against degeneracy, yet experience hath shewn, that, even under the best
forms, those entrusted with power have, in time, and by slow operations,
perverted it into tyranny; and it is believed that the most effectual means of
preventing this would be to illuminate, as far as practicable, the minds of
the people at large, and more especially to give them knowledge of those
facts which history exhibiteth, that, possessed thereby of the experience of
other ages and countries, they may be enabled to know ambition under all
its shapes, and prompt to exert their natural powers to defeat its purposes:
and whereas it is generally true that that people will be happiest whose laws
are best, and are best administered, in proportion as those who form and

---

⁵¹ Lipscomb: *Writings T. Jefferson*, I, 62.
⁵² *Ibid.*, 70.
⁵³ *Jour., H. Del.*, Dec. 15, 1778, 117; Dec. 16, 1778, 120; Messrs. Parker
and G. Mason were the members ordered to prepare and bring in the bill,
and Parker presented it the next day; G. Mason was a member of Jefferson's committee, and it is probable that the bill so quickly presented was
Jefferson's; *cf.* statement that some of the bills had been presented before
final report, in Jefferson's and Wythe's statement to the Assembly, June
18, 1779—Ford, P. L.: *Writings Thomas Jefferson*, II, 195–96; it is generally assumed because the final report was not submitted until June 18,
1779, that the first presentation of the bill was made at that time; *cf.* Maddox: *Free Sch. Idea Va.*, 12, where the date June 8, is obviously a typographical error; *cf.* La Rouchefoucauld-Liancourt: *Voyage Dans Les États
Unis*, IV, 327, the date 1776 in the Du Pont, Buisson, Pougens edition is a
typographical error; *cf.* Hoffman edition, Hamburg, 1779, *De la Rouche-
foucauld Liancourt Reisen*, III, 59.

administer them are wise and honest; whence it becomes expedient for promoting the public happiness that those persons, whom nature hath endowed with genius and virtue, should be rendered by liberal education worthy to receive, and able to guard, the sacred deposit of the rights and liberties of their fellow citizens, and that they should be called to that charge without regard to wealth, birth or other accidental condition or circumstances; but that indigence of the greater number disabling them from so educating, at their own expense, those of their children whom nature hath fitly formed and disposed to become useful instruments for the public, it is better that such should be sought for and educated at the common expense of all, than that the happiness of all should be confided to the weak or wicked:[54]

Here there is no reference to education as being directed in the interests of a state concern for religion; but, wholly in the interests of a state concern for liberty, as expressed in the free exercise of natural rights, with a strong emphasis on the lessons to be gleaned from history in illuminating the minds of the people—in pointing the way to defeat tyranny and ambition. The chief features of the bill were the provision for free local elementary schools; division of the state into twenty districts, in each of which was to be a grammar school, to which, by a certain winnowing process, a number of poor boys were to be sent gratis; and similarly, a smaller number later to William and Mary.[55]   The chief interest of the bill, however, lies not in the unique detail by which the new school system was to be brought into operation, but in the indication of the promulgation of a new educational philosophy for Virginia.   Turning to the curriculum, it is significant, that in accordance with the basic thought of the preamble, that history was to be taught in the very lowest schools, the three year elementary schools, to which all free children of both sexes, were to be required to attend, and at which tuition was to be gratis.   It was provided that in

. . . these schools shall be taught reading, writing, and common artihmetic; and the books which shall be used therein for instructing the children to read shall be such as will at the same time make them acquainted with Grecian, Roman, English, and American history.[56]

---

[54] *Sundry Documents*, 3–4; Ford: *Writings T. Jefferson*, II, 220–21.
[55] *Sundry Documents*, 4 *ff.*; Ford: *Writings T. Jefferson*, II, 220 *ff.*; Lipscomb: *Writings T. Jefferson*, I, 71; Jefferson in his *Autobiography* states there were to be 24 districts, but the bill enumerates only 20.
[56] *Sundry Documents*, Section 6.

Thus every child as it grew up was to consider its relation to society and the state in the light of the lessons to be learned from history.

At the time when Jefferson was drafting this bill, he still had hope of reorganizing the College of William and Mary in such fashion, that it would serve as the directing genius of the curriculum in the complete educational system which he had in mind. For this reason, the overseer in charge of ten of these elementary schools was to "see that any general plan of reading and instruction recommended by the visitors of William and Mary College shall be observed;" a similar provision held for the grammar schools.[57]

That Jefferson, in placing the plan of instruction in the schools under the direction of William and Mary, did not propose to have them under ecclesiastical control, appears from his *Notes on the State of Virginia,* written in 1781.[58] In explaining the object of the proposed elementary curriculum, he states:

. . . The first stage of this education being the schools of the hundreds wherein the great mass of the people will receive their instruction, the principal foundations of future order will be laid here. Instead therefore of putting the Bible and Testament into the hands of the children at an age when their judgments are not sufficiently matured for religious inquiries, their memories may here be stored with the most useful facts from Grecian, Roman, European and American history. The first elements of morality too may be instilled into their minds; such as, when further developed as their judgments advance in strength, may teach them how to work out their own greatest happiness, by showing them that it does not depend on the condition of life in which chance has placed them, but is always the result of a good conscience, good health, occupation, and freedom in all just pursuits. . . .[59]

It would be of interest to determine the temper of the people toward the bill, but the references to it seem meager, indeed. The bill was of course made known by the printing ordered in 1778. In 1779, Richard Henry Lee in a letter to Jefferson wrote:

[57] *Ibid.,* 5–9; Ford: *Writing Thomas Jefferson,* II, 223–27; Maddox: *Free Sch. Idea Va.,* 14, states that the direction of William and Mary was not to extend to the primary, only to the secondary schools, but see section 7 of the bill.

[58] Jefferson: *Notes on Va.,* Advertisement; Ford: *Writings T. Jefferson,* III, 68.

[59] Jefferson: *Notes on Va.,* 217–18.

I hope when the Assembly is preparing a system of law for [o]ur future felicity, that they will not neglect that noble and best foundation for public liberty, general diffusion of knowledge for which you had left with the House so excellent a System.[60]

The "Report of the Committee of Revisors" was not published until 1784, when 500 copies were printed.[61] The bill came up in the House in December, 1785, when the title was changed to "An act, directing the mode of appointing aldermen," and it was referred to the Senate for concurrence, where, upon a third reading, it was rejected.[62] No hint of the reasons for rejection appears in the Senate *Journal;* but Madison writing to Jefferson in December, 1786, states:

The bill on the subject of Education which could not safely be brought into discussion at all last year, has undergone a pretty indulgent consideration this. In order to obviate the objection from the inability of the Country to bear the expence, it was proposed that it should be passed into a law, but its operation suspended for three or four years. Even in this form however there would be hazard in pushing it to a final question, and I begin to think it will be best to let it lie over for the supplemental Revisors, who may perhaps be able to put it into some shape that will lessen the objection of expence. . . . [63]

Apparently, the chief objection to the bill was the expense involved in putting into operation the three year elementary school system. There is no hint of objection on the basis of curriculum, and as Jefferson's *Notes on Virginia* did not appear in an American edition until 1787, the significance of the nature of the curriculum was probably not generally realized. Subsequently, Jefferson's duties as a representative and minister to France from 1784 to 1789, and as Secretary of State, 1790–93, prevented his furthering his bill in the Assembly. That his continued interest in the problem of education was known, is evident from his having been invited, in 1795, by Mann Page to discuss the subject of "the education of our youth."[64] In November, 1796, when Jefferson was elected Vice-President of the United States, the Assembly took up the question of educa-

---

60 Ballagh: *Letters Richard Henry Lee*, II, 157.
61 Ford: *Writings T. Jefferson*, II, 196–97.
62 *Jour., H. Del.*, Dec. 21, 1785, 101; *Jour., Senate*, Dec. 29, 1785, 66.
63 Hunt: *Writings James Madison*, II, 292.
64 Lipscomb: *Writings T. Jefferson*, IX, 306.

tion. In their preamble to the resolution "that a plan for the general education of the youth of this commonwealth, ought to be adopted, & carried into immediate effect," the motives for education are indicated as political, ethical, and economic. Youth was to be

. . . impressed with a due respect for the government and laws, and rendered capable by a knowledge of the true principles of morality and virtue, as well as by habits of order & industry, of securing their own happiness, and maintaining and encreasing the glory, the strength, wealth and felicity, of their country.[65]

The bill was drawn up by a committee of eleven and passed December 22, 1796.[66] The preamble to the bill stressed the "use of letters" as a means whereby mankind, "availing himself in succession of the accumulated wisdom and discoveries of his predecessors" would be enabled "to illuminate and enoble his understanding, and his nature." Though this echoes the "heir of all the ages" theme of Jefferson's bill, there is no specific stress on history as the means whereby citizens were to be "rendered liberal and humane." The provision for instruction in the three year free elementary schools was limited to a direction that the children "be taught reading, writing, and common arithmetic."[67] It would be interesting to know whether the elimination of history as the core of the curriculum was due to a consideration of non-feasibility in the lack of suitable books, or to a consideration of the non-religious character Jefferson wished the curriculum to take, which would have been evident enough, by this time from a reading of his *Notes on Virginia.*[68] The inauguration of the system, the expense of which was to be assumed by the counties, was left to the county courts, who were to determine the first election of the aldermen and fill vacancies. In these features of the bill, according to Jefferson, were to be found the reasons for its failure; the connection between the county courts and wealth with its effect on education, is thus indicated by him:

---

[65] *Jour., H. Del.*, Nov. 15, 1796.
[66] *Ibid.*, Dec. 22, 1796, 203.
[67] *Acts of Assembly*, Dec. 22, 1796, 3–4.
[68] See p. 165; Du Pont: *National Educ. in U. S.*, 28 *ff.*, discusses the need of text books suitable for children and suggests that prizes be offered to the authors of suitable ones; *cf.* also Niles: *Register*, Nov. 1, 1817, XII, 145 *ff.*

And in the Elementary bill, they inserted a provision which completely defeated it; for they left it to the court of each county to determine for itself, when this act should be carried into execution, within their county. One provision of the bill was, that the expenses of these schools should be borne by the inhabitants of the county, every one in proportion to his general tax rate. This would throw on wealth the education of the poor; and the justices, being generally of the more wealthy class, were unwilling to incur that burden, and I believe it was not suffered to commence in a single county.[69]

The failure of the optional education bill of 1796, is better understood when it is known that at least 20 charters of incorporation for educational institutions had been granted between 1776 and 1796; that the impetus thus given to educational effort in schools under the direction of boards of trustees was steadily maintained, if not slightly accelerated, in the subsequent period to 1810, with over 30 incorporations for the period.[70] In the creation of these schools, resort was largely had to subscription, and lotteries, though some profited from glebes and escheated lands —taxation was thus avoided.[71] The most significant fact in connection with these incorporations was, however, that they surrendered education largely to the control of those interested in

---

[69] Lipscomb: *Writings T. Jefferson*, I, 71–72; for the point of view that education was opposed as being "incompatible with if not dangerous to slavery" see Hall, G. D.: *Rending of Va.*, 65.

[70] The list of incorporations as gleaned by the writer largely from the laws and *Journals* of the House and Senate is: 1782, Liberty Hall; 1783, Fredericksburg Academy, Transylvania Seminary, Hampden-Sidney; 1786, Alexandria Academy, Botetourt Seminary, Winchester Academy; 1787, Margaret Academy, Randolph Academy; 1788, Salem Academy, Warren Academy; 1790, Millfield Academy; 1791, Scottsfield Lodge Academy, Warminster Academy; 1792; Staunton Academy, Wythe County Academy; 1794, Martinsville Academy, Petersburg Academy; 1795, New London Academy; 1796, Fredericksburg Charity School, Ebenezer Academy; 1797, Charlestown Academy; 1799; Brooke Academy, Leesburg Academy, Stevensburg Academy—Culpeper County; 1800, Jefferson College; 1801, Banister Academy, Bellefield Academy; 1802, Halifax Academy, Washington Henry Academy; 1803, Albemarle Academy, Abingdon Male Academy, New Glasgow Academy, Richmond Academy; 1804, Norfolk Academy; 1805, Rumford Academy; 1806, Burr Academy, Dumfries Academy, Hampton Academy; 1807, Hallerian Academy, Richmond Female Academy; 1808, Ann Smith Academy, Centerville Academy, Franklin Academy, Fredericksburg Female Charity School, Stephensburg Academy—Frederick County, New Kent Charity School; 1809, Berryville Academy, Caroline Academy, Manchester Academy, (1810) Rappahannock Academy; Charles City Charity School; it is necessary to note that the Rappahannock Academy was a substitution for Caroline Academy.

[71] For gifts of escheated land, see p. 222, 235.

having education associated with definite religious training.[72] As individuals associated with religious interests, saw the advantage to be gained for denominational welfare in the control of education, took the initiative in providing educational facilities and teachers, it is not surprising that the energies of communities enlisted in this direction, did not turn to the county courts.

Then, too, the Legislature in granting these incorporations at the request of citizens, who usually came armed with petitions, probably felt that it was creating an educational system in accordance with the wishes of the citizens of the state.

After Jefferson's departure to France, no impetus of a constructive kind was given toward creating an educational system from a civil standpoint, unless the indirect effect of the glebe law of 1802 be considered, until Governor John Tyler's message to the Assembly in December, 1809.[73] Reviewing the educational status of Virginia, thirty-three years after its independence as a state, he laments that not an additional "single complete seminary" has been erected, that not in a single instance has the law of 1796 been complied with,

. . . to the disgrace of the County Courts, and to the great disadvantage of the people, . . . for in our present situation he must be a wealthy citizen indeed who can afford the means of educating one son, so as to place him in a condition to serve his country, either in the field or in its councils, whensoever his services might be called for. . . .[74]

This purely civil and political aim of education is further elucidated in the statement:

. . . It is also an opinion, that a government like ours cannot last so long as a mixed or single one, which, if admitted in its fullest latitude, only proves what I am endeavoring to prevent—the loss of the moral sense, of the love of country, of the adherence to sound principles, both in a civil and a political capacity, in consequence of the want of a timely regard to the diffusion of knowledge. . . .[75]

---

[72] See p. 214, n. 48, 218, 220 *ff.*, 239, n. 189.
[73] *Jour., H. Del.*, Dec. 4, 1809, 7; Tyler, L. G.: *Letters and Times of Tylers*, I, 238 *ff.*
[74] *Ibid.*, I, 238.
[75] *Ibid.*, I, 239.

It is evident that in Governor Tyler's opinion, the surrender of educational control as represented by the legislative diffusion of charters to boards of trustees, amenable to the state only with difficulty, had not served the interests of the state.

On December 15, 1809, a committee was appointed to prepare a bill "To appropriate certain escheats, penalties and forfeitures, to the encouragement of learning," and "so much of the governor's communication as related to the subject of education" was referred to the committee.[76] This bill which created the Literary Fund was passed on February 2, 1810.[77] Briefly, it provided that the auditor of public accounts take care of the fund; that the Legislature appropriate it for the promotion of literature as it should see fit, on condition that the appropriation was to be for the sole benefit of a school or schools in each county.[78] The bill reserved to future meetings of the general assembly, the specific details of operation.

The educational philosophy evolved by 1810, did not differ essentially from the basic principle, which had characterized the educational philosophy of the colonial period—that is, that education is primarily to serve the state. In the political philosophy of union of church and state, education was made to subserve the basic principle of that philosophy; in the evolving political philosophy of the supremacy of the civil state, education was made to subserve the new principle.

While Jefferson would have had the educational system operate through a large degree of local control,[79] the end to be achieved in his point of view coincided with that expressed by Governor Tyler in a message to the Assembly in December, 1810, when he said:

. . . But all these improvements must have for their foundation a good system of education, and a general diffusion of knowledge. The great imployments of civil and military officers, must of necessity be confided to some, while the rest of our citizens are engaged in their ordinary occupations. These are important trusts, and should be placed in wise and virtuous

---

76 *Jour., H. Del.*, Dec. 15, 1809, 25.
77*Acts of Assembly*, Feb. 2, 1810, 15.
78 *Ibid.*; the bill is attributed to James Barbour, Speaker of the House, in Tyler: *Lives and Times of Tylers*, I, 242; *cf.* Maddox: *Free Sch. Idea Va.*, 48.
79 Lipscomb: *Writings T. Jefferson*, XII, 393; XIV, 419-20.

hands. But how will a succession of such men be kept up without the aid of legislative patronage? The very sentiments, as well as services, of each individual belong to the public: The sacred trust of superintending and rightly directing these sentiments, by providing and maintaining a wise system of instruction, cannot be neglected without deservedly incurring the severest reproaches.[80]

The Facist-like statement of Governor Tyler was given a Platonistic tinge by Jefferson in a letter to John Adams, which, though written in 1813, may safely be taken as his view throughout this period:

. . . The law for religious freedom, which made a part of this system, having put down the aristocracy of the clergy, had restored to the citizen the freedom of the mind, and those of entails and descents nurturing an equality of condition among them, this on education would have raised the mass of the people to the high ground of moral respectability necessary to their safety, and to orderly government; and would have completed the great object of qualifying them to select the veritable aristoi, for the trusts of government, to the exclusion of the pseudalists; . . .[81]

Intrinsically, it was for the furtherance of a Utopian government that education was to serve; it was through education that the government was to purify itself.

Reaction Upon William And Mary College

For the College of William and Mary, separation of Virginia from Great Britain was a momentous event. The importance of the occurrence was further enhanced by the circumstances which brought about the separation of church and state, tending to take away the very reason for its existence as expressed in its charter. Though the full implications of the section on religion in the *Declaration of Rights*, with regard to its effects on education, were not immediately understood, there was almost immediately a realization that some modification of the original charter was in order if the college was to serve the state in the new order of things. The extent of the modification necessary became more apparent as the legislative program leading to complete separation of church and state unfolded.

---

[80] *Jour., H. Del.*, Dec. 4, 1810, 7; Tyler: *Lives and Times of Tylers*, I, 252.
[81] Ford: *Writings T. Jefferson*, IX, 428.

Among the articles on education in the *Virginia Gazette,* in 1776, was that of "A. M.," addressed to the Assembly. It concerned itself at length with the reforms necessary at the College of William and Mary, and stated "you will probably find it more expedient to favour it with a new charter, than to confirm the old one." It suggested that the visitors, reduced to twelve, and residing within forty miles of the college, be appointed by the Assembly. An enlargement of the faculty was also urged, for

. . . By the old charter, the College is to consist of only a president and six masters, or professors; but though this number might have been sufficient for the purposes intended when the College was founded, and for the views of those times, yet now, when opportunities of foreign education are cut off, when our divines, our lawyers, and physicians, in short, when all orders, both in church and state, are to receive their respective qualifications at our own seminaries, we shall find it necessary to enlarge our plan: . . . The necessary professorships, as they occur to me at present, are 14 in number, and as follows: Of Divinity, of Oriental Languages, of Moral Philosophy, Logick, Metaphysics, and Rhetorick; of Natural Philosophy, of Astronomy, of Mathematicks, of Humanity, of the Modern Languages, of History and Chronology; of Botany, of the Theory and Practice of Physick, of Chymistry, of Anatomy, and of Law. One of these might be appointed president, and have that title, and the powers thereto belonging, with an extraordinary allowance, but who should still perform the duties of his professorship. . . .[82]

"A. M." also wished the new charter to grant, besides the old power to confer degrees in arts, the degrees in "Law, physick, and Divinity." In order to prepare youth for the college, grammar schools were to be established in different parts of the country. It is evident from "A. M.'s" views that he saw nothing incompatible in retaining a school of Divinity with the section on religion in the *Declaration of Rights;* and—as he expected the Assembly to take the college under its financial protection— nothing incongruous in the state's contributing to meet the cost of religious training.

In the meantime, the question of educational legislation was being considered by the Committee of Revisors of the Laws,[83] and, particularly by Thomas Jefferson of that committee. The

---

[82] *Va. Gazette,* Nov. 22, 1776.
[83] See p. 163.

need of clearing up the college situation appears from the following notice of April 4, 1777, in the *Virginia Gazette*:

RESOLVED, that the Rector be desired to write to the Visitors and Governors requesting their attendance in Convocation, at the college on Tuesday the 6th day of May next, at 10 o'clock in the forenoon, informing them that this present Convocation of the Visitors and Governors, having assembled on Monday the 31st of March, agreeably to the charter, in order to inquire into the state and affairs of the college, and continued their inquiries by different adjournments to this day, find that there are many things of the utmost importance to the prosperity of the college which they are of opinion ought to be discussed and determined upon in a full meeting. That, amongst other things, several articles of accusation, for neglect and misconduct, have been exhibited against the President of the college, John Dixon, clerk, professor of divinity, and Mr. Emmanuel Jones, master of Brafferton, which render the request the more necessary; and, to prevent any inconveniences which may arise from the miscarriage of letters, it is ordered that this resolution be forthwith published in the Virginia gazette; and it is further ordered, that the President be furnished with a copy of this resolution, and acquainted that the said 6th day of May is appointed for him to make his defence.[84]

The next month, a lengthy memorial was presented to the House by the "Rector, Visitors and Governors of the College" representing "the ruinous state of the college funds."[85] They state that they were faced with the necessity of either increasing the charge to the students or resorting to voluntary contribution; in the former situation, they would keep all but those "born to wealthy inheritances from the advantages of the College," contrary to the design of the founders, "whose object it was to open the door of knowledge to all persons willing to enter;" in the latter situation, they would be compelled to act in an "indecent and unpracticable" manner,

. . . Indecent, because it wears the appearance of renouncing the protection of the Legislature, though uniformly given hitherto; and impracticable, by reason of the sum which the present exigence requires.[86]

It is evident from this plea, that the college hoped for the continued financial support of the Assembly—that it would be re-

---

[84] *Va. Gazette*, April, 4, 1777; *cf.* Tyler: *Williamsburg*, 166.
[85] *Jour., H. Del.*, May 28, 1777, 34 *ff.*
[86] *Ibid.*

tained as a state institution. The House took up the memorial
on several occasions without constructive action.[87] In November, 1778, the college called the attention of the House to their
memorial of the previous year,[88] and again without result.

Undoubtedly, delay was due not only to the monetary demands
of the war, but because the Assembly was awaiting the Report
of the Revisors. In June, 1779, the report was received. Aside
from "A Bill For The More General Diffusion Of Knowledge"[89]
and "A Bill For Establishing A Public Library," it contained
as part of a legislative trilogy for a complete educational system, "A Bill For The Amending The Constitution Of The College Of William And Mary."[90] In the "Bill For The More
General Diffusion Of Knowledge" the visitors of the college
were given the power to recommend the general plan of instruction of both the three year elementary and the grammar
schools.[91] The bill for amending the constitution of the college
proceeded first of all to review the ancient charter and history
of the college, and then, to recite the basis on which the charter
was to be amended. In view of subsequent opinion on the question as to whether the college was a public or private institution,
the following opinion as expressed by Jefferson is of interest:

And whereas the experience of near an hundred years hath proved, that
the said College, thus amply endowed by the public, hath not answered their
expectations, and there is reason to hope, that it would become more useful,
if certain articles in its constitution were altered and amended, which being
fixed, as before recited, by the original charters, cannot be reformed by the
said trustees whose powers are created and circumscribed by the said charters, and the said College being erected and constituted on the requisition
of the General Assembly, by the Chief Magistrate of the state, their
legal fiduciary for such purposes, being founded and endowed with the lands
and revenues of the public, and intended for the sole use and improvement,
and no wise in nature of a private grant, the same is of right subject to
the public direction, and may by them be altered and amended, until such
form be devised as will render the institution publicly advantageous, in proportion as it is publicly expensive; . . .[92]

[87] *Ibid.*, June 3, 1777, 58; June 6, 1777, 63; June 12, 1777, 74.
[88] Ibid., Nov. 9, 1778, 50.
[89] See p. 163.
[90] *Sundry Documents*: Ford: *Writings T. Jefferson*, II, 220–37.
[91] See p. 164–65.
[92] Ford: *Writings T. Jefferson*, II, 232–33; *Sundry Documents*, 55.

An indication of the reasons for legislative concern in the college is found in the statement:

. . . and the late change in the form of our government, as well as the contest of arms in which we are at present engaged, calling for extraordinary abilities both in council and field, it becomes the peculiar duty of the Legislature, at this time, to aid and improve that seminary, in which those who are to be the future guardians of the rights and liberties of their country may be endowed with science and virtue, to watch and preserve the sacred deposit; . . .[93]

A new direction was thus to be given to education—no longer was the state to concern itself with the spiritual life of the individual, but to endow "with science and virtue" the "future guardians of the rights and liberties of their country." Education in Jefferson's opinion was now to receive a civil and ethical, not a spiritual, direction. The welfare of the citizen was to be taken care of by the state; and the welfare of the state, by that ideal citizen whose serious concern it would be to guard the new principles on which the new political state was founded. From the standpoint of citizenship, the church had no function to perform. Education was for citizenship. The elimination of the church is to be found in the provision that the five visitors annually appointed by the Assembly, were not to "be restrained in their legislation, by the royal prerogative, or the laws of the kingdom of England; of the canons or the constitution of the English Church as enjoined in the said charter."

With regard to the curriculum, Jefferson wrote:

. . . There shall, in like manner, be eight Professorships, to wit, one of moral philosophy, and the laws of nature and of nations, and of the fine arts; one of law and police; one of history, civil and ecclesiastical; one of mathematics; one of anatomy and medicine; one of natural philosophy and natural history; one of the ancient languages, oriental and northern; and one of modern languages.[94]

Of particular interest is the designation of a professor of civil and ecclesiastical history—that the viewpoint was to be historical, not spiritual, is clear from the emphasis on the historical standpoint in the bill for the more general diffusion of knowledge.[95]

[93] Ford: *Writings T. Jefferson*, II, 233.
[94] *Ibid.*, II, 234.
[95] See p. 164.

No immediate action was taken on this bill, whether because of the difficulty of financing the plan at that time, or the alarm of the dissenters, as Jefferson indicated in a letter to Dr. Joseph Priestley, when in 1800, he wrote:

. . . I had proposed that William and Mary, under an improved form, should be the University, and that was at that time pretty highly Episcopal, the dissenters after awhile began to apprehend some secret design of a preference to that sect. . . .[96]

It is evident that in spite of the clause in the bill which was intended to eliminate the Anglican influence, there was a distrust of the possibility of rooting it out; nor did the appointment of Rev. James Madison, an Episcopalian, as President, in 1777, have a tendency to lessen the prejudice. A few months after the presentation of the Report of the Committee of Revisors, the college, again without effect, sent a memorial to the House asking for financial assistance.[97] As the legislature was evidently indisposed to take any action in behalf of the college, Thomas Jefferson, who was soon after his appointment as Governor, elected a visitor of the college, proceeded to effect some of the reforms he so ardently desired. In his *Autobiography,* he wrote:

. . . Being elected, also, one of the Visitors of William and Mary college, a self-electing body, I effected, during my residence in Williamsburg that year, a change in the organization of that institution, by abolishing the Grammar school, and the two professorships of Divinity and Oriental languages, and substituting a professorship of Law and Police, one of Anatomy, Medicine and Chemistry, and one of Modern languages; and the charter confining us to six professorships, we added the Law of Nature and Nations, and the Fine Arts to the duties of the Moral professor, and Natural History to those of the professor of Mathematics and Natural Philosophy.[98]

The transformation thus accomplished is described in a letter, December 9, 1779, by one of the students:

William & Mary has undergone a very considerable Revolution; the Visitors met on the 4*th* Instant & form'd it into a University, annul'd the

96 Lipscomb: *Writings T. Jefferson,* X, 147; cf. *Ibid.,* I, 71, ''The religious jealousies, therefore, of all the dissenters, took alarm lest this might give an ascendancy to the Anglican sect, and refused acting on that bill.''
97 *Jour., H. Del.,* Oct. 26, 1779, 25; Nov. 2, 1779, 35.
98 Lipscomb: *Writings T. Jefferson,* I, 74.

old Statutes, abolish'd the Grammar School continued Mr Madison President, & Professor of Mathematics Appointed Mr Wyth Professor of Law, Dr Mc-Clurg of Physick Mr Andrews of Moral Philosophy, & Monsr Belini of modern Languages. . . .[99]

The reasons for discontinuing the grammar school and the two professorships of Divinity and Oriental languages, which had played so important a part in the former life of the college are thus explained in a statement in the *Virginia Gazette,* December 18, 1779:

THE funds of the college being no longer competent to support so extensive an institution as that which the charter recommends; and where science at large cannot be cultivated, that scheme of education being most proper which is more immediately subordinate to the leading objects of society: The scanty stipend lately paid by each scholar for commons having occasioned a considerable expense: It being just, that students inducted into the several scholarships should be equally affected by the depreciation of money, with the college: since the original donations, on which they were founded, cannot be now disposed of, but at a depreciated rate: Experience having proved, that the rarer parts of science have been obstructed in their progress by the maintenance of a Grammar-School within the same; the learning of which may be acquired elsewhere, in a much shorter time: And the necessities of the college rendering it expedient to multiply the sources of revenue by every possible means: Let there be, therefore, six professorships: The 1st of which shall be, Law and Police; the 2d, Anatomy and Medicine; the 3d, Natural Philosophy and Mathematicks; the 4th, Moral Philosophy, the Laws of Nature and of Nations, and the fine Arts; the 5th, Modern Languages; and the 6th, for Brafferton.

In the statement "that scheme of education being most proper, which is more immediately subordinate to the leading objects of society," aside from the omission of the professorships of Divinity and Oriental languages, was found notification, particularly to the ecclesiastical world of Virginia, that education was to be in line with the new political philosophy of separation of church and state. Thus as a visitor of the college, Jefferson was able to go even beyond the point indicated in his bill for amending the constitution of the college, for that had retained the study of ecclesiastical history. When the college was reorganized in January, 1780, with five professors and no appointment in favor of religious study, a new direction was given

[99] *Wm. A. Mary Coll. Quart.*, IX, 22.

to educational history in Virginia, which was aptly enough described by the student cited previously, as a "revolution."

In 1784, the Assembly finally voted some financial assistance to the college by vesting certain lands and property near Williamsburg and Jamestown "in the president and professors of William and Mary university for ever," with power to sell or dispose as they saw fit for the advantage of the university, subject to control and direction of the visitors.[100]

Probably, owing to the retention of Episcopalians in the personnel of the college, the nature of the change being effected was not clear to all outsiders; and, it is perhaps not surprising that a man like George Washington, whose attention had been for many years directed largely to military matters, should write in April, 1788, in acknowledgment of his appointment as chancellor of the college:

. . . I confide fully in their strenuous endeavors for placing the system of education on such a basis as will render it most beneficial to the State and the republic of letters, as well as to the more extensive interests of humanity and religion.[101]

As a matter of fact, those interested in continuing the ecclesiastical tradition of the college were not content to give up their connection and influence without a struggle. In November, 1788, while Jefferson was in France as Minister,[102] there appeared in the *Virginia Gazette & Weekly Advertiser* a notice of a prospective meeting of the visitors and governors of the University of William and Mary, to consider the appointment of a principal and an assistant grammar master.[103] The real motives that inspired the closing of the grammar school, in 1779, are a matter of interesting speculation. Rev. John Bracken had been

---

[100] Hening: *Stat. at Large,* XI, 405–06; *cf.* also authority for lottery, *Acts of Assembly,* Jan. 28, 1805, 58; Feb. 11, 1811, 81; *Jour., H. Del.,* Feb. 14, 1811, 106; authority for lotteries for religious or educational purposes was not looked upon as rendering direct state support.

[101] *U. S. Bur. Educ., Circ. Inf.,* 1887, No. 1, 35; Sparks, J.: *Writings George Washington,* IX, 362; *cf.* Tyler: *Williamsburg,* 178, gives the date as 1794; *cf.* Randolph, J. W. & English: *History of College of Wm. & Mary,* 74, gives the dates of the chancellorship as 1788–99; the date as given in an authorized statement on p. 23, *The Richmond News Leader,* Dec. 31, 1925, is 1789.

[102] Malone, D.: *Life T. Jefferson,* 3.

[103] *Va. Gazette & Weekly Advertiser,* Nov. 27, 1788.

appointed its master on April 1, 1777; no fault was found with his conduct.[104] It might be argued that the elimination of the school of Divinity, the enthronement of sciences and modern languages in the college, did not call for the traditional grammar school training; or even, that by eliminating one source of classical learning, the road was being cut off to Episcopalian ecclesiastical study. However, Jefferson's remarks in his *Notes on Virginia* make it clear that he was not opposed to the classics in grammar schools,[105] but that he objected to the proximity of the grammar school to the college as tending to fill the college with children, thus discouraging "young gentlemen already prepared for entering on the sciences," and so limiting the usefulness of the schools for mathematics and moral philosophy.[106] It was probably the traditional connection of the grammar school with the college, its association of the humanities with ecclesiasticism which had tended to obstruct "the rarer parts of science," that it was intended, in 1779, to break down, in order to align the new education with the principle enunciated of making education "more immediately subordinate to the leading objects of society." In 1787, a suit was entered against the visitors for the restoration of Rev. Mr. Bracken to his former office of grammar master, but the case was adjourned to the Court of Appeals.[107] In January, 1789, the reopening of the grammar school was definitey announced.[108] There then arose a question as to the legality of this procedure, and action was suspended until the adjudication of the case in the November term, 1790, of the Court of Appeals.[109] The issue finally resolved itself into two questions—whether the institution was a private or public one, and the authority of the visitors in instituting changes and annulling appointments. In view of Jefferson's opinion in his bill amending the constitution of the college, that the institution was a public one, it is of interest to read the argument of John Marshall[110] that the public gifts, that is the financial support

[104] Call, D.: *Reports*, III, 577.
[105] Jefferson: *Notes on Va.*, 218–19.
[106] *Ibid.*, 223; *U. S. Bur. Educ., Circ. Inf.*, 1888, No. 1, 42.
[107] Call: *Reports*, III, 577.
[108] *Va. Gaz. & Weekly Advertiser*, Jan. 29, 1789.
[109] Call: *Reports*, III, 573 *ff.*
[110] *Cf.* p. 186, 297, 362.

formerly contributed by the Assembly, did not make the institution a public one—but that the public gifts as annexed foundations were governed by rules of the original foundation, that this had partaken of the nature of a private institution, and that the institution was therefore a private not a public one—that the visitors had the powers of general visitors of private corporations and could proceed as they chose. The court refused to require the restoration of Rev. Mr. Bracken.[111]   This decision was of serious consequence for the college, for while it enabled the visitors to have extensive powers, it tended to cut the college off, in its character as a private institution, from state support.   It probably explains, too, the statement of Rev. Mr. Madison to Thomas Jefferson in a letter of January 17, 1800, that there had been no meeting of the visitors for five years.[112] There was no longer any pertinent reason for not reorganizing the grammar school and this was done under Rev. John Bracken in 1792.[113]   In 1802, an advertisement in the *Virginia Gazette & General Advertiser* indicated that the curriculum, in addition to the humanities, was to consist of the reading of English books, writing, arithmetic, geography, and history.[114]   The grammar school was continued under Rev. Mr. Bracken until 1812, when he succeeded Rev. James Madison as President of the college; the grammar school was for a time discontinued.[115]

While the legal character of the college had changed from a public to a private institution, the elimination of the school of divinity effected, in 1779, continued, probably because the Episcopal Church did not feel that the time was ripe for any step looking towards its reintroduction.   At a convention, in 1787, the church resolved to

. . . recommend it to the parishes to provide funds for the education of two youths, from their early years, that they might be trained for the Christian

---

111 Call: *Reports,* III, 589 *ff.*
112 *Wm. & Mary Coll. Quart.,* Ser. 2, V, 93.
113 While the court had refused to award a writ of mandamus for restoration, the visitors were left free to proceed as they saw fit; Tyler: *Williamsburg,* 178.
114 *Va. Gazette & General Advertiser,* Jan. 15, 1802.
115 Tyler: *Williamsburg,* 182.

ministry: . . . and the selected youths were to be under the direction of the bishop and standing committee.[116]

In 1793, the presbyteries, consisting of not less than three nor more than ten ministers, were required "to take the oversight of all candidates for orders in their districts, to direct their studies, and to examine them."[117] The problem of clerical instruction solved for the time being, the Episcopalians were not disposed to force the issue of a theological department at William and Mary.

It is pertinent to discover what, in the meantime, had been the effect of the *Declaration of Rights* and the "revolution" of 1779 upon the spiritual life of the college.

It must not be thought that there was an immediate suspension in the college, of the mention of the name of God, of the reading or use of the Bible, of reference to religion. The extent of the preoccupation with religion and the attitude towards it may be gathered from evidence which will now be presented. It was an era of transition but the strength of traditional college attitudes is well known.

Three years before the "revolution" in the college, a number of students had organized the Phi Beta Kappa Society.[118] In their oath of fidelity, they swore "on the holy Evangelists of Almighty God" and called on "the Supreme Being" to attest their Oath.[119] In one of their early meetings they resolved, "That in every design or attempt, whether great or small, we ought to invoke the Deity, by some private sacrifice or devotion, for a fraternal prosperity."[120] In 1778, one of their declamations concerned "the advantages of an established church."[121] The following February, a sum received from a member "to purchase a Testament for the Society" was deposited in the Treasury, as the society was already provided in this respect. In November, 1779, the question for discussion was "Whether a General Assessment for the support of Religious Establishments

---

[116] Hawks: *Contrib. Ecc. Hist.*, I, 200.
[117] *Ibid.*, 221.
[118] *Wm. & Mary Coll. Quart.*, IV, 213–41.
[119] *Ibid.*, 216.
[120] *Ibid.*
[121] *Ibid.*, 22.

is or is not repugnant to the principles of a Republican Government.''[122] The subject for declamation in July, 1780, was "Whether Religion is necessary in Government.''[123] It is undoubtedly to these discussions of the Phi Beta Kappa Society that Bishop Meade refers in recounting conditions at the college at the time he presented himself to Bishop Madison for ordination:

. . . I was informed that not long before this two questions were discussed in a literary society of the College:—First, Whether there be a God? Secondly, Whether the Christian religion had been injurious or beneficial to mankind? Infidelity, indeed, was then rife in the State, and the College of William and Mary was regarded as the hotbed of French politics and religion. I can truly say, that then, and for some years after, in every educated young man of Virginia whom I met, I expected to find a skeptic, if not an avowed unbeliever. I left Williamsburg, as may well be imagined, with sad feelings of discouragement. . . .[124]

While the Bishop was speaking from rumor, a more accurate picture can be gathered from letters written by students in the closing years of the 18th century. Rob Michie wrote to David Watson on May 9, 1795:

Coming over to borrow your Greek testament I was sorry I could not have the satisfaction of seeing you. But believe me I experience no incompetent degree [?] from hearing of your attention to Divine Institutions. . . . But respecting religion, Mr. Causby a close reasoner and an implicit follower of Mr. Paine Reasonable Age. [sic] Has converted the whole Ducking Hole fraternity insomuch that we never think of such a thing. I asked the young gentleman at the time when he was very zealously opposing the faith if he had divested himself of even the most minute conscientious scruple respecting the Divinity of our Lord and Saviour Jesus Christ? Without hesitation he answered in the affirmative. But these are matters unfathomable by me for which reason I am resolutely determined to remain in the faith till I see cause to alter-which God forbid I ever should. They say he has so staggered the vestal faith of the vestal P. J. (if she ever had any) that she is resolved on a Revolution. . . .[125]

Three years later, William Brockenbrough, destined later to become one of the "pillars" of Monumental Church, Richmond, wrote to David Watson:

---

122 *Ibid.*, 232.
123 *Ibid.*, 237.
124 Meade: *Old Churches, Ministers and Families*, I, 29; Goodwin, E. L.; *Colonial Church*, 157.
125 *Va. Mag. Hist.*, XXIX, 134–35.

In conformity with the divine Doctrine expressed in the Decalogue, "Remember that thou keep *holy* the Sabbath Day" I take up my pen to do a deed a thousand times more holy than that of going to Church to observe the comings in, and the goings out, the Motions, the Actions, and the Dress, of Girls, or what is still worse the Ravings of an hypocritical Priest. For is not that amazing hypocricy which induces the recommending of Doctrine with earnestness, nay even with energy, which very Doctrines are not thought of, as soon as the pulpit is empty? This is a pretty beginning you will say. . . .[126]

The great disrespect into which anything associated with religion had fallen in the eyes of many of the students is vividly told in a letter, March 21, 1798, to the same correspondent by Isaac A. Coles:

. . . Your sentiments with respect to this College, accord perfectly with mine; the custom of pulling down steps, breaking carriages, etc. I think of all others the most detestable. Of late it has become vastly too fashionable. The other evening a large party made an attack upon the sacred property of God; the Communion Table was broken into a thousand pieces, all the prayer Books and Bibles scattered about the Church Yard, one winder entirely destroyed, and the pulpit itself bedaubed from one end to the other, . . . An offence so heinous, called aloud for punishment. The Bishop and professors talked high of expulsion, But the party was so numerous, and many of them so respectable, that, although they had direct proof, nothing was done. I once thought this old place might again survive, but I am convinced now that that time will never arrive; Were it not for the Bishop it would not now exist, without him, I make no doubt, it will expire.[127]

It was probably in an attempt to eliminate the possibility of episodes of this kind, that "A Statute For the wholesome Government of the College," which appeared in the *Virginia Gazette & General Advertiser* on April 10, 1802, was devised.[128]

The spirit of skepticism is thus defended by Coles in a letter, July, 1799, to Henry St. George Tucker; a defense which might serve as an answer to Bishop Meade's identification of inquiry with infidelity:

---

[126] *Ibid.*, XXX, 237; a note, *Ibid.*, states "The 'hypocritical Priest' certainly deserved no such epithet. He was the Rev. Dr. John Bracken, rector of Bruton, and President of William and Mary 1812–14 . . . elected Bishop of Virginia, but declined."

[127] *Ibid.*, 241.

[128] In this connection the comment of La Rouchefoucauld-Liancourt, *Voyage Dans États-Unis*, IV, 289–90, on the scattered housing system of the students is of interest.

The spirit of skepticism which so much prevailed & which every student acquired as soon as he touched the threshold of the college is certainly the first step towards knowledge; it puts the mind in a proper state not only to receive, but also to receive correctly. That it leads to Deism, atheism &c I will acknowledge, but on the same grounds we may object to reason. Skepticism indeed only gives it the reins.[129]

In the latter part of the same year another student, Chapman Johnson wrote to David Watson:

I was really somewhat surprised, to find the Bishop so firm a Christian, as I now believe him; after having so frequently heard, that he was a deist in sentiment. If he is not a Christian, he certainly is the most consumate hypocrite; and this I cannot believe of him; his firm belief is manifested in every action of his life.[130]

At the beginning of the nineteenth century, a student at the college, professing to find a less keen interest on the part of the student body in either religious or metaphysical speculation, wrote:

. . . It is really remarkable that the taste of the students here in favor of particular books and opinions varies as often as the fashions in the polite world. The Christian Religion is not as formerly a subject of general discussion, the science of metaphysicks no longer engages the affections of the young men, . . .[131]

It is clear from a review of the student correspondence of this period, that while the students allowed their speculations to be expressed at times in crude conduct, that fundamentally they were inspired by a spirit of inquiry, that spirit which is easily interpreted by the outsider as being equivalent to heterodoxy. It must be recalled that these were the years when the extensive legislative program looking to the separation of church and state was being carried through; that these were the years, also, of new political experiments at home and abroad, and of much political writing; as well as the years of a new interest in the sciences. During all this time the college was under the domination of a man who in many respects was characteristic of this transitional period. This man was the bishop referred to in Chapman Johnson's letter, Rev. James Madison,

---

[129] *Wm. & Mary Coll. Quart.*, IV, 107.
[130] *Va. Mag. Hist.*, XXIX, 266.
[131] *Ibid.*, XXIX, 278.

President of the college, from 1777 until his death in 1812.[132] He had been consecrated Bishop in 1790.[133] To understand somewhat the character of the man in charge of William and Mary College for thirty-five years, it is necessary to recall that he was elected to the faculty as President and professor of natural philosophy and mathematics, in 1777, at the age of twenty-eight.[134] Among the books introduced by him to his students, were Adam Smith's *Inquiry into the Nature and Sources of the Wealth of Nations*, Vatell's *Law of Nations*, Stewart's *Philosophy of Mind;* but he rather disliked to have his students read Godwin's *Inquiry Concerning Political Justice*.[135] Rouchefoucald-Liancourt wrote of him:

. . . L'évêque Madisson l'est beaucoup, en physique, en chimie, et même en littérature. Sa bibliothèque, bien moins nombreuse que celle du collège, est composée de livres d'un meilleur choix, sur-tout parmi ceux relatif aux sciences. Il augmente annuellement sa collection des ouvrages savans et nouveaux les plus estimés. C'est à lui que sont dûes des observations météorologiques très-bien faites en différens points de la Virginie, et auxquelles il a consacré beaucoup de tems.[136]

To be a political scientist, physical scientist, and at the same time a bishop in the Protestant Episcopal Church, was, in that day, as it would still be in this, sufficient to subject a man to a suspicion, on the part of some, as to his spiritual orthodoxy.[137] On this subject, Bishop Meade wrote:

. . . It has been asserted that Bishop Madison became an unbeliever in the latter part of his life, and I have often been asked if it was not so. I am confident that the imputation is unjust. His political principles, which at that day were so identified in the minds of many with those of infidel France, may have subjected him to such suspicion. His secular studies, and occupations as President of the College and Professor of Natural Philosophy,

---

[132] Tyler: *Williamsburg*, 194.
[133] Hawks: *Contrib. Ecc. Hist.*, I, 207–10; for a sketch of his life, see *Va. Mag. Hist.*, XXIX, 140, Goodwin: *Colonial Church*, 127–35.
[134] Tyler: *Williamsburg*, 170.
[135] *Ibid.; Va. Mag. Hist.*, XXIX, 140–41; *Wm. & Mary Coll. Quart.*, XIV, 76; *cf.* Wirt: *The British Spy*, 123 *ff.*, for the influence of Godwin upon Virginia youth.
[136] La Rouchefoucald-Liancourt: *Voyage Dans États-Unis*, IV, 294–95.
[137] Conway: *Barons of the Potomac and Rappahannock*, 143, calls Madison a ''rationalist.''

may have led him to philosophise too much on the subject of religion, and of this I thought I saw some evidence in the course of my examination; but that he, either secretly, or to his most intimate friends, renounced the Christian faith, I do not believe, but am confident of the contrary.[138]

Perhaps the question as to the Bishop's orthodoxy arose really from a kind of political prejudice. Though Rev. Mr. Madison had been asked, because of his well known republican principles, to supplant the former President, John Camm, a loyalist, and though the story is told of him, that in his sermons he never referred to "heaven as a kingdom, but as that *'great republic where there was no distinction of rank, and where all men were free and equal,' "*[139] yet, the fact that he had gone to England for ordination rankled in the minds of some of the super-patriots of the day—as is evident from a letter of Judge John Tyler, written July 10, 1795:

Remember, when I speak of the Bishop, I feel the highest veneration for his character as a man, but I like him not the better for his canonicals, they will not let men be enough of republicans; besides he went to *Great Britain* for the exalted station. Now who wou'd even be sent to Heaven by such a People? Even if it were possible they cou'd in the hight of human depravity work such a wonder, I am well assured that God will never make choice of such an agent.[140]

The writer of this letter when sending his message as governor, in December, 1809, to the Assembly, did not, however, allow any prejudice, if he still felt any, to stand in the way of recommending the restoration of the college to its former place of supremacy as a state institution. The chief recommendation was:

. . . to alter, amend, or do away with the present charter, so as to place it under the control of the Legislature in some shape or other. The visitors ought to be appointed by the Legislature, and vacancies supplied in a way to prevent them from degenerating into a self-created body.'"[141]

Referring evidently to the Marshall opinion,[142] the governor said:

Nor can there be a doubt of the right of the government in this respect, although a futile argument is advanced to prove the contrary, on the ground

---

[138] Meade: *Old Churches, Ministers, Families,* I, 28–29.
[139] Tyler: *Williamsburg,* 166–68.
[140] *Wm. & Mary Coll. Quart.,* II, 203.
[141] Tyler: *Letters and Times of Tylers,* I, 240–41; *Jour., H. Del.,* Dec. 4, 1809, 7–8.
[142] See p. 179.

of the charter by which it was established. All charters of a public nature are for public benefit, and whensoever they fail of their object, they should be altered or amended, or newly organized. No power should exist in our government but what emanates mediately or immediately from the people.

Why suffer a fragment of royalty to remain among us, unless "to create a longing after the fleshpots of Egypt?" Have not all the charters of our once humiliated colonies been done away, and those of a better order established and founded on the immutable principles of justice and the rights of man.[143]

Whether because the college preferred to cling to its ancient charter,[144] or the legislature and people dreaded increased taxes, or because of the prejudice of the other denominations towards a traditionally Episcopalian institution, or of the orthodox towards a reputed deistic or atheistic institution, nothing came of the governor's suggestion.

The history of William and Mary from the beginning of the Revolution to the inauguration of the Literary Fund is a curious one in its relation to the state. Regarded until 1790 as a state institution, it had been shorn of its ecclesiastical departments not by direct state action, but by its board of visitors; the state had permitted the retention of personnel who had strong ecclesiastical connections and influence; the state had given it, hesitatingly, it is true, financial support. As a private institution, after 1790, the loss of its former connection with the state, as a public institution, was regretted by those who saw the state left without a single public, that is, state dominated institution for education. On the other hand, no action was taken by the Episcopal Church, beyond restoring the grammar school, toward reëstablishing its character definitely as a Protestant Episcopal institution; an end which would have been logical enough, after the decision of 1790. As far as its cultural influence was concerned throughout this period, it is evident that in spite of a nominal ecclesiastical connection, that it was dominated not by an atmosphere of spiritual acquiescence, but by one of scientific inquiry. Of the students it was said in 1805:

---

143 Tyler: *Letters and Times of Tylers*, I, 241.
144 *Ibid.*, 243.

. . . One thing generally characterizes the gentlemen educated at William and Mary's College, is, their great liberality of sentiment; their minds are never cramped by local prejudices.[145]

In a sense the college represented, as will be shown, that transitional type of institution between Jefferson's ideal of a purely civil university and the denominational institutions that were arising to rival it.

Thomas Jefferson And A New Educational Philosophy

To understand Jefferson's ideal of a purely civil university, it is necessary to trace the development of Jefferson's educational philosophy, and the influences brought to bear upon its development. It will be recalled, that after presenting his Report of the Committee of Revisors when governor in 1779, Jefferson's retirement from that office in 1781, was marked by a considerable withdrawal until 1809, from contact with life in Virginia. In that period of almost thirty years, he had served as a representative in France, had been Secretary of State, Vice-President, and President of the United States, two terms, had been elected President of the American Philosophical Society, and had opportunity to come in contact with the keenest minds of those decades, both at home and abroad.[146]

As has been indicated in the review of the educational legislation proposed by Jefferson in 1779, education was to be brought into conformity with the new objects of society, which were no longer the mutual protection of the civil and religious aspects of society, but the protection of the individual in the free exercise of his natural rights.[147] The free exercise of these natural rights had evidently, in the opinion of Jefferson, been hampered by the views ecclesiasticism had imposed on the minds of the people; and it is clear that, in his opinion, he saw no solution for freedom from that ecclesiastical dominance, except by cutting religious influence as completely out of the field of education as it was being cut out of the field of government. Jefferson explained, as has been shown, the proposed elimination of re-

---

[145] Scott, J.: *Geographical Dictionary*, 1805, under *Williamsburg*.
[146] Malone: *Life T. Jefferson*, 3–4.
[147] See p. 164.

ligious influence from the elementary schools on the basis of immaturity of the students; a reason that no longer held for the elimination of the schools of divinity from the college. He undoubtedly realized immediately the illegality, in view of the *Declaration of Rights*, of obtaining state support for that institution, if those schools were retained; and he probably wanted, at the time, to save the institution to the state. It is clear from his views on the legitimate powers of government as given in his *Notes on Virginia*, that the government could not concern itself with education, unless education were divorced from religion. He declared:

. . . The error seems not sufficiently eradicated, that the operations of the mind, as well as the acts of the body, are subject to the coercion of the laws. But our rulers can have no authority over such natural rights only as we have submitted them. The rights of conscience we never submitted, we could not submit. We are answerable for them to our God. The legitimate powers of government extend to such acts only as are injurious to others. But it does me no injury for my neighbor to say there are twenty Gods, or no God. It neither picks my pocket nor breaks my leg. If it be said, his testimony in a court of justice cannot be relied on, reject it then, and be the stigma on him. Constraint may make him worse by making him a hypocrite, but it will never make him a truer man. It may fix him obstinately in his errors, but will not cure them. Reason and free inquiry are the only effectual agents against error. . . .[148]

If the legitimate powers of the government did not concern themselves with religious opinion, the corollary followed that the government could not concern itself with education, so long as education was concerned with religious opinion.

Jefferson's views in the *Notes on Virginia* were undoubtedly a further crystallization of the views to which he had given expression in *A Bill for Establishing Religious Freedom*.[149] This bill, presented in June, 1779, was postponed from session to session until passed during his absence from the country, in 1786.[150] The position taken by Jefferson in that bill, "that the opinions of men are not the object of civil government, nor under its

---

[148] Jefferson: *Notes on Va.*, 235–36; *cf.* Henley: *The Distinct Claims of Government and Religion*, 12–13, 14, 16.
[149] See p. 92 *ff.*
[150] Ford: *Writings T. Jefferson*, II, 237 *ff.*; Jefferson: *Notes on Va.*, 326 *ff.*

jurisdiction,'' that civil intrusion of that kind destroys religious liberty, that no one was to suffer financially, civilly, or otherwise because of religious opinion, rendered it impossible for the government legally to concern itself in the furtherance of education, if education was dominated by religious influence, for the government could not support one combination of this kind, without prejudicing the interests of another similar combination.   While the passage of this bill tended naturally to alienate Episcopal sympathy from Jefferson, it tended also with the lapse of years, when its logical implications became more and more evident, to alienate also other denominational influence.[151] The prejudices aroused against Jefferson by the enactment of this bill, common to the experience of all disturbers of the customary, lethargic social mind, were further increased as the views expressed in his *Notes on Virginia* had time to percolate through the public mind.[152]   An indication of the nature of the resentment aroused may be gleaned from certain passages in *Observations Upon Jefferson's Notes on Virginia,* printed in 1804.   Expressing surprise that a book containing so much infidelity, insidiously conveyed, should have circulated without a formal answer in a Christian country, the author writes:

. . . The intention of these pages is, to point out the passages, in his Notes on Virginia, which tend to the subversion of religion; and to examine whether, from brilliancy of invention, acuteness of investigation, or cogency of argument, they are entitled to the name of any other than modern French philosophy.[153]

After animadverting upon Jefferson's description of the junction of the Potomac and Shenandoah as contrary to Genesis,[154] the writer continues:

. . . But can any person who believes the testimony of his senses and reason, deny that the book which offers a theory of the earth contrary to the scrip-

---

[151] Bowers, C. E.: *Jefferson and Hamilton,* 103; for the Presbyterian position, see Rice, J. H. *Presbyterian Church Va.,* 48 *ff.;* for a highly favorable estimate of this bill by William Jennings Bryan, before he yielded to extreme fundamentalism, see Lipscomb: *Writings T. Jefferson,* VIII, i *ff.*

[152] Bowers: *Jefferson and Hamilton,* 103–04; Randall, H. S.: *Life Thomas Jefferson,* I, 494–95.

[153] [Moore, C. C.]: *Observations Jefferson's Notes,* 6.

[154] *Ibid.,* 7–8.

ture account of the creation; which denies the possibility of an universal deluge; which considers the Bible history as no better than ordinary tradition; which extols Voltaire and the French Encyclopedists, the imps who have inspired all the wickedness with which the world has of late years been infested; which says that the natives of America are older than those of Asia, though scripture says that the world was peopled from one pair, placed in Asia; which considers it as a doubtful matter whether the blacks be really men, or only an intermediate grade between us and the brutes; and which esteems all religions "good enough;" can he deny that this book is an instrument of infidelity?[155]

The consequences for the country in the promulgation of such views are then depicted by the writer:

. . . Wretched, indeed, is our country, if she is to be enlightened by these philosophers; . . . And for what? Is it to render more stable the uncertain condition of man? Is it to alleviate one of the miseries which afflict his nature? No; it is to banish civilization from the earth, that we may be reduced to the state of savages; to pluck from the wretched their sweetest consolation; to extinguish the only light by which the Christian hopes to cheer the gloomy hour of death; to quench the thirst for immortality which the Creator has attached to our nature; to degrade us from the rank of angels, to which we are taught to aspire, that we may complete the catalogue of brutes.[156]

The cry here made, that there was being foisted upon the country an execrable foreign religion, was one that was frequently echoed.[157] In the *Virginia Gazette and General Advertiser* of April 10, 1802, there appeared an extract from an address to the freeholders of Fairfax County, by George W. P. Custis, in which he defined Jacobinism for the benefit of his fellow citizens:

Jacobinism, Fellow Citizens, is in itself, a principle so vile, that its supporters are ashamed to acknowledge it. . . .
Jacobinism, Fellow Citizens, originated in impiety. The cause of the French Revolution may be justly attributed to Jacobinism. The modern philosophers disseminated principles destructive to the peace of France. —They began by despising religion, as incompatible with their exalted ideas; they found out that all men were equal, that government was a folly, and that a future state existed not. They pulled down the church to erect the temple of anarchy—They trampled the cross to raise the idol democracy—

---

155 *Ibid.*, 29.
156 *Ibid.*, 30.
157 Jones: *America and French Culture*, 407.

They destroyed the government to plant the tree of liberty:—In fine, they overturned the nation, to raise the republic. Behold, Fellow Citizens, the end of things—''The name of a modern philosopher, is now despised in France'' —The nation, seeing their error have subsided into an effective, energetic government; France from being a prey to faction, has become an envied nation: Philosophy has given place to national utility, and philosophers, like their systems, have become objects of contempt.

Reflect, my countrymen, on the awful end of Voltaire, D'Alembert, and Diderot—those were philosophers of the modern school. Voltaire died imploring mercy from the God he blasphemed. Listen to the groans which rend his soul; he sees the torments which justly await him, ''and in the deepest hell, a deeper yet, still gaping to devour him, opens wide.'' Yes, impious man, there is a final doom—receive thy just reward. Cast not thy eyes to heaven—invoke not mercy there—too long have you abused its inestimable gifts—repentance comes too late. Thou wilt find thy philosophy cannot save thee now. Listen to the pitiful confession of the dying infidel— ''If I have offended my God, and the church, I ask pardon of both.'' Yes, when wrung with agony; when vengeance was at hand, and horror stared him in the face, Voltaire endeavored to pray—he deigned to implore that God he had blasphemed. The scene must close—it furnishes an awful example—an improving lesson.[158]

It was undoubtedly from the snare of the views of Thomas Jefferson, who had spent five years (1784–89) in France, and who as president since 1796 of the American Philosophical Society, had excellent opportunity of meeting the exiled and visiting Frenchmen flocking to this country, that Mr. Custis wished to save his fellow-citizens.[159]

While Jefferson's thinking was very probably stimulated by his French experiences and contacts, some of his most important writing, *The Declaration of Independence,* the legislation of 1779, the *Notes on Virginia* had been done before he went to France—and his thinking on such questions as education, religion, and politics had received their definite bent before Jacobinism organized. The seeds of Jacobinism may have been sown in France by the writings of Montesquieu, Rousseau, and Voltaire, and Jefferson was familiar enough with their work, but familiarity with Jefferson's writings leads inevitably to the con-

---

[158] *Va. Gazette & General Advertiser,* April 10, 1802.
[159] Hansen: *Liberalism & Amer. Education,* 105, 107–09; Jones: *America and French Culture,* 402–03.

clusion that Jefferson did his own thinking.[160]   That Jefferson was an independent thinker is confirmed by a study of two French educational treatises, designed to influence education in Virginia, in particular.

It is necessary to speak first of Jefferson's contact with the educational scheme of Chevalier Quesnay De Beaurepaire.[161] The scheme itself is said to have been first suggested to Quesnay by John Page, of "Rosewell," in 1778.[162]   In its final form, its comprehensiveness compares well with any Utopian scheme in educational literature.   It was to have branch establishments in Baltimore, Philadelphia, and New York; it was to be in correspondence with the learned societies of Europe; it was to have professors, masters, and artists of various kinds; it was to concern itself with languages, sciences and arts; with mines, agriculture, printing; no human learning was to be foreign to it; it was well said of this plan *"ne se prescrit d'autres limites que celles de l'esprit humain.''*[163]   The scheme progressed to the point of receiving sufficient support in France, and particularly in Virginia, so that it was possible to celebrate the laying of the corner stone of Quesnay's Academy, on June 24, 1786, with the proper Masonic éclat.[164]   By the latter part of 1788, Quesnay, who had left Paris in December, 1786, succeeded in having printed a *Mémoire* of his project.[165]   Among the foreign associates of the enterprise, he lists in the *Mémoire* the name of "JEFFERSON, Ministre Plénipotentiaire des États-Unis de l'Amérique septentrionale, *à Paris.''*[166]   To assume from Quesnay's use of Jefferson's name, that Jefferson was actively behind the scheme is hardly warranted; in fact, Jefferson had written Quesnay in January, 1788, that he preferred to remain "abso-

---

160 For Jefferson's knowledge of these French writers consult index, Lipscomb: *Writings T. Jefferson*, XX; cf. also, Parrington, V. L.: *Romantic Revolution*, 10 ff; *The Colonial Mind*, 343 ff.

161 Quesnay de Beaurepaire: *Mémoire Statuts Et Prospectus, Concernant L'Académie Des Sciences Et Beaux Arts Des États-Unis de L'Amérique*, a translation of this publication by Rosewell Page, with an introduction by W. L. Hall, is to be found in the 18th Annual Report of the Library Board of the Va. State Library, 1920–21.

162 Grigsby, H. B.: *Hist. Va. Fed. Convention*, 1788, 68.

163 Quesnay: *Mémoire*, 108.

164 *Ibid.*, 23 ff.; *Va. Mag. Hist.*, XI, 253–54.

165 *Wm. & Mary Coll. Quart.*, Ser. 2, V, 85.

166 Quesnay: *Mémoire*, 83.

lutely neutral" in regard to the scheme.[167]   Jefferson probably
felt that the fate his far simpler educational scheme of 1779
was suffering, hardly warranted his extending encouragement
to such an elaborate scheme. Undoubtedly, as W. L. Hall has
said, "the scheme itself made a profound impression upon
him."[168]   No scheme since Bacon's Atlantis had perhaps so
much to recommend it to the Utopians. When Jefferson permitted the use of his name, he most certainly could not have
known that the published *Mémoire* was to contain a statement
that the acme of the whole achievement was to be found, after
inspiring Americans with a taste for the Beaux-Arts, and gaining their confidence in favor of French instructors, in "enfin
établir une Chapelle pour les Catholiques Romains, épars en Virginie."[169]   It was surely not for that consummation, the elaborate Masonic foundation ceremony had been held.   Many years
later, Archibald T. Robertson, in his *Life and Letters of John
Albert Broadus* said:

> . . . While there (1786) he had become interested in a gigantic scheme of
> the French savant, Quesnay, for the establishment of a national academy at
> Richmond, Virginia, which should be a reproduction of the great academy at
> Paris, with branches at New York, Philadelphia, etc. It was no less than
> an effort to reproduce French Catholic culture in the United States with
> Richmond as the center. . . .[170]

Whether the failure of the scheme is to be charged to the French
Revolution,[171] or to the Virginia preference for dancing, rather
than the severer discipline of the intellect,[172] is immaterial; its
doom was undoubtedly sealed upon the publication of the in-
criminating evidence of the *Mémoire*.[173]   As for the influence

---

[167] Bruce, P. A.: *Hist. U. of Va.*, I, 58; for a different view, see Jones:
America and French Culture, 477.
[168] Hall, W. L.: *18th Ann. Rep't. Lib. B'd. Va. State Lib.*, 1920–21, 7.
[169] Quesnay: *Mémoire*, 25–26.
[170] Robertson, A. T.: *Life and Letters of J. A. Broadus*, 57.
[171] Grigsby: *Hist. Va. Fed. Convention 1788*, 68; Hall: *18th Ann. Rep't.
Lib. B'd. Va.*, 1920–21, 9.
[172] Stanard, M. N.: *Richmond, People and Story*, 57.
[173] For other primary sources with reference to the scheme, see *Va. Gaz.
& Weekly Advertiser*, Nov. 15, 1787; April 16, 1789; *Va. Mag. Hist.*, XIII,
427, citing *Fredericksburg Va. Gazette*, Oct. 7, 1790, that the Academy had
been turned into a theater; Mordecai, S.: *Richmond in By-Gone Days*, 135;
cf. also *U. S. Bur. Educ., Circ. Inf.*, 1888, No. I, 21–30; Rosengarten, J. C.:
French Colonists in U. S., 73.

of the scheme upon Jefferson's educational thinking, it has been generally assumed that its grandiose scale had a considerable effect upon the development of Jefferson's scheme for the University of Virginia. It is true that he, at a later time, considered the possibility of importing a group of European professors, and that he sent for European professors for the University of Virginia;[174] but that Jefferson was in sympathy with this scheme which would have replaced the American Philosophical Society, fostered Catholicism, and imposed a French culture upon the country, is not in accord with what we know of his views. That he was probably in sympathy with the emphasis upon science, upon modern languages, upon technology, upon the arts, is substantiated by what we know of his attitude as expressed in his educational legislation of 1779, his procedure with regard to William and Mary, and the University of Virginia.[175]

Many years, however, were to elapse before the creation of the last named institution, and, in the meantime, as President of the American Philosophical Society, Jefferson had an opportunity of becoming acquainted with the best American and French thought on the subject of education.[176] In December, 1797, the society awarded prizes to Samuel Knox and Samuel Harrison Smith for their essays on a system of national education.[177] Jefferson was, however, undoubtedly too keen a student in the vital subject of education—impressed as he was with the

---

[174] See p. 367, 379, n. 258.

[175] The writer finds no authority for the view expressed by Jones: *America and French Culture*, 478, "But if the scheme failed, it was not without results. For the Academy was really a sketch for a graduate school, and when in 1779 Jefferson was developing his own ideas regarding the future of William and Mary College, he had Quesnay's ideas in mind, and he carried over the same notion in shaping the University of Virginia." All the evidence shows that Jefferson's scheme had been developed before Quesnay's; it is more likely that Quensay was influenced by Jefferson's scheme through John Page's knowledge of it, and as Quesnay was on military duty in 1777 and 1778, there is no evidence that the scheme had advanced to the point of influencing Jefferson in 1779; in the almost three decades before Central College was chartered, many other influences had been brought to play on Jefferson's educational thinking.

[176] Hansen: *Liberalism & Amer. Education*, 108; Jones: *America and French Culture*, 403.

[177] Hansen: *Liberalism & Amer. Educ.*, 110,286, 287; *cf. De Saint Méry, Moreau: Voyage Aux États-Unis*, 240–41, where he evidently criticises a plan submitted to the Society.

importance of the curriculum and organization of education in determining the character of the individual and social mind[178]— to believe that the final word had been said on the subject. Upon the arrival in this country, in 1799, of Pierre Samuel Du Pont de Nemours whom he had known in France, and whose familiarity with the subject of education had resulted in his being called to the post of secretary of the council of public instruction in Poland as long ago as 1772, Jefferson turned to Du Pont with the request that he write his views on the subject.[179]   In the preface to the second French edition of 1812, the author states that the treatise had the approval of Jefferson and that he consulted ''only his own mind for the suggestions he has written for the Americans.''   Before Du Pont had come to this country, Jefferson had already printed in French his first edition of the *Notes on Virginia*,[180] which clearly indicated his attitude toward education and religion; and likewise an English and French copy of the *Bill for Establishing Religious Freedom;*[181] and Du Pont had evidently seen the 1784 printed copy of the *Report of the Committee of Revisors.*[182]

Du Pont's treatise falls into three sections, primary schools, secondary schools or colleges, and ''the university, or rather the special schools for higher sciences.''   Jefferson in his bill of 1779 was able to give only the most summary features of his views on education, those views he elaborated somewhat in his *Notes;* Du Pont in his treatise was able to go into considerable detail.   In the first section, he concerns himself with the curriculum—reading, writing, arthmetic, and their method of presentation, also with morality and ethics, physics, mathematics and mechanics.   Physics here means, primarily, natural history of animals and common plants; ethics concerns the ideas of liberty, property, justice, mutual helpfulness, sacredness of agreements, benevolence.   Finally, Du Pont discusses the order of work—class rules and rewards.   There is no direct reference in this section to the place of religion.   Concerning history, his remarks may well be contrasted with Jefferson's:

---

[178] See p. 163 *ff.*
[179] Du Pont: *National Educ. in U. S.*, viii, xii.
[180] Ford: *Writings T. Jefferson*, III, 68 *ff.*
[181] *Ibid.*, II, 237.
[182] *Ibid.*, 197; Du Pont: *National Educ. in U. S.*, 56.

While the study of history is most important and should be a part of every education, I am uncertain where to place it in the primary course. It is so extensive and so engrossing! It is so easy to listen to its facts, to keep them in one's memory and repeat them to others, with no mental effort and with no reasoning, that I fear that so luxuriant a tree, of which the branches have so many tendrils and which grows so rapidly, might crowd out all the others.

I would wish, then, that in primary schools history should be a reward and not a study: that books on history should be given as prizes to the best students.[183]

In his consideration of the secondary schools or colleges, county institutions for children from 10 to 17 years of age, Du Pont approved some scheme as Jefferson's for making learning available to genius. With the professorship of Greek and Latin, he would associate that of literature; with that of French—ethics; with that of German—mental science; with that of geometry—algebra and the physico-mathematical sciences; with that of chemistry—physics, and natural history; with that of the law of nature—political economy, history, geography, and national law. What is of particular interest here, however, is the provision, in the daily regimen of the school, for religious observance. The requirement for the morning assembly is thus given:

A prayer shall be made by a pupil, head of his class. All the heads of classes shall have this duty in succession, each one reciting the prayer in a loud voice one day in each week. All the college, including the Principal, the professors, instructors, pupils and servants should be present and should repeat the prayer in a low voice. There should be no excuse except illness.

This prayer should be so worded as to be acceptable to all religious opinions and to offend no one, in order that no parent may object to hearing it repeated by his child. It should be inspired by *The Lord's Prayer*. We will offer one as a suggestion.[184]

The noon meal was to be preceded and followed by prayers, for which he gave a suggestion.[185] The eight o'clock supper was to be followed by a short prayer.[186] Du Pont goes on to say that the forms suggested,

---

[183] *Ibid.*, 26–27.
[184] *Ibid.*, 73.
[185] *Ibid.*, 75–76.
[186] *Ibid.*, 80–83.

. . . May very well be supplemented by those used in England and America for domestic occasions. There are many which may properly be used in families of any religion and those are all that are necessary.

It is a good principle in education never to begin the day or to sit down to a meal without a general prayer. Prayer is social. It teaches us to consider ourselves as brothers of one Father.

It is imperative that any prayer for general use shall be phrased in such terms that the maxims and sentiments expressed shall offend no sect. No one should be shocked or insulted. Let us give to those religions which seem most opposed some opportunities of seeing how much we all have in common and how easily bridges of tolerance may be built across the torrents of opposition.

General prayers, chosen with these precautions, suggest a brotherly union, remind us of the absent, warm our hearts, arouse thoughts that are wholesome for us all. But these very thoughts can never be helped by general discussion or controversy.[187]

Du Pont goes on to say, however, "If, therefore, we wish our young people to feel an honest piety they must not be compelled to attend religious ceremonies.[188] Du Pont does not make clear, whether he would excuse the pupils from attendance at these various prayers. The after supper prayer was to be "a preface to the self-examination that should end the day and precede sleep;" the purpose of this self-examination, he thus describes:

I hope, therefore, that we can persuade our children to make a careful and sincere examination of their own consciences after they have gone to bed. It will lead them to form good resolutions, helpful plans and mental prayers, dictated by personal conviction and by sentiment—the prayers that come from the heart and strengthen the soul.[189]

As it was Du Pont's thought that the separate states should have no university in our sense of the term, but that higher professional or "special schools" as he calls them should be at the national capital, the third section of his treatise does not concern us except in so far as there is an indication of his attitude toward religious instruction; he makes no provision for a school of theology.

In a section on free schools, Du Pont discusses the relation of private educational effort to public:

---

[187] *Ibid.*, 80–81.
[188] *Ibid.*, 81.
[189] *Ibid.*, 82.

If a man, or an organization, wishes to open a boarding-school, a secondary school, a college, a special school of greater or less scholarship, they should be quite free to do so; provided that before it opens they have submitted to the Committee of Education and the municipal magistrate the books or papers from which they expect to teach, and that these productions contain nothing harmful to morals or likely to inspire atheism; of this the Committee of Education shall judge. And, provided also, that such a school continues obedient to the supervision of the Committee of Education and to the Inspectors authorized by the Committees.

Of course, no one should be persecuted or insulted for his religious or irreligious opinions, any more than for the occupations or amusements that he arranges for himself in his own house, without harm to other citizens. But, since a school of atheism would be a school of false reasoning and would weaken one of the foundations of morality, which is the agreement of actions with universal reason and with supreme beneficence, I do not think that the government should permit that the doctrine which supposes that there is no HIGHER OR GREATER BENEFACTOR should be taught to young people *in class*. And I say the same thing of licentious books; they should not be printed nor offered for sale anywhere.

. . . .

But, in the case of children, an instructor whom no one may contradict, would have a terrible opportunity to warp their minds and pervert their hearts. Their education should no more be entrusted to an atheist than to a libertine.[190]

Summarizing Du Pont's views on religious instruction, it is noted that there is provision for ethical, but not for religious instruction in the elementary schools; instruction in ethics and a closely supervised religious life in the secondary school; and no provision in the university. The silence in the last instance was very probably due to the attitude toward religion as expressed in the national constitution; and in the first, Du Pont probably felt, judging from his observation that, "In America, a great number of people read the Bible, and all the people read a newspaper. The fathers read aloud to their children while breakfast is being prepared,"[191] that religious instruction for the early years would be sufficiently taken care of in the home.

In emphasizing ethical, not religious instruction, in the elementary schools, and in his suggestion that prizes be given for publication of suitable books, Du Pont indicates that he was in

---

[190] *Ibid.*, 148–50.
[191] *Ibid.*, 4.

agreement with Jefferson, that the Bible was not to be used as a text book in the elementary schools; it was through physics and natural history, that the children were to "learn to observe and to think" and to come to a realization of "the benevolence of the Creator."[192]   On the other hand, the uniformity of religious worship, which was to characterize the secondary school life, though qualified by the statement that there was to be no compulsion, finds no echo so far as known, in any of Jefferson's writings.   It seems to be wholly at variance with those statements concerning his attitude toward the relation that should exist between the individual and his religious expression;[193] it is at variance with the eternal hostility he had sworn "against every form of tyranny over the mind of man."[194]

As long ago as 1787, in a letter to Peter Carr, Jefferson had given at length his view that opinion in religion should come as the result of individual study of the subject; and it is clear from that letter, quoted here, that Jefferson would not save anyone, who had come to that position by reasons satisfactory to himself, even from atheism:

Religion.   Your reason is now mature enough to examine this object.   In the first place, divest yourself of all bias in favor of novelty and singularity of opinion.   Indulge them in any other subject rather than that of religion. It is too important, and the consequences of error may be too serious.   On the other hand, shake off all the fears and servile prejudices, under which weak minds are servilely crouched.   Fix reason firmly in her seat, and call to her tribunal every fact, every opinion.   Question with boldness even the existence of a God; because, if there be one, he must more approve of the homage of reason, than that of blindfolded fear.   You will naturally examine first, the religion of your own country.   Read the Bible, then, as you would read Livy or Tacitus. . . . But those facts in the Bible which contradict the laws of nature, must be examined with more care, and under a variety of faces.   Here you must recur to the pretensions of the writer to inspiration from God.   Examine upon what evidence his pretensions are founded, and whether that evidence is so strong, as that its falsehood would be more improbable than a change in the laws of nature, in the case he relates.   For example, in the book of Joshua, we are told, the sun stood still several hours. . . . Examine, therefore, candidly, what evidence there is of his having been inspired.   The pretension is entitled to your inquiry, because

---

192 *Ibid.*, 154.
193 *Cf.* Parton: *Life T. Jefferson*, 61.
194 Lipscomb: *Writings T. Jefferson*, X, 175.

millions believe it. . . . Is this arrest of the earth's motion, or the evidence which affirms it, most within the law of probabilities? You will next read the New Testament. It is the history of a personage called Jesus. Keep in your eye the opposite pretensions: 1, of those who say he was begotten by God, born of a virgin, suspended and reversed the laws of nature at will, and ascended bodily into heaven; and 2, of those who say he was a man of illegitimate birth, of a benevolent heart, enthusiastic mind, who set out without pretensions to divinity, ended in believing them, and was punished capitally for sedition, by being gibbeted, according to the Roman law, which punished the first commission of that offence by whipping, and the second by exile, or death *in furca*. See this law in the Digest, Lib. 48, tit. 19. §28. 3. and Lipsius Lib. 2. de cruce. cap. 2. These questions are examined in the books I have mentioned, under the head of Religion, and several others. They will assist you in your inquiries; but keep your reason firmly on the watch in reading them all. Do not be frightened from this inquiry by any fear of its consequences. If it ends in a belief that there is no God, you will find incitements to virtue in the comfort and pleasantness you feel in its exercise, and the love of others which it will procure you. If you find reason to believe there is a God, a consciousness that you are acting under his eye, and that he approves you, will be a vast additional incitement; if that there be a future state, the hope of a happy existence in that increases the appetite to deserve it; if that Jesus was also a God, you will be comforted by a belief of his aid and love. In fine, I repeat, you must lay aside all prejudice on both sides, and neither believe nor reject anything, because any other persons, or description of persons, have rejected or believed it. Your own reason is the only oracle given you by heaven, and you are answerable, not for the rightness, but uprightness of the decision. I forgot to observe, when speaking of the New Testament, that you should read all the histories of Christ, . . .[195]

---

[195] *Ibid.*, VI, 258–61; the direction here given by Jefferson may well be contrasted with the direction given by a father to his children in *The Poor Orphans Legacy*, a second edition of which was printed in Virginia, in 1792:

First then, in general, I intreat and charge you to make serious practical religion your main and principal work and business while you are in the world: . . .

Secondly, I exhort and intreat you to be much in reading the Holy Scriptures;

Thirdly, I exhort and [in]treat you, as a main and principal part of your work, to make sure of your conversion or regeneration; . . .

Fourthly, I exhort and intreat you, *my dear children*, personally to give up and bind yourselves to God by covenant, even according unto the terms of the new covenant of grace; . . .

5. I exhort and intreat you to embrace, not only the first, but also succeeding opportunities to seal your covenant by coming to the Lord's table; . . .

6. To intreat and beseech you, as dear children, with all care and watchfulness, to live and lead a truly pious godly life in the world, . . .

7. I intreat and beseech you, live near to God continually in the daily discharge of all holy duties, particularly secret prayer.

That Jefferson was now in sympathy with the thought of Du Pont that a group of young people in school should be subject to a uniform religious régime is indicated nowhere in his correspondence;[196] and is contradicted by the views he held at a later date when he was giving consideration to plans for the University of Virginia.[197]   Whatever the extent of agreement between Du Pont and Jefferson on other phases of the educational treatise, there is no likelihood that there was any on this.[198]   A study of Jefferson's correspondence indicates clearly that at heart he was opposed to even indirect civil connections with religion, and from that point of view it is not likely that he would have approved of uniform religious observance in public schools.[199]   In Jefferson's view, as expressed in a letter written in 1809, society's concern was with the ''moral precepts only in which all religions agree, . . . we should not intermeddle with the particular dogmas in which all religions differ, and which are totally unconnected with morality.''[200]   ''Reading, reflection and time,'' had brought him to this point of view.[201]   Jefferson's contacts had

8. Be not cold and formal in your prayers and other religious duties, . . .

9. Labour, I beseech you to have your souls deeply impressed with a religious regard for the sabbath day; . . .

10. *My dear children,* I also beseech you to strive to be spiritually minded, . . .

11. My next advice to you, . . . is to set the glory of God, and your own and others salvations, before you, as the chief ends of all that you do in the world; . . . Baker, A.: *The Poor Orphans Legacy,* 7 *ff.*

196 *Cf.* Lipscomb: *Writings T. Jefferson,* XVI, 281.

197 See p. 369.

198 For a somewhat different view, *cf.* Hansen: *Liberalism and Amer. Education,* 183–84—''Du Pont's plan for a national system of education might be considered to be not only consistent with Jefferson's ideas, but also an expression of Jefferson's greatest desires. By the plan coming from another, no undue prejudice would be raised because of party prejudice, and no political ridicule would be involved because of charges against him for apparent inconsistency. Du Pont's plan may be accepted as substantially Jefferson's view.''   The writer has already indicated Du Pont's statement that the treatise was the expression of his own views, and shown the points of contact between Du Pont and Jefferson; the writer can find no authority for the inference that Du Pont was being used to save Jefferson from political prejudice. For another review of Du Pont's work, see *U. S. Bur. Educ., Circ. Inf.,* 1888, No. 1, 49 *ff.; cf.* also Culbreth, D. M. R.: *U. of Va.,* 82, who declares that Du Pont's plan was ''too comprehensive for those unsettled days, but encouraged Mr. Jefferson in his own educational scheme for his State, that which he had formulated largely from French and German institutions, those fostering advanced instruction in distinct schools.''

199 Lipscomb: *Writings T. Jefferson,* X, 305; XI, 428.

200 *Ibid.,* XII, 314.

201 *Ibid.*

been important and stimulating, but served only to confirm his view that the concern of society need be only with morality, not with religion—a view that was derived from the thought that society, in its civil aspect, must not concern itself with religion—and hence education, under the state, must be divorced from religion. The attempt to make the state realize those views in definite action was his work in the years of his retirement to life in Virginia.

The Nature Of The New Struggle

It is evident from the facts presented in the initial efforts to bring education under civil control, that the mass of the people were still too much dominated by the ancient conception, that education was primarily the concern of the church, to understand the implications involved for education in the new political principle of separation of church and state. While it is true that many salient difficulties were alleged to make impossible the initiation of a state system of education, such as scattered population and taxation, yet it was the thought, as will be shown,[202] that education must be posited on a basic Christian conception of life, which tended to throw the direction of education into denominational hands, and hampered the realization of the efforts of those leaders, like Jefferson and Tyler, who thought of education as an instrument of the state.

The crux of the difficulty now concerned itself with a new problem in integration—that of integrating religious instruction with those forms of education which concerned the training of the individual for economic and political life—for a new type of citizenship—in a government which was legally divorced from all concern for religion.

Jefferson, in order to have education harmonize with the basic principles of the state, put forward the conception that the state should take over education, yet take no concern for religious training, leaving that to the home and the church. But it was, in fact, a far simpler matter to adjust the social-political life of the state on the principle of separation of church and state, than to adjust the religious-educational life. Centuries of ex-

[202] See p. 254 *ff.*, 283.

perience had gone into building up the conception that education must be posited on a religious foundation, not only for the welfare of the individual concerned, but also for the group as represented in the state.[203]   An attempt to supplant the church in the educational field meant the creation of a new teaching force. · Where was such a force to be obtained? From none of the existing educational institutions was it possible to turn out a group of teachers who would conceive education in terms of citizenship for the state, wholly divorced from a concern for the spiritual side of life.   As time went on, it became clear, that the fundamental problem in education was the question, which of two conceptions was to obtain primacy in education—the conception that education was for the state,[204] or the conception that education was a preparation for the life to come.

While, as will be shown, the religious-minded educational leaders came to assume the position that the ''other-worldly'' conception of education could and must be integrated with the notion of education for this life—for the state—the educators dominated by the civil motive for education refused, in theory, to compromise the civil position of the state in this matter, but, in practise, were compelled to make some concessions.   It will appear in the succeeding chapters of educational history in Virginia until the Civil War, that in the struggle for educational control, it was an easier matter, because the confidence inspired by tradition was back of them, for the religious interests of the state to dominate education than it was for the civil interests, which had to win the people over to a new point of view and to blaze a new path.

In a sense, the new struggle represented two forces, the state and the church, each intensely interested in education for the betterment, the perfection of the individual as a factor in consummating the perfection of society.   The new state, because of its very newness, was supremely conscious of its mission; the church, because its tradition was inseparably bound up with education, felt its very existence dependent upon maintaining its historical function.   The church might compromise, but it would not surrender.

[203] Haas: *Problem of the Christian State*, Ch. IV–VII, IX–X.

[204] State is here used from the strict constructionist standpoint of separation of church and state.

CHAPTER VI

INITIATION OF THE DENOMINATIONAL STRUGGLE FOR EDUCATIONAL CONTROL

While Thomas Jefferson was attempting to align education with what he conceived ought to be the educational philosophy in a state, which no longer legally concerned itself with religion, and Governor Tyler was declaring that the individual belonged wholly to the state,[1] the religious-educationally minded section of Virginia was setting about its own solution and adjustment to the problem of education in a civil state divorced from religion. The initial impulse to this movement had been given, as was shown,[2] in the Presbyterian effort just before the Revolution, to find a solution of its own educational problem in a state where the civil connection with religion was regarded as being to Presbyterian disadvantage. To properly evaluate their contribution, it is necessary to have in mind first that of other denominations.

The Baptists

The Baptists continued to feel their way more slowly in the problem of education. The General Committee of the Virginia Baptists consisting of delegates from constituent associations did not come into existence until 1784; the larger association being entered into, apparently, to strengthen the Baptists in their final efforts for complete religious freedom.[3] The first Baptist concern for education seems to have been limited to a resolution of the General Committee, in 1785, that the catechism, *Milk for Babes*, be printed.[4] In 1788, the General Committee took into consideration a letter from Rev. James Manning, founder and President of Providence College in Rhode Island,[5] urging a seminary of learning under the auspices of Virginia

---

[1] See p. 171.
[2] See p. 144 *ff*.
[3] *Cf.* Humphrey: *Nationalism and Religion*, 340, 345.
[4] Semple: *Hist. of Baptists*, 71-72.
[5] Humphrey: *Nationalism and Religion*, 325.

Baptists.[6] A resolution was passed, appointing ''a committee
of five persons on each side of James River'' to forward the business.[7] The committee, with some changes in personnel, continued from year to year, brought in a report at the meeting in
1793.   The plan submitted follows:

> . . . That 14 trustees be appointed, all of whom shall be Baptists: That these
> at their first meeting, appoint seven others of some other religious denomina-
> tion: That the whole 21, then form a plan, and make arrangements for
> executing it.[8]

Further light on the scheme is found in a paper prepared by
Rev. John Williams, one of the members of the committee:

> . . . ''Two seminaries of learning are proposed in our State, one on each
> side of James River. We have sufficient encouragement from our learned
> brethren in the North that we shall not want for able, skillful teachers.
> *This will also require very diligent efforts and liberal contributions.* And if
> we in this, as we ought in everything, do it with a single eye to the glory
> of God and the advancement of the Redeemer's interest, then shall we have
> sufficient grounds to hope we shall meet with the approbation of heaven.''[9]

A board of trustees was appointed, and held ''one or two meetings,'' but, according to Semple, ''apprehensive that they should
not be able to procure sufficient funds, with some other discour-
agements, they finally abandoned it.''[10] The failure is to be
explained, too, to the lessening authority and influence, after
1792, of the General Committee in Baptist counsels, and its re-
placement, in 1799, by a General Meeting of Correspondence.[11]
   Turning to the separate associations, it is found from the
records of the meeting of the Dover Association in 1793, that
they recommended ''that rules for family discipline and the instruction of youth, should be formed,'' but as late as 1809, no
adequate action had been taken;[12] the principle action having
been that of the meeting of 1796, when to its question, ''How

---

6 Semple: *Hist. of Baptists*, 78; Humphrey: *Nationalism and Religion*,
343.
   7 *Ibid.*
   8 Semple: *Hist. of Baptists*, 85–86.
   9 Taylor. *Baptist Ministers*, 131.
   10 Semple: *Hist. of Baptists*, 85–86.
   11 *Ibid.*, 86 *ff.;* Humphrey: *Nationalism and Religion*, 345.
   12 Semple: *Hist. of Baptists*, 97.

ought the religious education of children, to be conducted?'' the reply given was, *"By the use of catechisms; and we recommend for the present, such as may be judged useful."*[13] This answer was followed by the appointment of a committee ''to compose a suitable one.''[14] The work seems to have devolved, finally, wholly upon Rev. Robert B. Semple, the Baptist historian, who published it in 1809.[15] Though modestly failing to acknowledge its authorship, Semple comments upon it as follows:

. . . It however, met with great opposition, upon the principle, that nothing of the kind was necessary; that the Bible was sufficient; that things of that kind, had a dangerous tendency towards lessening the dignity of the scriptures; that the most corrupt and absurd sentiments, had been inculcated through catechisms.

The advocates for the recommendation replied, to these objections: that, corrupt men could communicate corrupt sentiments, through the most sacred channels: that the pulpit and the press, conversation and even public prayer, had been occasionally the vehicles of unsound doctrines; that, it could be no indignity to the scriptures, to inculcate upon the minds of children, principles and duties, completely sanctioned by the scriptures: that, such forms of instruction, greatly assisted parents in the discharge of their duty; seeing there could be few parents, capable of explaining the Bible suitably, for the instruction of children: that, the manners and morals of the children of Baptists, lately grown up, plainly evinced, that religious education had been too much neglected: that, the opponents to the measure, had probably fallen into the same mistake, that the cotemporary disciples of Christ had done, who forbade little children to be brought to their master, for which, they received his rebuke. After a lengthy and warm debate, the majority decided in favour of the recommendation. The same subject was taken up, a few weeks after, by the General Meeting of Correspondence, and by an unanimous vote, the catechism was recommended. It is devoutly to be wished, that this may be the beginning of a reformation, among the Baptists of Virginia, as to this duty: For, considering their exemplary piety in other respects, they have certainly been too remiss, in training up their children, in the nurture and admonition of the Lord.[16]

The sensitivity of Rev. Mr. Semple on this subject was perhaps the keener at this time, because the great gap between Presbyterian zeal and Baptist sloth in the direction of education had been such that it was becoming manifest, that Presbyterian-

---

13 *Ibid.*, 98.
14 *Ibid.*
15 Taylor: *Va. Baptist Ministers*, 317.
16 Semple: *Hist. of Baptists*, 106–07.

ism was about to achieve a position in the field of education which would outrival that of Anglicanism before the Revolutionary War. This sensitivity was further increased by the published statement of Rev. Mr. Rice, a Presbyterian preacher of Charlotte, "that, among the Baptists of this neighborhood, it is a maxim, very firmly established, that human learning is of no use."[17]   The assertion had been taken up by the Roanoke Association, in 1807, and an answer published,[18] and also by the General Meeting of Correspondence, in 1808, in a circular letter on the "calumny," as Semple calls it.[19]

The Baptist position on the subject of ministerial education, in this period, may be gleaned from the statement of Rev. A. Waller, who was ordained in 1793:

> . . . It is a lamentable mistake which some Christians labor under in supposing, that bécause the aid of the Holy Spirit is promised unto the Lord's ministers there is no reason for them to read and study. A minister who falls into this delusion is very apt to become cold and formal in the discharge of his duty and an Antinomian in principle.[20]

Whether inspired by Presbyterian criticism or by the feeling of satisfying a long felt need, as implied by Semple, it was not until 1809 that the General Committee of Correspondence took up the question of "religious education of children, and the establishment of some seminary or public school, to assist young preachers to acquire literary knowledge."[21]   The first problem was apparently felt solved by the recommendation of the Semple catechism, and the second by appointing a committee of two "to acquire information, and digest a plan for such a seminary."[22] It will be seen from the subsequent discussion of Presbyterian educational activity during this period that the Baptists, in limiting religious instruction to catechetical instruction, in their passing over in silence the creation of schools for the general education of youth under Baptist direction, form a striking contrast to the Presbyterians. Whether the Baptist position in this

---

[17] *Ibid.*, 245.
[18] *Ibid.*
[19] *Ibid.*, 86.
[20] Taylor: *Va. Baptist Ministers*, 292; *cf.* also p. 140.
[21] Semple: *Hist. of Baptists*, 89.
[22] *Ibid.*

matter at this time was due to any conception that education was a civil matter not to be tinged by religious influence does not appear definitely. Their historic position had of course been that the state was in no wise to concern itself with religion;[23] and there is some evidence that the process of incorporation necessary to protect property, whether in connection with schools or the activities of a religious society, was frowned upon. A test case, involving an annuity of £50 left for the education of young ministers, indicated to the Baptists, in 1807, that they would probably be compelled to resort to incorporation to protect their property. On this subject, the comment of Rev. Mr. Semple is illuminating:

> . . . If their becoming incorporated would be a dangerous precedent, leading in any wise to religious oppression, it is better to remain as they are, for it would certainly be more wise to jeopardize property than principles. . . .[24]

No one of the forty-five or more educational incorporations in the period to 1810 was sponsored, so far as known, officially by a Baptist association, in the sense that some were by Presbyterian presbyteries, although some Baptists, as individuals, may have appeared as trustees.

The Baptists although third in denominational importance during this period,[25] and probably not to be compared in wealth with the Presbyterians—considering the zeal with which they handled the problem of separation of church and state, would undoubtedly have found a way to meet Presbyterian educational ascendancy, if education under Baptist auspices had at the time loomed as sufficiently important to them. Even in the field of private education, the only important name seems to be that of Rev. Mr. Semple who for a number of years, after 1793, conducted a school at his farm called Mordington, in King and Queen County.[26] The Baptist reaction to the problem, while not one of total indifference, was characterized by an attitude of comparative passivity.

---

23 See p. 62 *ff.*

24 Semple: *Hist. of Baptists*, 193.

25 Scott: *Geographical Dictionary*, 1795, 1805, under Virginia; Morse, J.: *American Gazetteer*, 1798, 352, & 1804, under *Virginia;* Schermerhorn, J. F. and Mills, S. J.: *A Correct View of U. S.*, 8–10.

26 Taylor. *Va. Baptist Ministers*, 311; the name of Rev. Peter Nelson associated with Wingfield Academy does not come in at this time, as he did not join the Baptist Church until after 1808, *Ibid.*, 475–76.

The Protestant Episcopalians

With regard to the educational activity of the Protestant Episcopal Church during this period, the nature of their connection
with William and Mary College has already been discussed.[27]
The effect of the Revolutionary War upon the church is graphically told in its statistical decline from 91 clergymen in 164
churches and chapels in 95 parishes, to 36 clergymen in 36
parishes.[28]   The first convention of the clergy took place in 1785,
with Rev. James Madison, President of William and Mary
College, as presiding officer.[29]   This meeting had been preceded
the year before by a meeting of Protestant Episcopal clergymen
in New York, looking to the creation of a national organization.[30]
One of its decisions was to take steps to create a Bishop in each
state.   This resulted in selection of Rev. David Griffith as
Bishop-elect, in 1786, and entrance of the Virginia church into
the national union.[31]

However, the consecration of Rev. Mr. Griffith as bishop never
took place; and, in 1790, Rev. Mr. Madison was elected Bishop,
his consecration taking place in September of the same year.[32]
For more than twenty years, Bishop Madison directed the destinies of the church in Virginia.   One of the important concerns
of the church, through the greater part of this period, was, as
has been told elsewhere,[33] the attempt to retain the property
acquired during the colonial period; one of their very early conventions, however, took cognizance of the necessity of providing
a way for building up the ranks of the clergy.[34]   The resolution
of the Convention of 1787 with reference to this subject has already been noted.[35]

Instruction of children and ignorant persons, in the catechism
and principles of the church, by ministers, was declared obliga-

---

[27] See p. 171 *ff.*
[28] Hawks: *Contrib. Ecc. Hist.,* I, 153–54.
[29] *Ibid.,* 179.
[30] *Ibid.,* 183–84.
[31] *Ibid.,* 190, 192; Humphrey: *Nationalism and Religion,* 212–13, 228.
[32] Hawks: *Contrib. Ecc. Hist.,* I, 207, 210; Humphrey: *Nationalism and
Religion,* 229.
[33] See p. 93.
[34] Hawks: *Contrib. Ecc. Hist.,* I, Appendix, 22.
[35] See p. 180.

tory in one of the canons of the church as adopted at this convention.[36]

The Convention, in 1790, resolved to instruct its delegates to the General Convention for an amendment of the canon law to require candidates for the ministry to satisfy

> . . . the bishop that he hath a competent knowledge of moral philosophy, church history, and the belles lettres, and hath paid a particular attention to acquire rhetoric and pulpit eloquence, as the means of giving additional efficacy to his labours.[37]

It is interesting to find, in view of the case of *Bracken vs. William and Mary*, in 1790,[38] that the Convention, the following year, resolved,

> That it is the opinion of this committee, that as there are at present no divinity schools in our church, the instruction of students in divinity might very properly be made part of the business of each presbytery within its own bounds; . . .[39]

and prescribed the regulations under which the presbyteries were to act.[40]   Addressing the Convention in 1793, Bishop Madison earnestly recommended visiting of parishioners by ministers, "that, at these visits, children should be examined and instructed in their catechism; parents, when necessary, exhorted to lead Christian lives, and to be attentive to the religious instruction of their children; . . . "[41]   In view of the question as to the Bishop's orthodoxy,[42] it is interesting to note that one of his reasons for the above course, was that "it would afford the best opportunity of counteracting the great havoc which novel teachers are daily making, and which is carried on more successfully, I believe, by their private intercourse, than by their public harangues; . . . "[43]

The Convention of 1799 was notable for Bishop Madison's address to the members of the church, in which, appealing among

---

[36] Hawks: *Contrib. Ecc. Hist.*, I, Appendix, 25.
[37] *Ibid.*, Appendix, 31.
[38] See p. 179.
[39] Hawks: *Contrib. Ecc. Hist.*, I, Appendix, 46.
[40] *Ibid.*, see p. 181.
[41] Hawks: *Contrib. Ecc. Hist.*, I, Appendix, 56; Brewer, C. H.: *Episcopal Church*, 80.
[42] See p. 185.
[43] Hawks. *Contrib. Ecc. Hist.*, I, Appendix, 56.

other things for a moderate and certain financial support for the clergy, he takes up the importance, in his conception, of the function of the minister as an educator of youth:

. . . It is fortunate for you, for themselves, and for society, that to the ministerial office, your pastors generally add the office of instructors of youth. In this double capacity, they discharge duties the most interesting. It is certainly in the first period of education that the germe of future greatness is either fostered with a genial warmth which ensures its full development, or is bruised, stifled perhaps, or deadened, by the murdering hand of the instructor. Of what infinite importance, then, is it not to parents and to their children, to have in their own neighborhood, or in their parishes, schools under the guidance of men whose profession and whose duty is the inculcation and the practice of the sublimest moral duties, while they are instilling into the infant mind the first rudiments of science. Parents ought to have the highest security that the pastor of their church will be the faithful guardian of the morals and improvement of their children; while the vicinity also of the school enables parents to superintend the discharge of this most important trust. It is true, and I rejoice at it, that the pastor frequently derives from his labours, as instructor of youth, a reasonable competence; but it is no less true, that without this auxiliary resource, few could continue their ministerial functions. . . . But if this be the case, if it be a melancholy truth that the ministers of our church do not, as ministers, receive that support which their labours merit, or which will enable them to continue those labours, the inevitable consequence must be, so soon as this generation is passed, that there will be neither able pastors of our churches, nor confidential pastoral instructors of our children. But, I ask, who among us wishes to see the mournful period arrive, when the attendants at the altar shall no longer be men well instructed, well educated in all liberal sciences; men whose minds, enlarged by true philosophy, and exalted by sublime conceptions of the Deity, contain within themselves the strongest stimulus to virtuous action, as well as the surest antidote to a grovelling fanaticism, or a wild and extravagant enthusiasm, as inconsistent with the gospel as with reason? And yet arrive it must, unless the only preventive which the case will admit be strenuously applied.[44]

It was apparently with a yearning backward glance at the age of union of church and state, which, in the then depressed state of the church, probably seemed more glorious as it was receding; with a vivid memory, too, of the increasingly disrespectful attitude of the students toward religion, which had culminated in the outrage of 1798,[45] that the Bishop proceeds to discuss the

---

[44] *Ibid.*, Appendix, 80.
[45] See p. 183.

relation of the neglect of religious instruction to society and to the civil aspects of the state:

. . . Does not the entire neglect of parents in the religious instruction of their children manifest this truth? Does not the rapid growth of immorality in general, of profaneness and impiety; do not the beginnings of prodigious crimes; does not that party rage, which, not content with blasting, by slander's envenomed breath, the well-earned fame of honesty and worth, but, tiger-like, thirsts even for the blood of fellow-citizens; do not all these effects demonstrate that religion no longer dwells among us? . . . The unnatural state of man is certainly that which is diseased and polluted with moral turpitude; which is rendered loathsome by crimes rank and offensive to Heaven and earth. A state of religion and of virtue is his only natural state. The distinction between the religious and the moral man is a cobweb, which may entangle the sophist himself; but he who loves virtue, he who really practises moral duties, will never, without some violence offered to his nature, fall into the absurdity of neglecting the God by whose appointment they are made necessary to happiness. We need, then, to arrest the progress of irreligion, only assemble men once more as Christians; . . . let us snatch ourselves, our children, our country, from the madness of libertinism, from the vortex of impiety and irreligion, and let us revive the reign of truth and justice, of peace and righteousness, of love to God and man. . . . The cultivation of piety is ranked by the most eminent writers among the highest duties which a nation owes to itself. Perhaps the time may not be far distant, when the enlightened patriots of this country, in their legislative capacities, conscious of this duty, ''knowing that nothing is so proper as piety to strengthen virtue, and to give it its full extent;'' and preferring the prevention of crimes to the multiplication of sanguinary laws; or the perfection of citizens to their extermination; will bring forward some well-digested plan for the security of this great object. Whether a general assessment, upon principles suited to the nature of a free government, would not be the most happy expedient, and productive of really great and extensive public good, is a subject well worthy of the most serious consideration of every friend to virtue and genuine republicanism.[46]

It may be that the observant Bishop saw in the legislative support which the Presbyterians were obtaining for their educational institutions, a tendency that justified his hopes.

Probably due to the great struggle which now ensued for the retention of church property, and a depressed condition in the church, only one convention, that of 1805, at which nothing notable occurred with reference to education, seems to have been held before 1812.[47]

---

[46] Hawks: *Contrib. Ecc. Hist.*, I, Appendix, 81–83.

[47] *Ibid.*, 242, Appendix, 83, 87.

Except for the oratorical flight of the Bishop in 1799, there is evident, in the official expression of opinion and activity in the Convention records, a tendency to avoid the show of any inclination to tie the educational work of the church to the state. The educational concern is first with the duty of the minister, in his evangelical relation, to the family; second, with his duty as the instructor of youth, to permeate that instruction with a moral and religious tone; third, with his duty as the instructor of a successive ministry in the church.

Officially, the Conventions took no particular schools under their protection; nevertheless, in the history of the forty-five or more schools incorporated in this period, ministers and laymen, as instructors and trustees, took their part.[48]   Although the suit of Rev. Mr. Bracken resulted in the reëstablishment of the grammar school, no attempt was made to restore the theological department in the College of William and Mary.[49]   The Protestant Episcopal Church, though awake to the importance of the problem of educational control, was as yet too sensitive on the subject of church and state, to attempt any serious issue with the legislature on the subject of education.

The Methodists

As for the educational activity of Methodism during this period, it must be recalled that the official severance of the Methodist societies from the Anglican Church did not take place until the Baltimore Conference of 1784.[50]   At this conference, Rev. Francis Asbury, who, with Dr. Thomas Coke, had been appointed joint Superintendent, then the highest office in the Church, presented his long cherished scheme of a school, for which he had already received subscriptions.[51]   The object as indicated in a joint circular by Coke and Asbury is of interest as the first pronouncement of American Methodism on education, though the subsequent history of the institution founded near

---

[48] Among such schools may be listed Alexandria Academy, Norfolk Academy, Fredericksburg Female Charity School.

[49] See p. 180–81, 211.

[50] See p. 71; Bennett: *Memorials of Methodism*, 210 *ff.*; Humphrey: *Nationalism and Religion*, 190.

[51] Bennett: *Memorials of Methodism*, 215.

Baltimore under the name of Cokesbury College need not be followed here:

"The college is to receive for education and board the sons of the Elders and Preachers of the Methodist Church, poor orphans, and the sons of the subscribers, and other friends. It will be expected that all our friends who send their children to the college, will, if they be able, pay a moderate sum for their education and board; the rest will be taught and boarded, and, if our finances will allow of it, clothed, gratis. The institution is also intended for the benefit of our young men who are called to preach, that they may receive a measure of that improvement which is highly expedient as a preparation for public service."[52]

The Methodist organization of Virginia at this time consisted of a northern and a southern district. National Methodism carried on its work by an annual series of conferences; thus eleven were held from Georgia to New York in 1789, two of them in Virginia.[53] From 1775 until his death in 1816,[54] the most striking figure at the Virginia conferences was Asbury. It is due to his influence that the Methodist affiliation, after 1785, with the Sunday School movement in England, was transferred to Virginia.[55] Numerous statements have been made as to the first Sunday School in America or in Virginia. In a certain sense, the Sunday School movement may be regarded as a continuation of the catechetical instruction associated with the Anglican Church. Influenced by Dr. Bray, whose name is associated with the Society for the Promotion of the Gospel, Rev. Jonathan Boucher, of the Protestant Episcopal Church, while minister in Caroline County, 1763–70, had

. . . set up two or three serious and sensible black men as school masters to teach the children around them merely to read at their leisure hours, and chiefly on Sunday afternoons, something as Sunday schools now are here in England. . . .[56]

The use of Sunday leisure hours for the instruction of illiterates and negroes particularly, had also been taken advantage of by

---

[52] *Ibid.*, 215–16; Bangs, N.: *Hist. Meth. Episc. Church,* I, 230 *ff.*
[53] Bennett: *Memorials of Methodism,* 271 *ff.*
[54] *Ibid.*, 75, 615.
[55] *Ibid.*, 297.
[56] Wingfield, M.: *Caroline Co. Va.,* 20; Bouchier, J.: *Reminiscences of an American Loyalist,* 40–41, 59; Ford, W. C.: *Letters of Jonathan Boucher to George Washington,* 5.

the Presbyterian ministers, Davies, Todd, and Wright, in the period after 1750.[57] The Sunday School movement as introduced by Asbury into Virginia was, however, the outcome of his appreciation of the movement as inspired by Robert Raikes.[58] Methodist research seems to have established the fact that:

The first Sunday school to be founded in America, certainly the first one that can claim continuous existence, was begun by a layman, William Elliott, who emigrated from England to Virginia in 1724, and there became a Methodist convert about 1772. In 1785, he organized a Sunday school in his home, where each Sabbath afternoon he instructed the white boys "bound out" to him and girls in his charge, together with his own children. Soon the children of neighbors and friends were admitted. The Negro slaves and servants were similarly taught at another hour. "All were taught the rudiments of reading, in order that they might be able to read God's Word for themselves—the Bible being practically the only textbook in the school." . . . After sufficient advancement had been made, the catechism was studied, later Bible readings were prepared by the members of the class, and explanations and comments were given by the teachers. In January, 1801, the Burton-Oak Grove Methodist Church was built, and in due time William Elliott's home Sunday school was transferred to this church. Mr. Elliott came with it and became its first superintendent.[59]

Asbury himself is said to have organized the school opened, in 1786, at the home of Thomas Crenshaw in Hanover County.[60]

At the conference of 1790, the subject of instruction of poor children was given serious consideration:

"What can be done in order to instruct poor children (white and black) to read?"

"Let us labor, as the heart and soul of one man to establish Sunday Schools, in or near the place of public worship. Let persons be appointed by the Bishops, Elders, Deacons, or Preachers, to teach (gratis) all that will attend, and have a capacity to learn; from six o'clock in the morning till

---

[57] *Cf.* Davies: *Duty of Christians to propagate their Religion among Heathens;* Davies: *Letters, passim;* Campbell: *Hist. of Va.*, 529.

[58] Bennett: *Memorials of Methodism*, 295; *cf.* Graves, F. P.: *A Hist. of Educ. in Modern Times*, 49; *cf.* Brown, M. C.: *Sunday-School Movements in America*, 21.

[59] Wardle, A. G.: *Sunday School Movement Methodist Episcopal Church*, 46.

[60] *Richmond Enquirer*, Dec. 27, 1854; Bennett: *Memorials of Methodism*, 297; Wardle: *Sunday School Movement Methodist Episcopal Church*, 47; *cf.* Barnard, H.: *Amer. Jour. Educ.*, XV, 706, "The first school of the kind was established by Bishop Asbury in Virginia, in 1783;" Forrest: *Hist. Sketches Norfolk*, 149.

ten; and from two o'clock in the afternoon till six; where it does not interfere with public worship. The Council shall compile a proper school book
to teach them learning and piety.''[61]

In accordance with this resolution, a stronger impetus was
given to the movement, but it seems to have died out, whether
from neglect, or because ''the ardor of the teachers was damped
by persecution, and within a few years this interesting work was
altogether abandoned.''[62]   Perhaps the movement suffered particularly because of the known Methodist disapprobation of slavery, and their favorable attitude toward providing some instruction for negroes in these schools.[63]

The influence of Asbury is found in the creation of two other
schools in Virginia, under Methodist auspices; an English school
and an academy.   While these schools may have been typical
of the kind of schools Asbury wished established, only one example of each seems to have come down to us.

The English school was organized, in 1794, under Asbury's
direction at Harrisonburg, Rockingham County.[64]   There was a
board of seven trustees, with the elder of the circuit as president,
ex-officio.[65]   The rules formulated for the school by the trustees
in June, 1794, are of particular interest:

Rule 1. The Scholars shall attend at Eight O'clock in the Summer and
Half Past eight in the winter; and the Teacher Shall regulate the time of
attendance in Spring and Autumn, according to the length of the day.

. . . .

4. The School shall always be opened and closed with a prayer.

5. The Teacher shall appoint a weekly monitor, out of a Senior
Class, who Shall Call the list upon all Occasions, and see that the Scholars
be present at all times of Publick worship in the School; and give Information of all misdemeanors in the Teachers Absence. And also that all
Scholars of Seven Years old and upwards shall attend at publick service on
the Sabbath, wherever his or her Parents Guardians or Master may direct.

. . . .

9. In every case of Sinning against God, the trial shall be very
Serious, the facts proved, and the Sinner Properly dealt with, according to

---

[61] Bennett: *Memorials of Methodism*, 297–98.
[62] *Ibid.*, 298.
[63] Humphrey: *Nationalism and Religion*, 482–83; Bennett: *Memorials of Methodism*, 297, 547 *ff.*
[64] Wayland, J. W.: *Hist. of Rockingham County, Va.*, 283.
[65] *Ibid.*, 284.

the Judgment of the Teacher. If it should be near the time of a Visitation (of the trustees) let it be laid over till the meeting of the Board of Trustees.

. . . .

12. The Scholars Shall be examined in the "Instructions for Children" Once a week Except the Children of such parents as disapprove the same.

. . . .

17. There shall be no more than Forty Scholars admitted into the School.[66]

The trustees on the occasions of their quarterly visitations, on the last Fridays in November, February, May, and August, were to "Examine the Scholars in their knowledge of God and progress in Learning."[67] Colored servants of subscribers might be sent the first year on condition that "They shall be Classed & Seated by themselves."[68] Pupils attending public worship were to have a space reserved in the gallery.[69] In May, 1795, Asbury met the trustees of the school and read to them his "Thoughts on Education."[70] That same spring, the Board planned to add a grammar school, which was to "be under the same Rules & Regulations which have been made for the English School," except for the time allotted for vacation seasons.[71] There is no indication that this school was ever incorporated.

In 1796, the Virginia Assembly received a petition from a number of inhabitants of Brunswick County for the incorporation of Ebenezer Academy.[72] The act of incorporation, passed November 22, 1796, names among its trustees, John Easter, a well known Methodist preacher,[73] and Edward Dromgoole, at whose home Asbury seems to have been a frequent visitor, for it was there he spent the winter of 1797, whiling away the tedium of convalescence by hearing the children read and teaching them a little grammar. This school had been opened near

---

[66] *Ibid.*, 284–85.
[67] *Ibid.*, 285.
[68] *Ibid.*, 286
[69] *Ibid.*
[70] *Ibid.*
[71] *Ibid.*, no further definite reference to the school after 1796, appeared according to Wayland in the original records, the matter of securing a teacher for the school came up, however, in an 1820 quarterly meeting.
[72] *Jour., H. Del.*, Nov. 15, 1796.
[73] Bennett: *Memorials of Methodism*, 170.

Merritt's meeting house, in 1784, the year in which the Cokesbury scheme was initiated, and is regarded by some as the first Methodist school in America.[74] What the régime of the Academy was during this period does not appear, but its life was probably regulated under a system of rules similar to that of the Harrisonburg School. Asbury, in 1794, referred to the school as burdensome, and commented, that ''People, in general, care too little for the education of their children.''

The traces of Methodist educational activity that have come down to us indicate that their efforts from a denominational standpoint were of a character to bring them as little as possible into contact with the state. From a denominational standpoint, their concern was chiefly centered in providing some instruction for poor white and black children. The Sunday School scheme brought them into no contact with the state. The Harrisonburg school and Ebenezer Academy enterprises seem to have been matters of individual rather than conference concern, though undoubtedly inspired by Asbury's interest in bringing education under the Methodist ideal of life. Except for the incorporation of Ebenezer Academy, the efforts of the Methodists nowhere brought them into touch with the state.

It must be remembered that as late as 1810, the Methodists were the least in denominational importance of the four chief religious groups, the number of whites being reported as 18,864, and the number of colored as 6,150.[75] Essentially, a new church,

---

[74] *Ibid.*, 358; Cummings, A. W.: *Early Schools of Methodism*, 35, 38–39, 41; Morrison: *Beginnings of Pub. Educ.*, in his ms. notes, (Va. State Library) quotes Herbart F. Hutcheson in *Mecklenberg Times-Star*, July 13, 1917: ''Ebenezer Academy was the forerunner of Randolph-Macon College. The school was founded by Asbury and Rev. Edward Dromgool (father of Hon. George C. Dromgool) with the same purposes as those of the founders of R. M. C. When the movement for a college came to the point of fixing on a site, citizens of Brunswick County offered $20,000 if the college was placed at Ebenezer Academy.

Ebenezer Academy still stands in plain view on the Petersburg Road, twenty miles north of South hill.'' By 1809, the school was no longer under control of the church; such history of this school as we have is for a subsequent period—see Morrison: *Beginnings of Pub. Educ.*, 128–29; Bennett, the Virginia Methodist historian makes no reference to this school. Duvall, S. M.: *Meth. Episc. Church And Educ.*, 28, refers to a Cokesbury School, Surry Co., Va., should be, North Carolina, *cf.* Cummings: *Early Schools of Methodism*, 70.

[75] Bennett: *Memorials of Methodism*, 559.

concerned with questions of doctrine, of organization, of proselytism, and, in Virginia, for a number of years after 1792, torn by the O'Kellyan Schism,[76] it is not surprising that Methodism had not at this time, achieved so extensive a program for the control of education as Presbyterianism. Methodism had, however, awakened to a sense of the importance and desirability of furthering education under denominational auspices.

The Presbyterians

The point of view taken by the Presbyterians in founding Hampden-Sidney and Augusta Academy, that education should be given as adequate Christian, but not denominational, influence has already been indicated.[77] The degree of success in realizing this educational philosophy must now be considered.

In 1776, the trustees of Hampden-Sidney sent a memorial to the Assembly, stating that because of its rapid growth and general reputation, they hoped that their school was "not unworthy of the attention of the Legislature."[78] They enumerated the many reasons which made it appropriate for the Legislature to assist them in erecting their needed buildings; desiring, they said, "an opportunity of convincing the publick whether the interests of education are likely to suffer in their management." Finally, it was their opinion they could serve the institution better "if the Legislature should be pleased to erect the Board into a corporate body."[79] Their memorial was without immediate result, and in June, 1777, the trustees withdrew it,[80] probably in view of their wish to obtain authority from the Legislature to hold a lottery for the benefit of the Academy—a bill to that effect being passed the same month.[81] As lotteries were not regarded as direct state aid, the action was not subject to criticism. In 1783, the trustees again presented a petition for patronage by the Legislature, "praying that if the circumstances

---

[76] *Ibid.*, 313 *ff*; the schism was due to the opposition of James O'Kelly, to the growing influence of Asbury.

[77] See p. 144 *ff*.

[78] *Jour., H. Del.*, Nov. 17, 1776, 55 *ff*.

[79] *Ibid.*

[80] *Ibid.*, June 12, 1777, 74.

[81] *Ibid.*, June 28, 1777, 112; Hening: *Stat. at Large*, IX, 321; Burk: *Hist. of Va.*, IV, 227–29.

of the country will not admit of any other encouragement, they
may be granted a charter of incorporation.''[82]   The bill was
signed on June 28.[83]   The trustees were permitted

. . . to make and establish such bye-law, rules, and ordinances, not being
contrary to the constitution or laws of this commonwealth, as by them shall
be thought necessary for the good order and government of the professors,
masters, and students, of the said college.[84]

No professor was to be elected ''unless the uniform tenor of his
conduct manifests to the world his sincere affection for the liberty and independence of the United States of America.''[85]
The president and trustees were required to take an oath, to be
certified to the county court, that they would perform their
duties in accordance with the charter.   Of the personnel of the
twenty-seven trustees, five were ministers, and the rest for the
most part elders and members of the Presbyterian Church, ''and
all named by the Presbytery in her previous lists of Trustees,
but three.''[86]   A petition of the trustees to the Assembly, in
1851, thus refers to the Act of incorporation:

. . . although this movement originated with a body of christians dissenting
from the established church, and as such, in those days of civil and ecclesiastical oppression, forced to operate in their distinctive denominational
capacity, yet so soon as this oppression was removed, they renounced forever, in the year 1783, all connection with and control over the institution,
and committed its guardianship in perpetuity, to a board of trustees, appointed by the legislature of Virginia, and composed of individuals selected
from various denominations, and from *no denomination* indifferently, with
power to fill their own vacancies as they might successively occur.[87]

Though the academy by its act of incorporation became a college and dissolved ''all connection with the parent presbytery,''[88]
the preponderant influence in it continued Presbyterian, not
only because of the constituency of the Board of Trustees, but
because its Presidents were Presbyterians.   As there was, how-

---

82 *Jour., H. Del.*, May 16, 1783, 8.
83 *Ibid.*, June 28, 1783, 99.
84 Hening: *Stat. at Large*, XI, 273.
85 *Ibid.*, 274.
86 *Ibid.*, Foote: *Sketches of Va.*, 404–05.
87 *Jour., H. Del.*, 1850–51, Doc. No. 47, 3.
88 *U. S. Bur. Educ., Circ. Inf.*, 1888, No. I, 230.

ever, no technical affiliation, it was possible for the Board to appeal with greater hope of success to the Legislature for assistance. This they did the following year and obtained a tract of 412 acres which had escheated to the commonwealth.[89] In 1794, they obtained about 1200 acres of escheated land.[90] As far as the state was concerned, it was not using public wealth to support denominational or religious education.

Reconstructing the inner life of Hampden-Sidney from 1775 to 1810, we find that all its Presidents were Presbyterian ministers. The first President, Samuel Stanhope Smith, was afterwards President of Princeton College, New Jersey; his brother, John Blair Smith, who succeeded him, was afterwards first President of Union College, New York; the acting president, in turn, Drury Lacy, was in charge during the period immediately after the initiation of the great revival, of which, presently; the next President, Archibald Alexander, was later founder of Princeton Theological Seminary, and the name of Moses Hoge, President after 1807, is associated with the beginning of a Presbyterian seminary.[91] The presidency, during those years, carried with it the pastorate of Cumberland and Prince Edward Churches.[92]

With regard to the appointment of trustees during those years, Foote, the Presbyterian historian says:

> On the 16th of November, 1789, a Trustee was appointed to fill the vacancy occasioned by the death of Rev. Richard Sankey. The appointment was made by the Board without any official reference to the Presbytery, but was, in this case, as in the following years, in accordance to their well known wishes.[93]

A picture of the academic life of the college may be gleaned from an account of the commencement exercises in 1788. The class had previously been examined by the Board of Trustees and approved in the Latin, Greek, and French languages, and in the sciences. After prayer, there were a number of orations and

---

[89] *Jour., H. Del.*, June 1, 1784, 30; June 4, 1784, 35; June 30, 1784, 89; Hening: *Stat. at Large*, XI, 392.
[90] *Jour., H. Del.*, Nov. 26, 1794, 41; Dec. 8, 1794, 70; Dec. 23, 1794, 114.
[91] *Hampden-Sidney Catalog*, 1926, 12.
[92] *U. S. Bur. Educ., Circ. Inf.*, 1888, No. I, 236.
[93] Foote: *Sketches of Va.*, 406.

disputations among which was one on the question: "Is learning of any real advantage in a moral, political, or religious view?"[94]

The following account of student life, written by C. R. McIlwaine, an alumnus of the college and son of Dr. R. McIlwaine, President of the College, illuminatingly pictures the college life:

> A peculiar respect for gravity and decorum was characteristic of the old régime at Hampden-Sidney. The president, masters, and students were enjoined to appear at church in "distinguishing habits of black;" a requirement which, it is needless, to say, was soon dispensed with. The tutors resided in the college building in order to keep the students in proper obedience. The latter were strictly enjoined to remain in their rooms after the hour of nine at night. Attention to moral and religious duties was enforced by fines, provisions for which did not disappear from the code until 1809.[95]

Thus the public statement of 1775 that all would "be at liberty to attend that mode of publick worship, that either custom or concience makes most agreeable to them,"[96] had been translated into a regulation enforcing attention to religious duties by fines.

Perhaps this insistence upon attention to religious duties was the outcome of a religious revival which began in the college in 1787.[97] According to the account given by Foote, the attitude toward religion of the majority of the approximately eighty students in the college had been one of "contempt and ridicule." Students with religious inclinations were laughed at. It so happened that a student returning home for vacation experienced religion and was converted. Upon his return to college, he was put through a course of religious reading by the President, and was convinced of the genuineness of his conversion. Soon, a number of students were meeting together for religious study and experience. Their attempt to have a private religious meeting in one of the rooms in the college, however, precipitated a riot—so unusual was an attempt of that kind in the history of the college. The President, however, came to the rescue of the spiritually inclined students and decided to take charge of the meetings himself. Under his skillful leadership, it happened that "Within two weeks or thereabout, fully half of the stu-

---

[94] *Va. Gaz. & Weekly Advertiser*, Nov. 20, 1788.
[95] *U. S. Bur. Educ., Circ. Inf.*, 1888, No. I, 233.
[96] See p. 145.
[97] Foote: *Sketches of Va.*, 406.

dents in College appeared deeply impressed, and under conviction for their sins. Deep impressions and concern were generally made through the neighborhood.''[98]   The effects of the revival are thus stated by Foote: ''Many of the students were embraced in this revival, that, afterwards, became eminent in the church as ministers and elders.''[99]

There soon occurred some question in the public mind as to how to reconcile the events here described with the various statements as to the policy of the institution. In 1798, the Board felt it necessary to investigate a

... rumor that the faculty—''use unfair methods to proselyte the students to a particular sect,''—and examined several students to ascertain the degree of credit to be attached to it. After investigation, the Board reported the rumor to be without foundation, and directed their report to be published.[100]

It is, undoubtedly, difficult to determine when proselytism begins in connection with a revival. Referring to the article forbidding proselytism, Mr. McIlwaine said, in 1888, it was ''a law which had never been violated, and which had received but one interpretation within the entire history of the college.''[101]   On this subject the Episcopalian Bishop Meade commented:

... It was, in opposition to some fears expressed at the time, most solemnly pledged that it should not be a sectarian proselyting institution, though the forms of the Presbyterian Church would be observed in it; and the fact that Episcopalians have often been in some measure concerned, as trustees or professors, in its management, proves that the pledge has been redeemed as far as perhaps is practicable in such institutions.[102]

This revival which extended to Augusta Academy, then Liberty Hall Academy, and influenced Virginia Presbytery for half a century[103] must be placed in its relation to the ''baneful'' French influence which is generally spoken of as controlling

---

[98] *Ibid.*, 418.
[99] *Ibid.*, 406.
[100] *Ibid.*, *cf.* p. 432 where Foote hints that this investigation was due to Patrick Henry, one of the trustees.
[101] *U. S. Bur. Educ., Circ. Inf.*, 1888, No. I, 233.
[102] Meade: *Old Churches, Ministers, Families*, II, 30.
[103] Foote: *Sketches of Va.*, 406.

Virginia thought of this period.[104]   That Presbyterian zeal was banded to destroy it is indicated in the following letter:

> I must say, however, that I have never regarded either the Venables or Watkinses as 'bigots to Presbytery' as such. . . . The leading mind in that whole region, whether among the clergy or laity, was that of Colonel Samuel W. Venable, (eldest son of Colonel Nathaniel Venable above mentioned,) . . . Colonel V. was eminently a practical man,—a stern patriot and friend of good order in society, public spirited, and a patron of all improvement. Now, the bitter waters of infidelity, which had begun to appear in other parts of the State, were not unknown there, and on the outbreak of the French Revolution society in Virginia was menaced as it were with a deluge of false philosophy and its train of evils. It was to stem this tide that he and those who co-operated with him set themselves. It was not for a party that he contended, but for the substance of Christianity itself, which he believed to be in peril. As this was essential to the very existence of free society, all other questions were regarded as secondary.[105]

The influence of Hampden-Sidney and Presbyterianism in this connection is described by Foote:

> Hampden Sidney College was the center of religious action for the churches east of the Blue Ridge and south of James River, in connexion with the Presbyterian Church. In the Bounds of the same congregation which embraced the College, was a Law School of high standing, in which "free thinking," on the subject of religion, met with no check. The influences flowing from this fountain were a constant source of uneasiness to the pious people of Cumberland and the associated churches, and was an additional reason for their clinging together and using all means in their united power for mutual preservation, and the salvation of the young. The teaching of two such men as Lacy and Alexander was well calculated, under the divine blessing, to stop the progress of the evil, and guard the rising generation from its insidious effects.[106]

It had early become the custom for the President of Hampden-Sidney to take under his personal care students who were preparing for the ministry.[107]   Events were now shaping, looking to a more definite provision for theological training. Rev. Dr.

---

[104] Stanard: *Richmond, People and Story*, 71; Meade: *Old Churches, Ministers, Families*, I, 51 *ff.*; McCabe: *Va. Schools Before & After the Revolution*, 31–32; Morrison: *Travels in the Confederation*, II, 62–63.

[105] Meade: *Old Churches, Ministers, & Families*, II, 32; among the members of the Venable and Watkins families who were trustees of Hampden-Sidney, were Nathaniel & James Venable, Joel & Francis Watkins.

[106] Foote: *Sketches of Va.*, 502.

[107] *Ibid.*, 469.

Hoge who, in 1805, was conducting a classical school at Shepherdstown, in Jefferson County,[108] and had been training a number of men privately for the ministry, was trying to interest Presbyterians in a theological Seminary, on the model of the institutions of the pietist Franske, to be located in the Shenandoah Valley.[109] About the same time, a number of the members of the Hanover Presbytery started "a theological library at Hampden-Sidney for the purpose of mutual improvement."[110] The outcome was a resolution at a meeting of the Presbytery, in 1806,

. . . to establish at Hampden Sidney a complete theological library for the benefit of students in divinity. 2d. That an attempt to be made to establish a fund for the education of poor and pious youth, for the ministry of the gospel. 3d. That the Rev. Messrs. . . . be a standing committee to manage the business and make report to Presbytery at its annual meeting. 4th. That whatever funds are raised by the committee shall be vested in the Trustees of Hampden Sidney College; the appropriation of all such funds however shall forever remain with the Presbytery.[111]

$2500 was raised by the following spring. The resignation of President Alexander was followed by the election of Dr. Hoge to the presidency, in June, 1807. At the same time under the appointment of the Synod, he was elected Professor of Divinity. Dr. Hoge's services in his dual capacity are thus described by Mr. McIlwaine:

. . . Hanover Presbytery, in 1808, conveyed to Hampden-Sidney funds for founding a theological department, the latter simply acting as trustee to execute the behest of her venerable mother. Under the administration of Moses Hoge, the president performed the duties of professor of theology, although in an entirely separate and distinct capacity. . . . [112]

This development at Hampden-Sidney must of course be viewed in the light of her charter, and the policy enunciated at her founding; it may well be contrasted with the attitude of the

---

[108] Morrison: *Beginnings Pub. Educ. Va.*, 124.
[109] Graves: *Hist. of Educ. During Middle Ages*, 300 *ff.*; Foote: *Sketches of Va.*, 562–63.
[110] *Ibid.*, 562.
[111] *Ibid.*, 563.
[112] *U. S. Bur. Educ., Circ. Inf.*, 1888, No. I, 237.

Episcopalians during this period, in connection with the College of William and Mary, after the Marshall opinion of 1790.[113]

It is necessary to turn now to a consideration of some broader aspects of the Presbyterian attitude towards education. An appeal had been made by a member of the Hanover Presbytery to the Synod of 1779 for missionaries to be sent into Virginia to organize congregations,

> . . . and undertake the education of their youth, representing that there appears at present in many parts of that state, a very favorable disposition toward religion in general, and towards the Presbyterian church in particular; . . . that it is not desirable, nor to be expected that that most extensive country should continue long without some form of religion; that this Synod has now an opportunity of promoting the interest of religion extensively, which in a few years may be utterly lost by the prevalency and preoccupying of many ignorant and irreligious sectaries; . . . [114]

The matter was favorably recommended to the attention of the various presbyteries for their promotion.[115]

On the subject of the education of youth, the Synod of 1785 resolved

> . . . that it be enjoined on all congregations to pay a special regard to the good education of children, as being intimately connected with the interests of morality and religion; and that, as schools under bad masters and a careless management, are seminaries of vice rather than of virtue, the session, corporation or committee of every congregation, be required to endeavor to establish one or more schools in such place, or places, . . . and endeavor to induce the people to support them by contribution, being not only the most effectual, but eventually, the cheapest way of supporting them; that the Presbyteries appoint particular members, or if possible committees, to . . . visit the school, or schools, at least once in three months, to inquire into the conduct of the master, and the improvement of the children, and to observe particularly his care to instruct them, at least one day in the week, in the principles of religion; that the Presbyteries, in appointing ministers to supply vacant congregations, require it as an indispensable part of their duty, to visit at the same time the schools; and require at the next meeting of the Presbytery, an account of their fidelity in this respect, and of the state of the schools; and that, in these schools effectual provision be made for the education of the children of the poor; and that at the visitations of the schools, one or two of the most ingenious and virtuous of

---

113 See p. 179–81.
114 Humphrey: *Nationalism & Religion*, 266–67.
115 *Ibid.*

the poor children be annually selected, in order to give them a more perfect education, and thereby qualify these ingenious charity scholars, to become afterwards useful instructors in our congregational schools.[116]

This conception of creating their own teaching force for congregational schools is evidence of the carefully considered Presbyterian policy that education belonged to the church. It was a corollary of that conception, that inspection of schools was the function of ministers. In view of the extensive denominational program outlined, the fact that assistance had to be asked from the state, is not surprising; nor could a single school, like Hampden-Sidney, be relied upon to give a sufficient leadership. Other schools needed to be developed.

At a meeting of the Presbytery in 1776, it was decided to remove Augusta Academy from Mt. Pleasant to Timber Ridge, and change its name to Liberty Hall Academy.[117] By 1780, it was found necessary to move the Academy to the vicinity of Lexington. In 1782, the Presbytery, because of neglect of the school by the old trustees, appointed additional ones.[118] These trustees soon presented a petition to the Assembly representing that they possessed land and property and desired to more effectually encourage and promote literature.[119] The act of incorporation signed December 28, 1782, enjoined the oath of fidelity upon the faculty, and the oath or affirmation of faithful discharge of duty, in accordance with the charter, upon the trustees.[120] The majority of the trustees appointed had either been trustees formerly, or been active in connection with the Academy. The most important provision of the charter was, undoubtedly, the one forbidding any bye-laws, rules, and ordinances contrary to the

---

[116] *Ibid.*, 268; the Synod of New York and Philadelphia was divided into four synods, of which Virginia was one, in 1786, *Ibid.*, 279.

[117] Foote: *Sketches of Va.*, 448 *ff.; Wash. and Lee Catalog*, 1926, 20; Waddell: *Annals Augusta Co.*, 185; *cf. So. Lit. Messenger*, June, 1838, IV, 361 *ff.;* a conjecture that the change of name may have been inspired not by patriotic motives alone, but also by Rev. John Brown's memory of the name of his Ireland home, is made in *U. S. Bur. Educ., Circ. Inf.*, 1888, No. I, 306.

[118] Foote: *Sketches of Va.*, 457–58.

[119] *Jour., H. Del.*, Nov. 23, 1782, 34; Nov. 27, 1782, 39; Dec. 6, 1782, 55; Dec. 20, 1782, 74; Dec. 28, 1782, 90.

[120] *Ibid.*, Dec. 28, 1782, 90; Hening: *Stat. at Large*, XI, 164; *Wash. and Lee Catalog*, 1926, 21, erroneously gives October, 1782, as date of incorporation.

constitution or laws of the commonwealth.[121]   The trustees appealed to the Legislature for financial assistance, in 1786,[122] without result. In 1794, they requested the privilege of a lottery, that certain escheated lands in Rockbridge County be given them to assist them in rebuilding the academy which had been accidentally burnt, and also that the academy might be transformed into a college.[123] A bill in their favor was defeated that year,[124] and a petition again requesting an appropriation of public funds was received the following year.[125] It was not until December, 1796, that a bill "For erecting Liberty Hall Academy into a college" was passed.[126]

To understand the reasons for granting the charter at this time, the character of the charter granted, and certain circumstances in connection with the grant, it is necessary, first, to examine the internal history of the institution. The Rev. Mr. Graham, who was rector from 1782 to 1796, had been instrumental in bringing Presbyterian influence to bear in defeating the general assessment bill for religion in 1785.[127] This had not added to his popularity with a certain element in the Legislature. In the discipline of the school, particularly after the War, Rev. Mr. Graham had great difficulty.[128] An explanation is perhaps to be found in the character of the rules adopted, after the charter of 1782 was granted. Among these was one, that the school should be "opened with prayer at eight or nine o'clock, after which every student was to apply himself silently to his task, and never to go out without permission until dismissed with prayer in the evening."[129]

As a result of the revival which spread from Hampden-Sidney to Liberty Hall, Rev. Mr. Graham found, in 1789, that he could form a regular class of seven or eight students for systematic training in theology.[130] The consequence was that a meeting of

---

[121] Hening: *Stat. at Large,* XI, 164 *ff.*
[122] *Jour., H. Del.,* Nov. 3, 1786, 20.
[123] *Ibid.,* Nov. 24, 1794, 36; Nov. 29, 1794, 51; Rockingham—error.
[124] *Ibid.,* Dec. 8, 1794, 70.
[125] *Ibid.,* Nov. 24, 1795, 39.
[126] *Ibid.,* Dec. 27, 1796, 222.
[127] Foote: *Sketches of Va.,* 455–56.
[128] *Ibid.,* 459–60.
[129] *Wash. & Lee Hist. Papers,* 1890, No. I, 32.
[130] Foote: *Sketches of Va.,* 469.

the Synod of Virginia, in 1791, decided to establish at least one seminary for theological training in Virginia, that, under the care of Rev. Mr. Graham;[131] and a list of principles upon which the institution was to be conducted was drawn up.[132]   At a meeting of the Synod in 1792,

"Upon motion, Messrs. Graham, Hoge, and Houston, Ministers, and Mr. John Wilson, Elder, were appointed a committee to draft a minute, that may make the plan of education proposed by the Synod last year, coincide with the Act of Incorporation, instituting the Academy of Liberty Hall, and to make report before the rising of Synod."

The same afternoon, "the Committee appointed to draft a minute which may accommodate the plan of education proposed by the Synod to the Act of Incorporation, instituting Liberty Hall, report—that they examined wherein they do not coincide, and find that the following particulars appear necessary for Synod to adopt, in order to put it in the power of the Trustees of said Academy, to devote their property to the purposes proposed by Synod, agreeably to the proposals said Trustees have made in their petition to Synod. 1st. That instead of constituting the Presbyteries of Hanover and Lexington the Trustees of the Academy in Rockbridge, the Synod agree that they shall remain according to the direction of the Act; only that the Board is requested to fill up vacancies out of those two Presbyteries; and to agree to the direction of Synod that these two Presbyteries may attend at the examinations of the students.[133]

The action of the Synod in the following year is now given:

"Through the Committee of Overtures a petition was presented from the Trustees of the Academy of Liberty Hall, stating that they had agreed to the conditions in which the Synod proposed last year to patronise said Academy, and stating that, encouraged by this and other favourable considerations, they had contracted for buildings to the amount of £900, which are to be finished by the 1st of December, and praying the active aid and concurrence of the Synod. The Synod approved the vigorous exertions of the Trustees of the Academy, and earnestly recommend it to, and enjoin it upon the Presbyteries of Hanover and of Lexington, to exert themselves and to use their influence to raise money to aid the trustees in discharging the contracts already made, and to raise the Academy to as great a state of usefulness as possible."[134]

In 1794, the new buildings were ready, the school was flourishing, but "difficulties arose from the two offices of Mr. Graham,

---

131 *Ibid.*, 471.
132 *Ibid.*
133 *Ibid.*, 472–73; *Wash. & Lee Hist. Papers*, 1890, No. I, 44–45.
134 Foote: *Sketches of Va.*, 473.

Professor of Theology under the direction of the Synod of Virginia, and President of the Academy under the charter from the State."[135] In this statement, there is an indication of the crux of a real difficulty. It was, however, easy to attribute "the cry of bigotry and sectarianism" raised against Rev. Mr. Graham and the institution to Graham's unpopular political activity, or to the fact that "French principles" had become "popular in Virginia."[136] In April, 1797, the chairman of the trustees, in announcing the acceptance by the board, in the October previous, of Rev. Mr. Graham's resignation, was happy to observe that the Seminary had been "for many years, eminently useful in disseminating knowledge, and thereby subserving the general interests of literature and piety."[137]

In the meantime, other events were destined to reveal the religious-educational tendency of the institution in a new light. The Assembly had presented George Washington, in 1784, with fifty shares of stock in the Potomac River Company and 100 shares in the James River Company;[138] but Washington's resolution to shut his hand "against every pecuniary recompense" resulted in the Assembly's granting him permission, in 1785, to appropriate the gift as he saw fit to "objects of a public nature."[139] In September, 1796, Washington wrote to the Governor of Virginia his wish to confer the shares of the James River Company "upon the fullest consideration of all circumstances . . . to the use of Liberty Hall Academy. . . [140] In November, the House started its consideration of the proposal to convert the academy into a college; the bill was passed on the 21st of December.[141]

The preamble of the bill made no reference to any request on the part of trustees of Liberty Hall Academy for its conversion into a college. It indicated the basis of the action of the Assembly in the following statement:

---

[135] *Ibid.*, 474.
[136] *Ibid.*, 474–75.
[137] *Ibid.*, 477–78.
[138] Hening: *Stat. at Large*, XI, 525–26; Pickell, J.: *Potomac Co.*, 62.
[139] *Ibid.*, 64; Hening: *Stat. at Large*, XII, 44.
[140] Foots: *Sketches of Va.*, 482; *U. S. Bur. Educ., Circ. Inf.*, 1888, No. I, 297.
[141] *Acts of Assembly*, Dec. 21, 1796, 26–27.

WHEREAS, it has been communicated to this general assembly, that George Washington, President of the United States, has appropriated the shares which were directed to be subscribed, in his name, in the James River Canal Company, with the tolls and profits which shall accrue therefrom, to the use of Liberty Hall Academy, in the county of Rockbridge: And whereas the benevolent design of that most excellent citizen, will be better promoted by enlarging the nature of the said institution:

Section I. *BE it enacted*, That the academy, now stiled Liberty Hall Academy, shall be erected into a college, which shall be called and known by the name of the College of Washington, in Virginia.[142]

The bill made provision for four schools in the college—that of languages, of mathematics, of natural philosophy and astronomy, and of logic, moral philosophy and belles lettres. It will be noted that there was no place here for any activity like Rev. Mr. Graham's theological seminary. The system of education for the different schools, the rules and ordinances for the conduct of the students were entrusted to the president and professors. For the general government of the college, a board of visitors numbering among its members the governor of the commonwealth was appointed. Neither the board of visitors, nor the faculty, was at liberty to make any "bye-law, rule, ordinance, statute, or regulation whatever, contrary to the constitution or laws of this commonwealth."[143]

According to Presbyterian historians, the bill had been passed by the Assembly, "without the consent or knowledge of the Trustees of Liberty Hall,"[144] a statement seemingly confirmed by the preamble of the bill. The excitement created by this procedure is described by Rev. Mr. Henry Ruffner, President, 1836–48:[145]

A significant circumstance in this act is, that among the nineteen gentlemen named as visitors, not one was a clergyman, much less a Presbyterian clergyman, and scarcely one, if even one, was a member of the Presbyterian church. By whomsoever this new charter was contrived, one obvious part of the scheme was to deprive the Presbyterians of all share in the management of the institution, . . .

---

142 *Ibid.*
143 *Ibid.*
144 Foote: *Sketches of Va.*, 484; *Wash. & Lee Hist. Papers*, 1890, No. I, 68.
145 *Wash. & Lee Catalog*, 1926, 27.

By the first act of incorporation the Synod of Virginia and the Presbytery of Lexington had lost the control of it. To this they submitted without complaint; for the reason probably that the large proportion of Presbyterians, clergymen and church members in the board of trustees, gave assurance of a salutary degree of religious influence in the management of the institution. The agreement with the Synod of Virginia, by which a Theological school had been connected with it, was not only necessary at the time to raise the academy from its low condition, but was virtually dissolved by the resignation of Mr. Graham, several months before this new charter was enacted, and by the discontinuance of the ecclesiastical bodies to exercise the privileges derived from the agreement.

On the 21st of January, 1797, the board of trustees of Liberty Hall met and unanimously declared it as their opinion, ''that the late act of the Legislature of Virginia, erecting Liberty Hall Academy into a College, was an unjustifiable infringement of the rights of the corporation of Liberty Hall, and an instance of tyrannical imposition in the Legislature, and that, moreover, it did not repeal the act incorporating Liberty Hall Academy.''[146]

At a meeting on February 7, the Board asserted, ''We conceive the said Act to be a singular instance of infringement on the rights of a corporate body, which had not by any act of theirs violated tenure, or given cause for the abolition of their charter.''[147] As the trustees had not been officially informed of the Washington grant, and as the name of Bishop Madison, President of William and Mary, was rumored as the intended President,[148] the Board decided in April to appoint a committee to inform ''other corporations in the State, of the attempt to deprive us of our charter'' and to prepare a remonstrance to the Legislature.[149] The petition was considered by the House in December, and ''An act, for erecting Liberty Hall Academy, into a college'' was repealed on January 19th, 1798,[150] and its name changed to Washington Academy.[151]

To understand the action of the Legislature in its apparent attempt to wrest the charter from Presbyterian control, it must be recalled that Washington, in a letter to the Legislature in 1795, had indicated that it was his desire to appropriate the

---

[146] *Wash. & Lee Hist. Papers*, 1890, No. I, 68–69.
[147] Foote: *Sketches of Va.*, 484.
[148] *Ibid.; U. S. Bur. Educ., Circ. Inf.*, 1888, No. I, 297.
[149] Foote: *Sketches of Va.*, 485.
[150] *Jour., H. Del.*, Dec. 9, 1797, 12; Jan. 23, 1798, 101; *Acts of Assembly*, Jan. 19, 1798, 26.
[151] *Ibid.; Wash. & Lee Catalog*, 1926, 21–22; Foote: *Sketches of Va.*, 485.

shares of the Potomac River Company to a university in the District of Columbia, and those of the James River Company for a seminary in the state,

. . . upon an enlarged plan, but not yet coming up to the full idea of a University, . . . The students, who wish to pursue the whole range of science, may pass with advantage from the Seminary to the University, and the former by a due relation may be rendered co-operative with the latter.[152]

With this sentiment of Washington, the Legislature concurred in a lengthy resolution on December 1, 1795.[153] As soon as Washington had designated the particular seminary to be favored, the Legislature proceeded, undoubtedly having in view the fact that the gift to Washington had been a public one from the people of the state as a whole, and was now being returned for the benefit of the entire state, to change the charter of the institution, to make it in fact a public institution. As the Presbyterians were at this time, the most numerous religious denomination in the state,[154] and as they insisted that nothing had been done in violation of their original charter, they succeeded in having the charter which made the institution a public one withdrawn, and the college reverted into an academy. In 1926, the Washington gift still yielded an annual income of $3,000 to Washington and Lee University.[155]

Upon deciding to disband, in 1802, the Virginia branch of The Cincinnati Society decided to follow the example of its "late illustrious leader and hero, George Washington" and appropriate its funds to Washington Academy.[156]

Presbyterian educational activity during this period is repsented also in connection with the beginnings of another institution, Transylvania Seminary. In July, 1780, the House sent

---

152 *Ibid.*, 479

153 *Jour., H. Del.*, Dec. 1, 1795, 63; *Acts of Assembly*, 1795, 55.

154 Morse: *American Gazetteer*, 1798, 352; 1804, under *Virginia;* Scott: *U. S. Gazetteer*, 1795, 1805, under *Virginia.*

155 *Wash. & Lee Catalog*, 1926, 22.

156 *U. S. Bur. Educ., Circ. Inf.*, 1888, No. I, 298; Foote: *Sketches of Va.*, 485; *Wash. & Lee Catalog*, 1926, 22; *Va. Mag. Hist.*, I, 95–97; *Wm. & Mary Coll. Quart.*, XVII, 3; *W. Va. Hist. Mag.*, Jan., 1905, I, 1–9, 9–15; Adams, *U. S. Bur. Educ., Circ. Inf.*, 1888, No. I, 298, gives the amount "as about $23,000;" Foote, as $16,000; 1926 catalog, as about $25,000; *Va. Mag. Hist.*, as nearly $25,000.

to the Senate for its concurrence "An Act to vest certain escheated lands in the county of Kentucky, in trustees for a public school."[157] The act as passed, granted 8,000 acres of land to thirteen trustees, "for the purpose of a publick school, or seminary of learning;"[158] the Board of Trustees was, however, preponderantly Presbyterian, and the bill had been sponsored in the House by Colonel John Todd, nephew of Rev. John Todd, trustee of Hampden-Sidney.[159] The very meager indication of the original charter as to the authority of the trustees made it necessary to amend the charter,[160] The amended charter, passed on June 24, 1783, increased the number of trustees to twenty-five, and among important Presbyterian names may now be recognized Rev. David Rice, trustee of Hampden-Sidney, Rev. Caleb Wallace, and Samuel M'Dowell, trustees of Liberty Hall. The trustees were to have the right of perpetual succession "until the mode of electing trustees shall be otherwise directed by law." The name of Transylvania Seminary, with all the privileges of a college or university, was given to the institution. Leave to sell any of the lands must first have been obtained from the Legislature, and all regulations were required to be in accordance with the constitution or laws of the commonwealth. The oaths of fidelity and of office were to be taken by the trustees and faculty. The free donation was extended to 12,000 acres of land; and if as much as 20,000 acres were to be obtained for its use, that amount was to be forever free from taxes; if more than 20,000 acres were obtained, all lands above that amount were to be tax exempt until January 1, 1795. Degrees of Bachelor or Master of Arts were to be conferred only after stated examination before the trustees "in the presence of as many gentlemen of liberal education as may choose to attend." Finally, it was enacted, "That the said trustees shall, at all times, be accountable for their transactions touching any matter or thing relating to the said seminary, in such manner as the legis-

---

[157] *Jour., H. Del.*, July 4, 1780, 73.
[158] Hening: *Stat. at Large*, X, 287'-88.
[159] Peter, R., and Peter, J.: *Transylvania University*, 23–24; 54–56; William Christian, trustee of Liberty Hall was also a trustee.
[160] *Jour., H. Del.*, June 3, 1783, 33.

lature shall direct.''[161]   Thus the Legislature of Virginia made a splendid gift to the first state created University since its independence—an institution clearly intended as the provisions above cited indicate, to be for the public—subject through its trustees, though largely Presbyterian, in every matter to the Legislature.[162]   Most significant, however, was the tendency directed to the legislative control and safe-guarding of the institution from a civil standpoint.   The first meeting of the trustees was held in accordance with the charter in November, 1783, at John Crow's Station, in Lincoln County, one of the three counties into which Kentucky County had been divided in 1780.[163]   The actual start of the University was made in a resolution of the board on November 4, 1784,

''That one or more grammar schools be erected, as the funds would permit.

That the first be erected in Lincoln County, near the Reverend David Rice's dwelling.''[164]

As Rev. David Rice was one of the trustees, and chairman of its Board for a number of years, Rev. James Mitchell, a Presbyterian minister was chosen ''as master of the school at the Reverend David Rice's.''[165]   The district of Kentucky was, in 1785, erected into an independent state, to take effect September 1, 1787, but the law protected all land warrants previously issued and reserved Virginian authority over the disposition of unlocated lands until September 1, 1788.[166]   The trustees, therefore, petitioned the Assembly ''that further provision may be made to assure to them the 12,000 acres of escheatable lands heretofore

---

161 Hening: *Stat. at Large*, XI, 287.

162 William and Mary College had been created a University by its visitors, see p. 176.

163 Hening: *Stat. at Large*, X, 315; *U. S. Bur. Educ., Circ. Inf.*, 1899, No. 3, 36, 38; Peter: *Transylvania University*, 24; *U. S. Bur. Educ., Circ. Inf.*, 1888, No. I, 306.

164 Peter: *Transylvania University*, 28; *U. S. Bur. Educ., Circ. Inf.*, 1899, No. 3, 39.

165 *Ibid.;* Peter: *Transylvania University*, 29, referring to Rev. Rice, ''It will be noticed that its first grammar school was held in his house, and Davidson states he was its first teacher;'' Peter is evidently quoting Davidson, R.: *Presbyterian Church*, Ky., 67, ''He was chairman for several years of the Board of Trustees of Transylvania Seminary, and its first teacher, while yet a Grammar-School.''

166 Hening: *Stat. at Large*, XII, 37 *ff.*

appropriated to the said seminary, and a mode prescribed for
surveying and obtaining a grant for the same.''[167] They also
asked that ''one-sixth part of the legal fees received by surveyors
within the district of Kentucky, and heretofore reserved to the
use and benefit of William and Mary College, may be appropriated to the benefit of their seminary.''[168] The committee to
whom the petition had been referred, recommended that both
propositions be rejected, but the House on December 13, 1787,
transferred the surveyors' fees as requested from William and
Mary College to Transylvania Seminary.[169] There was some attempt in December to have a bill passed ''to repeal in part an
act, to vest certain escheated lands in the county of Kentucky,
in trustees for a public school''—whether the bill was favorable
or otherwise to the interests of the Seminary does not appear;
it was rejected by the Senate.[170] On the following day, December 18, 1789, the Legislature passed a new act ''concerning
the erection of the district of Kentuckey into an independent
state.''[171] Virginia land warrants were now to be recognized
when issued before September 1, 1791, and unlocated lands
were to be exempt from disposition by the new state until May
1, 1792.[172] As a result of petition by the Transylvania trustees,[173] the Legislature passed an act permitting seven trustees
to constitute a board to transact business;[174] a second act authorizing one or more lotteries not to exceed £500;[175] and a third act
strengthening the previous one concerning surveyors' fees.[176]
The act concerning Surveyors' fees was again amended to the
benefit of the Seminary in December, 1791.[177]

The liberality of the Legislature to an institution conceived
for the public benefit, but actually initiated in the house of one

---

[167] *Jour., H. Del.,* Nov. 22, 1787, 62.
[168] *Ibid.*
[169] *Jour., H. Del.,* Nov. 22, 1787, 62; Dec. 6, 1787, 84; Hening: *Stat. at Large,* XII, 642.
[170] *Jour., H. Del.,* Dec. 16, 1789, 133; *Jour., Senate,* Dec. 17, 1789, 75.
[171] Hening: *Stat. at Large,* XIII, 17 *ff.*
[172] *Ibid.*
[173] *Jour., H. Del.,* Nov. 6. 1790, 42.
[174] Hening: *Stat. at Large,* XIII, 147.
[175] *Ibid.,* 173.
[176] *Ibid.,* 180 *ff.; Jour., H. Del.,* Dec. 29, 1790, 167.
[177] Hening: *Stat. at Large,* XIII, 291; *Jour., H. Del.,* Dec. 10, 1791, 120.

Presbyterian minister and taught by another,[178] aroused the watchful interest of the public. An article in the *Kentucky Gazette*, September 1, 1787, "proposed, in order to remove the difficulty of contending sects, 'that they only furnish students with opportunities of knowledge and free inquiry,' and that truth would prevail; that they should 'appoint without regard to denominations.' "[179] Another article in the interest of "a liberal policy" on the part of the trustees was answered by "A Sectarian" with the statement "that it would not do to be 'liberal and disinterested' in matters of 'religion, morals, etc.' "[180] In 1787, Rev. David Rice discontinued his immediate connection with the institution.[181] The Seminary was moved to the neighborhood of Lexington in October, 1788.[182]

After a various experience with teachers, James Moore who had come to the Seminary, in 1792, while a candidate for the Presbyterian ministry, was displaced two years later, probably because his trial sermon had not been sustained, by Mr. Harry Toulmin.[183] As Kentucky was admitted into the Union in 1792, the affairs of the Seminary at this time are of interest only because of the Virginian interests which continued to be associated with it. The appointment of Mr. Toulmin, who was a minister in the Baptist Church, had been greatly seconded by strong letters from Thomas Jefferson.[184] Probably because of this fact, Mr. Toulmin was supposed to have a certain amount of sympathy with Jefferson in his views on spiritual matters. Further, Mr. Toulmin's brother, a minister in England, had published views "tainted with Socinian errors." According to Rev. Robert Davidson, Mr. Toulmin's appointment had been engineered by the "Deistical clubs," one of which was located in Lexington under the auspices of Genêt.[185] The appointment,

---

[178] *U. S. Bur. Educ., Circ. Inf.*, 1899, No. 3, 39.

[179] Peter: *Transylvania University*, 34.

[180] *Ibid.*, 34, referring to *Kentucky Gazette*, Dec. 22, 1787.

[181] Peter: *Transylvania University*, 38.

[182] Davidson: *Presbyterian Church, Ky.*, 289.

[183] Peter: *Transylvania University*, 44, 49.

[184] *Ibid.*, 52.

[185] Davidson: *Presbyterian Church, Ky.*, 290. As Genêt did not land in this country until April 8, 1793—Jones: *American & French Culture*, 546—French influence must have worked fast to affect an election in June, 1794.

immediately resented by a number of the Presbyterian trustees, was followed by their resignations, and subsequent creation of Kentucky Academy, where "their sons might enjoy the advantages of a liberal education without the contamination of their religious principles, and which might furnish the churches with able and faithful ministers."[186] The significance of this statement is better understood when it is known that the Synod of Virginia, in 1791, when creating the theological section at Liberty Hall,[187] had recommended it

. . . to the Presbytery of Transylvania, to institute and patronise a Seminary within their bounds, upon principles similar to those herein laid down, and for similar purposes; or to encourage either of those that are now recommended.[188]

Presbyterian educational activity during this period, however, is not summed up in the history only of Hampden-Sidney, Liberty Hall, and Transylvania Seminary, but in the history of many of the academies in that list of forty-five or more previously cited.[189] An attempt to go into the history of these institutions, except for a certain cumulative effect, would add little to the essential significence of Presbyterian activity.

The experience of Presbyterianism in attempting to conduct "public" education, for that had been the basis of their appeal to the people and Legislature for assistance, is of particular importance. They had had before them the experience of the Protestant Episcopal Church in connection with the College of William and Mary. It is clear from their public statement, at the initiation of the institution which was to be known as Hampden-Sidney, that they hoped to avoid the errors of the Anglican Church, to do what they thought that church had not done, to give an adequate Christian education without denominational bias. It has been shown that they were unable to avoid

---

186 Peter: *Transylvania University*, 49–52, 57, quoting Davidson: *Presbyterian Church, Ky.*, 291.
187 See p. 230.
188 Foote: *Sketches of Va.*, 472.
189 See p. 168; among academies associated at various times with Presbyterianism through teachers or trustees are Alexandria Academy, Staunton Academy, New London Academy, Washington-Henry, Ann Smith Academy.

the charge of sectarianism; that in their three most important experiments they tended to associate theological training; that when a crisis occurred which threatened to lessen Presbyterian influence, they preferred to withdraw.

From the point of view of the state, the Presbyterian experiment is likewise of interest. Each of the institutions had benefitted financially, though not to the extent desired by the interests concerned, either directly or indirectly from the state; nor did the state withdraw its support immediately after passing the *Bill for Establishing Religious Freedom,* in 1786—a clear indication that, while the legislature undoubtedly knew of the Presbyterian influence associated with these institutions, it had confidence in the expressed Presbyterian policy that education would be conducted not in the interest of the denomination, but in the interest of the general public. Though the state had attempted to throw rigid safeguards, to protect the interests of the public, around its creation of Transylvania Seminary, it was probably not until the test case of 1796, when it attempted to convert Liberty Hall into Washington College, that the state fully realized the direction into which its surrender of education to boards of trustees, representing largely a particular denominational influence, tended.

It is, of course, impossible, except for such a meager glimpse of the situation, as disclosed by the riot at Hampden-Sidney at the time of the revival—which may have been due merely to the effervescence of youth—to determine the extent to which, if any, students felt themselves aggrieved in conscience; to what extent, if any, they felt that the *Declaration of Rights* or the *Bill for Religious Freedom* had been violated by their compulsory presence at religious exercises; to what extent, if any, they felt that the rules of the institutions contravened the constitution and the laws of the state, agreement with which the charters of these institutions required.

As for the general public, it must be recalled that the denominational ascendancy during this period had gone to the Presbyterians, with Episcopalians, Baptists, and Methodists following in a descending order.[190] The Episcopalians were attempting to

---

[190] Morse: *American Gazetteer,* 1804, under *Virginia;* for a detailed statement, see Schermerhorn & Mills: *A Correct View of U. S.,* 8–10; the popula-

recover from the "slough of despond" into which they had been plunged by the Revolution; the Baptists and Methodists, as organizations, were as yet novices in the field of education.

The Status Of The Civil And Denominational Struggle For Educational Control By 1810

Two forces, civil and denominational, initiated a struggle for educational control in Virginia during the period of adjustment to the new political philosophy of separation of church and state.

Thomas Jefferson, the proponent of civil control of education, aligning his educational view with the new political philosophy, wished education to serve the principles fundamental in the new state constitution—principles guaranteeing freedom of conscience, exemption from financial, social, or political burdens because of religious views. Education was to be directed by the state in the interest of the preservation of these principles. To understand the importance of these principles for the preservation of human rights and the welfare of the state on its new civil foundation, history was essential; and so history, not theology, was to become the civil religion of the people.

To carry out so radical a program, one so completely at variance with the accustomed thought of the people, required education of the people, and that required time.

On the denominational side, the Episcopal Church, the downfall of whose supremacy, in the opinion of the dissenters, had been essential to the creation of the new state, was in no position to carry on its traditional control of education, except quietly, under private auspices; it hesitated to ask extensive favors from the state which had scorned it. The Baptists during the greater part of this period were too engrossed in the political aspects of their struggle to eliminate all traces of the former integration of church and state, to give attention to a comprehensive program of education. They began, however, to give some consideration to the problem of fundamental religious instruction. The Methodists, with a real appreciation of the importance of education for the masses, were too absorbed during this period

tion of Virginia for 1790, 1800, and 1810, was 747,610; 880,200; 947,600— *U. S. Bur. Census, Fourteenth Census,* 1920, *Abstract,* 1923, 19.

in proselytism in order to build up their new church, to attempt extensive control of education. It was the Presbyterians, with the oldest intellectual tradition behind them, among the dissenting groups, who, having now achieved the greatest numerical and economic importance, were enabled because of this position to make a serious attempt to prevent education from being dominated by purely civil control. The achievement of Presbyterianism in this connection was a highly important one; it was attained by compelling the Legislature to compromise its attitude looking towards a purely state controlled education. The most notable Presbyterian victory was that of 1798, when it compelled the repeal of the act of 1796 creating Washington College.

With Presbyterian success in enlisting support from the people for education under its auspices, it is only natural to find that the second important attempt of the Legislature, in 1796, looking to the civil control of education, by creating an elementary school system, proved a failure. It was not until the act of 1802 concerning the glebes was passed, providing a nontaxation source for schools, that serious experimentation with schools under civil control was begun.

The increasing importance of Presbyterianism in educational control, by the close of another decade, could not but be looked upon with alarm by those concerned in preserving in its integrity, the spirit expressed in the laws and constitution of Virginia. The direction of the education of youth, so that they would as citizens give serious thought to the preservation of those principles expressed in the legislation achieved in this period of adjustment, was by the close of the first decade of the 19th century, in the opinion of such Virginia statesmen as Tyler, an absolute essential in the further preservation of the constitution of the state.

The creation of the Literary Fund, in 1810, is important in Virginian educational history as marking the first attempt in Virginian history to create a fund applicable to general educational purposes for the state as a whole. Its greater significance lay, however, in the fact that it was the first attempt to give the direction of expenditures for the benefit of state-wide education, to officials of the state. Expenditure of state funds by state officials presupposes adherence to state laws.   An excellent gauge of how state laws are being interpreted is thus to be found in such expenditures.

Both the state and the church were conscious of the importance of education in its relation to the improvement of society. The state, however, was interested in furthering that improvement from an entirely different point of view from that of the church.   As will appear, the increasing religious strength of Virginia was soon to give a more articulate expression to the point of view of the church—that the improvement of society must be posited on an education that is a preparation for the life to come.

CHAPTER VII

CONTINUATION OF THE DENOMINATIONAL STRUGGLE FOR EDUCATIONAL CONTROL (1810–60)

Organized Religious Educational Activities

Randall, in his *Life of Thomas Jefferson*, tells how the announcement of Jefferson's election to the Presidency was received with such dread by pious New England females, that, fearing for the safety of their Bibles, they felt constrained to hide them "in the clefts of rocks."[1] The women of Virginia, with greater fortitude, greeted the return of Jefferson from the Presidency to retirement in their midst, by seconding most heartily a movement for placing a Bible in the hands of every man, woman, and child in the state. Apparently Virginia confidence in the future safety of these Bibles was sufficient to warrant certain citizens in requesting the Assembly for an act of incorporation for "The Virginia Bible Society"—a request granted in January, 1814.[2] The confidence of those behind the movement went even farther; they wrote Jefferson asking for a subscription, a request he complied with, while lamenting the change in the circumstances of society since his earlier days when so far as he could recall, he had never been in a home, where the wish for a Bible could not be gratified because of poverty.[3]

The year of the incorporation of the Virginia Bible Society was marked also by the completion of the Monumental Church[4] in Richmond, by members of the Protestant Episcopal Church.

---

[1] Randall: *Life of T. Jefferson*, I, 495.
[2] *Jour., H. Del.*, Dec. 18, 1813, 65; *Acts of Assembly*, Jan. 4, 1814, 120; Stanard: *Richmond, People and Story*, 110; the American Bible Society was founded in 1816; the American Sunday School Union in 1817, according to Morrison, A. J.: *South Atlant. Quart.*, Jan.–Oct., 1919, XVIII, 31; but *cf.* Brown: *Sunday School Movements*, 31.
[3] Lipscomb: *Writings T. Jefferson:* XIV, 81.
[4] Stanard: *Richmond, People and Story*, 69, 107; Meade, W.: *Brief Review Episcopal Church*, 7; Christian, W. A.: *Richmond*, 81.

Both events were probably the outcome of a deepened religious sense on the part of many Virginians—a feeling inspired by the tragic loss of a large number of lives in the disastrous fire, in December, 1811, of the Richmond theater located on Shockhoe Hill.[5]   The incorporation of the "Virginia Bible Society" was followed almost immediately by the creation of local supporting Bible societies, tract societies, "cent" societies, and most significantly, a revival of Sunday Schools, which formerly scorned, when under Methodist auspices, now arose to hamper the development of schools under the auspices of the Literary Fund.[6]

The "Norfolk Bible Society" was established in 1814, and by 1818 reported a distribution of 643 Bibles and 1241 Testaments.[7] The Protestant Episcopal Convention of 1816 organized a "Common Prayer-Book and Tract Society."[8]   The *Virginia Evangelical and Literary Magazine,* for 1818, notes the "Richmond Female Bible Society" as auxiliary to the "Virginia Bible Society," and the "Female Cent Society of Richmond and Hanover" for the education of poor and pious youth for the ministry.[9]   For this purpose, we are informed, cent societies, "principally female," contributed that year upwards of $3,000.[10] Five years after the incorporation of the Virginia Bible Society, Bible societies were to be found in all the leading towns in Virginia—Norfolk, Petersburg, Richmond, Lynchburg, Lexington, Staunton, Winchester, Fredericksburg, and other towns.[11]   In 1820, the "Richmond Tract Society" was founded.[12]   Bible and

---

[5] *Calamity at Richmond,* 26; *cf.* Hawks: *Contrib. Ecc. Hist.,* I, Appendix, 91; May, R.: *A Voice From Richmond,* 9 *ff.;* Rev. Robert May, an English missionary, en route to India, while in Philadelphia, in 1811–12, addressed large assemblies of children, and utilized this event in a lecture, entitled "A Voice From Richmond," to point a solemn warning against the theater and for a religious life; Morrison: *South Atlant. Quart.,* Jan.–Oct., 1919, XVIII, 31; *cf.* Michael, O. S.: *The Sunday School,* 59, 292; *Minutes of the Evang. Soc. of Phila.,* Feb. 24, 1812.

[6] See p. 217, 335.

[7] *Va. Evang. & Lit. Mag.,* I, 188.

[8] Hawks: *Contrib. Ecc. Hist.,* I, Appendix, 107; Brewer: *Episc. Church,* 143.

[9] *Va. Evang. & Lit. Mag.,* I, 94.

[10] *Ibid.,* I, 431; Bennett: *Memorials of Methodism,* 439, describes a female charity society organized, 1804, by Asbury, for the support of the missionary efforts of that church.

[11] *Va. Evang. & Lit. Mag.,* II, 139.

[12] *Ibid.,* VII, 323.

Tract Societies continued to flourish with an ever increasing vigor through the decades.[13]

Mere distribution, however, of Bibles and tracts will not make children or adults, religious, if they can not read them. It was only natural, therefore, that in the then inadequate school situation, the religious-minded people of Virginia should turn to the Sunday School as a solution of their problem. It seems that the tradition of the Methodist Sunday Schools had not died out altogether, and Virginians who were interested in education were of course familiar with the work of Raikes.[14] It would be an idle task to attempt to determine who was responsible for the initiation of the new movement.[15] By 1820, there is evidence that all the leading denominations were fostering the Sunday School movement.[16] The *Virginia Evangelical and Literary Magazine,* in 1818, stated that "It is known that Sunday Schools are established in all our large towns."[17] In 1819, the Richmond Sunday School Union, under Presbyterian and Methodist auspices had four schools with 640 scholars, and eight schools, in and about Goochland County, with 300 scholars affiliated with it.[18] Sunday Schools had spread to Lynchburg in the south and to Shepherdstown in the north.[19]

Margaret Mercer, who was later principal of a girls' school known as Belmont, described the Garnett Sunday School, established at Elmwood, where she was visiting, as then containing 160 scholars. Describing its success, she said, "many have been

---

[13] Royall, A.: *Black Book,* I, *passim; cf.* Morrison, A. J.: *Six Addresses—*Maxwell's *Discourse,* 16–17.

[14] *Richmond Enquirer,* Dec. 6, 1854.

[15] Maddox: *Free Sch. Idea Va.,* 33, gives James Mercer Garnett, the founder of a Sunday School at Elmwood, Essex County, in 1812, as one of the earliest in the movement; see p. 215 *ff.*

[16] *Va. Evang. & Lit. Mag.,* VII, 302; Hawks: *Contrib. Ecc. Hist.,* I, Appendix, 142; Bennett: *Memorials of Methodism,* 667; *Richmond Enquirer,* Dec. 6, 1854.

[17] *Va. Evang. & Lit. Mag.,* I, 95.

[18] *Ibid.,* II, 291, 340; Bennett: *Memorials of Methodism,* 667; Bennett states that "The Baptists were requested to unite in the enterprise, but they declined to have anything to do with such schools"—however, according to the *Richmond Enquirer,* Dec. 6, 1854, the Ground Squirrel Baptist Sunday School was organized in 1816.

[19] *Va. Evang. & Lit. Mag.,* II, 529; Christian, W. A.: *Lynchburg,* 59, 63; Cabell, M.: *Sketches Lynchburg,* 132.

dismissed, having learned, at even at an advanced age, to read their 'blessed Bible.' ''[20]

At an examination of the Shepherdstown school in September, 1819, there were distributed for good behavior and diligence, "16 New Testaments, 13 Watt's Psalms and Hymns, and 110 smaller books, among which were the Dairyman's Daughter, Sermons to Children, The Good Child's Petition, &c.''[21]

The common object of all these schools was that given as characterizing those of the Richmond Sunday School Union—"they are taught to read, and are instructed to fear and love God.''[22] Prayer, singing, and appropriate addresses were part of their common procedure.[23] The emphasis was not on a mere acquisition of reading ability; but rather, "to furnish the minds of the children with religious knowledge, to induce them to keep holy the Sabbath day, and, in short, to bring them up in the 'nurture and admonition of the Lord.' ''[24]

It is important to notice that Sunday Schools were getting well under way just at a time, when, because of the creation of the Literary Fund, there was every prospect that the state was about to devise some system of elementary instruction. While the President and Directors of the Literary Fund were concerned with a policy which should place "the foundations of scientific and moral improvement" in the state under civil control,[25] the religious-educationally minded section of Virginia were, by their successful efforts in providing the basic elements of learning, without cost, seemingly sweeping all before them. It is not surprising to find, therefore, that Jefferson spent the summer of 1817 in devising a plan for an elementary school system, free from all religious influence, and one, which would not draw upon the Literary Fund; nor, that all that could be accomplished by the Assembly of 1818 was a provision for the tuition of the poor, utilizing existing school facilities.[26]

[20] Morris, C.: *Memoir Margaret Mercer*, 48; *cf. Va. Evang. & Lit. Mag.*, III, 238 *ff.*
[21] *Ibid.*, II, 529–30.
[22] *Ibid.*, II, 291.
[23] *Ibid.*, II, 531–32; III, 239 *ff.*; Christian: *Lynchburg*, 63–64.
[24] *Va. Evang. & Lit. Mag.*, II, 530.
[25] *Jour.*, *H. Del.*, Dec. 19, 1815, 54.
[26] See p. 334–35.

The *Virginia Evangelical and Literary Magazine*, edited by a Presbyterian minister, Rev. John Holt Rice, which had always shown an interest in the Sunday School movement, published, in 1822, an article signed "Iota" which boldly came out with a plan for state subsidy of Sunday Schools, finding in them, the ideal elementary school system, worthy of support by the Literary Fund. This move may have been inspired as a reply to the action of the state in passing an act for the sale of the glebe lands in St. Ann's parish, Essex County, for the benefit of schools, with the proviso, "That no application of the said fund, or any part thereof, shall be made to the support and maintenance of any religious sect or denomination, or to any religious purpose whatsoever."[27]

Perhaps the alarm was taken that this was indicative of future legislation. In favor of Sunday Schools, "Iota" found that they were taught gratuitously, did not take children from their work, did not belong exclusively to any religious sect, were successful in discipline, in elevating the minds and manners of the poor, and in extending the reign of love between rich and poor. The Literary Fund, it was suggested, should supply the cost of twelve agents, who were to look after the schools in the twelve districts of the state, and the cost of a general depository for Sunday School books in Richmond.[28]   "A Friend To The Poor" replied that "Iota" was "endeavoring to prejudice the minds of the community against the education of the poor under the present organization."[29]

The suggestion of "Iota" was not wholly without result; while the Assembly did not venture directly to subsidize these schools, the school commissioners of Richmond, in 1825, declaring that "the object of the Literary Fund would be promoted by encouraging these institutions," distributed $50 among them for the purchase of books.[30] In the Report of the Second Auditor for 1828, the commissioners of Berkeley County announced that their clerk had turned over his salary to the Sun-

---

27 *Acts of Assembly*, Jan. 4, 1822, 54.
28 *Va. Evang. & Lit. Mag.*, V, 88 *ff.*, 240; Maddox: *Free Sch. Idea Va.*, 39–40.
29 *Va. Evang. & Lit. Mag.*, VI, 281.
30 *Jour., H. Del.*, 1825, Doc. L, 31.

day School in Martinsburg. A similar disposition of their salaries was made by the clerk and the treasurer of Hampshire County.[31] In defending their increase of aid for Sunday Schools to $100, the commissioners of Richmond, in 1828, gave an entended eulogy of these schools, emphasizing particularly the beneficent effects of the system of prizes upon the learning achievement of the students. The awards, they said,

. . . are of a literary character, consisting of books, designed to inculcate christian morality, and therefore free from the objection of exciting either cupidity or selfishness, while they are calculated to beget a fondness for reading.''[32]

Apparently there was no recognition, on the part of the advocates of Sunday Schools, of any impropriety in receiving appropriations from the Literary Fund for these schools. This was probably due to the fact that, in many localities, these schools represented combined denominational efforts, and there had arisen a tendency, upon the part of some in Virginia, since the Presbyterian pronouncement of its ''Christian'' education policy, to regard support for Christian, that is, non-sectarian, education, as a perfectly legitimate charge upon the state. It is quite probable that as no objections seem to have been raised by the officers of the Literary Fund, that the precedent set by the school commissioners of Richmond, in appropriating part of their quota to Sunday Schools, was followed in many places without being noted in the Reports of the Second Auditor. There was an evident disposition on the part of many commissioners to favor Sunday Schools.

The attitude is clearly indicated in the report of the school commissioners of Scott County, in 1828, who announced that a Sunday School Society had been formed in their county for the promotion of primary education, and that a petition had been sent to the General Assembly for pecuniary aid to purchase books.[33] The following year, the commissioners hope that if the Legislature make any change in the primary school laws,

---

[31] *Ibid.*, Second Auditor's Report, Sept. 30, 1828, 18, 21.
[32] *Ibid.*, 27.
[33] *Ibid.*

that it will further the Sabbath school plan, "if it can be done without promoting sectarian proselytism."[34]

To what extent Sunday Schools were non-denominational in character, is not definitely known. That the Baptists hesitated to join an inter-denominational effort has been shown.[35] It is known that the Protestant Episcopal Church did not look with favor upon the non-denominational character of these schools. In 1826, they formed the General Protestant Episcopal Sunday School Union with a view to publishing text-books and other literature distinctive of their church.[36]

In 1833, the school commissioners of Petersburg reported that there were four Sunday Schools with about 90 teachers and 600 scholars. In their opinion, the value of these schools to the community was nearly equal to the same number of common schools and they suggested that the Board appropriate money for text-books for their use.[37] At the same time, the commissioners of Northumberland reported that they had exceeded their quota because of having furnished books to the different Sunday Schools; but they are willing to refund the amount if "it be deemed that they have in this instance acted improperly."[38] A report from Norfolk County indicated that Sunday Schools were of value in taking care of the indigent children of laborers who flocked to the navy yard.[39] Reports testifying to the value of Sunday Schools appear as late as 1840, when Petersburg reported 700 children in its Sunday Schools.[40]

Probably the very fact that the educational efforts of Sunday Schools received such favorable publicity in the Reports of the Second Auditor encouraged some of the trustees of the Union Sunday School of Richmond County to ask, in 1843, for an act of incorporation.[41] The bill was indefinitely postponed that

---

[34] *Ibid.*, 1829–30, Doc. No. 4, 27.

[35] See p. 246, n. 18.

[36] Brewer: *Episc. Church*, 183; for its position in the church, *cf.* Meade: *Old Churches, Ministers, and Families*, II, 375; Hawks: *Contrib. Ecc. Hist.*, I, Appendix, 208.

[37] *Jour., H. Del.*, 1833–34, Doc. No. 4, 29.

[38] *Ibid.*, 27.

[39] *Ibid.*, 1836–37, Doc. No. 4, 25.

[40] *Ibid.*, 1839–40, 31.

[41] *Jour., Senate*, Jan. 9, 1843, 28.

year, and in 1844, it was resolved that it was inexpedient to report it.[42] This refusal of incorporation was in accordance with the tendency of that period to draw a line at what looked like encouragement of strictly denominational or theological education.[43]

Consideration must now be given to the effects of these organized religious-educational activities. Virginia, in the decade or more after the incorporation of the Virginia Bible Society, seems to have acquired rapidly a "godly" character. If we may trust the caustic account by Mrs. Anne Royall, in her *Black Book*, the once great state of Virginia, was now permitting herself to be plundered by a ravenous band of harpies whose object, under the guise of converting the heathen and extending religious knowledge to the poor, was to be avenged for the affront put upon them by the constitution in being excluded from civil privileges.[44] To Mrs. Royall, Richmond, swarming with missionary, Bible, and Tract societies, and newspaper agents to support them, seemed to have sunk into "ignorance and bigotry,"[45] nor were the cities of Petersburg and Fredericksburg in a much better position.[46] The Sunday Schools in her opinion were part of the scheme to extend the power of this religion-mad group, the real object being to establish a national religion.[47] Mrs. Royall's final thrust is to put the whole movement to the test of social progress, and she asks

. . . what effect all this pious preaching, and this ribaldry, of societies, and tracts, and Bibles, and Sunday schools, &c. has had on people in our own country. If they cannot reform themselves, how can they convert the heathen? How many have they converted? They have converted a great many into detestable hypocrites, but how many to Christianity? Look at the state of society in our towns—in every street. Old age is insulted, the poor are neglected, drunkenness, thefts, robberies, murders, debaucheries, divisions,

---

[42] *Ibid.*, Feb. 8, 1844, 152.
[43] See p. 286 regarding incorporations of theological seminaries.
[44] Royall: *Black Book*, I, 214; for articles on the author, see *The American Mercury*, Sept., 1927, XII, 87 ff.; *Va. Mag. Hist.*, VIII, 330; *Richmond Enquirer*, Oct. 4, 1854.
[45] Royall: *Black Book*, I, 156.
[46] *Ibid.*, 163, 147; cf. *Va. Evang. & Lit. Mag.*, V, 111–12, 166.
[47] Royall: *Black Book*, I, 165; cf. also *Va. Evang. & Lit. Mag.*, XI, 245 ff., where "Viator" ridicules the idea that the American Sunday School Union wished to foist a religious establishment upon the country.

broils, and strife abound. . . . It is mockery, and the height of impudence, to talk of civilizing the heathen, when you have not been able to civilize yourselves.[48]

In 1838, ten years after Mrs. Royal published her opinion, a writer in the *Southern Literary Messenger* gave his opinion of Sunday Schools:

I go for Sunday schools. Apart from religious edification, they have at least three distinct recommendations, even to the mere worldling, who looks to nothing beyond the temporal good of man. 1. Their lessons are learnt peculiarly well, and act with peculiar force upon the mind and character, from their coming but once a week. . . . 2. They afford opportunities for thousands, who (to the shame of Virginia be it spoken) have no other means of knowledge, to acquire much that may be useful. Some of these thousands cannot be spared from home on work-days: some, whose parents cannot afford to pay for their schooling, are not sent to the poor-schools, because pride will not let them consent to be singled out as objects of charity. Sunday schools avoid both these difficulties. The children of the rich and poor meet together there, without distinction—just as they would in those COMMON-SCHOOLS, the want of which has been so long and so justly a reproach to us. 3. Children who go to the Sunday School are kept out of mischief; saved from habits of vice and idleness. . . . Compare any number of regular Sunday scholars, with as many children of like condition, who have idled away their Sundays: and see which will furnish the larger number of good-for-nothing, or profligate people; if not criminals.[49]

He found, however, that many Sunday Schools had in recent years "been greatly perverted"; they had fallen from their former ideal of presenting a common Christianity. Instead of the good old books of *Sandford and Merton, Evenings at Home,* Edgeworth's *Early Lessons* and her *Parents' Assistant* and *Popular Tales,* Peter Parley's stories, and Sergeant's *Temperance Tales*—catechisms, essays, biographies, and tales, tending to illustrate mystic doctrines had been introduced. The writer asked:

Cannot the wise and good of every Christian denomination (including Unitarians and Catholics) determine, with some exactness, the great principles of religious truth in which they all agree; and then expel from Sunday schools, all books that teach any other religious tenets? The principles thus

---

[48] Royall: *Black Book,* I, 183.
[49] *So. Lit. Messenger,* IV, 224.

adopted, with moral duties, and the knowledge of Nature,—would present a range wide enough for the most active mind, during the longest life. . . .[50]

It would appear from the foregoing criticism, that other denominations gradually followed the stand taken, in 1826, by the Protestant Episcopal Church in favor of the use of denominational literature in their Sunday Schools.[51]   This development is particularly interesting in showing what seems to have been an inevitable tendency of denominationalism in handling educational matters.

That the Sunday School movement had a hampering effect upon the development of a civil elementary school system would appear from a study of the development of state legislation on this subject.   In spite of the opportunity for communities to benefit under the law of 1829 not only through free tuition and school buildings to be paid in part by the Literary Fund, only four counties, and those but in part, had taken advantage of the law by 1842.   It was only when it was evident to all observers that Sunday Schools were becoming denominational schools, that they were too limited in their curriculum to serve a society that was beginning to take an interest in science and industry, as is witnessed by the Mechanics Associations, Lyceums, and Library companies, incorporated after the thirties,[52] that the people were roused to express their opinion through conventions.[53]   But even then, as will appear, the religious interests of the state were not ready to surrender education wholly to the state.[54]

To many Virginians, the utilization of the one free day in the week for purposes of learning and religion—purposes far removed from the reputed idleness and dissipation characteristic of the colonial Sunday, had seemed an ideal solution of a social problem.   It seemed, too, to fit in with the economic situation of the poor; but except for such severe critics of society as Mrs.

---

[50] *Ibid.*, IV, 225.
[51] See p. 250.
[52] *Acts of Assembly, passim; cf.* Jan. 1, 1835, 155; Mar. 18, 1836, 249; Feb. 27, 1836, 252; Mar. 26, 1842, 101.
[53] See p. 345 *ff.*
[54] See p. 348 *ff.*

Royall and John Randolph,[55] there appears to have been little realization that the Sunday School, by approving child labor, was making poverty possible and respectable. While many were lauding the democratization of education and the fraternization of rich and poor as results of the movement, little heed was being taken of the fact that it was a movement adapted not to the real amelioration of society, but to keeping society in *statu quo.*]

That the movement did not succeed in keeping illiteracy down, even with the assistance given in that direction by the educational opportunities furnished by the Literary Fund, is evident from a statement of the Standing Committee of the Richmond Convention, in 1845, that "The ratio of those who cannot read in Virginia to her whole population, is as one to twelve and a half. While that of Massachusetts is as 1 to 164."[56]

The Sunday School movement, however, by its emphasis on a religious and moral literature for children was responsible for popularizing that type of literature in secular schools and helped to continue the tradition of the use of the Bible as a text-book. It probably contributed, too, to the continued insistence, on the part of the state, upon a good moral character in teachers paid by the state. The very limitations of the Sunday School made stand out in high relief the need of a more adequate system of education for the masses, the necessity of a public common school system.[57]

To appreciate fully the effects of the organized religious-educational activities represented in the movement initiated by the Bible societies and Sunday Schools, it is necessary to consider the literary propaganda of the religious-educational movement.

Views And Propaganda Regarding Religion In Education

Governor Thomas N. Randolph, in a message to the Senate in 1820, congratulating Virginia upon its increased religious fervor, in spite of the pessimistic prophecies at the time of separation of church and state, declared all that was necessary was to guard against "surreptitious endeavors to give a partial and interested direction to public opinion" upon the subject of religion by

---

[55] See p. 256.
[56] *So. Lit. Messenger*, Oct. 1845, XI, 605.
[57] *Cf.* Maddox: *Free Sch. Idea Va.*, 39–41.

means of an "indirect legislative sanction."[58]   The great difficulty in guarding legislation becomes evident when a review is
made of the literary propaganda designed to impress public
opinion with the necessity of permeating education with religious
influences.

The intention of the articles by "Iota" to influence legislation,
to which reference has been made,[59] appears also in his reference
to the religious prejudices arrayed against the University of
Virginia.   It was his opinion, that

. . . The whole religious part of the community will unite against any institution, which it is supposed will have influence in propagating error.   And
the opposition made by a warmly religious people is always formidable.   That
which smiles at the wheel and the stake, and triumphs in the flames, is not
to be trifled with or despised.[60]

The ease with which propaganda in favor of giving a religious
tone to education succeeded in influencing public opinion, was
probably due in part to the difficulty of comprehending how
education divorced from religious influence could operate in the
direction of inculcating those virtues and moralities which had
been associated with education when permeated, in the past, by
religion.   How could a perfect society be created without religion?   Rev. John H. Rice, in an address before the Literary
and Philosophical Society of Hampden-Sidney, in 1824, declared
that "nothing can supply the want of a body of well educated
men, led by professional duty to promote the interests of morals
and learning.   Such a body of men is furnished by the Christian
religion in its ministers."[61]   Without ministerial or religious
influences of some sort in education, it was difficult for many to
see how a moral society was to be created.   The popularity of
the Sunday School as an educational agency is to be explained
in part by its use of the Bible and a religio-moral literature presumed to be highly effective in inculcating all the virtues and
eradicating all the vices.   Further, the Sunday School was asso-

---

[58] *Jour., Senate*, Dec. 5, 1820, 7; for an example of English pessimism,
as late as 1827–28, with regard to separation of church and state, see Nevins,
A.: *Amer. Social History as Recorded by British Travellers*, 118.
[59] See p. 248.
[60] *Va. Evang. & Lit. Mag.*, V, 185.
[61] Morrison: *Six Addresses*, 12; *Va. Evang. & Lit. Mag.*, VIII, 7–8.

ciated with the opportunity for daily work, and a system of education that limited the opportunity of the poor to work was viewed by some as dangerous to society. The school commissioners of Williamsburg in their report for 1824, declared:

> . . . This committee are of opinion, that every system of education of the poor should be connected with labor: habits of indolence, and of course of vice, are not to be altogether overcome by the learning of schools. Humanity has to deplore the glaring and frequent vices of the learned. Employment, constant, regular and useful, united with proper instruction, may, and will enable the poor to supply their wants, know their rights and duties, and maintain and discharge them.[62]

Mr. William Maxwell, later President of Hampden-Sidney, in an address before the Literary and Philosophical Society, in 1826, gave as his ideal conception of Virginia society, that time when every man shall have his fowl or his ham in his pot, his Bible in his hand and in his heart, and understand "the principles of husbandry."[63]

There was one observer who looked with some misgivings upon this religious zeal and its interest in seeing that the poor worked six days a week. John Randolph in a letter in July, 1825, wrote:

> . . . Mammon is the true idol of our worship. The heart is with him. I see self-righteous people, who grind the faces of the poor, drive their slaves to the top of their speed, take the sacrament of the Lord's Supper, and then abuse their neighbors for worldly-mindness and want of religion, as if it were a piece of goods. . . .[64]

To John Randolph, like Mrs. Royall,[65] it seemed that fanaticism, not real religion, had spread over the land. Society, it appeared to him, in 1828, had deteriorated. Men of the vilest moral conduct were among the pillars of the church, he declared; women were neglecting their domestic duties—

> . . . many to the injury of their reputations, are running mad after popular preachers or forming themselves into clubs of one sort or another that only serve to gratify the love of selfishness and notoriety.[66]

---

[62] *Jour., H. Del.*, 1824–25, Sec. C, 30–31.
[63] Morrison: *Six Addresses*, 16–17.
[64] Bruce: *John Randolph*, II, 362.
[65] See p. 251.
[66] Bruce: *John Randolph*, II, 363; for Randolph's religious views, see Garland, H. A.: *John Randolph*, II, 62–64, 100; *So. Lit. Messenger*, XXVIII, 461; Niles: *Register*, July 30, 1836, L, 366–67.

Whether this harsh judgment was deserved, it is incontestable that the influence of women was an important factor in advanceing the spread of religion, from the standpoint, at least, of its formal prosperity, as seen in the building of churches, in the increased support for candidates for ministerial study, and in their contribution to the Sunday School movement and other religio-charitable efforts.[67]

While John Randolph and Mrs. Royall were regretting what they regarded as excessive religious zeal, "Olim," in the *Virginia Evangelical and Literary Magazine,* for 1828, gave it as his opinion that the leading influences in the country were against religion.[68] Colleges, he declared, afraid of the charges of sectarianism and bigotry were "cold in religion, and indifferent to all its interests." Where, then, could Christian parents send their sons to be educated? The only solution was to compel "a change in the management of public schools now established, or christians must unite, and build up others on truly christian principles."[69] Christians should not sit still when they did not know where to send their boys "without the imminent risque of their coming home to laugh at the Bible." This was a subject which involved not only Christians, but the entire well-being of society. The days of blasphemy in which the present statesmen grew up, might be gauged from the corruption of the body politic. With "another brood" growing up in the same principles, who see "infidelity and depravity . . . crowned with the honors of the country," "Olim" could no longer sit still and see the downfall of his country, his father-land, through vice and irreligion. It was necessary to correct the evil at the root, to begin with education. The solution was, first, to give emphatic expression on the subject of religion in colleges, by having it understood that parents required "instruction in the evidences, and general principles of christianity" to be brought into the course of study. In the second place, let the public be enlight-

---

[67] The contribution of women to the resuscitation of the Protestant Episcopal Church may be readily gleaned from the Appendix in Hawks: *Contrib. Ecc. Hist.,* I.

[68] *Va. Evang. & Lit. Mag.,* XI, 303 *ff.*

[69] *Ibid.,* 304.

ened by "strong, decided essays" on the subject to see its bearing on the best interests of the state. Third, Christians should seek

... the co-operation of intelligent and moral men, who, although not christians, yet are able to see the value of religious influences on the order and peace of society; and its absolute necessity in a government of laws.[70]

Fourth, Christians should give preference to institutions where the principles of Christianity are made the basis of education. Fifth, make the colleges a subject of special prayer. If, after trying these remedial measures, a reform cannot be effected, "there must be a complete secession of the church from the world in the matter of education" and Christians must institute their own system[71]

It is clear from "Olim's" argument that he would have Christians force upon the civil state a system of education that would distinguish it little, if at all, from any system that could be instituted under a union of church and state; that to him, the safety of society was posited on a religious foundation of life. Yet, if as John Randolph argued in the Virginia Convention of 1829–30, the admission of ministers as members of the Legislature would mean "*ipso facto* the union of Church and State," the program outlined by "Olim" would most certainly seem to indicate that very result.[72]

It was, undoubtedly, under the influence of propaganda like "Olim's" that Daniel Bryan, in 1828, recited his forty page poem on *Thoughts On Education In Its Connection With Morals* before the Literary and Philosophical Society of Hampden-Sidney. Bryan gave it as his opinion:

> Our favored land—the world itself—abounds
> With mournful proofs that virtue's sacred claims
> Command not in the nurseries of mind
> Their merited regards; that there the eye
> Of Discipline, though skilled and prompt to rouse
> The fervours of the youthful soul in quest
> Of classic glory, and the splendid ore

---

[70] *Ibid.*, 306.
[71] *Ibid.*
[72] Bruce: *John Randolph*, I, 628–30.

Lodged in the mines of Science, slumbers oft,
While siren passions wind their dangerous spells
Around the unguarded heart;—that doctrines there,
At war with the sublimest attributes
Of Christian truth, instil their fatal bane
Through tender breasts, and deeply taint the source
From which the streams of general morals flow.

.   .   .   .

THE appointed cure for these, and all the ills
That swell the catalogue of moral woes,
Is found within the Gospel's holy truths,
Let these be early on the mind impressed,
And carefully enforced from year to year
Until the character is formed mature
With their celestial doctrines deep imbued;

.   .   .   .[73]

Not only was the education of young men being impregnated
with the thought that all learning was secondary to that of the
Bible, that religion should receive the chief emphasis, but that
of young women was coming under a like educational philosophy.
At Mrs. Garnett's school at Elmwood, Essex County, pupils had
the benefit of a series of *Lectures on Female Education,* delivered by her husband, James M. Garnett. These lectures, in
printed form, ran through four editions in one year.[74]   Though
Mr. Garnett would not, remembering the Savior's parable of the
talents, have his youthful auditors believe that an ardent pursuit of science and literature was incompatible with true religion, yet he wished to impress them with the thought that the
eradication of all their vices, and the implanting of all the virtues was dependent upon accepting true religion as the only
principle of the soul.[75]

A strikingly similar evaluation of the objectives in education
appears in a valedictory address delivered by a principal of a
girls' school in 1829.   The proper educational emphasis was
neatly indicated in this recapitulation:

---

[73] Bryan, D.: *Thoughts On Education,* 9–10, 39.
[74] Garnett, J. M.: *Lectures on Female Education:* for a biographical note,
see Maddox: *Free Sch. Idea Va.,* 33; Morrison: *Beginnings Pub. Educ. Va.,*
93.
[75] Garnett: *Lectures on Female Education,* 295–99.

. . . That none may plead forgetfulness, let me briefly recapitulate once more, and for the last time, what our course has been. The primary objects always most earnestly pressed upon your attention have been, first and above all, to prepare yourselves for another and a better world, by a life of usefulness in the present; by the love and fear of God; . . . Your secondary objects have been the study of sciences and languages, physical and intellectual improvement, with a view, not to foster pride and vanity, but solely to increase your power of being useful. Lastly, you have been taught to acquire certain arts usually ranked under the head of ''accomplishments,'' but you have been invariably and perseveringly admonished to consider them merely as *recreations*, innocent if indulged in only occasionally, but sinful when made, as they too often are, the principal business of life. . . .[76]

Interestingly enough, objections to placing a supreme emphasis upon any single phase of educational development was voiced by Jonathan P. Cushing, President of Hampden-Sidney, a graduate of Dartmouth College. He had come to Hampden-Sidney, in 1819, as Professor of Chemistry and Natural Philosophy, and was President of the Institute of Education at the College in 1832.[77] In an address before the Virginia Historical and Philosophical Society, Mr. Cushing declared:

I would also observe, . . . that the common opinion of what ought to constitute a complete system of education, is, in some important respects, incorrect.

A system of education to be complete, should comprehend, the developing, strengthening, and maturing all the human powers.—These powers are divided into three great classes; *the physical, intellectual, and moral.* All of which in order to secure the highest degree of improvement, and the most perfect symmetry of which they are susceptible, should be fully and duly cultivated.[78]

---

[76] *So. Lit. Messenger*, I, 174; perhaps this valedictory was that of the Elmwood School, see p. 325; an advertisement of the school appeared in the *Richmond Enquirer*, Sept. 15, 1822; in this connection, may be quoted an excerpt from a letter of a ''President of the oldest college in Virginia,'' to his daughter, written immediately after her marriage: ''HISTORY, GEOGRAPHY, POETRY, MORAL ESSAYS, BIOGRAPHY, TRAVELS, SERMONS, and other well written religious productions, will not fail to enlarge your understanding, to render you a more agreeable companion, and to exalt your virtue. A woman devoid of rational ideas of religion, has no security for her virtue; it is sacrificed to her passions, whose voice, not that of GOD, is her only governing principle.'' *Ibid.*, I, 188.
[77] Morrison: *Beginnings Pub. Educ. Va.*, 54, 93.
[78] Cushing: *Va. Hist. Coll.* 1833, I, 28.

It was in the direction of developing all these aspects of education that Mr. Cushing wished the society to make investigations and prepare dissertations.

The very next year, however, Mr. Garnett came back with a defence of his own educational philosophy before Mr. Cushing's own Institute of Education. Expressing more succinctly the views of his *Lectures on Female Education*, Mr. Garnett declared that with whatever "rapidity and certainty" institutions indoctrinated youth in scholastic learning, "the paramount objects of all which deserves to be called education" would be missed unless moral and religious principles were "indelibly" fixed in the mind; only thus could humanity "form adequate conceptions of the great purposes for which they were created."[79]

The emphasis upon religion as being the only true basis for an understanding of life, for the perfection of society, and the assertion of a corresponding lesser value to be attached to scholastic learning, brought to the defence of the latter, a tactful champion in the person of Mr. George Tucker, Professor of Moral Philosophy in the University of Virginia. Speaking before the Virginia Historical and Philosophical Society, in 1835, Professor Tucker reviewed the contribution of philosophy, a synonym for which he seems to find in "reason," to religion. It is to philosophy that religion is indebted for freeing it from the superstitions imposed by fraud and credulity. As man's conception of what constituted the desirable features of morality in mankind changed—consonant, superior qualities were attributed to the Deity. In this transformation to superior virtues may be recognized the precepts of Christianity. The service of philosophy to religion was to separate from religion any dross which might cling to it, leaving "its own pure essence, undiminished and untouched." Those who fear, that, philosophy, which is hostile to superstition, is unfavorable to true religion, "have been too hasty in drawing general conclusions from particular facts." Professor Tucker went on to say:

. . . It is true that many of the philosophers of France, and some of those of Great Britain, during the last century, were not only opposed to the pre-

[79] Morrison: *Six Addresses*, 38–39; this address was reviewed in *Annals of Education*, V, 317 *ff.*

vailing creeds of their country, but seemed to have no very fervid religious feelings of any kind; but they were led first to make war on what they regarded as the abuses of religion, and then their attacks appear to be levelled against every thing which bore its name. It is highly probable that, by a natural process of the mind, from coming to hate the corruptions of christianity, they felt a prejudice against every thing which was associated with it. But on the other hand, we have seen some, occupying the very highest places in the scale of philosophers, who were sincere and zealous christians. Besides, the present age, which is the most philosophical the world has ever seen, is also the most generally and ardently devoted to christianity, as is evidenced by the extraordinary number of Churches, Bible Societies, Missionary Societies, Sunday Schools, &c. Let then the sincerely devout and pious dismiss their fears. . . .[80]

This recommendation to dismiss their fears found no response in the mind of Mr. Garnett, who apparently was not entirely impressed by the numerical strength of the religious activities enumerated by Professor Tucker. Instead, in a lecture before the Fredericksburg Lyceum, Mr. Garnett launched an attack upon the ''code of worldly morality,'' apparently his polite euphemism for ''anti-christian philosophy.'' He again asserted the necessity of a renewed emphasis upon making Christianity, religion, the basis of life.[81] Comparing the Christian code with the code of worldly morality, Mr. Garnett declared, that while the former could show thousands rescued from the lowest depths of profligacy and crime, the latter had not, by itself alone, effected a single case of restoration, its influence being at best *''preventive,''* not *''reclaiming.''* The worldly code sanctions much which the Christian code pronounces criminal.[82] The fact that many destitute of religion live exemplary lives, is no adequate proof, so far as education is concerned, ''of the sufficiency of the worldly code of morals, either to preserve or to reclaim mankind from vice and crime.'' While the worldly code of morality has no well defined standard of conduct—in the Christian code, ''everything is not only sure, but forever unchangeable.''

Further, in Mr. Garnett's opinion, practises in schools had been such as to minimize in the minds of youth, the importance

---

[80] *So. Lit. Messenger,* I, 407.
[81] *Ibid.,* I, 725 *ff.*
[82] *Ibid.,* 729.

of moral and religious knowledge. Unless this form of knowledge was given a supreme emphasis, the eternal welfare of the rising generation, a matter of infinitely deeper interest than anything which could possibly happen to the young in their present life, would be neglected.[83]   To strive to erect the edifice of education upon any other than a religious foundation might "possibly rear a very showy and even attractive house," but its materials would be "nothing better than "straw and stubble," continually liable to take fire from every flying spark—forever in danger of being blown down by every assailing wind."[84] Education was preparation for this life, "not as an *end*, but only as the means of attaining happiness in the next."[85]

Mr. Garnett was not alone in his zeal for the perfection of society as based on the Christian life.   A lengthy, unsigned article on "Christian Education" in the *Southern Literary Messenger*, some months before Mr. Garnett's, addressed to parents, begged:

> . . . O! ever while we live, let us make our children learn the Bible BY HEART, or not at all, that when they speak its language, they may speak as one whose "mouth speaketh out of the fulness of his own HEART."[86]

Mr. Lucian Minor, in 1835, delivered an "Address on Education," intended to emphasize the importance of education with respect to the permanence of republican institutions.   In discussing the curriculum, Mr. Minor, after urging that something of "Constitutional Law, and Political Right" might be taught even in childhood, placed his emphasis next on the importance of practical morals, "which teaches, and habituates us, to behave justly and kindly to our fellow creatures."   Mr. Minor fails, however, to suggest the Bible as a text-book, but declares, instead, that "No vehicle of moral instruction is comparable to the striking narrative."   He is confident no schoolboy will wish to rob an orchard after reading Miss Edgeworth's *Tarlton*, or fail

[83] *Ibid.*, 731.
[84] *Ibid.*, 732.
[85] *Ibid.*, 734.
[86] *Ibid.*, I, 433.

in facing with more than "Roman heroism" the daily occasions of life after reading *Sandford and Merton*.[87]

In a series of five lectures, in 1835–36, before the Fredericksburg Lyceum, Mr. Garnett gave a "Course on the Obstacles and Hindrances to Education, arising from the peculiar faults of Parents, Teachers and Scholars, and that portion of the public immediately concerned in directing and controlling our Literary Institutions."[88]   He found fault with teachers in compromising between a worldly code and the Christian code; in failing to implant morality in its appropriate soil, the heart.[89]   "Religious principle, consistently demonstrated by religious practice," must be taught and required.   He asked:

> . . . how many schools have we, where this is done? How many are there wherein not even *a pretence* is made of either public or private worship—of either moral or religious instruction? Numerous, deplorably numerous are the instances in which the poor pupils are all left to seek God or not, according to their own fancies; and where the miserable pretext for such criminal neglect is, that the Liberals of the present times, than whom, by the way, there are no greater bigots upon earth—bigots I mean in *unbelief*—would probably deem it an improper interference with the religious creeds of the scholars, if one word were ever uttered about religion at all.[90]

"Emulation," as one of the foundation stones for the superstructure of education, was vehemently denounced.   It led to the corollary that the object in education for boys was "money" and "distinction" in professions; while that, in education for girls, was "to get rich husbands."   In the meantime, "The great concerns of eternity are postponed to a less busy time."[91]

Trustees of schools were taken to task for not inquiring beyond the literary qualifications of teachers in charge of schools.[92] The failure of schools to insist on daily prayers and church attendance was a neglect which could be explained, according to Mr. Garnett, only by "a disbelief in the duty and utility of these practices."[93]

---

[87] *Ibid.*, II, 17 *ff.*, 20–21; Morrison: *Six Addresses*, 41 *ff.*
[88] *So. Lit. Messenger*, I, 725–34; II, 436–45, 477–86, 561–68, 613–22.
[89] *Ibid.*, II, 483.
[90] *Ibid.*
[91] *Ibid.*, II, 566.
[92] On actual practise in this respect, see p. 340 *ff.*
[93] *Ibid.*, 618.

Taking up the argument that even theological schools some-times turn loose upon society, infidels, hypocrites, and profligates, Mr. Garnett urged that a fair comparison could be made only by comparing this number with that of worthless young persons from all schools of every kind. He felt confident that the pro-portion from theological schools would be "almost beyond cal-culation smaller."

After all, according to Mr. Garnett, what, if there be no heaven, have scoffers to lose by the religious instruction of their children? The dread felt, by some marvellously scrupulous persons, of sectarianism is such that they refuse to teach the great fundamental truths in which all Christians agree. A negative attitude is as bad as open hostility. Mr. Garnett went on to say:

. . . The fact is, that in every school in the United States, wherein moral and religious instruction is neglected, many things are taught which *are contrary* to the principles of christianity. To prove this, look at the direction given to the conduct of the pupils. . . .[94]

Truly moral conduct can result only from genuine religious principles. Education on this basis alone can diminish the enor-mous mass of vice and crime. It is almost in every case the miserable victims of infidel opinions imbibed in early youth, who compose that motley, pitiable group which fill our jails and penitentiaries. Mr. Garnett asked whether it was "persons who have been morally and religiously educated from infancy, or such as have been most shamefully, most guiltily neglected in these all important respects," who restrained their "criminal passions?"[95] The only solution for the ills of society is to es-tablish schools which have as their basis "the Gospel of Christ as well as its divine morality."[96]

Rev. E. F. Stanton in an address, in 1835, at Hampden-Sidney, declared that religion was the only safeguard and stability of nations; without it, governments neither prospered nor endured.

---

[94] *Ibid.*, II, 620.
[95] *Ibid.*, II, 621; for the influence of George K. Taylor, of Virginia, in support of the penitentiary system as a remedial agent, see *Richmond Enquirer*, June 15, 1821.
[96] *So. Lit. Messenger*, II, 622.

Without the religious principle, educated people are but mad-men, ''accoutred for the work of mischief.'' The principle on which politicians act, that religion should be afforded no special encouragement, but left to spontaneous development, can have only one issue, ''an exuberant growth of noxious and destructive passions.'' It were better to rear youth ''in ignorance and barbarism,'' than to permit American academies and colleges to operate without a religious connection.[97]

The importance of religion to the safety and well-being of the state was taken up in a number of other addresses and articles during this period. That the Christian religion was the one principle which could sustain public virtue as well as private, that it acted as a restraint on vice, taught man humility, self-knowledge, and self-government, was the opinion of Thomas W. Gilmer in an address before the Virginia Historical and Philosophical Society, published in 1837.[98]

In 1838, there appeared a number of articles on ''The Influence of Morals on the Happiness of Man, and the Stability of Social Institutions,'' by a native of Petersburg, Virginia.[99] The theme of these articles was that toleration of opinions subversive of religion, and of publications destructive of morals, was injurious to the stability of society and the happiness of man. The Reformation of the 16th century, which ''erected a thousand different altars'' with its fostering of freedom of religious opinion paved the way for the infidel philosophy of the French Encyclopaedists, whose appalling doctrines were ''subversive alike of government, social order, morals, and religion.'' The corruption that ensued, melted the bonds of society ''as bands of flax before the flames of revolution.''[100] The Miltonic argument that truth was never known to be put to the worse in a free and open encounter, while sound in regard to political man, was, in the present condition of mankind, inapplicable to social man. For who would deny that the Bible with its every lesson of morality, with ''the most imposing truths, revealed by the Deity himself,'' had been unable, such was the perversity of

97 *Ibid.*, II, 245.
98 *Ibid.*, III, 97 *ff.*
99 *Ibid.*, IV, 145 *ff.*, 273 *ff.*
100 *Ibid.*, 145–46, 273, 276.

man, "to wrestle with error, that myriads have been and still are seduced from the paths of truth and morality, by the apostles of untruth and infidelity."[101] The Reformation, in freeing mankind from dominion by priesthood, by recognizing and establishing freedom of religious opinion, had raised a new and formidable enemy to religion "in the shadowy monster INFIDELITY." The rapid increase of infidelity and licentiousness "in these latter days" could only mean, finally, desecration of altars and broken charters. The lesson of history was plain, that licentiousness of morals and opinions is the prelude to catastrophe in nations as well as in individuals. The only hope of a republican government is to impress upon its youth that the prosperity of the nation depends upon the purity of its morals; that this is opposed to that indulgence of freedom in religious opinion which permits the preaching of infidelity.[102] Pure morality, essential to the preservation of social institutions, reposes upon revealed religion.[103]

The native of Petersburg did not remain unanswered. The reply, by a native of Goochland, centered in the thought that any system of morals or religion which was not due to the exercise of freedom of inquiry, but was forced upon a people, would inevitably prove to be degrading and corrupting.[104] Stability was not the most essential desideratum. While agreeing with the native of Petersburg that corrupt morals and licentiousness must be opposed, it was not in opposition to the Reformation, and support of Popery, that the remedy must be sought for staying these evils. The ancient popish doctrine that the tendency of knowledge was immoral and licentious, which represented that the fruit of the tree of knowledge brought crime and death, was a "libel upon the goodness of God."[105] Knowledge is the truth which leads men out of moral and intellectual darkness. The attempt to prostrate it, is the expedient of tyrants and oppressors. It is to knowledge that we are indebted for an understanding of the precepts of virtue and reading of the pages of

---

[101] *Ibid.*, 148.
[102] *Ibid.*, 150–51.
[103] *Ibid.*, 277.
[104] *Ibid.*, IV, 524 *ff*.
[105] *Ibid.*, 528.

religion. Evil in the world is not to be attributed to the culture of the reasoning power; any good, any blessing, may be perverted. In free and enlightened countries the triumph of knowledge perverted to the uses of evil is only momentary. It is freedom of thought, which leads to investigation, which leads to the discovery of truths, which exalts the condition of man as a rational being.[106]

The importance of religion in creating a pure literature, also, was the theme of occasional addresses. In 1838, Dr. D. L. Carroll, President of Hampden-Sidney, in an address before the Franklin Literary Society of Randolph-Macon College, emphasized "the duty of educated men *to bring the influence of the Bible to bear on the formation of our literature.*"[107] Commenting on this address, a reviewer in the *Southern Literary Messenger* said:

. . . Give the people religion, and give it to them early, and give it to them always. It will make them orderly, moral, thoughtful, intelligent, aspiring, enterprising and "ready unto every good work." Then schools will arise and learning will advance. . . .[108]

James E. Heath, the author of the novel, *Edgehill*, in an address before the Richmond Lyceum, in 1838, declared the maintenance of religious institutions and the adoption of wise systems of education, both, as necessary to avert danger to the country.[109]

Propaganda in favor of religious instruction or education controlled by religious interests received a new importance after 1840, because of the many conventions held with a design to improve the public school system. In 1841, the year in which Virginia was being stirred by the first of these educational conventions, Professor George E. Dabney, of Washington College, reviewed the educational situation in the *Southern Literary Messenger*.[110] Raising the question, whether Virginia was exerting herself to give her citizens that intellectual and moral power

---

[106] *Ibid.*, 778–79.

[107] Carroll, D. L.: *An Address*, 18.

[108] *So. Lit. Messenger*, IV, 694; for a resumé of an address, in 1848, on "The Importance of a Pure Literature" by Rev. S. J. P. Anderson, see James: *Lower Norfolk Co., Va. Antiquary*, IV, 27.

[109] *So. Lit. Messenger*, IV, 705 *ff.*

[110] *Ibid.*, VII, 631 *ff.*; Morrison: *Beginnings Pub. Educ. Va.*, 58–61.

necessary to give realization to freedom, Professor Dabney went on to say that the supineness of the Legislature might be ascribed to the desire to keep the masses in ignorance so that they might be more readily deceived and misled, or else to an insensibliity on the part of the Legislature to the evils of mental darkness and moral degradation. The defects of the present system were due to the absence of permanent schools and schoolhouses, and inadequate care in selection of teachers. The government which interfered to protect the public health had a right to protect the minds and morals of children from quack teachers. Another defect was the inadequate support of academies and colleges. The surplus of the Literary Fund voted in 1821, and made effective in 1836, had benefited, to date, because of the discretion given school commissioners, only about seventeen academies. The intermediate schools should be under the control of the State, and partly endowed by it. It was right that all should be taxed for the common benefit of all—for the maintenance of an educational system which was "at least equal to courts of justice, for the preservation of life and property."[111] It was necessary that the improvement of the mental and moral powers of the people should keep pace with the development of physical resources, if the development of the latter was to have a salutary effect on the people.[112] Apparently, Dr. Dabney seems to have felt that only by a larger element of state control of the educational situation was it possible to assure adequately the moral development of the masses. But to Mr. Garnett, who addressed the Richmond Educational Convention, in December, 1841, the radical defect of the entire school system, from the primary school to the University, lay not only in the question of control, but also in that of direction—in making the great end of education not merely the advancement of the worldly interests of the students, but that of their moral and spiritual natures. That Mr. Garnett, in his great zeal for the advancement of religion in education, seems to have preferred to ignore the real facts will appear from a study of the actual situation in schools.[113] In Mr. Garnett's opinion, the increase of the means of education had given a new

111 *So. Lit. Messenger,* VII, 635.
112 *Ibid.,* 636.
113 See p. 343.

direction to crime, diverting it from crimes against the person to crimes against property.[114]   Admitting the deficiencies of the educational system in Virginia, education was, nevertheless, certainly much more diffused over the state than it had been formerly.   If such education were in itself sufficient to make man useful and happy, and communities correspondingly virtuous— how was it, Mr. Garnett asked, that the criminal statistics of Virginia revealed such a different story?   Referring to the crime situation, he said:

> . . . These—unless I have greatly misunderstood them—exhibit a most alarming and increasing catalogue of swindling, theft, robbery, murders and assassinations, both public and private, besides many other crimes and atrocities, which are too shocking to mention, that are frequently perpetrated in almost every part of our country.   Many of them are not committed by such men only as can neither read nor write, but by vast numbers of those who have enjoyed all the advantages of what is commonly styled *"the best education,"* and have gone through the usual course of studies generally followed in all our schools and colleges.   Can this system then be perfect?   Nay, is it not radically defective?   And ought not the strong arm of the law to interpose for its correction—at least so far as law can effect this most desirable end? . . .[115]

Particularly severe was his denunciation of the inadequate care exercised in the selection of and supervision of teachers by school commissioners; public funds went either "to feed some of the drones or moths of the social hive, or a portion of the poisoners of the public morals."[116]   If Virginia was to have popular education as it should be, it must be founded on the basis of religion and morality.   It was in the Sunday Schools that a practical guide was to be found.   The preparation to meet the fortunes of life with true Christian fortitude is never given in the public schools, from the lowest to the highest.   Man indoctrinated with the religious spirit, is a truly noble and glorious being, without such indoctrination, "though possessed of all the learning of the schools," he is an utterly base, abject, despicable creature.[117]

What Mr. Garnett hoped to achieve was an integration of religion with the education which the state was furnishing.   It

---

114 *So. Lit. Messenger*, VIII, 116.
115 *Ibid.*, 118.
116 *Ibid.*
117 *Ibid.*, 120.

was his opinion that in the field of education, a union of church and state was not only desirable, but essential for the improvement of society. The advances already made, as will be shown,[118] in permeating education with a religious tone, were practically ignored by him, apparently because the results appeared to be so low in the scale of what he believed was possible, if education were posited wholly on the religious ideal.

The attitude of those impressed with the necessity of indoctrinating youth with religious principles is well illustrated in an address, before the Alumni Association of Washington College in 1843, by Rev. Archibald Alexander, D.D.[119] He declared the notion becoming prevalent of excluding religious instruction especially from common schools was a most dangerous error. That any objection should exist to making religion, the most important of all subjects, a part of every system of education, might seem strange to some, but there were, Dr. Alexander stated, some plausible objections, such as the alleged one

. . . that the minds of youth should not be prejudiced in favor of any religion, before the judgment has come to maturity; that the minds of children should be left unoccupied until they are capable of judging for themselves on this important subject.[120]

Dr. Alexander went on to say that if this plan were pursued in all subjects, there would be an end to the education of youth. But the human mind cannot be kept free from religious opinions and impressions, "and if we neglect to inculcate sound principles, such as are erroneous and dangerous will be adopted. The only way to keep out error is to pre-occupy the mind with truth."[121] Religion is as much needed by the young as by the old; to neglect the inculcation of its doctrines would be the greatest injury to the child. The more popular objection that since there are so many sects and denominations, religion cannot be made a part of the educational system "without interfering with the creeds or consciences of one sect or another," he held might be a valid reason for not giving peculiar denominational teaching in schools, but not a valid reason for refusing to teach

---

[118] See p. 340–44.
[119] *Wash. & Lee Hist. Papers*, 1890, No. 2, 113 *ff*.
[120] *Ibid.*, 124.
[121] *Ibid.*

those things "in which all Protestants agree." Dr. Alexander went on to say, "As all admit that the Bible is true and the source of all correct information on the subject of religion, there can be no reasonable objection to having it read in schools." Of course, the Doctor admitted that the Romanists did not approve the Protestant version of the Bible, but as they "are unwilling to have their children made acquainted with the contents of the Holy Scriptures, except such parts as their priests choose to communicate" they may be disregarded. "Happily," the Doctor declared, "in most parts of our country, this class of people are not found, or in numbers so small that no exceptions need be made to accommodate them." Where they are numerous, their children should be gathered into schools of their own, and not "allowed to interrupt that course of instruction which is judged to be the most efficient, in a country where four-fifths of the people are Protestants."[122] It is evident that Dr. Alexander's Christian point of view did not extend to having minority religious groups benefit in any way from the advantages of public education. Aside from ignoring the question of taxation in the system which he outlined as desirable—he failed to take into consideration the social and political aspects of a society divided under state auspices on a religious basis.

An anonymous writer "On Public Education in Virginia," in the *Southern and Western Literary Messenger and Review,* in November, 1847, after declaring that the recent interest aroused in education, by a set of philanthropists, was dying away, proceeded to discuss aims in education. He declared that the education which was wanted was one that would show man "that all he learns and does has reference to an eternal life."[123] With this as the ultimate end of education, he asks, "what means have been used for its attainment?" The statement that the amount of crime has not diminished with the increase in education, is not alarming when what that education has been, is considered. Its object has been to supply the intellect with knowledge, without considering its applicability to the formation of character. The writer was, however, no proponent of equali-

---

[122] *Ibid.,* 125–26.
[123] *So. & West. Lit. Messenger & Rev.,* Nov., 1847, XIII, 685 *ff.*

tarianism; where funds were insufficient for all grades of education, the preference should be given to the higher, as the graduates of these schools would be "centers of light to all around." Did not the principle of inequality run through all creation, exemplified by the greater light to rule by day, and the lesser by night? After noting with satisfaction the part taken by the Presbyterian church, in education, the writer wonders,

. . . that the ministry of other Protestant churches have not been more alive to its importance, in this they might learn much wisdom from the Roman Catholic priesthood; the great part they have had in the education of their church, is no doubt the chief source of their unbounded influence, an influence which, though badly used, has been nobly earned.[124]

If ministers could be awakened to the importance of uniting education to the duties of their ministry, "we might, perhaps, by associating them with our school commissioners, secure some officers more interested in the subject than those we have hitherto had." It is thus seen by what gradual steps, the religious-minded hoped, if unable to obtain full educational control, to, at least, secure some point of control which would assure giving a religious tone to education.

An article on "The North and The South" in *De Bow's Review* for 1849 discusses educational and criminal statistics. In this connection, it is of interest to note that Brissot De Warville who travelled through the United States, in 1788, was of the opinion that "Crimes are more frequent in Virginia than in the northern States. This results from the unequal division of property, and from slavery."[125] The writer in *De Bow's Review* found that the amount of crime in proportion to the white population was four times as great in New York as in Virginia, and that Massachusetts had twice the amount of crime that Virginia had. In proportion to population, all the New England States had twice the number of penitentiary convicts of Virginia.[126]

---

[124] *Ibid.*, 688.

[125] De Warville, J. P. B.: *New Travels U. S.*, 435.

[126] *De Bow's Review*, VII, 309; it must be noted that comparisons of this kind are apt to be fallacious, as the definitions of crimes and penalties are not the same in all states.

The favorable showing in Virginia was attributed by the writer to the fact that instead of Episcopalians, the Baptists who had a stricter form of religious discipline, were the predominant sect.[127] While the census of 1840 revealed only about 4,500 illiterates above the age of twenty in Massachusetts as compared with the more than 58,500 of Virginia, the writer went on to say that Virginia in her social intercourse had a system of oral instruction which compensated for the want of schools. Social intercourse, while it did not teach people to read or write, taught people to think and converse, to interchange opinions and diffuse intelligence. The writer noted that Virginia was about nine times as large as Massachusetts, that it would need that many times the number of schools and teachers that existed in Massachusetts to afford the same conveniences for attending school. As it was, in many places owing to the thinly settled character of Virginia, not ten scholars could be found in ten square miles. The writer did not, however, make any reference to the connection, if any, between the criminal and educational statistics, or the connection between density of population to crime.[128]

Moncure D. Conway in a pamphlet entitled *A Plea of Education, Virtue and Thrift, VS. Ignorance, Vice and Poverty,* addressed to the State Convention of Virginia, 1850, took up the negative view of the progress of society as expressed by Emerson, that "Society never advances," and declared it to be ignoble, tending to the belief that "ignorance alone is bliss." He held, on the contrary, "THAT IT IS TO THE INTEREST OF EVERY MEMBER OF A COUNTRY THAT EVERY OTHER MEMBER THEREOF SHOULD BE EDUCATED!"[129] Defective education meant the acceptance of pernicious principles. To the objectors to the district system on moral grounds, who "doubt if it's going to keep our penitentiary empty," he replied, by reviewing the educational history of the 27,948 criminals in New York for the period 1840–48.

---

[127] *Ibid.,* 311; as a matter of fact according to the census of 1850, the predominance was going to the Methodists; the writer estimated the Baptists as at 80,000, the Methodists at 30,000, see p. 312 for census figures for 1850; *cf.* also *De Bow's Review,* X, 543.

[128] *Ibid.,* VII, 311–12.

[129] Conway, M. D.: *Free Schools in Va.,* 6.

He declared that of this number only 1,182 had a common school education; 414, a tolerably good education; and only 128 were well educated; with about one-half of the rest able merely to read and write. As for the fact that a certain professor had committed murder, Mr. Conway answered, ''Very well: neither did being one of Christ's disciples hinder Judas from being a vile traitor; now shall I, for that renounce the Christian persuasion?''[130]

Mr. John R. Thompson, editor of the *Southern Literary Messenger* in an address before the Literary Societies of Washington College, in 1850, declared that the prestige of Virginia had declined considerably because of her failure to provide adequately for the diffusion of knowledge among her citizens. He asked:

. . . How many are there of those who make up the monthly assemblages upon our court-greens, whose minds are in the dark, not only as to the history of the past and the general condition of the globe they live upon, but as to the first doctrines of moral accountability and the benign truths of religion? . . .[131]

Mr. Thompson held with Mr. Garnett that when one had written himself a man of letters as far as scholarship could make him so, he would still need ''the safeguard of pure and lofty principles of character.'' It would be futile to diffuse knowledge without enlightening the people at the same ''time with the precepts of a Divine morality.'' To make a state great and prosperous, something more is wanted than mere knowledge among the people.[132]

In a commencement address at Richmond College, in 1850, John Howard, in reviewing the history of suffrage in Virginia, attempted to show that loss of universal suffrage was the corollary of ignorance. It was the right of every citizen to see to it that every child received an education

. . . if not commensurate with the numerous and responsible obligations it will be called upon to fulfil to itself, to society, and to its God, at least in-

---

130 *Ibid.*, 18.
131 Thompson, J. R.: *Education and Literature in Va.*, 13–14.
132 *Ibid.*, 29; *cf.* also Morrison: *Beginnings Pub. Educ. Va.*, 73; *So. Quart. Rev.*, III, 290.

struction sufficient to read the constitution and laws by which it is to be governed, and the Holy Volume whose teachings fill the mind with that wisdom which cometh down from above and illuminate the way from earth to Heaven.[133]

The free school system, he declared was the only one by which Virginia could ever hope to accomplish so noble an end.[134]

In an address at the opening of the Richmond Athenaeum, in 1852, John Robertson declared that reason and experience concurred "in proving that mental cultivation at once disseminates the seeds of virtue, and best prepares the mind to receive and mature them." It was owing to "the ignorance and the consequent immorality of the many," with its tendency "to demoralize the entire mass," that the best instructed became contaminated.[135]

Popular knowledge as a necessity of popular government, was the theme of James C. Bruce, in a lecture before the Danville Lyceum, in 1853. Mr. Bruce declared:

. . . Our laws are every day more and more relaxed, our children are more and more neglected, and the tide of ignorance and of vice is settling to our shores from the old world, with fuller and fuller volume. . . . The rights of property, the sanctity of marriage, and the truth of our holy religion are not now as formerly, covertly attacked but openly assailed. Secret foes, counting on their increased numbers, have assumed the attitude of undisguised enemies. They may be in a minority now as they doubtless are, but is there not danger that this minority may grow into a majority?[136]

Referring to the various charges against slavery, as being "a propagator of a false religion—a corrupter of morals—a despiser of law and order—a barrier to progress—a promoter of social inequality—an enemy to knowledge,"—it was the last

---

[133] Howard, J.: *An Address on Popular Education*, 30.

[134] *Ibid.; cf. So. Quart. Rev.*, III, 302; the extent of illiteracy in Virginia may be gathered from Howison's *History of Virginia*, published in 1848, in which he stated, basing his remarks on the census of 1840, that besides the more than 58,000 illiterates over 20 years of age, there were 166,000 children between 7 and 16 years of age, of whom about 28,000 attended the Free and Lancasterian schools, an average of 12 weeks in the year; 12,000 went to colleges, academies and classical schools; the remaining 126,000 attended no school at all, learned only what poor and ignorant parents could impart. *De Bow's Review*, X, 547; cf. also *So. Lit. Messenger*, XIX, 298.

[153] Robertson, J.: *Introductory Address Opening the Richmond Athenaeum*, 21.

[136] *So. Lit. Messenger*, XIX, 295.

which was the most serious indictment. But, argued Mr. Bruce,
if the people were educated in virtue and knowledge, then the
institution of slavery would stand the test of any tribunal.[137]
It was not in slavery which could furnish a source of revenue
to meet the cost of schools, nor the sparseness of population, but
in the apathy of the people, and the want of appreciation of the
vital importance of education, that the true reason for the poor
educational showing of Virginia as compared with Massachusetts
was to be found.[138] It was to the Christian that the subject of
education made a distinct appeal. The Bible was a sealed book
to 58,000 citizens. Mr. Bruce went on to say:

> . . . Missionaries are sent abroad on errands of mercy to distant continents,
> and to isles of the sea, the most remote and the most barbarous, for the
> purpose of proclaiming the doctrines of christianity; and yet the key to
> its mysteries and its hopes is with a marvellous inconsistency of benevolence
> refused to our own people. The church has in all ages been the steward of
> learning, and is its great patron by prescription. . . . Let the voice of
> religion, which I thank God is yet potential in this land, be heard in favour
> of general education. Let christians of every sect throw aside their rival-
> ries, their contentions, and their party strifes which disgrace them in the
> eyes of the world, and stand together in brotherly love on the wide platform
> of charity, and lend their united councils and their united strength to that
> cause on which hang the best hopes of philanthropy and religion.[139]

Mr. Bruce took hope from the Bible that a brighter epoch was
shadowed forth. "The reign of vice and ignorance cannot be
perpetual." Mr. Bruce was convinced that by making men
wiser, they were made better. While individuals in exceptional
cases might be found, who having intelligence, were without
virtue, history gave no account of a community of this kind.
"A wise people are a virtuous people, and a virtuous people are
a free people all the world over."[140]

While most proponents of education demanded it, because of
a passion for the creation of a Utopian society, some bold spirits,
tiring of the "Chambered Nautilus" argument, began to demand education as a right. The *Richmond Enquirer* quoted
with approval the editor of the *Leesburg Democrat*:

[137] *Ibid.*, 297–98.
[138] *Ibid.*, 299.
[139] *Ibid.*, 300–01.
[140] *Ibid.*, 302.

. . . We expect no lull of human passion, nor do we dream that temperance, social order and prudence, will thereby pervade the whole mass of the community. We do not look upon it as possessing any transmuting power, or as the infallible cure for all social and political diseases; yet none will question its beneficial power, and its inestimable blessings to those that will receive it. Every one is ready to admit its undeniable effects as a corrective and a paliative of many social evils—as a sedative against political disquiet—as a privilege, from which it is envious malignity to exclude any class—as a right, which it is not for us to withhold, because it may be abused by some or neglected by others.[141]

A rather unique explanation for the fall of college students from moral grace was offered by "C" in a letter to the *Richmond Enquirer*. It was in the imperfection of instruction, this correspondent argued that a fruitful source of dissipation at college and in after life is to be found. The student enters college, but

. . . Having been imperfectly *grounded* in his different studies, he falls in the rear of those who are his inferiors in *natural* talent. It is now too late to retrace his steps; and, too proud to have it said by his classmates that he studies hard and stands badly, he turns to his bottle! With liquor and cards he manages to kill *troublesome* time, and down tumble the magnificent aircastles of his fond father. . . .[142]

Mr. "C" was pleased to note a call for a "Convention of Teachers" to be held in Richmond where improvements in the art of managing or instructing boys were to be discussed.

A favorite argument of the proponents of free school systems was that education would serve as a deterrent from crime. Thus Mr. Conway in scanning the New York statistics had shown that the curve of frequency of crime was greatest among the least educated. A writer in *De Bow's Review*, for 1854, collated certain statistics from the census reports of 1850 and found that "The 'land of steady habits' is no longer with the New-Englanders and the people of the free States," that "the ten Northern free states had twice as many criminals as the ten Southern slave states, though the latter had four times as many

---

[141] *Richmond Enquirer*, Jan. 28, 1854.
[142] *Ibid.*, Feb. 24, 1854.

persons unable to read or write.'' The number of criminals in Massachusetts on June 1, 1850, were 301, in Virginia, 188.[143] The writer of the article stated that he gave the information without comment, leaving it ''as a nut for philosophers and moralists to crack.'' However, it is evident that while comparative statistics of this kind are interesting enough, they are not a reliable basis on which to draw conclusions. The same types of crimes may not be punished in the states compared, nor may the punishment of crime be pursued with the same vigor in the places compared.[144]

An editorial in the *Richmond Enquirer*, in June, 1854, discussed the question of the relation of education to crime, and of punishment to crime. The editorial declared that while education sharpened the sensibility to shame, and increased the control of the intellect over the passions and animal propensities, thus diminishing ''the frequency of the more brutal and atrocious offences against humanity,'' it did not relieve society of criminals. Whether because of a more vigilant police or because more things were listed as penal offences, crime did not seem to have disappeared in proportion to the advance of civilization.[145] The editorial went on to say that prompt and adequate punishment was the only security of society against crime. Until human nature has been ''disciplined and subdued by the morality of the christian faith,'' society must enact and rigidly enforce proper penalties against crime. Society in recent years had come to regard crime as ''less the result of ill-regulated passion and want of principle, than of a defective cerebral organization,''—with a consequent sympathetic attitude to criminals. The writer declared that

---

[143] *De Bow's Review*, XVI, 578–80; an article in the same *Review* for 1855, XIX, 282, gave the following statistics based on the census of 1850 for Massachusetts and Virginia respectively, native white population 819,144 and 871,393; free colored 9,064 and 54,333; foreign 163,598 and 22,952; number of prisoners in state prisons, native white 264 and 121; free colored 50 and 67; foreign 158 and 19.

[144] Articles of this type, appearing in a responsible journal cannot be ignored, because they played a part in forming public opinion.

[145] *Richmond Enquirer*, June 13, 1854.

In profession, at least, this theory of crime and punishment has made
but little progress in the South; but we are not sure that its spirit is not
sadly interfering with the execution of the laws against malefactors. . . .[146]

It is clear from this editorial, that if punishment of crime was
not pursued with the same vigor in all parts of the country,
that statistical comparisons such as in the articles in *De Bow's
Review,*[147] are not sound.   When it is kept in mind, too, that the
better policing of crowded urban areas will result in larger detection and punishment of crime, the difficulty of drawing conclusions from criminal statistics gathered under disparate conditions is clear.

That the editorial sentiment of the *Richmond Enquirer,* however, was friendly to the opinion that education was an ameliorating influence in the reduction of crime is indicated in their
approval of a House of Refuge for the 33 convicts, from 10 to
20 years of age, lodged in the Penitentiary.[148]   The editor hoped
that institutions would be established in Wheeling and Richmond,
"and that the reformed inmates may go forth in each division of
the State to bear testimony in favor of these beneficent institutions in Virginia."[149]

Other problems besides that of the connection between crime
and education occupied the attention of the *Richmond Enquirer*
in 1854.   There was the perennial topic of infidelity.   Referring
to the fact that astronomy and geology had been "successively
employed to discredit the authority of Scripture," the writer
declared that "more thorough research, . . . and a clear insight
into the mysteries of nature" had corrected rash and imperfect
generalizations so that "in the end, the discoveries of science
have confirmed the revelations of Scripture."   Now that astronomy and geology had deserted to the Bible, the apostles of infidelity had solicited the aid of Ethnography and pretended

. . . to have discovered that races are original and permanent types, and
not the modified forms of essential unity. . . . They affirm the impossibility

---

146 *Ibid.*
147 See p. 273.
148 *Richmond Enquirer,* Feb. 24, 1854.
149 *Ibid.*

of the descent of the various races of men from a single pair—denouncing the story of Adam and Eve as childish and absurd, and unworthy of respect among intelligent minds.[150]

The hasty generalizations and rash conclusions of such false science as is embodied in *Types of Mankind* are the foundation on which "infidelity takes its stand."[151]

The *Richmond Enquirer* took occasion to note in the summer of 1854 that "Know-nothingism," with its spirit of opposition to Catholicism and the foreign born, was contrary to the spirit of Virginia and could not flourish on its soil—"It is not forgotten that Virginia was the first to recognize *religious liberty* by legislative enactment, and the first to protest against an *alien law.*"[152]

While these were the sentiments of the *Richmond Enquirer,* Bishop Meade quoted a letter of B. B. Minor, written about this time to the effect that

. . . Whilst the motto of every patriot and Christian should be, "A religious nation, and not a national religion," yet a connection between Church and State is apt to confer upon the State the benefit of an express recognition, in all enterprises of public pith and moment, of God's supremacy and superintending providence. . . .[153]

Rev. M. W. Jackson, of Charlotte County, in a pamphlet, published in 1854, entitled *Wealth and Health or a Guide to Parents in the Education of Children*, while urging that youth "at an early period, should have their minds directed to the ways and means of support, and the best methods of promoting health," declared that religion was sadly neglected in the schools, and that its proper text-book, the Bible, was "now almost discarded." According to Mr. Jackson, this indicated a bad moral condition of teachers and patrons. He asked whether a wise people would endeavor "to blot out the sun," that they might "be guided by a feebler taper?" If the style of the Bible "is a little antiquated," compensation is found "in the sublimity of its doc-

---

[150] *Ibid.*, April 29, 1854.
[151] *Ibid.*
[152] *Ibid.*, July 13, 1854; *Richmond Coll. Hist. Papers*, June, 1916, I, 309–35.
[153] Meade: *Old Churches, Ministers, and Families*, I, 117.

trines and the purity of its precepts.'' As a power in securing subordination, the Bible was superior to the birch. He went on to say, ''If it cannot be systematically taught and expounded, at least let it be read with seriousness, and portions of it committed to memory.''[154] Sunday Schools, too, should be encouraged. ''Education'' is a misnomer when applied to a course of study which does not embrace religion. In Mr. Jackson's opinion, there had been very little improvement in common school books for the last half-century, except for Dr. McGuffey's series; however, he recommended also Webster's *Spelling Book* and Murray's *English Grammar*.[155]

Another pamphlet of clerical advice on the subject of education was the *Pastoral Letter* published by Bishop Meade in 1858. The Bishop took as his theme, the subject of ''Education, chiefly in its bearing on the moral and religious character of the children and youth of our State and Diocese.'' He noted with satisfaction the changed attitude of Virginia young men and women to the profession of teaching—former scorn had changed to respect, as evinced by the ''hundreds of the sons and daughters of Virginia thus engaged.''[156] The Bishop then traced the history of religious instruction in education from ancient times, showing that it had always been the duty of teachers to give instruction in morals and religion. ''The common consent of mankind,'' declared the Bishop, ''points to this truth, that religion, the greatest, most sublime and important of all sciences, is to be taught to the young.'' To exclude the Bible from the schools is ''most insulting to its Great Author.'' Let all the subjects that may exist be studied in schools, but only in light of the Bible. It was his opinion:

. . . This book should open our schools each day. Every teacher should read a well selected portion of its sacred contents each morning, and sometimes add a few plain words of explanation and affectionate exhortation. A brief view of the evidences of its Divine original should be studied in every high school and college in the land. . . .[157]

---

154 Jackson, M. W.: *Wealth and Health*, 17.
155 *Ibid.*, 18–19.
156 Meade, W.: *Pastoral Letter*, 6; for other evidence as to the changed Virginian attitude toward teaching as a profession, see ''The Confessions of a Pedagogue''—*So. Lit. Messenger*, XXX, 46.
157 Meade: *Pastoral Letter*, 10–11.

The Bishop went on to say, "Who would venture to raise any sectarian objection to so Godly a practice, through fear that a word might sometimes be used not in strict accordance with his church or system?" He noted the happy effects of the limited religious instruction in Sunday Schools and the "genuine revivals" which were the outcomes of the efforts of pious teachers in high schools, colleges, and female institutes.[158] He declared that where large numbers are thrown together, it is particularly important that government and discipline should be under religious influence.[159] As for punishment in school, it should "be administered after reflection and prayer, with tenderness and love." It was not because it was painful, to be dispensed with— "for it is the ordinance of God, and no divine appointment can be despised or neglected without provoking his displeasure."[160] The object of education, according to the Bishop was "to raise up amongst us a race of Christian patriots and philanthropists, . . . their hearts burning with love to God and man, and ready to spend and be spent in every good cause."[161]

Nature of the Religious Viewpoint

It is clear from the views on religion in education presented as having received publicity in addresses before lyceums and educational societies, in monographs, and in the press, in the decades before the Civil War, that Virginians had an increasingly keen interest in the problem; that, in the case of those strongly imbued with a religious conception of education, this interest frequently assumed the form of zealous propaganda in favor of their particular panacea. Significantly for the development of the treatment of the problem in the actual school situation, it will be noted that this discussion was largely from a theoretical standpoint, a philosophical treatment of the problem,[162] which, while it recognized as the central theme of the problem, the betterment of society, saw religion as the primary factor in that

---

[158] See p. 326.
[159] Meade: *Pastoral Letter*, 11.
[160] *Ibid.*, 12.
[161] *Ibid.*, 23.
[162] *Cf.* for a recent scientific approach to the problem, Hauser, C. A.: *Latent Religious Resources in Public School Education.*

problem, without a very clear realization of the limitation of that factor by other important factors, such as political, industrial, and social wrongs. The Virginia mind saw the end it wished achieved for society, it believed it had found the means in religion; but it was religion in the large, without reference to the careful analysis that is necessary to make any important factor function correctly in society if it is to be a truly ameliorating force.[163] However, as will appear from a consideration of the discussions at the educational conventions in the last two decades before the Civil War,[164] Virginians were beginning to see that in the proper treatment of the problem, a needed solution was the determination of the question of sphere of control of religion in education—whether that responsibility belonged to the state or to the church, or in part to both. Perhaps the most significant result of the discussion during this period was that by keeping the problem before the general public, church membership and denominational growth were stimulated. How these views and propaganda were reflected in the practises and activities of the various denominational groups is our next consideration.

---

[163] For a recent scientific approach to the problem, *cf.* Yocum, A. D.: "Standards for Judging the Material and Method of Religious Education"; *cf.* his "What Democracy Should Compel Through Religion."

[164] See p. 345 *ff.*

CHAPTER VIII

DENOMINATIONAL ACTIVITIES AND INFLUENCES IN EDUCATION

Anomalous Position of William and Mary

That the anomalous position in which the College of William and Mary had been left, with respect to its relation to church and state, would not be permitted to endure long, in view of the general movement, which began in the second decade of the nineteenth century, to strengthen the position of religion in Virginia, may be readily surmised. Further, the coming of Rev. Richard Channing Moore as Bishop of Virginia, in 1814, signified a renewal of life for the Protestant Episcopal Church.[1]

In July, 1815, the Board of Visitors of the College of William and Mary announced to the public that "This year, Students may, at their election, attend lectures on Municipal Law, and in a short time, Lectures on Theology also, it is hoped."[2] Manifestly, the Protestant Episcopal Church had not been an inattentive observer of the activities of the Presbyterian Church in the direction of advancing theological education.[3] The matter of providing a theological chair at William and Mary was first officially presented by the President of the college, Dr. J. A. Smith, to the Convention of the Protestant Episcopal Church in their May session, 1815.[4] The convention authorized the Bishop and standing committee to take measures for the promotion of this important object.[5] The matter was referred, in 1816, to the following convention,[6] but no action seems to have been taken until 1820, probably because both the college and the church were

---

[1] Hawks: *Contrib. Ecc. Hist.*, I, 251.
[2] *Wm. & Mary Coll. Quart.*, XXV, 240.
[3] See p. 225 *ff.*, 229 *ff.*, 302 *ff.*
[4] Hawks: *Contrib. Ecc. Hist.*, I, Appendix, 98, 108; *Semi-Centennial Celebration Theol. Sem.*, 21; *Richmond Enquirer*, June 1, 1821, "Literary & Religious Intelligence."
[5] Hawks: *Contrib. Ecc. Hist.*, I, Appendix, 98.
[6] *Ibid.*, Appendix, 108.

awaiting the outcome of the proposed legislation of the period of 1817–19 with regard to the conversion of colleges into state institutions, and the extension to them of the benefits of the Literary Fund.[7]

It may be, too, that the opposition aroused by the attempt of the Presbyterian Church to incorporate the Virgina Theological Seminary had instilled a sense of caution in the Episcopalians with regard to this movement.[8]   This would appear from the fact that the resolution of the convention of 1820 merely expressed a sense of due appreciation and called the attention of the members of the church to the intention of the college soon to employ a clerical professor for the benefit of theological students, and the "liberal offers of assistance" by the professors "to such students of all denominations."[9]   Apparently, the convention did not see its way clear at this time to establish a more definite connection with this venture of the college.   The convention of May, 1821, however, approved the following motion:

> . . . taking into consideration the deficient condition of the diocess ·as respects the means of theological instruction, and the importance of retaining among ourselves, for education, those young men who may be disposed to devote themselves to the sacred office of the ministry, recommend to this Convention the establishment of a theological school in Williamsburg; it being understood that the society of the college in that place is willing that such a step should be taken, and that the faculty have generously offered to afford gratuitously, to all *bona fide* students of theology, a course of lectures for the support of such school.
>
> It is therefore recommended, that a Board of Trustees, . . . be appointed to adopt the most efficient means for establishing the same, by raising funds and selecting one or more professors; the proceedings of which board shall be subject to the decision of the next Convention.[10]

A Board of Trustees, clergymen and laymen was appointed, and the solicitation of subscriptions authorized.[11]   Matters now progressed rapidly, and, in June, an announcement was made to the public through the Richmond Enquirer.[12]   The announce-

---

[7] See p. 333, 335.
[8] See p. 302 *ff*.
[9] Hawks: *Contrib. Ecc. Hist.*, I, Appendix, 141; *cf. Semi-Centennial Celebration Theol. Sem.*, 21.
[10] Hawks: *Contrib. Ecc. Hist.*, I, Appendix, 149.
[11] *Ibid.*
[12] *Richmond Enquirer*, June 1, 1821, "Literary & Religious Intelligence."

ment stated that Episcopalians, aware that "Without knowledge, religion degenerates into bigotry and superstition"; and that "without religion, the paths of learning are dark and cheerless," were planning to provide "for the publick education of candidates for the ministry."[13] The faculty of William and Mary had generously "proffered to permit the gratuitous attendance upon their lectures, of those who should intend to devote themselves to the ministry." Further, the college, an incorporated body, would "act as trustees for the pecuniary benefit of the infant establishment." The church by supporting one professor only, would reap the advantages of a college faculty. It must be kept clearly in mind, however, "there will be no connection between the college and the school, which will always be kept entirely independent of each other." While the new seminary was to be "essentially episcopal," since general theology and all the concomitant branches were to be taught, pupils of every religious denomination would be almost equally benefited and gladly welcomed. If Christians of every description could be induced to avail themselves of these advantages, science and piety, no longer confined to a class or sect, "would warm and lighten, and meliorate the land."[14]

It is evident from this statement of catholicity of purpose, that Episcopalians had taken a lesson from Presbyterian policy and were seeking to disarm any possible opposition. As a private institution, the college was, of course, free to extend its activities as it chose, but there was a possibility that the college would profit from the act of February 24, 1821, in regard to the distribution of the surplus of the Literary Fund.[15] This might complicate matters in the future. Then, too, the authorities of the college were not unaware that there was a considerable opinion in the state in disagreement with the decision of 1790 in the Bracken case.[16]

There does not appear to have been an immediate reaction in the press to this announcement; but, in the latter part of July, there appeared in the *Richmond Enquirer*, a lengthy article by

---

13 *Ibid.*
14 *Ibid.*
15 See p. 336.
16 See p. 179.

"A DISSENTING FARMER," addressed *"To the* PUBLIC *of* VIRGINIA, *and especially to the* EPISCOPAL CLERGY, *and the visitors of* WILLIAM *and* MARY COLLEGE."[17] The writer declared himself a friend to learning and the Protestant religion, but he feared the announcement concerning the theological professorship would "prove mischievous to both." He asked whether the faculty and visitors knew that every corporation is a trust for specified objects, not to be diverted to any other purpose; had they considered that there had been no such professorship in the college since the revolution; that "the exclusive patronage of any sect of religion in any body incorporated by law," was contrary to the *Bill of Rights* and the *Act for Religious Freedom?* The action of the Legislature in refusing permission to Hampden-Sidney to erect a chair of this kind was "decisive proof of its indisposition to allow any privileges to sectarians."[18] The incorporation of William and Mary by the crown did not give it rights and privileges not possessed by Hampden-Sidney. The commonwealth had succeeded to all the rights of the crown, and the charter was now held of the state. It was absurd to think, because the charter had been signed by William III, that, for example, "it might be converted into a college for the instruction of negroes only," and there would be no redress. Nor could it be urged that the "indulgences" granted the Episcopal clergy are given "by the professors in their individual character, and not as public functionaries." The property of the college, including the library, was public property and the visitors and professors were but trustees for the state:

They are to educate the free white youth of this country in the liberal and useful sciences, without regard to religious, or political opinions; and without favor or oppression to any denomination of men, entitled by our laws to equal privileges.[19]

The writer objected also, as having the appearance that religion and philosophy are at war, to the expression, "band of antichristian philosophers," as used in the Circular asking for funds. He advised the public "to contribute nothing, until the question

17 *Richmond Enquirer*, July 27, 1821.
18 See p. 303.
19 *Richmond Enquirer*, July 27, 1821.

of law be settled, whether William & Mary College can, consistently with our institutions, lend itself to any religious sect.''[20]

There was an immediate response by Bishop Moore who had perused the address ''with emotions of sorrow and surprise.''[21] The fact that the Circular addressed to the friends of the Episcopal Church appealed for money was incontrovertible proof that the school expected no pecuniary aid from the college, but would depend altogether upon the benevolent. Could the fact that all the professors but one had promised to instruct the theological students free of charge, and that these students would have the benefit of reading the theological works mouldering on the shelves of the library, be construed as an invasion of the rights of other denominations? Episcopalians claimed no exclusive right to the attention of the faculty, or to the library of the college, but thought that the youth of Virginia had a right to avail themselves of the benefits so generously extended. As for the *Bill of Rights*, the Bishop had been assured by one of the judges of the Court of Appeals that the plan was not in contravention of it. It was evident from the proceedings of the late convention, which he subjoined,

. . . that the Governors or Visitors of Wm. & Mary have nothing to do with the appointment or support of the Theological Teacher; but that the power to make the appointment, and the weight of his support centers in the Convention of the Church, and in that alone.[22]

An attempt to further support the Episcopal position appeared in the *Richmond Enquirer* of August 7, by ''One of those appointed to superintend the Episcopalian School to be established in Williamsburg.'' The writer admitted that the professors of William and Mary had no right in their public capacity ''to bestow exclusive patronage upon any one denomination of christians.'' However, he felt assured that any other Christian society desiring to do what the Episcopalians wanted to, would receive the same facilities and benefits. In fact, an informal offer of this kind had already been made to a member of the Baptist church. Other Christian groups were at liberty to endow chairs

[20] *Ibid.*
[21] *Ibid.*, July 31, 1821.
[22] *Ibid.; cf.* citation from Hawks: *Contrib. Ecc. Hist.*, I, Appendix, 149, p. 286.

and reap similar benefits. However, if the various denominations did not care to do this, the original announcement in June made it clear, it was not necessary to be an Episcopalian to enter. A profession of belief in the doctrine of the cross and declaration of sincere intention to be a minister, only were required. The material that was common ground to all could be gone over in common, peculiar tenets taken care of elsewhere.

The same issue of the *Enquirer* contained the reply of "A DISSENTING FARMER" to Bishop Moore.[23] His chief contention now was that the halls of the college, its apparatus, and library, were merely converted funds that had "changed their shape," belonging inalienably to the public. Neither they, nor the services of the professors, while in the college could be diverted from the general public use to the benefit of members of a particular religious faith, "while others, are made to pay for them."[24]

On the 14th, two articles appeared, one by "JUSTITIA," the other by "A Friend to William & Mary."[25] "JUSTITIA" appealed to the good sense of the "DISSENTING FARMER" whether it was not an injustice to deny Episcopalians the benefits of the proposed scheme, which were wholly in line with the original purpose of the college as expressed in its charter, when these identical benefits were available to every other denomination which wished them. He took occasion to comment, too, on the objection of the "DISSENTING FARMER" to the expression "band of anti-christian philosophers." While he believed "that the greatest philosophers that ever lived, were found in the ranks of Christianity," he nevertheless felt it important that students should have "all the aids of philosophy and science, that they may be enabled to meet anti-christian philosophers with their own weapons."[26]

"A Friend to William & Mary" entered into the difficulties facing denominations attempting to create theological seminaries. It was absolutely necessary in order to protect property that it be in the hands of incorporated trustees. Either the trustees of

---

[23] *Richmond Enquirer*, Aug. 7, 1821.
[24] *Ibid.*
[25] *Ibid.*, Aug. 14, 1821.
[26] *Ibid.*

the Episcopal Theological School must apply to the Legislature for incorporation or vest their funds in some corporate body already established. The Presbyterians had been unable with all the eloquence of Mr. Wirt to prevail upon the Legislature.[27] The habits and feelings of Virginia, the principles of the revolution, the *Bill of Rights*, the *Act for Religious Freedom*, the act of 1799,[28] were all opposed to *"legislative* encouragement, directly or *indirectly,* of any religious sect." An attempt looking to vesting of funds in the corporation of William and Mary had two objections: the corporation of that college could not be held legally responsible for the funds originally intended for the theological school;[29] secondly, to attempt this would be to sanction an evasion of the law. The prosperity of the institution was opposed to any scheme which would make it have "avowedly *"under its patronage,"* an Episcopal Theological School."[30]

A few days later "CAIUS" entered the controversy with a question as to how the professors could afford to teach gratis, unless it were, that the college was enabling them to do so by the salary it was paying, and that, in fact, it was the college that was paying for the instruction.[31]

The most serious injury to the cause was, however, the publication on August 21, of a lengthy statement by "A Visitor of William and Mary" to the effect that the President of the college had assured the visitors of the college at their meeting, in July, that the notice in the *Enquirer* of June 1 had not received the sanction of the President and Faculty of the college; and thus the statement that the college as an incorporated body would act "for the pecuniary benefit" of the theological school was an error in fact. The visitor was opposed to "the idea that a government or its corporations may interfere with matters of religion, because they profess to extend the like privileges to persons of every religion or denomination."[32] Granting the possibility

---

[27] See p. 302.
[28] See p. 156, n. 15.
[29] Apparently referring to attempt of Presbyterians to use a similar procedure at Hampden-Sidney, see p. 303–4.
[30] *Richmond Enquirer*, Aug. 14, 1821.
[31] *Ibid.*, Aug. 17, 1821.
[32] *Ibid.*, Aug. 21, 1821.

of equal treatment, were not the persons intended for the ministry obtaining under this plan exclusive privileges? The writer's argument, in view of subsequent action at the University of Virginia and other institutions,[33] in this connection, is not without interest:

> . . . If the college shall give these aids to *persons only who are intended for the ministry*, do they not in fact enjoy privileges which *all other students of divinity* do not enjoy? If so, it is in direct hostility to the spirit of the 4th art. of our bill of rights. Shall I be told that the objection will be obviated by reason that every one may study divinity? I have only to answer, that to offer an advantage on such terms would be to effect the very thing which is to be guarded against, to wit, an encouragement to any or every religious denomination of persons intended for the ministry, and that by giving them privileges which every other person in society does not equally enjoy—nor does it matter whether this encouragement comes directly by an act of the legislature.—The effect is the same, if they can do so through the many wealthy corporations under their control. . . .[34]

He urged Episcopalians to apply to the Legislature, if they wished a charter, saying,

> . . . Let them, at least, act openly and avow at once what is intended, lest the conjectures which are made (I hope without foundation) be realized, that William & Mary is acting only as the jealous rival of a distinguished individual: with these plans of the church, the visitors have had no connection. . . .[35]

Whether or not a feeling of rivalry and jealousy of Jefferson and his University of Virginia had entered into the question of creating a theological school at William and Mary, it seems true that the matter had been entered into with a view to strengthening both the college and the church.

The report of the trustees of the Theological School, at the convention, in 1822, indicated that correspondence from Maryland, whose support had been solicited, revealed there was a "difference of opinion as to the usefulness of the contemplated school, and its location at Williamsburg." A fund of over $10,000 had been collected from various localities in Virginia. A delay of another year was inevitable to gather further subscriptions. A constitution for the school, which contained no reference to

---

[33] See p. 390, 637.
[34] *Richmond Enquirer*, Aug. 21, 1821.
[35] *Ibid.*

William and Mary, was presented and adopted.[36] An election of trustees also took place.[37]

At the convention, in 1823, announcement was made that Rev. Mr. R. Keith, who had been rendering partial service in the institution during the year, had been appointed professor of divinity.[38] In the following year, the convention was informed that Mr. Keith had settled in Alexandria, in October, 1823, and had thirteen candidates for orders, under his charge.[39] In explaining the change, it was stated that Williamsburg was "too remote and inaccessible to justify the hope that students can be obtained for a theological institution at that place. The experiment was tried for one year without success." The experiment at Alexandria was very hopeful and it was moved that the school be located there.[40]

With the removal of the school to Alexandria, an episode of striking interest in Virginian educational history was brought to a close. It was not until after the Constitution of 1851, which, while forbidding charters of incorporation to any church or religious denomination, permitted churches or religious denominations to secure title legally to church property "to an extent to be limited by law," that the way was open for theological seminaries to seek incorporation.[41] In 1854, "An Act incorporating the Protestant Episcopal Theological seminary and high school in Virginia" was passed. It limited both the amount of land and money that could be held, but contained the usual provisions of incorporation of academic institutions.[42]

The failure to bring the Theological School to Williamsburg, the publicity of the controversy, the acknowledgment in the convention of Williamsburg's remoteness and inaccessibility, the prospective opening of the University, all reacted unfavorably upon the college. From an enrollment of 61, in 1821, when the

---

36 Hawks: *Contrib. Ecc. Hist.*, I, Appendix, 153–54.

37 *Ibid.*, 156.

38 *Ibid.*, 164.

39 *Ibid.*, 173.

40 *Ibid.*, 174; *cf. Semi-Centennial Celebration Theol. Sem.*, 21–22, where the removal is attributed in part to the influence of the "Maryland brethren."

41 *Acts of Assembly*, 1849–52, 332.

42 *Ibid.*, Feb. 28, 1854, 65.

controversy began, the numbers dropped to 33 for 1823, to approximately 20 for 1824, and 14 for 1825.[43]

In view of these circumstances, it is not surprising to find that Jefferson was informed by Cabell, who as a trustee of the University was interested in protecting its interests, that a movement was on foot in Williamsburg to remove the college to the capital, Richmond.[44] In support of the proposed change, Cabell indicated there would be the clergy, the Federal party, Richmond, the medical men of the state, "Chancellor Brown and others, of the Board of Visitors," and the faculty except Judge James Semple, professor of law.[45] He suggested to Jefferson that the movement be countered by a proposal to use the capital of the college to endow academies throughout the state—not that he did not feel some hesitation in thwarting the hopes of those who saw in the change a means of saving the institution—but he was unwilling to see the labors of so many years spent in the University project injured by competition.[46]

Jefferson's reply to Cabell indicated that he viewed the situation with hope rather than dismay.[47] Reviewing the situation, Jefferson reiterated his former opinion regarding the legal status of the college—that the Legislature could legitimately proceed to the transformation of its charter and the transfer of its location. As to the selection of Richmond, he reviewed and demolished the points in its favor. Since the Legislature had acknowledged the ineffectuality of the college by sanctioning the University, the obvious solution was to transfer its resources to the University.

---

[43] Tyler: *Williamsburg*, 269—Tyler gives "no record" for 1824; in *Letters and Times of Tylers*, I, 344, he gives the number as 18; the statement of approximate number is found in a letter from Jefferson to Cabell—Lipscomb: *Writings T. Jefferson*, XVI, 41.

[44] Randolph: *Letters Jefferson & Cabell*, 305.

[45] *Ibid.*, 305 *ff.*; *U. S. Bur. Educ., Circ. Inf.*, 1887, No. 1, 58; there is some question as to whether "Chancellor Brown" is to be identified as William Browne, elected a visitor of the college in 1812—Randolph & English: *Hist. of College Wm. & Mary*, 77, or as William Brown, who according to correspondence from E. G. Swem, Librarian of the College of William & Mary, was "a member of the General Court of Virginia about this time"; a discussion of these various factors in the movement will be found in Bruce: *Hist. U. of Va.*, I, 308 *ff.*

[46] *Ibid.*; *U. S. Bur. Educ., Circ. Inf.*, 1887, No. 1, 58.

[47] Randolph: *Letters Jefferson & Cabell*, 308 *ff.*; Lipscomb: *Writings T. Jefferson*, XVI, 35 *ff.*

However, he voiced his opinion, "it will not be removed," and suspected that there was a design by the professors, "the prime movers," to foist their incompetency which had "degraded and foundered the vessel whose helm was entrusted to them," upon the new University.[48]

The matter of removal was presented by President Smith to the convocation of visitors on July 5, 1824.[49] In urging the advantages of the step, Dr. Smith stated, "A medical school would be organized and attached to the College, and the theological school might be re-united to us."[50]

The proponents of the movement soon had to face not only the opposition of the supporters of the University, but the opposition in the Board of Visitors and faculty that represented the intrenched historical and family interests of Williamsburg as led by John Tyler, John B. Seawell, among the visitors, and Judge James Semple, professor of law in the college.[51] Before the end of the year, the situation developed to a point where a petition of the President and faculty in behalf of the transfer was referred to the Legislature.[52] Memorials in opposition were likewise presented. In January, the Committee of Schools and Colleges went into an examination of the entire project. It is clear from Jefferson's opinion already cited that there was an opinion current, that the deterioration in the position of the college as to numbers and influence was due to incompetency on the part of its staff. From a paper furnished the committee by Dr. Smith, it appears that a certain amount of opposition had arisen against him personally on the score of his reputed "deistical opinions." Dr. Smith appealed to his former pupils, some of whom were now in the House, as to whether there was the slightest truth in the allegation. On the contrary, he had avoided meddling "with points of faith," as having no commission to impart religious in-

---

[48] *Ibid.*, 41.
[49] "Report of the Committee of Schools and Colleges, On the Subject of the Removal of the College of William & Mary," *Jour., H. Del.*, 1824–25, 3 *ff.*
[50] *Ibid.*
[51] Tyler: *Williamsburg*, 184; Tyler: *Letters & Times of Tylers*, I, 344.
[52] "Report of the Committee of Schools and Colleges on the Subject of the Removal of the College of William & Mary," *Jour., H. Del.*, 1824–25, 3 *ff.*; Lipscomb: *Writings T. Jefferson*, XVI, 85.

struction. He had always pressed upon his pupils "the narrow limits of the human understanding" and had urged the importance

... of a *reasonable* degree of faith; a faith which requires not unattainable degrees of evidence, and which is equally removed from the incertitude of the sceptic on the one hand, and the blindness of the bigot on the other.[53]

For further proof as to his attitude, Dr. Smith referred to Rev. Mr. Keith, now of the theological seminary in Alexandria, who had honored him by attending his "entire course of lectures" and then sent him "a theological student, *(who has been since ordained,) to attend the very lectures now objected to.*"[54] Further, if it were not "for the importance and solemnity of the subject," Dr. Smith declared, he would "be tempted to smile at the reports" in which, at one time, he was called an "atheist," at another "a rigid Calvinist" and more recently "a bigoted episcopalian, who intends to subject the College and all its concerns to the very worthy and pious bishop who presides over that church," and now, a "deist."[55]

Mr. Seawell in his examination by the committee in January, contended that irrespective of the truth as to Dr. Smith's "entertaining and inculcating deistical opinions," the report had operated "very considerably to the depression of the College." He believed "no man would from choice bring up his son in these opinions," and was convinced "that many believed the report." Upon inquiry, however, as to whether the students were "free to form, and enjoy what opinions they please upon religious subjects?" Mr. Seawell answered he knew of no restraint which had been or could be imposed upon them.[56] Mr. Seawell further indicated that, in his opinion, Dr. Smith's former anxiety to retain the Rev. Mr. Keith in his position in the college, when that position had become a mere sinecure, was due to the fact that it

---

[53] "Report of the Committee of Schools and Colleges on the Subject of the Removal of the College of William & Mary," *Jour., H. Del.*, 1824–25, 12.

[54] *Ibid.; cf.* Smith, J. A.: *A Syllabus Of The Lectures Delivered To The Senior Students In The College Of William And Mary, On Government;* ... *To which is added, A Discourse* ... *On The Manner In Which Peculiarities In The Anatomical Structure Affect The Moral Character.*

[55] *Jour., H. Del.*, 1824–25, 12.

[56] *Ibid.*, 18–20.

would offset the rumors current about Dr. Smith's inculcation of deistical doctrines.

The appeal of the college to the Legislature was not without dramatic interest to Jefferson. In a letter in the latter part of December, he said:

> . . . I am glad the Visitors and professors have invoked the interference of the legislature, because it is an acknowledgment of its authority on behalf of the State to superintend and control it, of which I never had a doubt. It is an institution established for the public good, and not for the personal emolument of the professors, endowed from the public lands and organized by the executive functionary whose legal office it was. . . .[57]

Considering the possibility of removal, and following up the line of argument that the resources of the college belonged to the public, Jefferson stated, that since these resources were too large for an institution secondary to the University, that the surplus should be distributed to every part of the state for the creation of intermediate schools, or colleges, as originally proposed in the Rockfish Gap report.[58]

Madison, to whom the plan was made known, wrote Jefferson that he heartily approved of the plan to fill the gap between the primary schools and the University, but he declared,

> . . . I have little hope however that the College will accede to any arrangement which is to take from it a part of its funds, and subject it to the Legislative Authority. And in resisting this latter innovation, it will probably be supported by all the Sectarian Seminaries, tho' to be adopted as legal establishments of the intermediate grade. It is questionable whether the sectarian Seminaries would not take side with William & Mary in combating the right of the Public to interfere in any manner with the property it holds. The perpetual inviolability of Charters, and of donations both Public & private, for pious & charitable uses, seems to have been too deeply imprinted on the Public mind to be readily given up. . . .[59]

Cabell, who was watching developments in Richmond, now informed Jefferson that the proponents of the transfer scheme

---

[57] Lipscomb: *Writings T. Jefferson*, XVI, 85; this opinion was voiced, probably, not only because of reaction in Virginia on this subject, but also because of the decision in the Dartmouth College case, 1819; Cubberley: *Pub. Educ. U. S.*, 206; Brown, E. E.: *The Making of Our Middle Schools*, 289 ff.; see p. 179, 186.

[58] Lipscomb: *Writings T. Jefferson*, XVI, 86; see p. 369.

[59] Hunt: *Writings J. Madison*, IX, 213.

were apparently about to achieve their object, that in order to hinder them it was necessary for Jefferson to forward a bill embracing his intermediate school plan. Jefferson forwarded the bill to Cabell on January 22.[60]   Cabell, following the Jeffersonian argument that William and Mary was a public, not a private corporation, appealed, in the press, under the name of "A Friend of Science" to the Assembly to show no hesitation in using the resources of the college to the advantage of the public as it saw fit.[61]

Whatever the impression of this address upon the minds of the Assembly—Mr. Cabell thought it had a preponderant weight, in the final issue of the matter—a speech by Mr. Tyler, who was a member of the House, defeated the transfer project.[62]   Mr. Tyler succeeded in convincing the Assembly of the fact which Jefferson had suspected, that the waning fortunes of the college had been due, in large measure, to incompetency in its staff.[63]   The rigorous laws with respect to discipline put in practise by the President had resulted in the suspension, dismission, or expulsion, out of an attendance of 500 students, in ten years, of no less than 77.   Mr. Tyler also succeeded in repelling the old charge as to the unhealthfulness of Williamsburg.[64]

It is evident from the attempt first to associate a theological seminary with the college at Williamsburg, and then to accomplish its removal to Richmond, that there was a strong party in the Protestant Episcopal Church anxious to restore the college to an unequivocal position as a denominational institution.   The opposition in Williamsburg to its removal was undoubtedly based on historical pride.   As for the Assembly, it probably preferred to have the status of the college continue in its equivocal position rather than to offend an important denomination.

Dr. Smith resigned soon after the failure of his cherished plan.[65]   His successors, Rev. Wm. H. Wilmer, and particularly

---

[60] Randolph: *Letters Jefferson & Cabell*, 335, 499; Bruce: *Hist. U. of Va.*, I, 318.

[61] Randolph: *Letters Jefferson & Cabell*, 337, 508–11; Bruce: *Hist. U. of Va.*, I, 318–19.

[62] Mr. Tyler, later President Tyler, was the son of Governor Tyler, who had been responsible for the creation of the Literary Fund.

[63] Tyler: *Letters & Times of Tylers*, I, 344.

[64] *Ibid.*

[65] Tyler: *Williamsburg*, 184; *Wm. & Mary College Catalog*, 1926, 29.

Rev. Adam Empie, were successful in starting the college upon an era of comparative prosperity.[66]

At a convocation of visitors in July, 1830, a code for the government of the college was adopted. Provision was made for daily religious exercises in the chapel; attendance, however, was not compulsory.[67] The regulation with regard to religious observance on Sunday read:

> On the sabbath day, all the students and scholars have it in their power to attend some place of public worship; and both at public worship and in the chapel, every pupil is required to behave with all that decorum and solemnity which are due to the place and the occasion.[68]

The opening session of the college in October, 1836, was marked by an address to the students of the newly elected President, Thomas R. Dew, an alumnus of the college, and professor of moral and political philosophy, since 1828.[69] His address on this occasion is of particular interest because of his advice to the students on their attitude toward religion. After advising them to be punctual in attendance and attentive in church on Sunday, and referring to the pulpit as a source of religious instruction, morality and civilization, President Dew urged the students to

> . . . Be always respectful in your conversation towards religion, not only from regard to the feelings of others, but for the sake of your own reputation. Avowed infidelity is now considered by the enlightened portion of the world as a reflection both on the head and heart. The Atheist has long since been overthrown by the light of nature, and the Deist by that of revelation. The Infidel and the Christian have fought the battle, and the latter has won the victory. The Humes and Voltaires have been vanquished from the field, and the Bacons, Lockes, and Newtons have given in their adhesion. The argument is closed forever, and he who now obtrudes on the social circle his infidel notions, manifests the arrogance of a literary coxcomb, or that want of refinement which distinguishes the polished gentleman. . . .[70]

The confidence with which it was asserted that all opposition to Christianity and true religion was now vanquished is an interesting reflection of the advance in religious progress made in the

---

[66] Tyler: *Williamsburg*, 184: Hawks: *Contrib. Ecc. Hist.*, I, Appendix, 211.

[67] Report of Lit. Fund, *Jour., H. Del.*, 1835–36, 16.

[68] *Ibid.*, 21.

[69] Tyler: *Williamsburg*, 186, 197.

[70] *So. Lit. Messenger*, II, 768.

two decades since the incorporation of the Virginia Bible Society.[71] President Dew went on to say that if any of the students were ministers, "or professors of religion studying with a view to the ministry," that the college lectures were free to them of all expense, that the college would feel sufficiently recompensed, if the instruction would become "instrumental in promoting virtue and true religion."[72]

It was probably due to the precedents set by the practise of the University of Virginia since its foundation,[73] and by Washington College, in 1829, in this matter,[74] as well as the increasing religious sense of Virginia since the early twenties, with the likelihood that many voices would not now be found which would venture to express opposition to a procedure tending to advance the interests of religion, that this offer of free instruction to ministerial candidates was now made and incorporated into the regulations of the college. The catalogue of the college for 1843–44 stated that it was "by a resolution of the faculty" that all students studying for the ministry were to be "admitted without fee to all the lectures, including the classical department."[75]

The catalogue of that year said nothing of religious requirements, but stated that students had "an opportunity of attending Divine Service on every Sunday at the Episcopal, Baptist or Methodist Church."[76] Among books used in Professor Dew's department, the Moral and Political Department, were Paley's *Moral Philosophy* and Chalmers' *Evidences of Christianity*.[77]

In 1856, William and Mary College joined other denominational colleges in convention to obtain support from the Assembly.[78] Apparently, the college had benefited in no way from the proposed distribution of the surplus of the Literary Fund voted in 1836.[79] In February, 1859, the main building of the college was destroyed by fire. Ex-President Tyler, who was

71 *Cf.* Dr. Dew's Baccalaureate address in 1837—*Ibid.*, III, 405.
72 *Ibid.*, II, 768.
73 See p. 390.
74 See p. 309.
75 *Catalogue of the officers and Students of William and Mary College,* Session of 1843–44, 20; *Ibid.*, 1844–45, 19.
76 *Ibid.*, 1843–44, 20.
77 *Ibid.*, 8, 14.
78 See p. 359, 360.
79 See p. 337–38.

made chancellor of the college that year, the first to be honored with that office since Washington, took occasion, in an address to the alumni gathered to devise means for rebuilding the college, to review the history of the college in its attitude toward religion. He said:

It has been sometimes urged—and who or what in this world can escape censure or objection?—that the government of the college had been hurtful and injurious to youth. Even at the moment that she was sending out into society a large number of refined and cultivated minds, to sustain, by both precept and example, the great fabric of Christianity, because some one, or at most two of her distinguished sons, espoused the doctrines of Unitarianism, she was in some quarters denounced, notwithstanding her faculty was chiefly composed of distinguished divines, and was presided over by James Madison, the eminent president of the college, and bishop of the diocese of Virginia, as promulgating heretical doctrines, and elevating, after the manner of Paris in the wild outbursts of the French revolution, the goddess of Reason to the throne of the Universe. I take leave to say, not only upon the strength of my term of service, as one of her visitors, for forty-four years, but as one of her students, that no licentiousness of opinion or belief, can have been justly ascribed to her at any period of her existence. It is also proper to say, that, while she has taught the vital principles of Christianity, and derived her lectures from the purest sources of the moral law, she has done so in no spirit of sectarianism. A common shrine is established at which all, of whatever sect, may worship without question or restraint. So was it in the olden time, and so is it now. . . .[80]

The success of those interested in restoring the college was such, that despite the inaction of the Assembly with regard to a proposal for the state to donate $10,000 to the college, the college was enabled to be in full operation by February, 1860.[81]

There was, however, probably a doubt in the minds of some as to the future stability of the institution, for a petition to the Assembly in January, 1860, from the residents of the county of James City, requested that the College should "be taken under the protection and management of the Legislature, and endowed."[82] The issues of Civil War, however, prevented serious consideration to this petition, compliance with which would prob-

---

[80] *De Bow's Review*, XXVII, 146; Randolph & English: *Hist. of College Wm. & Mary*, 57; Tyler, L. G.: *The Making of the Union*, 20; Tyler: *Williamsburg*, 189, gives 1857 as date for chancellorship.
[81] *Ibid.; Jour., Senate*, Dec. 20, 1859, 100.
[82] *Ibid.*, Jan. 5, 1860, 112.

ably have cleared up the anomalous position of the college, since 1776, in its relation to church and state.

Presbyterian Educational Activities

Presbyterian anxiety to create a theological seminary in connection with one or another of their leading institutions has already been described.[83]   The success of Dr. Hoge in his work at Hampden-Sidney was such that Presbyterians decided to ask for the incorporation of the "Theological Seminary of Virginia." The presentation of a petition for this purpose in 1815, met with great opposition and was rejected by the House in February, 1816, though Rev. John Holt Rice, the future editor of the *Virginia Evangelical and Literary Magazine* appeared in its defence before the House, as did Mr. Wm. Wirt.[84]

From a pamphlet entitled "An Illustration Of The Character & Conduct Of The Presbyterian Church In Virginia," written by Mr. Rice, but not published until after the rejection of the petition, the nature of the opposition and defence may be gathered.   The opposition revealed five objections: 1. The incorporation of a theological seminary had "a squinting towards an establishment" of religion; 2. It would be granting exclusive privileges, contrary to the *Declaration of Rights;* 3. Holding property in *mortmain* is injurious to the State; 4. It would set a precedent to other denominations, the collision between varying interests would be felt in elections; and 5. The Legislature "has nothing, and ought to have nothing whatever to do with religion."   In reply, Mr. Rice held that the statement of purpose in the petition, that the seminary was intended for all denominations and for the furtherance of Christianity, not denominationalism, was sufficient answer to the first objection.   As for the second and third objections, Mr. Rice held that a school and not a sect was being incorporated; and incorporation of this school was no more a violation of the law than those of other schools, charitable societies, and industrial incorporations.   As for the fourth objection, "Let every society, without discrimination have their churches, and their schools, and we ask no more."

---

[83] See p. 225, 230.
[84] *Jour., H. Del.,* Jan. 2, 1816, 88; Feb. 1, 1816, 153.

As for the last objection, Mr. Rice argued there was no violation of law, as "the religion of every man will be as perfectly free after such incorporation as before." The real issue was whether the Legislature would encourage religion at all. Christianity was the religion of the nation, its truth acknowledged by the government in directing that "oaths should be administered 'on the holy Evangelists of Almighty God.'" Nothing remained for the Legislature to do, but to grant them what they "have a natural right to do, namely erect schools, and educate our youth for the highly important office of the ministry of the gospel."[85]

The fact that the Legislature had incorporated the Virginia Bible Society, in 1814, and refused this incorporation, shows clearly enough that it was not convinced that the Presbyterians would succeed in conducting a non-proselyting Christian theological seminary in distinction from a denominational one. It is evidence, too, of how denominational rivalry in Virginia was beginning to interpret Presbyterian educational activity. To Jefferson, the fact that the advocates of the seminary had received an audience in the Legislature seemed to be a mark of "unusual respect."[86]

The refusal of the Legislature to incorporate, did not halt the plans for the institution. The seminary was opened in January, 1824, under the care of Hanover Presbytery.[87] The proximity of the seminary to the college of Hampden-Sidney, led to some confusion in the public mind, upon its first establishment, as to its connection with that institution. A statement was therefore issued in 1826 to the effect the seminary was "in every respect separate and independent" from the college.[88] In order to solve the problem of safeguarding the funds of the seminary, Hanover Presbytery decided to request the General Assembly of the Presbyterian Church to extend "its patronage" to the seminary, and in turn to give the Assembly of the church such control as would be "sufficient to secure its being conducted on Presbyterian prin-

---

[85] Rice: *An Illustration Of The Character & Conduct Of The Presbyterian Church In Virginia*, 44–56.

[86] Lipscomb: *Writings T. Jefferson*, XIV, 406–07.

[87] *Treasurer's Report to the Board of Trustees of Union Theological Seminary*, 1883.

[88] *Va. Evang. & Lit. Mag.*, IX, 611.

ciples and consistently with the wish of the Assembly.''[89]   The
General Assembly of the church consented to the proposal and
proceeded ''to 'receive, manage and invest' any funds of the
institution, in the name of the corporation of the 'Trustees of
the General Assembly of the Presbyterian Church in the United
States of America.' ''[90]   After 1836, the General Assembly of
the church relinquished its ''management and tenure of the funds
(then about $27,000) to the Directors'' of the institution, who
thereafter made investments in the names of private parties.[91]

After the constitution of 1851 had established the principle
that religious organizations could secure title to property,[92] the
way was opened, looking to incorporation.   An act of incorporation was passed in December, 1855.[93]   Neither this act nor one
amending it in March, 1858, proved acceptable;[94] it was not until
1867, that a satisfactory act of incorporation was obtained.[95]

Before the seminary was formally organized in 1824, there
appear to have been quite a number of students in the college
who were pursuing, at least, preliminary studies for the ministry.
A ''Society on Missions'' whose membership consisted of ''students preparing for the Ministry'' is reported, in 1818, with the
object of gaining ''as accurate and extensive information as possible respecting the state of morals and religion, principally,
though not exclusively, in our own country.''[96]   The course of
study as given in a notice for 1818, designates for the grammar
school, ''Sacred History; . . . Greek testament, John, Acts,
Romans and Hebrews, or its equivalent''; but gives no indication
of religious work in the college course.[97]

---

[89] *Proceedings of the Presbytery of Hanover*, May 6, 1826, 196; *Va.
Evang. & Lit. Mag.*, IX, 330–32.
[90] *Treasurer's Report to the Board of Trustees of Union Theological Seminary*, 1883.
[91] *Ibid.;* cf. Martin, J.: *Gazeteer*, 267.
[93] See p. 365.
[93] *Acts of Assembly*, Dec. 20, 1855, 190, ''An ACT for the incorporation
of the Trustees of Union theological seminary in Prince Edward.''
[94] *Treasurer's Report to the Board of Trustees of Union Theological Seminary*, 1883; *Acts of Assembly*, Mar. 6, 1858, 210.
[95] *Ibid.*, Jan. 9, 1867, 507.
[96] *Va. Evang. & Lit. Mag.*, I, 171.
[97] *Ibid.*, II, 237–38.

The tremendous struggle between the denominational institutions and the University of Virginia that ensued, when it looked as if the Literary Fund was to be applied to educational efforts that were "public" in the most limited sense, of being entirely without religious connection, will be described elsewhere.[98] In this connection, a most interesting defence of the propriety of Hampden-Sidney College to appeal for funds appeared in the *Richmond Enquirer* in July, 1821. It was based on the thought, that since the character of the institution was determined by its charter, which had been drawn up by Mr. Madison at the close of the Revolution, when the principle of separation of church and state had already been established in the Legislature, and since that body, "able and disposed to guard against every restriction, and to grant no powers but such as are essential to the best interests of the people" had approved the charter, there was no reason why subsequent Legislatures should hesitate to appropriate money to the institution for fear of contravening the law. The article went on to declare that it was "confidently expected" that the Legislature would appropriate from the Literary Fund not only to Hampden-Sidney but to other colleges. Legislative patronage would need to be extended not only for buildings, but for the college library, for apparatus, for scholarships, and for endowment of professorships.[99]

The report submitted by the college to the state in accordance with an act of 1835,[100] included the "Laws of the College." It was the duty of the President to see that morning and evening prayers were held with the students and to attend to their religious instruction in such manner as he might deem expedient.[101] The tutors were required to attend the meals of the students, to ask a blessing and return thanks. The professors and tutors were required to attend chapel exercises, morning and evening, and to assist the President in the exercises of the Sabbath.[102] As for the students, they were required to attend morning and evening prayers at the appointed time and to "behave with

---

[98] See p. 336, 372.
[99] *Richmond Enquirer,* July 27, 1821.
[100] See p. 337.
[101] *Jour., H. Del.,* 1835–36, 33.
[102] *Ibid.*

gravity and reverence during the whole service.'' A similar rule held with regard to Sabbath worship, and ''when not engaged in the public duties of the Sabbath,'' the student was required to ''conduct himself in an orderly and decent manner,'' and attend such duties as the President might have prescribed for the day.[103] There is no doubt from the phraseology of the rules that attention to them was compulsory. Whether the services ever gave offence to the students as being too sectarian in character does not appear; an effort was made probably to prevent their being so in order to avoid criticism.

The hope of friends of Hampden-Sidney that the Legislature would at some time see fit to give it some measure of support never failed. The college in 1844 and 1845 did however receive loans from the Literary Fund, for the benefit of its Medical College at Richmond, and in 1850 was released from paying the interest.[104] In 1854, when a bill for ''creating a fund for the perpetual maintenance of a system of Primary or Free Schools''[105] was before the Legislature, an inquiry was made in regard to the expediency of appropriating $20,000 as an endowment fund for Hampden-Sidney on condition that the college agree to educate thirty-two students free of tuition fees; it was, however, reported ''inexpedient to legislate on the subject.''[106]

The year 1854 marked the incorporation of the ''Medical College of Virginia,'' as an institution separate from Hampden-Sidney.[107] This medical college had its inception as a branch of Hampden-Sidney at Richmond in 1837,[108] and was ''established under the charter and seal of Hampden-Sidney College'' in 1838.[109] The proposal to incorporate the medical department as a separate college aroused considerable discussion in the newspapers. The perennial question as to the desirability of transferring the medical department of the University of Virginia to Richmond, where it might have clinical facilities was can-

---

103 *Ibid.*, 36.
104 *Acts of Assembly*, Feb. 9, 1844, 23; Feb. 20, 1845, 18; Mar. 9, 1850, 36.
105 See p. 359.
106 *Jour., Senate*, Jan. 11, 1854, 116; Jan. 30, 1854, 185.
107 *Acts of Assembly*, Feb. 25, 1854, 26; Christian: *Richmond*, 180–81.
108 *Wm. & Mary Coll. Quart.*, XIX, 159; Heatwole: *Hist. of Educ. Va.*, 145.
109 *Hampden-Sidney Catalog*, 1926, 11.

vassed.[110] There were, however, other issues involved. A letter in the *Richmond Enquirer*, about a week before incorporation was granted, charged that an attempt was "being made to incorporate, out of State Funds, the *Episcopal Church*, under the name of the Medical School of Virginia."[111] It appears from the article that, in some way, control of the institution had passed from the Presbyterians to the Episcopalians, so that sixteen of the nineteen visitors were said to be Episcopalians. The article went on to say:

> . . . If there was a bill before the Legislature to charter a school of any kind, and there were sixteen out of nineteen of the visitors Roman Catholics, it would be called ''a Roman Catholic School.'' And I cannot see why this Medical School bill has not its proper title. Call it as it should be called, the Medical School of the Episcopalians of Virginia and the Whigs. It has been opposed by those who have thought upon the subject in Richmond, knowing full well that if it succeeds, it will add another powerful corporation to the overgrown Whig strength of the city of Richmond.[112]

It was for the people to "strike down this monster" and see to it that the visitors received their appointment from a representative of the people, the governor, and not through "Episcopacy or Federalism." For the state to "give $25,000 to sixteen Episcopalian visitors to a Medical School, in which the professors are all of the Episcopal persuasion, as rumour says, is outrageous."[113]

Another question which arose was whether the medical college had not in fact become a public corporation in view of the loans extended to it by the Legislature. This was denied in a speech in the Senate by Mr. Tazewell who held that since the loans had been made to a private corporation, the original character of the institution had no more been changed "than in the case of a gift or loan by an individual to a public corporation."[114]

In passing the act of incorporation, the lien which existed on the real estate in favor of the president and directors of the

---

[110] *Richmond Enquirer*, January and February, 1854. For Jefferson's point of view on this subject, see Lipscomb: *Writings T. Jefferson*, XVI, 36–38.

[111] *Richmond Enquirer*, Feb. 17, 1854.

[112] *Ibid.*

[113] *Ibid.*

[114] *Ibid.*, Mar. 11, 1854.

Literary Fund, because of previous loans was retained.[115]   An annual report to the Second Auditor was required.   A board of nineteen visitors with ample powers, particularly with reference to the appointment and removal of the faculty was instituted. Finally, as if to pour oil on the ruffled waters aroused by the controversy in connection with the incorporation, it was provided that the act was to take effect when assented to ''by the present faculty of the Medical College of Richmond,'' and nothing in the act was to ''be so construed as to express or imply any censure to either the trustees of Hampden-Sidney college or the faculty of the Medical School in Richmond.''[116]

Further light is thrown on Presbyterian educational activity, the reaction of the public towards it, and the effects of time and experience upon Presbyterian educational policy, in a consideration of the history of Washington College.

The Presbyterian Academy at Lexington, Washington Academy, was converted into Washington College by an Act of Assembly in 1813.[117]   The favor shown it by Washington in his grant of 100 shares of stock in the James River Company was now followed by an expression of favor on the part of the Society of Cincinnati.[118]   The society was contemplating dissolution and petitioned the Assembly to be permitted to dispose of its funds as a gift to the college on condition that it establish a military school.[119]   This permission was granted by the Assembly in 1814, with the proviso that until the military school be established, the funds be vested in the commonwealth.[120]   The subsequent history of that fund will be discussed later in connection with the history of the Virginia Military Institute.[121]

The college next came prominently before the public, as a rival of Central College for the favor of the state as a University.   It offered the Washington gift, the fund from the Cincinnati Society, and its entire property of 31 acres and buildings.

---

[115] *Acts of Assembly*, Feb. 25, 1854, 26; see p. 306.

[116] *Acts of Assembly*, Feb. 25, 1854, 28; for subsequent transition in control to the state, see p. 474.

[117] *Acts of Assembly*, Jan. 2, 1813, 90.

[118] See p. 231, 234.

[119] *Jour., H. Del.*, Dec. 20, 1813, 69.

[120] *Acts of Assembly*, Feb. 5, 1814, 73; *Wm. & Mary Coll. Quart.*, IX, 193–94.

[121] See p. 365.

There was also the promise of a gift from the people of Lexington and the gift of a considerable estate by a citizen of Rockbridge County. Aside from the fact that all of these did not amount in value to what Central College had to offer, the fact that Jefferson was able to convince the Commission that the Charlottesville neighborhood and not Lexington was the center of the State's population, resulted in the vote being cast for Central College.[122]

In the internal history of the college, we find that the trustees sought, in 1819, to further the religious welfare of the students by buying three pews in the Presbyterian Church for their use for Sabbath attendance; but it seems not to have been a successful effort, as the pews were sold not many years later.[123] The implied failure in church attendance would seem rather odd, but is perhaps explained by the publication of the course of study in 1821, which stated that the freshman, sophomore, and junior classes of the college were to be employed on Sundays "in the study of the scriptures," the senior class, in "studying the Evidences of Christianity."[124] It may be that these studies left little leisure for regular church attendance.

In 1829, the Board adopted new regulations for the school, presented by its acting head, Rev. Henry Ruffner.[125] It was now ruled that students were to rise at five o'clock in the morning, or as soon thereafter as the signal was given and assemble for prayer. On Sundays, students were to attend "to exercises of a religious nature, such as the study of the holy scriptures." Authority was given the faculty to admit poor students "of promising talents, and good moral character" without payment of fees.[126]

In view of the seeming compulsion in required attendance at prayers and attention to religious studies, it is of interest to read the following rule which heads the section on religious worship and moral conduct in the report submitted to the state in 1835:

---

[122] Bruce: *Hist. U. of Va.*, I, 216 *ff.*
[123] *Wash. & Lee Hist. Papers*, 1893, No. 4, 39.
[124] *Va. Evang. & Lit. Mag.*, IV, 320.
[125] *Wash. & Lee Hist. Papers*, 1895, No. 5, 5–6.
[126] *Ibid.*, 7.

Every student shall enjoy that right which is natural to all men, and which is so fully guarantied to its citizens by the laws of this state—to worship their Creator according to the dictates of their own consciences; and all sectarian influence is hereby prohibited.[127]

The rules went on with the customary requirements of morning and evening prayers to be attended "with the utmost decorum," to attend divine service on the Sabbath; and when not engaged in public worship on Sunday, to "abstain from their accustomed sports and amusements, as well as from every act unsuitable to the day," and to attend such duties on that day as might be assigned by the faculty.[128] It would appear difficult to reconcile these rules with the freedom of conscience guaranteed in the first rule, unless we are to assume that this freedom of conscience was taken care of in the prohibition of tinging the religious activities with sectarian influence. Freedom of conscience was most evidently interpreted as not extending to a freedom to deny Christianity or to a refusal to take part in a general Christian service.

While Virginia in the decades before the Civil War was becoming more strongly religious as was evinced by the increased number of churches in each of the leading denominations,[129] and educational institutions affiliated with the different denominations arose in greater numbers and had their being, yet the sentiment in the press liked to applaud any action which tended to show that an educational institution had so far reconciled its policy, as to proceed in consonance with the now accepted interpretation of the Virginia Constitution, that it was laudable in educational matters to be Christian but not sectarian. The action of the Board of Trustees of Washington College in 1854, in disclaiming by a resolution any right to make the College a sectarian institution, and denying the charge of having been governed by sectarian influence in the selection of professors, was favorably commented upon by the *Richmond Enquirer*.[130] The action taken was held as "worthy of imitation by every other Institution of learning in the country." The action was re-

---

127 *Jour., H. Del.*, 1835–36, 24.
128 *Ibid.*
129 See p. 321.
130 *Richmond Enquirer*, Aug. 19, 1854; Sept. 26, 1854.

garded as particularly meritorious in view of the fact that the majority of the Board were Presbyterians and might have used their position to advance the interests of their church. They had now relieved the institution "from the odium of a suspicion of being under the exclusive control of the Presbyterian Church." The trustees had yielded to the wiser and better policy of "managing the Institution solely for the promotion of the cause of education, and not with a view to the advancement or propagation of the creeds of any sect or denomination."[131] From 1854 on, Washington College was technically a non-sectarian institution. Whether in taking, this step, the trustees were influenced by the animus shown in the press against sectarianism in the Richmond Medical College controversy does not appear. There seems to have been no effort made by the friends of the college, as was the case by those of Hampden-Sidney in this year, to obtain support when it appeared that the whole question of financing education was to come before the Legislature.[132] Perhaps it was felt that the announcement of its non-sectarianism would automatically bring it into a more favored position for future aid. In an announcement of non-sectarianism the institution had little to lose, it could still exert a religious influence by inculcating general Christianity. In 1855, the college catalogue stated under the caption of "Religious And Moral Culture," that

This is accounted of primary importance; as the increase of intellectual power is not a benefit or a blessing, unless placed under the controlling influence of right moral feeling. Our means of securing this all-important end, are, the regular morning and evening worship of the College assembled as a family; this consists of reading of a portion of sacred Scripture, singing and prayer; Bible recitation on Sabbath; and the public lecture in the chapel. Students are also required to attend one other public exercise on Sabbath, in such place as their parents or guardians may direct.[133]

The transitional period of adjustment after the Revolution to 1810, when it looked as if the Presbyterian denomination was to take over the control of education in the state, was followed by a period less favorable to the continuation of Presbyterian su-

---

[131] *Ibid.*, Aug. 19, 1854.
[132] See p. 359.
[133] *Wash. College Catalog*, 1855, 14.

premacy. The attempt to incorporate their theological seminary aroused bitter criticism. The chief factor, however, in checking Presbyterian educational activity was undoubtedly the determined opposition of Jefferson, which prevented the acceptance of one of their institutions as the university of the state, and initiated a tendency in the Legislature opposed to granting aid from the Literary Fund to institutions with denominational affiliation.

The difficulty of financing the institutions already in existence, in order to have them keep pace with the University, was such that Presbyterians no more attempted any pretentious educational undertakings. At the beginning of the Civil War, the endowment of Washington College, which had been especially favored by various gifts, amounted to but little more than $100,-000.[134] By 1850, Presbyterianism ranked third in denominational importance, having been outstripped in growth by the Methodists and Baptists who held first and second rank respectively.[135] It was no longer in a position to undertake extensive educational ventures.

Probably the most interesting educational undertaking begun in this period was the creation, in 1842, of Augusta Female Seminary, the forerunner of Mary Baldwin Seminary and Mary Baldwin College.[136] The seminary had its inception in the suggestion of Rev. Rufus W. Bailey to the ministers and members of the denomination in Staunton, and Augusta County.[137] The declared purpose of the institution, in the constitution adopted, was "to afford the means of a thorough literary and religious education to the female youth of this portion of our country."[138] When the school had been in operation two years, a petition for incorporation was presented, which was granted in January,

---

[134] *Wash. & Lee Catalog,* 1926, 23.

[135] *U. S. Bur. Census Rep't,* 1850, 286, 292.

[136] Waddell: *Annals Augusta Co.,* 268; another institution which seems to have had Presbyterian affiliation was Leavenworth Female College, at Petersburg, incorporated in 1856, *Acts of Assembly,* Feb. 26, 1856, 197; it is cited by Hotchkiss, J.: *Va. Geog. & Polit. Summary,* 211, under the name of Leavenworth Seminary. Its founder was Abner Johnson Leavenworth, Amherst, 1825, and one of the founders of the "Virginia Education Association," 1863.

[137] *Mary Baldwin College Catalog,* 1925–26; Blandin, I. M. E.: *Higher Educ. Women,* 316–20.

[138] *Ibid.,* 317.

1845.[139] The cornerstone of the school building contained, appropriately enough, a Bible with the superscription—"The only rule of faith, and the first text-book of the Augusta Female Seminary."[140]

While Presbyterians did not undertake, during this period, any educational venture which was to loom for education in Virginia so significantly as had their activities in connection with Hampden-Sidney and Washington College, their activities as represented in those institutions are most illuminating for the problem of denominational affiliation in education. In view of their expressed policy to keep education "Christian" but not "sectarian," the fact that the trustees of Washington College decided finally to renounce all affiliation is most interesting and probably to be taken as indicative of the fact that there was a considerable question in the mind of the public as to the general Christian character of the religious activities in Presbyterian educational institutions.

Again, the assertion that the principle of the *Declaration of Rights,* guaranteeing freedom of conscience, was to be a cardinal rule of their institutions, while promulgating at the same time rules implying compulsory religious observances, shows the difficulty of reconciling education under denominational affiliation, with its implication of care for the religious instruction of youth, and a philosophy of state based upon the principle of separation of church and state.

Baptist Educational Activities

The great need of all the denominations in Virginia, in the first decades of the nineteenth century, was theological seminaries in which to train ministers, to build up their churches. The efforts of the Protestant Episcopal and Presbyterian churches to incorporate institutions of that kind met at first with failure. The Baptists, traditionally slow in educational ventures, made no effort to provide facilities for theological training until 1830, when at a General Association meeting in Richmond, a few of

---

[139] *5th Ann. Rep't Lib. B'd, Va. State Lib.,* 1907–08, 171; *Acts of Assembly,* Jan. 30, 1845, 105.
[140] Blandin: *Higher Educ. Women,* 318.

the members met "to devise and propose some plan for the improvement of young men who, in the judgment of the churches, are called to the work of the ministry."[141]   The "Virginia Baptist Education Society"was formed, and for two years aided young men placed in two schools in charge of Elders in the church. In 1832, a manual-labor school, the "Virginia Baptist Seminary" was organized, offering a four year intermediate course with theology as an optional study.   The school was established at Spring Farm near Richmond, and in the following year moved to Columbia, near Richmond.[142]   By 1840, the Society decided to apply for a charter.   At the suggestion of a Baptist member in the Legislature, Col. Edmund Broadus, the proviso not to authorize the establishment of a theological professorship was inserted in order to avoid difficulty in obtaining a charter.[143] The institution was incorporated as Richmond College.   The trustees were authorized "to admit gratuitously, in whole or in part, as their respective cases may require, such person or persons as they may think proper."[144]   The intention was, of course, to make possible the admission of prospective candidates for the ministry, for while specific theological instruction had to be given up, and other denominations besides the Baptist were represented among trustees and faculty, it was apparently felt that a sufficient denominational character could still be retained and such religious influences exerted as to make the institution a desirable preliminary training ground for future Baptist ministers.[145] The trustees of the college took over the property of the Society in 1843,[146] but the Society continued to extend aid to such students of the college as were planning to enter the ministry.[147]

In 1854, when it appeared that the question of financing public education was to be discussed in the Legislature, representatives of the college, as did friends of Hampden-Sidney, made an attempt to obtain an appropriation from the Literary Fund.[148]

141 *U. S. Bur. Educ., Circ. Inf.*, 1888, No. I, 271.
142 *Ibid.; Acts of Assembly*, May 4, 1840, 92.
143 *U. S. Bur. Educ., Circ. Inf.*, 1888, No. I, 272.
144 *Acts of Assembly*, Mar. 4, 1840, 95.
145 *U. S. Bur. Educ., Circ. Inf.*, 1888, No. I, 275.
146 *Ibid.*, 273.
147 *Ibid.*
148 *Jour., Senate*, Jan. 24, 1854, 166.

The request was met with the reply that it was "inexpedient to grant the prayer of the petition."[149] In the latter part of 1855, permission was granted to withdraw the petition from the files.[150]

In 1858, the charter of the college was amended and the proviso forbidding establishment of a theological seminary was omitted.[151] There was now no longer any point, since the provision of the Constitution of 1851 protecting the property of religious organizations, in particularly excluding theological departments, unless the group responsible for an educational institution wished particularly to assure its omission.

In western Virginia, Dr. Alexander Campbell, who was founding a church, known as "Disciples of Christian Baptists" but usually referred to in that day as "Campbellite Baptists" was responsible for the creation of Bethany College.[152] A charter was secured in 1840; it also contained a prohibition concerning the establishment of a theological professorship.[153] This, however, did not militate against the plan of the founder to have the Bible as the leading text-book of the institution, and to have a missionary and religious spirit pervade the institution.[154] Dr. Campbell, besides acting as President of the institution, was also "professor of mental philosophy, moral science, political economy and sacred history."[155]

Another college of Baptist affiliation was Rector College, established at Pruntytown, in Harrison, now Taylor County, and incorporated in 1842.[156] Its trustees had been incorporated, in 1838, as the Western Virginia Education Society.[157] In 1845, the college received a loan from the Literary Fund.[158]

---

[149] *Ibid.*, Jan. 30, 1854, 186.

[150] *Ibid.*, Dec. 15, 1855, 76.

[151] *Acts of Assembly,* April 7, 1858, 211.

[152] The church is now known as Disciples of Christ.

[153] *Acts of Assembly,* Mar. 2, 1840, 95–97; the catalogue for 1855, 9, lists a School of Sacred History and Moral Philosophy, with studies in Evidences of Christianity, Sacred History, Biblical Literature, Ecclesiastical History, and Moral Philosophy.

[154] Whitehill, A. R.: *Hist. of Educ. W. Va.,* 69, 71.

[155] *Ibid.,* 70.

[156] *Acts of Assembly,* Mar. 4, 1842, 88.

[157] *Ibid.,* Mar. 28, 1838, 174.

[158] *Ibid.,* Feb. 12, 1845, 18; Morrison: *Beginnings Pub. Educ. Va.,* 166.

A more important institution that had its origin in an education society was that now known as Hollins College.[159]   The enthusiasm of Rev. Joshua Bradley created "The Valley Union Education Society of Virginia" about the year 1840.   This society purchased an hotel property at Botetourt Springs, and opened a school in 1842.[160]   In 1844, the society was incorporated by the Legislature, as a joint stock corporation.[161]   Though the fact is not evident in the charter, one of the principles on which the society was established, as appears in its by-laws of that period, was that "requiring the Principal of the school to be a graduate of an American college and a member of the Baptist denomination."[162]   As this fact was seemingly well known, as was the fact that Prof. C. L. Cocke, who was called to the institution as its principal, in 1846, remaining in that capacity until his death in 1901, was a Baptist, the institution was assumed in public opinion to be affiliated with the Baptist denomination. It was not, however, a denominational institution in the sense of being under the care of any Baptist association.

The school was originally co-educational, but in 1852, at the suggestion of Prof. Cocke, it was made a school for girls, and by an act of Legislature empowered to confer degrees.[163]   In 1855, the school received a gift from Mr. and Mrs. John Hollins of Lynchburg.   Mrs. Hollins was a Baptist, but Mr. Hollins was not a member of any church.   The fact of Mrs. Hollins' affiliation with the Baptist church, and the change of name to Hollins Institute, in 1855, apparently confirmed the popular impression of Baptist affiliation.   As a matter of fact, when the charter was amended, in 1855, in respect to the name of the institution, and the property transferred from the Valley Union Education Society to a self-perpetuating board of trustees, Mr. and Mrs. Hollins made no stipulations as to denominational affiliation.[164]

[159] Hotchkiss: *Va. Geog. & Polit. Summary*, 211.

[160] Smith, W. R. L.: *C. L. Cocke*, 37; Cocke, C. L.: *Address, Fiftieth Anniversary*, June, 1893; *Hollins College Catalog*, 1926–27, 4; *Jour. of Educ.*, XVIII, 56; Blandin: *Higher Educ. Women*, 320–25.

[161] *Acts of Assembly*, Jan. 13, 1844, 88.

[162] Cocke: *Address, Fiftieth Anniversary*, June, 1893.

[163] Smith: *C. L. Cocke*, 46; *The Sewanee Review*, XXIX, 504; *Acts of Assembly*, June 2, 1852, 180.

[164] *From correspondence;* Smith: *C. L. Cocke*, 48; *Acts of Assembly*, Dec. 19, 1855, 203.

In 1860, when another gift was received from Mrs. Hollins, and Professor Cocke inquired whether it was her wish to change the status of the school, Mrs. Hollins' reply was "that it was not,— she wished the institution to be open to all Christian denominations and the general public."[165] A perusal of the records in the early history of the institution indicates that no mention was made, at the time of change of name to Hollins Institute, of denominational affiliation for any officer.[166] Nevertheless, it appears that Professor Cocke, in 1862, probably influenced by the by-law regarding the presidency, described the status of the school in these terms: "The organization of this school is unlike all others in Virginia. To some extent it is denominational, but decidedly anti-sectarian. . . . It is responsible to no religious body and its success depends solely on its merits."[167] As a matter of fact, according to the authorities of the college, "During all the history of the institution, no denominational distinctions have been observed, either in the selection of faculty, or the acceptance of students."[168] Protestant ministers of various denominations have always officiated at Sunday chapel services.[169]

As to the character of the internal conduct of education under Baptist auspices, very little information seems to have come down to us. The historian of Richmond College, referring to the omission of theological instruction in consequence of the act of incorporation wrote:

. . . This did not in any wise impair, it rather increased, the religious influence of the college, but it changed the main design, or as one might say, it shifted the centre of gravity. The seminary was designed especially for ministerial students and admitted others on payment of fees; the college aimed at a liberal education for any and all vocations, and granted certain privileges and exemptions to students preparing for the ministry. The seminary, moreover, was distinctively, in fact, as in name, Baptist; the college,

---

[165] *From correspondence.*
[166] *Ibid.*
[167] Smith: *C. L. Cocke,* 55.
[168] *From correspondence.*
[169] *Ibid.;* while technically not a Baptist institution, Prof. Cocke's admission that "to some extent it is denominational," justifies its inclusion in a consideration of Baptist educational activities.

though unquestionably denominational, had from the first other denominations represented in its trustees and faculty, as well as in its students.[170]

At Hollins, daily evening worship, consisting of prayers and hymns, with Professor Cocke in charge of the service, was the custom from the beginning.[171]   The place, religion held in the education of young women in the period before the Civil War, may be gathered from the commencement address of Alexander H. Sands, in 1859.   Mr. Sands was very explicit in his directions regarding the religious literature the fair graduates were to read in order to improve their minds, enlarge their hearts, and "more faithfully discharge some of the offices" they owed to themselves.   The names, he mentioned, are Taylor, Barrow, Chillingworth, Butler, Hall, Chalmers, Spurgeon, and Monod.[172]

It is evident that the Baptist Church, like other denominations, had succeeded in giving to instruction, under their auspices, a religious tone satisfactory to them from their denominational point of view.

Methodist Educational Activities

A new impetus to Methodist educational activity was given by the recommendation of a General Conference of the church in 1824, "that each Annual Conference establish a seminary of learning under its own regulations and patronage."[173]   The matter was taken up by the Virginia Conference in 1825.[174]   An offer of $20,000 from the citizens of Brunswick County, if a college were placed at Ebenezer Academy, was disregarded to place the college near Boydton in Mecklenberg County, probably because of the more advantageous offer of the Boydton Male and Female Academies at that place.[175]

The charter of the college granted, in 1830, contained a prohibition against the establishment of a theological professorship.[176]   As if in answer to this prohibition, the institution's first

---

[170] *U. S. Bur. Educ., Circ. Inf.*, 1888, No. I, 275.
[171] Smith: *C. L. Cocke*, 92, 94, 124.
[172] *So. Lit. Messenger*, XXVIII, 328.
[173] *Randolph-Macon College Catalog*, 1925–26, 23; Bennett: *Memorials of Methodism*, 707, 709.
[174] *Ibid.*
[175] See p. 219; *U. S. Bur. Educ., Cir. Inf.*, 1888, No. I, 240.
[176] *Acts of Assembly*, Feb. 3, 1830, 36 *ff.*; Martin: *Gazetteer*, 234.

president, Rev. Stephen Olin, in his inaugural address ventured to affirm, "that this generation has not given birth to another absurdity so monstrous, as that which would exclude from our seminaries of learning, the open and vigorous inculcation of religious faith which is acknowledged by our whole population, and which pervades every one of our free institutions."[177]

The following popular account of life at the college in the early days is not without interest:

> . . . In those days schedules were strenuous, and the day's work had to be begun with proper devotions. . . . The dim light of the study scarcely penetrated the dark corners, and the professor in charge would gravely remark, "We will dispense with the reading for obvious reason." If "Old Santy," the president, was leading, he would announce to the tittering benches, while he felt his pockets in vain, "We will omit reading, as I have left my specs at home." Somehow the boys did not have the heart to tell him that they were on his forehead in full view. But what they lacked in reading, they gained in praying. . . .
>
> Even the prayers had to have an end, and then the recitations dragged along wearily until the slow bell brought breakfast. Afterwards there were lectures and more recitations until the bell rang for evening prayer at five o'clock. . . . Even the Seniors had no very easy time, and in 1839, there was a "strike" against taking a course in "Evidences of Christianity" on Monday morning before breakfast. Like most strikes, it ended disastrously for the strikers, and several had to leave, not, however, without the sympathy of their fellow-sufferers. . . .[178]

In 1854, Randolph-Macon like other denominational colleges asked for an appropriation from the state. It was for the specific amount of $20,000 as an endowment; but it was declared "inexpedient to legislate" on the matter.[179]

A few years after the establishment of Randolph-Macon College, the members of the Holston Conference took steps to create an educational institution. At a meeting in Abingdon, in January, 1836, it was decided to establish the college at Emory, Va.[180] A charter was granted in March, 1839. Besides the pro-

---

[177] *Annals of Education,* IV, 546.

[178] *South Atlant. Quart.,* XX, 238–39; cf. *Randolph-Macon College Catalog,* 1854, 23.

[179] *Jour., Senate,* Jan. 11, 1854, 116; Jan. 21, 1854, 152; Jan. 30, 1854, 185.

[180] *Emory and Henry Catalog,* 1926–27, 16–17; Summers: *Hist. S. W. Va.,* 575–76.

hibition against a theological school or professorship, it was enacted:

> . . . That a majority of the said board of trustees shall, at no time consist of any one religious denomination, nor shall any person be ineligible to any office or trust appertaining to the college, or be secluded from a full and free participation in the privileges and benefits of the college on account of his religious tenets.[181]

Whether because the college attempted to operate at first as a manual labor college, it soon became involved in debt, and in 1843 it appealed to and received from the Legislature a loan from the Literary Fund.[182] In 1850, the Legislature permitted the trustees to discharge interest accrued and accruing on the loan by educating annually "sixteen indigent and deserving young men as state students, free of all charge for board, lodging and tuition."[183] The young men so educated were required upon graduation to teach in some school or college in the state for at least two years.[184]

An article in the *Richmond Enquirer*, in 1846, referred to the college as being "under the guidance of a very pious, able, learned and energetic Faculty." It made the following statement of the policy of the institution:

> The policy of the institution is, to send out upon the walks of after life perfectly educated men—not with intellects Angel-bright, and hearts as black as Lucifer, but men with well developed moral sentiments, highly cultivated mental faculties, properly regulated social affections—which, united in any single individual, give us the notion of a perfectly educated man. . . .[185]

As at Randolph-Macon, morning prayers were held by candle light. At evening prayer, singing was substituted for reading the Scriptures.[186]

In 1858, the Holston Conference took over Martha Washington College, a school for girls which had been projected by a lodge

---

[181] *Acts of Assembly*, Mar. 25, 1839, 136.

[182] *Ibid.*, Feb. 27, 1843, 26; Summers: *Hist. S. W. Va.*, 578; *U. S. Bur. Educ., Circ. Inf.*, 1888, No. I, 255.

[183] *Acts of Assembly*, Mar. 20, 1850, 36 *ff*.

[184] *Ibid.*

[185] *Richmond Enquirer*, July 28, 1846.

[186] *U. S. Bur. Educ., Circ. Inf.*, 1888, No. I, 257–58.

of the I. O. O. F. of Abingdon, and incorporated in 1854.[187]   The act of incorporation was amended, in 1860, to allow the Holston conference equal representation upon the board of trustees.[188]

Anticipating the Methodists in the southwestern part of the state in establishing a college for women, those in the southeastern part had established Danville Female College at Danville.   The college opened in the fall of 1854, and an act of incorporation was granted in March, 1856.[189]

In the northwestern part of the state, the Methodists in 1857 took over Marshall Academy, which had been incorporated in 1838, and secured a charter converting it into Marshall College.[190] A prohibitory clause against a theological professorship was included.[191]

The interest of Methodism, in the last three decades before the Civil War, in creating educational facilities with denominational affiliation is to be regarded as perhaps a very natural outcome of its phenomenal denominational growth in that period.   By 1860, its 1,403 churches with a value of $1,619,010, showed a decided gain in denominational strength over its nearest rival the Baptists, with 787 churches, representing a value of $1,243,505.[192] Though starting late in the educational field, it was through Randolph-Macon, and Emory and Henry already beginning to make a considerable impression in the educational world of Virginia.   According to a writer in the *Southern Literary Messenger*, in 1857, ''Randolph-Macon, and Emory and Henry are following close upon the heels of William and Mary, Washington and Hampden-Sidney.''[193]

The increased denominational strength of both the Baptists and Methodists had begun to exert its effect upon their attitude toward education, as the superior denominational position of the Presbyterians had in the decades immediately after the Revolu-

---

[187] *Acts of Assembly*, Mar. 3, 1854, 66; Jan. 22, 1856, 195; Summers; *Hist. S. W. Va.*, 567 *ff.*; cf. Blandin: *Higher Educ. Women*, 327–28.

[188] *Acts of Assembly*, Feb. 22, 1860, 458 *ff.*

[189] *Richmond Enquirer*, Aug. 28, 1854; *Acts of Assembly*, Mar. 1, 1856, 199.

[190] *Acts of Assembly*, Mar. 30, 1838, 167; Mar. 4, 1858, 212.

[191] *Ibid.*

[192] *U. S. Census Rep't*, 1860, 485–87.

[193] *So. Lit. Messenger*, Mar. 1857, XXIV, 168.

tion. The same writer in the *Southern Literary Messenger* referred to the fact that

. . . Any thing like a general opposition to educated preachers by the Methodists and Baptists, is among the things that have passed away, not to return. They now not only wish to have their young men *well* educated, but they wish to have them educated under their own denominational influence. They wish to add to parental influence, that of the school; and, when it may please the Head of the church to call their sons into his service, they feel confident that they will not forsake the paths which their fathers have chosen.[194]

Apparently the lesson to be learned from the history of denominational educational activity in Virginia is the desire not only to exert a religious influence—a christian influence—but if possible a denominational influence in education.

Religious Influences In Secondary Education

The influences exerted to give a religious tone to elementary education, supported from the Literary Fund, will be considered in the discussion of the civil struggle to control education. To understand fully the effects of the religious movement begun in Virginia as the result of the creation of the organized religious educational activities already discussed, it is necessary to see what was the attitude toward religion as exemplified in the prevalent practise of private secondary education.

It would be idle to draw any sharp lines of distinction among the various types of educational institutions, private schools, academies, seminaries, and institutes. While the last three types were largely incorporated institutions, and some, at various times received financial aid from the Literary Fund and were required to report to the state, thus partaking in part the character of public institutions, they were to all intents and purposes private institutions through their government of self-perpetuating boards of trustees—in many cases representing particular denominational influences.

There are comparatively few advertisements of schools of these types after 1810 that did not stress the fact that they would pay attention to the "morals" of their pupils. A clue to the inter-

---

[194] *Ibid.*, 167.

pretation of this term is not always given. James G. Waddell, principal of Spring Hill Academy, in an advertisement in May, 1818, stated, "None, but boys of correct moral deportment, will be received as pupils" and promised "an unremitting attention" to their improvement.[195]

In eleven advertisements of schools, for the years 1821 and 1822, which mention morals and religion, six merely refer to the fact that the "morals" of the students will be taken care of.[196] An advertisement in 1821, of Bremo Seminary stated the pupils must provide themselves with "a Bible or Testament."[197] The advertisement, in the same year, by Carter Berkeley announcing the opening of his school at Edgewood, Hanover County, left no doubt as to the attitude toward morals and religion he intended to inculcate in his school:

Convinced by his own experience and warned by that of ages, that without attention to discipline and moral order, no Seminary can ever answer its professed end, and that to assemble youth together without enforcing strict obedience to their instructor, and decency and propriety of conduct towards all with whom they associate, would be but to plant them in a hot bed of vice and immorality, the subscriber intends to establish rules for the government of his School founded upon the only true and certain basis of morality, the precepts of Him who "spake and acted as never man did, . . ."[198]

The advertisement of Newington Academy in 1822, besides referring to the attention given to "morals" indicated that the New Testament was studied in Greek.[199]

An advertisement for Rappahannock Academy, in 1822, after announcing that regard would be had to the "moral advancement" of the pupils, stated that prayers were held at nine in the morning, and at the same hour in the evening.[200] That the trustees of this academy had always taken serious thought for the morals of the young, is evident from the fact that they had, in

[195] *Richmond Enquirer*, May 19, 1818; *cf. Ibid.*, July 20, 1821.
[196] *Ibid.*, Feb. 15, 1821, Miss Clarke's School; Aug. 27, 1822, Mrs. J. Drew's school; Oct. 25, 1822, Edward Cannon's school; Nov. 1, 1822, Miss Jane Bell's school; Nov. 1, 1822, Mrs. Mary C. Garlick's school; Dec. 5, 1822, J. Silliman's school.
[197] *Ibid.*, Jan. 11, 1821.
[198] *Ibid.*, Jan. 13, 1821.
[199] *Ibid.*, Nov. 12, 1822.
[200] *Ibid.*, Oct. 25, 1822.

1812, petitioned the Assembly "that the practice of selling ardent spirits to children (so pernicious to morals and learning) be restrained by a moderate penalty."[201]

The advertisement, in 1822, of the Tappahannock Female Academy indicated that its object was to make the lives of its students "virtuous and happy."[202] Martin, in his *Gazetteer*, testifies to the seminary as being "of the first order" and that "every attention is paid to the moral and religious duties of the pupils, by the pious and accomplished lady who presides over the establishment."[203]

A rather unusual notice of a school of this period, because of the detail in which the course of study was presented was that of the "female Academy at Sturgeonville."[204] The system proposed was one which, while not neglecting the intellectual faculties, was intended "to form the virtues of the heart."[205] Unremitting care and exertion were promised in forming and guarding the characters of the young ladies. In the early classes, the Union Catechism was used. The studies in the first session of the Senior Class consisted of Paley's *Natural Theology*, and Parkhurst's *Moral Philosophy*, in the second session, Stewart's *Philosophy*, and *Ecclesiastical History*.[206]

The reports of the various academies to the state in compliance with the act of 1835 in reference to the distribution of the surplus of the revenue fund are quite illuminating as to the manner in which these schools were conducted. Margaret Academy reported as one of its rules that the students were to be called to religious worship at such hour every morning as the teachers from time to time prescribed.[207] Newington Academy reported that "dismission or expulsion is incurred by habitual neglect of study, wanton and repeated violation of established rules, pro-

---

[201] *Jour., H. Del.*, Dec. 16, 1812, 60.

[202] *Richmond Enquirer*, Nov. 5, 1822.

[203] Martin: *Gazetteer*, 167; for other advertisements of this acadamy, see *Richmond Enquirer*, June 19, 1846; Sept. 12, 1854.

[204] *Amer. Jour. Educ.*, Oct. 1828, III, 618; for a reference to its owner, Henry Clary, A.M., see Morrison: *Beginning Pub. Educ. Va.*, 128.

[205] *Amer. Jour. Educ.*, Oct. 1828, III, 618.

[206] *Ibid.*, 618–19.

[207] *Jour., H. Del.*, 1835–36, 49.

fane swearing, irreligious language and writings.[208] At North-umberland Academy, regular daily attendance at divine service was required, the rule adding "Neither happiness, usefulness, nor true politeness are to be expected without the love of God and good will towards man.[209] The rules of Washington Academy required the daily routine to be opened with prayer and attendance at divine worship on the Sabbath, "if practicable."[210] Students were not permitted without permission to leave the grounds on the Sabbath. The attitude of Danville Female Academy was indicated in the following statement:

. . . And while they have studiously avoided the inculcation of all sectarian doctrines, it has been their anxious desire, both in the construction of the laws which govern the institution, and in the selection of teachers, that the pure precepts of *christianity, morality* and *virtue* should be deeply impressed and strictly conformed to.[211]

That the emphasis on a moral and religious life was strong at Mrs. James M. Garnett's school may well be surmised from the writings of Mr. Garnett,[212] but is further evinced from a glimpse of her character, which we get from one of the boys at the school conducted by her husband about 1829, after Mrs. Garnett had given up her school for girls. The student wrote many years later:

. . . During my whole stay at Elmwood she was indeed a mother to me, chiding me gently when in fault, encouraging me in every way to press forward, calling me to her chamber to read a portion of the Scriptures, and afterwards whatever there might be of interest in the newspapers.[213]

The influence of the Garnett family was, however, most pronounced upon a kinswoman, Margaret Mercer, born in Annapolis, Md., 1791.[214] On a visit to Elmwood, Miss Mercer was very much impressed, as we have seen, with the Sunday School conducted by Mr. Garnett.[215] It would seem that she was a

208 *Ibid.*, 54.
209 *Ibid.*, 58.
210 *Ibid.*, 74.
211 *Ibid.*, 46.
212 See p. 259.
213 *Wm. & Mary Coll. Quart.*, XVIII, 27–28; *cf.* Garnett, J. M.: *Token of Regard.*
214 Morris: *Mercer*, 14.
215 *Ibid.*, 48; see p. 246.

young lady of decided spiritual gifts, for upon her return home, Mrs. Garnett wrote asking her "to send her some written prayers for the use of her school" recently opened.[216] Upon her father's death, Miss Mercer returned to Mrs. Garnett's home as an instructor in drawing and painting.[217] Miss Mercer immediately took her part in the Sunday School work.[218] After some years with Mrs. Garnett, Miss Mercer returned home and converted her ancestral home at Cedar Park into an academy. About 1834, she decided to return to Virginia and opened a school at Belmont near Leesburg. A picture of her school, until it was closed in 1846, may be gathered from the following excerpts from her letters:

. . . I have never seen my school half so pleasing as during this year—no wayward or refractory spirit among them, and most of them deeply interested in religion—I have the daily enjoyment of fostering and training gentle spirits for Heaven.

. . . I wish you could be here next Sabbath. Six of my pupils expect to unite themselves to the company of God's faithful people, in the communion of Christ, our passover. They expected to have been confirmed, but Bishop Meade having been prevented coming, they will unite in the sacrament.

. . . Soon after I came home I found a great seriousness growing among my scholars, and I have been entirely devoted to that subject for three weeks past. I wish I could describe the scenes I have had here around me. It pleased God on Sunday, the 28th of May, to send us truly a shower of blessing; no less than ten of my pupils seemed suddenly, and without any visible means sufficient to satisfy our minds, to be occupied with a sense of sin.[219]

These excellent spiritual fruits which seemed so mysterious to Miss Mercer are better understood when Miss Mercer's activities and preoccupation with the spiritual life of her pupils are known. Miss Mercer prepared a manual "Studies for Bible classes," and a series of lectures entitled "Popular Lectures on Ethics."[220] Their use is indicated in the following explanation in a letter:

---

[216] *Ibid.*, 53; see p. 259, 260, n. 76.
[217] Morris: *Mercer*, 94.
[218] *Ibid.*, 95.
[219] *Ibid.*, 155, 158, 163.
[220] *Ibid.*, 169, 174.

. . . I have taken the liberty of transmitting to you my first and only effort at authorship. The ''Ethics,'' you will readily see, have no other aim but to draw the attention of my pupils to the truth, that morality is the law of God, and to be found pure only in the Bible. The *arrangement* of the little volume of Bible studies you will understand. Our Sabbath occupations are light; . . . Before breakfast the girls recite verses and hymns; after breakfast we study the Bible lesson, which comes in regular succession according to the direction of the manual. We have always a Sabbath-School, in which the teachers and some of the young ladies engage as instructors. We have either morning or evening service, as we are favoured with public worship or not. When we have no minister, we read the evening service and a sermon, devoting the morning to Bible studies, reading, teaching, and good books. In the evening, before prayers, we recite the Bible lesson, in which, as each young person reads in regular succession the texts searched out, I make such remarks as I think expedient; . . . After our Bible lesson, the day is closed by evening prayer, . . . We always sing in family prayers.[221]

The impression made by Miss Mercer upon her pupils was such that at her death, her pupils erected a tomb with the inscription:

Sacred to the memory of Margaret Mercer, born July 1, 1791; died September 17, 1846. Her remains repose beneath the chancel of this church, built by her own self-denying labours. This monument is erected by her pupils, as a testimony of their admiration of her elevated Christian character, and of their gratitude for her invaluable instructions.[222]

The *Southern Literary Messenger*, in 1835, took rather extended notice of the Young Ladies Seminary at Prince Edward Court House conducted by Mr. E. Root, a graduate of Williams College.[223] The school, which at the time had 116 pupils, was recommended to the public for its ''discipline which combines kindness and gentleness with order and propriety—a careful attention to the manners and morals of the pupils.''[224] The studies of the third and last year of the course included Natural Theology, Evidences of Christianity, Moral and Political Philosophy. The books used were Youth's book on *Natural Theology*, and Paley's on the same subject, Abercrombie's *Moral Philosophy*, Alexander's *Evidences of Christianity*, and the Bible.[225]

[221] *Ibid.*, 174; *cf.* 177 *ff.*, for copies of lectures from the *Ethics;* Mercer, M.: *Popular Lectures on Ethics.*
[222] Meade: *Old Churches, Ministers and Families*, II, 275.
[223] Morrison: *Beginnings Pub. Educ. Va.*, 132–33.
[224] *So. Lit. Messenger*, I, 520.
[225] *Ibid.*—Advertisement on back cover; *cf.* Martin: *Gazetteer*, 269.

Whatever may have been the nature of the discipline which combined "kindness and gentleness" in schools for girls, it was sometimes a different kind of discipline that ruled in schools for boys.   At Berryville Academy, the story goes,—the principal,

. . . a Presbyterian preacher, Mr. Baber, was a most excellent man, but somewhat eccentric. He used to open with very long prayers, and one day a boy tiring of it said "Amen," and all arose. The old gentleman immediately proceeded to thrash every boy, and when through resumed his prayer and finished without further interruption. . . .[226]

At a convention of the Protestant Episcopal Church in 1837, a resolution was offered looking to the creation of schools in the diocese on the ground that the sons of Episcopal families were too often entrusted to local and irresponsible schools, which were either sectarian in their character or totally unorganized and desultory in their operations.[227]   The following year, the lack of candidates for the Theological Seminary at Alexandria was attributed to the want of an institution "for conducting the previous literary education of candidates."[228]   The school was opened in 1839, its object as stated by its first principal, Rev. W. N. Pendleton, was:

. . . To educate youth on the basis of religion. To apply the instructions of the Bible in the work of training the mind, influencing the heart, and regulating the habits; to provide boys during the critical period of middle youth and incipient manhood the safest and best superintendence, the soundest and most healthful moral influences, and the most faithful Christian guidance associated with the most useful and extensive course of learning practicable. In a word, it is to make full trial of Christian education in training youth for duty and for heaven.[229]

The school was incorporated in 1854.[230]   An excerpt from a letter of a student gives a picture of the religious activities in the period just before the Civil War:

---

[226] Gold, T. D.: *Hist. Clark Co.*, 33.
[227] Kinsolving, A. B.: *Story Southern School*, 20.
[228] *Ibid.*, 21.
[229] *Ibid.*, 25; *cf.* Meade: *Old Churches, Ministers and Families*, II, 489; *Episc. H. S. Catalog*, 1859–60, 9.
[230] Kinsolving: *Story Southern School*, 38.

. . . Other memories are welling up as I write—of the procession to the Seminary chapel on Sunday mornings and of the services in our own chapel Sunday evenings; of our Society and prayer meetings, and of the weekly lecture by a theological student; . . .[231]

In the two decades before the Civil War there seems to have been, if anything, a heightened desire on the part of schools to assure the public that the religious and moral welfare of the students would be taken care of.   An advertisement in 1846 of Mrs. Carrington's Boarding School for Young Ladies states, "The boarders are expected to attend church with the family, free of charge for pew rent."[232]   Peyton Harrison in an advertisement, the same year, assured the public that he had "obtained satisfactory evidence of Mr. Burt's competency to give instruction in the Latin and Greek Languages and Mathematics, as well as of his moral and religious character."   Further, the students would "be provided with a conveyance for attending public worship every Sabbath day, in the Presbyterian and Episcopal churches, alternately; and Sabbath exercises will be required of them at home."[233]   The alternate church attendance was to obviate the charge of conducting a sectarian school.   Occasionally no line is drawn between Christianity and morality, and the emphasis is placed on the combined idea in the term, "Christian morality."[234]

An attempt to combat the fears of parents in sending their children away to school, which explains at the same time, the large number of schools in Virginia which emphasized the religious influence, is found in an editorial in "The Southern Argus," February 21, 1848, on Norfolk Academy. This school, it will be recalled, was, in its original history, a free town school under the control of town officials, but until the close of the 18th century it had been to all intents and purposes under Protestant Episcopal Church influences.[235]   In 1804, the Assembly incorpo-

---

[231] *Ibid.*, 59.

[232] *Richmond Enquirer,* Aug. 18, 1846; *cf. Piedmont Institute Catalog,* 1860, 3.

[233] *Richmond Enquirer,* June 30, 1846.

[234] *Ibid.*, Sept. 26, 1846, advertisement, Miss F. T. Hughes Seminary.

[235] James: *Lower Norfolk C'y, Va. Antiquary,* I, 21–35; IV, 106–07; *Wm. & Mary Coll. Quart.,* III, 3–8; *Va. Mag. Hist.,* XIII, 426, cites *Fredericksburg Va. Gazette,* Oct. 23, 1788.

rated the school and control was vested in a Board of Trustees having perpetual succession.[236]   The editorial follows:

. . . We are acquainted with many excellent parents who prefer keeping their sons in comparative ignorance, deeming it a wiser alternative than sending them to the public institutions of the country where they run the risk of contracting such morals and habits of extravagance as would render them useless members of society and anything else but a pride and pleasure to their family.   These feelings we have always respected, and consider, of the two alternatives ignorance in the higher attainments of learning is vastly preferable to vice.   But no such apprehension need be entertained in sending a son to our institution in this city, where he would be surrounded by such moral and religious influences that he would find no flowers strewed in the path of dissipation, and little inducement to teach it unless from an innate and uncontrollable love to pursue the intricacies of its serpentine way.   It is proper to remark that there is no *Sectarian* preponderance controlling the institution, but that each scholar is permitted to attend such church as may be most agreeable to his parent or guardian. . . .[237]

An account showing the attention given to Bible study in a private home school of a dozen or so pupils is found in a letter from John A. Broadus who was to become famous as a Baptist preacher. He wrote:

. . . We have made a little beginning in the study of Scripture history; I divide all the boys into two classes, each reciting every other day—the smaller ones are to read some of the narratives, as the story of Abraham, of Jacob, of Joseph, of Moses, of Samson, etc., the other class are reading the history connectedly, with some little attention to chronology.   I do not want to try to teach them theology for more reasons than because I don't know it myself.   Nor do I seek to have them *study* the Bible particularly—it is only to induce them to *read* it with interest and attention and to give them such helps in understanding and remembering the history (for it is as sacred history that we read it) as my information and time will permit. I am glad to find that the boys take a good deal of interest in the reading, though I have not been able to get more than five or ten minutes to talk with them about what they have been reading. . . .[238]

In 1853, the Baptists obtained from the Assembly the incorporation of Richmond Female Institute,[239] reincorporated, in 1894, as Woman's College of Richmond. An article in the *Southern*

---

[239] *Acts of Assembly*, Mar. 2, 1853, 244.
[236] *Acts of Assembly*, Jan. 19, 1804; *Norfolk Academy Catalog*, 1926–27.
[237] James: *Lower Norfolk Co., Va. Antiquary*, IV, 30.
[238] Robertson: *Broadus*, 82.

Literary Messenger, in 1860, describes the institute as having three departments, "Preparatory, Collegiate, and Ornamental." Since its opening only four young ladies had been able to complete fully its extensive course, "yet, many, very many, have left its walls with a degree of mental and moral training, that, whether in the social circle or in the school room, must do honor to their Alma Mater and widen her benevolent influence."[240]

Rev. J. R. Moore, the principal of Woodburn Female Seminary, which was incorporated in 1858, and whose history was later to be associated with that of the University of West Virginia, wrote, some years after its founding, concerning the objects of the institution in the following terms:

> This institution was founded by a company of gentlemen of commendable liberality for the purpose of furnishing to North Western Virginia a permanent female school of high order; such as may meet the wants of the public, in securing to young ladies a thorough, elevated and refined education, and one which will qualify them not only for usefulness in all the domestic and private relations of life, but prepare them, if need be, for advancing the cause of learning and Christianity, and render them self-supporting and independent in some degree by fitting them for the profession a Christian woman so adorns—that of teacher.[241]

It is clear from the educational practise of the schools cited here that their distinguishing quality was attention to a moral and religious conception of education. If in the attempt to impress the students with the importance and necessity of a religious life, there was not exerted that form of pressure which could be regarded as legally contravening the principle of the constitution guaranteeing freedom of conscience, there was undoubtedly exerted that most difficult form of pressure to escape— whether that escape is desirable or not is another question—that of the social pressure of the group.

---

[240] *So. Lit. Messenger,* XXXI, October, 1860, supplementary section following, p. 320; References to this school before 1860 are found in *Richmond Enquirer,* June 3, 1854, June 30, 1854, July 18, 1854, Barnard: *Amer. Jour. Educ.,* I, 231; Robertson: *Broadus,* 129.

[241] Morgan, B. S. & Cork, J. F.: *Hist. of Educ. W. Va.,* 174–75.

CHAPTER IX

CONTINUATION OF THE CIVIL STRUGGLE FOR EDUCATIONAL CONTROL

The Development Of A Civil School System

The legislation of 1810, which created the Literary Fund, was followed the next year by an act defining more clearly its purpose and mode of operation.[1] The object of the fund was declared to be its appropriation solely for the benefit of schools to be held in every county—an object described as being "humane, just and necessary, involving alike the interests of humanity and the preservation of the constitution, laws and liberty of the good people of this commonwealth."[2] A board consisting of the governor and four other state officials was incorporated to transact all business in connection with the fund.[3]

The report of the President and Directors of the Literary Fund, in December, 1811, indicated that it had completed its organization and that the fund amounted to almost $13,000.[4] Efforts were made in the next few years to strengthen the financial condition of the fund, but nothing was done to define more closely the nature of the schools which were to benefit from the fund, or to create an integral school system.[5]

It was probably with a view to influencing public opinion in favor of such a system, that Jefferson, in 1814, taking advantage of the necessity of defining the position in the educational field, of the proposed Albemarle Academy in which he was interested, gave his views at length to Peter Carr, President of the trustees of the academy, through whom and Thomas Ritchie, they were given the necessary publicity in the *Enquirer*.[6] The system now

---

[1] *Acts of Assembly*, Feb. 12, 1811, 8; *Jour., H. Del.*, Feb. 14, 1811, 106.
[2] *Acts of Assembly*, Feb. 12, 1811, 8.
[3] *Ibid.*
[4] *Jour., H. Del.*, Dec. 16, 1811, 33.
[5] *Acts of Assembly*, Feb. 20, 1812, 16; Feb. 8, 1813, 35; Feb. 9, 1814, 27.
[6] *Sundry Doc's*, 12; for Ritchie's attitude toward education, see Ambler, C. H.: *Thomas Ritchie*, 62–63, 220.

proposed was to consist of elementary or ward schools, in which, seemingly influenced by Du Pont's criticism, geography replaced history of the 1779 scheme;[7] general schools, divided into three sections, comprehensively called those of language, mathematics, and philosophy; and a third group, professional schools of various kinds, including one of Theology and Ecclesiastical History.[8]

As a result of the propaganda thus initiated, the enthusiastic annual reports of the President and Directors of the Literary Fund, and the circularizing of leading educators of the country, by Governor W. C. Nicholas, the Assembly, in 1816, had a mass of data to be utilized in creating a complete state school system.[9] The possibility of effecting this object, at this time, was increased by the augmentation of the Literary Fund into a prospective "million dollar fund" as a result of adding to it certain sums due the state from the national government.[10] A bill "Providing for the establishment of Primary Schools, Academies, Colleges, and an University" was passed by the House on February 18, 1817, but was defeated by the Senate on the 20th.[11] A unique feature of the bill was provision for the conversion under certain conditions of existing academies and colleges into state institutions.[12] The bill was defeated by two opposing forces; those interested in maintaining the ascendancy of private and denominational education did not regard with favor the wresting of educational control from their hands by the state;[13] those favoring Jefferson's scheme for converting Central College, the former Albemarle Academy into the State University wished a pronouncement in its favor.[14]

The defeat of this bill left the way open for a further attempt of the Jeffersonian party in the Assembly to introduce another

[7] See p. 164, 197.
[8] *Sundry Doc's*, 12 *ff.*; Lipscomb: *Writings T. Jefferson*, XIX, 211 *ff.*
[9] *Jour., H. Del.*, Dec. 4, 1815, 5 *ff.*; Jan. 12, 1816, 113 *ff.*; Feb. 24, 1816, 199; Dec. 20, 1816, 101; *Sundry Doc's; The Academician*, Mar. 25, 1818, I, 39; Maddox, *Free Sch. Idea Va.*, 63 *ff.*
[10] *Acts of Assembly*, Feb. 24, 1816, 6; Maddox: *Free Sch. Idea Va.*, 55–56; Niles: *Register*, April 6, 1816, X, 89.
[11] *Sundry Doc's*, 35.
[12] *Ibid.*, 44.
[13] Maddox: *Free Sch. Idea Va.*, 69 *ff.*
[14] *Ibid.*, 68.

bill for a state educational system. The religious-education section of Virginia had already started its Sunday School movement looking to the control of the elementary education of the
masses.[15]   Jefferson saw elementary education operating in the
interests of the church rather than the state; and the late summer of 1817 found him busy in drawing up a bill for an elementary school system, which to meet the free tuition feature of the
Sunday School system, was to be carried on without drawing a
cent from the Literary Fund, leaving that fund intact at the
same time for colleges and his favorite University scheme.[16]

The bill as originally drawn by Jefferson is of interest also in
its clearly indicated opposition to the Sunday School movement.
Ministers were to be excluded from serving as visitors of elementary schools.[17]   Teachers were to see to it that "no religious
reading, instruction or exercise, should be prescribed or prac-
ticed inconsistent with the tenets of any religious sect or denomination,"—a provision which would have resulted in eliminating
all religious instruction and exercises.   These two features of the
bill were eliminated, however, before its introduction to the Assembly,[18] with the evident intention of obviating controversy and
of increasing its chance of passing.   The withdrawal of elementary education from the benefit of the Literary Fund, and the
application of that fund to the creation of nine collegiate districts
with a college in each, in addition to a central university, met
with opposition from those interested in utilizing the Literary
Fund to defray in part the cost of elementary schools, which they
held to have been "the *primary* object of its institution."[19]

The result was the introduction and passing of a substitute bill,
entitled "An act appropriating part of the revenue of the Literary Fund, and for other purposes."[20]   The overseers of the poor
were now replaced by school commissioners who were to pay for
the tuition of as many poor children as they deemed expedient in

15 See p. 246 *ff.*
16 Lipscomb: *Writings T. Jefferson*, XVII, 417.
17 *Ibid.*, 418–19.
18 Randolph: *Letters Jefferson & Cabell*, 96.
19 Maddox: *Free Sch. Idea Va.*, 59, cf. 49; *Acts of Assembly*, Feb. 21,
1818, 11.
20 *Ibid.*

elementary subjects, utilizing existing school facilities. Provision
was also made for a board of commissioners to prepare plans for
the creation of the University of Virginia, and an annual appropriation of $15,000 ordered to meet expense of building and
endowing the institution.[21]

The passage of this act left the Sunday Schools at no real disadvantage. While the law constituted writing and arithmetic in
addition to the reading which was emphasized in Sunday Schools,
as part of the curriculum, the necessary classification of the child
as a pauper, put him at a disadvantage when compared with his
unstigmatized admission into the Sunday School. The tendency
toward "democratization" of Sunday Schools increased with
their tendency to become denominational in character, resulting
to the advantage of the Sunday School movement.[22]

The act of 1818 which utilized part of the revenues from the
Literary Fund for elementary education for a limited social
group, and part for a University, which, in the nature of things,
could reach only another limited social group, left a large intermediate section of society wholly unprovided for. The existing
academies and colleges, finding themselves without a share in the
single fund, into which they saw it was the evident intention of
the Legislature to concentrate all revenues for educational purposes, began immediately a movement to obtain some share of
that fund. Resolutions offered in January, 1819, inquiring what
portions of unappropriated revenues from the Literary Fund
were available for William and Mary College, Hampden-Sidney,
and Warren Academy, were followed immediately by inquiry
into its applicability and availability for the colleges and academies of the State as a whole.[23] It was found that the revenues
of this fund were insufficient for any purpose of this kind.[24] The
discussion in February, 1820, indicated a disposition on the part
of some in the Legislature to divide any surplus of the Literary
Fund, after making an annual appropriation to the University
and for the education of the poor, among William and Mary

---

21 *Ibid.*
22 Brewer: *Episc. Church*, 210.
23 *Jour., H. Del.*, Jan. 19, 1819, 113; Jan. 20, 1819, 118.
24 *Ibid.*, Feb. 3, 1819, 159.

College, Washington College, and Hampden-Sidney College and any other incorporated colleges and academies.[25] In February, 1821, it was decided to grant an amount not to exceed $20,000, to the colleges and academies of the state, at such time as the annual income of the fund should provide such an amount above a basic $60,000.[26]

It is significant as indicative of an intended oversight by the state, that preliminary to more specific action upon this general law, a resolution directed the President and Directors of the fund to report to the Assembly, the colleges and academies endowed by the present or former government, or by private munificence, the state of their funds, their acts of incorporation and rules.[27]

The denominational interests of the state particularly were active in forwarding this movement looking to financial aid from the state. "Iota" in an article on the "Literary Fund of Virginia" in the *Virginia Evangelical and Literary Magazine* for 1822, clearly indicated the alarm felt by the religious element in the state at the news that Jefferson's Central College was to be the University of Virginia.[28] In defending the claims of the several colleges in the state upon the bounty of the Legislature, he said that the neighboring people were attached to them, that many of the most intelligent and influential citizens had received their education in them. The affection thus engendered resented the impression that "the University is intended to put down these old and valuable institutions to the level of mere Academies."[29] "Iota's" plan without eliminating the University idea for the state, altogether, besides favoring an appropriation for Sunday Schools,[30] included a permanently endowed academy for every 10,000 souls, aid to the existing colleges, and assistance to the people in erecting several others where needed.[31]

The limitation of the benefits of elementary education, in the act of 1818, to children who were stigmatized as poor was so objectionable that a remedy was sought in petitions and presenta-

---

[25] *Ibid.*, Feb. 19, 1820, 197.
[26] *Acts of Assembly*, Feb. 24, 1821, 15–16.
[27] *Ibid.*, Mar. 15, 1821, 143.
[28] *Va. Evang. & Lit. Mag.*, V, 185.
[29] *Ibid.*
[30] See p. 248.
[31] *Ibid.*, 240–41.

tion of other bills.[32] The reports of the Second Auditor, during the decade in which the act had operated, indicate that the Sunday School had become a serious rival of the efforts of the school commissioners under the Literary Fund.[33] Any scheme the state would have to offer, must have superior inducements.

In February, 1829, a new law affecting elementary education was passed. The school commissioners were authorized to divide the county into districts, to appropriate a certain portion of their funds to building schoolhouses, the rest to be raised by subscription, and another portion to paying a school teacher, the balance again to be met by subscription. Such schools were to be free schools without fee for every free white child in the district. The law was, however, optional, not mandatory, and school commissioners were at liberty to operate under the law of 1818.

While the religious forces of the state were organized to operate schools on a voluntary basis, the civil forces were not, and not even the inducement of a partial support for buildings and tuition was sufficient to popularize this act. By 1842, only four counties had taken advantage of this act, and in some of these, only to a limited extent.[34]

It was not until 1835 that the Assembly took up the law of 1821 providing for the distribution of surplus revenues of the Literary Fund by calling upon the President and Directors of the Literary Fund for information as to the condition of the university and colleges and academies of the state.[35] About forty academies were reported on.[36] The Assembly had already in 1833 made an appropriation of an annual grant of $100 from the Literary Fund for ten years, subsequent grants to be at the pleasure of the Assembly, to Margaret Academy, in Accomac County.[37] The discussion in 1836 of the bill proposed on the basis of the information received, indicates that besides the University—Wil-

---

[32] *Jour., H. Del.*, Jan. 22, 1820, 137; 1826–27, 7–8; *5th Annual Rep't, Lib. B'd Va. State Lib.*, 1907–08, 223; Morrison: *Six Addresses*, 11–12.
[33] See p. 249–50.
[34] *Jour., H. Del.*, 1841–42, Doc. No. 34, 2–4; *cf.* Morrison: *Six Addresses*, 47, in which Lucian Minor states only three counties had taken advantage of the law.
[35] *Acts of Assembly*, Feb. 26, 1835, 253.
[36] *Jour., H. Del.*, 1835–36, Doc. No. 31.
[37] *Acts of Assembly*, Feb. 27, 1833, 13.

liam and Mary College, Randolph-Macon College, Hampden-Sidney College, Washington College and 38 academies were to benefit from the surplus of the Literary Fund. The colleges were to receive sums from $1,000 to $3,000, the academies from $100 to $500.[38] The law, however, as passed was general in its terms and provided that the surplus revenues should be distributed by the school commissioners ''in the several counties, cities, towns or boroughs'' to the academies or colleges therein, provided no sum should be used for building purposes. The trustees of institutions receiving these funds were to report to the officers of the Literary Fund as to their use.[39] In 1838, the school commissioners were authorized to distribute surplus funds as they deemed most advisable.[40]

The extent to which academies received aid from school commissioners varied from year to year—four were reported as receiving aid in 1837, nine in 1840, eleven in 1844.[41] Acts in favor of appropriations from the Literary Fund for particular academies were also passed from time to time.[42] Loans were also occasionally made from the Literary Fund to academies.[43]

In the wide power thus given school commissioners to distribute state funds without reference to the question whether the institutions were free from objectionable denominational characteristics in the conduct of their educational activities may be seen the change in the temper of the people from the days when they fought to destroy Anglican church influence and to free the state from ecclesiastical domination. By 1830, the Methodist church had profited from Presbyterian experience. The state incorporated Randolph-Macon College, apparently satisfied that it was guaranteeing its non-denominational character by forbidding it to establish a theological professorship, and by the law of 1836,

---

[38] *Jour., H. Del.*, 1835–36, Bill No. 5.
[39] *Acts of Assembly*, Mar. 22, 1836, 7.
[40] *Ibid.*, April 6, 1838, 33; *cf.* also *Ibid.*, Mar. 9, 1841, 51.
[41] *Cf.* Various Second Auditor's Reports as *Jour., H. Del.*, 1839–40, Doc. No. 4; 1846–47, Doc. No. 4; 1847–48, Doc. No. 4.
[42] *Acts of Assembly*, Mar. 12, 1840, 104; Feb. 17, 1842, 94; Mar. 4, 1843, 28; Feb. 13, 1844, 25; Mar. 12, 1842, 89; Mar. 9, 1849, 252; also *5th Annual Rep't, Lib. B'd Va. State Lib.*, 1907–08, 177.
[43] *Acts of Assembly*, Feb. 9, 1844, 23; Feb. 28, 1846, 28.

Randolph-Macon was entitled to share equally with Hampden-Sidney in the surplus of the Literary Fund.[44] Technically, of course, it would probably have been difficult to prove that the various colleges and academies were infringing the law in their religious activities. By reducing all religious education taught in schools of this type to the common denominator of Christian education, it is probable that their activities would have been sustained by the courts and the bar of the then public opinion in Virginia. Governor John Floyd, of Virginia, writing in his diary in June, 1831, indicated the success of the Bible Society movement in the following description of the temper of the people:

> . . . Much preaching through the city today and has been for some time. It is fortunate that the Constitution permits everybody to preach and pray as they please else this fanaticism which has seized upon the minds of the people, . . . would seek to satisfy itself by shedding the blood of their fellow citizens ''for love of the Lord they adore'' as was done so often in England and most of the governments on the continent of Europe.[45]

Madison, the following year, likewise testified to the greatly increased religious character of Virginia in the fifty years since the withdrawal of the legal support of the State.[46]

There was probably a very considerable element in Virginia who agreed with the sentiments regarding the relation of religion to education expressed by Rev. Stephen Olin, President of Randolph-Macon College, on the occasion of his induction into that office, in 1834,

> . . . Christianity is our birthright. It is the richest inheritance bequeathed us by our noble fathers. . . . And are the guardians of public education alone 'halting between two opinions?' . . . Can wise and practical men who are engaged in rearing up a temple of learning to form the character and destinies of their posterity, for a moment hesitate to make ' Jesus Christ the chief corner stone?'[47]

In interpreting Mr. Olin's address, the reviewer writes,

> It is not to be supposed, however, that Mr. Olin is in favor of subjecting our public seminaries to the control of any particular religious denomina-

---

44 *Ibid.*, Feb. 3, 1836; see p. 338.
45 Ambler, C. H.: *Floyd*, 145–46.
46 Hunt: *Writings J. Madison*, IX, 486; *cf.* also IX, 101–03.
47 *So. Lit. Messenger*, I, 16.

tion, or that the faith of the student is either to be influenced or regulated by sectarian views. On the contrary, he considers that such a course would be a manifest violation of the principles of free government.[48]

With this surrender of the public opinion of the state largely to the interests of the religious-education section of the state, it is necessary to see whether the primary schools were conducted with regard to a civil or religious conception of education. The reports of the Second Auditor after the creation of that office in 1823 give us an intimate picture of the schools of the period.[49]

These reports indicate that the blank forms furnished the school commissioners in accordance with the law of 1822 required information concerning the moral character of teachers and moral instruction of pupils.[50] Thus the commissioners of Nicolas County in 1823 reported: ''Every attention has been paid by the teachers to the morals of their pupils. . . . Teachers, in every instance, have been procured of correct morals.''[51] In 1825, the commissioners of Harrison County resolved to select only such teachers as ''are persons of correct moral courses,'' and the treasurer was not to pay the teacher until the school commissioners had given the teacher a certificate stating that he had ''bestowed proper care and attention to the education and morals of said children.''[52] The practise of the different counties with respect to their insistence upon moral character in teachers varied—some stating they had not examined the qualifications of teachers, but believed them to be persons of moral character; some based their belief on observation; others stated that they had ''properly examined'' their teachers; others, again, excused their failure to do so because of the difficulty of getting teachers.[53] In 1835, Smyth County reported:

. . . The commissioners have appointed persons to examine into and certify as to the qualifications and moral character of every teacher wishing to

---

[48] *Ibid.*

[49] *Acts of Assembly*, Feb. 24, 1823, 50–51.

[50] *Ibid.*, Mar. 2, 1822, 14; the Assembly had required before this, in 1812, in passing a law creating ''a free school or schools'' from the sale of glebe lands of St. Paul's parish in King George County, that ''No tutor shall at any time be employed unless he produce satisfactory evidence of his qualifications and morality.''—*Ibid.*, Feb. 11, 1812, 104.

[51] *Jour., H. Del.*, 1823, 8.

[52] *Ibid.*, 1825, Doc. L, 23.

[53] *Ibid.*; see 1831–32, Doc. 4, Sec. K, for year 1830.

*obtain aid from the literary fund, and resolved that no teacher shall receive
any part of said fund unless he obtain such certificate.*[54]

Some school commissioners apparently did not relish the task
of certifying to the moral character of teachers. Amelia County
reported:

> . . . It is considered by the school commissioners an invidious task to
> undertake to examine into the moral character and qualifications of teachers
> employed by the communities around them, when others who employ them
> are satisfied as to both: they are generally, almost universally, gentlemen
> and ladies of high standing and unblemished reputation.[55]

That the school commissioners drew a sharp line between
"moral" and "religious" in their search for qualified teachers is
not apparent. The close alliance between these two terms in the
thought of the people is indicated in the report of Northumberland County for the year 1837 when they congratulated themselves,

> . . . *that the qualifications of most of the teachers employed the present
> year are much better than in any previous year, and that the moral char-
> acters of all of them are very good, they being, with but one exception, pro-
> fessors of religion.*[56]

The benefit of this alliance was particularly emphasized in the
education of girls. The commissioners of Patrick County gave
it as their opinion,

> . . . all history, and the progress of events in all the nations of christen-
> dom establish the fact, that every thing in morals, religion, and our habits,
> depends essentially upon the mother—she it is that gives *tone* to the feel-
> ings and energy of the child, and makes him either a worthy member of the
> community, or a miserable drone and outcast.[57]

Ohio County reported a considerable number of their teachers,
"are females, characterized for piety and intelligence, under
whose care and instruction a correct tone is given to the morals
of female pupils."[58]

Further light is thrown on the importance of the qualification
of "moral character" in a circular of the Second Auditor, in

---

[54] *Ibid.*, 1836–37, Doc. 4, Sec. L, 28.
[55] *Ibid.*, 1839–40, Doc. 4, Sec. L, 19.
[56] *Ibid.*, 30.
[57] *Ibid.*, 31.
[58] *Ibid.*, 1841–42, Doc. No. 4, 34.

May, 1841, to the commissioners explaining the meaning of "An Act authorizing additional compensation for the tuition of poor children."[59]   The act had provided that this additional compensation was to be allowed only when the teacher had been ascertained, "either by examination of a committee of the school commissioners, or in some other satisfactory manner, to possess a fair moral character, and other proper qualifications for conducting a school of respectable grade."[60]   The Auditor thus interpreted the act:

> The possession of a "fair moral character" ought never to be dispensed with in a teacher of indigent children.   Many of that class are so unfortunate as to be deprived of all moral and religious instruction and example on the part of their natural guardians, and it is therefore the more highly incumbent on the school commissioners to remedy the evil to the utmost of their power by the selection of teachers qualified and willing to perform that parental duty to the children.   That education which enlightens the mind and neglects to improve the heart, not only leaves unchecked the evil propensities of Nature, and the vicious habits resulting from bad company, but in fact tends to increase the ability of the pupil to indulge them to a wider and more destructive extent.   How essential then to the temporal and eternal welfare of the children is this qualification in the teachers![61]

The reason for financial encouragement of moral teachers at this time was undoubtedly a result of literary propaganda emphasizing the importance of morals and religion in education upon society, and marked particularly the first outcome of the Smith Report on the Prussian School System which had been presented to the Assembly the year before.[62]

It was obviously a sincere desire to protect the morals of youth which inspired the Assembly to pass "An act regulating and restraining the terms upon which credits shall be allowed by merchants, tradesmen and others to the students of the universities and colleges of the state."[63]   No longer could a merchant, confectioner, tailor, shoemaker, tavern keeper, keeper of any house of entertainment, or keeper of a livery stable, corrupt the youth of the state by leading them into extravagance.[64]   In 1848,

---

[59] *Acts of Assembly*, Mar. 20, 1841, 51.
[60] *Ibid.*
[61] *Jour., H. Del.*, 1841–42, Doc. No. 4, Sec. D, 49.
[62] See p. 345.
[63] *Acts of Assembly*, Mar. 10, 1838, 29.
[64] *Cf. Jour., H. Del.*, 1837–38, Doc. No. 29.

this law was modified to the extent of making it applicable to students under the age of twenty-one years in any incorporated educational institution of the state.[65] The most significant feature of the law was the fact that the state undertook to regulate the conduct of students of institutions, which though incorporated, in many instances, were regarded as being affiliated with particular denominational interests.

In bringing moral instruction to pupils, the use of rules, moral lessons drawn from readers, and scriptural readings and prayer were employed.[66] The extensive use of the Bible was of course in line with the colonial tradition of its use for school purposes; but its use had now undoubtedly received a still more important sanction from the emphasis in its favor created by the Bible Society and Sunday School movement. In reports from over 100 counties for the year 1834, about one-third report the use of the Bible or Testament.[67] Kanawha County, which did not mention the use of these books, reported as its elementary books "Webster's *Spelling Book, Pleasing Companion, Moral Instructor,* and Murray's *Reader*."[68] The reports for the books in common use, in 1840, indicate the *Bible* in 22 counties, the *Testament* in 49 counties and the *Moral Instructor* in 5. Among 35 books listed, the order of frequency was *New York Reader,* 58; *English Reader,* 56; *Testament,* 49; Murray's *Introduction,* 24; *Bible,* 22; Parley's *Works,* 18.[69] In the following year, the *Bible* was reported for 27 counties; *Testament* for 55; and *Moral Instructor* for 3. The list of frequency for that year in a list of 40 books was, *New York Reader,* 57; *Testament,* 55; *English Reader,* 49; Murray's *Introduction,* 27; *Bible,* 27; *United States Reader,* 13; Parley's *Works,* 13.[70]

In commenting upon a proposed plan for the purchase of books, the Second Auditor, J. Brown, said in 1836:

. . . special care should be taken to select such books as would be best adapted to facilitate the progress of the learner, to inculcate the true prin-

---

[65] *Acts of Assembly,* Mar. 14, 1848, 120.
[66] Addington, R. M.: *Old Time School in Scott County,* 20.
[67] *Jour., H. Del.,* 1835–36, Doc. No. 4, Sec. L.
[68] *Ibid.,* 23.
[69] *Ibid.,* 1841–42, Doc. No. 4, Sec. M.
[70] *Ibid.*

ciples of morality and religion, and to afford an acquaintance with the history of his native country, and the character of its political and social institutions.   These being uniform throughout the state, could not fail in time, under the active superintendence of the school commissioners, to raise up for the state a large body of useful, intelligent and virtuous citizens. . . .[71]

It is clear from the above statement addressed officially to the General Assembly, and intended to guide school commissioners, that in accepting the inculcation of morality and religion as features of the educational program, the state differed in no wise from the policy of the religious-educationally minded section of the people.   By the close of the 4th decade, the propaganda in favor of giving a religious tone to schools had been so successful that it is hardly likely that schools of any other character would have been tolerated by the people at large.

It was, of course, only a generalized kind of Christianity that the state was willing to sponsor.   It apparently tried to avoid giving encouragement to any activity that might be construed as giving an advantage to denominational Christianity.   While it did not hesitate to incorporate academies and colleges that had a certain amount of denominational affiliation,[72] probably because they emphasized general Christianity and claimed to avoid proselyting action in favor of their own denomination, it refused to encourage theological seminaries, as being obviously in the interests of denominational religion, encouragement of which, in the early decades of the nineteenth century, it seemingly was felt was illegal.   Thus in 1839, in ''An ACT concerning devises made to schools, academies, and colleges,'' it declared any devise or bequest to a theological seminary invalid.[73]

There began at this time a new movement which, looking to improvement of the educational status of Virginia, sought to enlist a heartier general public interest in it.   The impetus to this movement seems to have been given by the official acknowledgment of Governor Campbell, that the two decades, since the law of 1818 regarding elementary schools went into operation, had been practically negligible in reducing the amount of illit-

---

[71] *Ibid.*, 1836–37, Doc. No. 4, 4.
[72] See p. 168, 312 *ff.*
[73] *Acts of Assembly*, April 2, 1839, 13.

eracy in Virginia.[74] To emphasize the inadequacy of Virginia in the direction of elementary education, the governor submitted by way of contrast to the attention of the Assembly the *Report On The Prussian Primary School System* prepared by Rev. Benjamin M. Smith.[75]

This comprehensive report is of particular interest because of Rev. Mr. Smith's statement of the manner in which Germany handled the problem of religious teaching in schools and its applicability to Virginia. He had found that the "government" insisted on a strong religious influence. In actual practise, religious instruction was free from either "sectarian bigotry" or "licentious liberality." Sectarian views were left by the teacher to the clergyman for explanation.[76] With reference to the applicability of German experience to Virginia, Rev. Mr. Smith said:

> . . . I believe we might safely go this far,—to say in the proposed plan of elementary instruction,—"the bible shall be a class book, where the majority of the school patrons desire it." And lest I might be misunderstood, I will speak my sentiments in the language of a *French* philosopher, M. Cousin, "the less we desire our schools to be ecclesiastical, the more ought they to be *christian*. Religion is in my eyes the best, perhaps the only basis of popular education."[77]

It does not seem that the suggestion of local option with reference to the use of the Bible, in an attempt to obtain an official sanction for what, as is evident from the Second Auditor's Reports, was a common practise, received at this time any serious consideration.[78]

Far more significant were the suggestions made at a series of educational conventions held in the latter part of 1841, inspired by the revelation of the census of 1840, that nearly 60,000 white

---

[74] *Circulars*, 1870–76 Collection—*Governor Campbell on Public Free Schools*, Message of January, 1839—a survey of men's signature on marriage licenses between 1817 and 1837 had indicated only about a two per cent improvement; *cf.* also Morrison: *Beginnings Pub. Educ. Va.*, 63.

[75] *Jour., H. Del.*, 1839–40, Doc. No. 26; Morrison: *Beginnings Pub. Educ. Va.*, 55.

[76] *Jour.*, H. Del., 1839–40, Doc. No. 26, 16.

[77] *Ibid.*, 24.

[78] Rev. Mr. Smith had been connected with the Institute of Education of Hampden-Sidney College and could not have been unaware of the extensive use of the Bible in the classroom.

people in Virginia over twenty years of age could neither read nor write. The publication of this fact throughout the United States was, according to Mr. Garnett, in an address before the Richmond Convention, "replete with reproach, degradation and disgrace to Virginia."[79] The conventions were designed to influence the report concerning "a school system best adapted, in their opinion, to secure the benefits of education to the people of this commonwealth," which the Legislature had asked the President and Directors of the Literary Fund to submit.[80]

At the convention held at Clarksburg, September 8, 1841, representing northwestern Virginia and the Shenandoah Valley,[81] all clergymen present were invited to take their seats as members and officiate with opening prayer.[82] It is clear also from the papers presented at the convention that the clergy were regarded as having more than an idle concern in the problem of education. Judge E. S. Duncan forwarded a letter in which he indicated that the goal to be sought by the western part of the state was to diffuse education so widely that "there shall not be one of our children who cannot read the gospels and the constitution, and the history of our country." He urged that "the clergy with great propriety" might give their aid in forming local associations to further education. The people must be impressed with the idea that "knowledge is power" for good—a fact proved by the statistics of criminal jurisprudence which indicated that as education advanced, crime diminished.[83] John D. D. Rosset in submitting his plan for public education emphasized the importance of requiring the teacher to "prove his morality by authentic certificates,"[84] and he also would have "reading the Bible" as one of the subjects taught.[85] The Convention likewise received

---

[79] *So. Lit. Messenger*, VIII, 115.

[80] Barnard: *Amer. Jour. Educ.*, XVI, 173 *ff.*; *Acts of Assembly*, Mar. 8, 1841, 51; *Jour., H. Del.*, Feb. 7, 1838, 109.

[81] Barnard: *Amer. Jour. Educ.*, XVI, 173 *ff.*; *Jour., H. Del.*, 1841–42, Doc., No. 7.

[82] *Ibid.*, 4, 7.

[83] *Ibid.*, 8–9.

[84] *Ibid.*, 10; the necessity for improving the quality of teachers is indicated in Rev. Henry Ruffner's description of the teachers of country schools as being "sometimes lazy, drunken vagrants, who deserve to be whipped themselves, instead of being entrusted with the whipping of the poor children in their schools."—*Ibid.*, 12.

[85] *Ibid.*, 11.

an address from Rev. Alexander Campbell, founder of Bethany College,[86] which showed his indebtedness to the Smith Report and his agreement with Smith's approbation of the views of Victor Cousin.[87] On the importance of the Bible, and religious instruction in education, Rev. Mr. Campbell said:

The Bible, as a school-book and moral instruction, are made a part of every day's education in every good school in the old world and in the new. A few years have accomplished a truly marvellous revolution in public opinion on this subject. Even since the French Revolution, that era of terror, that age of atheism and infidelity, that triumph of lawless despotism and licentious majorities, enlightened minds have looked to the Bible with more intense interest and assurance than before, as the palladium of all human rights, as the only strong and safe guarantee of our social immunities and privileges, whether political, moral, or religious. The philosopher, the patriot, the statesman and the philanthropist, equally with the Christian, say intellectual without moral culture is a curse to each and every community. To educate the head and neglect the heart, is only giving teeth to the lion, claws to the tiger, and talons to the eagle to seize and devour their prey. The ablest politicians and the most profound philosophers of France, England and America, now affirm that education in universities, in high schools and common schools, without the Bible and moral training, is a national calamity rather than a public benefaction. Hence in Prussia, and in most of the German States, in France, England and America, there is but one voice to be heard on this subject. All concur, sectarianism with all her brood and all her rival fears to the contrary notwithstanding, all coalesce in recommending the Bible as a universal school-book from the first lesson in the reading class to the last recitation in the college course.

.   .   .   .

It is also becoming more and more evident, that notwithstanding all our sectarian differences, we have yet something called a *common* christianity— that there are certain great fundamental matters—indeed, every thing elementary, in what is properly called piety and morality, in which all good men of all denominations are agreed; and that these great common principles and views form a common ground on which all christian people can unite, harmonize and co-operate in one great system of moral and christian education.[88]

It is evident from the manner of Rev. Mr. Campbell's emphasis on utilizing the elements of *common* Christianity in the educational process, that he believed this was entirely legal in Virginia

---

[86] See p. 315; Whitehill; *Hist. of Educ. W. Va.*, 65 *ff.*
[87] For Victor Cousin's *Report on the State of Public Instruction in Prussia*, see Graves, F. P.: *Hist. of Educ., in Modern Times*, 148.
[88] *Jour., H. Del.*, 1841–42, Doc. No. 7, 36.

and not tending to contravene the law, as perhaps some might interpret the attempt to teach sectarian Christianity. It is clear that the Presbyterian emphasis on the teaching of a common Christianity had come to be accepted as a safe position on the subject of religion in education.

The convention closed its session with an address *"To our Fellow-Citizens of the Commonwealth of Virginia"* and a memorial *"To the Legislature of Virginia."* The address to the citizens emphasized the necessity of building up in the individual, by education, a sense of responsibility to the state, in its republican form of government, and to God.[89] It argued that the philosophic and the religious development of mankind is found "in the freedom and moral responsibility of the individual." In bringing the individual to a realization of his responsibility, society must utilize every agent, the church as well as the state. It was not just to expect the church by its mere sabbath ministrations to a group, a large percentage of whom had learned neither to read nor write, let alone *to think,* to achieve anything substantial against the "passions, prejudices and false interests" that have held sway during the other six. The address continued, "We may as well attempt to roll back the waves of the ocean with a bulrush as attempt to stay the tendency to crime, misfortune and misery which must result from a continued state of such society." Besides there was the large group which never went to church. The only solution was for the church not to "confine herself to the pulpit," she must come into the school room. "The union of the church and the schoolhouse is not impracticable, and their moral union is indispensable; . . ." The basis of this union would be found in the diffusion of a common Christianity on the part of the church, while the state "by the proper distribution of funds," and by other inducements would receive the advantages and aid to be obtained from the church.[90]

In arguing for an alliance between the church and state on a basis of a common Christianity, the committee of the convention were substituting an alliance between many churches and the

---

89 *Ibid.*, 17.
90 *Ibid.*, 18–19.

state for the colonial alliance between the Anglican church and state. Beyond indicating "There will be a union of the state to every church to the full extent of the ability of the church in a state of union to do good and promote the welfare of the community," as an outcome of this alliance, the report did not indicate how the state was to reconcile its judgment of what pecuniary reward should be granted the church, for its benevolent work in assisting the state, with what the church might regard as its due, particularly when it would be necessary to extend the reward to the church not as one church but as several denominational churches.

The memorial to the Legislature did not go so far as the address to the citizens in emphasizing the necessity for a union between church and state on the subject of education. It presented the "necessity of adopting a system of public education, which *shall fully develope all the mental facilities, physical energies, and moral and social affections.*" It stated that the then system left out two necessary features of a proper education, the moral and physical branches. It emphasized the fact that there was no provision for ascertaining the acquirements, the capacity to teach, and moral character of the teacher.[91]

The second important convention was that held at Lexington in October, with delegates representing the counties of Bath, Augusta, and Rockbridge in the Shenandoah Valley.[92] The Convention was marked by the presentation of a "PROPOSED PLAN FOR THE ORGANIZATION AND SUPPORT OF COMMON SCHOOLS IN VIRGINIA" drawn up by Rev. Henry Ruffner, President of Washington College.[93] Rev. Mr. Ruffner emphasized the great necessity of preventing the education of youth "from falling into the hands of immoral or incompetent men."[94] Unblemished moral character and sound principles of Christian piety were indispensable qualifications in a school teacher. The teacher, "If not in full communion with a chris-

---

[91] *Ibid.*, 27–28.
[92] Barnard: *Amer. Jour. Educ.*, XVI, 173 *ff.*; *U. S. Comm. Educ. Rep't*, 1899–1900, I, 381–99.
[93] *Jour., H. Del.*, 1841–42, Doc. No. 35; Knight: *Recons. & Educ. in Va.; South Atlant. Quart.*, Jan. & April, 1916, Reprint.
[94] *Jour., H. Del.*, 1841–42, Doc. No. 35, 5.

tian church," should "at least be free from religious infidelity
and profaneness of language or sentiment, and be well acquainted with the holy scriptures."[95]   An important auxiliary
qualification was that prudence "which will keep him from inter-
meddling with religious, political or personal disputes among his
employers."   Among the subjects to be taught the prospective
teacher in his Normal school should be natural theology, the evidences of Christianity, and the Bible.[96]

Regarding the auxiliary means of popular instruction, Rev.
Mr. Ruffner declared Sunday Schools were "in a moral and religious point of view of unspeakable importance."   While they
could not be included in the public school system, because of varying denominational connection, yet "where this sort of institution
is neglected by the religious community, and where no religious
worship is regularly attended to, the Sunday instruction of the
children should be provided for by the school trustees."   The
schoolmaster should undertake this task, or where none is employed, pious and benevolent persons should undertake it.   "The
bible and other books proper for teaching the common principles
of religion" should be used, thus the youth would be prevented
from falling into "idle and corrupting practices."[97]

The third convention in Richmond, in December, was dominated by the practical-minded editor of the *Richmond Enquirer*,
Thomas Ritchie, and had nothing pertinent to say on the question
of religion in education.[98]

Governor Rutherford, in sending his message to the December
session of the Legislature, referred to the subject of education as
the one of the most vital importance that could occupy its attention.   He declared it was necessary from the point of view of
humanity and sound policy "to rescue from ignorance thousands
who for want of timely instruction may be lost to society."   En-

---

95 *Ibid.*
96 *Ibid.*, 6; *U. S. Comm. Educ. Rep't*, 1899–1900, I, 381–97.
97 *Jour., H. Del.*, 1841–42, Doc. No. 35, 8.
98 *Ibid.*, 1841–42, Doc. No. 11; Doc. No. 53; Barnard: *Amer. Jour. Educ.*,
XVI, 175; Maddox: *Free Sch. Idea Va.*, 143 *ff.*; *Ambler: Thomas Ritchie*,
220, confuses the date of the publication of the report of this convention
with the date of the convention; Morrison: *Beginnings Pub. Educ. Va.*, 61;
for an example of the influence of these conventions in stirring public
opinion, see Morton, O. F.: *Annals of Bath Co.*, 140.

lightenment was the means to lessen crime and purify public morals, to advance religion and perpetuate free institutions.[99] He urged that the colleges and academies should receive that patronage from the state to which they were entitled.

The report of the President and Directors of the Literary Fund in compliance with the act of March 8, 1841,[100] was submitted by Governor Rutherford to the Assembly, February 21, 1842. It stated that the most "prominent obstacle" to the usefulness of the system then in operation was "the want of well educated and moral teachers."[101] The "Project For A District School System" which constituted part of the report, provided on this point that the school commissioners, or a committee thereof, or some person or persons deputed by them should examine into the qualifications of the teacher and his moral character, and a certificate to that effect must be produced to the trustees prior to appointment.[102] The report did not attempt to define what was desirable in "moral character" nor did it say anything on the subject of religion in education. A bill in accordance with the "project" passed the House but was defeated in the Senate, primarily, it would seem, because of its provision for creating the office of superintendent of common schools.[103]

In a sense there was nothing strikingly new in the proposed regulation to improve the moral character of teachers. The act of March, 1841, had provided for additional compensation of teachers rated as possessing "a fair moral character."[104] The report for the school year ending 1842 indicates a difference of opinion as to the effectiveness of this scheme. The school commissioners of Roanoke stated that the law had been considered, but that the conclusion had been that no good would result— "the character of the teachers would be the same, and the effect would be to lessen the number taught." Shenandoah decided to refuse pay to teachers who came to school under the influence of

---

99 *Jour., Senate*, Dec. 7, 1841, 8.
100 See p. 346, n. 80.
101 *Jour., H. Del.*, 1841–42, Doc. No. 53, 3.
102 *Ibid.*, 6.
103 *Ibid.*, Feb. 21, 1842, 163–64; Maddox: *Free Sch. Idea Va.*, 147; *Jour., Senate*, Mar. 15, 1842, 231; Mar. 17, 1842, 238; Mar. 23, 1842, 267.
104 See p. 342, n. 59.

liquor. Nottoway was able to report that her teachers were "men of good moral character, and most, if not all of them professors of religion.''[105]

The discouragement with regard to the educational situation which had been reflected in the conventions of 1841 was not shared by the Second Auditor, James Brown, Jr., who had held that office since 1823. His report for 1842 in reviewing the educational situation, declared,

. . . Is it nothing that a youth is enabled to *read*—to *write a letter*—to *cast up in figures* the quantity and value of the products of agriculture and art? This amount of knowledge, if it be accompanied by sound moral and religious principles, will introduce its possessor into the busy world with strong claims on the respect and confidence of his fellow-citizens, and will assuredly conduct him to wealth and distinction, if nature has endowed him with a mind susceptible of improvement, and a resolute heart determined on success. . . .[106]

In the emphasis of the various conventions of 1841 upon the necessity of improving the qualifications of teachers, the denominational colleges of the state saw an opportunity of being of service to the state and at the same time building up their institutions. In January, 1844, representatives of William and Mary, Hampden-Sidney and its branch, Richmond Medical College, Washington College, Randolph-Macon, Emory and Henry, Bethany, Richmond College, and Rector College were present.[107] The convention was presided over by Rev. Henry Ruffner. It forwarded a memorial to the Legislature asking for an appropriation from the Literary Fund. In lieu of $1500 each, they proposed to educate gratis a certain number of students to be selected in such way as the state should indicate. These students were to be required to engage in teaching as were the students at the Virginia Military Institute.[108] Nothing came of this memorial.

---

[105] *Jour., H. Del.*, 1843–44, Doc. No. 4, Sec. L, 27–31.

[106] *Ibid.*, 1842–43, Doc. No. 4, 4.

[107] The article in the *So. Lit. Messenger*, Feb. 1844, X, 121, reporting this convention refers to Wm. & Mary as being ''under no particular sect''; Hampden-Sidney & Washington as Presbyterian, Randolph-Macon, Emory & Henry, Bethany as Methodist; Richmond College as Baptist. Rector College was likewise Baptist, see Morrison: *Beginnings Pub. Educ. Va.*, 166; for Bethany's affiliation, see p. 315.

[108] *So. Lit. Messenger*, Feb., 1844, X, 121 *ff.*; *Jour., H. Del.*, 1843–44; Doc. No. 21; Gov. Thos. M. Randolph in Literary Fund Report, 1820, re-

The following year was marked by another serious attempt, initiated at Richmond, "to take into consideration the best means of effecting the immediate adoption by the Legislature, of some more efficient and extensive system of popular Education."[109] In introducing its report of that meeting held in August, the *Southern Literary Messenger* asked:

. . . Who can doubt, that the most efficient instrument of good, in all our States, is the moral and religious training of the rising generation, that they may be qualified to discharge the duties of freemen, and to enjoy the privileges and pleasures of intelligent beings?[110]

A resolution introduced at the meeting emphasized a well regulated system of "Popular Education" as "the most efficient means of securing that virtue and intelligence" on which depended the preservation of liberty and a republican form of government.[111] A Standing Committee was appointed who issued an address to the people of Virginia, in which they declared it to be "a subject of paramount importance to the patriot, the philanthropist and the christian" to endeavor the regeneration of Virginia by urging upon the illiterate the necessity of intellectual and moral cultivation.[112] After referring to the fact that the ratio of those who could not read in Virginia was as one to twelve and a half, the address declared:

It would be worthy of consideration, if we could compute the amount annually paid by the State for the punishment of crime, consequent upon that state of moral debasement, which is ever the offspring of ignorance, and then ascertain how much less it would require to introduce intelligence and virtue. . . . If we could tell how many millions ignorance and vice cost the State,

ferred to the University as a future source of teachers—*Ibid.*, Jan. 5, 1820, 100; the Report of the Literary Fund in 1830, suggested to the Assembly "a school in each county on the plan of Pestalozzi" to furnish better trained and "moral" teachers;—*Ibid.*, 1830, Doc. No. 4, 36–37; both Hampden-Sidney in 1831 and Randolph-Macon in 1839 had interested themselves in the problem of education from the professional standpoint, the former in its Institute of Education, the latter in its proposed Normal Department—Morrison: *Beginnings Pub. Educ. Va.*, 54, 58; in 1842, Washington College offered a course for "English teachers" *i.e.*, common school teachers—*Ibid.*, Ms. notes opposite p. 58; *cf.* also Culbreth: *U. of Va.*, 83, re J. C. Cabell and Pestalozzi.

109 Christian: *Richmond;* 152; *So. Lit. Messenger*, Oct., 1845, XI, 604.
110 *Ibid.*, 603.
111 *Ibid.*, 604.
112 *Ibid.*, 605.

we would then see the importance of educating every child within our territory.[113]

In closing the report, the committee invoked "the aid of the
Reverend Clergy."[114]

As a result of the Richmond meeting in August, a General
State Convention, consisting of 213 delegates representing 51
counties, assembled, in December, at the same place. The convention appointed a Central Committee of Education "whose
function was to influence the Legislature and spread propaganda
throughout the State in favor of a revision of the educational
system."[115]   In this the Committee was eminently successful.[116]
In February, 1846, the Assembly enacted legislation establishing
district free school systems in about 20 counties, for the most
part circling along the periphery of the state from the southeastern to the northwestern borders.[117]   The inauguration of these
systems was left to the voters of the various counties and was
responsible for the creation and continued activity of the education associations inspired by a January meeting in Richmond, as
well as publicity in the press on the subject of education.[118]   The
act provided that all white children from 5 to 21 years of age
were to receive tuition free of charge; no class distinction was
made. The funds for the system were to be derived not only
from the Literary Fund, from interest on glebe funds, and other
gifts or bequests, but also from taxation. The curriculum, which
went beyond the three R's to include English grammar and geography, and, when practicable, history, especially of Virginia and
the United States, and the elements of physical science, made no
reference to the inculcation of morality or religious training.

---

[113] *Ibid.*, 606.
[114] *Ibid.*
[115] Barnard: *Amer. Jour. Educ.*, XVI, 175; Maddox: *Free Sch. Idea Va.*,
149, gives the number of delegates as 113; Morrison: *Beginnings Pub. Educ.
Va.*, 66.
[116] *Cf. 5th Annual Rep't, Lib. B'd Va. State Lib.*, 1907–08, 207, for petition of Citizens of Central Virginia; *Jour., Senate*, Jan. 8, 1846, 47; publicity in *Richmond Enquirer*, Jan. 3, 17, 19, Feb. 13, 1846; Maddox: *Free
Sch. Idea Va.*, 150.
[117] *Acts of Assembly*, Feb. 25, 1846, 37; cf. Feb. 12, 1846, 41; Feb. 19,
1845, 19.
[118] *Richmond Enquirer*, Jan. 19, March 5, April 14, Aug. 8, Oct. 2, 1846;
Peyton: *Augusta Co.*, 222–23; Christian: *Lynchburg*, 135–36.

School commissioners, however, were forbidden to appoint teachers without examining either by themselves or by special deputy into the qualifications of teachers for teaching and their moral character.

This provision for specific district free school systems was followed in March, 1846, by two laws, one entitled "An ACT amending the present primary school system," the other "An ACT for the establishment of a district public school system."[119] The primary school act retained the indigent tuition feature of the law of 1818, but was different from it in making mandatory upon the courts the division of the county into districts, the appointment of district school commissioners, and the election by these in turn of county superintendents. However, if the voters cared to, they might discard this system, in favor of any district free school system already enacted, in favor of particular counties, or the general act passed under the same date for a district public school system.[120]

The general act provided for a district system whose business was conducted by a county corporate body of school commissioners.[121] The expense of the system was to be defrayed in part by the Literary Fund, and in part by taxation. The provisions for the curriculum and qualification of teachers were essentially the same as those in the acts for specific district free school systems.[122]

---

[119] *Acts of Assembly*, Mar. 5, 1846, 29 *ff.*; Mar. 5, 1846, 32 *ff.*

[120] *Ibid.*, Mar. 5, 1846, 29 *ff.* The reasons for this variety in educational procedure may be gathered from the explanation by Wm. M. Burwell in an "Address before the Society of Alumni," University of Virginia, in 1847: "The recommendation of a State system, supported by a tax upon revenue subjects, revived the quieted questions of taxation and distribution, by shewing the excessive contributions of the East and the disproportionate advantages of the West, and this would again bring up the question of the power of a Constitutional Government to impose an exclusive tax upon property for Education, . . . The first difficulty is not, therefore, in the want of a population sufficiently dense to furnish scholars; but in so adjusting taxation as to secure to all, the benefits of Education, by a proper apportionment of contributions for its support." Burwell, W. M.: *Address Before the Society of Alumni*, 12–13.

[121] The commissioners were elected as heads of precincts, consisting of a suitable number of districts, while the districts were under the immediate control of three trustees, two of whom were elected by the people and one by the board of school commissioners.

[122] *Acts of Assembly*, Mar. 5, 1846, 32 *ff.*; *Jour., Senate*, Mar. 3, 1846, 198; Mar. 5, 1846, 219.

The propaganda initiated, in 1841, with a design to influencing educational legislation in the direction of tying more closely the lines of church and state, had, in 1846, succeeded only in giving a legal sanction to the insistence that the teacher should be of moral character; it had been unable to influence the curriculum specifically. The term "moral character" was of course extremely elastic and was undoubtedly interpreted in many communities in a manner little differentiated from religious character.[123]

Before the legislation of 1846 had had an opportunity to be put into practise, amendatory legislation was enacted in favor of various counties.[124] This new legislation is interesting in its attempts to enact more specific legislation from the point of view of morality and religion. In a law for Loudoun, Fairfax, and Kanawha counties, the moral character of the teacher had to be approved, school commissioners were given the power to recommend text-books, but it was provided that no books were to be used "nor instruction given in the public schools, calculated to favor the doctrinal tenets of any religious sect or denomination."[125] The principles of truth, justice and benevolence were to be enforced by precept and example.[126] The law passed shortly after, for Frederick and Jefferson counties included "moral philosophy" as one of the courses to be given when practicable, and provided that no books of an immoral or irreligious tendency, and none of a strictly sectarian character was to be used.[127] The moral character of the teacher had to be approved, and children of "grossly reprehensible conduct or incorrigibly bad habits" could be expelled.[128] Similar legislation was enacted

---

[123] *Cf.* Report from Smyth County in *Jour., H. Del.*, 1849–50, Doc. No. 4, 87–88.

[124] A hint as to reasons for this is given in *Acts of Assembly*, Jan. 22, 1847, 238; and Feb. 4, 1847, 238, in failure to appoint school commissioners, etc.

[125] The criminal Code of 1848 made importation, printing, publishing, selling, distributing, introduction into any family, school or place of education, of any printed matter tending to corrupt the morals of youth, a criminal offence.—*Ibid.*, Mar. 14, 1848, 110–11.

[126] *Ibid.*, Mar. 10, 1847, 34 *ff.*

[127] *Ibid.*, Mar. 20, 1847, 29 *ff.*

[128] *Ibid.*; *cf.* also Mar. 27, 1848, 64 *ff.*

in January, 1848, for Patrick County; in March, 1849, for King George County, and also for Albemarle County.[129]

It is of interest to find that an article in the *Southern and Western Literary Messenger and Review* in November, 1847, suggested that the school commissioner should be empowered to grant licenses to teach, but not unless the teacher could show a certificate from the college or university where he had been educated, indicating not only his literary attainments, but certifying also as to his moral character—the writer justifying this procedure on the basis that the salaries were furnished by the government.[130]

It was apparently in answer to those insisting upon these high standards, that Mr. Brown replied in his report for that year, saying that, if compelled to wait for "competent teachers," there would be fine and intelligent children compelled to remain "ignorant of the alphabet, and of course of their bibles, for the remainder of their lives."[131]

The report of the Second Auditor for the year 1848 is of particular interest because of the picture given with regard to the interpretation of religion and morals in education as it was worked out in Smyth County. This county working under the primary system act[132] had a county superintendent, who in that capacity, visited many of the schools. He reported:

Many of the teachers are professors of religion, and with one or two exceptions, all are of good moral character; and to these one or two, notwithstanding they were qualified to teach, the superintendent has refused the necessary certificate in order to enable them to receive any portion of the school fund, as he conceives it would be improper to employ the Sabbathbreaker, the profane swearer, or the drunkard, in our schools, no matter how well qualified in other respects.[133]

It is evident from the attitude expressed in the above report and in those of other counties, such as Giles and Hanover, that education was being regarded as effective only when allied with religious influences and the moral influences derived from that

---

[129] *Ibid.*, Jan. 24, 1848, 71; Mar. 8, 1849, 63; Mar. 14, 1849, 57; *cf.* also November 27, 1852, 227.
[130] *South. & West. Lit. Mess. & Rev.*, Nov., 1847, XIII, 687.
[131] *Jour., H. Del.*, 1848–49, Doc. No. 5, 9.
[132] See p. 355.
[133] *Jour., H. Del.*, 1849–50, Doc. No. 4, 88.

source.[134]   That a procedure such as pursued in Smyth County could readily be used by school commissioners to operate to the disadvantage of teachers of a minority religious denomination in a community will be granted.   In submitting his report for 1850, Auditor Brown again emphasized the importance of having school commissioners examine the moral character of teachers they employ, but did not define the term.[135]

In 1850, the anticipated State Convention for the revision of the State Constitution again brought before the public the subject of education.[136]   The educational statistics at that time were not flattering to Virginia pride.[137]   Likewise, notwithstanding the efforts to improve the religious condition of Virginia during the last few decades, Assistant Bishop Meade had told a congregation in Richmond that neither a clergyman nor a church was to be found in a certain county within a day's ride from Richmond.[138]

In an address intended to influence the Convention, Moncure Daniel Conway emphasized the importance of reducing illiteracy, if an extension of the right of suffrage was to be granted.   In answer to those who were opposed to the extension of the free school system on the ground that religion must be ignored, he answered:

. . . Now this is the theme most harped upon—and very dishonestly—by the opponents of this system.   Education goes on the ground that any *peculiar religious tenets* shall be taught AT HOME, and that general doctrines of virtue and morality shall be the limit of the School.   Well, now, this is RIGHT.   Where is the parent who would surrender the *privilege* of teaching his children, on those momentous questions, himself?   How do you expect the child to study the precepts of the Bible, if he be not taught to read?   What set of School-books on earth are there which are not replete with reading of a Religious character?[139]

---

134 *Ibid.*, 46, 49.

135 *Ibid.*, 1851, Doc. No. 4, 9; Norfolk, in 1855, in announcing the opening of a free school, which it hoped would "become a useful institution to the community in rescuing many friendless children from ignorance and vice," advertised also for a teacher "of good moral character."—James: *Lower Norfolk Co., Va. Antiquary*, IV, 38, 39.

136 Morrison: *Beginnings Pub. Educ. Va.*, 75.

137 Barnard: *Amer. Jour. Educ.*, I, 368; statistics as given by Barnard based on the census of 1850—number of white persons over 20 years who could not read or write, 77,005.

138 Thompson: *Educ. and Literature in Va.*, 14.

139 Conway: *Free Schools in Va.*, 27.

The Convention beyond debating the subject of education, took no action.[140] The Assembly continued to pass special legislation creating local free school systems as the desire for them arose,[141] and amendatory acts on education in general.[142]

The criticism to which Virginia was subjected upon the publicity of its educational status in comparison with other states in the union,[143] while it at first had led to the efforts to extend education for the masses which culminated in the legislation of 1846, now began as the North and South were facing each other as opponents on the slavery question, to lead to a certain degree of reaction in seeking to defend southern educational institutions and procedure.[144] [In 1855, an article in *De Bow's Review*, on a comparison of "Common Schools and Universities, North and South" argued that a statistical comparison of educational results in Virginia and Massachusetts showed that the University system of Virginia with its emphasis on colleges was superior to the common school system in producing that type of men which would redound to "the honor, reputation, and glory" of a country.[145]

In 1854, a Select Committee which had been ordered by the Senate to take up the subject of free schools throughout the Commonwealth "presented a bill 'erecting a fund for the perpetual maintenance of a system of Primary or Free Schools throughout the Commonwealth.'" The bill after a third reading was tabled.[146] It was in consequence of the prospects opened up by the consideration of this bill that the various colleges sought once more for an adequate assistance from the state.[147]

In December, 1855, Governor Johnson sent to the Assembly a plea that constructive action be taken in accordance with the law of 1821, granting a certain surplus from the Literary Fund to

---

[140] Morrison: *Beginnings Pub. Educ. Va.*, 75.

[141] *Cf. Acts of Assembly*, Mar. 29, 1851, 37; Mar. 15, 1851, 41; Feb. 25, 1851, 38; May 11, 1852, 173–75; April 2, 1853, 234.

[142] *Ibid.*, June 3, 1852, 117.

[143] Niles: *Register*, Aug. 29, 1829, XXXVII, 2; Feb. 26, 1848, LXXIII, 416; June 6, 1846, LXX, 214.

[144] *De Bow's Rev.*, XVI, 551.

[145] *Ibid.*, XVIII, 554.

[146] *Jour., Senate*, Jan. 5, 1854, 100; Jan. 24, 1854, 166; Feb. 9, 1854, 232; Feb. 24, 1854, 286; Feb. 27, 1854, 295.

[147] See p. 300, 306, 314, 319, *cf.* 311.

colleges.[148]   As the credit to the Literary Fund for the last fiscal year had amounted to upwards of $117,000, he suggested that a certain portion be given to aid the colleges that were not already endowed.   The justification for this grant was that the colleges "confessedly contribute largely to the intelligence, wealth and power of the commonwealth, and furnish a large portion of those who develop its resources, guard its honor and wield its destiny." He suggested that when a college had raised $50,000 by subscription and invested that amount in state securities, an appropriation should be granted from the Literary Fund equal to the interest of $25,000.[149]   With this official encouragement to further the interests of the colleges, defenders of the collegiate system of education took new heart in educational conventions held at Richmond, in July, 1856, and August, 1857.[150]   Governor Wise in his address at the latter convention taking up the subject of sectarianism in the colleges, and arguing for a system of university supervision, said:

Again: It may be urged that the most of our established colleges are sectarian in their character and influence. And I say, what if they are? The Literary fund is the people's fund, and the religions of the schools are the people's religions. The evangelical sects all have institutions of learning under their patronage. I don't know one of them which proslyte[s] through the schools, and it is well for us that we had religious sects to establish and foster colleges, for without them there would have been but few if any established. They have nurtured our institutions of learning and done the most for public and private instruction; they deserve the meed of our bounty. God forbid that we should not have a variety of sects of religion, and that all should not be tolerated. I ask only that they will acknowledge "Christ crucified," and that each in its own way will worship the only true and living God. Sectarianism will keep alive that rivalry and competition in the churches and schools which will forever prevent the green scum of a state of stagnation. . . . Christianity is a part of our republicanism, not by law, but by faith, and habit, and history, and I would deeply deplore to see any institutions, religious or literary, in our land, inscribed to the "unknown God." The only limitation to patronage of any should be that they are christian. . . .[151]

---

148 See p. 336.
149 *Jour., Senate*, Dec. 3, 1855, 16.
150 *Jour., H. Del.*, 1857–58, Doc. No. I; Maddox: *Free Sch. Idea Va.*, 167; Barnard: *Amer. Jour. Educ.*, XVI, 176.
151 *Jour., H. Del.*, 1857–58, Doc. No. I, 68.

It is interesting, after this defense of sectarian colleges and state support on the basis that "the religions of the schools are the people's religions," to read a message by the same governor to the Assembly in which he defended his refusal "to acknowledge Divine Goodness" in his messages or to appoint Thanksgiving Days on the ground that "State officers have no authority or power to interpose in religious matters belonging exclusively to private individuals and their voluntary church organizations."[152] In recognizing the sectarian influence of the colleges, the governor was not ignorant of the line drawn between church and state by the constitution, for he now said:

> ... But, there is no church establishment, and ought to be none; and there ought to be no meddling of the State with matters of religion and faith, except to protect and defend the freedom of conscience and voluntary worship, and to enforce sound morality and common decency. ... Any recommendation of worship from the State or its officers, in any form, is to some extent a constraint upon the people, who have forbidden by their constitution the intermeddling with such matters by political power. Politics and religion ought not, in any way, to be brought into contact. They pollute and destroy each other. Two of the worst evils of the times are *political-religion* and *religious-politics.* ... [153]

Apparently in the opinion of Governor Wise, an acknowledgment of "Divine Goodness" or a Thanksgiving proclamation was a greater tax on conscience than expenditures from the Literary Fund in behalf of colleges with denominational affiliation.

In 1856, the Assembly passed an act empowering circuit or county courts to incorporate institutions for educational purposes upon compliance by the incorporators with certain regulations.[154] It is interesting to note that in this act, as in an earlier act of 1848 concerning the educational activities of benevolent associations, there were definite limitations upon the amount of property and land that could be held, implying an attempt on the part of the state to curb the power of these private educational efforts.

---

[152] *Jour., Senate*, 1857, 107.

[153] *Ibid.*

[154] *Acts of Assembly*, Mar. 11, 1856, 33; this law has made difficult the tracing of incorporated academic institutions after that date; the act was amended in 1858.—*Ibid.*, Mar. 15, 1858, 54.

It is necessary to turn now to a consideration of the attitude of the assembly in regard to the extent of authority and privilege it was willing to grant educational institutions. This attitude appears to have changed in the direction of greater limitation as time went on, and experience, such as in the cases of William and Mary College and Washington College,[155] indicated the necessity of safeguarding the future interests of the state. The result was a tendency to restriction in the character of the general provisions enacted in charters.

While the early incorporations of educational institutions, after the separation from Great Britain, beginning with Liberty Hall, in 1782,[156] placed no restraint upon the authority and privileges of the trustees, other than that they were not to act "contrary to the constitution or laws" of the commonwealth, by the second decade of the 19th century, this proviso was extended to include the United States.[157]   In the following decade, seemingly influenced not only by its own experience with regard to chartered institutions, but also by the Dartmouth College decision of 1819, given by Chief Justice Marshall, recalling too, the case of Bracken vs. William and Mary,[158] the Assembly began to assert specifically its right to control chartered educational institutions. Thus, in 1826, in incorporating Rockingham Academy, whose original trustees were members of the Primitive Baptist and Dunker persuasions,[159] the Assembly provided "That the said 'academy shall, in all things and at all times, be subject to the control of the Legislature."[160]   The real intention of this proviso was more clearly expressed in the incorporation of New Baltimore Academy in 1827, when it was enacted "That nothing in this act contained, shall be so construed, as to restrain the General Assembly of this Commonwealth, from amending, altering, or abolishing, at any future period, the said corporation."[161]   In 1838, the Assembly had up for consideration, "An Act, pre-

---

155 See p. 189, 297, 233.
156 Hening: *Stat. at Large,* XI, 164.
157 *Cf. Acts of Assembly,* Jan. 31, 1814, 121, and subsequently.
158 See p. 179; Brown: *The Making of our Middle Schools,* 289–90.
159 Wayland: *German Element Va.,* 158.
160 *Acts of Assembly,* Feb. 18, 1826, 79.
161 *Ibid.,* Jan. 4, 1827, 100;—Rev. John Ogilvie, was principal of this academy from 1835 to 1855, Morrison: *Beginnings Pub. Educ. Va.,* 156.

scribing certain general conditions for the incorporation of academies and other literary institutions.''[162] Among the features of the bill indicating the tendency of the Assembly to control chartered institutions was, aside from the usual phrase forbidding conduct and procedure contrary to the laws of the state and the United States, the right to amend or repeal the charter and the requirement to report to the state, upon penalty of fine for failure in two successive years.[163] This bill was ordered printed, but was not passed. The right asserted by the Assembly ''to modify or repeal'' charters was, however, a common feature of incorporations after this time.[164] It was, of course, a device that enabled the Assembly to incorporate, without criticism, institutions which must have been known to be controlled predominantly by a single denomination;[165] it did, however, serve to protect the future interests of the state. Gradually, in incorporating institutions of this type, further limitations were placed upon them. In incorporating, in 1842, Northwestern Virginia Academy, at Clarksburg, an institution of Methodist affiliation, the charter declared:

. . . That no person shall be ineligible to any office or trust appertaining to the academy, or be excluded from a full and free participation in the privileges and benefits of the academy, on account of his religious tenets.[166]

In addition, it was forbidden to establish any theological school or professorship in connection with the institution.[167] A similar provision occurs in other incorporations; but that of the Academy of the Visitation, Mont De Cantal, an institution of Catholic affiliation is unique in having a prohibition against the establishment of a nunnery in connection with it.[168]

The provision sought by the act of 1838 with regard to reporting was enacted into the code of 1848, which required trustees

[162] *Jour., Senate*, Feb. 8, 1838, 55.

[163] *Ibid.*, April 9, 1838.

[164] *Acts of Assembly*, Dec. 15, 1840, 121.

[165] *Cf. Ibid.*, Dec. 15, 1840, 121; Feb. 23, 1849, 174; *Va. Sch. Rep't*, 1885, 151.

[166] *Acts of Assembly*, Mar. 26, 1842, 91.

[167] *Ibid.*; Miller, T. C.: *Hist. of Educ. W. Va.*, 42; Brown: *Secul. Amer. Educ.*, 66.

[168] *Acts of Assembly*, Feb. 21, 1845, 103; Mar. 14, 1850, 126; *Jour., Senate*, Mar. 13, 1850, 170; Whitehill: *Hist. of Educ. W. Va.*, 98; *Morgan & Cork: Hist. of Educ. W. Va.*, 165–66.

of all academic institutions to report to the Second Auditor, who was to withhold any revenue from the Literary Fund from institutions who were receiving funds from that source, if they failed to comply.[169]

The tendency to place limitations upon chartered institutions, making their existence dependent upon the will of the Assembly, and the attempt to avoid, by forbidding theological professorships, an appearance of lending aid to particular denominational interests, may be regarded as an effort on the part of the Assembly to protect the principle of separation of church and state.

With the great onward sweep of religious interest in Virginia after 1815, with the struggle of the various denominations to extend their influence, particularly by building up schools and colleges in affiliation with them, it became necessary for the state to impose safeguards as it was able, in face of the prevailing temper of the people, to protect that principle which not so many decades ago it seemed impossible could ever be possibly endangered in Virginia. The activity of the Methodist, Presbyterian, and Baptist ministers in the decades of 1830 and 1840 is thus described by a writer:

. . . Every licensed minister of these three denominations were agents [sic] for their colleges, working for their endowment, making educational speeches, soliciting students, and stirring up the people generally on the subject of education. . . .[170]

The state not only attempted, through the form of charter granted, to limit denominational activities through educational institutions, but, as has been indicated, in 1839, forbade devises to educational institutions for the benefit of theological seminaries.[171] In 1842, conveyances or devises for the benefit of religious congregations were limited, and no congregation was permitted to hold more than two acres of land in an incorporated town, or thirty acres in the country.[172] An attempt, in 1844, to bring up the question of the amount of property to be held by literary, charitable, and religious associations was defeated.[173]

---

[169] *Code of Va.*, 1848, 383.
[170] *Va. Sch. Rep't*, 1885, Part III, 88.
[171] See p. 344.
[172] *Acts of Assembly*, Feb. 3, 1842, 60; *Jour., Senate*, Jan. 5, 1842, 35 *ff.*
[173] *Jour., H. Del.*, Jan. 15, 1844, 95.

The Constitution, adopted in 1851, forbade the General Assembly to grant a charter of incorporation to any church or religious denomination, but permitted it to secure title to church property "to an extent to be limited by law."[174] It was in consequence of this provision, that charters were obtained by the various theological seminaries, and that institutions which formerly had prohibitions in their charters against theological professorships now sought amendments, if they thought the change desirable, omitting the prohibition.[175]

While these were the legal principles by which the state sought to protect the principle of separation of church and state, as it endeavored to extend its control over education, it is most illuminating to see what happened in actual practise in the conduct of state institutions.

The only institution of collegiate rank which was created durin this period, aside from the University, as a state institution was the Virginia Military Institute. The gift of the Society of Cincinnati to Washington College[176] remained in the treasury of the state, accumulating interest. In 1835, an act was passed authorizing its transfer when the conditions upon which the gift was made had been complied with.[177] The following year, it was proposed that since the funds were still insufficient to appropriately endow a military professorship, that the public arsenal near Lexington be converted into a military school, and the funds used to defray the cost of maintaining the arsenal be combined with the gift to effect the object proposed by the Society. An act was accordingly passed, the important feature of which was that the General Assembly was authorized to appoint the board of visitors, thus making it in a sense a state school. It was, however, to "be regarded and taken as a part and branch of Washington College."[178] Provision was made for admission of cadets from

---

[174] *Acts of Assembly,* 1849–52, 332; this action which forbade incorporation of churches, but allowed it to their agencies was the result of a movement in favor of church incorporation, sponsored by the Protestant Episcopal Church, some years before—cf. *Debates Cont. Conv.,* 1901–02, 764.

[175] See p. 293, 304, 315.

[176] See p. 308, n. 118.

[177] *Acts of Assembly,* Mar. 12, 1835, 8.

[178] *Ibid.,* Mar. 22, 1836, 12 ff.

the senatorial districts and for a state annuity of $6,000.[179]   In 1837, the appointment of the visitors was vested in the governor.[180]   Two years later, another act was passed which erected the school into a separate institution to be known as the Virginia Military Institute with the privilege granted the visitors of making any arrangements with Washington College for reciprocal relations as to instruction which might be mutually agreeable.[181] In 1842, cadets received as state students were required upon graduation to serve as teachers for two years in one of the schools of the state.[182]

Considering that it was a state institution in its beginnings, the character of the school in the early period of its career, as revealed by Superintendent Francis H. Smith, is not without interest:

. . . Besides the regular course of instruction above noticed, each class is required to attend recitations in the Bible, or the Evidences of Christianity, on the Sabbath. These classes are under the care of the professors. The cadets are also marched in a body, when the weather will permit, once every Sabbath, to one of the churches in Lexington—an equal distribution of their attendance being made among the four existing denominations. The cadets have also formed themselves into a Bible society, auxiliary to the Virginia Bible Society, and promote this cause by annual contributions.[183]

One wonders what choice the students of the state had in their distribution ''among the four existing denominations.'' The compulsory recitations in the Bible or in the Evidences of Christianity are probably not to be regarded as having been sectarian. Further light on the problem of religion in education in a state posited on the principle of separation of church and state is obtained from a study of the University of Virginia.

The University of Virginia

Jefferson's hope, that the College of William and Mary could be transformed into a civil university, faded with the judicial

---

179 *Ibid.*
180 *Ibid.*, Mar. 22, 1837, 20.
181 *Ibid.*, Mar. 29, 1839, 17 *ff.*
182 *Ibid.*, Mar. 8, 1842, 21.
183 *Jour., H. Del.*, 1844–45, Doc. No. 28, 7; *cf.* 1859–60, Doc. No. 11, 30; *Va. Hist. Reg.*, II, 227.

decision of 1790 that it was a private institution.[184]   In 1794, the President of the college, in a letter to James Madison, referred to a scheme proposed to him by Jefferson two years before for "establishing an University for this state, in some central Position upon a liberal & extensive Plan."[185]   A scheme for transferring the College of Geneva from Switzerland to Virginia was given up by Jefferson, in 1795, as involving too many difficulties.[186]   An opportunity for creating his ideal civil university came to Jefferson, however, with the development of events in connection with Albemarle Academy, an academy intended for Charlottesville, a town near his home, and incorporated in 1803.[187]   The academy seems to have had a paper existence only, when, in 1814, an attempt was made by the trustees to set it in motion.   As the story is told in the *Old Dominion Magazine*, Jefferson, happening to ride past while the trustees were in session, his counsel was invoked, and he surprised the trustees by urging them to secure subscriptions and convert the academy into a college.[188]   Jefferson now became a trustee.[189]   Steps were immediately taken to secure aid from the public and the Assembly, and on February 14, 1816, an act establishing a college by the name of Central College, in the county of Albemarle, was passed.[190]

While this was the period in which the leaders of the Protestant Episcopal Church and the Presbyterian Church were interested in getting their theological seminaries under way,[191] and the Virginia Bible Society had already undertaken its work, there seems to be no definite evidence that the opposition of the religious forces, which was to reveal itself with increasing strength

---

[184] See p. 179.

[185] *Wm. & Mary Coll. Quart.*, XI, 75.

[186] Lipscomb: *Writings T. Jefferson*, IX, 297; Bruce: *Hist. U. of Va.*, I, 60–63.

[187] *Ibid.*, I, 116; Morrison: *Beginnings Pub. Educ. Va.*, 136; *Old Dominion Magazine*, V, 2, in back of volume.

[188] *Ibid.*

[189] *U. S. Bur. Educ., Circ. Inf.*, 1888, No. I, 56; Morrison: *Beginnings Pub. Educ. Va.*, 136; Bruce: *Hist. of U. of Va.*, I, 121, 125–26.

[190] *Old Dominion Magazine*, V. 2, in back of volume; Randolph: *Letters Jefferson & Cabell*, 381; Culbreth: *U. of Va.*, 90; *Jour., H. Del.*, Dec. 7, 1815, 23; Dec. 14, 1815, 38; Dec. 15, 1815, 43; Jan. 5, 1816, 104; Feb. 27, 1816, 205; *5th Annual Rep't, Lib. B'd Va. State Lib.*, 1907–08, 33; *Acts of Assembly*, Feb. 14, 1816, 191; *Va. Mag. Hist.*, XXIX, 445.

[191] See p. 285 *ff.*, 302 *ff.*

after the next few years, existed at this time. The chief opposition which had manifested itself in the Legislature to the scheme was that feature of the petition which had requested that the appropriation of the Literary Fund due Albemarle County should be transferred to the new institution, and this need not be regarded as necessarily due to any religious opposition.[192] The most significant feature of the incorporating act was that tending to make it a public or state institution; for the act made the governor the patron of the college with power to appoint the six visitors who were to serve only for limited terms of three years.

It was quite natural, therefore, that as dealing with a public institution, the governor should, in January, 1818, present to the Legislature the report of the trustees which embodied the suggestion that in view of the disposition of the Legislature to create a system of general education, with a university as a component part, that the trustees of Central College were ready to turn over its resources to the state for that purpose.[193] The act of February 21, 1818, regarding appropriations from the Literary Fund, provided a board of commissioners to consider the details and submit a plan for the University of Virginia.[194]

On February 26, Jefferson wrote Joseph C. Cabell that he felt that the success of the proposal to have Central College converted into the University, would, if he were named one of the commissioners, be endangered. He declared:

> There are fanatics both in religion and politics, who, without knowing me personally, have long been taught to consider me a raw head and bloody bones, and as we can afford to lose no votes in that body, I do think it would be better that you should be named for our district.[195]

By this time, the opposition, which had been manifested toward the incorporation of the Theological Seminary of Virginia,[196] had

192 *Jour., H. Del.*, Dec. 14, 1815, 38; *U. S. Bur. Educ., Circ. Inf.*, 1888, No. I, 67; and Culbreth: *U. of Va.*, 90–91, attribute the defeat of this proposition to the opposition of the religious forces representing the older colleges—but a study of the attitude of the Legislature toward the Literary Fund reveals that there was a consistent opposition to diverting it from the use of elementary schools to higher institutions, see p. 334, 335.

193 *Jour., H. Del.*, Jan. 14, 1818, 118.

194 See p. 335.

195 Patton, J. S.: *Jefferson & Cabell*, 47.

196 See p. 302 *ff*.

made the religious forces of the state bolder in their efforts to maintain their position. The gathering of the religious forces of the state to carry on a campaign of religious propaganda as evidenced by the creation of the Virginia Bible Society, and the events in its train, apparently inspired in Jefferson a certain hesitation to associate himself in a prominent capacity with the university scheme, whose success he wished to assure. His name, however, headed the list of commissioners in the Rockfish Gap report submitted to the Assembly, in December, 1818. In reviewing the objects of education, the report emphasized the cultivation of moral character as an essential part of a well-directed educational scheme, which should be "moral, political and economical."[197] With regard to religious education, the report submitted the following view:

In conformity with the principles of our constitution, which places all sects of religion on an equal footing, with the jealousies of the different sects in guarding that equality from encroachment and surprise, and with the sentiments of the Legislature in favor of freedom of religion manifested on former occasions, we have proposed no Professor of Divinity; and the rather, as the proofs of the being of a God, the creator, preserver, and supreme ruler of the universe, the author of all the relations of morality, and of the laws and obligations these infer, will be within the province of the professor of ethics, to which adding the developments of these moral obligations, of those in which all sects agree, with a knowledge of the languages, Hebrew, Greek and Latin, a basis will be formed common to all sects. Proceeding thus far without offence to the constitution, we have thought it proper at this point, to leave every sect to provide as they think fittest, the means of further instruction in their own peculiar tenets.[198]

It was not intended, however, to eliminate the exercise of all religious functions at the University, for the plans called for a building "in which may be room for religious worship, under such impartial regulations as the Visitors shall prescribe."[199]

---

[197] *Jour., H. Del.*, Dec. 8, 1818, 9–11.
[198] *Ibid.*, 14.
[199] *Ibid.; U. of Va. Alum. Bull.*, Nov., 1895, II, No. 3, 87; Feb., 1897, III, No. 4, 93; Randolph: *Letters Jefferson & Cabell*, 463, 472; *U. S. Bur. Educ., Circ. Inf.*, 1888, No. I, 130, refers to Edward Everett's article in North American Review, Jan., 1820, in which the absence of a theological department in the University, is referred to as probably the first instance of the kind in the world.

The report closed with the offer of all the property of Central College to the state on condition that its site be made that of the University.

On January 25, 1819, the Assembly having accepted the offer, passed "An act for establishing an University."[200]   The act retained the principle of state control in the Board of Visitors and made the University "in all things, and at all times" subject to the control of the Legislature.   Its lengthy curriculum made no reference to theology or ecclesiastical history, though it retained instruction in Latin, Greek, and Hebrew.

The act of incorporation had hardly been signed, when Mr. Jefferson had to face a serious issue in connection with the appointment of Dr. Thomas Cooper as a proposed professor of the University.[201]   Dr. Cooper had been Jefferson's second choice as professor of Central College.   His first choice had been Rev. Samuel Knox, recipient of a prize in December, 1797, from the American Philosophical Society for his *Essay On The Best System Of Liberal Education, Adapted To The Genius Of The Government Of The United States.*[202]   Knox had been President of the Frederick Academy in Maryland and was regarded as an experienced educator.   His views in his *Essay* indicate that he agreed with Jefferson in divorcing theological education from public education, leaving it to the various denominations to erect their own schools, his recommendation being that there should be "One institution of this kind in each state, for each particular denomination."[203]   The offer of appointment was decided upon in July, 1817;[204] but, in October, the board was informed that Knox had "withdrawn from business" and the appointment was now offered to Dr. Cooper.[205]   With the transfer in January, 1819, of Central College to the state as its university, Jefferson

---

[200] *Acts of Assembly*, Jan. 25, 1819, 15.
[201] For articles on the life of Dr. Cooper, see *South Atlant. Quart.*, XVIII, 6 *ff.*; XIX, 24 *ff.*; XXII, 139; Niles: *Register*, Dec. 31, 1831, XLI, 326; June 22, 1839, LVI, 261; cf. Beard: *Rise Amer. Civilization*, I, 452; *Students U. of Va., Semi-Cent. Catalogue*, "Mr. Jefferson's Pet."
[202] See p. 195; Knox: *Essay On Best System*, Advertisement.
[203] *Ibid.*, 78.
[204] Lipscomb: *Writings T. Jefferson*, XIX, 365.
[205] *Ibid.*, 367; Bruce: *Hist. U. of Va.*, I, 194–95, referring to Knox seems to be unaware of the connection between Knox and Jefferson and refers to him as a "shadowy figure."

was anxious to assure the retention of Cooper's appointment. In February, Jefferson wrote Cabell, "Our engagements with Dr. Cooper oblige us to receive him,"[206] and proceeded to a consideration of organization plans. The reply by Cabell informed Jefferson that Cooper was "rather unpopular in the enlightened part of society," and that his appointment was "one of great delicacy and importance."[207] It is evident from Jefferson's reply that he assumed the opposition to be on the basis of Dr. Cooper's personal habits, for the propriety of which he could vouch. The fact that New York, New Orleans, Philadelphia, and even William and Mary were competing for his services, seemed to Mr. Jefferson sufficient assurance of his desirability.[208] The visitors of the University at their March meeting confirmed the appointment.[209]

The news of this appointment was received by the *Virginia Evangelical and Literary Magazine,* which had shown a favorable attitude toward the idea of a state university,[210] with a statement of decided disapproval.[211] They had their reasons: this was a matter of public concern; visitors and professors were public officers; "their conduct and their avowed principles are fair subjects of enquiry."[212] In their subsequent explanation of their attitude, they reviewed Dr. Cooper's observations on the writings of Dr. Joseph Priestley; not to do so, they felt would be to "sin against the common good;" to fail in the duty they owed their country.[213] With Dr. Priestley's objection to an alliance between church and state, they were in hearty accord; but they were opposed to his views on materialism and to Dr. Cooper's concurrence in his views, particularly as his argument was applied to a denial of the separate existence of the soul.[214] Especially objectionable was Dr. Cooper's statement that a man

206 Randolph: *Letters Jefferson & Cabell,* 164.
207 *Ibid.,* 165–66.
208 *Ibid.,* 167 *ff.*
209 Lipscomb: *Writings T. Jefferson,* XIX, 377.
210 Randolph: *Letters Jefferson & Cabell,* 157; *Va. Evang. & Lit. Mag.,* II, 46–47, 179; *U. S. Bur. Educ., Circ. Inf.,* 1888, No. I, 107.
211 *Va. Evang. & Lit. Mag.,* III, 49.
212 *Ibid.*
213 *Ibid.,* 64.
214 *Ibid.,* 67.

might be a good member of society, irrespective of the number or
fractional number of Gods in which he believed, and his question,
if he is a good man, "what more has society to require?"[215]   Offensive as was Dr. Cooper's opinion that "the doctrine of the
immateriality and immortality of the human soul" had originated in ignorance and been supported by imposture, the reviewer was struck with the impiety of his statement, "But if it
do lead to Atheism, what then?"   In the reviewer's opinion, it
must surely "require immeasurable hardihood and insensibility
to rob the universe of its maker, and man of his heavenly father,
because a philosopher is at a loss how to account for the generation of a worm!"[216]   To permit Dr. Cooper to come to the University would "alienate a very considerable part of our
people."[217]   It was not without a sense of vexation that Jefferson felt it necessary to surrender on this question.[218]   Dr.
Cooper's resignation was accepted by the Board,[219] and Jefferson
took occasion in his report to the Legislature, under date of October 3, 1820, to remind them that funds were lacking to proceed
in accordance with the commissioners' report of 1818 for a building in "which may be rooms for religious worship,"[220] disavow-
ing inferentially any intention to foist an irreligious university
upon the state.

The prejudice engendered by the Cooper incident was reflected
in the greatly increased opposition of the denominational forces
of the state, and particularly in their determination to receive
financial support from the state for their institutions.[221]   The
opposition to Jefferson, personally, is acknowledged by "Acade-
mus," an ardent advocate of the University, in letters to the
Enquirer.[222]   A loan from the Literary Fund to the University
was obtained in February, 1821, only by a compromise looking
to future appropriations from the same source to the various col-

---

215 *Ibid.*, 70.
216 *Ibid.*, 71–73.
217 *Ibid.*
218 Barringer: *U. of Va.*, I, 263; Bruce: *Hist. U. of Va.*, I, 204; Patton:
Jefferson & Cabell, 69–70; Randall: *Life of T. Jefferson*, III, 465–66.
219 Culbreth: *U. of Va.*, 108.
220 Lipscomb: *Writings T. Jefferson*, XIX, 394.
221 See p. 336.
222 *Richmond Enquirer*, Jan. 25 & Feb. 10, 1821.

leges and academies of the state.[223] But the denominational
forces of the state could not be conciliated by promises looking
so far into the future. Their temper is indicated by Cabell in a
letter to Jefferson in August, 1821, in which he refers to the talk
of the Presbyterians and Episcopalians at "their synods and
presbyteries" to the effect that "Socinians are to be installed at
the University for the purpose of overthrowing the prevailing
religious opinions of the country," and hence their increased
activity to strengthen their own institutions.[224] In the following
January, Cabell in his correspondence urged Jefferson "to show
a friendly disposition towards the colleges," referring to the
fact that the friends of Hampden-Sidney were anxious for aid,[225]
and that the clergy were "spreading the belief of their intended
exclusion."[226] Cabell finally reported a conference with Rev.
Mr. Rice, in which they "agreed in the propriety of a firm union
between the friends of the University and the Colleges, as to the
measures of common interest, and of postponing for future discussion and settlement points on which we differ."[227] In January, 1823, Jefferson wrote Cabell he still differed from him as to
the advisability of "giving a dollar to Hampden-Sidney." To
single out this one institution, he felt would be a departure from
principle, making the rest "enemies." It were better to let
Hampden-Sidney take its chance with the rest.[228]

The meeting of the visitors of the University held in October,
1820, which concurred in the arrangement to annul Dr. Cooper's
contract, was authorized to enter into arrangements for engaging
the services of Mr. Nathaniel Bowditch of Salem and Mr. George
Tichenor (Ticknor) of Boston.[229] The appointment of these

---

[223] For articles and reports of debates on this loan bill, see *Ibid.*, Feb.
15, 27, April 20, 24, May 18, 1821.

[224] Randolph: *Letters Jefferson & Cabell*, 215; Bruce: *Hist. U. of Va.*, I,
299, would attribute this rumor to opponents of further loans to the University—see p. 334, for opposition to diverting the Literary Fund to higher
education.

[225] Randolph: *Letters Jefferson & Cabell*, 227.

[226] *Ibid.*, 230.

[227] *Ibid.*, 233.

[228] *Ibid.*, 271.

[229] Lipscomb: *Writings T. Jefferson*, XIX, 390; Bruce: *Hist. U. of Va.*,
I, 329; *U. S. Bur. Educ., Circ. Inf.*, 1888, No. I, 71; the name is given as
Tichenor in original citation.

professors from Unitarian New England was no more successful than that of Dr. Cooper's. According to Cabell, it was through the correspondence of the Bible Societies that the discovery was made of the objectionable religious opinions of the two professors.[230]

It was becoming clear to Jefferson that effective action must be taken to save the University from the determined opposition of the religious groups.[231] He accordingly took advantage of the October, 1822, report to the Assembly to present his views on the question of religion at the University. He referred once more to the fact that the building, which according to the commissioners' report of 1818, was to contain rooms for public worship was not yet begun for want of funds, and to the statement in that report concerning the omission of a professorship of divinity in accordance with the constitution.[232] He explained, however, that the omission was not intended to indicate that "instructions in religious opinion and duties" was excluded by the state as "indifferent to the interests of society." It had been felt to be safer to leave to each sect, its own instruction as less inimical to religion, than for the state to show a concern in it. A plan had been suggested which promised to give the various sects the benefit of public aid without public interference. The plan was for the various religious groups

. . . to establish their religious schools on the confines of the University, so as to give to their students ready and convenient access and attendance on the scientific lectures of the University; and to maintain, by that means, those destined for the religious professions on as high a standing of science, and of personal weight and respectability, as may be obtained by others from the benefits of the University. Such establishments would offer the further and greater advantage of enabling the students of the University to attend religious exercises with the professor of their particular sect, either in the rooms of the buildings still to be erected, and destined to that purpose under impartial regulations, as proposed in the same report of the commissioners, or in the lecturing room of such professor. To such propositions the Visitors are disposed to lend a willing ear, and would think it their duty to give every encouragement, by assuring to those who might

---

230 *Ibid.;* Randolph: *Letters Jefferson & Cabell,* 233–34.
231 *Cf. Richmond Enquirer,* Mar. 12, 1822, for opposition in House; also *Ibid.,* Mar. 19, 1822.
232 See p. 369.

choose such a location for their schools, that the regulations of the University should be so modified and accommodated as to give every facility of access and attendance to their students, with such regulated use also as may be permitted to the other students, of the library which may hereafter be acquired, either by public or private munificence. But always understanding that these schools shall be independent of the University and of each other. Such an arrangement would complete the circle of the useful sciences embraced by this institution, and would fill the chasm now existing, on principles which would leave inviolate the constitutional freedom of religion, the most inalienable and sacred of all human rights, over which the people and authorities of this state, individually and publicly, have ever manifested that most watchful jealousy.[233]

The salutary effect of Jefferson's proposal, which may be regarded as his extension of Knox's plan to the particular Virginia situation, and a modification of the Episcopal plan with regard to William and Mary,[234] was described by Cabell in a letter to Jefferson as "the Franklin that has drawn the lightning from the cloud of opposition."[235] Jefferson, himself, in a letter to Dr. Cooper, in November, 1822, indicated that he hoped

. . . by bringing the sects together, and mixing them with the mass of other students, we shall soften their asperities, liberalize and neutralize their prejudices, and make the general religion, a religion of peace, reason and morality. . . .[236]

The sincerity of Jefferson and the visitors of the University in this proposed solution is attested by the fact that at a meeting on April 5, 1824, when regulations for the University were drawn up, provisions were made taking cognizance of this plan, and providing for a room in the rotunda to be used for religious worship, "under the regulations allowed to be prescribed by law."[237]

James Madison in defending the University of Virginia plan in a letter to Edward Everett[238] wrote:

---

[233] Lipscomb: *Writings T. Jefferson*, XIX, 415–16; Patton: *Jefferson & Cabell*, 72 ff.

[234] See p. 286; *cf.* also the subsequent Pesbyterian plan with regard to Hampden-Sidney, see p. 302.

[235] Randolph: *Letters Jefferson & Cabell*, 273; Culbreth: *U. of Va.*, 120.

[236] *Ibid.*, 117.

[237] Lipscomb: *Writings T. Jefferson*, XIX, 449–50; Randall: *Life T. Jefferson*, III, 470–71; *Jour., H. Del.*, 1826–27, 14.

[238] See p. 369, n. 199.

A University with sectarian professorships, becomes, of course, a Sectarian Monopoly: with professorships of rival sects, it would be an Arena of Theological Gladiators. Without any such professorships, it may incur for a time at least, the imputation of irreligious tendencies, if not designs. The last difficulty was thought more manageable than either of the others.[239]

It was Madison's opinion that the "X*n* mind" of Virginia would, because of its acceptance of the principle of separation of church and state, soon become reconciled to the University of Virginia plan.[240]

The position arrived at, by 1824, on the subject of religion at the University was, for those who like Jefferson and Madison defended the integrity of the principle of separation of church and state, the only logical one. While it had the color of yielding to the religious interests of the state, it sacrificed no principle of Jefferson's, as the student was free to accept or disregard a religious association as he chose and the state in no way contributed to the plan except to furnish space in the Rotunda—to cavil at which as long as the place was free to all religious groups might be interpreted as prohibiting the right to religious worship.

It is probable that if it could have been done without tending to a denominational bias that Jefferson would have rather favored a professorship in ecclesiastical history; for, in preparing his catalogue of books for the University, he indicated the following basis for his selection of religious books:

. . . In Religion, divided as it is into multifarious creeds, differing in their bases, and more or less in their superstructure, such moral works have been chiefly selected as may be approved by all, omitting what is controversial and merely sectarian.[241]

---

239 Hunt: *Writings J. Madison*, IX, 126; *U. S. Bur. Educ., Circ. Inf.*, 1888, No. I, 138.

240 Hunt: *Writings J. Madison*, IX, 126–27.

241 *U. of Va. Alum. Bull.*, Nov., 1895, II, No. 3, 79; Barringer: *U. of Va.*, I, 277; Bruce: *Hist. U. of Va.*, II, 186–87; that Jefferson was inclined to guard students from political "heresies" by censoring the text-books used is revealed in his letter of Feb. 3, 1825 to Cabell—Randolph: *Letters Jefferson & Cabell*, 339; Jefferson, in his classification of books for the library had "Religion," and under history, "Ecclesiastical" history; and under law, "Ecclesiastical" law. *Alum. Bull.*, Nov. 1895, II, No. 3, 79–80; Jefferson had asked the views of Madison—*cf.* Hunt: *Writings J. Madison*, IX, 202 *ff.*; Rives, W. C.: *Madison*, I, 641.

In 1826, one year after the opening of the University to students,[242] "Philodemus," in the *Virginia Evangelical and Literary Magazine*, published a series of letters to the President and Directors of the Literary Fund, in which he reviewed the educational situation of Virginia. He objected to the distribution of the Literary Fund to elementary schools and the University, as neglecting the middle strata of society.[243] He believed, too, that the University would tend to force other colleges into the status of preparatory schools for the University.[244] Further, the indiscriminate admission of boys above 16 to the University would work an injury to preparatory schools.[245] The Legislature, he held, should have given more patronage to colleges, which meant, of course, the denominational colleges.[246] It was, however, in the discussion of morals in schools that "Philodemus" showed his real animus against Jefferson and the University, in the implication that morality and virtue were not necessarily the concomitants of an "intellectual" education, when divorced from religious influences. He said:

. . . Many a promising youth, the light of his parents' eyes, the joy of their hearts, and the subject of their fondest hopes, has brought on them the bitterest disappointments, and hastened their sorrowful progress to the grave, merely because the due culture of his moral feelings had been totally neglected. A cold and callous-hearted philosopher heeds not this suffering. He has formed his theory. He steadfastly maintains that learning and science will ensure virtue and wisdom; and pursues his plans while the morality of the state is continually lowering its standard, and she is daily losing her influence.—We commenced this course at the close of the revolution; and now we begin to see its results. Gentlemen, we have been long enough misled by this error. It is time to attempt a change. When infidelity spread its poison through the land, then many of the practical maxims, which made our fore-fathers equal to the foremost men of all the world, were abandoned; . . . The work of education is only half performed, when man's moral powers are uncultivated. . . . Arguing then on what is admitted; permit me to ask, in tones of deepest earnestness, is the banish-

---

[242] The University was opened Mar. 7, 1825, according to statement in *Students U. of Va., Semi-Cent. Catalogue;* for announcement concerning opening, see Niles: *Register*, June 26, 1824, XXVI, 279; Mar. 26, 1825, XXVIII, 50.

[243] *Va. Evang. & Lit. Mag.*, IX, 83 *ff.*

[244] *Ibid.*, 196 *ff.*

[245] *Ibid.*, 204.

[246] *Ibid.*, 207.

ment of religion from seats of learning, likely to subserve the true interests of virtue, science and literature among us?[247]

The occasion for this lecture on the morals of students at the University was probably found in reports of disturbances at the institution, and expulsion of students.[248]

The articles by "Philodemus," in 1826, were not followed up until 1828, when "Olim" took up the question of "Religion In Colleges" by asking the question, *"Is it safe for a pious parent to send his son to College?"*[249] While the article referred to colleges in general, there is no doubt that the University was included, if not particularly intended. In the opinion of "Olim," "the error must be exploded, that moral and religious culture may safely be let alone."[250] The licentiousness of infidelity would inevitably lower the standards of morals.[251] Christians everywhere must work together to insist upon the introduction of religious instruction and observance in colleges.[252]

An event now occurred which to many of the religious-minded of Virginia justified their anxiety to introduce religion into educational institutions. In January, 1829, a typhoid fever epidemic, which closed the University from February to May, was looked upon by many as retribution for the insufficient godliness of the place.[253] Of all the consequent criticisms, that felt most keenly was one made on the occasion of a solemn memorial service in the Rotunda.[254] Rev. William Meade, later Protestant Episcopal Bishop of Virginia, was selected to deliver the sermon on the occasion. In the presence of a large audience of faculty, students, clergymen, then attending the Protestant Episcopal convention in Charlottesville, and neighbors, he preached on Amos (3rd chap., 6th verse) "Shall a trumpet be blown in the city and the people not be afraid? Shall there be evil in the

---

[247] *Ibid.*, IX, 352, 354.
[248] Niles: *Register*, Nov. 26, 1825, XXIX, 195; *Amer. Jour. Educ.*, Nov., 1826, I, 697; Ambler, C. H.: *Correspondence R. M. T. Hunter*, 27; Lipscomb: *Writings T. Jefferson*, XIX, 478–79, 98.
[249] *Va. Evang. & Lit. Mag.*, XI, 303 *ff.*
[250] *Ibid.*, 305.
[251] *Ibid.*, 307.
[252] *Ibid.*, 305.
[253] Barringer: *U. of Va.*, I, 146; Bruce: *Hist. U. of Va.*, II, 244, 370.
[254] *Ibid.;* Meade: *Old Churches, Ministers and Families*, II, 53 *ff.*

city and the Lord hath not done it?''[255] The doctrine of an overruling special providence in opposition to atheism or chance was the theme. A warning was given to ''heed'' the judgment of God, to study ''the divine philosophy of the Bible'' and teach the morality of the Bible in the institution. Finally, ''The importance of literary institutions was dwelt upon, and especially the great duty of calling in the aid of Heaven in the conduct of them.''[256] Great offence was taken at the sermon. Rev. Mr. Meade said:

> . . . It was charged against it that, besides undertaking to interpret and apply the judgments of God in a way which had been most carefully avoided, a personal attack had been made on the Professors and Visitors of the University, and especially on its chief founder, whose opinions, having been published to the world, were known to be contrary to those expressed in the sermon.[257]

Rev. Mr. Meade published the sermon and found, he said, ''Many were astonished to find that any in a Christian land could object to its doctrines, or expect any other improvement of the occasion from a Christian minister.''[258]

Resentment of Rev. Mr. Meade's use of the epidemic as a visitation from God was the greater, upon the part of some connected with the University, because through the interest of James Madison, now Rector, and probably Chapman Johnson, one of the trustees who had used his influence against the Cooper appointment, and other religious-minded persons of the University, an arrangement had been entered into the year before with the

---

[255] Meade, W.: *Sermon . . . May 24, 1829.*
[256] *Ibid.;* Meade: *Old Churches, Ministers, and Families,* II, 54.
[257] *Ibid.,* II, 56.
[258] *Ibid.;* Rev. Mr. Meade in closing his discussion refers to the fact that for some time after this event he was not invited to the University and attributes the opposition to him as coming not from ''Virginians'' and ''Americans'' but from ''foreigners,'' evidently referring to the professors who had been selected from European institutions. According to Trent in *English Culture in Virginia,* 22, ''All of the first faculty seem to have been Episcopalians except Dr. Blaetterman, who was a Lutheran.'' Cf. *U. S. Bur. Educ., Cir. Inf.,* 1888, No. I, 138; but, irrespective of that fact, the governing board was made up of Virginians, and it was probably the shock to their Virginia sense of courtesy which was responsible for Rev. Meade's being regarded as ''*persona non grata.*'' For the selection of the first professors, see Bruce: *Hist. U. of Va.,* I, 356 *ff.,* 369.

Episcopal and Presbyterian clergymen of Charlottesville to conduct religious services on alternate Sundays in the Rotunda.[259] This movement was probably an attempt to meet Presbyterian criticism as expressed in the articles of "Philodemus" and "Olim." As the arrangement for these services was a purely voluntary one, with no guaranteed salary, for the ministers, it was felt not to be in violation of the law. In 1829, arrangement was made for a regular chaplain to be paid by voluntary contribution. Insufficiency of funds resulted in the abeyance of the chaplaincy during the next two years and the invitation in turn of various preachers. By 1833, the determined efforts of a group of the faculty and students resulted in the institution of a regular annual chaplaincy to 1848.[260] The chaplains were selected in turn from the four leading denominations, Presbyterian, Episcopal, Methodist, and Baptist.[261]

By 1835, the religiously inclined had undertaken the work of a Sunday School and a Bible Society.[262] In referring to an address delivered before the society that year by the Hon. H. L. Pinckney, of South Carolina, a writer in the *Annals of Education*, speaks of the University as "an institution designed by some of the projectors, to furnish an example of the power of *unassisted human philosophy*," but now imbued by its officers "with the spirit of Christianity."[263]

It would, indeed, have been surprising that the University twenty years after the movement for the religious indoctrination of Virginia, begun by the Virginia Bible Society, should have escaped that influence wholly. By 1835, the room in the Rotunda was no longer able to hold those who wished to attend the services there and a movement was begun for the erection of a chapel.[264] The Board of Visitors while approving the scheme, apparently were not ready to sanction a site within the limits

259 *Ibid.*, II, 369–71; Patton: *Jefferson & Cabell*, 315–16; Metcalf, J. C.: *Cent. of U. of Va.*, 7–8; for a list of chaplains, see *Students U. of Va.*, *Semi-Cent. Catalogue*, and *U. of Va.*, *Alum. Bull.*, Feb., 1897, 94–95.
260 Bruce: *Hist. U. of Va.*, II, 373; Metcalf: *Cent. of U. of Va.*, 8.
261 *Ibid.*
262 Bruce: *Hist. U. of Va.*, II, 380; *U. of Va.*, *Alum. Bull.*, Feb., 1897, III, No. 4, 101; *cf. So. Lit. Messenger*, VIII, 53–54.
263 *Annals of Educ.*, V, 302–03; *cf.* Martin in his *Gazetteer*, pub. 1836, 123, who gives publicity to the religious exercises of the University.
264 Bruce: *Hist. U. of Va.*, II, 377.

of the campus.[265]   A petition of the students, drawn up by Prof. Bonnycastle, in 1837, was never formally presented to the Board, though they were informed of it.[266]

By 1840, the religious atmosphere at the University had so increased that a foreign religious observer, Rev. John D. Lang, noted with satisfaction that:

. . . The University of Virginia, founded and endowed through the influence and exertions of President Jefferson, languished and became almost extinct, till a Christian influence was infused into its management; *then* it ''practised and prospered.''[267]

The increasing religious spirit of the institution was, however, no more able to cope with or solve the disciplinary problems of the institution, than the philosophic appeal to reason had been in the days when Jefferson was alive.[268]   In 1840, a riot at the University had resulted in the murder of Professor John A. G. Davis, who had come out to quell it.[269]   In 1842, there appeared an unsigned article on the University of Virginia, in the *Southern Literary Messenger*, which referred to the special public attention drawn to the University by that event.[270]   The writer's opinion was that the event ought not to induce any one to withdraw his confidence and support from the University.   He said:

No institution should be encouraged where vice and immorality are not put down, or where any thing allied to them, is tolerated.   Are they tolerated at the University?   Far from it.   They are severely rebuked and punished; whilst every means of prevention is anxiously sought and adopted.   Examine the laws of the University of Virginia, and learn how they are enforced, and it will appear that the discipline, though mild, is firm, moral, and to a certain degree, religious.   There is scarcely an institution in the country, whose statute book contains more moral and salutary regulations.   Many persons, remembering a period in her history, to which none of her friends revert with satisfaction, look upon her as a horrid school for the morals of young men.   They have not read her late history; they even forget what

---

[265] *Ibid.*, II, 377 *ff.*

[266] *U. of Va., Alum. Bull.*, Feb. 1897, III, No. 4, 101 *ff.*

[267] Lang: *Religion and Educ. in Amer.*, 284.

[268] Niles: *Register*, Nov. 26, 1825, XXIX, 195; *So. Lit. Messenger*, VIII, 52.

[269] Niles: *Register*, July 10, 1841, LX, 304; Bruce: *Hist. U. of Va.*, II, 309; Minor, L.: *Discourse On The Life Of John A. G. Davis.*

[270] *So. Lit. Messenger*, VIII, 52; the article was by B. B. Minor who had been a student in 1837.—*U. of Va., Alum. Bull.*, Feb., 1897, III, No. 4, 101.

important reformations a few years may bring about. The system of discipline instituted by Mr. Jefferson proved, even in his day, to be impracticable; . . .[271]

Jefferson's greatest error in the opinion of the writer was that of "banishing religion from her walls." The disapproval with which a non-religious University was regarded is indicated in the following statement:

. . . The whole should have been planned and executed in reliance upon Divine aid and direction; for nothing can be truer than "except the Lord build the house, they labor in vain who build it." Without being superstitious, the over-ruling hand of Providence must be acknowledged; and apprehensions sometimes arise lest Heaven has decreed the fall of the University, in order to prove to man the folly and impiety of founding such institutions, without invoking its blessing. Religion cannot be safely separated from any human undertaking. For literature and science to produce their salutary effects upon the mind and heart—to make man better as they make him wiser—they must be associated with, and tempered by, religion; nor should their connection be slight and incidental, but designed and intimate. . . .[272]

Mr. Jefferson's system, the writer tells us, was now abandoned, regular religious services are conducted twice-a-week, but a chaplain is insufficient; religion must be made a primary concern. Neither must the externals of religion be decried; the religious services of the University must be conducted so as to make an impression upon the youthful mind; "The first thing to be done is to erect a suitable chapel."[273]   The annual rotation of chaplains was ineffective. "Get a good one and retain him longer," was the advice of the writer.[274]

Undoubtedly, the anxiety of the friends of the University to defend it was all the greater at this time because the appointment, in 1840, of Charles Kraitser, an Hungarian and a Roman Catholic, and, in 1841, of J. J. Sylvester, an Englishman and a Jew, had brought the University somewhat more than the usual amount of orthodox Protestant criticism.[275]   The Board of Visitors, however, while they permitted the use in 1841 of an enlarged

271 *So. Lit. Messenger*, Jan., 1842, VIII, 52.
272 *Ibid.*, 53.
273 *Ibid.*, 54.
274 *Ibid.*; Jefferson was not without defenders in Albemarle County, see Niles: *Register*, Aug. 22, 1840, LVIII, 392.
275 Bruce: *Hist. U. of Va.*, II, 160–61; III, 73–77.

gymnasium for religious services, saw apparently no way of reconciling the presence of a chapel on the campus with the law, and probably feared that it would mean the presence on the campus of undesirable sects such as the Unitarians.[276]

While the Board of Visitors was trying, on the one hand, to keep to a Jeffersonian interpretation of the separation of church and state, perhaps particularly inclined to that point of view when it was a question of expenditures from their limited funds, and, on the other hand, endeavoring to conciliate the enormous pressure of the increasingly religious-minded forces in the state, they found that the University was being threatened with the loss of its annuity of $15,000 granted to it by the original act establishing a university in 1818.[277] The report of the Committee of Schools and Colleges as given in the *Journal* of the House for 1844–45 makes it clear that the poor discipline in the University was still associated in the public mind with the ancient reputed irreligious tendency of the University. The committee in declaring it inexpedient to repeal the annuity gave their opinion of the religious reputation and actual religious condition in the college. It acknowledged there had been "Injurious impressions as to the irreligious tendencies of the institution." This opinion they were happy to say was "now very generally abandoned" though some prejudice still lingered with a few. They were able to say on the authority of "numerous pious divines" that in no similar institution was to be found a greater degree of voluntary respect "to ministers and ordinances of christianity" and so much devout piety. As evidence of the religious disposition of the University, they pointed to its chaplains, supported wholly by "voluntary contributions," as were a Bible Society and Sunday School. The arrangement for an annual succession of chaplains of different denominations secured the university from sectarian influence which would "not fail to impair its usefulness as a state institution."[278]

---

[276] *Ibid.*, II, 378.

[277] *Acts of Assembly*, Feb. 21, 1818, 14.

[278] *Jour.*, *H. Del.*, 1844–45, Doc. No. 41, 5; *cf.* Bruce: *Hist. U. of Va.*, III, 120; *cf. Richmond Enquirer*, Mar. 18, 1846, article by "Common Sense" in which he argues against withdrawing $15,000 appropriation as not helping to establish common school system.

Either because there is no necessary connection between religion and morals or because the religious activities did not embrace a sufficiently large proportion of the students, to be effective, the session of 1844–45 was marked by a series of riots of such proportions as to finally compel a temporary suspension of lectures during April.[279]

Seemingly, the religious sentiment of the state now finally succeeded in convincing the Visitors that the ungodly conduct of the students would be eliminated, if a still stronger religious force were introduced into the University. The resignation of George Tucker, professor of moral philosophy, now opened the way for bringing a minister into the University. The choice fell upon Rev. W. H. McGuffey, of Ohio, Presbyterian minister. With one stroke, the Board conciliated a powerful denomination and bridged the gap between religion and morals at the University, for Dr. McGuffey's strength in the field of morals is recognized, at once, when it is known he was the author of the McGuffey *Readers*.[280] With Dr. McGuffey, a new religious era began at the University. Dr. McGuffey lost no time in instituting morning prayers.[281] In 1849, the *Virginia Historical Register* quoted from the *Watchman and Observer* the account of "Clericus" who had visited the University.[282] He found that about one fifth of the 260 students were professors of religion in communion with various churches. There was daily morning prayer in the chapel by candle light. Four of the professors were in communion with the Christian church—the other five were "uniformly and decidedly in favor of religion." The chaplaincy by a recent arrangement had been extended to two years.[283] There was a Sab-

[279] Niles: *Register*, April 26, 1845, LXVIII, 119; May 3, 1845, LXVIII, 144; Bruce: *Hist. U. of Va.*, III, 112–18.

[280] *Ibid.*, II, 176; III, 90 *ff.*, 135; Bruce indicates the date of McGuffey's original connection with the University as 1846; Horner, F.: *Autographs of U. of Va.*, 21, gives the dates of McGuffey's connection as 1845–73; Culbreth: *U. of Va.*, 429; for other references to McGuffey and his influence, see Sullivan, M.: *Our Times*, II, 22–23; *South Atlant. Quart.*, XVI, 1 *ff.*; Gordon, A. C.: *W. F. Gordon*, 382; an advertisement of "Dr. McGuffey's Eclectic Series" of reading and spelling books appears in *Richmond Enquirer*, Sept. 9, 1846; McIlwaine, R.: *Memories Of Three Score Years and Ten*, 91–92.

[281] Bruce: *Hist. U. of Va.*, III, 135.

[282] *Va. Hist. Register*, II, 56.

[283] See p. 380.

bath School of some thirty children. The reference to Rev. Mr. McGuffey's presence is characteristic of the activities of ministers of his denomination: "The professor of Moral Philosophy performs an extra service in conducting a small class of five in a Theological course of instruction for the ministry." A colporteur was making sales of books to the students and an agent of the American Bible Society had recently collected in the chapel about $150. "Clericus" doubted whether there was to be found in the country, a college having "a more decided, strong, and salutary religious influence." In the thirty years since its founding, Jefferson's ideal civil university, in which religious or denominational influence tending to exert a certain social pressure in its favor was to have been strictly barred, had been transformed by the pressure of the religious sentiment of the state into a college which was beginning to exert upon the state probably as much religious influence as Hampden-Sidney.

McGuffey's labors were soon seconded by the chaplain, Rev. Wm. H. Ruffner, subsequently Virginia's first State Superintendent of Schools, who planned a lecture series on the "evidences of Christianity" to be given by the "most learned ministers of the Presbyterian church."[284] The sermons in book form later appeared on the tables of pious Virginians and received due praise in the *Virginia Historical Register*.[285] McGuffey seems, too, to have secured the assistance of various members of the faculty in spreading religious influence.[286] In particular, he had the efficient help of John B. Minor, chief professor of law, who conducted a course of lectures on the Bible, on Sunday mornings, at 9 o'clock. To these lectures, all his students were invited. A student who attended these lectures, has written:

. . . It was well understood that Professor Minor recognized the Christian life as the only one, and that he considered an acquaintance with the Bible essential to every lawyer, looking with special favor and interest upon those in his department of like opinion—who earnestly attended and studied these Scriptural lectures. Realizing this, few law students inclined to incur his

---

[284] Bruce: *Hist. U. of Va.*, III, 135–36; *W. Va. Hist. Mag.*, Oct., 1902, 33–43.

[285] *Va. Hist. Reg.*, V, 231.

[286] Bruce: *Hist. U. of Va.*, III, 142.

disfavor through what apparently seemed at the beginning of the course a slight extra tax upon time, that which, however, developed into no little responsibility as the session advanced, owing to the thoroughness of instruction and amount of material included.[287]

The social pressure which was responsible for Mr. Culbreth's entrance into the class is thus indicated:

. . . I did not connect myself with the class until the beginning of my third year and then at the solicitation of that congenial boon companion, Davis, whose religious precepts and example I so much admired as to permit a positive influence—that for which I am deeply grateful—over many of my University doings.[288]

With the religious forces at the University tending continually to become intrenched more strongly, it is not surprising to learn that the Board of Visitors, in 1851, not without some misgivings as to the legality of their action, granted permission for the building of a parsonage, the funds to be raised by voluntary contribution.[289] The permission was modified the next year—but as it did seem illogical, if the University was to have a chaplain, that he could preach, but not live on the campus—the matter reached a successful issue for the chaplain by the completion of a parsonage in 1855.[290]

In 1853, John A. Broadus, an alumnus of the University, whose graduation address, "Human Society in its Relation to Natural Theology," was to forecast his brilliant career as a minister, delivered in the Baptist church of Charlottesville a series of lectures on the Apostle Paul.[291] According to his biographer, "This series created a sensation and thronged the church to overflowing with professors and students from the University."[292] Whether because of the influence of the presence of Rev. Mr. Broadus in Charlottesville, and at the University as an assistant instructor,[293] or because of the accumulated effects of the other good works at the University, the *Richmond Enquirer* in April, 1854, was able

[287] Culbreth: *U. of Va.*, 432; *cf. U. of Va.*, *Alum. Bull.*, Feb., 1897, III, No. 4, 97.
[288] Culbreth: *U. of Va.*, 431.
[289] Patton: *Jefferson & Cabell*, 316; Bruce: *Hist. U. of Va.*, III, 143–44.
[290] *Ibid.*
[291] Robertson: *Broadus*, 74, 106.
[292] *Ibid.*
[293] *Ibid.*, 94.

to quote the good news of the *Charlottesville Jeffersonian,* that "Twenty or more of the students of the University profess to have been converted during the revival which has been progressing in that institution for several weeks past."[294] The article stated that one fifth of the students in the previous year had been professors of Christianity and believed the number greater that year.[295]

It would appear, that in spite of the attestation of the revival to the excellent religious influences now dominating the University, the report of which had reached as far south as the *Augusta* [Ga.] *Times,* a writer in the *Southern Literary Messenger* was not quite satisfied with the religious status of the University.[296] There was, he complained, "no provision for a *school of Theology.*"[297] The original lack of provision for religious teaching had been "remedied under the demand of a public sentiment." The religious sentiment, one of the strongest of man's nature, demands recognition. Consequently,

We must have religion in our education, because we cannot separate it from our nature. We must have it in our schools, colleges, universities. It is a necessity. Our relations to God are universal. They create obligations which are everywhere and in all the same, unchangeable. Prayer is not a sectarian enactment. It is the demand of nature; and no man, remaining a man, can live absolutely without it. . . . No man can object to the Lord's prayer. We have common wants. . . . The petition "forgive our sins" is of universal application. . . . We must, as a religious people, have the forms of prayer. We cannot have a public religion without it. We cannot honor God suitably without it—in family, in the church, in the legislative hall, in our schools and colleges.[298]

Comparing the public and denominational institutions, in respect to their religious atmosphere, the writer finds little difference. He declares that the experiment to conduct educational institutions "without prayer, without religion, even with the teaching of infidelity" had resulted in uniform failures.

---

294 *Richmond Enquirer,* April 29, 1854.

295 *Ibid.;* Bruce: *Hist. U. of Va.,* III, 138, places this revival after the typhoid fever epidemic of 1857–58.

296 *Richmond Enquirer,* June 14, 1854; *So. Lit. Messenger,* Feb., 1854, XX, 72.

297 *Ibid.*

298 *Ibid.,* 73–74.

. . . They have either become extinct or re-vivified by the incorporation of the religious element. Society demanded it—public opinion required it—discipline could not be maintained without it. There will always be a failure where man is attempted to be educated, elevated, governed well, without religion. . . .[299]

The article as an indication of the position achieved by the religious forces in connection with public education and an indication of a contemplated movement is not without significance.

A writer quoted in *De Bow's Review*, the following year, spoke of the prosperity of the University as a most gratifying instance of southern progress. He mentioned with satisfaction that

. . . Of late years, a large proportion of the students have been young men of decided moral or religious character. Reliable men have informed us, that the best social influences prevail in the institution and the deportment of the students is much above that of most of our colleges.[300]

Occasional disturbances had marked the conduct of the students since the Davis episode,[301] but as Bruce, the historian of the University, says, "The spirit of turbulence had, however, been steadily waning since 1850."[302] However, it was apparently difficult for the students always to approach the standard hoped for by those interested in their moral or religious welfare. Rev. Broadus who was chaplain, in 1856, wrote in a letter,

. . . The Christmas holiday appears to have destroyed all special seriousness in college, as I feared it would. I can find no heart to hope now for any general revival during this session. Yet, oh, if it might be so! I know of some eight students who have professed conversion during the session; three in connection with the Baptist meetings; three with the Presbyterians; and two without any special influences. . . .[303]

A writer, in *De Bow's Review*, in 1857, reviewing Randolph's volume of correspondence between Mr. Jefferson and Joseph C. Cabell, again referred to the absence of a Divinity School at the University.[304] This unwise exclusion had been the cause of much

---

299 *Ibid.*, 74.
300 *De Bow's Review*, Aug., 1855, XIX, 218.
301 See p. 381.
302 Bruce: *Hist. U. of Va.*, III, 128.
303 Robertson: *Broadus*, 131.
304 *De Bow's Review*, Jan., 1857, XXII, 68.

misrepresentation of the University in the past. Mr. Jefferson's purpose, clear from the correspondence, was "to prevent the University from falling into the hands of any one religious denomination, and thereby to preserve it free from sectarianism." This was an erroneous view; professorships in theology could be established, without touching upon "disputed points of christian doctrine or church government." Without a school of theology, the University was not complete. "One great branch of human learning, inferior to no other, is ignored." The writer was evidently more sanguine of his proposed experiment than Madison had been of such a scheme.[305]

In the session of 1857–58, a second typhoid fever epidemic occurred which was even more disastrous than in the reputed infidel days of 1829.[306] According to Barringer, who was a student at the time, this epidemic could not in view of the religious advance of the University be regarded as "a token of divine displeasure."[307] However, the knowledge of sanitary science which had progressed along with religion at the University, had proved ineffective.

Whether because of solemn reflection induced by this tragic event, or because of a culmination of the religious activities of the University which now included a "Society of Missionary Inquiry," or because the year 1858 was one "in which the religious feeling was greatly quickened among Christian communities over the world," a movement now took place looking to the establishment of a branch of the Young Men's Christian Association.[308] The object as stated in the constitution was "the improvement of the spiritual condition of the students and the securing of religious advantages to the destitute points in the neighborhood of the University."[309] The standing committee were expected "to

---

305 See p. 376; *cf.* Hunt: *Writings J. Madison*, IX, 210.
306 Barringer: *U. of Va.*, I, 146–47, gives the number of dead in the first epidemic as 6, in the second as at least 14; Bruce: *Hist. U. of Va.*, III, 138, gives the number in the second as 20.
307 Barringer: *U. of Va.*, I, 147.
308 Metcalf: *Cent. U. of Va.*, 8 *ff.*; Bruce: *Hist. U. of Va.*, III, 138 *ff.*; Barringer: *U. of Va.*, I, 147; a similar organization of this type existed before this time under the name of "Adelphian Society" at Bethany College, see *Bethany College Catalog*, 1855, 22.
309 Metcalf: *Cent. U. of Va.*, 10.

induce all suitable young men to connect themselves with it; to endeavor to bring their fellow students under moral and religious influences by securing their attendance at prayer meetings, and also to take in charge all contributions for benevolent objects."[310] It is significant of the success of the activities of the organization that of its 92 original members, 26 became ministers.[311] It is interesting to note, too, the University claims to be the first institution of its type to associate with it a Y. M. C. A.

With the increased impetus to attendance at religious meetings given by the new organization, the need for a chapel was more keenly felt than ever. In 1860, approval was given for a collection from the students for this purpose. Collections were also made from outside sources. A site was chosen in 1861, but further action was held in abeyance on account of the Civil War.[312]

The history of the exemption from tuition fees at the University of students for the ministry finds its origin apparently in the spirit of co-operation with theological seminaries suggested by Jefferson.[313] It was not, however, intended as part of the scheme as stated, to place students studying for the ministry in a privileged class. The enactments of the rector and visitors of the University as stated in their published pamphlet, in 1825, merely declared students of such religious schools, when attending the University, should be considered as students of the University, "subject to the same regulations, and entitled to the same rights and privileges."[314] According to a resolution offered at a meeting of the faculty in September, 1837, it had been the

. . . Practice of the Professors since the first establishment of the University to allow Ministers of the Gospel and Students of Theology to attend the Lectures in their respective schools free of charge—but the Faculty has hitherto adopted no formal Resolution on the subject.[315]

---

[310] *Ibid.*

[311] Bruce: *Hist. U. of Va.*, III, 139–40.

[312] *Ibid.*, 145–46.

[313] See p. 374.

[314] *Enactments By the Rector* . . . 1825, 10; for consideration by the Presbyterian Church of the Jeffersonian scheme, in 1859–60, see Barringer: *U. of Va.*, I, 153.

[315] Resolution of Faculty, Sept. 6, 1837—*from correspondence; cf.* Whittet & Shepperson: *Sketch U. of Va.*, 11.

A statement of exemption had, however, appeared in the catalogue for the year 1833–34; and, as a result of the formal resolution of the faculty, in 1837, similar statements appeared in subsequent catalogues.[316] With the publication of the catalogue of 1850–51, this statement was slightly changed to require those seeking exemption to bring proper certificates from their congregations as to character and standing.[317] These students were now classified as "privileged students."[318]

The Legislature was, of course, kept informed of the religious developments at the University through the reports of the Rector and Visitors of the University.[319] There seems to be no suggestion that as a group they were not in sympathy with the movement to bring religion into the University. Probably many were inclined to believe with James C. Southall, who addressed the Alumni in 1860 on the "Subject of Democracy," that the change had been a desirable one not only for the University but also for the state. Mr. Southall declared:

. . . I think I can observe the most marked change in this institution. I have understood that one-fourth or one-third of the students now are usually pious. They hold daily prayer-meetings. By this token, I am persuaded that Virginia shall prosper.[320]

In view of the gradually increasing extension of religious interests and influences at the state's most important educational institution, it will be seen that certain tendencies which characterized the treatment of the problem of religion in education, in the period after the Civil War, were the natural consequents of an "historical environment" created by the principle of separation of church and state, and the experience of a society dominated by a theistic conception of the universe and man's place in it.

---

[316] *U. of Va. Catalog*, 1839–40, 19; 1841–42, 18; 1847–48, 27.
[317] *Ibid.*, 1850–51, 33.
[318] *Ibid.*
[319] *Cf. Va. Documents*, 1859–60, Doc. No. 12.
[320] Southall, J. D.: *An Address on the Subject of Democracy*, 28.

PART III

DURING THE PERIOD OF CO-OPERATION WITHOUT ALLIANCE

(FROM THE CIVIL WAR TO 1926)

CHAPTER X

INAUGURATION OF THE POLICY OF CO-OPERATION WITHOUT ALLIANCE

The New Virginia

From many points of view, the separation of western Virginia from "the Old Dominion," and its entrance into the Union on June 20th, 1863, as West Virginia may be regarded as one of the serious consequences of the Civil War for Virginia.[1] While the loss of approximately one third of her territory may have contributed to the subsequent social and economic unity of the remaining section, this gain has been at the expense of vast potential wealth in the lost territory.[2] Various factors, generally listed as geographic, ethnic, religious, and economic, have been noted by historians as contributing to the "disruption" of Virginia; but, in the sixty years since the Civil War, the greatly improved means of communication have tended to lessen considerably the significance of these factors, which loomed so large before the War, and to make important the loss represented in the actual and potential wealth of West Virginia.[3] It would be a futile task to attempt to evaluate these various factors in creating that attitude of sectionalism which resulted in separation. The spirit of dissent in the section west of the Blue Ridge and in the Shenandoah Valley, which had in the colonial period contributed so largely to the downfall of the Established Church and the separation of church and state, spreading westward, now gave expression to that feeling of hostility, which the failure to recognize in adequate fashion the demands for free and universal education, suffrage and representation, had, since the early part of the nineteenth century, inspired in that section. It

---

[1] McGregor, J. C.: *Disruption of Va.*, 320.
[2] *Ibid.*
[3] Maddox: *Free Sch. Idea Va.*, 17–20, 93 *ff.*; McGregor: *Disruption of Va.*, 17; Ambler: *Sectionalism in Va.*, 175 *ff.*; Sweet, W. W.: *The Meth. Epis. Church*, 54.

is a fact that since the close of the eighteenth century, western Virginia had been fairly consistent, as demonstrated by the vote of its representatives in the Assembly, in its favorable attitude toward free elementary education, in opposition to the tendency of the East to favor higher, at the expense of lower education.[4] In the opinion of Ambler, the small proportionate enrollment of students from western Virginia in the University of Virginia and eastern colleges of the state, as compared with their enrollment in colleges in Ohio and Pennsylvania in the two decades before the Civil War, should be attributed largely to the growing sectional feeling and antagonism of western to eastern Virginia on this subject of educational policy—spurning, when it did yield to the lure of higher education, to avail itself of the opportunities in the home state.[5]

Students of the causes leading to "disruption" have also found in the attitude of the various denominations, particularly of the Methodist Church, to slavery, a more potent factor, in the separation of western Virginia, than the differences on the question of educational policy.[6] The establishment of the Wesleyan Methodist Connection of America, in 1843, with the resulting schism in the Methodist Episcopal Church, in 1844, the consequent creation of the Methodist Episcopal Church, South, in 1845, and the subsequent rendering of western Virginia as "the real "dark and bloody ground" of the church conflict" between the old church and the new, for retention or acquisition of membership and prestige, contributed, according to an historian of that conflict, to the intensification of the "existing sectional feeling in Virginia and paved the way for the new state of West Virginia."[7]   The definite stand, since 1856, of the ministers of

---

[4] Maddox: *Free Sch. Idea Va.*, 92; Ambler: *Sectionalism in Va.*, 273 *ff.*

[5] *Ibid.*, 275, 282. Ambler states that out of 112 Virginia students at the University, 1841–42, only 12 came from counties west of the Blue Ridge; in 1859, only 17 out of 370 Virginia students were from West Virginia; *cf.* Maddox: *Free Sch. Idea Va.*, 92; *Branch Hist. Papers*, III, 133.

[6] Ambler: *Sectionalism in Va.*, 282 *ff.*; *Va. Literary Museum*, I, 333; for a statement of the attitude of the Presbyterian, Baptist, and Protestant Episcopal Churches toward slavery, see Sweet: *Meth. Epis. Church*, 26–28; for brief statements concerning divisions in the Baptist, Presbyterian, and Protestant Episcopal churches on the slavery question, see *The Encyclopedia Americana*, III, 223, and XXII, 535, 536, 683.

[7] Norwood, J. M.: *The Schism in the Meth. Epis. Church, 1844*, 48, 99, 131, 135, *cf.* 187; Buckley: *History of Methodists*, 414, 459 *ff.*; Sweet:

the old church against dis-union contributed to the separation of western Virginia.[8]

With the separation of western Virginia, "the Old Dominion" lost about 361,000 out of an approximate population of 1,600,000.[9] The history of education in Virginia in the decades immediately after the Civil War is the history of education in a Virginia shorn of a considerable proportion of its former territory, population, and wealth. With the separation of western Virginia, and the emancipation of its slaves, it was a "new" Virginia which re-entered the Union, in May, 1865.[10]

The New Civil School System
(1860–1902)

To understand the relation between religion and education in the "new" Virginia of the reconstruction period, it is necessary to give first, at least, a cursory account of the new civil school system inaugurated after the War. It was not until the Constitutional Convention of December, 1867, that serious official consideration was given to the further development of the public school system of Virginia—no important modifying legislation having been passed since 1846.[11] Under the "reconstruction" Constitution of April, 1868, Virginia was ruled until the Constitution of 1902 was adopted; and the educational history of Virginia during the period of the "Underwood Constitution," 1868–1902, may well be studied as a unit.

While official consideration of the educational problem was lacking during the War, the professionally minded among the educators of Virginia, as represented by the Educational Associations of Richmond and Petersburg, had called for a conven-

---

Meth. Epis. Church, 22, 36, 46, 53–55; Sweet, p. 53, gives the membership in western Virginia of the Methodist Episcopal Church, as 21,792, of the Methodist Episcopal Church, South, as 10,898; *U. S. Bur. Census, Mortality and Misc. Stat.,* 1860, 487, gives the number of Methodist churches for Virginia as 1,403, with aggregate accommodations as 438,244.

8 Sweet: *Meth. Epis. Church,* 53–55.

9 McGregor: *Disruption of Va.,* 11.

10 Taylor, A. A.: *Negro in Reconst. of Va.,* 9.

11 See p. 355; the education issue had come up before the Constitutional Convention of 1864, but no action had been taken; *cf.* Eckenrode, H. J.: *Political Reconst. Va.,* 93.

tion of teachers, in December, 1863.[12]   The meeting was held
in Petersburg, and an "Educational Association of Virginia"
was organized, which was to meet annually, but did not meet
again until 1866 at Charlottesville.[13]   At this meeting, a committee was appointed to address a memorial to the General Assembly, proposing the creation of a "Department of Public Instruction."[14]   An address on this subject was delivered by Rev.
Dr. B. Sears, of the Peabody Education Fund, at the annual
meeting in 1867.   Aside from these efforts, the Educational Association of Virginia apparently made no attempt to influence
the legislative program with regard to the administrative features of the proposed educational system; the Association concerned itself largely with the curriculum and professional problems.[15]   With respect to the curriculum, it manifested a keen
interest in the problem of the relation of moral and religious
instruction to education.[16]

The chief educational problem presenting itself to the Constitutional Convention of 1867 was that of extending educational opportunity.   Not only did the enfranchisement of the
negro make a consideration of this phase of the problem important from his standpoint and that of society in general, but a
review of the census figures of 1860, with regard to illiteracy,
made it an equally important consideration from the standpoint
of the whites.   Of an approximate total population, in 1860, of
1,600,000, about one third was colored.[17]   Of the white population, over 7 per cent of those over twenty years of age could
neither read nor write.[18]

The Convention was addressed, in January, by Dr. Sears, who
explained the reasons of the trustees of the Peabody Education

---

[12] *Minutes Educ. Assoc. Va.*, 1863, 3.

[13] Barnard: *Amer. Jour. Educ.*, XXII, 551; *Va. Educ. Jour.*, Dec., 1891,
529–30; the Educational Association of Virginia continued its existence until
1882, and was reorganized in 1891, *Ibid.*

[14] Barnard: *Amer. Jour. Educ.*, XXII, 552; *Minutes Educ. Assoc. Va.*,
1866.

[15] Barnard: *Amer. Jour. Educ.*, XXII, 552 *ff.*; *cf.* various annual *Minutes
Educ. Assoc. Va.*

[16] See p. 418, 421, 427 *ff.*

[17] *U. S. Bur. Census, Population*, 1860, 511–13.

[18] *Ibid., Mortality and Misc. Stat.*, 1860, 508; the actual figures for this
illiterate group were 74,055.

Fund in concentrating their resources and labors on elementary schools.[19] Dr. Sears held it impossible to be satisfied with the education of the few, seeing that God had scattered talents liberally among the people. He demolished the argument that poverty of the parents was a sign that God did not intend the children to be educated, that it was irreverent to interfere with God's purposes by taking the education of children from the hands of the parents and giving it to the community—by denying that children belonged exclusively to the parents. They belonged to the community as well. What the state saved in withholding education, it paid in the more revolting form of criminal jurisprudence. It was the responsibility of the government to educate those "who are so materially to affect its safety and prosperity." What the state could do better and cheaper than the individual ought to be done by the state. Education came thus within the province of the state. So highly was Dr. Sears' address regarded that ten thousand copies were ordered printed; it received wide publicity in the press.[20]

The central feature of the educational system as provided by the constitution, adopted in April, 1868, was a uniform system of public free schools to be inaugurated in every county by 1876. The control of the Second Auditor over education, except in his capacity as accountant of funds, was eliminated. The administration of education was turned over to a State Board of Education which was to include a superintendent of public instruction to be elected by the General Assembly.[21] In addition to adequate supervision, the new stystem was distinguished by a specific taxation system, rendering education free to all and eliminating the pauper system. The Constitution was ratified in July, 1869,

---

[19] Samuel: *Debates & Proc's*, 1867, I, 604 *ff.*; *Jour. Convention*, 1867, 112; Sears, B.: *Education: An Address; cf. N. E. A. Proc's*, 1900, XXXIX, 91, article by Oscar H. Cooper, who places Dr. Sears, after Francis Wayland, as the second greatest Baptist educational leader.

[20] *Jour. Convention*, 1867, 112; Samuel: *Debates & Proc's*, 1867, I, 726 *ff.*; for an indication of objections raised against public schools in the South, see Dr. Sears' *Objections to Public Schools Considered* in connection with his annual Report to the Peabody Education Fund, 1875.

[21] *Acts of Assembly*, 1869-70, 624-25; Feb. 28, 1870, 13.

and Rev. William Henry Ruffner was elected state superintendent of public instruction on March 2, 1870.[22]

Superintendent Ruffner, in accordance with the Constitution, was requested to present a bill for a uniform system of public free schools. He had for his guidance not only the general section on education in the Constitution, but also a resolution, by the Senate, which stated that the object of the constitutional provision for education was the better preparation of posterity for "the discharge of the duties of an American citizen." To this end, the state sought to replace the "wide-spread ignorance" which cursed the commonwealth, by "intelligence, morality, and honesty."[23] In formulating his plan, Superintendent Ruffner asked also for the views of those interested in education to be submitted in writing.[24] The characteristic features of the plan seem, however, to have received their impression from the scheme proposed by his father, Henry A. Ruffner, at the Lexington Convention, in 1841.[25] The bill presented by Superintendent Ruffner was accepted July 11, 1870.[26]

The type of system created can be gauged from the fact that it was to be administered through a state board of education, state superintendent, county superintendents, and district school trustees.[27] Licensing of teachers was the function of the county superintendent, who was to include "morals" in a consideration of their fitness.[28] The curriculum provided for "orthography, reading, writing, arithmetic, grammar, and geography." No other branches were to be introduced "except as allowed by special regulations to be devised by the board of education." On the subject of religious instruction, there was silence. The board of education was likewise to provide gradu-

---

22 Knight, E. W.: *Reconst. and Educ. Va.*, in *South Atlant. Quart.*, XV, 34–35; Taylor: *Negro in Reconst. of Va.*, 146; *U. S. Comm. Educ. Rep't*, 1871, 357.
23 *Jour., Senate*, Oct. 19, 1869, 32.
24 *Richmond Enquirer*, Mar. 10, 1870.
25 See p. 349; Maddox: *Free Sch. Idea Va.*, 140–41; *South Atlant. Quart.*, XV, 37; *cf.* Heatwole: *Hist. of Educ. Va.*, 219.
26 *Acts of Assembly*, July 11, 1870, 402.
27 *Ibid.*
28 *Ibid.*

ally for the uniformity of text-books.[29] Separate schools were to be maintained for negroes, an issue which the section on education in the Constitution had passed over in silence.[30] The Constitution had authorized the Assembly to establish, as soon as practicable, normal schools, agricultural schools, "and such grades of schools as shall be for the public good."[31] Superintendent Ruffner's bill was confined, however, to inaugurating an elementary school system, though the age limit was extended to persons twenty-one years of age.[32]

The school system was put into operation about the middle of November.[33] At the end of the scholastic year, in 1871, there were more than 2,900 schools, and 3,000 teachers, and about 130,000 pupils.[34] While the years immediately after the inauguration of the system saw modifications of the law, particularly with regard to the administrative phases of city and county school organizations,[35] the main features of the system remained unchanged throughout the period of the Underwood Constitution.

In 1875, district school boards were permitted, upon sanction of county school boards, to admit an "intermediate grade of instruction between that of the common school and that of the college" into the public schools.[36] A fee not to exceed $2.50 per month for each pupil was permissive.[37] Special legislation, in 1873, had authorized high schools in Elizabeth City County and in Tazewell County.[38] As a consequence of the law of 1875, public high schools were to be found, within the next decade, in leading cities and in scattered county towns.[39] With the law of

---

[29] *Ibid.*, *Richmond Enquirer*, April 5, 1870.

[30] *Acts of Assembly*, July 11, 1870, 413; Taylor: *Negro in Reconst. Va.*, 146.

[31] *Acts of Assembly*, 1869–70, 625.

[32] *Ibid.*, 413.

[33] A law regulating and supervising elections for school purposes was not passed until December. *U. S. Comm. Educ. Rep'ts*, 1871, 357; *Acts of Assembly*, Dec. 23, 1870, 14.

[34] *U. S. Comm. Educ. Rep'ts*, 1871, 357.

[35] *Acts of Assembly*, Mar. 31, 1871, 405; Feb. 21, 1872, 81.

[36] *Ibid.*, Mar. 25, 1875, 269.

[37] *Ibid.*

[38] *Ibid.*, Mar. 27, 1873, 236; April 2, 1873, 346.

[39] *U. S. Comm. Educ. Rep'ts*, 1881, 260; 1884, 274; cf. *Acts of Assembly*, Feb. 24, 1876, 93; Feb. 19, 1880, 70; Feb. 27, 1880, 86; Mar. 6. 1882, 275.

1875, Virginia had in outline, for the first time under state auspices, a complete system of public instruction from the elementary school to the University.

To round out this system, it was necessary, however, to provide facilities for the training of teachers to man the system, and to create higher institutions to meet specific social and economic needs.

One of the objects in encouraging, in 1875, an intermediate grade of instruction was "to qualify pupils to become teachers in public schools."[40]   Though Dr. Ruffner's bill had passed over in silence the constitutional authority to create normal schools, he was not unmindful of the great need for these schools. It was felt, too, that the creation of these schools would serve as compensation for the neglect of higher education of women.[41] In the meantime, mushroom normal schools sprang up over the state to supply the need for trained teachers. These schools were usually held in summer. The Valley Normal School at Bridgewater, Rockingham County, opened in 1873, and in 1878 had 10 normal and 116 other pupils, and received aid from the county.   Another normal school was the Shenandoah Valley Normal School at Strasburg, Shenandoah County, which received both a state and county appropriation.[42]   Training for colored teachers was available after the Civil War, at Hampton Institute; at St. Stephen's Normal School, Petersburg, under the Protestant Episcopal Church; at the Normal School for Colored Students in connection with the Richmond public school system; and at the Richmond Institute under the Baptist Home Mission Society.[43]   Under the Peabody Fund, summer normal schools were held at the University of Virginia and at Lynchburg, for white and colored teachers respectively, in 1880.[44]   In addition, county superintendents frequently held teachers' institutes.[45]

In the late seventies, the topic of higher education for girls was a frequent subject of discussion before the Educational Associa-

---

40 *Ibid.*, Mar. 25, 1875, 269.
41 *U. S. Comm. Educ. Rep'ts*, 1873, 398.
42 *Ibid.*, 1878, 247.
43 *Ibid.*
44 Heatwole: *Hist. of Educ. Va.*, 236–37.
45 *Ibid.*, 238; *U. S. Comm. Educ. Rep'ts*, 1878, 247; 1882–83, 261.

tion of Virginia.[46] In the earlier part of the decade, Dr. Ruffner had written:

> Although Virginia has made large contributions to higher education . . . yet from no source, so far as I know, has the State ever given anything to advance the education of her daughters. Nor has private liberality taken that direction to any considerable extent. The religious denominations have raised small amounts for this purpose, but the means furnished have, in nearly all cases, been exhausted in the erection of imperfect buildings, leaving nothing for endowment or literary apparatus.[47]

By 1879, sufficient interest had been aroused to call forth a resolution from the Senate of Virginia, acknowledging that the commonwealth had never made any provision for the higher education of her daughters, and requesting the Superintendent in his next annual report to furnish "such information and views in regard to higher female education as might be useful in considering the propriety and practicability of making by this State some provision in this direction."[48] From the supporting speech of the sponsor of this resolution, Mr. C. T. Smith, of Nelson County, one gathers that the proposition was interpreted by some as a thrust at private schools. This he denied, stating that it must be remembered that many had not the means to patronize first class schools.[49] As far as can be gathered, the opinion, at that time, of the head of one of the most important schools for girls in Virginia, that of Charles L. Cocke, of Hollins Institute, was highly in favor of state intervention in behalf of the education of girls.[50] As a result of Dr. Ruffner's favorable report, the Legislature of 1883 authorized a state normal school for girls.[51]

For the establishment of the first Normal school for white girls, the property of the Farmville Female College was given to the

---

[46] *Ibid.*, 1878, 249; Barnard: *Amer. Jour. Educ.*, XXII, 553 *ff.*; *Va. Educ. Jour.*, X, Sept., 1879, 385 *ff.*

[47] *U. S. Comm. Educ. Rep'ts*, 1873, 398; *cf.* Morrison: *Beginnings Pub. Educ. Va.*, 32–33.

[48] *U. S. Comm. Educ. Rep'ts*, 1898–99, II, 2344; *Va. Educ. Jour.*, X, May, 1879, 212.

[49] *Ibid.*, 213.

[50] *Richmond Enquirer*, Mar. 16, 1876; for a reactionary view, see p. 447; *cf.* also *Va. Educ. Jour.*, XI, Nov., 1880, 348, 362, 365–66.

[51] *Va. Educ. Jour.*, April, 1883, 98, 101; *U. S. Comm. Educ. Rep'ts*, 1883–84, 273, 1898–99, II, 2345; *cf. Va. Sch. Rep't*, 1885, 35.

state.[52]   The act of incorporation of the State Female Normal School was passed in March, 1884, and the school opened that year with Dr. Ruffner, former state superintendent, as President.[53]

While the opening of the normal school for girls may be regarded as the outcome of propaganda since the War, in favor of provision for the higher education of girls, particularly with a view to meeting the need for trained teachers for the public school system, its establishment was undoubtedly hastened by the creation of the Virginia Normal and Collegiate Institute for colored male students.   This school decreed by the Assembly, in 1882, was one of the results of the "readjuster" era in Virginia politics.[54]   A state which could find funds to establish a school of this type for negro boys, and appropriate one third of the land scrip granted by Congress to Hampton Institute, was compelled to find means for the higher education of its women.[55] The school for colored students was incorporated under the name of "The Virginia Normal and Collegiate Institute" and established at Ettrick, near Petersburg.[56]   The superintendent of public instruction was made ex-officio chairman of the board of visitors.   The school was to have a college as well as a normal department.   State students were to be admitted free of charge on condition of carrying out an agreement to teach for two years.[57]   In creating this school, the state created the first specific training school for teachers, though the Virginia Military Institute had since 1842 been sending out its graduates as teachers under the same conditions.[58]   In 1884, provision was made

---

[52] The history of this institution went back to the incorporation of the Farmville Female Seminary Association in 1839.   *Acts of Assembly*, Mar. 5, 1839, 120.   In 1860, the charter of the association was amended to permit the incorporation of Farmville Female College, with authority to confer degrees.   *Ibid.*, Mar. 21, 1860, 463.

[53] *Ibid.*, Mar. 7, 1884, 417; Heatwole: *Hist. of Educ. Va.*, 248; *U. S. Comm. Educ. Rep't*, 1883–84, 273.

[54] See p. 434; Heatwole: *Hist. of Educ. Va.*, 361; Taylor: *Negro in Reconst. Va.*, 283, attributes it to "Mahone's pledge that the Readjuster party would establish a higher institution of learning for Negroes."   *Va. Normal and Indust. Institut. Gazette*, XXXII, No. 5, 18.

[55] See p. 405.

[56] *Acts of Assembly*, Mar. 6, 1882, 283.

[57] *Ibid.*

[58] Maddox: *Free Sch. Idea Va.*, 123.

for a summer school course of eight weeks at this institution for the colored teachers of the state.[59]   In 1902, the name of the school was changed to the Virginia Normal and Industrial Institute, and an industrial department was substituted for the college department after forty-nine persons had received the degree of B.A. during the period from 1889 to 1902.[60]

The history of this period is not complete without reference to the action of the state in accepting, in 1866, the land scrip authorized by the Morrill Act of 1862.[61]   The income from the sale was appropriated in 1872, in the proportion of two thirds to one third, to the Virginia State Agricultural and Mechanical College, later known as the Virginia Polytechnic Institute, a school for white students, and to the Hampton Normal and Agricultural Institute, a school for colored students.[62]   The history of the Virginia Polytechnic Institute at Blacksburg, Montgomery County, which now ranks with the College of William and Mary, the University of Virginia, the Virginia Military Institute, and the various state Teachers' Colleges, as one of the higher state institutions goes back to the Olin and Preston Institute incorporated in 1854.

The appropriation to this school and Hampton Institute was made only after ignoring the strong pleas of the friends of existing state and denominational higher institutions.[63]   An alumnus of the University urged, in 1870, that there could be no real conflict of interests between the University and the denominational colleges with respect to the land grant fund.   To divide the fund among a large number of colleges would be contrary to the spirit and letter of the law providing for the gift; to give the fund to the University would be ''to give it to all the denominations, to the people, and to the best advantage for all.''   The

[59] *Acts of Assembly,* Mar. 7, 1884, 442.

[60] *Ibid.,* Mar. 29, 1902, 397; Heatwole: *Hist. of Educ. Va.,* 360; *Va. Normal and Indust. Instit. Gazette,* XXXII, No. 5, 19–20.

[61] *Acts of Assembly,* Jan. 27, 1866, 224; Cubberley: *Public Educ. in U. S.,* 210–11.

[62] *Acts of Assembly,* Mar. 26, 1872, 451; *cf. Ibid.,* Feb. 5, 1873, 38; Mar. 19, 1873, 180; Feb. 23, 1894, 408–09; Virginia was also very much interested in obtaining land grants for public free school purposes and furthered the Blair Bill, *cf. Ibid.,* Mar. 10, 1873, 196; Dec. 14, 1887, 579; Reisner, E. H.: *Nationalism and Education,* 435.

[63] Heatwole: *Hist. of Educ. Va.,* 204.

University had demonstrated by the presence of its alumni as professors in denominational colleges that it was the "great normal school" of the state. Its prosperity meant the prosperity of the colleges.[64]

The Legislature turned from these pleas to approve the taking of a vote of the citizens of Montgomery County to determine whether they would subscribe to the enterprise of establishing a college there. As a result, $20,000 and the property of the Olin and Preston Institute were transferred to the state, which bought some adjoining property.[65] The Institute has since shared in the benefits of grants made by Congress to land grant colleges.[66]

Hampton Institute, which shared in the appropriation in behalf of the colored population of the state, had been established with a view to improving the condition of the negro race, as the result of its being placed upon its own responsibility by the Civil War. Hampton, in the early part of the War, had been one of the many centers in the South where the American Missionary Association had undertaken its work.[67] In 1865, the national government created the Freedmen's Bureau, and, in 1866, the Bureau placed General Samuel Chapman Armstrong in charge of Eastern Virginia with headquarters at Hampton.[68] Through the co-operation of the American Missionary Association, which purchased, in 1867, a considerable property at Hampton, the Hampton Normal and Agricultural Institute was begun, in 1868, with General Armstrong as Principal.[69] A county charter was obtained from the Circuit Court of Elizabeth City County in September, 1868.[70] In 1870, the American Missionary Association surrendered its control, and a charter was obtained from the Assembly.[71] A self-perpetuating board of trustees was created.[72] The statement is usually made that by this charter,

[64] *Richmond Enquirer*, April 16, 1870.
[65] Heatwole: *Hist. of Educ. Va.*, 204 ff; *Acts of Assembly*, Mar. 21, 1872, 338.
[66] *Va. Polyt. Instit. Catalog*, 1926, 5.
[67] Peabody, F. G.: *Hampton Institute*, 42; cf. *N. E. A. Proc's*, 1884, XXIII, 98.
[68] Peabody: *Hampton Institute*, 43; Peabody, F. G., and Ludlow, H. W.: *Armstrong's Ideas*, 13.
[69] *Ibid.*, 14; *Hampton Instit. Catalog*, 1926, 14.
[70] *Hampton Normal and Agricultural Institute Act of Incorporation*, 3.
[71] *Ibid.*, 5; *Acts of Assembly*, June 4, 1870, 164.
[72] *Ibid.*

the Institute "became independent of any denominational organization.[73] According to the account of one historian of the Institute,

> . . . an independent Board of Trustees was created, without sectarian limita-
> tion or other condition than that "the teaching should be forever evangeli-
> cal." The good-will of the Association was, however, perpetuated by mem-
> bership of some of its officers in the first Board of Trustees, a relationship
> of confidence and intimacy which has continued for nearly a half century.[74]

Neither the limitation concerning "evangelical teaching," nor the
connection with the American Missionary Association appears by
reference in the charter. In 1872, the Assembly voted one third
of the agricultural college land grant to the school, eventually
amounting to $95,000.[75] It was apparently in consequence of
this appropriation that the Assembly, in 1873, designated the
board of education and the president of the Virginia Agricultural
Society as ex-officio members of the board of curators of the
school; this board was to consist of five members, three of whom
were to be of African descent.[76] In 1874, the superintendent of
public instruction was made an ex-officio member of the board.[77]
These curators appointed by the governor were accustomed to
meet with the trustees at their annual meeting, and sit with
them upon invitation,[78] thus creating an impression in the minds
of many that Hampton Institute was a state institution, particularly, as its reports appeared among those of other state institutions in the reports of the state superintendent.[79]

With the establishment of a free elementary school system,
provision for intermediate instruction, the establishment of Virginia Normal and Collegiate Institute, the Normal School at
Farmville, the Virginia State Agricultural and Mechanical College, the partial control in Hampton Institute, and assumption
by the state of the Medical College in Virginia, in 1860, which

---

[73] *Hampton Instit. Catalog*, 1926, 14; Peabody & Ludlow: *Armstrong's
Ideas*, 14.

[74] Peabody: *Hampton Institute*, 100.

[75] Taylor: *Negro in Reconst. Va.*, 168.

[76] *Code*, 1873, 674, 676; *Acts of Assembly*, Feb. 6, 1877, 50; *cf.* Mar. 27,
1876, 221.

[77] *Ibid.*, Mar. 14, 1874, 94.

[78] *From correspondence.*

[79] *Cf. Va. Sch. Rep't*, 1904–05, 260; 1914–15, 597.

will be discussed in another connection,[80] the state had in the first three decades after the war obtained a fairly well rounded system of educational institutions. It will only be necessary before closing this account of the new educational system to give a brief consideration to two aspects of the public school system—necessary in the later understanding of the problem of religion in education—namely, the provision for and procedure in regard to text-books and the curriculum.

The act of July 11, 1870, creating the free public school system, provided that uniformity of text-books should be taken care of on some gradual system by the board of education.[81] The board resolved in February, 1871, that when it should decide upon the school books to be taught in the public free schools of the state, all the schools must use the books prescribed; and that from and after September 1, 1871, the schools were to use only the books prescribed by the board.[82] The feeling for uniformity of text-books prescribed by state authority had probably grown in Virginia owing to a conviction that the state had been too much dominated before the War by northern text-books. At the meeting organizing the Educational Association of Virginia, in 1863, expression had been given to the feeling that, while much might be said in compliment of many northern schoolbooks, the South must ultimately have a system of text-books of her own. The feeling was voiced that ''No intelligent and progressive people can afford to employ foreigners to provide the intellectual pabulum of their children, or to give shape to their young minds and morals through the plastic agency of rudimentary and higher school books.''[83]

In his report for 1874, Dr. Ruffner, under the caption, ''STATE UNIFORMITY OF TEXT BOOKS: TENDING TO DESPOTISM, CORRUPTION, AND INTELLECTUAL DEATH,'' published also as a circular, took up the question of censorship of books taught in schools. Dr. Ruffner's opinion was that the ''central Board ought simply to *make regulations*

---

[80] See p. 474.
[81] *Acts of Assembly*, July 11, 1870, 414.
[82] *Circulars—Review of the School Law*, 1871, 23.
[83] *Minutes Educ. Assoc. Va.*, 1863, 4.

providing for uniformity of textbooks in the various schools, and excluding in general terms all books containing false or offensive statements.'' Thus, history books unfair to Virginia or books containing sentiments unfit to be taught to children should be barred. This disposition of the subject, he believed to be consistent with the statutory and organic law of the state. If the State Board insisted on making selections, it should choose a considerable number on the same subject, permitting local choice.[84] The request of the County School Board of Henrico County to be permitted to use books not on the prescribed list was denied by the Board of Education. This resulted in the presentation to the Legislature of an appeal for more liberty, and ''A Bill to regulate uniformity of text-books.'' The bill stated in part:

No book containing immoral, irreverent, false, unpatriotic or otherwise seriously objectionable statements or sentiments, shall be chosen for use in our public schools, or be tolerated therein; and any parent, teacher or school officer discovering such objectionable statements or sentiments in any book licensed or used in a public school, shall have the privilege of complaining, and of appealing in the manner provided in the general law, from one school authority to another, until the case be finally decided by the Board of Education.[85]

Dr. Ruffner commented on this bill as embodying the soundest and best views on the subject, and guarding against all possible evils.[86] It was not passed.[87] This failure need not be ascribed to any scruples on the part of the Assembly to legislate directly on the subject of text-books, for, in 1884, it directed that two works, by J. Esten Cooke, entitled *Virginia: A History of Her People* and *Stories of the Old Dominion* be placed on the prescribed list by the Board.[88]

The curriculum received no substantial modification until almost the close of the period, when, in 1900, the Assembly enacted legislation broadening its content. Morality and religion were not mentioned. No other than the specified subjects were

---

[84] *Circulars—Extract from Annual Rep't of Sup't Pub. Inst.*, 1874, 156–57.
[85] *Circular No. 132, Dep't Pub. Inst.*, Mar. 20, 1875, 8.
[86] *Ibid.*, 9.
[87] *Ibid.*
[88] *Acts of Assembly*, Mar. 8, 1884, 456.

to be introduced except as allowed by special regulations of the Board.[89]

The extension of educational opportunity, the creation of an integral public school system which was accomplished during the period of the "Underwood Constitution" by provision for a uniform system of free schools, intermediate, and higher instruction, was brought about as far as enactment in law was concerned without any special reference to the religious element in education. In creating this system, the state seems to have been dominated by the ideal of training youth in the duties of American citizenship, for the safety and prosperity of the state; it apparently did not feel it necessary to specify, in law, the relation of religion or the church to the consummation of this ideal, to be achieved by education. What the state permitted in practise, what its attitude was to religion in general, will be considered presently.[90] Its use of the Congressional land script grant for the creation of a new institution for white students, instead of creating a special school at the University, seems to have been animated in part by the desire to avoid a sense of injury on the part of denominational schools, and in part to avoid any entangling alliance with denominational interests. Its grant to Hampton Institute, and the dual control necessitated thereby, seem to have been dictated largely by expediency; by the fact that justice demanded part of the grant for the instruction of colored youth, and Hampton Institute was the most available institution, unless the state were to create a new one. With the establishment of the Virginia Normal and Collegiate Institute, it would have been logical to transfer the funds from Hampton to the new school, but it was many decades before this was done.[91] The characteristic repugnance of the state to legislate on the subject of religion in education is evident from the defeat of the bill to regulate uniformity of text-books.

The Constitutional Convention Of 1867–68 And Religion

In giving consideration to the problem of education, to what extent did the Constitution Convention of 1867–68 give thought

---

[89] *Ibid.*, Jan. 24, 1900, 134.
[90] See p. 412–17.
[91] See p. 592–93.

to the problem of religion in education? What forces in the state attempted to influence the consideration of the problem of religion in education?

As indicated previously,[92] the Educational Association of Virginia was well organized before the meeting of the Constitutional Convention. At its meeting, in 1866, at the University of Virginia, in a long list of subjects proposed for its attention, a committee referred to the association as the two paramount subjects for their attention:

1st. The necessity and best modes of Moral and Physical training and development.

2nd. The necessity and best modes of conveying a thorough knowledge of the *facts* and *practical precepts* of the Bible.[93]

The first subject was passed over for that session, but the second was presented for consideration in addresses delivered by Mr. J. B. Minor, who urged the vital importance of the introduction of the Bible into the schools as a text-book, and by Dr. McGuffey,[94] who cited instances within his own experience ''of the most lamentable ignorance of the plainest facts of the Bible History.''[95] So important were the two subjects with reference to moral and Biblical instruction regarded by the Association, that special committees were appointed to report on them at subsequent sessions. At the session, in 1867, at Lynchburg, the committee on ''The Necessity and best modes of Moral and Physical training and development'' was continued and a general discussion of the subject participated in.[96] In spite of its lively interest in the subject, the Association apparently made no attempt to influence the Constitutional Convention with respect to some recognition of its views on the importance of moral and religious instruction in education.

[92] See p. 397.

[93] *Minutes Educ. Assoc. Va.*, 1866, 6.

[94] See p. 384.

[95] *Minutes Educ. Assoc. Va.*, 1866, 8; Barnard: *Amer. Jour. Educ.*, XXII, 551; at the Southern Educational Convention of 1863, called by the North Carolina State Educational Association, and meeting at Columbia, S. C., in April, 1864, a committee was appointed to report at the next meeting how far the Bible should be introduced as a text-book into schools and colleges.— *South Atlant. Quart.*, VIII, 354, 359.

[96] *Minutes Educ. Assoc. Va.*, 1867, 7; Barnard: *Amer. Jour. Educ.*, XXII, 552.

A review of the *Journals* and *Debates* of the Convention indicates that the subject of religion and its importance to society
were given serious discussion but once, and that in connection
with the question whether an acknowledgment of the Deity
should be made in the preamble to the Constitution.[97]   The debate on this question continued several days and resulted in a
victory for the proponents of recognizing the Deity in affairs of
state.   The section added to the previous preamble of the Constitution read:

> We, therefore, the delegates of the good people of Virginia, elected and
> in convention assembled, in pursuance of said acts, invoking the favor and
> guidance of Almighty God, do propose to the people the following Constitu-
> tion and form of government for this Commonwealth.[98]

While the *Declaration of Rights* passed in 1776, and regarded as
part of the Constitution had referred to religion as "the duty
which we owe to our Creator," this was the first acknowledgment,
in the constitution of Virginia, of the Deity as an agent whose
favor and guidance were to be invoked in behalf of society and
the state.[99]   It is highly significant not only as a civic acknowledgment, but also as an expression of the changed attitude
wrought by the religious fervor in the decades before the War.
Above all, it may be taken as a herald of the attitude that was to
characterize the state in its relation to religion in the period
after the Civil War—an attitude which may be described as
seeking the co-operation of the church, but without establishing
a definite alliance.

The connection between education and religion was presented
to the consideration of the Convention twice.   The first occasion
was upon a communication from the conference of the Methodist
Episcopal Church of Virginia and North Carolina, meeting in
Richmond, in January, 1868.   The report of the Committee of
Education of that Conference stressed education for the masses

[97] Samuel: *Debates & Proc's*, 1867, I, 358 *ff.*, 382 *ff.*
[98] *Ibid.*, 402–03; *Acts of Assembly*, 1869–70, 612.
[99] The Assembly had, however, in 1863, in a resolution expressing its high
appreciation of the patriotic fortitude and devotion displayed by the women
of Virginia during the War, referred to the sublime spectacle exhibited by
the women of the whole community elevated and purified by a high Christian
civilization—"beautifully blending a holy zeal for their country with humble
piety to God."—*Acts of Assembly*, Mar. 26, 1863, 121.

as most important for progress both in church and state, and urged members of the church to further the development of common schools and to patronize them, as well as institutions of a higher grade.[100] The report was received without official comment.

The second occasion was upon the presentation of the report of the Committee on the Prevention and Punishment of Crime. Among the propositions submitted for incorporation into the Constitution, as tending to the prevention of crime, were proposals to empower the General Assembly to pass laws to secure a proper observance of the Christian Sabbath, and, under the caption of "Moral and Religious Education," a recommendation that the course of study should "embrace moral as well as intellectual culture."[101] With regard to reform prisons for juveniles, the report recommended that such institutions should give inmates "the benefit of industrial, educational, and religious training."[102]

As far as the actual work of the Convention was embodied in the Constitution, there was no hint that the state in any way concerned itself with the problem of religious training in education. Neither the interest of the Educational Association of Virginia in the problem of morality and religion in education, nor the favorable attitude of the Methodists, the state's strongest denominational group, toward public education, was sufficient to elicit a definite reaction of the Convention on the subject of religion in education. In a sense, its constitutional recognition of the Deity marked its most significant reaction, symbolic of turning from a negative, towards a co-operative attitude to religion and the church.

Co-operative Attitude Of the State Toward Religion In General

To understand the attitude of a state toward religion in education, it is necessary first to arrive at some conception of its interpretation of the relation between church and state, of its attitude toward religion in general—and this can, perhaps, best be gauged from its procedure in handling various religious prob-

---

[100] Samuel: *Debates & Proc's*, 1867, I, 237; *Jour. Convention*, 1867, 70.
[101] *Ibid.*, 332.
[102] *Ibid.*, 333.

lems as they affect the social, economic, or church life of the people.

In 1862, while the War was at its height, the Assembly took up the question of amending previous Sabbath legislation.[103] An effort to regulate the working of railroads in the state on the Sabbath was tabled on the ground that it was inexpedient to legislate at that time; undoubtedly, due to the fear of hampering military movements.[104]   On the question of hunting on Sunday, an attempt to protect from the proposed penalties of the act, those who conscientiously believed that the seventh day of the week alone ought to be observed as the Sabbath, was marked with defeat for the conscientious objectors.[105] The bill as passed, levied a fine of not less than five nor more than twenty dollars for hunting on the Sabbath; this was considerably higher than that which had been imposed for violating the Sabbath by engaging in other callings.[106]   In 1878, the penalty for violation of the Sabbath, placed at $2 for each offence, was excepted for those handling the transportation of mail, passengers, and baggage.   A less narrow note was introduced, too, in the exception of any one who, believing the seventh day ought to be observed as the Sabbath, actually refrained from all secular business and labor on that day, on condition that the person thus favored did not compel an apprentice or servant not of his belief to work on Sunday, and that he did not disturb any other person.[107]

In 1872, citizens of Lynchburg had asked for a law to prevent work on the Sabbath day by railroads.[108]   The Assembly finally passed an act, in 1884, restricting the running of railroad trains on Sunday.   The limitation was placed specifically on the movement of trains after 9 o'clock Sunday morning.   It may be that this restriction was an attempt to curb the Negro penchant for excursions.[109]   In 1890, an act was passed to prohibit the load-

---

103 See p. 156–57.
104 *Jour., Senate*, Jan. 29, 1862, 109; Feb. 1, 1862, 118; Feb. 19, 1862, 152.
105 *Ibid.*, Mar. 6, 1862, 190.
106 *Acts of Assembly*, Mar. 12, 1862, 93; *cf. Ibid.*, 1846–48, Mar. 14, 1848, Ch. VIII, sec. 16, 112.
107 *Ibid.*, Mar. 14, 1878, 304.
108 *Jour., Senate*, Feb. 10, 1872, 251.
109 *Cf.* Taylor: *Negro in Reconst. Va.*, 65–66.

ing and unloading of steamships' and steamboats' cargoes on Sunday.[110]

Protection to religious meetings was extended in 1874, by a penalty for disturbers, of not more than six months in jail and a fine not to exceed $100.[111] In 1878, provision was made for the appointment of temporary police to protect religious meetings.[112]

An amendment to the *Code*, in 1867, validated all conveyances and devises made since 1777 to religious congregations. It validated likewise all future conveyances of land for religious congregations or societies, and residences for bishops or ministers as long as they continued officers of a church or religious society. Books and furniture were to be vested in the same trustees as those in which the land was vested.[113] The constitution, the following year, confirmed the rights of ecclesiastical bodies in, and to, church property.[114] An attempt, in 1871, to strike this section from the Constitution failed.[115] Such organizations wishing to borrow money or to sell and convey property were permitted to proceed only by special enactments of the Assembly, or by appeal to the circuit court for trustees to handle the matter.[116] The amount of land to be held was restricted by law to no more than two acres in an incorporated town, and to no more than two hundred acres out of such town.[117] This legislation seems now to have been inspired not merely to protect the interests of the civil as against the ecclesiastical arm of society, or to give a measure of protection to the property of religious interests, but as much to facilitate the settlement of ecclesiastical property because of the schism in the churches resulting from the difference in opinion on the slavery issue.[118]

The practise of exempting church property from taxation continued, but an attempt was made in 1876, to take away this privi-

---

[110] *Acts of Assembly*, Feb. 7, 1890, 38.
[111] *Ibid.*, Mar. 14, 1874, 93.
[112] *Ibid.*, Mar. 14, 1878, 306; *cf.* also *Ibid.*, Feb. 23, 1875, 102.
[113] *Ibid.*, April 26, 1867, 907.
[114] *Ibid.*, 1869–70, 628.
[115] *Jour., Senate*, Jan. 20, 1871, 119–20.
[116] *Cf.* numerous acts of this type passed almost yearly; *Acts of Assembly*, Mar. 3, 1879, 161; Jan. 31, 1884, 79; Jan. 31, 1890, 28; Mar. 4, 1898, 977.
[117] *Ibid.*, Mar. 10, 1864, 57.
[118] See p. 396.

lege, which brought from the *Enquirer* the comment that, "Of course so radical an innovation upon our old fashioned way of raising revenue will not be permitted without an earnest protest by representatives of every part of the State."[119]   The proposal was defeated.[120]

With regard to the law forbidding incorporations of religious bodies[121]—incorporations of various activities, such as publishing and missionary societies belonging to the various denominations, and in practise, of course, used to further their religious activities and practises, were made by the state, apparently without any feeling of violation of law.   Thus the Assembly chartered the "Trustees of the Presbyterian Committee of Publication" in 1873, whose object was described as "the dissemination of religious truth by means of the printing and circulation of books, tracts, papers, cards, etc.," a strictly denominational activity for the extension of denominational welfare.[122]   Other incorporations, practically equivalent to incorporating religious bodies were, in 1876, that of the Virginia Christian Missionary Society, whose object was declared to be "to promote the spread of the gospel within the limits of the state of Virginia,"[123] and, in 1888, that of the Baptist State Mission Board, whose object was "the purpose of disseminating christianity in the state of Virginia.[124]   The object of incorporation of the Disciples Union of Richmond and Manchester was plainly stated as being to "foster mission Sunday schools and churches."[125]

During this period, numerous local Young Men's Christian Associations were incorporated, the movement probably being forwarded by the establishment of the Y. M. C. A. at the University of Virginia.   Such an organization had been incorporated for Lynchburg, in 1858; it now appeared in Luray, Fincastle, Portsmouth, Danville, Roanoke, Norfolk, Hampton, Newport

119 *Richmond Enquirer*, Mar. 17, 1876.
120 *Ibid.*, Mar. 19, 1876; *cf. Acts of Assembly*, April 2, 1877, 302.
121 See p. 365.
122 *Acts of Assembly*, Mar. 8, 1873, 116.
123 *Ibid.*, Mar. 18, 1876, 154.
124 *Ibid.*, Jan. 18, 1888, 22.
125 *Ibid.*, Feb. 29, 1892, 795.

News, and other places.[126] In 1894, the State Executive Committee of the Young Men's Christian Association was incorporated.[127] The purpose of the Association was generally stated as being the promotion of ''religion, morality, education and social culture'' or the equivalent. At times, the acts, like those for Luray and Fincastle, limited the privileges of voting and office to male members of ''the evangelical christian denominations, that recognize in their doctrines the divinity of Jesus Christ, the Lord and Saviour of mankind, and a future state of the eternal reward and punishment.''[128] By 1892, the total number of Y. M. C. A.'s in the state was given as 63; local, 35; college, 18; railroad, 9; army, 1.[129]

With regard to the Assembly practise relative to the use of chaplains,[130] it appears that procedure after the War was influenced by precedents established just before the War. In 1853, an attempt to provide payment for ministers to open the sessions of the Senate was defeated, but a resolution to have them attend by invitation was approved.[131] Ministers of the various denominations in Richmond were invited by resolution to officiate in 1857 and in 1858.[132] Ministers of Richmond still continue by invitation to open the sessions of the Assembly with prayer, doing this without compensation.[133]

It is apparent from this review of legislation, affecting in one way or another, the religious life of the people, that the legislature did not hold itself aloof from co-operating with the church in such matters as concerned its interest. While from one point of view much of this legislation may be regarded as enacted from the point of view of law and order, and protection to property, its essential nature was the protection and extension of the interests of the church.

---

[126] *Ibid.*, Feb. 24, 1858, 263; Mar. 22, 1872, 386; Mar. 19, 1884, 722; Mar. 6, 1886, 540; Feb. 18, 1888, 179; Mar. 3, 1890, 765; Mar. 5, 1890, 969; Mar. 5, 1894, 730; Jan. 11, 1896, 52; Mar. 3, 1896, 709.

[127] *Ibid.*, Feb. 15, 1894, 281.

[128] *Ibid.*, Mar. 19, 1884, 722; 1886, 541.

[129] *Va. Sch. Jour.*, Jan., 1892, I, 24.

[130] See p. 154 *ff.*

[131] *Jour., Senate*, Dec. 8, 1853, 45–46.

[132] *Ibid.*, Dec. 9, 1857, 3; Mar. 12, 1858, 514.

[133] *From correspondence.*

Conflicting Views Concerning The Reaction Of The Public School System Upon Religious Instruction

The silence of the Constitution on the subject of religion in education seemed, particularly in view of the prospective launching of a new public school system, only to enhance the interest of educators and religious-minded people in Virginia in the problem.

The Educational Association of Virginia at its meeting, in 1868, appointed a new committee to report on the question of Biblical instruction.[134] At the meeting in 1869, it was decided that the theme of the opening address, in 1870, should be *"The necessity and best method of Bible instruction in the schools of Virginia."*[135]

In the meantime, there now appeared to give publicity to the work and views of Virginian educators, the *Virginia Educational Journal.* In an early number, the writer of an article on "The Bible in Public Schools" gave it as his opinion that the proposed establishment of public schools meant that the problem of reading the Bible in those schools would need to be faced and solved.[136] After referring to the controversy in northern and western cities on this subject, and the exclusion of the Bible from the schools in Cincinnati, the writer proceeded to state his views. The home and not the school was the place for pious instruction. Among the insuperable objections to compulsory reading of the Bible was the fact that it was not suitable for school lessons. The principle that the majority have a right to prescribe the religious instruction in schools has for its corollary the right to prescribe the reading of other works consonant with it, and will result in inculcating the religion of the majority and establishing religious tyranny. The benefits from the introduction of the Bible would be outweighed by the dangers; public schools to be acceptable to all classes of the community should be "subservient, not to religious, but literary and scientific culture."[137]

With the proponents of this view, that a public school system and religious instruction therein were incompatible, the largest

---

[134] *Minutes Educ. Assoc. Va.*, 1868, 7.
[135] *Ibid.*, 1869, 14.
[136] *Va. Educ. Jour.*, Jan., 1870, I, 88 *ff.*
[137] *Ibid.*, 89, 90–91.

religious denomination in Virginia at that time, the Methodist, expressed its disagreement. At their conference in the spring of 1870, in opposition as they declared to the views of Romanism, they passed a resolution to support with all their influence the common school system and to "seek the education of all the people of Virginia."[138] As the strongest denomination in Virginia, the Methodists apparently felt confident of preventing the schools from becoming altogether irreligious.[139]

The agitation in various sections of the country to eliminate the Bible from the public schools reacted unfavorably upon the proposed public system for Virginia.[140] Since 1820, the Virginia public mind had been nurtured on an increasingly favorable attitude toward turning a very large part of the religious instruction of youth over to the school, whether public or private. In some strongly inclined denominationalists, the attitude of Catholicism in its insistence on a purely denominational education found a sympathetic echo; in others, the Catholic attitude inspired a feeling that the public school must be fostered as an expression of opposition to Catholicism, and yet in some way be given a sufficiently religious tone.

There was, however, a considerable current of anxiety and distrust of the proposed public school system, due, in part, because some professed to see in it, northern influence; and, in part, because the possible elimination of the Bible and religious instruction from schools ran counter to the whole course of thought and experience of Virginia. Dr. Ruffner, consequently, in his report to the Assembly in March, 1870, in connection with his bill on the public school system, felt called upon to recognize the current objection to the public school system on the ground that it inclined "people to religious error and impiety." To this, he entered an emphatic denial, declaring it would be strange, if well ordered schools in Christian neighborhoods would lead

---

138 *Richmond Enquirer*, Mar. 4, 1870.

139 *U. S. Bur. Census, Pop. and Social Stat.*, 1870, 557; the Methodist Church had 1,011 organizations, 270,617 sittings; the Baptist, 849 and 256,830 respectively; the Presbyterian, 204 and 70,605; the Episcopal, 185 and 60,185.

140 See p. 418; *cf.* Pearson, C. C.: *Readjuster Movement*, 60–62; Knight: *Reconst. and Educ. Va.*, in *South Atlant. Quart.*, Jan. & April, 1916, Reprint, 18.

to such results. The moral influence in a school would be that pervading the neighborhood. While immoral teachers might be found in private schools, they never were in public schools. It was an established fact that the vast majority of teachers in public schools were religious and active in promoting Sunday Schools. Careful study of the subject had convinced Dr. Ruffner that piety had everything to hope for and nothing to fear from public schools.[141]

In reply to Dr. Ruffner, "L" declared in the *Virginia Educational Journal*, that if the object of education be to make men better Christians as well as better scholars, that the less said about the wonderful benefits from public schools the better. He asserted that more beastly crimes against the laws of God and man were committed in one month in Massachusetts than in all the southern states together in one year; and of course, he found no difficulty in citing cases from northern newspapers disproving that all the teachers in public schools were moral.[142]

A plea for public schools on the basis that there was no irreconcilable conflict between the aims of the state and the church in education was made in the May, 1870, number of the *Virginia Educational Journal*. The writer argued that their practical reconciliation was secured by confining each to its proper sphere and by co-operation on their common ground. He urged that the state "educate with reference to time, the Church, with reference to eternity, and both co-operate in securing sound morals and a pure life." Guided by these principles, the various parts of the public school system might be organized not to conflict with but to aid the legitimate claims of religious education.[143]

At the meeting of the Educational Association of Virginia, in 1870, Rev. B. M. Smith, of the Union Theological Seminary, whose "Report on the Prussian Primary School System," in 1839, had established his reputation among Virginia educators,[144]

---

[141] *Circulars*, Doc. No. 6, *Rep't Sup't Pub. Inst.*, Mar. 28, 1870, 4; *Va. Educ. Jour.*, I, Doc. No. XIII.
[142] *Ibid.*, May, 1870, I, 223–25.
[143] *Ibid.*, I, 207–09.
[144] See p. 345.

delivered an address on the "Merits and Defects of Prevailing Schemes of Common School Education in the United States."[145] Dr. Smith declared that the increasing association, since the War, of the development of public schools with New England was not justified by a study of the history of its development.[146] As to the charge that moral degeneracy resulted from the admixture of various sorts of children in a school, the same charge might be applied to such assemblings, entirely apart from school, or even be attributed to a decline in the purity and scripturalness of religious faith taught in church, school, and family.[147] All true lovers of real religious liberty commended the forbidding of all sectarian interference in the control of public schools. To allow the civil authority to prescribe the reading of the Bible in schools gave it the right to proscribe; and, if allowed "to define the Bible as a reading book, to define *what* Bible, or what translation, or with what aids and comments."[148]

Unconvinced by Dr. Smith's arguments, a resolution expressive of the opinion of one group, was offered in the Association the following day, which, after referring to the efforts in New York and Ohio to exclude the Bible, recommended to the principals of the primary schools, academies, and colleges of the state, "to institute as a part of the services of said institutions the reading of the Holy Scriptures and to consider the Bible as a text-book."[149] The resolution was tabled, and a report of the action appeared in the *Richmond Enquirer,* under the caption, "The Holy Bible Laid On the Table."[150] The Association, apparently not ready to take a definite stand, again appointed a special committee to consider the question of religious instruction in schools.[151]

While the Methodist Church went on record to support the proposed system of public schools,[152] the Protestant Episcopal

---

[145] Smith, B. M.: *Merits and Defects*, also in *Va. Educ. Jour.*, Aug., 1870, I, 318 *ff*.
[146] Smith: *Merits and Defects*, 5.
[147] *Ibid.*, 10.
[148] *Ibid.*, 13.
[149] *Minutes Educ. Assoc. Va.*, 1870, 11.
[150] *Richmond Enquirer*, July 16, 1870.
[151] *Minutes Educ. Assoc. Va.*, 1870, 13.
[152] See p. 412.

Church, as it had favored strictly denominational Sunday Schools in the twenties,[153] now favored church schools, aligning herself in principle with the Catholic Church. A committee, appointed to consider the establishment of a system of church schools throughout the diocese, submitted a report which was accepted, indicating that, in their view, all instruction for the young must be distinctly Christian.[154] As state schools, perhaps unavoidably, could admit no special concern for piety, they could not but prove detrimental to the religious character of children and ultimately of the entire people. Schools from which the Bible and the wise inculcation of its lessons were excluded must be regarded as being against Christianity. Though taxed for such schools, and hence the means for the creation of church schools lessened, the committee felt, in view of their convictions on the subject of religion in education, that they must recommend two kinds of church schools:

. . . 1. Such as are ordinarily known as parish schools, where the benefits dispensed are entirely gratuitous, the expense being borne by such contributions as can be secured. 2. Schools no less under control of Parochial authorities, yet admitting the principle of compensation on the part of parents who patronize them.[155]

It was accordingly resolved that the churches and parishes of the diocese do their utmost to establish such schools, to be under the supervision of their rectors, and subject to parochial authority, and that reports be submitted of the condition of these schools annually.[156]

In view of the fear of the Protestant Episcopal Church, and a rather general public sentiment, that public schools would be withdrawn wholly from religious influence, it is interesting to find, upon investigation, that not only was the state superintendent of public instruction, himself, a Presbyterian minister,[157]

---

153 See p. 250.

154 *Richmond Enquirer*, July 19, 1870, from the *Southern Churchman*, July 14.

155 *Ibid.*

156 *Ibid.*

157 For biographical notices and articles on Rev. W. H. Ruffner, see *W. Va. Hist. Mag.*, Oct., 1902, 33–43; *Branch Hist. Papers*, June, 1910, III, 124–44; Heatwole: *Hist. of Educ. Va.*, 243–44; *South Atlant. Quart.*, XX, 25 *ff.*, 137 *ff.*; *The Va. Teacher*, Oct.–Nov., 1924, V, 268 *ff.*

but that many of the county superintendents, who were elected to administer the county systems, were ministers. Thus, Prince Edward County elected Rev. B. M. Smith, whose address before the Virginia Educational Association has been referred to.[158] In commenting upon his nomination, the *Richmond Enquirer* noted also the report that clergymen were in the same county to be voted for as trustees of school districts, "because from culture and character they are regarded as eminently fitted for the positions indicated."[159] Of the ninety county superintendents elected in 1871, seventeen or a little over eighteen per cent were ministers.[160]

The motive in their election and the effects can be gauged from a statement by Mr. Wayland, historian of Rockingham County, and a letter from Rev. W. T. Price, which he quotes; Mr. Wayland declared:

Although there was less prejudice against the free school system of 1870 and following years in the Valley than in most other sections of Virginia, many even in Rockingham looked upon it with misgiving, fearing an aggravation of the race problem, a weakening of the moral code, and various other undesirable things.[161]

The statement by Rev. Mr. Price follows:

When the public system [of 1870] was first mooted, the feeling quite prevalent among the more influential people was that the effect would be a very serious one upon the religious interests of the people, through secular education. . . . The first superintendent of schools [in Rockingham] was the Rev. Mr. Loose. He favored all efforts to have the teachers realize their moral responsibility. The result was that a predominating element of officers

---

158 See p. 420.

159 *Richmond Enquirer*, Jan. 29, 1870.

160 These were Rev. H. T. Darnall, Amelia County, *Va. Sch. Rep't*, 1885, Part III, 149; *U. S. Comm. Educ. Rep't*, 1871, 360; Rev. Wm. Hicks, Bland County, *Ibid.*, 1872, 348; Rev. G. Gray, Botetourt County, *Ibid.*; Rev. J. A. Waddel, Charles City and New Kent, *Ibid.*; Rev. W. E. Wiatt, Gloucester County, *Ibid.*, 1871, 361; 1872, 348; Rev. W. A. Hill, Greene and Madison; Rev. W. A. A. Taylor, Lee County; Rev. L. J. Haley, Louisa County; Rev. E. L. Baptist, Mecklenburg County; Rev. T. W. Sydnor, Nottoway County; Rev. G. W. Dame, Pittsylvania County, *Ibid.*, 349; *Va. Sch. Rep't*, 1885, Part III, 157; Rev. W. W. Walker, Richmond and Westmoreland, *Ibid.*, 262; *U. S. Comm. Educ. Rep't*, 1871, 361; 1872, 349; Rev. G. W. Holland, Rockingham County, *Ibid.*; Rev. J. Lyons, Tazewell County; Rev. A. L. Hogshead, Washington County; Rev. J. D. Thomas, Wythe County, *Ibid.*

161 Wayland: *Hist. Rockingham Co.*, 302.

and teachers were in control of the system who realized this. The institutes were opened with prayer, the Bible was read in all the schools as a preliminary exercise, and in numerous instances the school would be led in extempore prayer, or the Lord's Prayer would be recited in concert. As time passed it was to be noticed that the moral and religious features became more evident, and the baneful effects of mere secularism were in great measure prevented.[162]

It is probable that the attitude and experience of Rockingham County were duplicated in other counties where ministers were in charge; and it is not unlikely that investigation of the administrative personnel at this time in many towns and cities would show that the clergy were in partial control. Thus in the organization of schools at Lynchburg at this time, the names of Rev. C. C. Bitting, and Rev. T. H. Early appear.[163]

That ministers should now play a prominent part in the inauguration of the public school system, in view of the religious development in Virginia before the War, is not surprising. In the organization of the Educational Association of Virginia, in 1863, ministers had a prominent part. Rev. Dr. J. M. P. Atkinson, President of Hampden-Sidney was chosen president, and the offices of corresponding and recording secretaries went to ministers. Opening and closing prayers were made by ministers, and names of the clergy appear on various committees.[164] The War had not weakened the influence of the clergy in Virginia. The Bible Society of Virginia was still in existence, holding annual meetings.[165] The two most venerated heroes of the War were Stonewall Jackson and Robert E. Lee, as distinguished for their pious Christianity as for their heroic valor.[166]

---

[162] *Ibid.*, 302–03; Mr. Wayland and Rev. Mr. Price are incorrect in stating that the first superintendent was Rev. Mr. Loose—according to the *U. S. Comm. Educ. Rep't*, 1871, 361; 1782, 349, the first county superintendent was Rev. G. W. Holland; the name of Rev. J. S. Loose first appears in the report for 1873, 406.

[163] Christian: *Lynchburg*, 286–87.

[164] *Minutes Educ. Assoc. Va., passim.*

[165] *Cf. Richmond Enquirer*, April 5, 1876.

[166] Beard: *Rise Amer. Civilization*, I, 139; see p. 590; General Lee received part of his secondary eductaion at the Alexandria Boarding School, conducted by a famous Virginia Quaker teacher, Benjamin Hallowell—*cf. Circular of the Alexandria Boarding School*, 1853, and Morrison: *Beginnings Pub. Educ. Va.*, 115–16.

The conflicting views concerning the possible effects of the public school system upon the religious life of the state represented in the opposite stands taken by the Methodist and Protestant Episcopal churches, the apparent inability of the various groups in the Educational Association of Virginia to adopt a definite position in the matter of religious training in public schools, the contrasting views of Dr. Smith and Dr. Ruffner, as to the compatibility of a public school system with religious instruction, are all indicative of the necessity faced by Dr. Ruffner of crystallizing these various views into a policy on the subject which would make it possible for the public school system to function.

Dr. Ruffner's Initiation Of A Policy Of Co-operation Without Alliance

The school system had hardly been inaugurated when an attempt was made to get an official expression of interpretation from the Assembly on the subject of reading the Bible in public schools. It appears that Mr. R. L. Carne, county superintendent of Alexandria County and City, had attempted to exclude the Bible.[167] The matter was finally referred to Dr. Ruffner, whose duty it was according to the bill creating the public school system,

. . . to determine the true intent and meaning of the school laws and regulations, and to explain to the county superintendents and other school officers the several duties enjoined thereby upon them, and his decision shall be final, unless and until reversed by the board of education.[168]

The decision was published in the *Virginia Educational Journal* and is important as still being the official, and, in a sense, the legal opinion on the subject of religious worship in the public schools of Virginia.

DEAR SIR—The subject of religious worship in the public schools is one which has occasioned great trouble in other States, and I thought it best for the school law to be silent on the subject. I felt sure that our Virginia doctrine in regard to the rights of conscience is correct. Whilst it is proper for the State reverently to acknowledge the authority of the Supreme Being, it has no right to use, or allow to be used, its authority

---

[167] *Jour., H. Del.*, Feb. 17, 1871, 199.
[168] *Acts of Assembly*, July 11, 1870, 405.

or its means to aid particular sects, or to inculcate any particular religious doctrine, or to enjoin any particular form or mode of worship. Yet it does not follow from this that all religious exercises should be rigidly excluded from public free schools any more than from the University, the Military Institute or the halls of Legislation. Where it is agreeable to those concerned, and conducive to order and morals to have such exercises, I can see no objection to its being allowed, provided the exercises are fit and becoming as to manner and time, and no one is required to attend upon them whose conscience would be offended thereby. But if serious complaint, disorder, or trouble of any kind would be likely to result from their introduction, they ought not to be allowed. This can be decided only by the local authorities.[169]

It is clear from this statement, that the question of reading the Bible or religious instruction in public schools was to be left for determination to the direction of local authorities. The decision is characteristic of the attitude foreshadowed by the expression invoking the aid of the Deity at the promulgation of the Constitution, an attitude seeking co-operation without definite alliance.[170] The historic position of the legal separation of church and state was not to be marred by a legal incorporation of anything that would tend to establish a definite alliance between church and state. There was to be no definite legal alliance, but where the people wished to co-operate in permitting the Church to exert a religious influence in education, it was to be allowed.

Dr. Ruffner took occasion, too, in his *Report* for 1871, to enter at length into the question of moral and religious training.[171] He started with the premise that education is conducted by the state "on account of its politico-economical advantages." However, in the complete educational scheme, the parents, the state, and the church, each had a particular part to perform which it could do "better than either of the others."[172] While the state cannot properly teach religion, it does not follow that all incidental allusions or observance of a religious character should be forbidden. The central principle was that "the true theory of civil government forbids the use of state money or state authority

---

[169] *Va. Jour. Educ.*, II, 197.
[170] See p. 412.
[171] *Va. Sch. Rep't*, 1871, 56 *ff*.
[172] *Ibid.*

in any way that contravenes individual rights of conscience.''
The enunciation of this principle is important and it will be of
interest to investigate the extent to which it subsequently operated in the actual conduct of public education in Virginia.[173]
Dr. Ruffner deprecated the whole controversy as detrimental to
both education and religion.[174]

But, so keen was the general interest in the problem, that it
was not possible for Dr. Ruffner to ignore it subsequently. At
the meeting of the Educational Association of Virginia, in 1871,
two members of the Special Committee on Religious Education
in Public Schools, Prof. J. B. Minor, of the University, and Rev.
Wm. F. Gardner, of Prince George County, submitted reports.
Mr. Minor recommended Bible teaching in schools, and addressed
his attention to the details of the procedure necessary in connection with the adaptation of the Bible to school methods.[175] Rev.
Mr. Gardner undertook a philosophical discussion of the problem. He was an advocate of free public instruction as the cheap-
est and best means for the prevention of vice and crime, and for
securing the material welfare of the masses.[176] While it was not
desirable that public schools, maintained by the state, should
be under church control, it was desirable that people should become more pious as they became more intelligent. Though the
state did not educate for the purpose of increasing church membership, yet the result was ''the means of getting religious information.'' The aim of the state, ''good citizens,'' was obtained
''in proportion, as they are governed by the principles of christianity.''[177] In schools, under the control of the majority of
voters, it was imprudent and unjust to have any religious instruction except Bible-reading. Children sent to public schools
must not be permitted to grow up in irreligion. The proper
agencies for that religious instruction were the home and the
church.[178]

The Association, apparently wearied with the theoretical discussion of the problem, requested the committee to find out defi-

[173] See p. 525, 638, 643.
[174] *Va. Sch. Rep't*, 1871, 56–58.
[175] *Va. Educ. Jour.*, Aug. 1871, II, 362.
[176] *Ibid.*, 364.
[177] *Ibid.*, 365.
[178] *Ibid.*, 366–67.

nitely from the teachers of the state, the number of schools in which Bible reading had been adopted and with what results.[179]

In view of the interest still manifested in the problem, Dr. Ruffner, in his report for 1872, discussed the question from the point of view of the relation of the state and church to education. Theoretically, education was the function of neither, but since education among the people was essential to the well-being of both, each had a right to step in to see it was done. The state as a secular organization charged with promoting the public good in temporal things might more readily enter upon the work of education. If, individuals and the state were, however, to inculcate anti-christian sentiments or to interfere with healthful religious training, then the church was bound to step in and carry on secular as well as sacred instruction. As between private and public systems, the question was one of expediency.[180]

Elsewhere, in the same report, Dr. Ruffner discussed the denominational character of the various colleges in the state, and held that it was natural and proper that the various denominations should maintain colleges where the influence would be in harmony with their own religious views. In his opinion, they were "none the less valuable as instruments of public education because of their denominational character." But the fact that an institution, "whether State or chartered," was without denominational character, was not presumption against its usefulness, or its Christian character. He recalled the fact that people formerly were as uneasy about the religious influences of, and within, the University, as many were now in regard to that influence in connection with public free schools.[181]

The conciliatory attitude of Dr. Ruffner in which he sought to give expression to his *laissez faire* policy of permitting the people to co-operate, or not, with the church as they chose, so long as there was no commitment to the principle of definite alliance, or union between church and state, did not strike a wholly responsive chord. The *Virginia Educational Journal* published a lengthy article, in 1872, on the educational advantages of the

---

179 *Minutes Educ. Assoc. Va.*, 1871, 7; the report of this investigation, if made, does not appear in subsequent Minutes of the Association.

180 *Va. Sch. Rep't*, 1872, 100–01.

181 *Ibid.*, 105–06; Hotchkiss: *Va. Geog. & Polit. Summary*, 211.

use of the Bible. In the writer's opinion, its exclusion from schools in favor of heathen authors was the most "monstrous absurdity" of the age. "A Christian country must assert and enjoy its privileges—must not be ashamed to act out its belief."[182]

After years of discussion, an attempt was made, in 1873, at a meeting of the Educational Association of Virginia to place it on record on the subject. A resolution was offered indicating the conviction of the association that, while the introduction of sectarian questions into public institutions was to be deplored, yet, such a daily recognition of Almighty God as would impress upon youth a sense of the paramount claims of religion was to be desired. Therefore, the daily use in the public schools, of the Lord's prayer, and the daily reading of a selection from the Holy Scriptures, was, in the judgment of the Association, a safeguard against infidelity, "and that such a practice might be universally introduced by a wise and judicious scheme of lessons, without giving offence to the peculiar tenets of any branch of the Christian Church." After some discussion, the resolution was tabled for consideration at the next meeting.[183]

The Association at its next meeting, however, contented itself with listening to an address by Dr. Ruffner on "Moral Instruction in Schools." The difficulty, according to Dr. Ruffner, lay in determining how far public education might proceed with due regard to the rights and scruples of citizens. The war on the subject, he felt, was one concerning forms rather than substance; it was not an opposition to religion and morals, but the manner of teaching them, due to the jealousy of parties or sects, and in part to a change in the educational temper and system of the day.[184]

Shortly before this, Dr. Ruffner had delivered an address on "Religion in the Public Schools," before the Grace Street Church, Richmond, as a part of the program of the week of prayer for colleges, recommended by the Presbyterian General Assembly, the concluding day of which it was decided to dedicate to schools of every grade. In many ways this address so

---

[182] *Va. Educ. Jour.*, May, 1872, III, 253, 257.
[183] *Minutes Educ. Assoc. Va.*, 1873, 11.
[184] *Va. Educ. Jour.*, Nov., 1874, VI, 6–10.

expressive of his policy of conciliation, during this period, may
be regarded as Dr. Ruffner's most important contribution to the
subject in the first period of his control of the public school
system.[185]   Dr. Ruffner, referring to the 175,000 primary school
children in Virginia, said that they were at a most impressionable
age, but one which was the seed time, not the harvest time of the
church, and that the public schools in belonging to no church belonged to all.   Schools were morally and religiously what the men
were who controlled them.   Religious instruction for childhood,
which was unsuited to public schools, could be given at home, in
the Sunday School, and in the church.   What was needed was to
have school authorities and school teachers impressed with the
responsibility of establishing within the child the power of conscience and the fear of God.   In Virginia, the Christian people
of the state had a controlling influence in the management of the
public school system, because the people were a Christian people.
It was by no special management that the majority of the ninety-
four school superintendents were Christian professors—many of
them Christian ministers.[186] While ''no unreasonable proscrip-
tion; no union of Church and State; no form of sectarian proga-
gandism; no interference with the conscientious scruples of
anybody'' was wanted, it was desirable to have pervading the
school system that personal influence that comes from sound
principles and the fear of God.   With reference to the rules to
be followed, in practise, in regard to religion in public schools,
Dr. Ruffner reiterated the principles laid down in his letter to
County Superintendent Carne.[187]   In closing, he enunciated his
doctrine of mutual co-operation, which whether followed as a
deliberate policy or not, has been, as will be subsequently
shown,[188] of real importance in the actual development of the
problem.   The church, he declared, could not afford to stand

---

[185] *Ibid.*, April, 1874, V, 258 *ff*. The editor of the *Journal* in quoting
this address from the *Richmond Dispatch* commended it in a special note
to the careful attention of his readers, because of ''The official source, the
dispassionate treatment of delicate questions, and the vast importance of
the subject.''
[186] See p. 423.
[187] See p. 425.
[188] See p. 525.

aloof from the public schools, nor the public schools be without
the sympathy of the churches.[189]

While the Educational Association of Virginia could not, or
did not care to, come to any definite conclusion on the problem
of religious training in education, Dr. Ruffner by his letter to
Superintendent Carne, by his recognition of the place of denominational institutions in the educational scheme, and a general
conciliatory attitude toward opposing views and forces, to which
he gave expression in various writings and addresses, succeeded
in crystallizing for the state a policy of co-operation without
committing it to any entangling legal alliance. This diplomatic
solution of the problem was not met, however, by that popular
accord which one might suppose it merited; instead, Dr. Ruffner
soon saw himself and the public school system placed on the
defensive.

The Public School System On The Defensive

With the year 1875, Dr. Ruffner found that his free school
system was being threatened by a serious opposition led by a
group who were opposed ostensibly to state support for negro
education, particularly, in view of the fact that the state was
unable to meet the demands of its creditors. Careful consideration of the controversial writings of the leaders of the opposition indicates, however, that the real crux of the opposition lay
in the question whether private, that is, denominational education or public education was to dominate in Virginia.

The opposition opened battle by a series of articles in the
Religious Herald in the spring and summer of 1875, under the
signature of "Civis" who was later revealed as Dr. B. Puryear,
of Richmond College.[190] These articles were followed by a series
of articles in the *Southern Planter and Farmer*, beginning in December, 1875.[191] As summarized by "Civis" himself, his articles
in the *Religious Herald* were designed to demonstrate that the
political principles which were invoked for public school support

---

[189] *Va. Educ. Jour.*, April, 1874, V, 258–62.

[190] The *Religious Herald* was a Baptist publication; its editorial policy
at the time liberally opened its columns apparently to all phases of controversial questions.

[191] Civis (Puryear, B.):*The Public School In Its Relations To The
Negro; cf. South Atlant. Quart.*, XX, 143–44.

were foreign to free institutions and fatal to liberty; harmful
to the energies of the people and to public morality. Education
was the sacred and imperative duty of parents, not of government. The assumption by the state of the duties, privileges, and
prerogatives belonging to the parental relation was a dangerous
denial of the reciprocal relations of parent and child, and contrary to Scripture. The cost of public instruction, he argued, to
those whose money supported it, was greater than better instruction at the private school. Enforced charity was an injury to
the party receiving it, and to the party wronged by unjust taxation. Finally, Virginia was forbidden by simple honesty to
carry on such a system when compelled to do it with money belonging to the creditors of the commonwealth.

As the last objection was one which for a time threatened to
wreck the public school system, and was used not only by the
staunch advocates of private education, but by politicians,
claiming to be disinterested in the controversy as it affected the
issue of public versus private education, it is necessary to digress
sufficiently to indicate briefly the relation of the financial situation to public education.

In 1861, the Assembly had passed an ordinance that, until
otherwise provided by law, all the revenues accruing to the
Literary Fund, except for appropriation to the University and
the Virginia Military Institute, should be appropriated to the
military defence of the state.[192] Before the Civil War, several
of the incorporated colleges and seminaries of the state had invested their funds in the bonds and other securities of the Commonwealth, and, as early as 1866, the Assembly had passed an
act that the interest due on these bonds should be paid by the
state.[193] Similar enactments were passed in subsequent years,
and thus these educational institutions were protected.[194] In the
serious financial situation of a $45,000,000 debt, which con-
fronted the state, in 1870, public officials began to divert some of
the tax returns for school purposes to payment of the state

---

[192] *Acts of Assembly*, June 26, 1861, 57.
[193] *Ibid.*, Feb. 22, 1866, 438.
[194] *Ibid.*, Feb. 23, 1867, 667; July 9, 1870, 322; July 11, 1870, 431; Mar.
20, 1872, 327; Mar. 3, 1882, 203; Pearson: *Readjuster Movement*, 44.

debt.[195] By 1873, Dr. Ruffner, in order to protect the public school system, secured an act authorizing the funding of the bonds belonging to the Literary Fund, and requiring the auditor to pay the constitutional quota of school funds in cash.[196] Dr. Ruffner sought to further defend the public schools in an article "Poverty VS. Education" by declaring that, in view of the well-known fact that Virginia spent about twenty millions a year in whiskey and dogs, while only one million was asked for education, the plea of poverty was fallacious.[197] In spite of Dr. Ruffner's efforts to protect the public schools, the amount due the schools increased yearly, until, by September, 1878, about $850,000 was due.[198] In 1879, conditions were such that enrollment dropped from 140,472 to 72,306 for whites, and from 61,772 to 35,768 for negroes.[199] As far as Dr. Ruffner could determine, the diversion of funds and enforced reduction in availability of public education had created a reaction favorable to public schools, the people refusing to yield their patronage to private schools which were started, or to pay a small tuition fee in public schools.[200]

In the meantime, there had been formed, in 1877, within the conservative political party, a new group calling itself the Readjuster party, which sought relief from the burden of debt through partial repudiation.[201] Dr. Ruffner finally decided that the interests of the schools rendered it advisable for him to join the moderate section of this group, which, in the spring of 1879, passed two acts, known as the Henkel and McCulloch bills. These bills gave a proportionate protection to public school funds and provided for adjustment and funding of the debt.[202] The McCulloch Bill was, however, attacked by the more extreme group

---

[195] Taylor: *Negro in Reconst. Va.*, 156; *Va. Normal & Indust. Instit. Gazette*, XXXII, No. 5, 18; Pearson: *Readjuster Movement*, 24.

[196] *Acts of Assembly*, Mar. 29, 1873, 267; Pearson: *Readjuster Movement*, 62.

[197] Ruffner, W. H.: *Public Schools—Difficulties Removed*, 1.

[198] Pearson: *Readjuster Movement*, 62.

[199] *U. S. Comm. Educ. Rep't*, 1879, 242.

[200] *Ibid.*, 244.

[201] *South Atlant. Quart.*, XX, 149.

[202] Pearson: *Readjuster Movement*, 85–87; *South Atlant. Quart.*, XX, 148–49.

in the Readjuster party, with the final result that Dr. Ruffner's support of the bill cost him his re-election to office in 1882.[203] What share the determined opposition of a section of the clerical group, which began with the opposition of Dr. Puryear, in 1875, to manifest itself toward the public school system and its chief defender, and which, in 1878, had resulted in a number of ministers joining a "society to preserve the credit of the state,"[204] had in Dr. Ruffner's defeat is, as yet, a matter of conjecture.

The temper of those who found in the financial condition of the state, a reason for opposing the public school system can be gauged from the statements of "Civis" in the *Religious Herald,* in 1878:

> . . . It has been left to Virginia, with piteous pleas of poverty on her lips, to offer to every boy within her limits, whether rich or poor, and without distinction of race, color or previous condition, free tuition from the alphabet up to and through the University! Well, she does not do it with her own money, and perhaps that makes the thing defensible!
>
> .   .   .   .
>
> On the wages of sin, we are educating into sin, the rising generation. The basal lesson of their education, which they cannot fail to imbibe, is that plighted faith and public honor and private rights are vile; for all these are contemptuously spurned and set at naught by the policy we are now pursuing.[205]

The financial situation as affecting the schools was not cleared up, however, until the passing in 1882, of the "Riddleberger bill," which placed the Literary Fund in the most favored class of creditors, and the "Granstaff Act," which protected the local estimated quota of the state's appropriation for school purposes.[206]   School funds benefited also from the sale of the state's interest in the Atlantic, Mississippi, and Ohio Railroad.[207]   As Pearson, the historian of the Readjuster Movement declares:

---

[203] *Ibid.,* 149–50; Pearson: *Readjuster Movement,* 115.
[204] *Ibid.,* 83–84.
[205] *Religious Herald,* Feb. 14, 1878; there were two correspondents writing for the *Religious Herald* in 1875 under the name of "Civis" and it is not certain that the articles from which these citations are made were by Dr. Puryear, hence the *nom de plume* "Civis" is retained, without making a definite attribution; *cf.* editorial note, in Puryear's *The Public School in its Relations to the Negro,* 5.
[206] Pearson: *Readjuster Movement,* 145.
[207] *Ibid.*

"Public education received such generous treatment that some feared the ruin of the denominational schools."[208]

Reverting now to Dr. Puryear's articles in the *Southern Planter and Farmer*, it will be seen how the readjuster issue served as a convenient peg on which to hang his opposition to the development of the public school system, and the negro race the cloak to conceal his antagonism to state intervention in education. Discussing the public school system in its relation to the negro, Dr. Puryear argued that it was not by accident, but by the act of God, that the negro was placed in an inferior position to the Caucasian. His proper economic position was that of a laborer; to educate him, would unfit him for his calling.[209] The real animus of these articles comes out, however, in the statement that the government was drifting into Prussian absolutism, as evinced by the fact that the President had recommended to Congress compulsory education, proposing "to tax the church to support the school," and in this matter was being backed by the feeble support of the Governor of Virginia.[210] What the President was proposing was that the Federal government should lay its "cold and heavy hand" upon the children, prescribing what they shall and shall not learn, "forbidding the reading of the Bible and the bare mention of the name of Christ," constituting itself as a sort of "wet nurse" in forming the minds, morals, health, and habits of the little urchins, a procedure which would result in "relaxation of parental and filial obligation and manifold forms of atheism and irreligion." But parents cannot surrender education to either the federal or the state government without guilt, as to do so is in irreconcilable conflict with the

---

[208] *Ibid.; cf.* the impetus given to the creation of higher state institutions, see p. 404; for a further explanation of the financial situation as it related to schools, see Mahone, Wm.: *Attitude of the Readjusters of Virginia. . . . The public debt of Virginia examined; cf.* also *Richmond Enquirer,* "The Cost of the Free School System in Virginia," Mar. 30, 1876; "The School Fund Muddle," May 2, 1876; *Religious Herald,* XIII, Jan. 31, 1878, "Letter from Civis," No. 3, in a series of letters on necessity of Virginia's paying her debt, and *Ibid.,* Feb. 14, Mar. 14, Mar. 21; *Va. Educ. Jour.,* IX, 550.

[209] Civis: *The Public School In Its Relations to the Negro,* 8–9.

[210] *Ibid.,* 12; *cf.* Smith, S. M.: *Relig. Educ. in Mass.,* 262, 302; these were also the years of agitation concerning the Hoar Bill, see Reisner: *Nationalism and Education,* 429 *ff.*

Biblical doctrine of parental duty and responsibility.[211]   The public school system and the theory of separation of church and state could not exist together.   If religious instruction is given in the public school, some will hold that they are taxed to propagate religious error.   If religious instruction is excluded, then "in the clear opinion of the great bulk of Protestants," it becomes an institution in the interests of atheism and infidelity. Who would be taxed to have their children taught to trample upon the lessons of religion?   Since the state cannot prescribe a religious creed, the Bible cannot be read in the public school. When the Bible, the only infallible source of ethics is excluded, and emphasis placed upon the cultivation of the intellectual powers without the proper cultivation of the moral faculties, no safe-guard against vice and crime is furnished.   Summing up the insuperable difficulties that belong to the public school system, Dr. Puryear said they were two—compulsory attendance and religious instruction.[212]   Besides, "The attempt to lift our whole population, white and black, into a literary atmosphere would be supremely silly, even if we possessed the fabled gift of Midas."[213]

On this issue, Dr. Puryear does not seem to have been able to carry some of the more representative Baptist opinion with him, for both the Dover Baptist Association and the *Religious Herald* declared themselves in favor of public schools.[214]   Though Dr. Puryear was answered by Dr. Ruffner, who unmasked his *nom de plume*, it will be sufficient to consider Dr. Ruffner's defence of the public school system as stated in his controversy with Rev. Dr. R. L. Dabney.[215]

The Ruffner controversy with Dr. Dabney, of the Union Theological Seminary, was initiated by an article on "The Negro and the Common Schools" by Dr. Dabney in the April number of *The Southern Planter and Farmer*.   It was followed by a series of articles by Dr. Ruffner and Dr. Dabney in the *Richmond Dis-*

---

[211] Civis: *The Public School In Its Relations to the Negro*, 12, 26; for a discussion of President Grant's views, see *Va. Educ. Jour.*, X, 452.

[212] Civis: *The Public School System In Its Relations to the Negro*, 35.

[213] *Ibid.*, 26.

[214] *South Atlant. Quart.*, XX, 147; for a later article in which Dr. Puryear modified his views, see *Va. Educ. Jour.*, Mar., 1889, 125.

[215] *Richmond Enquirer*, July 21, 29, 1876.

patch and the *Richmond Enquirer,* the whole controversy thus receiving ample publicity.[216] In answer to Dr. Dabney's declaration that the negro's business was "to work and not read," Dr. Ruffner reminded him that his position was contrary to that of Samuel Davies,[217] "the Patrick Henry of the Presbyterian church," who believed that the poorer the class the more reason for furnishing them with religious literature and the Bible, and who, moreover, did not draw a line at the negroes.[218] Dr. Ruffner then summarized Dr. Dabney's argument concerning religion in schools into four points: 1. Religious truth should form a prominent part of the subject matter of every child's education; 2. that it should always form a part of the subject matter of primary school education; 3. that it cannot be properly taught in schools supported by public money; 4. hence the present public school system should be exchanged for the "old Virginia" system.[219] On the first point, Dr. Ruffner was in agreement, and particularly with Dr. Dabney's view that it belonged to the parent; and, if so, why complain of the state for not teaching religion. On the second point, Dr. Ruffner held Dr. Dabney to be inconsistent and impracticable, for it would necessitate the delegating of religious instruction to a teacher, thus depriving the parent of his inalienable right; nor was Dr. Dabney's qualification that the teacher was to be a professing Christian, a practicable one, for a professing Christian might not be always your sort of Christian. On the third point, Dr. Ruffner held that the public schools as a matter of historical fact taught religion more regularly, thoroughly, and soundly, than it had ever been taught in private schools.[220] Going back for support to the report of the Rockfish Gap Commission,[221] Dr. Ruffner gave it as his interpretation that

---

[216] Reprints of Dr. Ruffner's articles are to be found in a bound volume of *Circulars,* 1870–76, under the title of "The Public Free School System," in the Virginia State Library; the dates for Dr. Ruffner's articles in the *Richmond Enquirer* are April 5, 6, 8, 12, 13, May 10, 17, 24, 28, June 2, 1876; for Dr. Dabney's articles in the same paper are April 20, 22, 26, May 6, 1876.

[217] See p. 142.

[218] Ruffner, W. H.: *Pub. Free Sch. System,* 14.

[219] *Ibid.,* 25.

[220] *Ibid.,* 29.

[221] See p. 369.

. . . The State may formally teach the recognized morality of the country, and the will of God as the standard and ultimate authority of all morality, but distinctively religious teachings shall be left to volunteer agencies; and these volunteer agencies, including the teachers, may engage in any amount of teaching or worship which is agreeable to the parents, and which does not interfere with the rights and convictions of those who differ.[222]

As for the cry, that "if the Bible be cast out," children will grow up infidels, Dr. Ruffner asked whether the fifty years of trial with the University of Virginia, and thirty-seven years with the Virginia Military Institute had proven them to be vehicles of infidelity?[223]   There was no need to legislate Christianity into the schools of a Christian people, it would "go in of itself."[224] As for the relation of education to crime, Dr. Ruffner referred to the experience of Scotland and contrasted the Scotland of the eighteenth century after the Parliament at Edinburgh had re-created the dead public schools with the Scotland of the seventeenth century.[225]   In view of all these considerations, how could Dr. Dabney argue in his fourth point for a return to the "old Virginia" system, in which the state paid the tuition of poor children in any convenient schools, in which they would either get no religious teaching, or, if they did, the state would after all be using public money for religious teaching.[226]   Dr. Dabney might have his choice: "No religion, or religion taught by State money!"[227]

As to the effects of the controversy upon the public school system, there have been various estimates. Professor Knight who has carefully studied Virginian and southern educational history states:

. . . In the end the controversy may have had the effect of stimulating the feeble-hearted, though in a few instances there is evidence that Dr. Dabney's arguments caused some discontent with the system.[228]

---

[222] Ruffner: *Pub. Free Sch. System*, 32.
[223] *Ibid.*
[224] *Ibid.*
[225] *Ibid.*, 34; *cf.* Morgan, A.: *Rise and Progress of Scottish Education*, 62, 70.
[226] Ruffner: *Public Free School System*, 31.
[227] *Ibid.;* Knight: *Reconst. & Educ. Va., South Atlant. Quart.*, Jan. & April, 1916, Reprint, 33.
[228] *Ibid.*

A correspondent of the *Richmond Enquirer* declared, when the controversy was at its height, that if it were not for the Presidential canvass, "the existence of the common-school system would be most seriously imperilled, judging from the sympathy expressed for Dr. Dabney."[229] H. Waddell, in an article on Dr. Ruffner, in 1924, declared that this controversy and the public addresses made by Dr. Ruffner "informed the people of the merits of the new system, resulting in a steady growth of the schools in popular support."[230] The report of the United States Commissioner of Education in discussing the status of public schools in Virginia for 1876, declared:

> The school system was never so prosperous, so well managed, or so strong in public favor as at present, notwithstanding that during the year covered by the report an organized movement was made for its overthrow. Writers of ability attacked it virulently and an attempt was made to assemble a convention of opponents. The State superintendent, under the authority of the law which imposes upon him the "general supervision of the public free school interests in the State" entered freely into the discussion, circulating a large number of educational tracts. He expresses the belief that while a small class of worthy opponents have been led by the debate to be more open and decided in their opposition to the school system than before, far more has been gained than lost by the discussion.[231]

With the close of the Dabney-Ruffner debate, a distinct period in the early history of the newly established school system came to a close. The school system had been placed on the defensive, and though it had to weather until 1882 the stormy discussions raised by the readjuster issue, Dr. Ruffner had succeeded in creating a reaction favorable to the public school system, as is evidenced by the triumph of the system in the adjustment of the readjuster issue.[232] The opposition had been unable to present a solution more desirable than that of Dr. Ruffner's policy of co-operation without alliance.

---

[229] *Richmond Enquirer*, May 12, 1876, article by "Hilclymer."
[230] *Va. Teacher*, Oct.–Nov., 1924, V, 271.
[231] *U. S. Comm. Educ. Rep't*, 1876, 402.
[232] See p. 434–35.

CHAPTER XI

GRADUAL ADJUSTMENT TO THE CO-OPERATION
POLICY

Favorable Progress Of The Public School System

Although no discussions of the problem of religion in education in the subsequent régime of Dr. Ruffner loomed so large in
public interest as had the controversies with Dr. Puryear and
Dr. Dabney, there was nevertheless manifested a continued concern in the problem. Some of the expressions of this concern
are not without significance in indicating the trend of opinion
on this subject, helping to crystallize the attitude to which expression was given in the formulation of the Constitution of 1902,
and the practises in the period under that Constitution.[1]

Dr. Ruffner's bold stand in the defence of the public school
system, the able manner in which he attempted to advance his
conciliatory policy, attracted the attention of educators in the
country at large. In the summer of 1876, he presented an address on "The Moral Element in Education" before the National
Education Association. Typical of his desire to conciliate his
opponents was the declaration that "Deference for eccentricities
of religious opinion will have become an intolerable vice when
any school teacher hesitates to acknowledge the existence or the
authority of the blessed God and Father of us all."[2] As for
moral instruction, it was up to the schools to systematize the right
principles given by the church and to develop for society those
details which will serve to inform and guide men in their daily
life and form part of the scheme under which the young are educated.[3]

Another example of Dr. Ruffner's effort to conciliate denominational opinion was his address before the English Lutheran
Church of Richmond, in October, 1876. Referring to the work

---

[1] See p. 473 *ff.*
[2] *N. E. A. Proc's,* 1876, XVI, 41.
[3] *Ibid.,* 43.

of Roanoke College, affiliated with the Lutheran Church, Dr. Ruffner again declared that the usefulness and popularity of a college were not necessarily diminished because controlled by a particular denominational influence.[4] While home teaching and influence in religious matters might be sufficient for children going to school at or near home, and the mature young man going to a University might be trusted to keep himself under wholesome influences, the immature youth going from home before his habits had become firmly established needed to be placed under guaranteed influences of the most healthful sort—for this purpose nothing was better than a denominational college.[5]

During this period, the question of state appropriations to denominational institutions began to receive attention in the press, due undoubtedly to a question in the public mind as to how the state was going to dispose of the land scrip granted by Congress.[6] Dr. J. L. M. Curry, who was later to be associated with the Peabody Education Fund, in an article in the *Religious Herald* in June, 1878, dwelt upon the evil which had grown up in some states of appropriating public money, usually under the guise of charity, to denominational institutions. He held that no religious denomination should receive one cent from the public treasury, but that all denominational enterprises should take care of themselves. Appropriation to sectarian institutions was at variance with the entire freedom of religious belief and action that was a distinguishing characteristic of the government. To tax a citizen of one faith to encourage the tenets and doctrines of another was a flagrant wrong. While taxation for the public school system on the basis that a certain amount of education is necessary for the preservation of the state was justifiable, that principle could not be extended to appropriation for denominational higher education.[7] The position taken by Dr. Curry is characteristic of the attitude which apparently had influenced the Assembly to assume a share in the control of Hampton Institute.[8]

---

[4] See p. 428.
[5] *Va. Educ. Jour.*, Nov., 1876, VIII, 32.
[6] See p. 405.
[7] *Religious Herald*, June 27, 1878.
[8] See p. 407.

This article seems to have been in line with the position taken by the *Religious Herald* in a previous editorial, in May, on the relation of taxation to religious instruction in public schools. The *Herald* declared that its position in maintaining the principle that it was unjust to tax Roman Catholics, Jews, and sceptics to support Bible reading in the public schools had received no support from the Protestant religious press. It held that while there might be no objection to a pious teacher reading the Bible in public schools, where there was no opposition from patrons, that on the whole, the Bible was not a proper school book for children. To enforce Bible reading would lead to the establishment of Christianity by law, taxing the public for its support, and finally enforcing its claim, by penalties, sword, and fire. This was held to be "anti-republican, anti-Christian, unreasonable, and at war with the best interests of society."[9] This attitude of the Baptist publication on the question of Bible reading in the public schools is of significance in view of the Baptist position on this question a half century later.[10]

While the Baptist position tended to a complete cleavage in interest between the church and state on the question of religious instruction in education, favoring the limitation of all religious instruction to the church, and denominational schools, Dr. Ruffner still believed in the possibilities of co-operation without definite legal affiliation between church and state in the treatment of this problem. His views appear rather strikingly in his caustic comment, in the *Virginia Educational Journal,* upon the address of William Allan, principal of McDonogh Institute, Maryland, before the Virginia Educational Association, in July, 1878. Colonel Allan had held that it was not possible to look to the public schools for religious instruction, and that they were uncertain and imperfect agencies for moral training. In providing for secular education, the state had undertaken only half the educational task; the proper work to be done by the Church was not lessened, for the public schools could do little in teaching morals, nothing in teaching religion, thus contributing "only feebly or indirectly to that virtue without which the intelligence

---

9 *Religious Herald,* May 2, 1878.
10 See p. 513, 516.

of a community is worthless, or worse." Whatever virtue was to be attributed to the educational system of Massachusetts, it was to be found not primarily in her free school system, but rather in her admirable academies and college and the University which crowned all. The business frauds and the social scandals of northern cities did not indicate that public school education had helped society. Virginia should develop first her higher institutions, then her public system of elementary instruction.[11]

To this address, Dr. Ruffner replied that Colonel Allan should have read a little more of the history of public schools, and should have given one good reason why morals could not or ought not to be taught in public schools. Nor could he see how a private teacher who opened his door to the public could with propriety act differently from a public teacher in respect to either morals or religion. As for the teaching of religion, he felt that was rarely done wisely and properly in any type of school. Nor could Dr. Ruffner follow Colonel Allan in his argument, which, while reducing the influence of primary schools to an infinitesimal quantity, still found in them the cause of economic and social depravity, while attributing the prodigious intellectual influence of New England only to her colleges.[12]

Elucidating his views further in his annual report, for 1878, Dr. Ruffner declared that the public school was far from being morally neutral. The discipline of a well regulated school was, in itself, highly ethical, and this effect was often enhanced by the tone and direct teaching of text-books, and the precept and example of the teacher.[13] In the effort of some, who would keep the masses in ignorance, in order to protect them from religious error, Dr. Ruffner discovered a reactionary tendency which could lead only to mediaeval darkness. While education was not religion, or a substitute for it, it was the handmaid of religion.[14]

Dr. Dabney did not cease his opposition to the public school system with the close of his debate with Dr. Ruffner. In answer to an article by Dr. Dabney in the January number of the

---

11 *Va. Educ. Jour.*, Sept., 1878, IX, 483–93.
12 *Ibid.*, 499–500.
13 *Va. Sch. Rep't.*, 1878, 60–61.
14 *Ibid.*, 62.

Southern Planter and Farmer, Wm. N. Nelson, superintendent
of schools for Clarke County, denied that the Virginia school had
anything to fear from the supposed "Yankeeizing" tendency of
public schools. On the whole, the efforts of the Northerners in
pouring their millions of dollars into the South, and in coming
personally into the South to assist in its rehabilitation, was evidence that Christianity need not fear to trust itself into the hands
of free schools.[15]

In answer to an article by Dr. Dabney, in the September number of the *Princeton Review* in which he attempted to convince
Northerners that public schools were making of them a nation
of infidels, and that their only hope of salvation lay in adopting
the "old Virginia" system,[16] a writer in the *Virginia Educational Journal* declared that Dr. Dabney knew well enough that
infidelity has its source from college and university men and
from theological seminaries, and that the simple, old fashioned
gospel was nowhere so much valued as among the masses of the
very people who were educated in public schools. It was not from
McGuffey's *Readers* and Maury's *Geographies,* but from literature like that of the *Princeton Review,* that people were seduced
from the old faith. After all, as Dr. Philip Schaff's article in
the same *Review* had indicated, the effects of the public school
system had not been such as to prevent the fusing of the
heterogeneous materials of the country "into a Christian population equal in its proportion of Christian people to the best
community that ever existed, and at least equal (no doubt superior) to what the country has known at any time in the
past."[17]

Of the effects of the public school system upon the moral and
religious life of the country, no one perhaps was in a better position to speak than Rev. A. D. Mayo, a New England educator,
and, after 1880, Associate Editor of the *New England Journal of
Education,* who by travel, observation, and study was conversant
with educational conditions all over the United States. In
an article for the *Virginia Educational Journal,* in 1879, on

---

[15] *Va. Educ. Jour.,* Feb., 1879, X, 68–71.
[16] See p. 334–35, 438, 450.
[17] *Va. Educ. Jour.,* Oct., 1879, X, 449 *ff.*

"The Charge of Godlessness and Shiftlessness Against the Public Schools," Dr. Mayo found the sources of the charges against the public school system to lie in its rapid expansion over a large area, and its direction largely by local intelligence and zeal, resulting in certain local defects, not necessarily inherent in the system itself. Among the various grounds of opposition, it was natural that proprietors and teachers of private seminaries should oppose public schools because of personal interests. While municipal reformers interested in cutting down public appropriations, and social reformers ready to prophesy the downfall of the Republic, found various reasons for opposing the public school system, yet "the most insidious assault on the American system of Public Education, comes in the name of good morals and pure religion."[18] Opposition was coming primarily from two sources—first, from the Catholic Church, upon orders from Rome, seconded by a portion of the Protestant Episcopal Church, which was bringing pressure to bear in favor of the old time English system of church parochial schools,[19] and a guerilla force composed of recruits from all Christian denominations; second, from those who demanded what was called "industrial education." In answer to the first group, Dr. Mayo held that while the public school system could not by its very nature be a specifically religious agency, yet its influence was always in the direction of the universal Christian religion. In bringing together children of all classes and in instructing them in respect for each other's rights, order, law, and good manners, it was a seminary of the common moralities of public and private life. Dr. Mayo further declared that "A people educated solely by the clergy would be what the people of Europe have always been, always ready to burst out into religious wars, nation against nation, race against race, church against church." To test the effects of the public schools on moral training, it was only necessary to compare the records of the free high, and normal schools for general deportment with that of sectarian academies and colleges. Hazing and rebellion against authority were unknown in public schools. The fearful denunciations of the clerical group and the secularists

[18] *Ibid.*, Jan., 1879, X, 2.
[19] See p. 422, 489.

against public schools were due to the fact that they could not capture them as an attachment for their own religious or anti-religious sect. If the growth of children in the virtues that make up the character of the good citizen in a modern Christian state was a mighty power on the side of true religion, then our public schools were eminently religious. In most of them, the Bible still remained, like the Dictionary, a hand-book of practical morality. "In all, even the most secularized city, extracts from religious writings, besides the Bible abound in the school-books; religious hymns are sung, and the character and influence of the teachers is most carefully guarded." Taking the teaching body as a whole, there was no group in the country which could be compared with it in sincerity, self-sacrifice and rectitude of moral purpose; nor would the ministerial profession be "at all disparaged by comparison with these ministers of public education."[20]

The meeting of the Virginia Educational Association, in 1880, was marked by further discussion of the reaction of the public and denominational school systems upon the moral and religious development of society. Prof. S. C. Wells in a paper on "The Strong Points in Southern Society" defended denominational colleges as bulwarks of morality; on them depended the hopes of the future for the conservation of the truer and higher interests of southern society.[21]

Rev. T. W. Sydnor, superintendent of schools of Nottoway County, in his address, at the same meeting, discussed the relation of the Sunday School and public free school. While having in common the fact that they were public and free, the one was kept up under the auspices of the church, in the interest of good morals and pure religion; the other, under the auspices of the state, in the interest of good morals and sound learning—neither

---

[20] *Ibid.*, X, 11–12; *cf.* also Dr. Mayo's statement—"Thus when any portion of the Church or clergy assails the American state and schools as 'godless,' and charges it with oppressing the people by its common school-tax, it is only another way of asserting the old medieval proposition,—that theology and ecclesiasticism are the essence of religion; that there is no common element in Christianity; and that the clergy have a divine right to shape the education of a whole people in the interest of their own special studies and professional advantage. . . ." *New Eng. Jour. Educ.*, Sept. 28, 1882, XVI, 198.

[21] *Va. Educ. Jour.*, Nov., 1880, XI, 359.

could take the place of the other. The Sunday Schools had long since abandoned the idea that they were primarily to teach children to read and spell, they now did this only incidentally, realizing that their business was to teach religion, and in so doing to make the Bible their text-book. The public schools must not invade the domain of the Sunday School, nor teach religion, except in its great moral principles. While Rev. Mr. Sydnor would have nothing taught in schools at variance with the Bible, it need not be made a text-book. That he, like Dr. Ruffner, saw nothing incompatible in maintaining a public school system along with a denominational system, may be gathered from his further suggestion that the various denominations might elevate one of their seminaries for girls into a first class college comparable with that for boys, while the state should go on with the movement on foot for a state University for girls.[22]

On the subject of the rival claims of denominational and public education in respect to the general welfare of society, the comment of the *New England Journal of Education*, in April, 1880, upon the receipt of Dr. Ruffner's annual report is of interest; the *Journal* stated that:

Perhaps there has been too much parading of statistics of Southern illiteracy, and too great a flood of gratuitous advice on Southern education, if not too large expectations on the part of sectarian educational enterprise in the South, during the past dozen years. With all gratitude for the great denominational agencies, Catholic and Protestant, that are seeking the mental reconstruction of this sorely-afflicted realm, we have no faith in anything but a thorough and complete system of public education to meet the great want of these States. . . .[23]

The strong hold, the denominational and the "old Virginia" system had upon those interested in the development of private schools, established before the War, confirming the accuracy of Dr. Mayo's observation on this point,[24] may be gathered from an address in 1881, before the Virginia Educational Association, by Prof. C. L. Cocke, Principal of Hollins Institute.[25] In his

---

22 *Ibid.*, XI, 344 *ff.*; and 348–49.
23 *New Eng. Jour. of Educ.*, April, 1880, XI, 217.
24 See p. 445.
25 See p. 403.

opinion, the "old Virginia" system made the moral and spiritual, as it should, most prominent; and a maintenance of that system was made necessary for the future preservation of society. Virginia, which had secured perfect religious freedom to the state and nation, could not "go back on herself and her great principle, and through a school system invented and imposed by others," deny the right to worship, depriving youth "of their Bible and their God."[26]

Prof. J. D. Dreher, President of Roanoke College, at the same meeting, in an address, on "The Benevolent Spirit And The Higher Education" declared that benevolent persons recognizing the power of education in the progress of the race, were profoundly concerned about the spirit fostered at educational centers. Believing that the best interests of the state and the happiness of coming generations required a decided religious element in education, and feeling that the state could not guard the interests of morals and religion so well as corporate boards of trustees, they preferred that the state should not have full control over higher education. The argument for public free schools as being the only assurance that the mass of the people would receive elementary education and the state be thus protected against the dangers of an ignorant population, with its argument of necessity and protection to the state, did not hold with reference to higher education.[27]

Without entering into the question of the relation of higher education to the safety of the state, the *Virginia Educational Journal* in December, 1881, chose to emphasize the principle of the relation of common schools to the public safety. While not forgetting the superior mission of the church and of the family, it felt that the only instrumentality which could be made to include all the people and be depended on to give the type of instruction required for the public safety was the common

---

[26] *Va. Educ. Jour.*, Jan., 1882, XIII, 9; see p. 442–43.

[27] *Va. Educ. Jour.*, Jan., 1882, XIII, 53–54; *cf.* also *Ibid.*, Oct., 1890, XXI, 452, quotes articles in *The Independent* by Howard Crosby, D.D., LL.D., "Religion and the Schools"—opposed to state providing education in normal schools and state colleges. "The State has no right to furnish any citizen gratis with the luxuries and remunerative advantages of the higher education."

schools. The cultural level of thought in Virginia, at that time, with respect to the relation of the public school system to social and economic development, may be gathered from the statement that if the work of the public school system were properly done, it would be effective in making the masses followers of right principle, law and order, justice, peace and patriotism, protectors of the home, property, and government. ''The rich must be taught that poverty has rights as well as property—that oppression must cease, and the poor must be taught where their rights begin and where they end.''[28]

While by the close of Dr. Ruffner's régime, in 1882, there seemed to be a pretty well established acceptance of the principle, even by denominational leaders, that in regard to the question of desirability of turning over elementary education to the state or to the church, that public safety demanded its surrender to the state, the question of the merit of extension of this principle into the realm of secondary education was yet far from receiving any conclusive opinion favorable to state control.

In a paper on ''The Proper Relation of Secondary Schools to the State System of Public Schools and to Denominational Control—The Work of Secondary Schools in the Past, and Their Future,'' Prof. Wm. T. Thom, of Hollins Institute, took up the question of the extension of the public school system into secondary instruction. He found that one serious difficulty in that development was the place to be assigned to religion. Any state system, he declared, must refuse to recognize Christianity as an element in the state scheme of school life. If true to themselves, the various denominations must follow the Catholics in creating schools of their own. In his opinion, the people of Virginia preferred secondary schools to be non-sectarian, but were utterly averse to their being non-religious. When the parents of Virginia sent their children away to secondary school life, they wished to be assured that the religious training of their children would not stop at a time when they were entering upon higher intellectual ground, when the restraints of home influence were removed. With this pre-disposition of Virginia, the religious question would immediately become an issue upon the

---

[28] *Ibid.*, Dec., 1881, XII, 369–70.

extension of the public system into secondary education. When children were going to the elementary school, religious instruction was not so essential, because as compared with home life, school life was incidental. Were the public school system extended into the secondary grades, the determination of the people to have religious instruction would be confronted by the determination of the sects to have this instruction conform to their wishes; and both groups would be "confronted by the logical obligation of the State not to have any religious instruction if anybody objects." The only solution was for the state utilization of private schools, paying per capita for instruction, and, in turn, having the privilege of examination and inspection.[29] What Prof. Thom was advocating, was, in reality, the application of the old pauper principle, formerly associated with elementary education in the "old Virginia" system, to secondary education. While the opinion of professional educators on this question was inconclusive, it is of interest to note that, since the act of 1875,[30] the enrollment in public high schools had steadily increased, going from 7,262 pupils in 1879–80 to 8,139 in the following year.[31]

In a decade after the inauguration of the public school system and the enunciation of the Ruffner policy of co-operation, certain tendencies were beginning to be marked. The policy of state funds for state institutions only was receiving important support. There was a general recognition that a parallel system of public and denominational education was possible, and that public safety required state control of elementary education. The extension of state control into the secondary field was still a debated question. In the gradual development of a tendency favorable to state control of elementary education, Dr. Ruffner's conciliatory policy in assigning a real place in the educational scheme to denominational institutions, and in leaving the question of religious instruction to local decision had an important part.

---

29 *Ibid.*, Jan., 1882, XIII, 20–31.
30 See p. 401, n. 36.
31 *U. S. Comm. Educ. Rep't.*, 1879–80, 329; 1880–81, 260.

Interest In Outside Opinion Regarding Religion in Education

The period following Dr. Ruffner's withdrawal from the super-intendency was characterized by an increasing interest in obtaining the reaction of outside opinion to the subject of religion in education. While the *Virginia Educational Journal* and its successor, the *Virginia School Journal*, gave considerable space to the views of Virginia educators on the subject, they also quoted liberally, apparently without reference to any partisan bias, from other sources.[32] Among the more important writers, to whose opinion space was given, was Dr. E. E. White, Superintendent of Schools, Cincinnati, Ohio.[33] Dr. White held that what was needed to give efficacy to any system of moral training was not formal religious instruction, but religious influence.[34] What was important was the quickening of conscience and the influencing of the will by the wise use of religious motives and sanctions, and not formal religious instruction.[35] This position, he believed, was actually achieved in the majority of American schools, so that they might be regarded as being religious without being sectarian.[36]

The desire to receive outside opinion on this subject was responsible for the invitation to Dr. J. P. Wickersham, Superintendent of Schools in Pennsylvania, to address a conference of county and city superintendents at Richmond, in 1883. Dr. Wickersham declared it as his opinion that one of the essentials of a system of public instruction was that *"its administration should be unsectarian and unpartizan,"* on the ground that the public schools were for the children of all sects and all parties, and that all classes were compelled to support them.[37]

---

[32] *Va. Educ. Jour.*, Mar., 1883, XIV, 71; July, 1883, XIV, 205; Oct., 1884, XV, 419; Dec., 1884, 513; April, 1886, XVII, 165, 166; May, 1886, 193; July, 1886, 289; Feb., 1887, XVIII, 49; Aug., 1888, XIX, 356; Sept., 1889, XX, 396; Oct., 1891, XXII, 443; *Va. Sch. Jour.*, April, 1893, II, 132; Nov., 1893, 313; and April, 1895, 114.

[33] Dr. White held a number of important positions, including the state superintendency of Ohio, and was a prolific educational writer, the author of many text-books, the best known being his *School Management*.

[34] *Va. Educ. Jour.*, Oct., 1884, XV, 420.

[35] *Ibid.*, Feb., 1887, XVIII, 57.

[36] *Ibid.*, *cf.* also *Va. Sch. Jour.*, Sept., 1893, II, 229.

[37] *Va. Sch. Rep't.*, 1883, 104–05.

In his report for 1888, State Superintendent Buchanan took cognizance of the current criticism of public schools as revealed by the addresses at the meeting of the National Education Association in San Francisco, and discussed the applicability to Virginia schools, of the criticism that they failed to teach morality or cultivate religious sentiment.[38]   Taking up the position held by some that the schools must necessarily fail to teach morality or offend against the cardinal principle of government—the absolute separation of church and state—Mr. Buchanan held that the basic principles of morality were nevertheless taught in school by that very régime which enforced order, obedience to rightful authority, and industry.   Granting that the Bible furnished the essential basis, the ultimate ground of morality, there were certain fundamental principles of morality and of religion, such as were embodied in the Ten Commandments and the Golden Rule, which could be taught without sectarian bias and without trespassing on liberty of conscience.   The various virtues of truthfulness, honesty, reverence, self-respect, self-control, regard for the rights and feelings of others, sobriety, and decorum, which constitute the practical side of religion, and are the essential elements of good character and good citizenship could be best taught not by systematic lectures, but informally and incidentally. Such instruction need not be inconsistent with the home or church life of children.   No scholastic training could be considered a satisfactory substitute for that which the family and the church ought to give, but many children in the public schools were not reached by church influence, and many were in a better moral atmosphere in their public school life than in their home life. On the whole, Mr. Buchanan was of the opinion that the facts did not seem to warrant the criticism in the unqualified form in which it had been made, that public schools failed to teach morality or cultivate religious sentiment.[39]

An editorial in the *Virginia Educational Journal* called the particular attention of its readers to a series of articles in the *Forum* for 1888, in which Rev. M. J. Savage, a Unitarian, and Bishop R. Gilmour, a Roman Catholic, had taken opposite points

[38] *N. E. A. Proc's*, 1888, XXVII, 127–65.
[39] *Va. Sch. Rep't.*, 1888, 34–35; *U. S. Comm. Educ. Rep't.*, 1887–88, 1112.

of view on the vitally important subject of morality and religion.[40] Rev. Mr. Savage had held that morality concerned this life chiefly, and was justice and right between man and man, while religion was chiefly concerned with the salvation of the soul in another world, and was a matter between the soul and God; thus making morality and religion separable in fact, and so, in thinking and teaching. Bishop Gilmour, on the other hand, held that religion and morality were inseparable and depended on each other as cause and effect, that the morality which must be taught was Christian morality, having its origin in the Christian religion, that to pretend to teach morality without religion was nonsense.[41]

Apparently impressed with Rev. Mr. Savage's view, space was given in the *Journal* of February, 1890, to his declaration that it was a misfortune for any one to attend parochial and private schools, as they tended to give people a narrow view of their religious opinions and were not so broadening as the public schools.[42]

The heightened interest manifested in the subject of religious instruction in public schools at the meetings of the National Association in 1889,[43] and the conferences of the United States Senate Committee on Education and Labor, in February, 1889, on a proposed amendment to the Constitution, respecting the neutrality of the states on the subject of religion, and the exclusion of all institutions where sectarian doctrines, tenets, ceremonies, *et cetera*, were taught, from any participation in funds raised by taxation, and the consequent organization of a "National League for the Protection of American Institutions," with the object of preventing all sectarian or denominational appropriation of pub-

---

[40] *The Forum*, IV, 460 *ff*., Rev. Mr. Savage's article, 573 *ff*.; V, 47 *ff*., 146 *ff*., 289 *ff*., 454 *ff*., Bishop Gilmour's article, 574 *ff*., 682 *ff*.; VI, 92 *ff*., 204 *ff*.; these articles were by various contributors on the general subject, "What Shall The Public School Teach." Rev. Mr. Savage, at first a Congregationalist, was then a minister of a prominent Boston Unitarian Church; Bishop Gilmour was Bishop of Cleveland; *cf.* Smith: *Relig. Educ. in Mass.*, 262 *ff*.

[41] *The Forum*, IV, 460 *ff*.; V, 454 *ff*.; *Va. Educ. Jour.*, May, 1889, XX, 227.

[42] *Ibid.*, Feb., 1890, XXI, 70.

[43] *N. E. A. Proc's*, 1889, XXVIII, 111–79; *cf.* 1890, XXIX, 179 *ff*., 690 *ff*.

lic funds, resulted in a questionnaire being sent by the United
States Commissioner of Education in August, 1890, to educational
leaders, on the subject of adjustments between public and
parochial school authorities.[44]   On this subject, the agent for
Virginia, of the Peabody Education Fund, Dr. J. L. M. Curry,
wrote that there was no example of adjustment between public
and parochial schools which involved a division of school funds.
He declared that this would not be in accordance with the public
school system as established, and would involve a hateful connection between a church or sect and the state, and, that however
plausible such a division might be made to appear, it involved
the overthrow of free schools.[45]   The State Superintendent, John
E. Massey, wrote that he did not recall any examples of adjustment between public and parochial school authorities, and that
such adjustments would be illegal.[46]

It would seem that the city of Lynchburg was the only place
where, upon the inauguration of the school system, difficulty arose
on the score of Catholic parochial education.   The school system
opened in April, 1871, with separate schools for boys and girls,
Protestants and Catholics, and black and white.   By 1874, the
Catholic insistence that separate schools be continued under Rev.
J. J. McGurk for the children of their faith, aroused considerable
controversy and became a matter of municipal politics.   It was
finally decided not to retain separate Catholic schools in the
public school system, and Catholic schools went outside of the
system.[47]

The question of the conversion of public school funds for
denominational education, which stirred the country in 1889–90,
and which was followed a few years later by an attempt to have
the New York legislature appropriate funds for denominational
and private education, received editorial comment in the *Virginia
School Journal,* in January, 1894.   It was held that such a policy
would split the population of the state into as many factions as
there were church organizations, each insisting on having their
separate schools and upon receiving their proportionate share of

---

[44] *U. S. Comm. Educ. Rep't,* 1888–89, 429 *ff.*
[45] *Ibid.,* 433.
[46] *Ibid.,* 434.
[47] Christian: *Lynchburg,* 286–87, 399; Magri: *Cath. Church, Richmond,* 99.

the school fund raised by general taxation. The result would be that the state would become the "nursing mother" of warring sects, religious animosity would revive, and genuine Christianity suffer. In Virginia, it would mean that the public funds would have to be divided in at least nine different ways, with the consequence that the public school system inaugurated for all would soon fall into disrepute and have to be abolished. If a choice were necessary between a distribution of public funds to sectarian schools and no public schools at all, it were better to choose the latter. Parents and churches should provide religious instruction, the public schools existed simply to impart secular instruction which was needed "to fit the citizen for the discharge of his civic duties, and to make him a useful member of society." Those dissatisfied with the public schools conducted on a non-sectarian basis were at perfect liberty to have their children taught in sectarian schools which they alone should support. It were better to abolish the public school system than to introduce into it an element of discord which would disrupt society.[48]

The Virginia desire during this period to get the best expert opinion in regard to the problem of the relation of morals and religion to education is indicated in their extending an invitation to Dr. W. T. Harris, United States Commissioner of Education, to address a meeting of county and city superintendents, in May, 1897. Dr. Harris, taking for his subject "The Relation Of School Discipline To Moral Discipline," declared that the general assumption was that moral instruction meant moral philosophy, and that since philosophical instruction was out of the question in the elementary schools, the supposition was that there was no moral instruction in elementary schools. To correct this situation, suggestions had been made to prepare a preliminary catechism to moral philosophy, or that religious instruction should be introduced, or that Bible reading without note or comment be used. In answer, he drew a line between intellectual and moral instruction, and held that moral instruction should secure the formation of moral habits. In studying existing school systems in America, it is soon realized that moral instruction belongs to the side known as discipline, and not to instruction in books and

[48] *Va. Sch. Jour.*, Jan., 1894, III, 6.

theories. The four cardinal principles of school discipline were regularity, punctuality, silence, and industry, in other words, the subjugation of the will. Beginning with mechanical obedience, moral education gradually develops out of this stage to individual responsibility, which implies a sense of freedom. The higher moral duties are those that relate to the individual himself and to his fellows; but beyond the secular virtues of justice, prudence, fortitude, and temperance, relating to the self and others, were the ecclesiastical ones of the theologians, faith, hope, and charity. But as faith is also a secular as well as a theological virtue, and hope and charity have their practical sides, instruction in these virtues can be given which is not sectarian. The final aim of instruction in morality should be to have the pupil assimilate the law of duty and make it his own.[49]

The solicitation of the expression of outside expert opinion on the subject of morality and religion in education, and the attention paid to reported expressions of such opinion, show the continued Virginian interest in this subject. While this may be taken as a recognition on the part of Virginians of the fact that the problem was a universal, not a local, one, it is indicative that the problem was felt to be far from definite determination in the minds of Virginians. Nevertheless, in spite of this feeling of the indeterminateness of the problem, it will be seen that the tendency to adjustment to the public school system as an accepted institution was making progress.

Adjustment To The Public School System As An Accepted Institution

A review of the Virginian expression of opinion in the period after Dr. Ruffner's withdrawal as Superintendent reveals that there was considerable attention to those aspects of the problem which concerned a diagnosis of the problem from the point of view that the public school system was here, and that it was here to stay, and what was necessary was to diagnose both the school and social situation so that proper adjustments might be made. As representative of outside opinion during this period tending

---

[49] *Ibid.*, Dec., 1897, VI, 324–30.

to influence this attitude, the propaganda of Dr. Mayo[50] in favor
of the public school system may be cited. The necessity of
accepting the public school system as a permanent social institution was emphasized by Dr. Mayo in an article on "Southern
Women In The Recent Educational Movement In The South,"
written for the national government. He declared that what the
clergy of all sects, North and South, needed, was a conversion
from the theory that a "christian education" could be given only
by the establishment of expensive, prolific academies and colleges,
with their drain upon overtaxed denominations, and at the best
available only to a small proportion of either white or black,
and an acceptance of the public school system as the people's
university which would reclaim the South from "white illiteracy" and "colored barbarism."[51]

The tendency to regard the problem as a concrete one had
started, however, before this particular expression of it by Dr.
Mayo. It is seen in an address by Prof. W. D. Thomas, before
the Albemarle Association, in which he diagnosed the inadequate
accomplishment of society as being due to the failure to educate
the pew up the educational standard of the ministry. The influence of a Christian amounted to but little, if he was an uneducated Christian.[52]

Prof. F. V. N. Painter, of Roanoke College, reviewing the
"Educational Tendencies Of The Present" before an educational
conference in Richmond, in 1885, declared that, while a heterogeneous population had seemed to render expedient the exclusion
of specific religious teaching from public schools, the ancient
tendency inaugurated by Harvard and William and Mary to
associate higher education with denominational institutions was
being well maintained. The religious spirit, perhaps less sectarian than formerly, was still interested in founding and supporting colleges.[53]   Dr. Painter did not seem to find in the public

---

[50] See p. 445.
[51] *U. S. Bur. Educ., Circ. Inf.*, 1892, No. 1, 160.
[52] *Va. Educ. Jour.*, Sept., 1883, XIV, 270.
[53] *Va. Sch. Rep't.*, 1885, Part III, 41; Dr. Painter was author of a formerly
popular *History of Education*.

school system any unfavorable reaction upon the denominational system; it was being well maintained.[54]

A more serious concern in the moral situation, as it actually was developing in the public school, was expressed by Superintendent Massey, in an article in the *Virginia Educational Journal*, in April, 1890. He raised the question whether all public free school teachers exerted a strictly moral influence over youth by being themselves truthful, honest, sober, punctual, industrious, good mannered, regardful of legally constituted authority, loyal and patriotic. It was his opinion that teachers who did not measure up to this standard should resign.[55]

The importance of the teacher was likewise emphasized in an address on "Character Building" by Mr. J. P. Britt, of Norfolk, at a meeting of the State Educational Association and Conference of Superintendents of Schools, in 1891. Mr. Britt stated that teachers could not shift their responsibility in this matter to the home and the church. To do so, would be to lose sight of the fact that the moral nature was being developed in school life, whether for good or for evil. The root of morality rested in obedience to constituted authority, to the parent, teacher, state, and to God. The tendency of the age was to permit too loose a rein in the name of Liberty. Virginians of right belonged to conservative stock, there was still left some respect for time honored customs and principles, they had no free-love communities, no theaters open on Sunday, no Sunday baseball, no Haymarket riots, and marriage was still an ordinance of the church and not a civil contract determinable at pleasure. As long as Virginia's sons and daughters were taught that "he who rules must first learn to obey," Virginia would still remain "the conservator of good morals and the home of high and noble principles."[56]

This emphasis upon the importance of the teacher in exerting a proper moral influence continued to be a popular theme of Virginia educators. Thus, Anne L. C. Brickhead argued in an article in the June, 1892, number of the *Virginia School Journal*, that school teachers stood preëminent as public conservators of

---

[54] *Cf.* rise of denominational institutions, Ch. XIII.
[55] *Va. Educ. Jour., April*, 1890, XXI, 178–79.
[56] *Va. Sch. Rep't.*, 1891, 224.

morality, as no class had such opportunities for impressing moral lessons upon minds that were at the proper stage of development to receive and retain them—the impressions of childhood being most enduring.[57]

That, for the most part, adjustment to the public school system as an accepted institution, was being definitely reached by the close of the nineteenth century, may be gathered from articles which treat the problem of moral instruction as a purely curricular problem without consideration of its theoretical bearings on the progress of society. An example of this type of discussion may be found in an article on "Moral Force" in the *Virginia School Journal*, in January, 1897, by F. B. Watson, superintendent of Pittsylvania County. Mr. Watson discussed the importance of utilizing school assemblies as an agency in emphasizing the view that character must be the capstone of the educational structure. To combine moral instruction with the course prescribed by the state, it was not necessary "to deliver lectures on ethics, sermons on the Bible, or theological discourses; for in nearly every school study, the great underlying truths of Scripture are easily deducible, and susceptible of comprehension by the dullest mind." He then goes on to find in various school studies, ideas and principles which are applicable in morals.[58]

A similar insistence that moral training was a concrete problem was expressed by E. G. Matthews, Roanoke County, who urged his brother teachers upon entering the school room to be mindful of the fact that they were "at the head of a seminary where mortal minds are trained for usefulness and happiness."[59]

In the gradual, though, as will be shown,[60] not complete, acceptance of the public school system, the clever conciliatory policy initiated by Dr. Ruffner continued to play its part. It made possible the development of the public school system without any seriously detrimental effect upon higher denominational education. This may be gathered from an address, in December,

---

[57] *Va. Sch. Jour.*, June, 1892, I, 186; *cf.* also *N. E. A. Proc's*, 1894, XXXIII, 136–37.
[58] *Va. Sch. Jour.*, Jan., 1887, VI, 10–11.
[59] *Ibid.*, April, 1897, VI, 124.
[60] See p. 473.

1894, by C. E. Vawter, before the Immigration Convention of
Virginia. Mr. Vawter referred to the work of the denominational colleges, Randolph-Macon, Hampden-Sidney, Richmond
College, and Emory and Henry, and declared that they were
all deeply rooted in the educational system and in the love and
veneration of the people. This, he declared, was abundantly
proven by their success since the War, for, in face of free tuition
in all the state schools, and without state appropriation, they
were living to a great extent on their tuition fees.[61]   Of course,
probably one of the greatest factors in the survival of institutions
of this type, which Mr. Vawter failed to note, was that the state
had not attempted to provide a super-abundance of equivalent
rival institutions, as strategically scattered over the state for the
reception of students as were these institutions. Whether by
design or by force of economic necessity, the net result was to
calm the fear of these institutions as to their continued existence.

As far as the relations between the state and the denominational forces were concerned, at the close of the century, in
regard to control of higher education, it may, perhaps, be sufficient to refer to an article, in 1900, in *World's Work*, a journal
particularly interested in all phases of southern educational
progress. In commenting upon the work of President William
L. Wilson, of Washington and Lee University, the article compared the support given to state universities in the South with
that of the West and declared that generous support of state
universities in the South was not so common as in the West, for
"in too many of the states the ecclesiastical bodies discourage the
public maintenance of universities." This attitude it declared
unfortunate, as few of the churches were in a position to equip
their own colleges well.[62]

It was also as an outcome of Dr. Ruffner's policy which had
left the question of the religious program in education to local
decision, that the public school system, particularly after the
settlement of the readjuster issue, continued to make such progress as it had. Toward the close of this period, this treatment

61 *Va. Sch. Jour.*, Dec., 1894, III, 331.
62 *World's Work*, Dec., 1900, I, 130; see p. 314, 530, 549.

of the problem in view of the preponderant Protestantism of Virginia seems to have been accepted as satisfactory by that group; at least, there was a gradual lessening of the reiterated cry by the former ardent denominationalists that religion in public schools was impossible because of separation of church and state. As the Catholics had turned to the parochial school system as their solution of the problem of adequate religious instruction in education, the Jewish people were perhaps the most important minority group affected by the development of the Ruffner policy. It is therefore of some interest to get the reaction of one of their most prominent leaders to this problem. In an article on "The Democracy of the Public Schools," in the *Journal*, in May, 1897, Dr. Edward N. Calisch, Rabbi of a prominent Richmond congregation, declared that for public schools to remain essentially *public* schools, it was necessary for them to be essentially and completely under public and secular control and be supported by the public morally as well as materially. As the creation of the state, they must be kept from sectarian tendency. The introduction of even the simplest kind of religious exercise in a public institution jarred upon the harmony of national independence. In order not to disturb the rights of individuals, the recognition of which rights had led in the historical events creating the nation, it was essential not to cross the line that lies between the parallel paths of church and state— the public schools must be completely and purely secular. Further, as it is in the public schools alone that the true democracy of the country is displayed, it is essential for the future citizenship of the individual that a child should not be sent from the public to the private school except for the most cogent of reasons. The people must recognize that the public schools are part of the machinery of government, applicable to all of the people and not a part of them.[63]

To understand Dr. Calisch's view, the emphasis upon the elimination of even the simplest kind of religious exercise, it must be remembered that religious instruction with the Jews has for centuries been in the home and in the synagogue, and these

---

[63] *Va. Sch. Jour.*, May, 1897, VI, 152–53.

agencies are still regarded by their leaders as the most desirable agencies.[64] With the home and the synagogue furnishing a sufficient Jewish religious instruction, Dr. Calisch, naturally, wished the elimination of specific Christian instruction and religious exercises from the public schools.[65]

The opinion at the close of the century, as to the effect of separation of church and state upon religion, may be gathered from an editorial in the *Virginia School Journal.* Reviewing the world progress of the century, it found that in nothing had there been a greater departure from the past than in education and the science of pedagogy; reforms in civil and religious liberty were, however, resisted. In support of that statement, it cited the fact that the union of church and state, in Great Britain, was more powerfully intrenched than ever, notwithstanding that the example of her own colonies and the United States showed that "the separation of churches from government control and support had purified religion, increased spirituality in churches, enlarged contributions, given greater power to Christianity, and constituted one of the prime elements in the permanence of free institutions."[66]

Apparently adjustment to the public school system as an accepted institution was reaching a fairly satisfactory status; the fear which had existed upon its inauguration, that it would prove detrimental to religion, or incompatible with separation of church and state, was, in view of the actual situation as it developed, rapidly vanishing in many quarters.

Practise With Regard To Religious Instruction

In view of Dr. Ruffner's declared policy as to the procedure to be followed in regard to religious instruction, what evidence do we have as to the actual practise? Reference has already been

---

[64] Cohen, S. M.: *An Inquiry Into The Tendencies Of The Week Day Religious Education Movement In Its Relations To The Public Schools.*

[65] Dr. Calisch's congregation belongs to the Reform wing of American Jewry. For the development of a later Virginia Jewish attitude toward this problem, see p. 510.

[66] *Va. Sch. Jour.,* Jan., 1899, VIII, 4.

made to the important place the clergy took in holding key administrative positions upon the inauguration of the system.[67] While this fact need not be taken as indicative of a forced religious influence upon school instruction, it may, at least, be regarded as not tending to the creation of an anti-religious sentiment and influence in public schools.

Dr. Ruffner's enunciation of his policy in reply to Superintendent Carne's attempt to exclude the Bible, was highly favorable to the introduction of the Virginia custom of religious school exercises into the new public school system, the attempts to exclude such exercises by regulations being very few.[68] Judging from the regulations adopted for Nelson County, in 1877, the teacher was required to carefully exclude from the school room all questions of a sectarian or partisan character and to make a diligent and constant effort to promote the moral as well as the mental culture of his pupils; general religious instruction, apparently, such as Bible reading, prayer, and singing of hymns, in keeping with the Virginia tradition was not excluded, the regulation being designed evidently to eliminate denominationalism.[69] Along with this regulation, a list of prescribed books is given with the statement that no others must be used except by special permission of the county superintendent. The Bible is not on the list, but that does not necessarily indicate that it was not used, but merely that it was not regarded as a reading textbook, that function being supplied by the Holmes' *Speller* and *Readers*.[70]

While the *Virginia Educational Journal*, which was at first the organ of the Educational Association of Virginia, and, in 1874, by special arrangement placed in part at the disposal of the State Board of Education,[71] devoted large space to the various phases of the controversy regarding religion in education, it contained practically nothing in the way of specific suggestion to show what should be the actual classroom procedure with regard to the

---

[67] See p. 423.
[68] See p. 425.
[69] *Va. Educ. Jour.*, Nov., 1877, IX, 41–42.
[70] *Ibid.*; cf. investigation by *U. S. Comm. of Educ.*, p. 464.
[71] *U. S. Comm. Educ. Rep't*, 1874, 426.

handling of this problem. With the passing of the *Journal,* in
1892, to be replaced by the *Virginia School Journal,* suggestions
as to classroom procedure became more frequent. Thus, in the
very first issue, there appeared an unsigned article, "Exercises
for Opening School," which consisted first of a responsive religious service by the teacher and pupils, then the Lord's Prayer
by both, and finally the roll call of the pupils, each pupil to answer with a quotation.[72]

There soon appeared, also, definite suggestions for utilizing religious holidays in the school program. These suggestions began
in December, 1894, when there appeared in the editorial column,
under the caption of "Christmas," specific suggestions to use the
occasion in teaching the children; first, to teach the calendar, then
Christ—his influence on civilization, and similar points, and
finally to use the occasion for providing appropriate supplementary reading.[73]   Greater stress was placed on the utilization
of holidays, however, in the twentieth century.[74]

A more definite idea as to the actual status of religious instruction in Virginia may be gathered from reports by the United
States Commissioner of Education.   In 1896, he sent a questionnaire on religious instruction to city school superintendents. The
replies from Virginia, for 10 cities of 8,000 population and over,
indicated that 9 had religious instruction; in one, it was prohibited by regulations; in eight, it was not prohibited; in none
was it limited to reading the Bible; in 8, the Bible was read; 7
had prayers; 5 had sacred song; in none was comment forbidden.[75]   Only 2 cities with a population of over 4,000, but less
than 8,000, reported; both cities had religious instruction; in one,
it was limited to the Bible, the other, besides the Bible, had
prayer and sacred song.[76]

An article on "The Bible In The Public Schools And State Universities" quoted Superintendent Massey's opinion to the effect
that he believed the Bible to be read in nearly all the Virginia
schools and that this had been the custom since their organiza-

---

[72] *Va. Sch. Jour.,* Jan., 1892, I, 9.
[73] *Ibid., Dec.,* 1894, III, 330.
[74] See p. 472.
[75] *U. S. Comm. Educ. Rep't,* 1896–97, II, 2189.
[76] *Ibid.,* II, 2190.

tion. Reports to the writer of the article indicated that the Bible had been read in Richmond schools from the beginning.[77] Regulations in Manchester and Roanoke required Bible reading, and Roanoke specified also the singing of a suitable hymn, and the Lord's Prayer. The Bible was read in all the schools of Staunton, and two other cities reported the custom as general, but not universal.[78] The superintendent of schools of Roanoke, Mr. B. Rust, thus described his position:

> I am strongly opposed to setting aside the dear old Bible as its stands for all the books in Christendom. . . . I believe in having the entire work at hand and in reading such selections as would "establish our youth in habits of truth, purity, uprightness, and goodness." I believe in being absolutely nonsectarian in and around our schools, and at the same time I would have all our teachers be godly men and women, exemplifying all the graces of the Christian character in their daily lives before the pupils. This would tend to the building of high character and good citizenship.[79]

It is clear, from the evidence cited, that Dr. Ruffner's policy of leaving to local decision the question of religious education had resulted in an almost universal inclusion of a certain amount of formal religious observance in the public school program. This adjustment of the issue was making it more difficult for even ardent supporters of the denominational system to charge that public schools were completely godless. There was, however, still the old question whether education received in the public school system was an effective deterrent from crime.

The Public School System As An Agency Against Crime

The creation of the free public school system, in 1870, revived the question of the relation of crime to education. Reference has already been made to Mr. Ruffner's argument that morality was safe with the public school, and "L.'s" answer that more crime existed in Massachusetts than in the whole South.[80] In his report for 1871, Dr. Ruffner took occasion to show, by quoting vari-

---

[77] *Cf.* also *Annual Rep'ts of the Sup't, Richmond*, 1899, XXIX, 38, and subsequent reports, where Bible is listed as to be used for all schools.
[78] *U. S. Comm. Educ. Rep't*, 1897–98, II, 1550.
[79] *Ibid.*
[80] See p. 419–20.

ous authorities, that the illiteracy of prisoners was greater than that of the general population, both in this country and in England; that in New York, there was eleven times more ignorance among prisoners than among the outside adult population; that in Ohio, 81 per cent of prisoners were illiterate, and 74 per cent ignorant of a trade; in England, illiteracy among prisoners was estimated at 95 per cent.[81]

The popular cry of the opponents of the extension of public education, that education was not a preventive of crime, was taken up by the *Richmond Enquirer* in an editorial on September 1, 1874, and applied to the negro race. That journal, which had shown its hostility to the negro from the Convention days of 1868,[82] declared that the negroes now showed themselves as a mass more ignorant, vicious, and unqualified for service to society than they were upon the 5th of April, 1865. Some, having learned to read and to write, but without the moral training of family government that should go with such knowledge, had used their acquired information for purposes of crime, such as forging their employers' names for store orders. Their learning had enlarged their capacity as well as inclination to crime, and disqualified them for their natural position as laborers.[83] Turning from consideration of the negro, the editorial went on to express the opinion that the craze for education in Virginia had proven anything but beneficial to the white race. While not objecting to, and in fact advocating, the giving to every white boy, by State aid, a rudimentary education, consisting of a sound knowledge of reading, writing, and arithmetic, the writer would leave it to the boy's capacity or genius to make his way beyond that point. The editorial asked:

How many educated loungers, college graduates and the like, above manual labor in consequence of their advantages, and yet unable to find places suited to their training and supposed dignity afflict society? It must be acknowledged that a large number of young men are ruined annually for all purposes of good to Virginia by over-education.

---

[81] *Va. Sch. Rep't*, 1871, 59–61.
[82] Taylor: *Negro in Reconst. Va.*, 237, *et passim*.
[83] For an understanding of the negro and labor situation at this time, the reader is referred to Taylor: *Negro in Reconst. Va.*, Ch. VI and VII.

As professional teachers as a class had no practical sense, it was important to select, for the control and management of public education, practical men of common sense, who would remember the nature and constitution of society, that it must have a bottom and top to it.[84] In an editorial, in November, however, the *Enquirer* felt that it was a cause for congratulation that crime had not kept pace in Virginia with its rapid increase noted in other sections of the country.[85]

It is interesting to note in view of the discussion of the relation of religious instruction to education, and the bearing of this upon crime, that the Assembly recognized by a joint resolution, in 1879, that there was a real value in religious instruction, at least, for prisoners. The resolution provided for furnishing "accommodation of the prisoners on the Sabbath day in the religious services conducted by the chaplain and the Sunday-school association of said penitentiary," on the ground that it recognized "the great value of the religious instruction given to the convicts for years past by gentlemen who have voluntarily contributed their time and service to that end."[86]

The State Superintendent's Report for 1884 quoted from an address of Prof. M. A. Newell, Secretary of the State Board of

---

[84] *Richmond Enquirer*, "Popular Education In Virginia," Sept. 1, 1874; cf. *Ibid.*, Sept. 4, 1874, "The Cause Of Education In Virginia," referring to State Superintendent's Report, showing that there were more young men in Virginia in college in proportion to white population than in any other country in the world; the editorial questioned whether the prevalent idea of the necessity of college education was not erroneous and injurious—what Virginia needed was educated mechanics, educated workmen, aristocrats of labor.

[85] *U. S. Bur. Census, Pop. and Social Stat.*, 1870, 568, shows that the total number of persons in prison on June 1, 1870, was 1,244, consisting of 331 native white, 901 native negro, 12 foreign born. A number of general articles on the relation of crime to education appear in the *U. S. Comm. Educ. Rep'ts*, 1872, 586–95; 1874, cx–cxx; 1877, cciii–ccv; the conclusions of the rather careful article in the 1872 volume, 594, by E. D. Mansfield were: "*First*. That one-third of all criminals are totally uneducated, and that four-fifths are practically uneducated. *Secondly*. That the proportion of criminals from the illiterate classes is at least tenfold as great as the proportion from those having some education." Cf. *N. E. A. Proc's*, 1881, XX, 45, 48; 1894, XXXIII, 342 *ff.*; *U. S. Comm. Educ. Rep't*, 1871, 32–37, 548–52; 1888–89, I, 600–01; *U. S. Bur. Educ., Circ. Inf.*, 1893, No. 4; Wickersham, J. P.: *Education and Crime, U. S. Bur. Educ. Pamphlets*, 1881.

[86] *Acts of Assembly*, Feb. 15, 1879, 90; *cf.* recommendation to Constitutional Convention, see p. 413.

Education of Maryland, delivered at the conference of county superintendents at Richmond, that year. Prof. Newell had referred to an article by Rev. James Conway, in the *American Catholic Quarterly Review,* which had spoken of the pernicious moral effects of state or secular education, attributing to it the catalogue of crimes chronicled in the newspapers.[87] Prof. Newall held that religious instruction was the duty of the church, and if crime was on the increase, it was not because of too much secular, but of too little religious instruction; that the church had not effectually performed the work which it had undertaken; further, that since the school claimed only three out of the twenty-four hours, it could not be asserted that the church had no opportunity to do its proper work.[88]

In 1901, the *Virginia School Journal,* apparently with the design of influencing public opinion, which was about to have the whole question of public education brought anew before it, in view of a proposed Constitutional Convention, reprinted at length one of the most interesting and important contributions made during this period on the subject of the relation of crime to morals, religion, and education, namely, the address on ''School Statistics and Morals'' delivered by United States Commissioner of Education, W. T. Harris, in 1893, before the National Education Association.[89]

Dr. Harris took the position that if the habits taught in school reënforce the virtues, and, if the intellectual studies aid in spreading Christian doctrines, the secular school has a moral tendency, though not undertaking any direct functions of the church. He then considered the appeal to statistics in the attack and defense of education in respect to moral influence. Briefly the arguments on the subject had run as follows: 1. Purely secular instruction in ideas and habits must be anti-religious and consequently tend toward vice and crime, and 2. purely secular instruction reënforces religion and exerts an influence repressive of vice and crime. The appeal is then made to statistics to show that states having the oldest and most efficient school systems have the larg-

---

[87] *Amer. Cath. Quart. Rev.,* Jan., 1884, 117–18.
[88] *Va. Sch. Rep't,* 1884, 119–20.
[89] *N. E. A. Proc's,* 1894, XXXIII, 342.

est number of criminals, and that education has merely changed
the character of crime, from robbery and theft in the case of
the illiterate, to forgery or breach of trust, in the case of the
educated. Dr. Harris next referred to that section of the Mansfield report, which made it appear that three-fourths of a large
group of prisoners were literate, and only one-fourth illiterate, a
fact which would appear damaging to public schools.[90] But the
real approach to the problem was to find out whether a given
number of illiterates in the population furnished as many criminals as the same number of persons who could read and write.
A study of the problem from this angle showed that the illiterates
furnished more than six times their quota, while the literate furnished one-fifth less than their quota.

The defenders of secular education could also point significantly, according to Dr. Harris, to the statistics of religious
education among criminals. In an inquiry covering two hundred jails made by the United States Bureau of Education, in
1892, out of an aggregate number of about 55,000 prisoners,
10,376 prisoners were reported with no religious training, while
18,612 were reported as having had it. Statistics of the Detroit
jail for 25 years showed 37,089 out of 40,338 as having religious
training as against 2,249 who had none. To interpret statistics
correctly, however, it was necessary to consider that the 92 per
cent of the criminals in Detroit who had religious instruction,
had been furnished by the 98 or 99 per cent of the whole population who had been under religious instruction, while the 8 per
cent without it, represented one or two per cent of their class in
the state. But, after all, criminals did not become such through
their religious teaching, but because they neglected its advice.
As for the type of crime, investigation showed that person and
property had become more secure on the whole, and that it was
offences against order and decency, mostly cases of drunkenness
that had increased.[91]

---

[90] See p. 467, n. 85; *U. S. Comm. Educ. Rep't*, 1872, 590; Dr. Harris is
referring here to Dr. Mansfield's presentation of the raw figures, not to his
interpretation nor to his conclusions.

[91] *Va. Sch. Jour.*, May, 1891, X, 134–37.

It would seem, that as far as expert opinion was concerned, that the existence of the public school system was justified to society, by its contribution in reducing the extent and severity of crime. As for the relation of religious instruction to the problem, the opinion seems to have prevailed, that, probably because of the hitherto inadequate and ineffective presentation of much of the religious instruction, its effectiveness as a deterrent from crime could hardly be satisfactorily measured. At least, the *Virginia School Journal* seems to have felt that on the basis of an effective agency for the diminution of crime, the public school system was justified in appealing to the continued support of Virginians.

In the years since its inauguration, the public school system had had to meet the fears of those who believed that it would prove injurious to denominational education, detrimental to the religious welfare of the people, and an ineffective agency against crime. It had been placed upon the defensive. That it was able to triumph over these fears, this opposition, was due to the genius of Dr. Ruffner in correctly gauging Virginia sentiment, in reconciling conflicting views, by the enunciation of a policy of co-operation without alliance. That the reading of the Bible, saying the Lord's Prayer, and singing hymns might be construed by some strict constructionists of separation of church and state, as a violation of that principle, is another matter. Dr. Ruffner's policy made possible a *modus operandi*. This policy, while resulting in a parallel educational system, made possible a gradual adjustment on the part of society to the public school system, to its recognition as an accepted institution. If, in the three decades of its existence, the public school system had not completely won the affection of all Virginia, it had, at least, proven its place as an important institution in society.

CHAPTER XII

VINDICATION OF THE CO-OPERATION POLICY IN EXPERIENCE

Survey of the School Situation, 1902

The beginning of the twentieth century was marked by agitation for a new Constitution. While relief was thus sought in a number of matters, the chief object appears to have been the qualification of the negro vote.[1] The educational situation, too, came in for a certain amount of attention. The educational conferences begun at Capon Springs, W. Va., in 1898, and designed to study the problem and improve the educational situation of the educationally backward sections of the South, had led, in 1901, to the creation of the Southern Education Board and the appointment of Dr. Robert Frazer, formerly president of the Farmville Normal School as agent of the Board.[2] In the early part of 1902, the General Education Board was created, and Dr. Frazer was also associated with it, along with Henry St. George Tucker, formerly dean of the law faculty of Washington and Lee.[3] The outcome of the propaganda of these various agencies and the newspapers was the organization within the state of the Co-operative Education Association of Virginia.[4]

What was the educational status of Virginia as these organizations found it upon investigation? While the per cent of school population, 5 to 18 years of age, enrolled, had risen steadily from 32.34% in 1870–71, to 45% in 1879–80, to 60.51% in 1889–90, to 63.19% in 1899–1900,[5] and the average number of days the schools were kept during the year had increased for those dates

---

[1] Taylor: *Negro in Reconst. Va.*, 285; *The Times*, Jan. 26, 1902, letter by "H"; cf. *U. of Va. Rec., Ext. Ser.*, VII, No. 3, 16.

[2] Heatwole: *Hist. of Educ. Va.*, 306 ff.; *The Times*, Jan. 30 and Mar. 13, 1902.

[3] *Ibid.*, Feb. 16, 1902; Heatwole: *Hist. of Educ. Va.*, 316–17; *General Educ. Board*, 1902–14, 3.

[4] Heatwole: *Hist. of Educ. Va.*, 217; see p. 481.

[5] *U. S. Comm. Educ. Rep't*, 1910, II, 670.

from 93.2 to 112.8, to 118.2, to 120.0,[6] closer inspection revealed that education while making consistent progress had not made adequate progress in the last decade.

The editor of *The Times*, on a tour of the state, reported for his paper the educational situation as he saw it upon personal inspection and upon report from various educators. He was particularly impressed by reports of Dr. Frazer with regard to the bad housing and poor teaching.[7] Subsequent editorials, articles on education, and correspondence in *The Times* revealed that the apparent acceptance of the public school system as a social institution, in spite of its general progress, had in a sense been only a specious acceptance. A review of the references to education in *The Times* indicates that there was a feeling that the real cause of the backward educational status of Virginia, particularly as reflected by the condition and status of the rural public schools, was due to the difficulty in overcoming the prejudice against public education. The people who patronized private schools, paid their taxes, but did not concern themselves with the public school system, and evinced no appreciation of the importance of popular education to the state.[8] At a conference of the Southern Education Board, in 1902, Dr. Frazer declared "it is by no means uncommon to find men of intelligence and influence who are out and out opposed to free public education for all the people."[9] Thus old prejudices lingered. One correspondent declared that the fact that private schools and public schools existed side by side simply meant that Virginia taxpayers were subjected to a double tax and the remedy was to have the public school of such a character that the private school would have no chance to exist in the same community.[10]

It does not appear that the favor extended to private schools was based wholly on the belief of a better religious tone in those schools, but rather to a prevalent idea that the teaching, particu-

---

6 *Ibid.*, II, 674.
7 *The Times*, Feb. 2, 1902; W. S. Copeland, editor.
8 *Ibid.*, Feb. 9, 18, 1902.
9 *Proc's 5th Conf. Educ. South*, 1902, 35.
10 *The Times*, Feb. 22, 1902, letter by J. W. Weiser; *cf. Ibid.*, Mar. 9, letter by Maria P. Duval.

larly in the rural schools was not satisfactory—a condition that seems to have been attributed by some to the entrance of politics, nepotism, and sectarianism in the selection of school officials and teachers. Dr. Curry, who as the agent of the Peabody Education Fund, was conversant with conditions, writing on the steps necessary to improve public schools, declared:

> Politics and sectarianism should be vigilantly excluded in the selection of superintendents and teachers. Nepotism, family ties, agreement in partisan politics, in church fellowship, have been the bane of schools and of school officers.[11]

On this subject, Rev. S. H. Thompson wrote:

> . . . I have not found as much denominationalism as some would have us suppose, yet I know of one instance where the [county] superintendent in every case showed special favors to the members of his church.[12]

The extent to which denominationalism entered into the selection of school officers is difficult of determination, but that it existed to an extent such as to be one of the contributing factors in the inefficiency of schools there seems to have been no doubt.[13]

The stimulus to discussion of the educational situation given by the revision of the constitution, by the creation of educational organizations to investigate the educational situation and to advance educational progress, resulted in a flood of publicity, as to the actual school situation, which made it apparent that the public school system had not been receiving the whole-hearted support of the people. As a concomitant of that situation, evidence appeared that the public school system had been permitted to drift into the hands of those who were using it for party ends, whether political, family, or sectarian. The situation called for remedies.

Constitutional Provisions, 1902, Affecting Civil and Denominational Education

The large issues raised by the publicity in the press, regarding actual conditions in the public school system, though seemingly

---

11 *Ibid.*, Feb. 9, 1902.
12 *Ibid.*, Mar. 2, 1902.
13 *Cf. Ibid.*, Mar. 9, 1902, letter signed ''Teacher.''

such as called for remedial action, received little attention from the Constitutional Convention, which concerned itself primarily with only two phases of the educational problem—appropriations, and reorganization of the central administrative system.

One phase of the appropriation issue concerned itself with the question whether the subject of appropriations for educational institutions should be decided by the Constitutional Convention or left to the Legislature. It was precipitated by the action of the University College of Medicine, a medical institution in Richmond, in attempting to secure a constitutional prohibition of appropriations to its rival, the Medical College of Virginia;[14] and by the attempt of the University to secure a constitutional provision for an annual appropriation of $50,000. In order to assist in its building program in 1844–45, the state had given the Medical College two loans totalling $25,000. In 1860, the state granted an additional loan of $30,000 on condition that a deed be executed conveying all property of the college to the Literary Fund as state property.[15] Before this, the act of incorporation, in 1854, had, in appointing the board of visitors, reserved to the governor authority to fill vacancies by death, resignation, or otherwise.[16] The property was now deeded to the state.[17] From 1865 to 1890, the college received an annual appropriation of $1,500; the amount was then raised to $5,000.[18] Apparently the state regarded the college as a state institution; and the college usually submitted an annual report to the state.[19] The University College of Medicine now sought a constitutional prohibition of further appropriations on the ground that the financial status of the college was satisfactory without such aid, and that the money should go into the elementary school system.[20] The convention refused to take any action, holding that both this matter

---

[14] See p. 306–08.

[15] *Acts of Assembly*, Mar. 1, 1860, 104.

[16] *Ibid.*, Feb. 25, 1854, 27.

[17] *Debates Const. Conv.*, 1901–02, I, 796; Hansbrough, G. W.: *Reports Supreme Court of Appeals*, LXXVII, 415.

[18] *Ibid.; from correspondence;* a statement in *The Times*, Jan. 25, 1902, gives the total appropriation up to that time as $44,000, which seems to be in error.

[19] *Cf. Va. Sch. Rep't*, 1894–95, 381 *ff.*

[20] *The Times*, Jan. 25, 1902.

and the question of appropriation to the University of Virginia should be reserved to the Legislature.[21]   The issue between the two institutions was settled, when the University College of Medicine, founded in 1893, joined the Medical College of Virginia in 1913.[22]

It was, however, on the question whether the bonds held by educational institutions, many of them denominational, which according to an act of 1892 were to be redeemed at the pleasure of the state, should be redeemed, or the interest formerly paid on them, be continued, that the chief fight was waged.[23]   It was charged that those members of the Convention, who had been opposed to an appropriation for the University of Virginia, were now championing an appropriation to sectarian and non-state institutions—it being held by some, that the fact that all other bonds had been refunded in 1892 at three per cent, while the state continued to pay five or six per cent on these bonds, constituted an appropriation of the difference by the state.[24]   This phase of the appropriation matter was finally ruled by the Convention to be a matter for legislative decision.[25]

The section on appropriations as it was written into the Constitution provided that no appropriation was to be made to any educational institution, unless owned or exclusively controlled by the state or some political subdivision, leaving it to the discretion of the General Assembly to continue its appropriations

---

21 *Ibid.*, Jan 26, 1902; *Debates Const. Conv.*, 1901–02, I, 783 ff.; Magruder, F. A.: *Recent Admin. Va.*, 73, writes ''The Medical College of Virginia receives an annual grant of $5,000 from the state, though it is not a state school.   To obviate the constitutional prohibition against supporting non-state schools, a board of visitors is appointed for the school.''   As a matter of fact, the courts have at different times held it to be a state institution; the board of visitors was appointed by the state in consequence of the loans, and before appropriations were made.   *From correspondence;* see Hansbrough: *Reports Supreme Court of Appeals*, LXXVII, 415; the decision cited declared visitorial authority resided in the state.

22 *Med. College Va.*, *Catalog*, 1927, 7.

23 *Debates Const. Conv.*, 1901–02, II, 2005–08; *The Times*, Sept. 10, 11, 1901; Jan. 26, 28, 1902.

24 *Ibid.;* Magruder: *Recent Admin. Va.*, 73–74; for discussion relative to Constitutional vs. legislative appropriations to the University, see, *Debates Const. Conv.*, 1901–02, II, 1712–21, 1751–52, 1761, 1842—the discussion was of interest in giving expression to the opinion that the denominational colleges were in positive, aggressive hostility to the University—*cf.*, 1716–18.

25 *The Times*, Jan. 28, 1902.

to the College of William and Mary, and leaving to the same
body the question of continuance or discontinuance of the payment of interest on certain bonds held by certain schools and
colleges.[26]   The limitation in the Constitution of the appropriation of public funds to state or civic controlled institutions, the
impulse for which accomplishment had been given in the discussion of the preceding period,[27] was a great step forward in
putting into actual realization the spirit of the *Declaration of
Rights* and the *Bill for Religious Freedom.*[28]

Among the more important changes provided by the Constitution, in the section on education, was the enlargement of the
State Board of Education.   It was now to include, in addition
to the Governor, Attorney General, and State Superintendent,
three experienced educators to be elected quadrennially by the
Senate from the faculties of certain of the higher institutions
supported by the state.[29] . The state superintendent was to be
elected by the people instead of by the Assembly as formerly.[30]
The selection of text-books was again left to the Board.[31]   The
duties of the superintendent were to be prescribed by the Board,
of which he was to be ex-officio president.[32]   It was the Board

[26] *Constit., 1902*, Sect. 141; *The Times*, July 3, 10, 1901; *Jour. Const.
Conv., 1901*, Rep't of Comm. On Reduction Of Expenses On The Department
Of Education: McDanel, R. C.: *Va. Const. Conv., 1901–02*, 96; the incorporation of this section was inspired largely by petitions from numerous
Baptist Associations, though some Methodists also petitioned, as did various
chapters of the Junior Order United American Mechanics, see, *Jour. Const.
Conv., 1901*, 121, 142, 174, *et passim;* the interesting debates on this subject, *Debates Const. Conv., 1901–02*, I, 800 *ff.*, revealed the opinion that such
appropriations were in violation of the act of 1785—were an ''indirect assault upon the public free school system of Virginia,''—that denominational
institutions could not rid themselves of an ''all persuasive'' atmosphere in
favor of their particular institution; *cf.* also *The Times*, Sept. 6, 1901,
editorial, ''A Religious Paper's View,'' which declared that consistency
would require the *Religious Herald*, in its opposition against appropriations,
to come out against tax exemption.

[27] See p. 441.

[28] *Cf. Constit., 1902*, Sect. 58.

[29] *Ibid.*, Sect. 130; the Board was to associate with itself also one city
and one county superintendent; there had been some discussion as to whether
representatives of private institutions, which would have presented an opportunity for denominational schools, should be given places on the board,
see, *Debates Const. Conv., 1901–02*, II, 1794; *The Times*, Dec. 20, 1901.

[30] *Const., 1902*, Sect. 131.

[31] *Ibid.*, Sect. 132.

[32] *Ibid.*, Sect. 131.

which was to have authority to make rules and regulations which were to have the force and effect of law, subject to the authority of the General Assembly to revise, amend, or repeal.[33]

With reference to religious matters, in some respects, the most interesting debates of the Convention centered around the question of omission from Section 18 of the *Bill of Rights* of the word "Christian" in the phrase, that it is "the mutual duty of all to practise Christian forbearance, love and charity towards each other." The sponsor for omission, John Garland Pollard, held that its inclusion was offensive to those who regarded the word as having a sectarian meaning. It soon became apparent that opposition to its omission was formidable enough to endanger the acceptance of the entire work of the Convention, and by a vote of 7 to 4, the Committee, on the basis of its not being "politically expedient," reversed its former action to omit.[34]

A most significant achievement of the Convention was the reënactment of the constitutional provision forbidding a charter of incorporation to any church or religious denomination, but securing the title to church property to an extent to be limited by law. This was accomplished only after very elaborate discussion of a proposal to extend the provision of the Constitution of 1851 which permitted the incorporation of agencies of churches to apply to the incorporation of the churches themselves. The incorporation of such church agencies had been held constitutional. The new proposal met with opposition from the *Christian Advocate,* spokesman for the Methodist Church, from the *Central Presbyterian,* spokesman for the Presbyterian Church, and in the Convention, both by Dr. Dunaway, Baptist, to whose "masterly effort," Dr. McIlwaine, Presbyterian, attributed the defeat of the proposition, and by Dr. McIlwaine, who held that all spiritual agencies were "incorporated by our Lord Jesus Christ" and need "no incorporation from man."[35]

---

[33] *Ibid.,* Sect. 132. In the financial support of the system, the former reliance on appropriations from general revenues was eliminated, and reliance was placed on the Literary Fund and specific taxation. *Ibid.,* Sec. 135.

[34] *Jour. Const. Conv., 1901,* 92; *Debates Const. Conv., 1901–02,* 88, 738–39; *The Times,* July 2, 14, 17, 18, 20, Sept. 10, 1901.

[35] *Ibid.,* Sect. 59; see p. 416; *Debates Const. Conv., 1901–02,* I, 355, 732–82; *Jour. Const. Conv., 1901,* 79, Minority Rep't of Comm. on Legislative Department; *The Times,* Oct. 13, 1901; McDanel: *Va. Const. Conv., 1901–02,* 95; McIlwaine: *Memoirs Of Three Score Years And Ten,* 365.

The Constitution likewise provided that the General Assembly was to make no appropriation of public funds, personal property, or real estate to any church or sectarian society, association or institution, which was entirely or partly, directly or indirectly controlled by any church or sectarian society, nor to any charitable institution except owned or controlled by the state.[36]   It thus definitely settled in law the question of appropriation to denominational educational institutions.

On the question of tax exemption, the Constitution granted an exemption on buildings and land actually occupied or held by churches or religious bodies for worship or for the residence of ministers, or for educational purposes, and to incorporated educational institutions.   Exemption was also extended to Young Men's Christian Associations, and other similar religious organizations conducted as charities.[37]

The most significant feature of the Constitutional provisions of 1902, affecting civil and denominational education, was, undoubtedly, the clear cut decision to eliminate any state appropriation to institutions associated in any manner with religious organizations.   Tradition was, of course, too strong to include in this prohibition, tax exemption to such institutions.   In the re-organization of the central administrative system, the wide legislative power given the State Board of Education, subject though it was to reversal by the Asembly, was, as will appear, of supreme importance.[38]

Dr. Ruffner's Policy Furthered By Educational Organizations

Discussion of the relation of morality and religion to education continued with unabated vigor after the acceptance of the new Constitution, the discussion being stimulated largely by the consideration of numerous aspects of the educational problem by the various organizations created to study and improve the southern educational situation.[39]

---

[36] *Const., 1902*, Sect. 67.
[37] *Ibid.*, Sect. 183; *Debates Const. Conv., 1901–02*, I, 792, 799; *The Times*, Sept. 1, 1901, Feb. 26, 1902.
[38] See p. 500–01.
[39] See p. 471.

In 1903, Dr. Wallace Buttrick, Secretary of the General Education Board, declared before the National Education Association, that while public education had gained in favor, "a careful observer of conditions and sentiment in the South sees that the old aristocratic ideal of society still hinders the progress of universal education at public expense."[40] While acknowledging that the "past, present, and future value of the denominational schools must not be underestimated," and granting that they were established for public rather than sectarian ends, and furnished a supply for teachers of free schools and leaders of public thought, yet, he concluded, "both the private and the denominational schools have retarded somewhat the growth of public education by meeting the needs of their respective communities with such satisfaction that the larger needs of free, democratic, all-embracing schools were overlooked."[41]

Judging from the evidence furnished by the newspaper letters of 1902,[42] it would appear that there were many who would have felt that Dr. Buttrick's statement regarding the satisfaction of the needs of their respective communities by private and denominational schools should be qualified, as being applicable only to a certain section of society, though in agreement with him that these schools had in reality been a somewhat hampering influence in the development of public education.

In fact, keen students of the relation of education to social progress were becoming convinced that universal education was the task solely of the state, that it never could be satisfactorily taken care of by private or denominational effort. Dr. Curry declared on this subject:

. . . Free universal education never yet, in the history of the world, has been provided by families, individuals or religious denominations. The Government must undertake and carry [it] out or it will be hopeless, ... If one human being has an inalienable God-given right to moral and intellectual development, so have all.[43]

As a member of the Southern Education Board, General Education Board, agent of the Peabody Education Fund and Slater Fund, Dr. Curry was in a position to speak authoritatively.[44]

[40] *N. E. A. Proc's*, 1903, XLII, 118.
[41] *Ibid.*, 120.
[42] See p. 472–73.
[43] *The Times*, Feb. 9, 1902; *cf.* Bruce, P. A.: *Rise New South*, 377, for denominational control of higher education of women in the South.
[44] *Cf. Proc's Conf. Educ. South*, 1903, 251 *ff.*

The propaganda started by the Southern Education Board and echoed in the newspapers of the state began to awaken the denominational interests of the state to the necessity of a broader attitude toward the educational problem confronting the state. In his reports to the Conference of the Southern Education Board, in 1903 and 1904, Dr. H. B. Frissel, agent of the Board, acknowledged the good will and interest shown, in the presentation of the cause of public education, by religious gatherings, particularly by the Baptist District Associations, through whom the General Association was favorably influenced.[45] Hopeful, too, was the almost general response of religious papers in opening their columns to educational news and their publishing of valuable editorials on the needs of the schools.[46] The work of the conference was placed upon a broad basis by Dr. S. C. Mitchell, of Richmond College, in a declaration that the educational revival for which the conference stood was "a friend to religion and patriotism" and "a foe to sectarianism and sectionalism."[47] At the conference in 1904, Dr. Mitchell asked for co-operation of the various denominations in furthering activities of the Board.[48] At the conference in 1906, it was reported that ministers of every denomination in Virginia had agreed with the Co-operative Educational Association to preach one or two sermons a year on education.[49]

In an address before this same conference, Dr. E. A. Alderman, President of the University of Virginia, in reviewing the educational progress of the South, declared that "It has been demonstrated that while the public schools do not infringe upon religious liberty, their instruction does not make for Godlessness or irreligion."[50] While the principle had been settled that there should be no organic relation between the church and the state, he felt, that there was after a period of confusion and difference, "a gratifying unity of purpose on the part of both church and

45 *Ibid.*, 52; 1904, 68.
46 *Ibid.*, 1903, 56.
47 *Ibid.*, 190.
48 *Ibid.*, 1904, 163.
49 *Ibid.*, IX, 36.
50 *Ibid.*, IX, 148.

State to build up an adequate school system free from sectarianism and partisan bias."[51]   There was, however, not yet, "a clear understanding of the inter-relations between the public schools and the private schools, and the State colleges and those that depend upon private beneficence and religious zeal."[52]

Among the associations launched during this period in which a number of Virginians were interested was the Religious Education Association, a national organization.   It held its first meeting in Chicago, in 1903.[53]   It was founded by educational and religious leaders interested in advancing the interests of religious instruction in the educational concept.   As stated in their publications, their purpose was to inspire the educational forces of the country with the religious ideal; the religious forces with the educational ideal, and to keep before the public mind the need and value of the ideal of religious education.[54]   It is not without significance for the relation between religion and education in Virginia, that there were soon among the officers of the Association such prominent Virginian educational leaders as Dr. Alderman and Dr. Mitchell.[55]

In Virginia itself, an organization of real influence, because of its immediate contact with the people, sprang up as one of the outcomes of the work begun by the Southern Education Board, in 1902.   It was the creation, in 1904, of the Co-operative Education Association of Virginia.[56]   In 1905, it conducted a campaign usually referred to as the "May Campaign" in which propaganda of various kinds was utilized to advance a more effective interest in public education.[57]   The Association came under the direction of the Governor, representatives of various state departments and higher institutions of learning, and a group of citizens.   The state superintendent of public instruction was made chairman of the Executive Committee.[58]

[51] *Ibid.,* 151.
[52] *Ibid.,* 153.
[53] *Proc's, Relig. Educ. Assoc.,* I, 402.
[54] *Relig. Educ.,* I, 2.
[55] *Ibid.,* 37, 39.
[56] *Proc's Conf. Educ. South,* 1904, 73–74; see p. 471.
[57] *N. E. A. Proc's,* 1922, LX, 1203; Heatwole: *Hist. of Educ. Va.,* 317.
[58] *N. E. A. Proc's,* 1922, LX, 1203; *Proc's Conf. Educ. South,* 1904, 74.

To carry on its work, the Association proceeded to organize the whole state by means of community leagues. At the end of the year 1914–15, 957 leagues had been formed with a total membership of over 30,000, and over $56,000 had been raised in actual money and gifts during the year. The leagues were distributed in every county in the state.[59] The object of these community leagues as stated in bulletins of the Association is "to advance the educational, social, moral, physical, civic and economic interests of the community."[60] To effect the purposes of social and moral improvement, a committee on moral life should be formed "to encourage regular attendance at the church and Sunday school service, and young people's religious services, and seek to bring about co-operation of all christian forces. It should discourage every immoral feature or influence in the community."[61] The "Moral life Committee" was particularly urged to foster closer co-operation between denominations and the various religious activities of the community, including Sunday School work and the observance of Better Church Day.

In 1917, an editorial in the *Virginia Educational Journal* called the attention of teachers to the fact that the Co-operative Education Association, the Virginia State Sunday School Association, and the Extension Department of the University of Virginia were united in encouraging the observance of "Better Church and Sunday School Day," and urged the co-operation of teachers.[62] Teachers were also urged in a hand-book issued jointly by the Department of Education and the Co-operative Education Association to organize Boys' and Girls' School Clubs. A suggested constitution for these clubs gave scripture reading, and the Lord's Prayer in concert, as part of the opening exercises of regular meetings.[63]

In 1920, the State Department of Education issued a bulletin prepared by the Co-operative Education Association, which in addition to urging that communities co-operate with the Y. M. C. A. and Y. W. C. A. officials in Richmond, to replace immoral

59 *Va. Sch. Rep't*, 1914–15, 137.
60 *Community League Bull. Co-op. Educ. Assoc.*, 1916, 2.
61 *Ibid.*, 5.
62 *Va. Educ. Jour.*, April, 1917, X, 359–60.
63 Eggleston, J. D., & Munford, B. B.: *School Clubs for Va.*, 3.

by wholesome moral meeting places, discussed ways and means of co-operation with church and Sunday School activities.[64] It declared that "One of the best methods for developing the clean, moral life of both young and old in any community is to have vigorous Sunday school and church work in every church."

Under the caption of "Regular Chapel Services In The School," the bulletin stated:

Our State not only permits but encourages the reading of the Bible in the school. This committee should co-operate with the teachers in providing for regular chapel services. It would be well to have the ministers of the different denominations assist in this by taking their regular turn in conducting service. It is not necessary to have any special creed presented. A passage of Scripture may be read, prayer offered, and appropriate songs used. This will prove a moral and spiritual blessing to the children.[65]

This statement is an obvious reflection of the introduction not many years before, of the study of Bible courses in the high schools;[66] in sanctioning the one, there was apparently no hesitation in giving an official, if not a strictly legal, sanction to the other—to what was common practise anyway.

It appears from a study of the reaction of the educational organizations, created at the beginning of the century to study and advance educational progress, that there was a feeling that the attitude of denominational education, in its aloofness from the broader aspects of education, affecting the state as a whole, had been prejudicial to public education. The remedy, it seemed to the educational leaders of these organizations, lay in closer cooperation between the representatives of denominational and civil education in advancing educational progress. What happened, because supported by definitely organized effort, was a more effective realization of Dr. Ruffner's policy of co-operation without alliance. Co-operation meant the yielding of the religious influences to the support of public education, on condition that the civil arm of society extended assistance in bringing a larger measure of moral and religious education into public education. This is seen in the work of co-operation between the

---

[64] *Bull. State B'd Educ.*, Sept., 1920, III, No. 2, Supp. No. 1, 20–21.
[65] *Ibid.*, 21.
[66] See p. 500.

representatives of the state and the Co-operative Education Association; it comes out still more clearly in the study of the development of moral and religious instruction during this period.

Failure Of Systematic Moral Instruction To Achieve A Place

That the status, at the beginning of the century, of moral and religious instruction in both elementary and higher education, was regarded with misgiving by some, may be gathered from a review of educational progress in an article, in 1903, in the *South Atlantic Quarterly* by Dr. Wm. E. Dodd, professor of history in Randolph-Macon College. Dr. Dodd charged that moral training was next to impossible, because, 1. the teacher was an underpaid officer, and 2. tenure was precarious, depending on the good will of his patrons. Attempts to discipline children resulted in refusal to patronize the school, and the teacher found it safer to ''make all his ideals of discipline both mental and moral accord with those of a half dozen of his patrons.''[67] As for higher education, should a pupil be fortunate enough to be brought up in a Christian home, he, then, went to a college where the form but not the essence of Christianity prevailed, where student life was almost anti-Christian, and, in place of an abiding faith, left the institution finally with nothing but an egotistical infidelity.[68]

In spite of this gloomy outlook of Dr. Dodd, definite efforts to improve the situation from the point of view of those desiring that greater pressure be brought to bear in behalf of extending moral and religious instruction were soon to be made. The Constitution of 1902 had eliminated the requirement of uniformity of text-books and had left the selection of text-books to the discretion of the State Board.[69] In 1906, the Assembly passed a law that no text-books once adopted were to be changed, or substitutes made, until used for a period of not less than four years.[70] It also provided, among other new subjects in the curriculum, that moral instruction should be given in the public schools, to be extended throughout the entire course.[71] This in-

---

[67] *South Atlant. Quart.*, II, 327–28.
[68] *Ibid.*, 329–30.
[69] *Va. Sch. Rep't*, 1904–05, xxxii *ff*,
[70] Cf. *Ibid.*, xxxviii; *Acts of Assembly*, 1906, 433.
[71] *Ibid.*, 443.

struction was to be imparted "by reading books and text-books inculcating the virtues of a pure and noble life." These text-books were also to be selected by the State Board.[72] The books selected were Emma L. Ballou's *Guide Right* for the primary grades, and Benjamin B. Comegys' *Primer of Ethics* for the grammar grades and high school.[73] The chapter contents of Miss Ballou's book concerned obedience, kindness, punctuality, truthfulness, honesty, temperance, studiousness, work, purity, courage, conscience, habit and character, and duties toward God; those of Mr. Comegys' book, which was an adaptation of Jacob Abbott's *The Rollo Code of Morals,* were truth, obedience, industry, honesty, fidelity, justice, politeness, duties at school, duties to playmates, benevolence, duties to dumb creatures, treatment of enemies, profanity, conscience, conscientiousness, duty to parents, forgiveness, gratitude, purity, repentance, duty to God. Commenting on the introduction of this subject, in his *State Report,* 1905–07, Superintendent Eggleston said:

. . . It ought not to be expected that these additional subjects would, at the start, be deemed as important as those of long standing in the curriculum, but they have been introduced to a gratifying extent. The teaching of these subjects will prove of great benefit to the children, and should become a part of every course of study.[74]

The introduction of this subject was followed in November, 1907, by publishing, in the *Virginia Journal of Education,* the course of study for moral instruction, prepared under the direction of the State Board of Education. Beginning with the first grade and extending through the seven grades of the elementary course, politeness, orderly behavior, and gentleness were to be stressed. Then, the various virtues or vices were allocated for specific instruction in each grade; in the second—kindness, truthfulness, duty, obedience; in the third—gratitude, forgiveness, confession, honesty; in the fourth—courage, self-respect, self-control, bad language; in the fifth—health, temperance, bad habits, industry; in the sixth—patriotism, civic duties, training;

---

[72] *Ibid.*
[73] *Cf. Form X—No. 46—Text Books and Educational Appliances For The Public Schools,* October, 1910.
[74] *Va. Sch. Rep't,* 1905–6 and 1906–07, 33.

in the seventh—patriotism, civic duties, general lessons. The nature of the teaching may be gathered from the instruction in teaching duty—to teach fidelity to duty, duty to parents, to teachers, to those about us, to God; in teaching obedience—to teach obedience to God; in teaching gratitude—to teach thankfulness to God, the giver of all good. In the seventh grade, in giving general lessons, the teacher was to recall legends, stories, and biographies already read, to draw practical lessons from the same, particularly from old Bible stories.[75] It is seen that in setting up a course in moral instruction, the state did not intend to draw a sharp line between ethical and religious instruction.

To what extent consistent training was given in morals, in accordance with the 1907 program, does not appear in official sources, the reports of the state superintendents throwing practically no light on this question. A report, in 1911, by Dr. Bruce R. Payne, of the University of Virginia, to the Religious Education Association, based on an inquiry made to the members of the State Board of Inspectors, who during the past five years, had visited practically all the schools of the state, revealed that as far as the moral instruction required by law was concerned, that there were various differences in procedure. One inspector found that it was taught by example and general guidance of conduct of the students, with not many schools giving special lessons on the subject; another reported that about 75 per cent of the teachers gave talks on morals, using story telling and illustrations; still another, that manners and morals were taught in the majority of high schools. Dr. Payne's conclusion was that while the educational code required systematic training in morals, only half the schools at that time had taken up the subject. He declared, however, that ''the moral tone of the schools is all that could be desired, and morality in many incidental ways is taught and applied.''[76]

Opportunities and procedures in regard to moral training in the classroom were discussed by Gertrude B. Bass, in the March, 1915, number of the *Virginia Journal of Education*. The writer

---

[75] *Va. Jour. Educ.*, Nov., 1907, I, 10–11.
[76] *Relig. Educ.*, April, 1911, VI, 99–101; *cf. U. C. Comm. Educ. Rep't*, 1912, I, 144, lists Richmond, Va., as having a system of moral instruction.

declared that while the common school was the place to inculcate the great industrial, social, and civic virtues, all the moral safeguards of national life—yet creeds and principles, learned by rote, would not eradicate vicious propensities, though parents and teachers persisted in hoping they would.[77] It was the sympathy and influence of the teacher which were important. As to the reading of the Bible, as a formal morning exercise, its value as an aid in moral training depended on the manner and spirit in which the exercises were conducted. The child needed to be impressed with the sincerity of the teacher. Methods of conducting moral lessons must be gathered by experience and observation, though the use of stories was a most effective medium.

In the bulletin giving the state course of study for elementary schools, in 1918, "morals and manners" were assigned only for the fourth year, specifically.[78] In 1922, the Assembly, in legislating on "what shall be taught in schools," again enacted that moral instruction should be given throughout the entire course, "by reading books and text-books inculcating the virtues of a pure and noble life."[79] The bulletin giving the state course of study for rural and elementary schools, in 1923, in listing the subjects to be taught, did not list moral instruction as a separate subject, but stated:

. . . It is required that teachers shall give very great emphasis to moral instruction in order that a strong moral fibre may be woven into the whole instructional program.[80]

From the general programs suggested, it appears that "morals and manners" were regarded as part of the work in the social study group section for the first two grades.[81] The subject, however, was nowhere outlined in the fashion of the 1907 program, and seemingly the older formal presentation of moral instruction was giving way to centering "the formation of right habits, attitudes, and ideals necessary for good citizenship" in the social study group section of the curriculum.[82]

---

[77] *Va. Jour. Educ.*, Mar., 1915, VIII, 358.
[78] *Bull. State B'd Educ.*, Oct., 1918, I, No. 2, 39–40.
[79] *Acts of Assembly*, Feb. 25, 1922, 69.
[80] *Bull. State B'd Educ.*, April, 1923, V, No. 4, 7–8.
[81] *Ibid.*, 286.
[82] *Ibid.*, 36.

It is not to be assumed, however, that all interest had been lost in the question of formal moral instruction in schools. The *Virginia Journal of Education*, in 1923, printed "A Moral Code for Girls and Boys" drawn up by Mrs. Hazel B. Douglass, of the Alexandria schools, interest in codes having been undoubtedly stimulated by the competition under the auspices of the Character Education Institution, Washington, D. C.[83] The code by Wm. J. Hutchins, which received the Donor's prize of that institution, in 1916, was reprinted by *The Virginia Teacher*, in 1924.[84]

The continued interest in character education may be gathered from a report on a conference on "Character Education In The Public Schools" led by Superintendent F. E. Clerk, of the Winchester schools. It appears that Winchester had a Committee on Character Education for the public schools, in which, the home, the church, and the school were represented. Mr. Clerk was particulary interested in finding some plan which like the Iowa plan would offer a means of teaching honesty, consideration for the rights of others, loyalty, and the moral virtues that pertain to childhood, and grow in after life into different but still proper associations.[85] Mr. Clerk declared himself as interested in specifically moral training as distinguished from such religious training as was available during the high school age in the state courses in Bible study.[86]

As in any conference on moral education, the discussion could not be limited to the question of purely moral instruction. In answer to a question, Mr. Clerk gave it as his opinion that the Gary plan which dismissed the children for religious instruction had not worked well in practise. He felt that the great danger in handling religious instruction in public schools was the danger in being misunderstood in terms of teaching denominationalism

---

[83] *Va. Jour. Educ.,* Feb., 1923, XVI, 256.

[84] *Va. Teacher,* Mar., 1924, V, 79 *ff.* For the report of the Committee on Character Education, of the N. E. A. in 1922, see *N. E. A. Proc's,* 1922, LX, 457–59.

[85] *Cf. Educational Council, Iowa State Teachers' Association, Report of Committee on School Credit for Bible Study, Religious Instruction and Moral Training,* Nov. 2, 1916; also in *Proc's Sixty-second Annual Session of the Iowa State Teachers' Assoc.,* Nov., 1916, 56 *ff.*

[86] See p. 502.

instead of religion. Mr. Clerk then referred to the fact that there was a statute which made moral instruction compulsory, and suggested that if ministers in a community would get together, they could help the school superintendent to comply with the law;—a statement which was indicative of the fact, that by 1923, the law of 1906 requiring moral instruction was not generally being complied with in the sense of offering formal moral instruction.

In answer to a question by Bishop Brown, of the Protestant Episcopal Church, as to whether there was any real reason why he should not attempt to have just a few church schools throughout his diocese, Mr. Clerk declared that, in principle, there was no need for conflict between private and public schools and that he was very much for the private school in the field where it could function better than the public school, particularly where parents were, for various reasons, unable to be at home to supervise the child, in which case, he felt that the character side of education was better protected in a private than in a public school.[87]

The *Virginia Journal of Education,* in 1924, published an article by Dr. H. H. Horne, of New York University, on "Moral and Religious Instruction in the Public Schools," which had been written with the Virginia situation in mind. Dr. Horne, drawing a line between instruction and education, stated that every Virginia teacher should be encouraged to carry out the state law with regard to moral instruction. He declared that only about 2 per cent of American public schools gave moral instruction, though it was one of the indispensable means of the formation of moral character. As for moral education, the public schools provided this, in that the whole school was in itself an "ethical instrument." He then went on to say that while there was a place for religious education, there was none for religious instruction in the public schools; reading the Bible, common prayer, and hymns had a place, being regarded by Dr. Horne as educational; but the communication of religious ideas in instructional form had no place in the American public school. Religious instruction was incompatible with separation of church

---

[87] *Va. Teacher, June,* 1923, IV, 147 *ff.*

and state, and freedom of religious conscience. Religious education, Dr. Horne interpreted as education conscious of its true goal, the knowledge and love of God, and the service of man. It was by the enlargement of personality through ideals of health, skill, integrity, justice, love of beauty, truth and God, that religious education was to serve as a medium in harmonizing the relation between the child, society, and God.[88]

The most interesting outcome of the law of 1906 for moral instruction was the fact that, within less than two decades, it was clear that the program of systematic moral instruction had failed to achieve a place in the public school curriculum. As no sharp line was drawn between the ethical and the religious in the program of 1907, its failure to achieve a secure position can hardly be attributed to the fact that it was too coldly ethical. Whether because there was a feeling that the subject of morals did not lend itself to learning by rote, there was a tendency away from a formal presentation as a separate subject to embodiment in the general development of the school routine, or in the social group in the curriculum. Though there were not wanting educational leaders to the close of the period, in favor of systematic instruction, yet experience seemed to favor its being "woven into the whole instructional program." Apparently the religious forces of the state had no clear cut point of view with respect to a program of moral instruction in the public schools, and saw their way but dimly in respect to co-operation with the state in effectively realizing such a program without first enlarging the religious program in education.

Propaganda For Religious Instruction

In view of the legal recognition and actual introduction of moral instruction, during this period, though it does not seem to have achieved a very distinct or prominent place, it is not without interest to see what was the status, and what the progress of religious instruction during this period.

The question of Bible reading in public schools was again[89] investigated by the United States Commissioner of Education in

---

[88] *Va. Jour. Educ.*, Mar., 1924, XVII, 270.
[89] See p. 464.

February, 1904. In Virginia, among cities of 8,000 population
and over, seven reporting, all reported religious exercises at
opening of school, consisting of reading either the Old or the
New Testament, prayer by teacher or class, and hymns or sacred
song. Comment on the Bible was forbidden in five cities.[90]
In the group of cities of over 4,000, but less than 8,000, four reported; though religious exercises were prohibited by none, one
city did not hold them. In the three conducting exercises, the
usual Virginia custom of Bible reading, prayer, and songs prevailed. In two of the cities, comment on the Bible was
forbidden.[91]

In view of this general recognition, in practise, of the Bible
as having a place in schools, and in view of the fact that the
moral instruction legally placed in the school program, was related not merely to purely ethical concepts of conduct, but also
to the proper attitude to the Deity to be inculcated in children,
it is not surprising that there should be advocated the next step
of more extensive and more definite instruction in the Bible.

In an editorial in the *Virginia Journal of Education,* for December, 1908, reference was made to the prevalent ignorance of
the Bible by youth throughout the country, as revealed in discussion before .the National Education Association and in an
article in the Pennsylvania School Journal.[92] The editorial declared that youth could not be expected to learn Biblical history,
so long as so few elementary and secondary schools in the United
States had courses in the English Bible. In Virginia, aside from
the custom in many of the schools of reading some selection from
the Bible as an opening exercise, the Bible was not taught. The
editorial went on to say:

We plead for the introduction of Bible stories and Bible history into our
schools, not in any sectarian or doctrinal sense, but in order that our boys
and girls may know the history of a religion, and the men who made it—a
religion which is the foundation-stone of our civilization.[93]

---

[90] *U. S. Comm. Educ. Rep't,* 1903, II, 2444, 2446.
[91] *Ibid.,* II, 2447; *cf.* similar report for 1905, I, 204.
[92] *Va. Jour. Educ.,* Dec., 1908, II, 18; *N. E. A. Proc's,* 1908, XLVI, 448–
57; *Pa. Sch. Jour.,* Oct., 1908, LVII, 153.
[93] *Va. Jour. Educ.,* II, 19.

In view of the prominence of this journal in the educational life of the state, this expression of opinion may be regarded as significant, and as indicative of a contemplated policy, on its part, in regard to the question of religious instruction in public schools.

With the sanctioning of the course of moral training, which was linked to a religious conception of morality, and with its announced policy favorable to Biblical instruction, the *Journal* now began to give concrete expression to its policy, by publishing suggestive articles along the line of moral and religious training, not from a theoretical standpoint, but from the definite one of class-room instruction. While in the previous period, there had been some slight suggestion regarding the utilization of holidays, far more attention and space were now given to this idea. The nature of this suggestion may be gathered from an article entitled "Happy Easter-Tide," suggesting that Easter in the primary grades be made a joyous, happy festival, that the morning talks and stories for a week before, be on the origin and customs of Easter, that Biblical stories, myths, fairy tales and flower legends be told, that Easter carols could be found in any Sunday School collection, and pictures like Plockhorst's "He is Risen," "Mary Magdalene," and Hofmann's "Easter Morning" be used.[94]

In an editorial on Christmas, the *Journal* declared, in December, 1909, that it was its chief desire "that the true meaning of Christmas be taught by all true teachers." It contained that month a number of Christmas songs, and, in December, 1910, elaborate suggestions for the utilization of the holiday.[95] An editorial on Christmas, in 1911, again urged that "All teachers should instruct their pupils why this is a holiday."[96] In making suggestions for the Thanksgiving holiday in 1910, an editorial suggested responsive reading of Psalms 96, 98, 100, and 103 as appropriate.[97]

---

[94] *Ibid.*, April, 1909, II, 24; *cf. Ibid.*, Dec., 1907, I, 14, on "The Christmas Holidays."

[95] *Ibid.*, Dec., 1909, III, 145; Dec., 1910, IV, 136 *ff.*

[96] *Ibid.*, Dec., 1911, V, 98; for other articles on holidays, *cf.* Nov., 1912, VI, 72–77; Dec., 1914, VIII, 161, 162, 193, 199–201; Dec., 1917, XI, 167–73.

[97] *Ibid.*, Nov., 1910, IV, 66.

A bolder suggestion was that in an editorial in the *Journal,* in October, 1909, which stated that it wished to be placed on record as rating character above scholarship, and that it agreed with Dr. J. P. McCaskey, Mayor of Lancaster, that teachers ought to see to it that pupils are able to repeat the Ten Commandments.[98]

The following year, an editorial expressed the opinion that no one should be permitted to teach who did not believe in the existence of God, and that the keeping of the Ten Commandments was essential to good citizenship and correct living. All teachers should not only believe in the efficacy of prayer, but should open their schools with scripture reading and a prayer for God's guidance and blessing. It even went to the point of suggesting the form of a private prayer for the teacher and that every teacher should use it or a similar one.[99]

That the association of Virginians with the Religious Educational Association[100] was not without bearing upon this movement for more definite religious instruction in Virginia may well be concluded. That Virginians were at least giving careful thought to the problem was made evident to the Association by an article on "How To Provide For The Spread of Religious And Ethical Teaching In The Local Community," written for their journal, in 1910, by Dr. Payne of the University of Virginia.[101] The problem according to Dr. Payne divided itself into a consideration of: (1) how to reinstate religious training in the home; (2) how to improve religious teaching in Sunday Schools; (3) how to guarantee Bible reading and Bible teaching in the day school; and (4) how to reinstate religious life and renew ethical ideals in rural communities. The local press, summer schools, ministers and Sunday School teachers were the agencies suggested by Dr. Payne to spread propaganda to provide more and improved religious and ethical teaching.[102]

The following year, Dr. Payne in an article on "Moral Education And Training" reported for the same journal the results of his inquiry to the members of the State Board of Inspectors.

---

98 *Ibid.,* Oct., 1909, III, 2–3.
99 *Ibid.,* Nov., 1910, IV, 65; *cf.* Dec., 1911, V, 122.
100 See p. 481.
101 See p. 486.
102 *Relig. Educ.,* June, 1910, V, 131 *ff.*

The answers indicated that reading of the Bible, prayers, and hymns were the prevalent practise in opening the morning exercises of schools, and Dr. Payne's conclusion was that the Bible was read in practically all the schools of Virginia, while systematic moral instruction which had been provided for by law, prevailed in only about half the schools.[103]   The results of this investigation furnish interesting evidence of the greater potency of Dr. Ruffner's policy, as compared with the effectiveness of law.

An article in the *Virginia Journal of Education*, in 1911, by Willis A. Jenkins, declared that the question of religious instruction in the public schools was one of the biggest that could be proposed to advancing civilization, and that human progress depended largely on its proper solution.[104]   The writer was of the opinion that consideration for differences in religion was essential, and that spreading of Christianity by compulsion was contrary to the Bible.   The aim of the public schools was the upbuilding of character.   As this was, however, a Christian country, the standards by which the public schools were endeavoring to shape character, the ideals taught, and the atmosphere of the schools were dominantly Christian.   Along with this, must be taught the brotherhood of man, and consideration for the difference of religious views, otherwise no public education, no freedom of religious thought was possible.   The public schools may lead to the door of the church, but must stop there, or else violate the essential principles of Christian religion.   This violation resulted when "Christian people will demand that the Jew, who is one of our very best citizens, shall be forced to send his child to schools where he is taught religious tenets inconsistent with his belief."   Consideration for the rights of others, the writer felt, made it necessary not to go, in public schools, beyond reading the Bible, singing Christian songs and reciting the Lord's Prayer;[105] the writer apparently regarding that much Christian instruction as not violating Jewish conscience.

There was, however, a concerted movement, as is evidenced by the propaganda just indicated, to do more than this in the public

---

103 See p. 486; *Relig. Educ.*, April, 1911; VI, 99–101.
104 *Va. Jour. Educ.*, July, 1911, IV, 663.
105 *Ibid.*, 634.

schools, particularly, the movement which will next be considered, to bring more definite study of the Bible into public schools. Mr. Jenkins' effort, as will appear, was merely an ineffectual gesture to keep the *status quo* in regard to this issue; a hint, as it were, that, in his opinion, the saturation point had been reached in the policy of co-operation without alliance.

The Movement For Bible Instruction In Public Schools

The Constitution of 1902 had left to the State Board the making of rules and regulations regarding the conduct of schools; and, though the General Assembly had legislated, in 1906, on the subject of the curriculum,[106] there was nothing to prevent the Board from legislating on the same subject, until reversed by the General Assembly.[107]

That the pressure of the propaganda brought to bear after 1902 in favor of more extensive religious education was not without result, is evident from the steps now taken by the State Board. In 1910, it adopted Nettleton's *Old Testament Narratives* for elementary schools.[108] At a meeting in November, 1911, a resolution was adopted, and ordered to appear in every issue of the *Virginia Journal of Education,* deploring the ignorance of the Bible and its neglect in homes and in schools. This neglect was regretted, as the Bible, aside from its religious and ethical teachings, was important from a literary standpoint. Commenting on this resolution, the editor declared:

> We regret that the study of the Bible, as literature, has not found a place in our public schools, and we can see no valid reason why Biblical history should be excluded when Pagan history is included in the course of study in every state of this Union.[109]

With the stated purpose of arousing the interest of teachers in possible solutions of the problem, an article, entitled "The Bible and the Rising Generation," by Dr. Vernon P. Squires, Professor of English, in the University of North Dakota, was reprinted at the same time from the *New England Journal of*

---

[106] See p. 484.
[107] *Constit. 1902,* Sect. 132.
[108] *Form X – No. 91,* Revised Aug. 1, 1911.
[109] *Va. Jour. Educ.,* Feb., 1912, V, 201.

Education.   Dr. Squires, in order to remedy the situation of inadequate knowledge of the Bible among high school graduates,
suggested a syllabus or outline of Bible study, the following out
of which would involve serious study well worthy of academic
recognition.   It should include the mastery of important historical facts, the life-stories of the chief Biblical characters,
geography of Bible lands, and memory passages.   With the syllabus and a Bible, the student, aided by his parents or Sunday
School teacher, could prepare for an examination for which he
would receive proper credit towards his diploma and admission
to college.   This plan being optional, and the course not being
taught in school, would avoid charges of compulsion and sectarianism.[110]

With the tendency to emphasize the need of more extensive religious instruction in public schools, there arose also a larger
demand for religious character in teachers.   J. H. Kile, of Newcastle, in discussing the qualifications of a teacher, declared that
the moral and religious welfare of children demanded that teachers tainted with infidelity, or Doctors of Divinity inclining to
higher criticism, must be ruled out as teachers of youth—no one
should be permitted to teach that Moses did not write the Pen-
tateuch or that the Book of Job is an allegory.   The only kind
of education, worthy of the name, was Christian education received "by learning at the feet of Christian men and women."[111]

Continuing its policy in favor of injecting a greater and more
definite religious influence into the public schools, the *Journal*
came out in April, 1914, with a statement that it would like to
see a Young Men's Christian Association organized in every rural
high school in Virginia, as an opportunity would thus be created
for developing the moral and physical life of the boys of the
state.   In this work, the principal, because of his familiarity with
the students, would be an ideal leader particularly in his approach to the religious side of youth.   Y. M. C. A.'s and ath-
letics went hand in hand; by making the schoolhouse the headquarters of both, and the principal the leader, the higher and

---

110 *Ibid.*, 202 *ff.; cf. Ibid.*, May, 1912, V, 390 *ff.*, an article designed to
influence teachers in favor of religious instruction in public schools.
111 *Ibid.*, April, 1912, V, 319.

finer moral attributes could be developed.[112] This advocacy of
the association of the school principal, an individual paid by
public funds, with an evangelical church movement is interesting
in showing how lightly it was contemplated, in spite of the constitutional separation of church and state, to forget the rights of
minorities. In a sense this proposal may be regarded as an inevitable outcome of the strengthened movement for co-operation,
between the educational and religious forces of the state, begun
in 1902.[113]

Following up its advocacy of the movement, the *Journal*, the
next month, published an article by Harry T. Baker, the State
Boys' Secretary of the Association. Mr. Baker stated that scores
of schools had found in the Student Young Men's Christian Association, or in the high school club affiliated with the "High
School Student Christian Movement," an answer to the problem
of maintaining and extending throughout the school a high
standard of Christian conduct. Mr. Baker then gave a description of these activities and invited co-operation in extending the
movement.[114]

In 1915, Rev. Thomas Dean Lewis, Professor of Biblical History and Literature at Sweet Briar College, discussed at length
in the *Journal*, "Religious Education: The Need And The Remedy."[115] Rev. Mr. Lewis started with the premise that no conception of education was complete, which, beyond imparting
knowledge, did not have power to inspire higher ideals of character. It was his opinion that the educational world was practically agreed that religion was a necessity in training our moral
natures.[116] Instruction in morals, he held, was no substitute for
religion.[117] No nation could be strong morally, which was not
religious. Religious instruction was particularly important at
the impressionable period of elementary and secondary school
life, and it was just this period that American children spent in
public schools, where there is no religious training. The intro-

---

[112] *Ibid.*, April, 1914, VII, 314–15.
[113] See p. 480.
[114] *Va. Jour. Educ.*, May, 1914, VII, 419–20.
[115] *Ibid.*, May, 1915, VIII, 466.
[116] *Ibid.*
[117] *Ibid.*, 467.

duction of religious instruction would give a new beauty, and
value to all the other subjects of the curriculum; introducing a
unifying principal into education.　Instead, everywhere evidence
was accumulating of the ignorance of the Bible, as attested by
a study made in the University of Michigan.[118]　The causes of
this ignorance, Rev. Mr. Lewis attributed: 1. to the decadence
of home life; and 2. to the fact that religious knowledge had been
eliminated from the educational system under which the majority of children were taught.　This omission resulted in a pernicious distinction, with a resulting wide cleavage, between
secular and sacred life.[119]　As for the remedies proposed, not
one had been found free of great difficulties.　Among such remedies were: 1. parochial schools; 2. reading of Bible and use of
the Lord's Prayer; 3. Sunday schools; and 4. excusing students
on Wednesday afternon for denominational religious instruction.
Rev. Mr. Lewis then suggested, as an approach to the solution
of the problem, to incorporate in the regular curriculum a course
of definite theistic teaching, emphasizing the existence of God
as a personal Creator and Father, and the duties and responsibilities that grow out of our relationship to Him, together with
a simple course in ethics, rooted in religion rather than in morality; this course to be given one hour a week on Wednesday
morning.

The real interest of the *Journal* in bringing the problem from
merely theoretical discussion to practical application in the classroom may be gathered from the fact that it published a series
of opening exercsies covering a period of five weeks.　This scheme
embraced moral lessons to be derived from scriptural selections
of both the Old and the New Testaments, also the use of hymns,
and prayers.[120]

The propagandic efforts of the *Journal* were now beginning to
bear fruit.　In 1915, at a meeting of the Virginia State Teachers'
Association, the following resolution was adopted:

Resolved, that this association, recognizing the value of a knowledge of
the Bible in any scheme of general education, and desiring that Bible teach-

---

[118] *Ibid.*
[119] *Ibid.*, 468.
[120] *Ibid.*, Oct., 1915, IX, 71 *ff*.

ing by the various religious agencies of the State shall be encouraged and raised to higher efficiency, recommends that the State Board of Education adopt some plan whereby the pupils of our public high schools who shall master a prescribed course of Bible study and pass an examination upon the same, shall receive credit toward their graduation, such action by the State board being of a character to protect the sacred principles of religious liberty, and to leave in the hands of our churches or other religious organizations the responsibility for Bible teaching.[121]

The "Rural Life Conference" meeting at the University of Virginia,[122] also passed a similar resolution, stating their belief "that the time has come for the Church and Public Schools of Virginia to co-operate for the more effective teaching of the Bible to the young." This resolution was given publicity in the journal of the Religious Education Association.[123]

In April, 1916, Mr. Flint Waller reviewed in the *Virginia Journal of Education* the status of Bible study for school credit throughout the United States, and suggested a modification of the Oregon plan for Virginia. The Virginia plan was to consist of four years of work, with 45-minute recitation periods. Each year's work was to represent one-fourth unit of credit. Separate classrooms were to be used. The Oregon syllabus was to be adopted, unless a better be found or prepared. The teachers were to have training equivalent to that required of high school teachers, and to be acceptable to the principal and to the board. The acceptance of the student's work for credit was to be in the hands of the principal, subject to review by the board. Class work and examinations were to be in the hands of the teachers, but under the supervision and direction of the principal.[124] The pertinency of this article is apparent when it is known, as will be shown presently, that definite steps had already been taken to introduce Bible study into the public school system.[125]

This step was the logical outcome of the resolution of the Board, in 1911, deploring the ignorance and the neglect of the

---

121 *Va. Sch. Rep't*, 1914–15, 124; cf. *Va. State Teachers Quart., Annual Proc's*, 1915, II, No. 1, 16.
122 See p. 622.
123 *Relig. Educ.*, Feb., 1916, XI, 76.
124 *Va. Jour. Educ.*, April, 1916, IX, 407.
125 See p. 500.

Bible. Sufficient pressure had apparently been brought to bear, since 1902, so that the civil side of the state was now ready to take cognizance of the opinion of the religious forces of the state, that the policy of co-operation without alliance, which so far had permitted a certain amount of formal religious instruction, needed strengthening, if religious instruction was to become an effective force in education.

Introduction Of Bible Study Into The Public High School

That Mr. Waller's article was designed to guide those interested in the problem of bringing more definite religious instruction into the public schools is evident from the fact that the State Board of Education had already taken action looking to the introduction of Bible study as a course for credit in the high school curriculum.   On February 2, 1916, the Board assigned to a committee of seven, representing educational and religious interests associated with the Jewish, Roman Catholic, and Protestant faiths, the task of preparing the various courses.   At a meeting of the committee on August 8, the syllabus was declared ready for presentation to the State Board of Education.[126]   Extracts from the minutes of the meeting of the State Board, held on August 29, indicate that three courses, two in the Old Testament, and one in the New Testament, were submitted by Professor W. M. Forrest, holder of the chair constituting the John B. Cary Memorial School of Biblical History and Literature at the University.[127]   The report was accepted and the following resolution unanimously adopted:

In response to a widespread desire throughout the State, voiced by resolutions adopted by various religious and educational organizations, the State Board of Education of Virginia hereby authorizes High School principals to give such pupils as fulfil the requirements set forth in the Official Syllabus of Bible Study prepared by the committee appointed by the Board, not less than half a unit, nor more than one unit of credit for Bible courses in lieu of regular High School electives of like credit value.[128]

In this resolution is to be found, without doubt, the most significant action taken by the state since the separation of church

---

[126] *U. of Va. Rec., Ext. Ser.*, Sept., 1916, II, No. 1, 4.
[127] See p. 616.
[128] *U. of Va. Rec., Ext. Ser.*, Sept., 1916, Ser. II, No. 1, 3.

and state, one hundred and forty years before, in moving in the direction of definite co-operation with the church. This movement cannot as yet be said to constitute a union with the church, for there is as yet no connection with the church, in constitutional law. It is, however, the outcome of the policy advised by Dr. Ruffner in the seventies, of co-operation without definite alliance in law. It is evidence of his keen understanding of Virginia sentiment and character.

In taking the action indicated, the State Board acted upon the authority granted in the Constitution to make all needful rules and regulations for the conduct of schools.[129] But there was at the same time, the question of reconciling this action with the *Declaration of Rights* and *Bill for Religious Freedom* which had been incorporated into the Constitution, and it was necessary in order not to contravene these aspects of the Constitution to issue certain directions in connection with the syllabus. These directions stated that the courses were not intended to be made a part of the public school teaching, nor were the public school funds to be used to provide this Bible teaching. The responsibility for pupils' entering upon this work must rest with their parents and religious advisers.

The directions indicated further that teaching might be done under almost any auspices, and classes meet once a week or oftener, but ninety recitation periods of forty minutes per period must be devoted to each course, and the teacher must do and require faithful work. Those certifying to the fitness of pupils to take examinations were to make sure that pupils had been thoroughly prepared and tested. While teachers were at liberty to supplement the courses with any tenets of their faith, or moral and spiritual applications, examinations would deal only with the historical, geographical, and literary matters outlined. References in the syllabus were given to the King James, the Douay, and Leeser versions of the Bible, in use among Protestants, Catholics, and Jews. For admission to the examination, pupils had to present a certificate signed by the teacher and superintendent of the religious school that the course had been covered in the prescribed manner and that the student was prepared.

---

[129] *Constit. 1902*, Sect. 132.

Those pupils passing the examination would be granted half a
unit credit in Bible study, and a maximum of one unit for passing the examination in two courses; pupils passing in all three
courses would be given a certificate. As the three courses consisted of two courses in the Old Testament and one in the New
Testament, Protestant and Catholic pupils were at liberty to
choose either two in the Old Testament, or one in the Old and
one in the New Testament; Jewish pupils, the two Old Testament
courses.[130] All examination papers were to be sent to the State
Superintendent at Richmond to be graded by the Committee, except in the case of seniors needing credit for graduation, in which
case the principal was to grade ''with such aid from local religious leaders, as he may desire''—the papers to be forwarded
later to Richmond.[131] From this description of the Viriginia
plan, the debt due to the articles by Dr. Squires and Mr. Waller[132] is apparent.

The character of these courses may be gathered from the summary description here given. Course I, Old Testament History,
consisted of ten prescribed passages, scattered from Genesis to
Isaiah, to be memorized; as were also the names of the Old Testament Books. The rest of the course was divided on a ninety
lesson plan into ten sections, each covering a definite consecutive
section of the Old Testament, as for example, Section I. The
Beginning of History, Genesis I to XI; Section II. The Hebrew
Patriarchs, Genesis XI, 27, to L. Course, II, Old Testament Literature followed along the same general plan, its subject matter
was divided into four sections; 1. Biblical legislation, codes and
covenant, general laws and holidays; 2. The Psalms; 3. The Wisdom books (Proverbs, Job, Ecclesiastes) ; and 4. The Prophets.
Course III, New Testament History and Literature also followed
the same general principles; its subject matter consisted of: 1.
The Life of Christ (divided for consideration into nine sections) ;
2. Leading features of the four Gospels; 3. The early history

---

[130] *U. of Va. Rec., Ext. Ser.*, Sept., 1916, II, No. 1, 6–7; *Va. Jour. Educ.*,
Oct., 1916, X, 75.

[131] *U. of Va. Rec., Ext. Ser.*, Sept., 1916, II, No. 1, 8.

[132] See p. 495, 499.

of the Church; and 4. Leading features of early Christian literature.[133]

Dr. Forrest, in writing of the new subject in the curriculum for the *Virginia Journal of Education,* October, 1916, discussed the value of this provision for Bible study. He declared that for the high schools, and for the colleges in which the pupils would continue their study, there would be a broad intellectual gain. Because of the extent to which the Bible had entered into our laws, institutions, history and literature, a knowledge of it was essential to a comprehension of tasks set students. Class work treating the Bible as seriously as other subjects would command respect; high school credit would give a definite goal. He concluded this phase of the subject, by saying that ''The worth of such an elevation of Bible class standards, and such a chance to hold young people to loyal and continued allegiance to religious organizations and teachers cannot be overstated.''[134]

This statement is of particular interest. It will be recalled that the State Board of Education in its directions,[135] had not ruled out instruction in denominational tenets. As far as the state supervision of the examinations was concerned, these courses were to be historical and literary in purpose. Prof. Forrest's statement makes clear that in the actual conduct of the course, it was hoped and expected, that these courses, being given under denominational auspices, would increase denominational strength. In this connection, it becomes necessary•to note that the syllabus, when first printed, was printed as a Bulletin of the Bureau of Extension of the University of Virginia, apparently to eliminate any criticism that the Board was using public funds to inculcate religious or denominational instruction.[136] But, as in order to make the plan effective, it was necessary to have copies of the syllabus for wide, annual distribution throughout the state, the

---

[133] *U. of Va. Rec., Ext. Ser.,* Sept., 1916, II, No. 1, 9–48; a syllabus of the various courses of study may also be found in the separate Bulletins of the State Board of Education; Course I in *Bull. State B'd Educ.,* Oct., 1924, VII, No. 2, Supp. No. 1; Course II, *Ibid.,* June, 1921, IV, No. 1, Supp. No. 2; Course III, *Ibid.,* Oct., 1924, VII, No. 2, Supp. No. 2.

[134] *Va. Jour. Educ.,* Oct., 1916, X, 76.

[135] See p. 501.

[136] For the University policy in furthering the religious interests of the state, see p. 621 *ff.*

Board in the following year had separate syllabi for the various courses, I, II, and III, printed.[137]   This necessitated the subsequent omission of the direction which had appeared in the first syllabus, saying that, "Teachers are at liberty to supplement the courses as outlined with any tenets of their faith, or moral and spiritual applications that they desire, . . . "   Probably it was felt that this statement was giving too strong a state sanction to denominationalism, or too much encouragement to a religious or spiritual purpose in giving the course.[138]   The great difficulty of reconciling a policy of co-operation in religious instruction with the nature of the Virginia Constitution is evident.

In connection with the plan, it is also necessary to point out that there was originally no requirement as to the educational standard of the teacher, and no limitation upon the quality of teaching, except that the class had to be in charge of a teacher who would do and require faithful work.[139]   By 1926, however, Dr. Forrest was called on to pass on teachers' qualifications, the final decision resting with the Supervisor of Teachers' Certificates.

The question of examination of the students was, the first year, taken care of by the chairman of the committee, Prof. W. M. Forrest, who drew up a set of questions on the courses, and, after submitting it to other members for criticism, gave the questions on Courses I and III to be printed by the State Board.[140]   At the end of the first school year, 1917, papers were received from three high schools and 31 pupils; 26 passed.   The courses had been given in Draper, Roanoke, and Whitmell.[141]   The examination consisted of ten general questions, all of equal value, one of ten memory passages, and the naming of certain books of either the Old or the New Testament.[142]

137 *Va. Jour. Educ.*, Dec., 1917, XI, 162.

138 *Cf. U. of Va. Rec., Ext. Sec.*, Sept., 1916, II, No. 6, Sect. 5, with *Bull. State B'd Educ.*, June, 1921, IV, No. 1, 4; it is interesting to note, however, that this statement was retained in the announcement of the State Department of Education by J. N. Hillman, Secretary, given in the *Va. Jour. Educ.*, Nov., 1921, XV, 102–03.

139 Athearn, W. S.: *Relig. Educ. and Amer. Democracy*, 89.

140 *Va. Jour. Educ.*, Dec., 1917, XI, 161.

141 Draper is in Pulaski County; Whitmell, in Pittsylvania.

142 *Va. Jour. Educ.*, XI, 161–62; *Relig. Educ.*, April, 1918, XIII, 136; cf. *Bull. State B'd Educ.*, Oct., 1924, VII, No. 2, 5, which implies that the first year's work consisted of one class with 27 pupils.

As a principal object of the Virginia plan, which was for the most part a modification of the North Dakota plan, was to find some way of getting public school pupils to study and know the Bible, without making possible the charge that a union between church and state was being fostered, the examinations and a large amount of the work connected with the administration of the scheme were shifted from the office of the State Board of Education and the office of the State Superintendent of Schools, where it would seem logically to have belonged, in view of the credit recognition given by the State Board, and placed in charge of Dr. Forrest at the University of Virginia. Later, Prof. Forrest was given the title of State Bible Study Examiner,[143] and he continues to serve in that capacity without salary from the State Department.[144]

In November, 1919, Prof. Forrest reported that the record showed 175 pupils in 15 classes, in 5 different counties had taken the examinations. There had been six classes in Course I, Old Testament History; one, in Course II, Old Testament Literature; and eight classes in Course III, New Testament History and Literature. Nearly all papers submitted had won a passing grade of 75. In Roanoke, the various churches had employed an instructor who taught pupils of all denominations. At Whitmell, the principal had taught pupils in the school building. In regard to the use of a public school building indicated here, it may be said that the plan, of course, did not contemplate use of public school buildings and school time for teaching these courses, but in a few cases this has been done on motion of the local school board.[145] The examination, because of the provision for credit, had to be given in the high school building or under some arrangement, approved by the principal.[146] By the end of 1921, 572 pupils in 43 classes had taken the prescribed examinations for credit, and the *Virginia Journal of Education* urged school and church officials to co-operate "that this fundamental type of instruction may be extended in Virginia."[147]

---

[143] *Ibid.*, VII, No. 2, 7.
[144] *From correspondence.*
[145] *Ibid.*
[146] *U. of Va. Rec., Ext. Ser.*, Nov., 1919, V, No. 2, 40–42.
[147] *Va. Jour. Educ.*, Nov., 1921, XV, 107–08.

A bulletin of the State Board of Education, in 1919, in discussing the ''Reorganization of Secondary Education,'' declared, apparently in justification of the attempt to extend the program of studies to include Bible study and 18 units of work, that:

> . . . The Church, as a whole, figures less effectively in the education of the child than it did in former years. Parents, under the high pressure of our exacting economic life, have ceased to equip their children with many of the values of life that they received when our economic and social life centered in the home.[148]

The general attitude of the teachers of the state to this work may be gathered from the following resolution passed in November, 1921:

> WHEREAS, We believe that character formation is a fundamental objective of public education, and that additional opportunities should be provided in connection with our public schools for affording our pupils religious education, free from sectarian objections:
>
> *Be It Resolved*, That we commend to teachers the wider use of the program of Bible study as outlined by the State Board of Education.[149]

It should be noted in connection with the introduction of the courses in Bible study that the Assembly had taken no part. This was not because it did not feel free to legislate on the curriculum, for it did, in February, 1922, amending the code as to the subjects to be taught in free schools.[150] In doing this, however, it made no reference to Biblical instruction, perhaps because it was legislating in behalf of the elementary schools.[151]

The reaction of a teacher, who had given the Bible study course, was published in the *Virginia Journal of Education*, in March, 1923. W. W. Arrowood, writing on his experience in Tazewell High School, felt that a knowledge of the Bible should be stressed: 1. for an understanding of English literature; and 2. for the safety of the Nation through its influence on the morality of the young. His experience in teaching high school pupils had convinced him that the Bible was not being properly taught to young people, either in the home, or in the Sunday School.

---

[148] *Bull. State B'd Educ.*, Sept., 1919, II, No. 2, 5, 7.
[149] *Va. Jour. Educ.*, Jan., 1922, XV, 192.
[150] See p. 484.
[151] *Acts of Assembly*, Feb. 25, 1922, 69.

He felt that the study ought to be made compulsory, instead of optional, in every high school.[152]

In October, 1923, the *Journal* again reminded its readers of the Bible study courses, stating: "It should be encouraged and fostered with the greatest care.[153] A bulletin of the State Board announced at the same time that more than 500 students had pursued the various Bible courses for high school credit in 1922–23; a number almost as large as the total number applying for examination during the previous six years. The State Board had also authorized the original commission to make a careful study looking to the further improvement, if possible, of the courses and methods of instruction.[154]

The following year, it was reported that during the eight years in which the courses had been offered, 2,350 students had taken the course for credit. In the year 1923–24, 933 students had taken the examination. Since 1917, 128 classes had taken the course; in some counties over 100 students were taking the course in their high schools.[155] In 1924–25, the enrollment was 799 students in 32 high schools.[156] It is interesting to note, however, that all schools were not using the official state syllabus.[157] Apparently, the State Board was not restricting credit to the users of the official syllabus, but giving credit upon the basis of ability to answer the examination questions.

This development, taken together with the tendency to utilize school buildings and school time for this instruction, is most interesting as indicating the difficulty of legislating on this subject. In this connection, it may be said that Dr. Horne, in his article on "Moral and Religious Instruction in the Public Schools,"[158] classed the state course in Bible study as religious instruction, but he assumed it to be given under religious auspices and outside of the regular public school activities, and that its object was for the sake of devotion and character formation, an object

---

152 *Va. Jour. Educ.*, Mar., 1923, XVI, 294.
153 *Ibid.*, Oct., 1923, XVII, 71.
154 *Bull. State B'd Educ.*, Oct., 1923, VI, No. 2, 18.
155 *Va. Jour. Educ.*, Sept., 1924, XVIII, 16 *ff.*
156 The figures as stated were given in an official interview; *Bull. State B'd Educ.*, July, 1925, 41, is incorrect, as it represents an incomplete list.
157 *Ibid.*
158 See p. 489.

which he cautioned was inharmonious with the emphasis on winning scholastic credit.[159]

It is not surprising to find that this optional scheme with regard to Bible study should be regarded as inadequate to the situation. In November, 1925, Mr. H. Augustus Miller, head of the English department, Petersburg High School, reviewed in the *Virginia Journal of Education* the results of a test in the Bible given 70 seniors in the Petersburg High School by the Virginia Sunday School Association.[160]   He found the reasons for ''the appalling ignorance of the most vital Book in the world'' thus revealed to lie in the fact: 1. the Sunday School is the most glaring failure in the educational system; and 2, ''the great bugaboo of 'the union of church and state' has made it impossible for the public school to teach the Bible.''[161]   The failure of the Sunday School he attributed: 1. to the fact that only one-half of the one hour is given over to the real business of teaching the Bible; and 2. that the situation was not conducive to real discipline. The only solution was to ''forget the 'church-state' terror and give the teaching of the Bible into the hands of the public schools.''   There, let the Bible be taught from literary and ethical standpoints, from which it could be objectionable to no sect or faith; and let the Sunday School's real purpose be fulfilled in teaching denominational doctrine.[162]

While the optional feature of the Bible study course was thus being criticized as inadequate to meet the needs of the situation, and the sponsors of the scheme, on the other hand, were congratulating themselves on the consistent progress in interest in the courses, as evinced by enrollment, certain tendencies were appearing in the actual conduct of the courses revealing the great difficulty in having the work function on the basis originally outlined.   Complete elimination of the use of state funds as represented by printing of materials, use of public school buildings, time and work of public school officials, was found hardly possible.   As far as official recognition by the Assembly was concerned, these courses did not exist.   Attempt to secure such

---

159 *Va. Jour. Educ.*, Mar., 1924, XVII, 270.
160 *Ibid.*, Nov., 1925, XIX, 94 *ff*.
161 *Ibid.*, 96.
162 *Ibid.*

recognition would have raised in an extreme form the question of separation of church and state.[163]

That the introduction of these courses had been possible at all was due to the co-operation of representatives of the Roman Catholic and the Jewish faiths. What was the significance of this co-operation? Is it to be assumed that the spokesmen for these groups were ready to find in the introduction of these courses a solution of the problem of religious instruction as it affected their adherents? Hardly. Rather, judging from pronouncements by the leaders of both groups as to their real position in the matter of religious instruction in education, this movement for co-operation is to be looked upon as an expression of good-will upon the part of minorities. As long ago as 1889, Cardinal Gibbons, of Baltimore, under whose jurisdiction Catholic Virginia was, had made clear that Catholicism saw in denominational schools the only practicable solution for the proper combination of religious and secular education.[164]

In 1925, after a careful survey under its auspices of the week-day religious education movement, The United Synagogue of America, the conservative wing of the Jewish faith adopted the following resolutions:

RESOLVED, that the United Synagogue of America take this opportunity to reaffirm the Jewish principle that no education is complete without religious education, and that it is the duty of all parents to provide their children with spiritual as well as secular training. We stand also within the American tradition which maintains the complete separation of Church and State as a means of safeguarding the liberty of its citizens and according to which the secular training of the child and his preparation for citizenship is within the province of the public school system, whereas religious training remains the task of the parent and the church with which he is affiliated.

RESOLVED, That in accordance with the American tradition we reaffirm that the curriculum of the public schools shall in no wise be made to include the element of religious education.

---

[163] *Cf.* the raising of this issue in connection with the Bible Bill, p. 517.

[164] *N. E. A. Proc's*, 1889, XXVIII, 113; for the Catholic position on church and state, *cf.* Encyclical Letter, Nov. 1, 1885, by Pope Leo XIII, in Ryan, J. A. and Millar, M. F. X.: *The State and The Church*, I *ff.;* also *Cath. Educ. Assoc. Bull.*, Nov., 1916, 53, 58; *Amer. Cath. Quart. Rev.*, Jan., 1884, 105–26; Marshall, C. C.: *The Roman Catholic Church*.

That in the conduct of the public schools the religious conviction and observances of the pupils shall in no way be interfered with or denied.

That the public school day shall be so arranged as to leave time for week-day religious instruction after school hours in places other than the public schools, and without any public school supervision whatsoever.

We realize that such an attitude places upon all Jews the added obligation of increasing the concerted effort to supply the needed spiritual training in every Jewish child.[165]

It is clear from the position here taken that while representatives of Virginia Jews may have co-operated in the introduction of the Bible study courses that a large representative Jewish opinion does not find in these courses either an ideal or an adequate solution of its problem.[166]

Dr. Ruffner's Policy Vindicated In The Experience With The Bible Reading Bill

Virginians interested in introducing religious education into schools, having introduced a chair of the Bible into the state university, and courses in the study of the Bible into the high school curriculum, began to devise means of obtaining a definite legal sanction for the introduction of religious education into elementary public schools.

In August, 1922, the *Virginia Teacher* published a lengthy article on "A Workable Plan For Religious Education In Our Schools," by Dr. Henry A. Converse, of the faculty of the State Normal School at Harrisonburg. Starting with the premise that religious instruction received by children is inadequate, that the Sunday School is failing, the writer declared that religious instruction must be had somewhere. The introduction of religious instruction into the public schools had seemed impossible, partly because of the idea of religious liberty, and partly because of denominational jealousy, but more so because of Protestant narrow-mindedness which would not admit that the religious instruction of the Catholic and of the Hebrew is better than none at all. The

---

[165] *From correspondence; cf.* Cohen: *An Inquiry Into The Tendencies Of The Weekday Religious Education Movement In Its Relations To The Public Schools.*

[166] The Jewish representative on the Commission on Bible courses was a member of Dr. Calisch's synagogue, see p. 462; *Bull. State B'd Educ.,* June, 1921, IV, No. 1, 3.

writer then explained that when the Inter-Church World Movement took form in 1919, the time was thought propitious for introducing religious instruction into the public schools of Virginia. The "Committee on Cooperation with the Inter-Church World Movement" introduced the following resolution as part of its report:

Resolved, that a committee of five be appointed to consider the advisability of asking the I. C. W. M. to consider with us a means of introducing religious instruction into the public schools—such instruction to be given to their adherents by the various religious bodies, or by persons authorized by the authorities thereof, one hour each week during regular school hours, the State Board of Education concurring.[167]

With the disintegration of the Inter-Church World Movement, nothing was done by the Committee, but discussion had brought out the fact that the State Board of Education had already provided a plan by which religious instruction might be given in the high schools.[168] At the State Sunday School Convention in Harrisonburg, in 1920, a resolution in harmony with that of the "Committee on Co-operating with the Inter-Church World Movement" was adopted. The writer then described a number of plans in operation throughout the country, based on the principle that pupils were to be dismissed at certain times to attend various churches for religious instruction.[169] Some such plan would work out well in towns and cities, but in the country it would probably be more advisable for the clergy of the various churches to go to the school one day a week to give the desired instruction.[170] The co-operation of the state, in the opinion of Dr. Converse, seemed very likely in view of the fact that Governor Davis at the Rural Life Conference, in May, 1921, had called on the clergy and school officials to co-operate in the teaching of ethics and morality. If the sentiment of the people in the state were sufficiently strong in favor of the plan, any legal difficulties could be removed. While the reports of the courses in Bible

---

[167] *Va. Teacher*, Aug., 1922, III, 206.
[168] *Ibid.*
[169] *Cf.* Lotz, P. H.: *Current Week-Day Religious Education*, 23; Lotz uses the term week-day religious schools without any distinction as to place where this instruction is given, or to the teacher giving it.
[170] *Va. Teacher*, Aug., 1922, III, 209.

study in high schools had indicated they were highly successful—
the town of Broadway, in Rockingham County, for example, reporting that a number of pupils who had taken the course had
connected themselves with the church of their choice—this course
could not be regarded as sufficient to satisfy the needs of any
community,

> . . . because if religious education is put off until our boys and girls enter
> the high school, we do not reach more than ten per cent of our children, as
> they leave school before they reach the high school.   Hence, if we wish to
> reach all our children we must begin in the lower grades.[171]

As a result of the cumulative efforts of the propaganda to
strengthen the religious elements in community and school life,
voiced in journals and by various organizations, the Extension
Division of the University contributing its part,[172] a serious effort
was now made to introduce a bill requiring the reading of the
Bible in the public free schools of the state.   In view of the fact
that opinion and evidence concurred in indicating that reading
of the Bible, along with prayer, and singing of hymns was the
common practise in either daily morning opening exercises of
schools, or at such times as assemblies were held, three or four
times a week in some schools, the introduction of a bill of this
kind would seem gratuitous.   There was, however, a group in the
state which felt that a legal enactment of this kind was desirable
to make certain that no school omitted the reading of the Bible;
and, at the same time, that the practise should have the prestige
of a legal sanction.   A bill to require the reading was consequently introduced in the Assembly, in February, 1924;[173] it
passed the House on March 3, with a vote of 83 to 5.[174]   The bill
was referred to the Senate, the next day,[175] but was defeated,[176]
one of its strongest opponents being Rev. George W. McDaniel,
pastor of the First Baptist Church of Richmond.[177]

---

[171] *Ibid.*
[172] See p. 621.
[173] *Jour., H. Del.*, Feb. 16, 1924, 318.
[174] *Ibid.*, Mar. 3, 1924, 607.
[175] *Ibid.*, Mar. 4, 1924, 611–12.
[176] *Ibid.*, Mar. 8, 1924, 612 *ff.*
[177] *Richmond News Leader*, Feb. 1, 1926, "Sincere, But Wrong."

The attitude of the Baptists on this question may be gleaned from the following resolution passed in July, 1925, by a meeting of the Dover Baptist Association:

Whereas, there is an effort being made to induce the next legislature of Virginia to pass an act requiring the COMPULSORY reading of the Bible in every public school; and

Whereas, the Bible is primarily a book of religion and as such its use should be left to the individual conscience free from legislative compulsion, and the duty of teaching it is a function of the home and the churches and not of the State; be it

Resolved (1), That the Dover Association on behalf of the twenty-six thousand members of its churches reaffirms the historic opposition of Virginia Baptists to any meddling by the State in matters concerning religion, and respectfully protests to the General Assembly against the passage of any such law on the grounds that it would be an improper interference by the State in the realms of religion, and a violation of the principles of religious liberty, and the complete separation of the spheres of church and State as embodied in the constitution of the Commonwealth.

(2) That a copy of these resolutions be transmitted by the Executive Committee of the General Assembly at its next session; and that the clerk send a copy to the moderators of the other Baptist district associations in Virginia with the request that they cooperate with us by the passage of similar resolutions.[178]

The position here taken against the passage of any such law as an infringement of religious liberty is particularly interesting, in view of the fact that the sanction of the State Board of Education for the study of Bible courses by high school students is as binding in law, until the Assembly chooses to amend, revise, or repeal it, as any act of the Assembly. From the Baptist position, the action of the State Board in sanctioning Bible study in high schools was, of course, partially redeemed by its optional feature.

The forces behind the movement for the introduction of compulsory Bible reading into the public schools would not suffer defeat, however, and prepared to introduce a similar bill to the Assembly in 1925–26. Before the bill actually came up for discussion, the press began to be deluged with letters on the subject. Writing to the *Richmond News Leader,* "Justice And Fair Play" declared that Protestant Christianity seemed to have im-

---

[178] *Min. 142nd Annual Session, Dover Baptist Assoc.,* 31.

proved "but very little on the past antics of Catholic Christianity."[179] It was the great principles of religious liberty which were responsible for 99 per cent of the wonderful progress America had made in the past century. The Baptist Convention in protesting against the attempt to introduce a further source of friction by the measure for Bible reading was to be commended. Apparently the "Klu Klux Klan, the Fraternal Order of Americans, and other self-styled patriotic orders" back of the measure, after objecting to Catholic parochial schools were forgetting fair play.[180]

Letters favoring the measure were not wanting, one writer quoting with satisfaction, as defining his position, an article in the *Christian Herald* to the effect that "the teaching of behavior, of reverence to God and right treatment of one's fellowmen ought to have place in the schoolroom of every State, and the time is coming when it will have a place there." This article had further declared that the Bible must be used as a text-book of morals in schools, as the essential element in character training. It referred with satisfaction to the decision of the Supreme Court of Kansas favorable to the reading of the Bible in that state.[181]

Another writer argued that there was a wide difference between reading the Bible, and being compelled to adhere to some religious belief. If the histories of Buddhism and Mohammedanism and the theory of evolution may be taught in schools, why may not the Bible be read? Aliens applying for citizenship must swear on the Bible to abide by the Constitution, and, in doing so, obligate their descendants. It is necessary to stand up for and proclaim "the basis of our moral and civic laws—the Bible."[182]

A writer opposed to the bill declared if public school teachers be compelled to read the Bible daily, why should not the State extend its beneficence by compelling every citizen of the state to do likewise, and to worship God publicly once a week at least?

179 *Richmond News Leader,* Nov. 30, 1925.
180 *Ibid.*
181 Lee G. Crutchfied, in *Richmond Times Dispatch,* Feb. 21, 1926; *cf.* also H. C. Baur, *Ibid.,* Feb. 22, 1926.
182 D. W. Weaver, *Ibid.,* Feb. 19, 1926.

Why should not the state take the next logical step and compel all teachers and pupils to be members of some Christian church or even name the church which they must join, and finally, why not compel the support of that church by taxation? The pending bill was "the first logical step to a State church." A special enactment is not necessary for reading the Bible in public schools; on the voluntary principle every school teacher may open school with the reading of the Bible. A law that would destroy this principle would defeat the very purpose of Bible reading, it would secure the letter, but destroy the spirit of Bible reading.[183]

Dr. McDaniel, who had opposed the Bible Bill in 1924, preached a sermon on January 31, 1926, under the title "Sincere, But Wrong" in which he declared that religion did not need the prop of the state, that it was a voluntary act, or it was not religion. Those who thought to advance the cause of religion by compulsory Bible reading were mistaken in their method.[184]

Baptist opposition to the bill soon found expression in specific action designed to defeat it. As in the days before the Revolutionary War, when Baptists fought for the principles of religious liberty and separation of church and state, so now they resorted to the use of the memorial. The bill introduced into the Assembly on February 5, had provided:

Be it enacted by the General Assembly of Virginia that at least five verses of the King James version of the Holy Bible shall be read, or caused to be read, without sectarian comment, at the opening of every public school on every school day by each teacher in charge. This section shall be construed to mean that the Bible shall be read to all students of all classes in the public school and that wherever there is a general assembly of school classes at the opening of such school day then such reading of the Bible shall be read by the principal or teacher in charge of such assembly.[185]

It differed from the 1924 measure in omitting provision for excuse from the class-room during the reading upon written request of parents; it also omitted the provision of that bill which limited it to reading and prohibited study.[186]

---

[183] Amos Clary, *Ibid.*, Feb. 14, 1926.
[184] *Richmond News Leader*, Feb. 1, 1926.
[185] *Richmond Times-Dispatch*, Feb. 7, 1926.
[186] *Richmond News Leader*, Feb. 6, 1926; *cf.* House Bill No. 353, 1924.

On the day after its introduction, the committee appointed by the Baptist General Association of Virginia sent a memorial in opposition to the Legislature. This memorial had been drawn up after fourteen district associations had gone on record as unanimously opposed to compulsory Bible reading and after the Baptist General Association had at a meeting on November 12, 1925, listened to an address on ''Soul Liberty Some Of Its Implications'' by Dr. R. H. Pitt, editor of the *Religious Herald.*[187] The committee drawing up the memorial consisted of seven Richmond Baptists and twenty-nine others from the state at large; they represented 1,175 churches with a total membership of 219,166 citizens.[188] The memorial presented its protest on the basis of the following eight objections: 1. The Bible properly read is an act of worship which cannot rightfully be enforced by law; 2. Compulsion to read a single version of the Bible, not regarded as the true Bible by others, is an invasion of the rights of conscience, an indefeasible natural right of man, which even the majority cannot take away; 3. To permit a pupil to withdraw from the exercise is unjust in that it will subject the pupil to embarrassment; 4. It is beneath the dignity of true religion to ask or receive any peculiar recognition from the law; 5. The scriptures cannot be separated from their sacred religious character; to advance their acceptance through pressure of law is an unworthy attempt to shift upon the state a duty divinely commissioned to the church; 6. Religious training should be given in the home and in the church; while religious instruction should be given along with secular training, it does not follow that it must be given by the same person and in the same place; 7. Baptists, as knowing historically what religious discrimination

---

[187] Pitt, R. H.: *Soul Liberty; Richmond Times-Dispatch*, Feb. 7, 1926; *Richmond News Leader*, Feb. 6, 1926; *cf.* Robertson, W. J.: *Changing South*, 145, who refers to the Virginia Baptist attitude as ''Probably one of the strangest things that has happened in the South in recent years, . . .''—while strange, perhaps from the point of view of the general southern attitude, the Baptist attitude, is, of course, in consonance with their historical position; *cf. N. E. A. Proc's*, 1900, XXXIX, 89.

[188] *Richmond News Leader*, Feb. 6, 1926; Pollard, J. G.: *Memorial Against Compulsory Reading of the Bible;* the total population of Virginia in 1920 was 2,309,187, *U. S. Bur. Census*, 1920, *Abstract*, 1923, 18; the Baptists were about 10 per cent; the memorial was drawn up by John Garland Pollard, *cf.* the *Richmond News Leader*, Feb. 23, 1926.

means, feel compelled in assisting to protect the rights of others; and 8. The issue is of tremendous import, not perhaps in itself, but because it is a violation of principle, and one violation leads to another until the principle itself is in danger, so that Bible reading will lead to Bible teaching until it may be expected that public school funds will be appropriated to Catholic schools so as to give them an equal opportunity to teach their Bible at public expense. The memorial, therefore, appealed to the legislature

. . . to adhere to the doctrine, peculiarly bound up with the history of the Commonwealth, which completely separates church and State, which refuses to exercise force in the realm of religion, and which places all religions on a plane of absolute equality before the law.[189]

In elaborating the second point, regarding the material differences in the various versions of the Bible and the attitude which regarded the version of a differing group as a sectarian book, the memorial pointed out the fact that the selection of the text-book of any sect to be read in schools was conferring a peculiar advantage upon that sect prohibited by the constitution. It called attention also to the fact that it was a mistaken idea that the Protestant religion or even Christianity had any peculiar rights in Virginia, and quoted the decision of the Supreme Court of Appeals to the effect that the *Declaration of Rights* and the act for securing religious freedom had placed the Christian religion "where it stood in the days of its purity, before its alliance with the civil magistrate."[190]

The *Richmond Times-Dispatch* on February 7, 1926, in an editorial, "No Church and State," declared that the bill for com-

---

[189] *Ibid.*, Feb. 6, 1926; Pollard: *Memorial Against Compulsory Reading of the Bible*, 7; *Richmond Times-Dispatch*, Feb. 7, 1926; in connection with the prescription of a single version of the Bible, it must be remembered that the Scofield Bible is the preferred version of many southern Baptist fundamentalists.

[190] Pollard: *Memorial Against Compulsory Reading of the Bible*, 4; referring to Perry's Case, Grattan: *Reports*, III, 641; there has been some divergence of judicial opinion in the U. S., as to whether Christianity is a part of the law. The highest courts of Pennsylvania and New York, the U. S. Supreme Court have supported the principle that Christianity is a part of the common law; but the decision of the highest court of Ohio in the case of the Board of Education V. Minor, and the treaties of the U. S. Senate with Tripoli (1796 and 1805) are cited as opinion indicating that Christianity is not a part of the common law, see, Levinthal, L. E., in *Jewish Exponent*, Aug. 5, 1927.

pulsory reading of the Bible should "be defeated by an avalanche of votes cast by men sitting as representatives of the people of Virginia, sitting in the very building designed as the State Capitol by Thomas Jefferson, author of the statute for religious freedom in Virginia." It declared the bill to strike at the very root of religious freedom and to be in violation of section 58 of the Constitution which forbids compulsion in attendance upon or support of religious worship, and the conferring of peculiar privileges or advantages on any sect or denomination. Further, the bill would imperil the long-held determination of Virginia to keep forever separate church and state. Religious freedom would be destroyed in Virginia, if the state dared to compel the reading of the Bible in the public schools. It could not believe that the General Assembly would be "induced to reject, crush and throw away one of the most fundamental pillars of American liberty."[191]

The Baptist position on this issue did not go unchallenged in the correspondence to the press. One writer, referring to Dr. McDaniel's sermon, while conceding that religion does not need the support of the state, very emphatically submitted that the state needed the support of religion in order to stand, and that there was no place where the teaching of religion would be so effective as in the public schools. The writer believed that the present standard of morals, as well as many phases of depravity, deplored by ministers and good citizens, to be largely caused by lack of knowledge of the basic principles of unselfish and right living as taught in the Bible. While no attempt should be made to force every one to be religious, yet it should be possible to point the way; and if this is harmful, then perhaps the Bible should be removed from courts of justice, legislature, and all other public activities.[192]

An article on the "Bible Reading Bill" by George Ainslie, who regularly reviewed the legislation pending in the Assembly for the *Richmond News Leader*, declared that the opposition to the bill rested not so much on the Bible named, or to its reading, as

---

[191] *Richmond Times-Dispatch*, Feb. 7, 1926.
[192] *Ibid.*, Chas. P. Taylor.

to its compulsory feature.[193] He pointed out that school authorities in high position stated that as a matter of fact the Bible was read every day in practically every public school in the state. It was feared that should a Bible-reading bill be declared to be in conflict with the state constitution, the question would at once arise whether the school authorities had the right to permit it to be read as was now the case.[194]

So great was the interest aroused by the Bill, that its author, Senator John M. Parsons, Grayson County, declared that he had never received so many letters on any bill as on this—that they came in large numbers from secret and patriotic orders and ministers personally endorsing the bill.[195]

On the 23rd of February, the *News Leader* printed an editorial under the caption "Withdraw the Bible Bill." It declared that since the measure would not pass, "why should not tolerance prevail and Virginia be saved from a controversy that will divide Christian people and arouse no end of bitter feeling—all to no purpose?" The reasons for not passing the bill had been set forth with "demolishing logic" in the Baptist memorial which breathed "the spirit in which the Virginia statute for religious liberty was enacted." That statute representing the principle of "soul liberty" as distinguished from political liberty was America's greatest single contribution to the world. The proposed bill would limit soul liberty. The editorial declared that in 90 per cent. of the schools of the state, the day was begun with religious exercises, and since there was no compulsion or formality, those not of the Protestant Christian denominations often shared in them, or did not protest. Prescription would involve freedom of conscience, "and thousands of Protestant people, along with all Catholics and Jews and rationalists, would feel that the state was dictating to them in a sphere where resistance was a duty."[196]

On February 25, the *Times-Dispatch* in an editorial entitled "Dangerous Tendencies" referred to the address of the Right

[193] *Cf.* Letter of Rev. H. H. Street, "Opposes Compulsion," *Ibid.*, Feb. 25, 1926.
[194] *Richmond News Leader*, Feb. 10, 1926.
[195] *Richmond Times-Dispatch*, Feb. 13, 1926.
[196] *Richmond News Leader*, Feb. 23, 1926.

Reverend James E. Freeman, Bishop of Washington, Protestant Episcopal Church, before the Department of Superintendence of the National Education Association,[197] and took exception to his suggestion that religion as well as morals be inculcated as part of the public school curriculum. It felt that the Bishop should have stopped with his emphasis on moral training. It declared:

> . . . Even the dignity of his position and the brilliance of his mind are insufficient to convince this nation that it should abandon its constitutional separation of church and State, cast overboard the teachings of Thomas Jefferson and embark on the dangerous experiment of a church and State united in the schools. The inculcation of morals in the schools is sound; the teaching of religion in the schools would be an error so grave that it might overthrow the public school system and perhaps imperil the nation itself.[198]

In the editorial opinion, Virginia, the home of Thomas Jefferson, could not be otherwise than "adamant" against the Bishop's suggestion.

The bill for compulsory Bible reading came up for a hearing in the Senate Committee on Public Institutions and Education, on February 25. Before a crowded audience in the Senate chamber, including representatives of various fraternal organizations sponsoring the bill, Dr. George E. Booker, formerly pastor of Methodist Monument Church, and then presiding elder of the district, was the principal speaker in favor of the bill.[199] Dr. McDaniel appeared in opposition, as representative of the Committee of the Baptist General Association of Virginia. The bill was defeated, 10 to 4, in committee, and thus ended its career in the legislature.[200]

As far as can be determined, the forces behind the Bible Bill were a group in the Methodist Church, and representatives of fraternal and patriotic orders.[201] Virginius Dabney writing in the *American Mercury*, November, 1926, stated:

---

[197] *N. E. A. Proc's*, 1926, LXIV, 667 *ff.*

[198] *Richmond Times-Dispatch*, Feb. 25, 1926.

[199] *Ibid.*, Feb. 26, 1926; other speakers in favor were Dr. J. Y. Downman, rector of All Saints Episcopal Church, who spoke at the request of a member of The Patriotic Sons of America, and Mrs. Emma Gregory Dyson, who claimed to represent the true Baptist sentiment.

[200] *Ibid.; Richmond News Leader*, Feb. 26, 1926.

[201] *Richmond Times-Dispatch*, Feb. 26, 1926.

. . . The principal advocates of the Bible Bill were the Methodists and the
self-styled Patriotic Welfare Committee, which last was also behind the
Constitution and Anti-Evolution Bills. This body of 100 per cent Americans
is composed of representatives of the Ku Klux Klan, Daughters of America,
Patriotic Order of Sons of America, Junior Order of United American
Mechanics, Order of Fraternal Americans, and Sons and Daughters of Liberty. It has failed in everything it has undertaken.[202]

The Methodist position in this matter may be regarded as the
outcome of the position taken by the Virginia Conference of the
Methodist Episcopal Church, South, at their annual conference
in 1916, at which they resolved to give greater attention to the
spiritual education of youth, not only through organizations, particularly the Sunday School, but to endeavor also "to influence
all institutions of learning to establish a distinct department of
spiritual education . . . which shall have for its great aim the
systematic development and training of the spiritual nature.
. . ."[203] In 1922, the Virginia Conference memorialized the
General Conference to create a commission for investigating and
recommending such reforms in the existing educational system
as would give to "the spiritual nature of man a place of as much
prominence at least as the intellectual," and which "will provide
that the education of the spiritual nature shall begin at the same
time as that of the intellectual, and shall continue co-ordinate to
the end of the course of education."[204] It was in accordance
with this resolution that the introduction of compulsory Bible
reading was regarded as an entering wedge in the program.

The defeat of the bill was heralded with satisfaction by the
press. The *News Leader* referring to the way the matter had
been handled declared that "The Virginia way has always been
the way of tolerance and of understanding. Any departure from
it is severance of the ties that link the present-day commonwealth
with the most splendid period of her past."[205]

The *Times-Dispatch*, in an editorial, gave great credit to the
Baptist Church, and declared that if the bill had become law,

[202] *Amer. Mercury*, Nov., 1926, IX, 354.
[203] Wingfield: *Hist. Caroline Co., Va.*, 145.
[204] *Ibid.*, 146.
[205] *Richmond News Leader*, Feb. 26, 1926.

"Virginia would have been shamed forever," and one of Thomas Jefferson's greatest achievements, "religious freedom would have become a hissing and a byword in this State." It stated that while there had been sincere religionists and publicists in support of the bill, the arguments before the committee had been of the type employed in the Dayton case; members of the Legislature had been asked in horrified tones whether they did not believe in the authority and inspiration of the Bible. Most of the newspapers in Virginia had opposed the bill, and many letters from able and informed persons, in opposition, had been printed; and while Governor Byrd was regarded as being opposed to the bill, yet the greatest single factor in its defeat was the Baptist church. And, it declared, in that church particular credit had to be given to Dr. R. H. Pitt and Dr. G. W. McDaniel. Virginia had "been saved from a step toward co-ordination of church and state."[206]

The position of the *Times-Dispatch* did not go unchallenged. A lengthy letter by one of its correspondents reviewed the situation from the point of view of the advocates of Bible reading. It stated that all educators realize that the goal of right education is character, and that "the culmination of life is not in the intellectual, but in the moral and spiritual." Reading the Bible would add as nothing else will to the moral tone of schools. The writer then quoted Woodrow Wilson, President Grant, Huxley, and Horace Greeley, and other prominent people, to show their emphasis upon the importance of the Bible for the progress of civilization, and Matthew Arnold as strongly urging the reading of the Bible in the public schools of Great Britain. As for the suggestion that it is un-American to read the Bible in the public school because of the Constitutional provision for separation of church and state, he declared no true American would advocate a union of church and state, and quoted Professor Weigle of Yale to the effect that "The principle of the separation of church and state must not be so construed as to render the state a fosterer of non-religious teaching or atheism."[207] This, the writer

---

[206] *Richmond Times-Dispatch*, Feb. 27, 1926.
[207] Prof. L. A. Weigle, since 1924, Sterling Professor of religious education, Yale University.

felt, was what was happening in America. As for the fact that there were three principal versions of the Bible, the writer felt that no difficulty was presented; it seemed to him "that one can easily determine what Bible ought to be used in Protestant Christian America." The argument that the reading of the Bible could not be done without sectarian bias, he regarded as puerile. If teachers cared to, they could exert a sectarian influence in the interpretation of historic and scientific facts. If questions concerning the Koran, the sacred stories of India and China, the religions of Greece, Rome, and ancient Israel are permitted in class-rooms, why not the reading of the Bible? It was "merely the propaganda of Satan, the arch-fiend of humanity, who, under the guise of religious tolerance, suggests that we should not teach the Word of God in our schools for fear of offending some over-sensitive fanatic or under-religious bigot." As children spend only about forty days in the Sunday School, and about one hundred and sixty in the public schools, it was the public schools that furnished the best opportunity for Biblical instruction. Any form of religious organization opposed to receiving aid from the state in the instruction of children was not worthy the name of church.[208]

The association of certain fraternal and patriotic orders with the movement to bring the Bible into the schools was resented by a writer, signing himself "Ex-Dane," who wished to know whether the action of one of these organizations in presenting a Bible and national and state flags to a certain school, in which they had pointed out that 75 per cent of the school children involved were of foreign birth, was intended "to insinuate that persons of foreign (presumably European) birth do not possess Christian religion, and that it is necessary to acquaint them with the fundamentals of Christianity as well as with our principles of government?" As the Bible is not and can never be part of the equipment of public schools, why should this Order go into public schools with Bibles which are perhaps not entirely acceptable to the creed of these "foreign-born" children?[209]

---

[208] E. Peabody Dahl, *Richmond Times-Dispatch*, Feb. 28, 1926.
[209] *Richmond News Leader,* May 14, 1926.

Whether the action of the Legislature in ruling out the compulsory reading of the Bible has closed the question seems doubtful. As late as December, 1927, Dr. McDaniel wrote an article entitled "The Bible In Its Place" for *Plain Talk*. He reiterated his opinion that the desire for compulsory Bible reading was well-meaning, but misconceived. A cherished principle made it necessary to part company with those desiring compulsory reading. Separation of church and state was the distinctive contribution of the United States to civilization. This principle meant that the state had no religious function; but that is not to disparage religion. The foundation of the state is force, that of religion is choice. "Religion and government are both strengthened when they are recognized as two distinct spheres." It is because the Bible is a religious book that the adherents of compulsory Bible reading wish it read. Dr. McDaniel then declared that "Every time Christianity has united with the State, corruption has set in on both sides. Christianity prospers most when freest." Christian dominance in Virginia is really the outgrowth of Jefferson's statute for establishing religious freedom; it is therefore necessary for citizens to be all the more mindful of the free principles under which they have grown to greatness, and to be very regardful of the rights of the minority.

Aside from the fundamental principles of freedom of conscience and the separation of church and state, compulsory Bible reading was, in Dr. McDaniel's opinion, open to the objection that it violates the Golden Rule; it violates that equality which ought to be the basis of every law. The attempts of various Bible bills to remain within constitutional guarantees by exempting from its operation those making written requests violates the principle on which general statute laws are enacted and winds up in governmental folly. Compulsory Bible reading, also, according to Dr. McDaniel, violates the right of the teacher who cannot conscientiously comply with the law; it may place the reading in the hands of those who may not believe in the Bible; it mars the religious harmony existing among various sects; it wrongs children by using the principle of compulsion; it wrongs those excused by throwing upon them the reproach and insult of the majority. Finally, it transfers to or divides with the

State, responsibility belonging properly to the home and church. While the churches should go everywhere with their message of salvation and service, it should do so without the aid of the state. It did not follow that because education, which once belonged exclusively to the church, was now under the state, that the state ought to compel Bible reading. Education, as dealing primarily with the mind, was the proper function of the state; the Bible dealt "with conscience, and that is inviolable."[210]

An interesting feature of the discussion in connection with the attempt to obtain a legal sanction for Bible reading was the practically complete silence respecting the Bible study courses in the high school. Whether because these courses were operating merely at the sanction of the State Board of Education, and hence not regarded as infringing upon the separation of church and state in the same way as enactment by the Legislature; or whether because of their optional character as distinguished from the compulsory nature of the Bible reading bill; or whether because an attempt to inject the fact of these courses into the discussion was felt likely to endanger their continuance, reference to these courses was discreetly omitted in discussion.

The most interesting reflection that comes from the defeat of the Bible reading bill is the evident correctness of the Ruffner viewpoint on the subject of religious instruction in education, as it affects Virginia, in finding in a policy of co-operation without alliance the true Virginia sentiment on this issue—the limits of action possible under a constitutional separation of church and state. Experience has demonstrated that Virginian historical pride in separation of church and state may yield a sanction for co-operation, but not for legal alliance.

Reaction To Anti-Evolution Proposal

In view of the great publicity given to the question of teaching evolution in the public schools, as the result of the Scopes trial at Dayton, Tennessee, in 1925, it is not surprising that a movement was started to bar the teaching of evolution in the schools of Virginia.

---

[210] *Plain Talk,* Dec., 1927, 95 *ff.*

The movement was formally launched by the organization of a committee known as the Patriotic Welfare Committee, and it was said those in the movement were

. . . members of the Ku Klux Klan, women of the Ku Klux Klan, junior order of United American Mechanics, Sons and Daughters of Liberty, Patriotic Order Sons of America, Patriotic Order of Americans, Daughters of America, and the Order of Fraternal Americans.[211]

The question, however, did not receive the attention and public interest which the compulsory Bible reading bill had, the reaction to the Dayton trial being most unfavorable. It was said that a Methodist clergyman was to have been responsible for sponsoring a bill in the Assembly outlawing the doctrine of evolution; but, he never presented it, as the opinion was that it would certainly be defeated.[212] A former Baptist preacher of a Richmond church, but then of Florida, who had given notice, in the summer of 1925, that he would introduce an anti-evolution resolution in the 1926 Southern Baptist Convention, wrote to the *Religious Herald*, in January, 1926, that he would no longer sponsor such a resolution.[213] After trying "to get the will of God about it," and thinking through the great Baptist denominational problem, he had arrived at a very clear opinion, that the convention should lose no more time debating the evolution question, but that it should allow nothing to sidetrack Baptists from the great missionary spirit that had called them into being and had held them together.[214]

In August, 1925, Joseph Roy Geiger, Professor of Philosophy and Psychology, at William and Mary College, discussed in *School and Society* the dangers involved in making a distinction between teaching evolution as a working hypothesis and as an established fact. He declared that:

If, . . . it is believed that the fact of evolution would be a rock on which religious faith must be wrecked, only two courses appear to present themselves. Either one must, as Bertrand Russell advises, look the universe in the face and bid it to do its worst; or, one must set about to prevent the

---

211 *Philadelphia Inquirer*, Aug. 13, 1925; *cf. American Mercury*, Nov., 1926, IX, 354; *School and Society*, Aug. 29, 1925, XXII, 273.
212 *Amer. Mercury*, Nov., 1926, IX, 354.
213 *Richmond News Leader*, Jan. 30, 1926.
214 *Ibid.*

fact of evolution from becoming a matter of general knowledge. In the latter case, prohibition must go the whole length and outlaw the teaching of evolution as hypothesis; to prohibit the teaching of it as a fact will not suffice. For so long as a hypothesis ''works,'' there is always the probability to be faced, that it will work itself up to the status of a fact.[215]

The greatest danger, in Prof. Geiger's opinion, however, lay in placing the ultimate fate of religion at the mercy of controversies dependent upon sense experience, upon what is or is not true in the realm of physical nature; rather, its ultimate security should be sought in the testimony of an ethical and spiritual consciousness.[216]

According to Virginius Dabney, writing in 1926, ''educators in Virginia are free to embrace Darwinism, and they do not hesitate to do so, even in the sectarian institutions. Anyone who attempts to hamper scientific research by an appeal to Scripture receives only loud guffaws and is speedily laughed out of court.''[217]

The failure of the Patriotic Welfare Committee or of any other group in the state to obtain a favorable reaction in public opinion to a proposal for an anti-evolution law is quite comprehensible in view of Virginian distaste to enact in specific legislation anything which may be regarded as having a bearing on purely instructional questions affecting religion, or which may be construed as raising the issue of separation of church and state.

The history of the development of moral and religious instruction in the quarter of century since the adoption of the Consti-

---

215 *School and Society*, Aug. 22, 1925, XXII, 245.

216 *Ibid.*; as an indication of the former attitude of the Virginia farmer to science in agriculture, reference may be made to an article in the *Virginia Journal of Education*, June, 1914, VII, 469–70, in which Mr. T. O. Sandy, State Agent for the Farmers' Co-operative Demonstration Work, appealed to the ministers of Virginia to assist in overcoming the prejudices of many farmers against scientific men and scientific agriculture. He suggested their attending meetings and in opening them with prayer.

217 *Amer. Mercury*, Nov., 1926, IX, 355; the course in General Biology and Invertebrate Zoology at Hampden-Sidney is thus described in the catalogue of 1926–27, 49; ''This course is designed to acquaint the student with the fundamental generalizations that are the product of modern research in Biology. Comparative morphology, physiology, and ecology of animal and plant life are illustrated by a detailed study of types of several groups. Attention is paid to the groupings of forms and to comparison of these groups. Laboratory work follows the class work and gives the student first hand knowledge of the objects of his study. . . .''

tution of 1902 makes it clear that every attempt in Virginia to contravene the historical principle of separation of church and state by the enactment of legislation looking to an alliance between church and state on this question has resulted in failure. What has been achieved in extending religious instruction in the public school system, and much more has been achieved, as an account of religious instruction in state controlled institutions will presently show,[218] has been achieved by a policy of cooperation which has in no way been grounded in legislative enactment—in recognition by the Assembly. As long as the religious forces of the state have been willing to work on a *laissez faire* policy as far as the question of separation of church and state is concerned, they have succeeded in obtaining much in the way of concession from the civil arm of the government. As to whether the policy of co-operation, or a stronger development of that policy has in it, or will reveal, the possibilities of contravention of the historical principle of separation of church and state is a matter that may well be left to speculation or future history.

---

[218] See p. 607 *ff.*

CHAPTER XIII

ACTIVITIES AND TENDENCIES OF DENOMINATIONAL EDUCATION

Criteria For Significance And Influence Of Denominational Developments

The feeling which existed in 1902, that denominational and private education had contributed to the continuation of the prejudice against public schools, has been described.[1] It is important, however, from many angles, but particularly from the point of view of determining the attitudes of those controlling denominational and private schools toward religion in education, to discover the procedures instituted in their schools, what was their influence upon the public school system, in what way religious life in these schools differed from the religious life developed in state-controlled institutions, to be described later.[2]

It would be most illuminating, if it were possible to trace accurately the growth or decline of denominational and private education after 1870, but because of the difficulty in past decades of obtaining complete statistics from these schools, no accurate conclusions can be drawn.[3] It is probably safer to gauge the signifi-

---

[1] See p. 472.

[2] See p. 607 *ff*.

[3] For example, the reports of the United States Commissioner of Education gave for 1871, six private secondary schools in Virginia, which, of course, was far from the correct number, for the enrollment of those in private schools was given as 27,372, which, while it represented elementary pupils also, obviously covered more than six secondary schools. Aside from this, anyone attempting to check schools known to exist, with figures in these reports will find various discrepancies. Only an approximate idea of the real situation can be given. The number of private secondary institutions given in the reports of the United States Commissioner of Education for 1871 are 6; for 1880,—30; for 1889–90,—60; for 1899–1900,—82; for 1909–10,—62; for 1919–20,—60. Of these, 5 in 1871; 14 in 1880; 28 in 1889–90; 33 in 1899–1900; 40 in 1909–10; 44 in 1919–20, are given as denominational—but while it will be shown that the various denominations established many new schools in the period after the Civil War, it is by no means certain that these figures tell the story accurately at any date, though

cance and influence of the work of these schools by showing the various denominational developments and the actual practices in the schools.

Educational Activities And Tendencies Of The Protestant Episcopal Church

With respect to the Protestant Episcopal Church, the most interesting development in its educational policy during this period, was its definite renunciation of any connection with the College of William and Mary, which, in 1906, became a state institution;[4] and its inauguration of a system of church schools.

The Civil War had been completely disastrous to William and Mary College. In May, 1861, it suspended its exercises;[5] it reopened in 1865, with an enrollment of 65 students. The damage done to buildings and equipment during the war was such that the college had to incur a heavy debt, and it found itself in a poor position to provide that instruction and equipment necessary to carry an enrollment sufficient to assist in its recuperation. The enrollment during the next ten years, varying from 42 to 86, dropped from 86 in 1875 to 27 in 1880; and between 1881 and 1888, the college had to discontinue instruction until it could improve its financial status.[6]

In 1888, the Board of Visitors of the college suggested that application be made to the Legislature for aid, on the basis that a system of normal instruction and training be connected with the collegiate course. The Assembly on March 5, 1888, approved this arrangement, and granted an annuity of $10,000 on condition that the college educate and train white male teachers for

---

accuracy has probably increased in recent decades. The number of pupils attending private schools for 1871 is given as 27,372; for 1879–80,—26,470; for 1899–90, figures are lacking; for 1899–1900,—6,998; for 1909–10,— 6,972; for 1919–20,—9,299. *U. S. Comm. Educ. Rep't*, 1871, 632, 359; 1880, 564–65, 325; 1889–90, II, 1566–68, I, 16; 1899–1900, II, 2430–33, 2145; 1909–10, II, 1160–62, 1153; *U. S. Bur. Educ. Bull.*, 1923, No. 29, 548–49, 543.

[4] See p. 531.

[5] Tyler: *Williamsburg*, 190.

[6] *Ibid.*, 192, 269; *U. S. Bur. Educ., Circ. Inf.*, 1887, No. 1, 65, 89; for efforts to influence Congress to assist in the rehabilitation of the college, *cf. Jour., Senate*, Mar. 26, 1874, 350; Mar. 27, 1874, 351; *U. S. Bur. Educ., Circ. Inf.*, 1887, No. 1, 62; Tyler: *The Making of the Union*, 26.

the public free schools of the state, giving gratuitous instruction and board at a nominal rate, to a certain number of state students on the basis of county and city representation.[7] Such students were to pledge themselves to teach for at least two years in the public schools of the state.

A most important feature of the new arrangement was that a new board of visitors was authorized to consist of ten appointees under the charter, and ten appointees by the governor, with the superintendent of public instruction as a member, ex-officio.[8] By giving the institution a semblance of partial state control, it was probably felt that criticism on the score of appropriations of public funds would be obviated. A new faculty was organized with Lyon G. Tyler as President.

Because of the basis on which the college was reorganized, it reopened, in 1888, with an enrollment of 102; and in 1905, the year before it was again reorganized, reached the highest enrollment to that date in its history, of 244.[9]

More than a century had elapsed since the separation from Great Britain, before the initial step was taken in the action which seemed the logical outcome of that separation. Contributory to this action was probably the fact that the Protestant Episcopal Church was not in a position to give the college that financial assistance which real rehabilitation required; and that an attempt to remove it to Alexandria would stir up again the intrenched historical prejudice in favor of Williamsburg, and that to remove the college to Richmond would now be to meet the rivalry of the Baptist, Richmond College.[10] The wisdom of affiliation with the state was justified by events.

With the partial state control inaugurated in 1888, it was only a question of time before the college became a state institution. By an act of March 7, 1906, the property of the college was transferred from the ancient corporation of "The President and Mas-

---

[7] *Acts of Assembly*, Mar. 5, 1888, 512.
[8] *Ibid.;* Tyler: *Williamsburg*, 192.
[9] *Ibid.*, 269.
[10] There was not wanting opinion that removal to one or the other of these places was a desirable solution—*cf. U. S. Bur. Educ., Circ. Inf.*, 1887, No. 1, 66.

ters or Professors of the College of William and Mary in Virginia" to "The College of William and Mary in Virginia."[11] The new corporation, to be appointed by the Governor of Virginia, was to consist of eleven members, including the superintendent of public instruction, their terms to be for four years each.[12] The subsequent history of the college concerns its career as a state institution.[13]

Aside from the Theological Seminary at Alexandria,[14] it will be recalled that the chief educational venture of the Church in the period before the War, was the establishment of the Episcopal High School in Virginia, near Alexandria, in 1839.[15] With the coming, in 1870, of Mr. Launcelot Minor Blackford, who served as principal until 1913, a number of interesting changes took place in the religious life of the school. Morning prayers were changed by the principal to after breakfast, that the boys might not associate prayers with demerits, the "sleepy-headed boy" being marked not "late prayers" but "late breakfast."[16] A Bible class was held on Sunday afternoons; not only was there an elucidation of some Bible passage, but its application in "direct, practical counsels as to the conduct that becomes a gentleman and a Christian."[17] The object of the school at that time was declared to be: "To provide an institution of learning where youth can be thoroughly educated on Christian principles, and where their morals and habits can be preserved from the dangers of evil associations."[18]

The religious observances of the school more recently include morning and evening prayers; Sunday morning services in the Theological Seminary Chapel, and in the school chapel in the evening; also a voluntary devotional Friday evening service held by the students from the Theological Seminary.[19] Bible studies are required in each of the six forms; beginning with the Old

---

[11] *Acts of Assembly*, Mar. 7, 1906, 94 *ff.*; Tyler: *Williamsburg*, 193.
[12] *Ibid.*
[13] See p. 636 *ff.*
[14] See p. 293.
[15] See p. 328.
[16] Kinsolving: *Story Southern School*, 105.
[17] *Ibid.*, 179.
[18] *Ibid.*, 112–13.
[19] *Episc. H. S. Catalog*, 1926, 21.

Testament in the first, and ending with a study of St. Paul in the last.[20]

In explaining the necessity for this type of school, Kinsolving, the historian of the school, declared, that

> It is because it is no part of the function of a University to teach religion, or for that matter to have an oversight of either character or manners except in a general and ineffectual way that the function of the Christian school is becoming increasingly important.[21]

In a school of this type, he declared, "the faith which underlies character may be freely and definitely taught." In establishing religious attitude before entrance to college, in his opinion, lay the chief hope of escape from a secularized state with its laxity of morals and corruption.[22]

The results of these religious activities and this attitude may be gathered from the Principal's "Report" for 1926, when, in an enrollment slightly less than 200, of whom 169 were Episcopalians, the rest of varying denominations, 14 students were confirmed that year.[23]

Another school for boys, affiliated with the church is the Stuyvesant School, founded 1912, at Warrenton, Fauquier County. Its religious exercises and influences are in accordance with the general principles of the church.[24]

There are affiliated with the church besides these two schools, two other schools for boys, Christchurch School, Christchurch, Middlesex County, and St. Christopher's School at Westhampton, Richmond. In 1920, there was formed a corporation by the Diocese of Virginia, known as the "Church Schools in the Diocese of Virginia."[25] The creation of this corporation is in line with the policy of the church which has been in favor of church schools for the youth of its own church.[26] As the general

---

[20] *Ibid.*, 13 *ff.*
[21] Kinsolving: *Story Southern School*, 258.
[22] *Ibid.*
[23] *Episc. H. S. Catalog*, 1926, 35–36.
[24] *Stuyvesant Sch. Catalog*, 1926, II, 17.
[25] *St. Christopher's Sch. Catalog*, 1926, 2.
[26] See p. 422; the Episcopal High School and the Stuyvesant School are not under this corporation.

character of all the schools under the corporation is similar, a description of the religious life at St. Christopher's will suffice.[27] As a church school, the school emphasizes the fundamental importance of religion in every department of school life. Not only are there morning devotional exercises, but "before every athletic event the boys of the whole School kneel together in prayer to ask God's blessing upon those who are about to represent them in the contest." Boarders must have a Bible and Book of Common Prayer, attend family prayers every evening, and Sunday School and church on Sundays.[28] All students must take two hours a week in the Bible studies of their form.[29] In 1924, a Missionary Society was organized, the objects of which are "self-sacrifice and service."[30]

A reduction in fees which is commonly made in the schools of the church to sons of clergymen, is in this school also extended to sons of teachers, and officers in the U. S. Army and Navy.[31] The enrollment of the school increased from 16 pupils in 1920 to 223 in 1925.[32]

Under the same church corporation are three schools for girls, St. Anne's School at Charlottesville, St. Margaret's School at Tappahannock, and St. Catherine's School at Westhampton, Richmond.

The nature of the religious life of these schools may be inferred from that at St. Catherine's School.[33] It is like St. Christopher's, a Country Resident and Day School. While a church school, it is open to all girls who meet the entrance requirements, which include compliance with the religious regulations. Each student, as in similar schools of this church, is required to have a Bible, Prayer Book, and Hymnal.[34] Religious studies are re-

---

27 This school opened, in 1911, as the Chamberlayne School, and was taken over by the corporation in 1920.

28 *St. Christopher's Sch. Catalog*, 1926, 11, 16.

29 *Ibid.*, 11, 45, 47 *ff.*

30 *Ibid.*, 27–28.

31 At the Episcopal School at Alexandria in 1926, discounts in costs were given to 20 boys who were sons of clergymen—*Epis. H. S. Catalog*, 1926, 35; *St. Christopher's Sch. Catalog*, 1926, 13.

32 *Richmond News Leader* Dec. 23, 1925.

33 This school was founded, in 1890, as the Virginia Randolph Ellet School and acquired by the church in 1920.

34 *St. Catherine's Sch. Catalog*, 1926, 3, 14.

quired in every class, and daily religious exercises are held. A substantial reduction in fees is made for a limited number of daughters of clergymen or missionaries of the diocese. The enrollment in 1925 was 275 girls. The purpose of the school is "to exalt the Christ," to interpret to its students "ideals of purity, of grace, and of loyalty to every cause worthy of Him and calling for their devotion."[35]

In the winter of 1925–26, a campaign for $350,000 in behalf of St. Christopher's and St. Catherine's was conducted in Richmond. The campaign was interesting because of the sentiment it revealed, at least among some of the wealthy business men of Richmond, regarding schools of this type. One prominent citizen was quoted as being particularly in favor of these schools

... because our children are not receiving any religious instruction in the public schools and very little in their homes, and were it not for the one hour a week supplied by the Sunday-schools they would learn very little of the Bible and its teachings.[36]

Another business man was in favor of the campaign because he thought, "that the children of Episcopal families should be educated and nurtured in church schools, just as those of other denominations are brought up in the schools of their respective bodies."[37]

Two other schools for girls are affiliated with the church, but do not come under the control of the corporation. They are Stuart Hall and Chatham Episcopal Institute. Stuart Hall, located at Staunton, was incorporated, in 1844, as the Virginia Female Institute, but its history goes back to the boarding school opened in 1831 by Mrs. Maria Sheffy at her residence, Kalorama.[38] From 1848 to 1880, the school was under the charge of Rev. R. H. Phillips, D.D., and achieved the position of being one of the most flourishing secondary schools for women in the state.[39] In 1874, the property was transferred to the Protestant

---

[35] *Ibid.*, 3.

[36] "Church Schools Are Needed Now, Says Mr. Taylor," *Richmond News Leader*, Feb. 1, 1926.

[37] *Ibid.*, Feb. 4, 1926—"High Ideals in Local Schools, Says Litchford."

[38] *Stuart Hall Catalog*, 1926, 44; Waddell: *Annals Augusta Co.*, 268; Blandin: *Higher Educ. Women*, 313–16.

[39] *Stuart Hall Catalog*, 1926, 9–10; *Richmond Enquirer*, June 17, 1870; *Relig. Herald*, Aug. 15, 1878.

Episcopal Church, on condition that it would pay off the debts and continue the school.[40]   In 1896, it was placed under the control of the two dioceses into which the church in the state had divided.[41]   In 1907, the name was changed to Stuart Hall, in memory of Mrs. J. E. B. Stuart, who had been principal from 1880 to 1898.[42]

Chatham Episcopal Institute was founded, in 1892, by the Danville Convocation of the diocese of Southern Virginia of the Protestant Episcopal Church.[43]   It was incorporated in 1894. In 1902, it was made the Diocesan School of Southern Virginia for Girls.   A recent statement of the purpose of the school declares it to be "to stimulate and guide growth through the active participation of each girl in the every day life of work, play and worship."[44]

The policy of Stuart Hall claims to be not narrowly sectarian. Students of various denominations attend.   They may attend the church of their choice once a month, at other times they are required to attend the nearest Episcopal church.   Morning and evening chapel attendance is required.   Visits may not be received on Sunday.[45]   Bible study is provided throughout the four year course and is required.[46]   The purpose "is to give a general knowledge of the original founding, and extension of Christianity, thus stimulating an intelligent interest in the Old and New Testaments and Church History.[47]   At both Stuart Hall and Chatham Episcopal Institute, daughters of clergymen are allowed special discounts.[48]

The outstanding feature of the educational policy of the Protestant Episcopal Church as seen from this survey is its complete renunciation of collegiate education, except for the special field of theology represented in the Seminary, and its complete devotion to the program, indicated by Bishop Brown to Mr.

---

[40] *Acts of Assembly*, Mar. 14, 1874, 100.
[41] *Ibid.*, Jan. 18, 1896, 110.
[42] *Stuart Hall Catalog*, 1926, 10.
[43] *Chatham Episc. Inst. Catalog*, 1926.
[44] *Ibid.*
[45] *Stuart Hall Catalog*, 1926, 13, 39.
[46] *Ibid.*, 19–20.
[47] *Ibid.*, 20.
[48] *Ibid.*, 43; *Chatham Episc. Inst. Catalog*, 1926, 6.

Clerk,[49] in favor of church schools embracing elementary and secondary education, established at strategic points over the state.[50] The church apparently feels, in view of the strong position established by other denominations in the college field in the years before and after the Civil War, that it can be of greatest service in influencing the ideal of a stronger position for religion in education by developing the secondary field.[51] It has now nine well established schools, four for boys, and five for girls, besides two institutions for colored students, Bishop Payne Divinity School, at Petersburg, and St. Paul Normal and Industrial School, at Lawrenceville; and also the Blue Ridge Industrial School, a mountain school for boys and girls at Dyke, Greene County. It is probably only a question of obtaining greater resources before this number will be increased.[52]

Educational Activities And Tendencies Of The Presbyterian Church

The most interesting development in the educational activity of the Presbyterian church is the tendency in recent years to do away with the self-perpetuating boards under which its affiliated institutions functioned, and to bring them under direct control of the synod and presbyteries—a tendency which may be taken as the initiation of a policy looking to closer denominational control. The program of Presbyterian educational activity has gradually, since the formation of the Presbyterian Educational Association of the South, been coming more and more in recent years under standards that control the activities and extension of the educational movement of the church as a whole.[53] The elaborate educational system which, shortly after the Revolution, it seemed that the Presbyterians were about to launch, it will be recalled, never materialized.[54] With the removal of Washing-

---

49 See p. 489.
50 *Cf.* "To Ask $350,000 For Schools Here," *Richmond News Leader,* Dec. 23, 1925.
51 *Ibid.*
52 Membership in the church increased from 33,593 in 1916 to 58,403 in 1926—*Press Summary, U. S. Bur. Census,* May 5, 1928.
53 *Cf. Minutes, 15th Annual Meeting, Presbyt. Educ. Assoc. South,* 6.
54 See p. 220 *ff;* 302 *ff.*

ton College from its list,[55] Presbyterian education after the Civil War was at a low ebb. Though Presbyterianism, in contrast to Episcopalianism, still maintains an interest in collegiate education, it is less strong than that church in the secondary field. It is, however, showing a strong interest in the development of mountain schools, which though now regarded as a mission activity of the church, has in it some interesting possibilities.

The institution which still looms largest in Presbyterian thought is Hampden-Sidney. Apparently as a consequent of its experience in the decade before the beginning of the Civil War,[56] Hampden-Sidney seems to have given up serious concern for rivalry with the University. In the period following the War, it assumed, on the whole, a quiescent attitude toward the increasing civil development of higher education in Virginia. It contented itself with stressing the fact that it maintained a union of religious and mental training, and made its appeal to those interested in that philosophy of education. At the centennial of the college, in 1876, Rev. M. D. Hoge, in referring to the claims of Hampden-Sidney upon the interest of the public, declared that the modern scientific attitude, which, while not specifically denying the Deity, made God an automaton, made more important than ever the reunion of religious and mental training emphasized at Hampden-Sidney. The founders of Hampden-Sidney knew nothing about evolution, but they believed that credence should be given to the Scripture and that the religious faculties were the noblest.[57]

The opinion that the tendency of higher institutions was largely skeptical and that "their spirit was far from what serious Christians deem safe for immature youth to come in contact with," was expressed by Dr. R. McIlwaine in his inaugural address in 1883.[58] In an address before the Second Presbyterian Church, in 1888, Dr. McIlwaine declared that Hampden-Sidney was the only institution in Virginia which made the history and literature of the Bible a requisite for graduation. The instruc-

---

[55] See p. 310.
[56] See p. 306.
[57] *Richmond Enquirer*, June 18, 1876.
[58] McIlwaine, R.: *Addresses*, 12.

tion made the students "acquainted with the facts of Scripture history, and somewhat with the Bible from Genesis through apostolic times."[59]   In the senior class, a thorough course on the Evidences of Christianity was given in which the students were instructed in the grounds on which Christianity rested, and thus were "fortified against skeptical objections brought against it." As Dr. McIllwaine expressed it:

. . . Our young men are thus not left to be carried away with the wild vamperings of an Ingersoll, or the learned sophistries of a Renan, a Strauss, or a Baur, or the scientific vagaries of a Darwin, a Spencer, or a Huxley, but are guarded and instructed as to the real foundations on which our religion is based.[60]

In the present religious life of Hampden-Sidney, the Y. M. C. A. holds its characteristic place; it conducts Bible classes, Mission Study classes, Wednesday and Sunday evening prayer services, and, at intervals, evangelistic services.[61]   Attendance at daily morning chapel services and upon church, Sunday morning, is required.[62]   It is stated, however, that reasonable provision is made for necessary absences.   It is altogether unlikely that a student who is unwilling to affiliate himself with the organized Christian life of the institution could comfortably continue his studies at Hampden-Sidney.

The aim of the courses in Bible study may well be contrasted with that of the courses at the University of Virginia.[63]   At the latter place, the courses are presumed to be given chiefly from historical and literary standpoints.   The object here is largely religious, as may be gathered from the statement of purpose "to lead the individual student into a Christian experience," and the fact that during the first two years much attention is given to Scripture memory work.   The passages are carefully selected: "(1) to meet the student's own present and future spiritual needs; and (2) to equip him for active Christian service." Three hours' work is required in each of the first two years; two alternate courses of two hours each are given as an elective for

[59] *Ibid.*, 34.
[60] *Ibid.*
[61] *Hampden-Sidney Catalog*, 1926, 77.
[62] *Ibid.*, 69.
[63] See p. 617, 618.

either Juniors or Seniors, and a fifth course of one hour in Christian Doctrine is likewise given as an elective for them. The description of the various courses indicates a larger emphasis upon the spiritual, devotional, and theological aspects of the Bible than in the course at the University of Virginia.[64] A definite attempt seems to be made to strengthen the student's conception of the Bible from the spiritual aspect, in order to withstand any assaults from either the philosophical or the rational standpoint.[65]

The whole emphasis at Hampden-Sidney is upon a Christianized education.[66] As a consequence of this fact, and also, in part because candidates for the ministry, who present an official statement from the proper church authorities, and sons of ministers of any denomination, are exempt from the payment of tuition fees, 12.5 per cent. of her graduates have in the century and a half of her existence become ministers or missionaries.[67] In 1926, 38 of her 232 students were avowed candidates for the ministry or missionary volunteers.[68] Because of this interest in the ministry, the college has a "Ministerial Association" composed of students looking forward to some form of Christian service as a life calling.[69]

In regard to the status of the college with Presbyterianism, Mr. McIlwaine, in 1888, declared, that while a majority of the Board had always been associated with Presbyterianism, the college was "only responsible for the duties imposed by a charter which renders her absolutely free from the undue influence of any denomination of Christians."[70] After having had for almost a century and a half a nominal liaison with Presbyterianism, through its original self-perpetuating board of trustees, Hampden-Sidney, in 1918, took steps to come under direct Pres-

---

[64] See p. 618.
[65] *Hampden-Sidney Catalog*, 1926, 48; the closest approach to study of the Bible from a theological standpoint at the University is the more advanced graduate course—*U. of Va. Catalog*, 1925–26, 141.
[66] *Hampden-Sidney Catalog*, 1926, 67; Stephenson, L. B.: "Why I Believe In Hampden-Sidney" leaflet.
[67] *Ibid.*; *Hampden-Sidney Catalog*, 1926, 80.
[68] Squires, W. H. T.: "The Turret's Twirl," leaflet.
[69] *Hampden-Sidney Catalog*, 1926, 78.
[70] *U. S. Bur. Educ., Circ. Inf.*, 1888, No. I, 237.

byterian control. On February 14, 1919, its charter was amended so as to transfer the control of the college to a Board of twenty-five trustees, directly appointed by the Synod of Virginia, to serve in groups of five from one to five years. Vacancies in the Board of Trustees, for any reason, were to be filled by the Synod.[71] The college now became unequivocally a denominational college. It was thus in a stronger position to impress Presbyterians with the importance of not sending "their sons at the most impressionable age to non-Christian colleges," where "Under the influence of cultured but skeptical professors seeds of doubt are planted in the hearts of many promising young Christians who come home educated but agnostics."[72]

Aside from Hampden-Sidney, the only other important Presbyterian educational activity in behalf of boys is in connection with the Danville Military Institute. This school was founded, in 1890, at Danville;[73] in 1921, the school was turned over to the Presbyterian Synod of Virginia.[74] A recent statement describes the school as "a preparatory school for boys and young men, where Christian influence prevails and where the development of character is placed above all other considerations."[75] The school is not intended, however, to be a sectarian school,[76] the purpose being to give a thorough preparation for college, under conditions most favorable among other objects for the "development of manly, Christian character." Morning chapel exercises are held and work in the Bible is required.[77] The courses offered in the first two years are in the Old, and in the last two years, in the New Testament.[78] Cadets are required, upon entrance, to register their Church preference, and to attend Sunday morning services of their church. All cadets attend Sunday evening service in a body.[79] The school hopes "By holding forth the

---

[71] *Hampden-Sidney Catalog*, 1926, 8.
[72] Squires: "The Turret's Twirl," leaflet.
[73] Originally this school was a military school, this feature being later discarded, but restored again in 1918.
[74] *Danville Milit. Inst. Catalog*, 1926, 9.
[75] *Ibid.*, 11.
[76] *Ibid.*, 12.
[77] *Ibid.*
[78] *Ibid.*, 25.
[79] *Ibid.*, 14.

Christian ideal as the true aim of life, . . . to teach that it is the duty and privilege of each one to become a Christian.''[80]

The recent tendency of Presbyterianism to bring its educational institutions under direct Synod control is seen also in the history of Mary Baldwin College, one of its institutions for girls. This school formerly known as Augusta Female Seminary,[81] came under the charge of Miss Mary Julia Baldwin and Miss Agnes McClung, in 1863, at a time when conditions threatened to close the school.[82] On March 14, 1895, its former charter was amended to allow a change of name to Mary Baldwin Seminary and the conferring of degrees upon graduates.[83] In 1916, the State Board of Education directed that Mary Baldwin Seminary be placed on the list of Junior Colleges.[84] In 1923, the trustees obtained such changes in the charter as to permit the transfer of the institution from the control of its self-perpetuating Board of Trustees to a Board of Trustees nominated by the Synod of Virginia.[85] One object of this change was to establish a standard college for women to be known as Mary Baldwin College. With the approval of the Synod, the Board hopes to conduct on the old property in Staunton, the Mary Baldwin Seminary; and on a new site in the country, near Staunton, to establish Mary Baldwin College.

The prescribed work for the A.B. degree includes six hours of Bible work. The aim of this work ''is to develop Christian character and practice based upon a study of the Word itself in its literary and historical setting, and to prepare students for teaching the Bible in Sabbath schools and secular institutions.'' Five courses varying from one to three hours a week are given in the department. In Mary Baldwin Seminary, two courses are offered, five times a week throughout the year.[86]

Regarding the religious life of the college, opening exercises are conducted each morning by the chaplain. The Y. W. C. A.

---

[80] *Ibid.*, 15.
[81] See p. 312.
[82] *Mary Baldwin College Catalog*, 1926.
[83] *Acts of Assembly*, Dec. 14, 1895, 5.
[84] *Mary Baldwin College Catalog*, 1926.
[85] *Ibid.*
[86] *Ibid.*, 23, 25–26; *Mary Baldwin Seminary Catalog*, 1926, 26.

is conducted by the students under the supervision of a member of the faculty. Attendance at the various religious activities, such as Sunday morning Bible class, Sunday morning and evening church services is also required. Attendance at other than the Presbyterian church, of which the college President is pastor, is permitted only according to prescribed college regulations. It is stated, that while every effort is made for the spiritual and moral development of the students, attempts to imbue their minds with sectarian prejudices are avoided;[87] that no attempt will be made to win to the Presbyterian Church students who come from other denominations; the control by the Synod being intended to give assurance that evangelical Christianity will hold a very high place.[88]

A second important Presbyterian institution for girls is Stonewall Jackson College. This school was opened in Abingdon, Washington County, in 1868, under the auspices of the Sinking Springs Presbyterian Church. The school was incorporated, in 1870, under the name of Jackson Female Institute.[89] In 1896, the trustees of this church transferred their interest to the Abingdon Presbytery, and a charter was obtained under the name of Stonewall Jackson Institute.[90] In 1914, it was decided to have Montgomery Presbytery join in ownership with the Abingdon Presbytery and to change the name to Stonewall Jackson College. This was accordingly done, and a new charter obtained.[91] The college is now under the control of the Synod of Appalachia and the Presbytery of Montgomery.

Though Presbyterian in its management, the school claims to be free from all narrow sectarianism. No attempt to alienate a student from the faith of her parents, it is said, will be tolerated. Students of other denominations have the privilege of attending the church preferred by their parents.[92] Faculty selections are made with a view to Christian character, as well as scholarship.[93]

---

[87] *Mary Baldwin College Catalog,* 1926, 63.
[88] *Ibid.,* 1926.
[89] Summers: *Hist. S. W. Va.,* 573; *Acts of Assembly,* June 27, 1870, 206.
[90] Summers: *Hist. S. W. Va.,* 574.
[91] *Stonewall Jackson Catalog,* 1927, 10.
[92] *Ibid.,* 13.
[93] *Ibid.*

The college has a Y. W. C. A., organized in 1900. Morning devotional exercises are held in the chapel. Sunday visiting is discouraged, as students are required to observe quiet hours in the afternoon.

In addition to the work of the Junior College, there is a four-year high school. Bible study is prescribed in every year of the preparatory department and the freshman year of the college. The aim of the one hour courses in the preparatory department is "not only to make the Bible interesting and instructive to the students, but helpful and regulative in their lives."[94]   The Old Testament is studied in the first two years "as a basis for the study of the development of the great Plan of Redemption." The New Testament study "is made to emphasize the fact that while the Old Testament is "unfolded" in the New, the New Testament is "enfolded" in the Old."[95]   The courses in the Junior College consist of two hours a week in the Life of Christ in the first semester; and, in the second, in Church History during the apostolic days.[96]

Under the direct auspices of Roanoke Presbytery, a co-educational secondary boarding school known as Central Academy is conducted at Stuart, Patrick County. It is an incorporated institution, and like all other Presbyterian institutions here described, accredited by the state. No tuition fee is charged residents of Patrick County, and only a nominal fee is charged non-residents. As the board also is very low, students are expected to assist in the work of the school. Students are not allowed to leave the grounds except to attend church services or by special permission.[97]   This school is apparently intended as a mission school in the mountains of southwestern Virginia,[98] though it is not actually referred to as such in the church literature, as are the schools known as Blue Ridge Academy, at the Hollow; Grundy Presbyterian School, at Grundy; Franklin High School, at Indian Valley; the Girls' Industrial School, at Foster

---

[94] *Ibid.*, 35.
[95] *Ibid.*, 35.
[96] *Ibid.*, 26.
[97] *Central Academy Announcements For 1926–27.*
[98] *Cf.* Ferrum Training School.

Falls; Hoot Owl Hollow Mission School, and Lewiscot Presbyterian Institute, both at Big Stone Gap.[99]

The co-educational school at Grundy is typical of these mountain schools. At the time of its founding, in 1909, as a missionary effort of Rev. F. E. Clark, there was not a Presbyterian minister in Buchanan County, and the largest school was a two-room school in Grundy.[100] Recent enrollment in the Presbyterian school is approaching the 200 mark. The general management of the school rests with a Board of Trustees elected by Abingdon Presbytery. As at Central Academy, the nominal fee paid by students is supplemented by required work in the conduct of the school. About sixty per cent of the students, because they are orphans or come from poor homes pay nothing. In the religious life of the school, the study of the Bible is an outstanding feature; it is taught in all the grades, and four years' work is required in the high school.[101] This emphasis upon the Bible is supplemented by activities of various religious organizations, and the religious routine characteristic of denominational schools.

An important educational activity sponsored by the church, through the Presbyterian Educational Association of the South, is the assignment of Presbyterian ministers to higher state institutions. Ministers are assigned to the University, the Virginia Polytechnic Institute, the Virginia Military Institute, and the State Teachers' Colleges.[102] This policy is based on the ground that there are more Presbyterian students in state and independent institutions than in the Church colleges.[103] Aside from the students at the Union Theological Seminary and the General Assembly's Training School for Lay Workers at Richmond, the number of students in Presbyterian schools of all kinds in Virginia in 1928, totalled 1,619,[104] and, of course, not all of these students were Presbyterians. The number of Presbyterians, in

99 *Minutes, 15th Annual Meeting, Presbyt. Assoc. South,* 18.
100 *Grundy Presbyt. Sch. Catalog,* 1928, 9.
101 *Ibid.,* 11.
102 *Minutes, 15th Annual Meeting, Presbyt. Educ. Assoc. South,* 7, 31.
103 *Ibid.,* 7, 14.
104 *Ibid.,* 20–23; calculated from figures there given, representing the 11 Presbyterian schools mentioned in this section.

Virginia, in 1926, was 67,463.[105]   It is apparent from these figures that denominational education is not having a very strong
hold on Presbyterians, in Virginia, for practically half this enrollment represents the number of students at the mountain
schools.[106]   With the present policy which has resulted in bringing most of these schools under the control of the Synod or Presbyteries, it may be that a wider appeal to Presbyterianism will
be possible.

Educational Activities And Tendencies Of The Baptist Church

One of the most interesting developments in Virginia denominational educational history is the concern which Baptists began
to feel, as they increased in numbers and wealth, for education
under Baptist auspices.   Regarded in the early part of the 19th
century as a group not particularly interested in education,[107]
their leaders have in more recent years shown a very keen interest in fostering denominational education.   Their present attitude to education may be judged from a "Report Of The Committee On Christian Education" at a meeting of one of their
strongest associations in 1925:

> As civilization advances and human life steadily becomes more complex
> there is increasing need for education in order that we may understand
> this modern world and be able to guide to spiritual ends the great forces
> in modern society which so profoundly affect human life.   As the educa-
> tional task of our colleges steadily grows and their opportunities for service
> to humanity are multiplied there is an ever increasing need for larger
> resources in buildings and equipment and endowment.   This should be
> accepted not as a burden but as an enlarging opportunity for promoting
> the cause of Christianity.
>
> Virginia Baptists have made gratifying progress in building and equip-
> ping a system of schools for the training of our young people. . . .[108]

The most important institution in this system is the University
of Richmond, whose history goes back to Richmond College.[109]

---

[105] Belonging to the Presbyterian Church in U. S., 63,598; to the Presbyterian Church in the U. S. of America, 2,911; to the Associate Reformed
Presbyterian Church, 954; *U. S. Bur. Census, Press Summaries*, April 30,
1928, May 1, 1928, Oct. 20, 1927.
[106] Includes Central Academy.
[107] See p. 208.
[108] *Min. 142nd Annual Session, Dover Baptist Assoc.,* 19.
[109] See p. 314.

After a period of suspension during the Civil War,[110] steps were taken at a meeting of the Baptist General Association in Richmond, in June, 1866, for the reorganization of the college;[111] it was opened in October, and by the end of the session the attendance was ninety.[112] An unusual innovation, at this time, was the decision to make attendance upon religious exercises purely voluntary.[113] By 1870, the attendance was approximately 160 students, of whom about 20 per cent were studying for the ministry, and more than one half of the students were classed as "professors of religion."[114] A statement issued by the college, at that time, urged that "Every minister and member of the churches should become a voluntary and zealous agent to advance the prosperity and influence of the college," if they wished it to become what many of its friends desired "the great Baptist University of the South."[115]

Though a large number of students looking forward to the ministry matriculated at the college, theology was not taught in it. These students were received free of tuition charges, irrespective of denominational bias. In 1877, there were forty such students on the roll.[116] The temper of the Baptists at this time with regard to a learned ministry may be gathered from an essay written, in 1875, by Dr. John A. Broadus at the request of the Trustees of the college.[117] Dr. Broadus started with the premise that education has to work from above downwards. While he felt that the Baptist position in the past in encouraging some uneducated men to preach had been quite right and necessary, in order to reach the masses so largely illiterate—that need would gradually diminish. In order to keep pace with the times, an increasingly large proportion of Baptist ministers must be thoroughly educated men.[118] Not only an educated ministry, but also

[110] Robertson, D. A.: *Amer. Univ. and Colleges*, 746.
[111] *U. S. Bur. Educ., Circ. Inf.*, 1888, No. 1, 276.
[112] *Ibid.*, 277–78.
[113] *Ibid.*, 278.
[114] *Richmond Enquirer*, Mar. 10, 1870.
[115] *Ibid.*
[116] *Jour. of Educ.*, April 19, 1877, V, 190; Brock, R. A.: *Richmond*, 21–23.
[117] Broadus, J. A.: *College Education.*
[118] *Ibid.*, 5.

an educated membership of both sexes was necessary to "give interest to Sunday Schools and prayer-meetings, diffuse correct ideas of Christian benevolence, and give sympathetic appreciation and moral support to an intelligent and active pastor."[119] In order to produce a membership of this type, having an education in the highest, broadest sense, it was necessary, according to Dr. Broadus, to keep boys and girls longer in school.[120]

With regard to the religious life of the college at this time, it was found that voluntary chapel service was well attended.[121] Bible instruction was a feature of the religious efforts of the college. The Sabbath was strictly observed.[122]

In 1890, the charter was amended to require trustees to admit free of all charges, except board, all preachers and candidates for the ministry belonging to the "regular" Baptists, and recommended by the education board of the Baptist General Association of Virginia, to which the former Virginia Baptist Education Society had transferred its rights.[123] The trustees were permitted to receive gratuitously such other students as they thought proper, and also to found and maintain other schools and colleges.[124]

It was under this authority that the trustees sought ways and means of enlarging the activities of the college; particularly was a need felt, it was stated, to have a well-equipped college for women in Richmond.[125] The Richmond Female Institute,[126] continued to flourish after the War.[127] At the commencement exercises in July, 1879, the degree of M.A. was conferred upon three of the students.[128] In 1892, a reorganization of the college took place, a new Board of Trustees was appointed, and a charter,

---

119 *Ibid.*, 11.
120 *Ibid.*, 13.
121 *Ibid.*, 21.
122 *Ibid.*, 23.
123 *Acts of Assembly*, Mar. 3, 1890, 789; see p. 314.
124 *Ibid.*, 790; *cf.* same principle, Randolph-Macon System, p. 560.
125 *Greater Richmond College.*
126 See p. 330.
127 *Richmond Enquirer*, June 30, July 14, 1870; *Relig. Herald*, July 18, Aug. 29, 1878; *Va. Educ. Jour.*, July, 1879, X, 319.
128 *Ibid.*

incorporating the school as the Woman's College of Richmond, was obtained in 1894.[129]

At the beginning of the century, it was declared that the very success of the college made it desirable to consider means of providing "better facilities for the education of women in Richmond."[130] In 1906, an agreement was made with the Education Commission of the Baptist General Association of Virginia, in the event the pending plans for a "Greater Richmond College" should succeed, that the "disposition of the franchise and property" of the Woman's College should be governed by the wishes of the Education Commission.

The efforts of the Baptists in the direction of the "Greater Richmond College" were now stimulated by the interest of the General Education Board in Virginia education.[131] The Board subscribed $150,000 on condition that $350,000 be raised by the Baptists.[132] The Woman's College was turned over to Richmond College, in 1914,[133] and thus gave way to Westhampton College, the new co-ordinate college for women, established, in 1914, in the suburbs of Richmond, where it adjoins the men's college.[134]

Westhampton College regards itself as a new creation based on an agreement made in 1906 between Richmond College and the Education Commission that the college would "establish and maintain a new college for women of equal grade with the college for men."[135] Richmond College had before this, in 1898, "admitted women to its advanced classes and to degree privileges,"[136] thus instituting a limited system of co-education which lasted until 1914,[137] and the new college looks to this fact as the origin of its history. In 1921, a new charter was obtained for Richmond College and Westhampton College under the name of

---

[129] *Greater Richmond College*, 7; *Acts of Assembly*, Feb. 7. 1894, 171.
[130] *Greater Richmond College*, 7.
[131] See p. 471.
[132] *Greater Richmond College*.
[133] It was operated until the close of the session of 1915–16, when the obligations to its students were considered as discharged.
[134] *From correspondence; Westhampton College Catalogue*, 1926, 14.
[135] *Ibid.*
[136] *Ibid.*
[137] *From correspondence.*

the University of Richmond, which includes, in addition, "The T. C. Williams School of Law."[138]   After a half century, "the great Baptist University of the South" was achieved.[139]

The University of Richmond, though it maintains a Baptist denominational relationship, has other denominations also represented on its Board of Trustees and in its faculty.[140]

With regard to the recent religious life of the men's college in the University, accounts indicate that the voluntary principle in regard to chapel services has not survived.   Attendance is required of all students unless specifically excused, one absence a week being allowed.   Prayer meetings held once, or oftener, every week, are conducted by the students.   A Sunday evening vesper service is held in common by Richard College and Westhampton College.[141]   The department of Biblical History and Literature offers four, three-hour courses, "Old Testament History and Literature," "New Testament History and Literature," "Modern Church Problems," and "Church History, Comparative Religion, Missions."   The aim is "to put the student into possession of a first-hand working knowledge of the Bible and to create an interest in the prosecution of these vital themes."[142]

Westhampton College has the usual religious activities of denominational colleges, including a Y. W. C. A.   The Young Woman's Auxiliary aims to foster a missionary interest and "to keep Baptist girls in touch with their denominational program."[143]   Attendance at chapel service is compulsory, but is regulated by Student Government.[144]   The department of Biblical History and Literature is under the direction of the same professor as at Richmond College, and exactly the same courses are offered.[145]

In an appeal for funds, in December, 1925, the University gave its enrollment as more than one thousand students, and stated

---

138 Robertson: *Amer. Univ. and Colleges*, 746; *U. of Richmond A Brief Sketch.*
139 See p. 547.
140 Robertson: *Amer. Univ. and Colleges*, 746.
141 *U. of Richmond Catalog*, 1926, 14, 16.
142 *Ibid.*, 40.
143 *Westhampton College Catalog*, 1926, 16.
144 *Ibid.*, 18.
145 *Ibid.*, 37–38.

that of its seven thousand living alumni, one thousand were in Richmond.[146]

The colored Baptists have their own higher educational institution in Virginia Union University. This institution is the result of a combination of a number of schools. Its history begins, in 1865, with Richmond Theological School for Freedmen, established under the auspices of the American Baptist Home Mission Society.[147] In 1867, it was reopened by the National Theological Institute, a Baptist organization, which had decided to merge its work into that of the American Baptist Home Mission Society. The school was placed by the Institute, that year, in charge of Dr. N. Colver, and called Colver Institute in 1869.[148] In 1876, the Assembly incorporated the school as Richmond Institute.[149]

In 1880, a limited number of young women were admitted, and this was continued until 1883, when Hartshorn Memorial College was opened. About thirty women had been in attendance, in that time.[150]

The school was reincorporated, in 1886, as Richmond Theological Seminary, and trustees were required to be members in good standing of a regular Baptist church.[151] In 1896, the Seminary and Hartshorn Memorial College were incorporated under the name of Virginia Union University.[152] The University was to provide a separate college for men. The board of trustees was to be under the control of the American Baptist Home Mission Society and the state convention of the colored "regular" Baptist churches; three-fourths of the trustees were to be regular Baptists.

In the meantime, Wayland Seminary, which had been opened, in 1865, in Washington, by the American Baptist Home Mission

---

[146] *Richmond News Leader;* Dec. 31, 1925; *cf.* Robertson: *Amer. Univ. and Colleges,* 747, apparently based on year 1926, gives enrollment, Richmond College, 492; Westhampton College, 333; T. Williams School of Law, 153; Summer School (1925), 204.

[147] Corey, C. H.: *Richmond Theol. Seminary,* 52–53.

[148] *Ibid.,* 54, 64–65.

[149] *Ibid.,* 88; *Acts of Assembly,* Feb. 10, 1876, 44.

[150] Corey: *Richmond Theol. Seminary,* 103, 135.

[151] *Ibid.,* 130; *Acts of Assembly,* Feb. 5, 1866, 60–61.

[152] *Ibid.,* Mar. 4, 1896, 800.

Society was united in 1899, with the University, and an act amending the charter passed in 1900.[153]   The act provided that the University, so long as it received financial assistance from the American Baptist Home Mission Society, was to be subject to visitation by its representatives; the society was also to have the privilege of approving the selection and dismissal of teachers.[154]

In 1923, the college department of Hartshorn Memorial College was co-ordinated with the University in such fashion as to permit its students to recite at the University, and get their degrees there.[155]

Recent accounts of the school emphasize the fact that it is Christian, rather than denominational; that unlike a state school, however, "it definitely aims to develop religious character no less than intellectual ability and culture."   The purpose of the school is to prepare for Christian life and service.   Great stress is placed upon right habits of conduct.[156]   Attendance at chapel, and service on Sunday afternoon is required.   On Sunday mornings, students have a choice of attending Y. M. C. A. Bible class at the school or going to the church of their choice.   There are also weekly prayer and devotional meetings by religious societies.   Two hours' work, each year, is required in the Bible in the college course.[157]   Bible work, usually consisting of a two-hour course, except one semester of five hours in Bible History, is also required in the last three years of the high school department.[158]   The University has a separate theological department leading to the degree of B.D.[159]

Hartshorn Memorial College, established in memory of Rachel Hartshorn, was incorporated in 1884, for the purpose of maintaining an institution of Christian learning of collegiate grade for colored women.[160]   Instruction in Biblical and Christian learn-

153 *Ibid.*, Feb. 17, 1900, 420; *Va. Union Univers. Catalog,* 1926, 10—historical outline in catalog is incorrect in stating that the name was first changed to Virginia Union University by the act of 1900.
154 *Acts of Assembly,* Feb. 17, 1900, 420–23.
155 *Va. Union Univers. Catalog,* 1926, 10; *Hartshorn Memorial College Catalog,* 1926, 11.
156 *Va. Union Univers. Catalog,* 1926, 17; *cf.* 1920–21, 15.
157 *Ibid.*, 1926, 18, 23–24.
158 *Ibid.*, 61–62.
159 *Ibid.*, 50.
160 *Acts of Assembly,* Mar. 13, 1884, 522.

ing was especially mentioned in the charter.   Various Baptist Home Mission societies were to have representation on the Board as long as they contributed to the college.[161]   The college aims to exert a strong Christian influence upon its students, and the "religious life is carefully developed."[162]   The courses of study extend from the sixth grade through the college.   In the high school, a five-hour course in the Bible is required in both the second and third years; in the college, two hours' work is required, each year, in the Bible or religion.   Among the religious organizations of the college are a missionary society, Sunday School, and a Christian Endeavor Society.

In addition to these two Universities for white and colored students, the Baptists have two junior colleges for girls, two academies for boys, and five mountain schools—these institutions are for white students.[163]   Averett College, the older of the two colleges for girls, is located at Danville.   It was originally incorporated as the Union Female College in 1859.[164]   Averett College claims it is not "narrowly sectarian;" its aim being "Christian Education."[165]   Attendance is required at daily chapel services, at Sunday School and Sunday morning service of the church of the student's choice.   Religious organizations are the Y. W. A. and the Volunteer Band.[166]   In the college, two, three-hour courses are offered in the Old and the New Testaments respectively, and a one-hour course in Sunday School pedagogy. Three hours' work is required in the Bible.[167]   No Bible courses are offered in the high school department.

The other junior college for girls is Virginia Intermont College.   This school was founded, in 1884, by Rev. J. R. Harrison, D.D., at Glade Spring, Washington County.   In 1893, it

---

161 *Ibid.*
162 *Hartshorn Memorial College Catalog*, 1926, 11, 12.
163 *Bull. State B'd Educ.*, July, 1925, VIII, No. 1, 36.
164 *Acts of Assembly*, Dec. 22, 1859, 448.   In 1864, its charter was amended, and the name changed to Roanoke Female College; *Ibid.*, Feb. 13, 1864, 68; it then had successively the names of Roanoke College for Women, Roanoke Institute, and now Averett College; *Averett College Catalog*, 1927, 13.
165 *Ibid.*, 13, 22.
166 *Ibid.*, 19–20.
167 *Ibid.*, 39, 42.

was moved to Bristol. It is under the control of a Board of Trustees appointed by the Baptist General Association of Virginia.[168] However, the school authorities state no attempt ''to influence pupils in their denominational preferences, will be exercised or tolerated.''[169] It endeavors in its atmosphere and teaching to create a positive Christian influence. The ''cultured Christian'' woman is the ideal of the school.[170] A statement by the authorities of the school declares: ''Give us intellect and righteous women and we can have model homes; these form the only sure basis for prosperity in the institutions of church and state.''[171] One-half hour chapel exercise is held, each morning; these exercises, in addition to the usual hymns and scripture reading and prayer, consist of voluntary Scripture quotations, and brief comments on select passages.[172] Pupils are required to attend Sunday mornings the churches designated by their parents or guardians; Sunday evening service is at the college. The college has a Y. W. C. A. A strong missionary sentiment is fostered among the students by a study of mission fields and special missionary meetings.[173] Two hours' work in the Bible is required in the college. Two courses, two hours a week are offered, one in the Life and teachings of Christ, the other in the Old Testament.[174] As at Averett College, systematic work in the Bible is not offered in the high school. Apparently, this is due to the fact that sixteen units of work are required to have this department accredited, and the nature of the required work does not allow much opportunity for adding systematic work in the Bible. In view of the injection of the Bible courses for credit into the public high school system, this situation in denominational schools is most interesting. It may, of course, be held that this lack is compensated by the general religious life of the school. At both Averett College and Virginia Intermont College,

---

168 *Va. Intermont College Catalog*, 1926, 17.
169 *Ibid.*, 24.
170 *Ibid.*, 4.
171 *Ibid.*
172 *Ibid.*, 23.
173 *Ibid.*
174 *Ibid.*, 40–41.

daughters of ministers receive a reduction in fees.[175]   Both institutions are accredited by the state.[176]

The two academies for boys are Fork Union Military Academy, at Fork Union, Fluvanna County, and the Hargrave Military Academy, at Chatham, Pittsylvania County.   The Fork Union Military Academy was founded in 1898 and turned over to the Baptist Church in Virginia in 1912.[177]   Its authorities state ''all forms of religious beliefs are tolerated and sincerely respected— Jew or Gentile, Catholic or Protestant.''   Cadets are required to attend Sunday School and church service on Sunday, but are excused upon written request of parents.[178]   A four-year course in both the Old and the New Testament is offered, and required for graduation, unless specific exemption is asked for, by the parents.[179]   The school is an accredited school.   Its appeal to the public is based on the ground that ''The State, the Nation, the World is calling for trained Christian men.''[180]

Hargrave Military Academy was originally organized, in 1909, as the Chatham Training School.   It has been associated with the Baptist denomination since 1913.[181]   Its new name was adopted in 1925.[182]   The Academy emphasizes its Christian influence, and the fact that, though denominational, it is not sectarian.   Students are allowed to attend the church of their parents' choice; but must attend services regularly at one of the five churches in the town.[183]   A Y. M. C. A. conducts its regular program, and there are the usual daily chapel exercises.   A two-year Bible course is given.   In the junior year, the work covers the Old, and in the senior year, the New Testament.   The Sunday School follows the course of study prescribed by the Sunday School Board.[184]   At both Fork Union Academy and Hargrave Acad-

---

[175] *Averett College Catalog,* 1927, 34; *Intermont College Catalog,* 1926, 69.
[176] *Bull. State B'd Educ.,* July, 1925, VIII, No. I, 35, 42.
[177] *Fork Union Milit. Acad. Catalog,* 1927, 12.
[178] *Ibid.,* 19.
[179] *Ibid.,* 52.
[180] *Fork Union Military Academy,* leaflet.
[181] *Hargrave Milit. Acad. Catalog,* 1926, 23.
[182] *Ibid.*
[183] *Ibid.,* 24, 55.
[184] *Ibid.,* 39.

emy, there are special considerations with regard to fees for sons of ministers and approved candidates for the ministry.

Since 1911, the Virginia Baptist Board of Missions and Education has co-operated in the establishment and maintenance of four co-educational mountain schools—the Buchanan Mission School, at Council, Buchanan County, the Blue Ridge Mission School, at Buffalo Ridge, Patrick County, the Oak Hill Academy, at Kindrick, Grayson County, and the Piedmont Baptist Mission School, at Alhambra, Amherst County.[185] While mission schools, these schools are not entirely free schools. Some scholarships and opportunities to meet expense by work at the school are available. For days pupils, the cost for tuition, is as a rule nominal. The cost for board in the dormitories in recent years has been between $120 and $140. Both elementary and secondary instruction are given, and in the secondary work the standards of the State Board of Education are set up. According to a leaflet of the Buchanan Mission School, the chief differentiation lies in this, that "A study of the Bible and kindred subjects is included in the course. These, of course, cannot be taught in State schools." These schools are frankly denominational schools, as is indicated by the co-operation of the Blue Ridge Mission School with the neighboring Baptist Church, and a statement of the Buchanan Mission School that "Our denominational schools must be maintained at whatever cost, and schools dealing with children at the most impressionable age must be maintained." It is apparently no pampering kind of Christianity that is inculcated. The gospel of work is emphasized, particularly for scholarship pupils. According to the authorities of the Blue Ridge Mission School, "Strict obedience to authority, good manners, studious habits and an aptness to learn will be required of all pupils. No pupil will be retained who shows an unwillingness to obey the rules of the school."

Justification for the existence of these schools is found in the statement of the Buchanan Mission School, that "The lives of hundreds of boys and girls of this mountain section have been helpfully touched. Many entering its halls have found Him

---

[185] A fifth mountain school is that of Lee Baptist Institute, at Pennington Gap, Virginia; its first graduating class was in 1911.

who has turned their lives into paths of Christian service, and have had their inspirations lifted.''[186]

An interesting feature of the development of the Baptist educational activity is the compactness of the system, with its five co-educational mountain schools, its two secondary schools for boys, its two junior colleges for girls, and its two Universities for white and colored students. It is, however, apparent from a comparison of enrollment in these institutions with figures of Baptist church membership, that these schools by no means reach that membership in any proportionate sense. The white Baptist membership, in 1926, was 236,867;[187] and yet, the number of children at the Buchanan Mission School, first opened in 1911, in 1928 was 174; the number of students at Fork Union Military Academy, in 1926, was 161; at Hargrave Military Academy, in 1927, 168; at Virginia Intermont College and Averett College, in 1927, 375 and 234, respectively; and these figures include students from outside of Virginia. At the University of Richmond, the enrollment, in 1926, was less than a thousand.[188] The number of colored Baptists in 1916, was 316,-531;[189] and the number of students at Virginia Union University, which includes a preparatory department was less than 700.[190] While some leaders in the Baptist Church may seek to stress the importance from a denominational standpoint of a system of schools ''actively engaged in the business of Christian education, interpreting education in terms of Christian character, and striving to make the whole process contribute to the moral and spiritual development of their students and training for service to the world,''[191] the Baptist layman, on the whole, seems content to avail himself of the educational opportunities furnished by the public school system, apparently satisfied to find com-

---

186 *Buchanan Mission School,* Leaflet; *Blue Ridge Mission School,* Leaflet; *Piedmont Baptist Mission School,* Leaflet.

187 *U. S. Bur. Census, Press Summaries,* Aug. 15, 1928, June 20, 1928, May 29, 1928, Mar. 20, 1928—Southern Baptists, 232,270; Primitive Baptists, 9,745; Regular Baptists, 3,387; Free Will Baptists, 465.

188 *Fork Union Milit. Acad. Catalog,* 1927, 63 *ff;* *Bull. State B'd Educ.,* Nov., 1927, X, No. 2, 110; Robertson: *Amer. Univ. and Colleges,* 747.

189 *U. S. Bur. Census, Press Summaries,* July 24, 1928, June 19, 1928—Negro Baptists, 316,095; Colored Primitive Baptists, 436.

190 *Va. Union Univers. Catalog,* 1926, 89.

191 *Min., 142nd Annual Session, Dover Baptist Assoc.,* 19.

pensation in any lack of religious training in that system, even complete absence of Bible reading, by supplementing it with religious instruction in the home, the church, and the Sunday School.

Educational Activities And Tendencies Of The Methodist Church

The most interesting development in Methodist educational activity in the period since the Civil War is the creation of the Randolph-Macon System. While there are a number of Methodist institutions outside the system, the two colleges for men and women, the two academies for boys, and the school for girls, which comprise the system, may be said to hold the center of Methodist educational interest.

Randolph-Macon College, the college for men, it will be recalled,[192] was the first Methodist venture in collegiate education before the Civil War. The War closed its doors, and the college was not reopened until 1866.[193] Various circumstances, such as the acquisition by the Methodists of North Carolina, in 1859, of the institution, subsequently known as Trinity College,[194] and particularly the fact that as a result of the War, Boydton had no nearby railroad, made it desirable, in the view of a number of those interested in the college, to transfer it to some other location. In September, 1868, the college was opened at Ashland, Hanover County.[195]

The removal of the college aroused considerable opposition among a minority group of trustees and citizens interested in keeping the college at Boydton. An attempt to legalize the transfer to Ashland, by amending the charter brought the matter before the Assembly. The minority group in their memorial, in 1870, attempted to show that the action of the Methodist Conference, *"a body of men unknown to the laws of the State,* and certainly not recognized in the charter,"* had exceeded their authority in adopting resolutions at various conferences from

---

192 See p. 318.
193 *Randolph-Macon College Catalog,* 1926, 24.
194 Now Duke University.
195 *Randolph-Macon College Catalog,* 1926, 24; Robertson: *Amer. Univ. and Colleges,* 409; Ashland was being boomed as a resort.

1863 to 1865, looking to the removal of the college.[196] To this the majority group answered that the college had been erected for no one section of Virginia, nor in particular for the section in which the buildings happened to be located; even, if defeated on the transfer question, they were determined to have a college at Ashland.[197] In July, the Assembly passed an act, amending the old charter, and quieting all doubts as to the validity of the transfer.[198]

At a conference of the Methodist Episcopal Church, South, in 1870, the proposition of the trustees to provide free tuition to the sons of ministers of the Conference was accepted.[199] The college prospered at its new location, and, in 1874, it was reported that 45 out of its 235 students were preparing for the ministry.[200]

In 1875, an act was passed for a self-perpetuating board of trustees, consisting of 24 to 44 members.[201] In 1888, in an account published by the college, it was stated that the college though denominational in the sense that it was supported and patronized mainly by the Methodist Church was, nevertheless, not sectarian in its instruction. No proselyting influences were used on students whose families were connected with other churches. The college sought, however, "to combine religious influences with scholastic advantages, believing that learning divorced from religion is a dangerous accomplishment to any one who receives it, and that such divorcement made general will be injurious to the State."[202]

One of the very interesting features of the instruction at that time was the course in Greek, in which, in addition to the usual work in that language, work in translations of the best Greek writers was also assigned. The object was to bring home to the pupils "the belief that God and Christ are in history," and that individuals and nations were to be warned by Greek sins and

---

[196] *Richmond Enquirer*, April 11, 1870.
[197] *Ibid.*
[198] *Acts of Assembly*, July 9, 1870, 339.
[199] *Richmond Enquirer*, Mar. 12, 1870.
[200] *Ibid.*, Mar. 11, 1874; *cf. Ibid.*, Mar. 12, 1870—over 100 students—of which 25 were preparing for the ministry.
[201] *Acts of Assembly*, Mar. 31, 1875, 422.
[202] *U. S. Bur. Educ., Circ. Inf.*, 1888, No. I, 243.

disasters. A further object was to bring to the students what
light the study of the Greek language and literature might cast
upon the New Testament.[203]

In 1890, an act was passed amending the charter and authorizing the board of trustees to erect and maintain schools.[204]   On
the basis of this act, there have been established since, under
the same board of trustees, Randolph-Macon Woman's College,
Lynchburg, 1893; Randolph-Macon Academy, at Bedford, Bedford County, 1890; Randolph-Macon Academy, at Front Royal,
Warren County, 1892—both academies for boys; and Randolph-
Macon School for Girls, at Danville, 1897.[205]   Since 1909, the
governing board of the system has been under the control of the
Baltimore and Virginia conferences of the Methodist Episcopal
Church, South.[206]

The recent religious life of the men's college includes required
chapel attendance.   Students are expected to avail themselves of
the opportunity to attend one of the five denominational village
churches on Sunday.   Bible classes are conducted on Sunday
morning by the professors, officers of the college, or other selected
teachers.   The Y. M. C. A. supervises various religious exercises
in the dormitories, and several Sunday Schools in the neighborhood.[207]   Three courses, three hours per week, are offered in the
study of the Bible; and one, preferably to be taken in the sophomore year, is required for the B.A. or B.S. degree.[208]   The college
emphasizes the realization in the student body of "the Christian
ideal of manhood."   Accordingly, it is the policy to require that
the officers and teachers not only be competent, but also that they
be "by life and experience, Christian men of the highest type."
It is interesting to note, also, that the positive Christian moral

---

203 *Ibid.*, 250–51.
204 *Acts of Assembly*, Feb. 7, 1890, 273.
205 *Randolph-Macon College Catalog*, 1926, 81; Robertson: *Amer. Univ.
and Colleges*, 577.
206 *Ibid.*, 576; Robertson gives the date as 1908, but *Carnegie Foundation for Advancement of Teaching, 4th Annual Rep't*, 41, indicates 1909 as
the date; date confirmed by correspondence.
207 Robertson: *Amer. Univ. and Colleges*, 576; *Randolph-Macon College
Catalog*, 1926, 28–29.
208 *Ibid.*, 37–39, 45–46.

and religious instruction instilled, is "in accordance with the teachings and practices of the Methodist Church."[209]

The founding of Randolph-Macon Woman's College was suggested by George M. Jones, of Lynchburg, to Dr. W. W. Smith, when the latter was on a visit to that city, in the interest of Bedford City Academy.[210] A land boom in Lynchburg facilitated Dr. Smith's obtaining from one of the land companies a site for the college, and $100,000 for buildings on condition that he obtain a similar amount.[211] In 1891, the fund was turned over to the Board and work was begun. The college was opened in 1893, and the purpose in establishing it was declared to be the creation of a college in Virginia, where young women might "obtain an education equal to that given in our best colleges for young men," in an environment suitable to the highest ideals of womanhood.[212]

Perhaps the most interesting episode in the history of the college from the joint of view of its religious affiliation, was its brief connection with "The Carnegie Foundation For The Advancement Of Teaching." A feature of the work of the Foundation, created in 1905, was the establishment of a retiring pension system for members of faculties of colleges and universities accepted by the Foundation, upon compliance with certain conditions. One of the conditions was that these retiring pensions should be paid to such teachers only, whose connection had been with institutions which were not under the control of a sect, or which did not require their trustees, officers, faculties, students, or a majority thereof, to belong to any specified sect, and did not impose any theological test as a condition for entrance or connection with the institution.[213] In 1906, Dr. Smith, the founder of the college, and the chancellor of the Randolph-Macon System of Colleges and Academies, presented an application for admission of Randolph-Macon Woman's College.[214] Dr. Smith

---

[209] *Ibid.*, 29.
[210] Christian: *Lynchburg*, 388.
[211] *Ibid.*
[212] *Randolph-Macon Woman's College Catalog*, 1926, 20.
[213] *Carnegie Foundation for Advancement of Teaching, 1st Annual Rep't*, 47.
[214] *Ibid.*, 12.

stated that the only formal relationship the college had with the Methodist Episcopal Church, South, lay in the fact that it was under the charter of Randolph-Macon College, and had the same trustees. This board, while denominational, "was a self-perpetuating board with no legal connection with the church organization." The Woman's College, Dr. Smith explained, was not under the control of the denomination, and received no support from it. In answer to the application, the Executive Committee of the Foundation informed Dr. Smith that they were ready to accept the institution, on the passage of a resolution by the Board of Trustees in accordance with the ruling regarding denominational control, already referred to. The Board accordingly, in August, 1906, passed a resolution

. . . that in the conduct of the Randolph-Macon Woman's College no denominational test is imposed in the choice of trustees, officers or teachers, or in the admission of students, nor are distinctly denominational tenets or doctrines taught to the students.[215]

Before final action was taken, the Foundation pointed out that certain matters of administrative usage pointed in public opinion, at least, to a denominational control by the church. Dr. Smith declared that in one case, at any rate, such announcement had been made without the authority of the college, and agreed that in future publications, and at the next Virginia Annual Conference, to point out that the college was governed by an independent board. Consequently, the Executive Committee of the Foundation voted on March 28, 1907, to include Randolph-Macon Woman's College in the list of those institutions, whose teachers were entitled to the benefits of the retiring allowance system.[216] At a subsequent conference of a committee of trustees of the college with the Executive Committee of the Foundation, regarding the relations between the college and the Foundation, the Executive Committee explained that they interpreted the resolution, on the basis of which the college had been admitted, to mean that the question of a prospective trustee's denominational affiliation or belief would not be considered.[217] The trus-

---

215 *Ibid.*, 13.
216 *Ibid.*, 14.
217 *Ibid.*, *4th Annual Rep't*, 7.

tees of the college must "make clear to the conference the board's independence in choosing trustees, or aquiesce freely in a choice of trustees under supervision of the conferences."[218]   The passing of the resolution which had been the basis for admission of the college into the benefits of the Foundation had raised a storm of protest in the Baltimore and Virginia Conferences, which insisted that "while the board of trustees was legally independent, the conferences, as representing the denomination, ought to control the college through the choice of trustees."[219]   At a meeting, in June, 1908, between the trustees and representatives of the conferences, the trustees, besides making clear that they regarded the Randolph-Macon Colleges as agencies of the church, adopted a resolution that future vacancies in the Board of Trustees should be filled by the Board, only after names proposed for such vacancies had been submitted for approval to the Conference within whose bounds the vacancy occurred, and had been approved.[220] A copy of these resolutions was sent to the foundation with the request, that, if such action rendered the institution ineligible, its name be removed.[221]   In closing the discussion of the episode, the report of the Foundation declared: "there has never been a better opportunity to show that a body of Christian people interested in education can amply support the institutions which they prefer to control."[222]

The aims of the college have been declared to be the promotion of the highest type of Christian womanhood and the development of a spirit of Christian service.[223]   As at Randolph-Macon College, the faculty are selected not only on the basis of competence, but also on that of moral and religious character.   Daily compulsory chapel services are held.   One of the seven Bible courses offered is required for a degree.   A Y. W. C. A. conducts Bible and mission study classes.[224]   Sunday vesper services are generally conducted by ministers from the city.   Attendance at pre-

---

[218] *Ibid.*
[219] *Ibid.*, 41.
[220] *Ibid.; from correspondence.*
[221] *Carnegie Foundation for Advancement of Teaching, 4th Annual Rep't*, 42.
[222] *Ibid.*
[223] *Randolph-Macon Woman's College Catalog*, 1926, 21.
[224] *Ibid.*, 21–22, 33.

ferred church and Sunday School is encouraged.[225]   Free tuition
is offered to daughters of ministers of all denominations.[226]   In
1925–26, the college enrollment was 841 students.[227]

The proposed establishment of the Randolph-Macon Academy
at Bedford was heralded in the *Virginia Educational Journal,* in
1890, with the statement that the establishment of a first class
academy for the thorough preparation of students for college
challenged "the admiration and the imitation of others."[228]   The
encouragement given the undertaking in southwestern Virginia
seemed to the Methodists to warrant their establishing, in 1892,
another academy in the northwestern part of the state at Front
Royal.   The religious life of these schools follows the same general principles.   A constant effort is made in the school at Bedford "to create and maintain an atmosphere helpful to the growth
of virile Christian character."   Morning and evening devotional
services are held, and students are required to attend Sunday
morning church services.[229]   The school has a Y. M. C. A.   Two,
five-hour courses in the Bible are offered; one in the Old Testament History, the other in the Life of Christ and the Life of St.
Paul.[230]   At the academy at Front Royal, three courses in Bible
study are offered, apparently following the state syllabus of Bible
study for high schools.[231]   At both schools, sons of ministers of
conferences contributing to the funds of the system, and candidates for the ministry of an evangelical church receive a reduction in fees.[232]   The authorities of the Academy at Front Royal
declare, "Worldly amusements that weaken and destroy the
spiritual life of young people and are contrary to the teachings
and practices of the Methodist Church are forbidden."[233]

The Randolph-Macon School for Girls at Danville was formerly the Danville College for Young Ladies.[234]   It was pre-

---

225 *Ibid.,* 22.
226 *From correspondence;* Robertson: *Amer. Univ. and Colleges,* 577.
227 *Ibid.*
228 *Va. Educ. Jour.,* July, 1890, XXI, 316.
229 *Randolph-Macon Academy, Bedford, Catalog,* 1926, 8–9.
230 *Ibid.,* 20.
231 *Randolph-Macon Academy, Front Royal, Catalog,* 1926, 33.
232 *Ibid.,* 43; *Bedford, Catalog,* 21.
233 *Front Royal, Catalog,* 45.
234 See p. 321.

sented by its owners, in 1897, free of all encumberance, to the Randolph-Macon System.[235] The authorities of the school declare that though denominational, its teaching is non-sectarian. Its influence is Christian, and only active members of Christian churches are engaged for the faculty.[236] Students are required to attend Sunday morning service at the church of their parents' choice; attendance at any other church being only by parents' permission in writing.[237] Attendance at Sunday School is required, as also at the morning and evening devotional exercises. The school has a Y. W. C. A. Two courses in the Old Testament, and one in the New are offered as electives. The object of these courses is stated as two-fold: "to give the student a better idea of the Bible as history and literature and to assist her in seeing how its truths have influenced for good the thought and life of mankind." The various church doctrines are not discussed.[238]

The authorities of the Randolph-Macon System declare that it is not desired in any of their institutions to influence the denominational preferences of students. The officers do, however, "consider themselves under obligations to conform to the moral standards and religious uses of the Methodist Episcopal Church, South, under whose auspices the institutions were established." It is because of various advantages and economies that the schools are conducted under one system.[239]

The schools not under the Randolph-Macon System are Emory and Henry College, formerly for men, now co-educational, and Martha Washington College for Women, both in Washington County; Blackstone College for Girls, in Nottoway County; the Ferrum Training School, in Franklin County; and the Triangular Mountain Institute, at Mt. Heron, in Buchanan County.

During the Civil War, Emory and Henry College, which was the second higher Methodist institution in the state,[240] yielded its buildings for hospital purposes to the Confederate government. In 1865, the college was again opened to students. While

---

[235] *Randolph-Macon School Catalog*, 1926, 13.
[236] *Ibid.*, 17.
[237] *Ibid.*
[238] *Ibid.*, 50.
[239] *Randolph-Macon College Catalog*, 1926, 81.
[240] See p. 319.

the enrollment before the War had reached 280 pupils,[241] after the War, it varied for a time from 80 to 150; in 1926, its enrollment was 329, consisting of 271 men and 58 women.[242]

In 1890, the charter was amended to require 13 of its 27 members to be appointed by the Holston Annual Conference of the Methodist Episcopal Church, South.[243] In 1918, the Holston Conference decided to consolidate Emory and Henry College and Martha Washington College under one Board of Trustees.[244] An amendment to the charter was obtained, and the two colleges were operated under the same president from 1919 to 1922. Since 1922, each college has had a separate president and administration, but control by one Board of Trustees continues. At Emory and Henry College, women have been admitted since 1922 to the Junior and Senior classes; daughters of members of the faculty and young women living in the community may be admitted to the freshman classes.[245]

With reference to the religious life of the college, "all students are *required* to be present with the professors" at the daily chapel services.[246] This requirement is based on the ground that the assembly "for instruction and devotion has been found promotive of that sympathy and good spirit essential to harmony and good order." Attendance on Sunday morning services in the college auditorium is also required, except for students who attend church elsewhere.[247] The college services are usually conducted by the regular college pastor or by other distinguished ministers. Students are also urged, but not required to attend one of the various classes of the Sunday School which meets for service and Bible study. Every effort is made according to the school authorities "to interest our students in religion and religious work." A series of special services with the object of endeavoring to bring students to a realization of a religious life is conducted every session.[248] So seriously are the religious ac-

241 Summers: *Hist. S. W. Va.*, 578.
242 Robertson: *Amer. Univ. and Colleges*, 413.
243 *Acts of Assembly*, Feb. 4, 1890, 235.
244 *Emory and Henry Catalog*, 1926, 18.
245 *Ibid.*, 19.
246 *Ibid.*, 30.
247 *Ibid.*, 33, 36; Robertson: *Amer. Univ. and Colleges*, 413.
248 *Emory and Henry Catalog*, 1926, 33–34.

tivities regarded that students having a total of seven unexcused absences from chapel and church, or five from chapel, or four from church are liable to suspension from college for one week, during which they may return home, or be compelled to remain on the campus. All class work and special tests must be made up. A fee is charged for the tests and examinations missed.[249] This imposition of a penalty by fine for failure to attend a religious service is of interest, in view of the principles enunciated in its original charter, and the fact that the Virginia Constitution guarantees freedom from compulsion or penalty with respect to religious worship.[250]

The college has a Y. M. C. A. with its varied activities of Sunday evening services, Bible classes, and missionary work. There is also a combined college and community mid-week prayer service conducted by the college pastor.[251] Bible study equivalent in amount to one hour a week for each of the four years is required for a degree;[252] but all students, whether or not candidates for a degree, are required to take at least a one-hour a week course in the Bible each year. Eleven courses are offered in Religious Education. Their chief concern is with various aspects of instruction and training in that field; among these courses are some that deal with the moral and religious development of the child and the adolescent, and a consideration of a national program of religious education.[253] Six courses are given in addition in the Old and the New Testament. Not all these courses are given each year, and as the college is on a quarter session basis, some are given only for certain quarters.

The college remits tuition fees to the following classes of privileged students: 1. those intending to preach and regularly endorsed by their denominations—the college will collect the tuition fees of those who do not carry out their expressed intention; 2. sons of ministers in service of any denomination; and

---

[249] *Ibid.*, 36.
[250] See p. 320; the college may perhaps justify these penalties on the basis of a necessity for obedience or uniformity.
[251] *Emory and Henry Catalog*, 1926, 45.
[252] *Ibid.*, 54–55.
[253] *Ibid.*, 73–75.

3. sons of superannuated or deceased members of the Holston Conference.[254]

Martha Washington College, which came under the control of the Holston Conference in 1858, was closed for a few months only, in 1862.[255]   In 1867, the charter was amended to give the Holston Conference power to appoint annually a board of visitors, equal in number to the board of trustees, to constitute with that board a joint board to manage the institution.[256]   Since 1918, the college has been consolidated, by the Holston Conference, under the same board of trustees as that of Emory and Henry College.[257]   The change in the status of the college from that of a degree conferring college to that of a junior college, was made in 1922.[258]

A statement by the college declares that an ''effort is made to strengthen and stimulate every impulse toward Christian life and service, but sectarianism is avoided.''   While all students are required to attend Sunday School at the Methodist Episcopal Church, South, denominational church loyalty is fostered by the requirement to attend the church of one's choice at the Sunday morning hour of worship.   Daily chapel attendance is also required.[259]   A Y. W. C. A. contributes its share to the religious life.[260]   Four hours of work in the Bible are required for completion of the Junior College Literary Course.[261]   The courses offered are ''The Bible itself in the Old and New Testament,'' ''The Worker and His Bible including the Organization and Administration of the Sunday School,'' ''A Study of the Psalms,'' and ''The study of a Harmony of the Gospels.''[262]

A second junior college for girls is Blackstone College, established by the Methodists of the Farmville District of the Virginia Conference.   A charter incorporating the school, then known as the Blackstone Female Institute, was obtained in February,

---

[254] *Ibid.*, 38.
[255] See p. 320; Summers: *Hist. S. W. Va.*, 570.
[256] *Acts of Assembly*, Feb. 9, 1867, 624.
[257] See p. 566.
[258] *From correspondence.*
[259] *From correspondence; Martha Washington College Catalog*, 1926, 18.
[260] *Ibid.*, 20.
[261] *Ibid.*, 33.
[262] *Ibid.*, 35.

1892.[263]   The school having made consistent progress, the Board of Trustees decided, in 1915, to extend its work by adding a junior college program.[264]   The school holds that "All morality must be founded upon religion; the best results, therefore, can only be gained under positive Christian influence."[265]

Religious life at Blackstone College appears to be less sectarian in tendency than at some other Methodist institutions.   Students are permitted to attend the church to which they belong or that of their parents' choice.   The school has its own Sunday School, divided into two departments, Young People and Intermediate-Senior.   Following a worship service in common, students attend classes arranged according to age groups and taught by faculty or student teachers.   Sunday evening denominational group meetings are held for study of the work of individual churches, a union meeting being held the first Sunday of each month. This plan of study is under the auspices of the World Fellowship Department of the Y. W. C. A.   Other features of the religious program are a Sunday School training school held at the college under the auspices of the town churches, and a week devoted to the study and discussion of the practical phases of Christian living.   Visitors are not received on Sunday.   Three hours' work in the Bible for one year is required for graduation from the college, and one unit in the college-preparatory department.   The work in the college is devoted to a study of the New Testament.   A three-hour course in Religious Education is also offered.   In the preparatory department, the first semester is devoted to Paul, the second to the Life of Christ.[266]

There are two mountain schools under church control; the more recently established is Triangular Mountain Institute, located at Mount Heron, and chartered in 1922.[267]   It was preceded by the school at Ferrum, which is rapidly outgrowing its former character.   Ferrum Training School, originally, like Central Acad-

---

[263] *Acts of Assembly,* Feb. 15, 1892, 359; *Blackstone College Catalog,* 1929, 15; land for the school was donated by the Blackstone Land Company; in 1906, Mr. Andrew Carnegie gave $17,500 to an expansion fund, *Ibid.,* 17.
[264] *Ibid.,* 17–18.
[265] *Ibid.,* 21.
[266] *Ibid.,* 26, 29–30, 41–42, 51.
[267] *Christian Educ. Mag.,* Aug., 1927, XVII, No. 3, 60.

emy, in the Presbyterian Church,[268] was a missionary venture of
the church. It was opened in September, 1914, under the Virginia Conference of the Methodist Episcopal Church, South,
and the Woman's Missionary Society of the Conference. The
Conference elects fourteen of the trustees, the Missionary Society,
seven.[269] It has gradually expanded until at present it is offering the work of a Junior College. The school places its emphasis
upon training looking to teaching, preaching, and missionary
work. A resident pastor preaches to the students on Sunday.
Every pupil is expected to attend Sunday School. An Epworth
League, a Young People's Missionary Society, and other religious
activities are part of the school life. The faculty are members
of the church. One of the features of the religious work is a
special service, in order to bring the students "to a definite decision for Christ and the meetings always result in the professing
of faith on the part of nearly all of the students in the School."
Regular and systematic study of the Bible is required. Students
are required to sign a contract upon entering the school and
failure to observe its terms is punished in various ways which
may include dismissal. Visitors are not allowed to come on
Sunday, but may come Saturday, and stay over the week-end.[270]
As the charges for board and tuition are very low, all students
must agree to work ten hours per week.

In the high school, courses in the Bible are required in the first
and second years. In the third and fourth years, elective courses
are offered leading to the diploma in the "Cokesbury Course in
Religious Education for training of Sunday School workers."[271]
Two courses are given in the Bible in the college department,
and are planned for students who are preparing for either the
ministry or missionary work of the church. This work is required of all ministerial and missionary volunteers, and leads to
the Diploma in Religious Education given by the General Sunday School Board. In the Education department, a course is
given in Ethics and Religious Education.[272]

---

[268] See p. 544.
[269] *Ferrum Training School Catalog*, 1926–27, 8; leaflet, "A True Story
that Reads Like a Romance."
[270] *Ferrum Training School Catalog*, 1926–27, 10–11.
[271] *Ibid.*, 22–23.
[272] *Ibid.*, 19–20.

It is seen from this account of Methodist educational activity that there has developed in the church, two systems of schools; one closely co-ordinated in the Randolph-Macon system; the other, a scattered system under various regional conferences. Their chief unifying feature lies in the fact that they come under the direction of principles and policies emanating from the Board of Education, Methodist Episcopal Church, South.[273] From the description of the religious life at these Methodist institutions, it is apparent that at most of them the feeling of obligation "to conform to the moral standards and religious uses of the Methodist Episcopal Church, South," tends to lead somewhat toward sectarianism, in the conduct of, at least, part of the religious life.

It is rather interesting to find that the mountain school movement has made so little progress in a denomination which is so much larger in numbers and wealth than is the Presbyterian church, or the Baptist.

Like the Presbyterian Church, the Methodist Episcopal Church, South, has inaugurated a system of pastors at state institutions, two recent appointments being to the University of Virginia and William and Mary College. It is the intention to extend this system to all state institutions as funds are available. The church is also furthering the extension of Bible chairs at state institutions, and the possibility of establishing one at the University of Virginia is being discussed.[274]

The question of the extent to which the three senior colleges, the three junior colleges and four secondary schools meet the needs of the church is worthy of consideration. In 1926, it was estimated that the white Methodists of the state numbered 266,-081.[275] The total number of students attending, in 1927, at the

---

[273] *Cf. Christian Educ. Mag.*, Aug., 1927, XVII, No. 3.

[274] *Ibid.*, 25, 27–28, 41; with one Bible chair already there, apparently this would involve some scheme along the line of the Jeffersonian proposal. see p. 374.

[275] *U. S. Bur. Census, Press Summaries*, July 13, July 13, June 19, 1928, Dec. 9, 1927, Jan. 30, July 19, June 29, May 24, 1928;—Methodist Episcopal Church, South, 237,903; Methodist Episcopal Church, 22,841; Methodist Protestant Church, 5,004; Wesleyan Methodist Connection, 230; Free Methodist Church, N. A., 103; according to the same source, the colored Methodists numbered 32,402;—the African Methodist Zion membership being 17,592; African Methodist Episcopal, 14,635; the Colored Methodist Epis-

schools described, was 3,887.[276]   Interestingly enough a survey of
the church affiliation of the students at Emory and Henry College, the two Randolph-Macon Colleges, Blackstone, and Martha
Washington College, reveals that out of their total enrollment
of 2,301 students somewhat less than half, 1,040 students, belong
to the Methodist church—and these figures represent also students from outside of Virginia. Apparently in spite of the
efforts to promote denominational education, and the opinion of
some Methodist leaders as evinced by their desire to introduce
compulsory Bible reading, that the public school system is not
sufficiently godly, Virginia Methodists are not flocking to their
own schools. It is conceded that one reason for the existence
of these schools is the training of ministerial students; a total of
105 students was registered at all the institutions in 1927.[277]

Educational Activities And Tendencies Of Minor Evangelical
Groups

While the educational activities of the four leading denominations loom largest, because of the number and range of their
schools, the educational activities of some of the smaller denominations hold a certain interest and importance because of the
various contributions that they have made to the educational and
professional life of the state. The general principles under
which they operate their schools, do not differ very essentially
from those of the leading denominations, except in the case of
the Mennonites.

---

copal, 2,175—there have been and are a number of colored schools under
the various Methodist churches—space has limited any consideration of
colored schools to the more outstanding ones; those interested in denominational colored schools should consult, *U. S. Bur. Educ. Bull.*, 1916, No. 39,
607 *ff*; Brown, W. H.: *Educ. Negro in Va.*; Earnest, J. B.: *Relig. Devel't
Negro in Va.*; Jones, C. C.: *Relig. Inst. Negroes.*

276 *Christian Educ. Mag.*, Aug. 1927, XVII, No. 3, 58–61; calculated
from figures there given.

277 *Ibid.*; in this connection it may be stated that taking the Methodist
Episcopal Church, South, as a whole, it was reported, in 1927, that four per
cent of its ministers were graduates from theological schools in comparison
with thirty-two per cent in the Methodist Episcopal Church; eleven per cent
were college graduates as compared with forty-five per cent in the other;
sixty-nine per cent, high school graduates, compared with eighty-two per
cent in the other; the discipline in both churches is practically the same.
Ibid., 8.

Among the smaller denominations which operate one or more schools are the Lutheran, the Reformed Church, the Mennonites, the United Brethren in Christ, the Church of the Brethren, the Disciples of Christ, and the Friends.

The Lutherans have been interested in developing Roanoke College for boys, and Marion Junior College for girls. Roanoke College, now at Salem, Roanoke County,[278] was the work of Rev. David Frederick Bittle and Rev. Christopher C. Baughman. It was incorporated in 1853; the establishment of a theological professorship was forbidden.[279] Its charter was amended in 1888, to require two-thirds of its board of trustees to be members of the Evangelical Lutheran Church.[280] Though a denominational institution, about two-thirds of its enrollment was estimated, in 1888, to be from other denominations.[281] It was stated, at that time, as an indication of the liberal tendencies of the college, that it had in 1886–87, representatives at seven theological seminaries.[282]

Marion Junior College, at Marion, Smyth County, was founded in 1873, by the Lutheran Synod of Southwestern Virginia as Marion Female College. Incorporated in 1874, it was conducted as a liberal arts college until 1912, when the trustees voluntarily fixed its standard as that of a junior college, but it still operates under its original charter.[283] Though the President and the majority of the Board of Trustees are, in accordance with the charter, members of the Lutheran Church, no denominational restriction is placed on the faculty or student body. The authorities state, however, that it is "a church institution and in its policies and teachings is loyal to the Church."[284] The usual activities and requirements of denominational colleges, including work in the Bible, appear in the religious life of both

---

[278] Originally located near Staunton in 1842, under the name of Virginia Institute, changed in 1845, to Virginia Collegiate Institute.

[279] *Roanoke College Catalog*, 1926, 14; *Acts of Assembly*, Jan. 30, 1845, 104; Mar. 14, 1853, 238; Gilbert, D. M.: *Lutheran Church*, 41–42; Wayland: *German Element*, 159; *Jour. of Educ.*, June 28, 1883, XVIII, 11.

[280] *Acts of Assembly*, Feb. 3, 1888, 65–66.

[281] *U. S. Bur. Educ., Circ. Inf.*, 1888, No. I, 263.

[282] *Ibid.*

[283] *Acts of Assembly*, Jan. 23, 1874, 10; *Marion College Catalog*, 1925, 9.

[284] *Ibid.*, 9, 16.

Roanoke College and Marion Junior College.   They are both accredited by the state.[285]

The Virginia Classis of the Reformed Church in the United States has one school, Massanutten Academy for boys, at Woodstock, Shenandoah County, chartered in 1899.[286]   Representation on the Board of Trustees is not limited to the members of the Reformed Church.   The school aims to be thoroughly Christian, without being sectarian.[287]   One of the features of the school life is a week of prayer, which is made "an occasion of deep spiritual value to the life of the school."[288]

Shenandoah College was founded, in 1875, at Dayton, Rockingham County, under the auspices of the United Brethren in Christ, as a co-educational institution.   Chartered in 1876 under the name of Shenandoah Seminary, it has subsequently been known as Shenandoah Institute, and Shenandoah Collegiate Institute and School of Music.[289]   It has been a junior college since 1922, and accredited by the state since 1924.   Its religious life follows the general principles of other denominational schools. In its Bible work, it stresses "the great doctrines of salvation as opposed to the modern 'isms.'"[290]

The Disciples of Christ control Lynchburg College, a co-educational institution chartered in 1903, under the name of Virginia Christian College; the name being changed to its present form in 1919.   It follows the declared policy of most Virginia de-

---

[285] Statistics according to *U. S. Bur. Census, Press Summaries*, April 6, Mar. 23, May 7, Feb. 1, May 31, 1928—for the various branches of the Lutheran Church in Virginia, for 1926, are: The United Lutheran Church in America, 19,252; The Evangelical Lutheran Synodical Conference of America, 1,729; Evangelical Synod of Missouri, Ohio, and other States, 1,372; The Evangelical Lutheran Joint Synod of Ohio and other States, 364; Norwegian Lutheran Church of America, 334; Total, 23,051.

[286] *Bull State B'd Educ.*, Nov., 1927, X, No. 2, 109, indicates that it is beginning to admit girls, as the enrollment is given 124 boys, 12 girls.

[287] *Massannutten Acad. Catalog*, 1926, 23; Wayland: *German Element*, 162.

[288] *Massannutten Acad. Catalog*, 1926, 38; according to booklet $\frac{No. 5,}{174}$ "Reformed Church in the United States," 7, issued by Bureau of the Census, 1928, the membership for Virginia of the "Reformed Church in the United States" was 2,669; *cf. Ibid.*, 11.

[289] Wayland: *German Element*, 161; *Shenandoah College Catalog*, 1926, 10; *U. of Va. Rec., Ext. Ser.*, Sept., 1924, IX, No. 1, 77–78.

[290] *Shenandoah College Catalog*, 1926, 38.

nominational colleges in avoiding sectarianism. A recent statement by the college declares it "is proud of the large number of students prepared for the ministry and missionary work."[291]

Bridgewater-Daleville College is a union of two institutions of the Church of the Brethren. Bridgewater College had it origin, in 1880, under the name of Spring Creek Normal and Collegiate Institute at Spring Creek, Rockingham County. Two years later it was moved to Bridgewater and called the Virginia Normal School, under which name it was incorporated in 1884.[292] In 1889, it was chartered as Bridgewater College.[293] The history of Daleville College goes back to a private school started in 1890, by B. F. Nininger, of Daleville, Botetourt County. In 1893, the school was called Botetourt Normal School, and, in 1894, it was chartered as Botetourt Normal College.[294] In 1909, the charter was amended, and the name changed to Daleville College. In 1914, it became a junior college. It was decided, in 1923, in the interests of the church to concentrate on a secondary school program in co-operation with Bridgewater College.[295] Both institutions are accredited by the state. While students of its own affiliation in the academy at Daleville receive special instructions in church doctrine and practisé, students of other denominations are encouraged in their own affiliations.[296] The college offers at graduation in addition to the regular diploma, a certificate in Religious Education to those students who have taken thirty hours' work in various courses in Biblical literature and religious education.[297] Attendance at daily chapel service, at Sunday School and the church of one's choice is compulsory.[298]

---

[291] *Lynchburg College Catalog*, 1926, 17; *from correspondence.*

[292] *Acts of Assembly*, Mar. 3, 1884, 286; *Bridgewater College Catalog*, 1928, 11–13.

[293] Wayland: *German Element*, 162; *U. of Va. Rec., Ext. Ser.*, Sept., 1924, IX, No. I, 77.

[294] *Bridgewater-Daleville Academy Catalog*, 1926, 10.

[295] *Ibid.*

[296] *Ibid.*, 16.

[297] *Bridgewater College Catalog*, 1928, 30; a Bible School had been organized in 1898, "but a definite course of study was not offered until years later." *Ibid.*, 12.

[298] *Ibid.*, 35, 37; the membership of The Church of the Brethren in Virginia for 1926 is given as 16,875 in Booklet $\frac{No. 10}{026-030}$, "German Baptist Brethren," 9, issued by the Bureau of the Census, 1928.

The interest of the Society of Friends in education for negroes, characteristic of that religious group from the early days of its history, has resulted in their development of the Christiansburg Industrial Institute, at Cambria, Montgomery County. This school founded, in 1866, by Captain Charles S. Schaeffer as a primary school for colored children was aided by the Friends' Freedmen's Association.[299]   At the close of the century, it was decided to follow the example of Hampton Institute, and to transform the school into an industrial institute;[300] the school was incorporated, in 1900, under its present name.[301] Its present organization consists of an elementary school, secondary school, and provision for teacher training, home economics, agriculture, and industrial arts. It is now supported by the Friends' Freedman's Association of Philadelphia, by funds from Montgomery County, and private contributions.[302]   The religious life of the school is that characteristic of other denominational schools.[303]

Of all evangelical, denominational schools in Virginia, that of the "Eastern Mennonite School" is perhaps the most interesting in the absolute frankness with which it acknowledges itself as a strictly denominational school, and the consistency of its policy in that direction. It is a co-educational school, near Harrisonburg, and had its inception in 1913; the project being furthered by the favorable action of the Virginia Conference of Mennonites in 1914.[304] The curriculum, originally consisting of short Bible terms, was extended in 1917 to that of an academy and separate Bible department. The academy was accredited by the

---

[299] *Christiansburg Catalog*, 1926, 7.

[300] *Ibid.*

[301] *Acts of Assembly*, Feb. 27, 1900, 706.

[302] *Christiansburg Catalog*, 1926, 7.

[303] The number of Friends in 1926, in Virginia, is given as 1,157, for the Orthodox Branch, and as 347, for the Hicksite Branch, in Bulletin $\frac{No. 11}{086-089}$, 8, 17, "Friends" issued by the Bureau of Census, 1928; in view of these small numbers, Friends in Virginia "are now throwing their energy into the public school system for white children. At Lincoln, Va., in Loudoun County, the Friends School was given to the school district and is now an up to date rural high school with Friends participating in the management." *From correspondence.*

[304] Hartzler, J. E.: *Educ. Menn. Amer.*, 170; *U. of Va. Rec., Ext. Ser.*, Sept., 1924, IX, No. 1, 78.

state in 1921. Since that date, there has been a gradual extension of the work into a junior college,[305] and the school now consists of a Bible School, Academy, Junior College, and Correspondence Department.

In 1924, an amendment was secured to its original charter,
granted in 1917, giving the Virginia Conference of the Mennonite Church legal power to appoint a governing board having
direct responsibility for the conduct of the institution. Neighboring conferences, however, have been granted the right to
appoint two members each, on the Board, and the school thus is
regarded as the church school of the Eastern wing of the Mennonite Church.[306]

The school is particularly interesting because of the strictness
with which it holds to denominational lines. The position taken
by the authorities of the school is, that

... If a denomination has a rightful claim to an existence, she also has
the right to indoctrinate and establish her young people in her Articles of
Faith and doctrinal standards; nay, it is her bounden duty, if she wishes
to maintain, propagate, and perpetuate them.[307]

It holds further, that mental discipline and knowledge have
value only as contributing "to the necessary comforts of life, to
the salvation of souls, and to the glory of God." The purpose
of the school is not only to save their young people to the
church while they are getting an education, but to give them
such knowledge of God's Word as will strengthen them in their
moral and spiritual life.[308] A recent catalogue of the school gives
in full the eighteen articles of Faith of the Virginia Conference
of Mennonites, and states that at the opening of each school year,
the entire faculty express their assent and pledge their loyalty
to the principles enunciated in the articles of Faith.[309]

Though a strictly denominational school, all students of good
moral character who are willing to comply with the general
rules, regulations, and discipline are heartily welcomed. In the

[305] *Eastern Mennonite School Catalog*, 1926–27, 10.
[306] *Ibid.*
[307] *Ibid.*, 8.
[308] *Ibid.*, 12.
[309] *Ibid.*, 13.

management of the school, the discipline of the church with regard to standards set up in conduct and apparel is adhered to. Students are required to attend Sunday School and preaching service each Sunday.[310]   A Young People's Christian Association was organized in 1922.   Students may not graduate from any department, unless they have had two units of Bible.[311]   In the Bible School, the Elementary Bible Course is a two-year course for students having no preparation beyond the public or high school.   The Advanced Bible Course is a two-year course of college grade.   A Special Bible Term is held for six weeks in winter—it is along doctrinal and inspirational lines, and intended for those not able to attend school regularly.[312]   Both the Elementary and Advanced Bible work consist of a series of required and elective courses.   The objects of the work in the Bible school are to furnish properly trained workers for the church, to give the students "a keener appreciation of the doctrines and practices of the Mennonite Church," and to aid them in solving the perplexing problems of life from the informed church standpoint.[313]   In the junior college, 18 courses, including New Testament Greek, are offered in the Bible department, but all courses are not offered every year.[314]

The purpose in providing a college was to furnish an education, in its broadest sense, under distinctly denominational influence.   It was held that an introduction to the great fields of knowledge is of value, not only in life, but of greater worth in "revealing to the individual the glory of God as manifested in His handiwork."[315]   The school finds no difficulty apparently, from its theological standpoint, in offering courses in biology, both in its Academy and Junior College.[316]   The great harm in pursuit of a college education lies not in "an inherent evil of the knowledge gained," but in the influence of teachers, and the school atmosphere.   In view of the fact that Mennonites in

---

310 *Ibid.*, 23.

311 *Ibid.*, 27.

312 *Ibid.*, 28.

313 *Ibid.*, 27–28.

314 *Ibid.*, 37–40; a third year's college work is offered to those desiring it; *U. of Va. Rec., Ext. Ser.*, Sept., 1924, IX, No. 1, 79.

315 *Eastern Mennonite School Catalog*, 1926–27, 33.

316 *Ibid.*, 40, *cf.* 13, Article III.

America have not been very much inclined to favor higher education,[317] this expression of interest in the subject represents a new attitude.[318]

Educational Activities And Tendencies Of The Catholic Church

Because of the hostile attitude toward Catholicism during the colonial period,[319] and the consequent slowness of Catholics to migrate to that state, Catholic education had had but a slow development in Virginia.[320] The first serious effort in the direction of Catholic education was made by the Sisters of Charity of Emmittsburg, Maryland, when two sisters went in 1832 to establish the St. Francis Xavier's School, at Alexandria, Virginia. This was followed, in 1834, by the opening of St. Joseph's Asylum and School at Richmond,[321] and schools at Norfolk and Martinsburg in 1837 and 1838.[322] A second school at Norfolk was opened in 1848.[323] In 1833, St. John's Academy, a school for boys, was opened at Alexandria.[324] Bishop Whalen founded St. Vincent's College and Seminary at Richmond in 1841.[325] In 1848, the Sisters of St. Joseph opened St. Joseph's Cathedral School, a co-educational secondary school at Wheeling; this was followed, in 1855, by establishing in the same town, St. Vincent's School, and, in 1858, St. Alphonsus' School.[326] A school for German Catholic children was opened in Richmond, in 1851.[327]

An impetus to further development of the Catholic educational program was now given by the first diocesan synod ever held in Virginia, in 1855, which urged the erection of schools

---

[317] Hartzler: *Educ. Menn. Amer.*, 51–52.

[318] The number of Mennonites given for Virginia, in 1926, by *U. S. Bur. Census, Press Summary*, Dec. 9, 1927, is 1,894.

[319] See p. 45 *ff.*

[320] Magri: *Cath. Church, Richmond*, 45–46—mentions a school taught by Bishop Kelly, the first Bishop, at Norfolk, 1821–22; also a classical school for boys taught by Rev. T. Hore, at Richmond, 1824–28.

[321] *Cf. Ibid.*, 52, 55.

[322] *Ibid.*, 61, 58.

[323] Burns: *Cath. Sch. System U. S.*, 222–23, 257–58.

[324] *U. S. Comm. Educ. Rep't*, 1880, 564.

[325] Cassidy, F. P.: *Cath. College Foundations*, 90; Magri: *Cath. Church, Richmond*, 60, indicates opening was in 1840; it was discontinued in 1846, *Ibid.*, 68.

[326] *Ibid.*, 70; *U. S. Comm. Educ. Rep't*, 1873, 613; 1875, 657.

[327] Magri: *Cath. Church, Richmond*, 78.

wherever possible.[328]   Before the Civil War, free and parochial schools existed at Richmond, Petersburg, Lynchburg, and Harper's Ferry.[329]   The Catholic population, at that time, was estimated at 12,000.[330]

Following a depression in educational activities caused by the Civil War, extension of Catholic education was furthered by the coming in of various teaching orders.   Thus, at Richmond, the Nuns of the Visitation, in 1866, established the Academy of Monte Maria for girls; the Sisters of Charity, in 1867, St. Patrick's School; the Benedictine Sisters, in 1868, an academy and school—subsequently establishing themselves at Bristow, where they now conduct a private grammar school for boys; the Xaverian Brothers, after 1881, secondary schools at Richmond, Norfolk, Fort Monroe, and Newport News.[331]   From 1868 to 1881, St. John's Seminary was conducted at Norfolk.[332]   After 1881, Franciscan Sisters from England, who had established themselves in Baltimore, extended their work to Richmond and Norfolk, concerning themselves chiefly with schools for colored Catholics.[333]   Apparently, those schools which desired incorporation had no difficulty in obtaining it, thus St. Mary's Female Academy, at Norfolk, was incorporated in 1852, and the Academy of the Visitation, Monte Maria, at Richmond, in 1868.[334]

With the coming of the various teaching orders, Catholic education appears to have made consistent progress.   The establishment of the public school system, in 1870, seems to have stirred up only one noteworthy controversy affecting Catholic schools— that at Lynchburg, to which reference has been made.[335]   It seems that Catholics, as they were able, either sent their children to the schools established by the various teaching orders or set

---

[328] *Ibid.*, 82.

[329] *Ibid.*, 83.

[330] *Ibid.*, 88.

[331] *Ibid.*, 96, 119; Burns: *Growth and Devel't Cath. Sch. System*, 90, 121; the Benedictine Sisters formerly conducted St. Edith's Academy for girls at Bristow.

[332] Magri: *Cath. Church, Richmond*, 101, 119.

[333] Burns: *Growth and Devel't Cath. Sch. System*, 343; for opposition to extension of Catholicism among negroes, see Magri: *Cath. Church, Richmond*, 119.

[334] *U. S. Comm. Educ. Rep't*, 1880, 564–65.

[335] See p. 454.

about establishing, as at Lynchburg, parochial school systems. Before the Civil War there were six parochial schools in the diocese.[336] By 1906, the year in which the Sacred Heart Cathedral, Richmond, was consecrated, Catholicism, in Virginia, was represented by 30,000 Catholics, with fifty-four priests to serve them. Educational activity was represented by Old Point Comfort College, established by the Xaverian Brothers, in 1899, and four other schools under their control;[337] four industrial schools, two for white, and two for colored boys, conducted by various teaching orders; a school for colored girls; seven academies for girls, with an attendance approximating 1,000; parochial schools with an attendance of about 5,000 white and 400 colored children distributed over twenty-one parishes; and four orphan asylums caring for about 300 children.[338]

A school survey, made in 1926, showed that there were in Virginia, one college for boys, with 165 students; three colleges for colored boys and girls with 840 pupils; thirty-two parochial schools with 5,672 white, and 1,509 colored pupils; and two boarding academies for girls with 126 boarders, or a total of 8,312 children under Catholic instruction.[339] Ten teaching orders furnish the instruction for these schools.[340] According to the latest census reports, the Catholic population in Virginia in 1926, was 38,605.[341] If one may characterize the distinguishing quality of Catholic education, it is the frankness of emphasis upon strictly sectarian training for Catholic students. A review of their school programs indicates that it is not their custom to

---

[336] Magri: *Cath. Church, Richmond,* 88.

[337] A catalogue of Old Point Comfort College for 1920–21, 5, gives the date of opening as Feb. 1, 1898; it was incorporated Mar. 3, 1898, *Acts of Assembly,* Mar. 3, 1898, 951.

[338] Magri: *Cath. Church, Richmond,* 138–39; *U. S. Comm. Educ. Rep't,* 1903, I, 1090, gives 16 parochial schools with an attendance of 2,000 children; as late as 1916, *Ibid.,* 1916, I, 417, statistics for attendance in 27 schools of the diocese was placed at 4,692; yet *cf.* same for 1912, I, 239, where the figures for 1911 and 1912 are 5,400 and 4,440.

[339] *From correspondence.*

[340] The Benedictine Fathers; Xaverian Brothers; Visitation Sisters; Daughters of Charity, St. Vincent de Paul; Sisters of the Blessed Sacrament; Benedictine Sisters; Franciscan Sisters of Baltimore City for Colored Missions; Sisters of the Holy Cross; Sisters of St. Benedict; and Sisters, Servants of the Immaculate Heart Of Mary. *Ibid.*

[341] *U. S. Bur. Census, Press Summary,* July 24, 1928; the figures for 1916 in the same report are 36,671.

require non-Catholic pupils, whom they express a willingness to
receive, to take their systematic courses in religion; such students
are, however, required to attend all public religious exercises, on
the ground of "maintenance of discipline and uniformity."[342]
The attendance at the public exercises for such students is seemingly regarded as a mere formality.

The nature of the religious instruction given at these institutions from the first primary grade through the fourth year of
the high school may be gathered from an account of the work
as given at St. Mary's Academy, founded, in 1869, at Alexandria,
under the direction of the Sisters of the Holy Cross.   In the
primary department, a prayer class is held the first year, catechism and Bible stories feature the work of the next three years;
in the following four years, catechism and Bible history are
studied; in the classical course in the high school, two and one-
half hours' work per week in religion is given.   This work covers:
"1. Present Organization and Status of the Church, II. Origin
and Development of the Church, III. Exercises of Teaching
and Ruling Authority, IV. The Work of Sanctification in the
Church."[343]   In the grades, the Standard Catholic series of
reading books is used.   At the Monte Maria Academy, in Richmond, the religious studies of the graduating class, the work of
which year is equivalent to the first year of college, covers in the
first semester, "Apologetics, revelation, tradition and scripture;
Christianity and the non-Christian religions; the Church and
the Churches;" and in the second semester, "General Introduction to the Old Testament, number and classification of books,
the Hebrew Bible, Greek, Latin and English versions, analysis
of contents, peculiarity of matter and form of sources of the
Old Testament books."[344]   In addition, students have a one
semester course in Natural Theology.[345]   At the Benedictine

---

342 *Monte Maria Academy Catalog,* 1921–22, 6, 26; *Linton Hall Catalog,*
1928, 7; *St. Mary's Academy Catalog,* 1926–27, 13; *Old Point Comfort
College Catalog,* 1920–21, 6–7; Old Point Comfort College is now the Novi-
tiate and Aspirant House of the Xaverian Order, and conducts only a high
school for day scholars and aspirants—*from correspondence; St. Emma
Industrial and Agricultural Institute Catalog,* 1928, 6.
343 *St. Mary's Academy, Catalog,* 1926–27, 5, 8.
344 *Monte Maria Academy, Catalog,* 1921–22, 10.
345 *Ibid.*

College, in Richmond, a military day school for boys, two periods of religious instruction a week are given. In the first year, the course comprises: "Faith, its necessity, qualities; the Apostles' Creed, commandments, violation of the commandments, virtue and Christian perfection. Grace, the sacraments, indulgences, prayer, ceremonies and liturgy of the Holy Mass and of the sacraments. The sacramentals, Text: Deharbe, Large Catechism, Complete;" in the second year, "God, the Father and creation. God the Son and the redemption. The Holy Ghost and the work of sanctification. Christian morals. General principles of morality. Virtue and sin. Commandments of God. Text: Complete Catechism, Deharbe, to pg. 161;" in the third year, "The Commandments of the Church. Evangelical counsels and beatitudes. Means of sanctification. Grace. Prayer. The Sacraments. The Liturgy. Devotions. Confraternities. Text: Complete Catechism, Deharbe, complete;" in the fourth year, "Christian Revelation and Its Credentials, The Church the Teacher of Revelation, God in Unity and Trinity, The Creation, The Incarnation and Redemption, the Sacraments, Duties in General, the Ten Commandments, the Commandments of the Church, the Last Things, Errors."[346] It is apparent from the nature of the courses here outlined, that there is a greater tendency than in evangelical churches, to a study of purely church liturgy and forms, and the relation of theology to the practical issues of sin and virtue; the Bible itself is less a text book.

The expressed ideal that animates these educational institutions does not differ essentially, except for the strongly denominational tone of the systematic religious instruction, from that which characterizes evangelical institutions. The aim of the Benedictine College is to give its students "such a general, vigorous and well-rounded development of all their faculties, mental and moral, as will enable them later to take up their chosen life's work with pleasure and profit.[347] At St. Mary's, the object is to combine thorough academic training with "a solid moral and Christian training."[348] The authorities of Monte Maria Academy declare, that

---

[346] *Benedictine College Catalog*, 1924, 13–18.
[347] *Ibid.*, 6.
[348] *St. Mary's Academy, Catalog*, 1926–27, 3.

. . . throughout the careful ordering of the academic discipline, with its
religious influences and its uplifting associations, a two-fold idea is kept
in view. First, the *formation of the pupil's character*, gently moulding
her young heart, broadening and strengthening her best impulses, and training her in the practice of the womanly virtues. Secondly, to ensure to her
the benefits of a solid and refined education.[349]

The fact that with a membership of somewhat over 38,000,
Catholicism in Virginia has a school population of over 8,000 under distinctively Catholic instruction is due, undoubtedly, to the
zeal of the teaching orders of the church and to the fact that the
priesthood have been able to impress the people with the necessity of a separate education for Catholic youth, both from the
standpoint of their individual preservation and that of the
Church. Apparently the people are in agreement with their
leaders that the only practicable solution for religion in education is denominational schools.[350]

Significance Of Denominational Educational Activity In Its Relation To Church And State

By far the most interesting outstanding conclusion, which this
investigation of the history of denominational educational activity in Virginia since the Civil War reveals, is that this activity, as
far as the four leading evangelical denominations are concerned,
if intended as an ideal solution of the problem of religion in education is practically negative from the point of view of reaching
their membership in any adequate fashion. While the opposition which was manifested at the time of the inauguration of the
public school system, in the seventies, was said to have lingered on
until the beginning of the present century and to have prejudiced
its adequate development, yet, if the figures of the extent of the
school systems developed by the churches, and the attendance at
them, at the close of the first quarter of this century, have any
significance, it is that of the triumph of public education in
popular favor. While the fact that the major educational load
of society is being carried by the state, not by the church, may be
attributed to the fact that the state can compel by taxation, the

---

[349] *Monte Maria Academy, Catalog,* 1921–22.
[350] See p. 509.

church use only moral suasion, the crux of the matter lies, seemingly, not so much in the question of financial support, but in this, that the larger proportion of church membership finds in the public school system a sufficiently satisfactory solution of its educational problem.

Careful analysis of the religious life of denominational schools shows that many of their activities such as morning and evening prayers, grace at meals, mid-week and Sunday religious services, are possible to any Christian family that desires to stress such activities by the ordering of Christian living at home and through church affiliation. Not only is this possible, but ministers and Christian parents must acknowledge that this has been, and is being achieved, in countless Christian homes. It is only in the element of a certain social compulsion, in the stimulus to religious life by their collective life, and close supervision, that these schools achieve more than is accomplished in homes where a less strictly Christian religious tone prevails. In fact, it has been seen that in many secondary denominational schools, the exigencies of the regular course work required for accrediting by the state or other agencies are such that the amount of systematic religious study is no larger, if as large, than that available in the public high schools where co-operation offers the State Bible-study course, or, where that is lacking, the student avails himself of affiliation with the church. Of course, where for any reason a well ordered family life, centered with proper relation to education in public school and church is impossible, it is apparent that a denominational school in taking the place of the home has an important function to perform.

Perhaps the most important reason for existence of denominational schools, from the denominational standpoint, has been their service as a nurturing ground for future workers of the church, but the churches of America, since the Civil War, would never have reached their present status, unsatisfactory as some may find it, if this source had not been supplemented by workers coming from non-denominational private, and public schools.[351]

---

[351] See p. 621, regarding U. of Va. graduates; yet, discussion at the Presbyterian Educational Association of the South, in 1928, revealed the opinion: "That the interest of the student body in State Schools was toward fitness

One of the rather unique developments in denominational educational activity, in the last quarter of century, has been the mountain school. As experimental schools in rural education, they will undoubtedly play, if continued support is granted, an important rôle in pointing to the state possible solutions of problems affecting rural education, particularly in mountain districts.

Another important denominational activity concerns the extension of church work into state institutions. This work, which seems to be in line with the Ruffner policy of co-operation has interesting possibilities in its reaction upon the relations between church and state. It would appear to be along the line of development of the Ruffner policy that the major development of denominational educational activity of the future points. In fact, if the history of the present status of denominational education in Virginia has one significant lesson, it is that the major problem of denominational educational activity of the future lies not in private denominational schools, where the greater financial outlay is at present—but in supplementing the public school system, where their larger membership is, and from which their future strength must be drawn.[352]

A feature of the development of evangelical denominational education which deserves some comment is the very frequent claim of non-sectarianism in the conduct of these schools; in this respect, such schools tend to become little differentiated, if at all, from private non-denominational schools which stress their Christian tone,[353] or, in fact, from many of the Virginia public

for business and not in religious matters, and therefore the Church College was still needed.'' *Minutes, 15th Annual Meeting, Presbyt. Educ. Assoc. South,* 15.

[352] In this connection, it is interesting to note that an attempt of a Protestant Episcopal Rector of a Richmond church to establish week day religious instruction in that city, after receiving approval of various religious interests in that city, had to be dropped because, it was said, of the opposition of the Baptists, as it was felt that because of their large numbers, the movement ''would not succeed without their co-operation.'' *From correspondence.* The Baptist opposition was, of course, in line with their traditional opposition to any connection between church and state, and such schools, as usually conceived, would naturally involve co-operation with the civil arm of the government. *Cf.* Cohen: ''An Inquiry Into The Tendencies Of The Week Day Religious Education Movement In Its Relations To The Public Schools.''

[353] See p. 589–607.

schools, which, as has been shown,[354] by their morning assemblies, and stress on Christian holidays, certainly create quite a Christian atmosphere.

One feature of denominational educational activity is the liberality extended to families of ministers, and to prospective ministers, in the way of furnishing educational opportunity at small or no cost—a practise common enough in state and private non-denominational institutions. At a recent church educational conference, the question was raised whether financial aid to such candidates "did not tend to injure the character of the ministry." A very authoritative opinion was given that it did and that the solution lay in seminaries raising their standards of education and being more careful in admitting students.[355] That free education by the church for the church should prove any more harmful than that by the state for the state or church seems strange; rather, one wonders whether the difficulty lies not so much in free education, as in the tendency to create and extend a class privilege.[356] Many institutions would seem to be recognizing this fact, and are apparently attempting to remedy this situation by imposing restrictions and limitations of various kinds.

There is one further interesting matter which should be noted in connection with the development of denominational schools in their relation to the problem of church and state; namely, the issue of property held for religious purposes. Reference has already been made to the Virginia tendency to limit property for purely religious purposes.[357] The most recent legal expression on this subject still limits church property to two acres of land in a city or town, and to not more than seventy-five acres out of a city or town, and money or other personal estate, exclusive of books and furniture, to $30,000.[358] A review of the amount of property held by denominational, educational institutions soon makes it apparent that this limitation does not apply to churches

---

[354] See p. 494, 492.

[355] *Minutes, 15th Annual Meeting, Presbyt. Educ. South*, 10.

[356] See p. 612.

[357] See p. 415.

[358] *Code of Va.*, 1924, par. 43; 1887, par. 1403; *Acts of Assembly*, Mar. 28, 1902, 336–37.

in their guardianship of schools;[359] a distinction apparently being made in Virginia law between purely church holdings and "property devoted to educational purposes although controlled by a religious denomination."[360] The same section of the law which forbids the incorporation of any church or religious denomination[361] is taken as authority for incorporation of denominational educational institutions.[362]

In the "liberal policy of the State," as one legal authority has described it, [363] in the matter of incorporation of denominational, educational institutions is to be found an important partial explanation of the success of the co-operation policy, however objectionable this "liberal policy" may be to some strict constructionists of the principle of separation of church and state. After all, while denominational colleges may require a certain amount of Bible study for obtaining their degrees, it is the state which grants them the authority to confer the degrees.

---

359 St. Emma Industrial and Agricultural Institute, Rock Castle, has 1,700 acres of land, including a two-mile frontage on James River—*St. Emma Indust. & Agric. Catalog*, 5–6; Hampden-Sidney College has 250 acres— Robertson: *Amer. Univ. and Colleges*, 437; Emory and Henry about 100 acres—*Emory & Henry Catalog*, 1926, 24.

360 *From correspondence.*

361 *Code of Va.*, 1924, Sec. 3872, 872; *Pollard's Code*, 1904, 1105 d.

362 *Ibid.;* cf. also *The Virginia Law Register*, I, N. S., 161, 163; *Code of Va.*, 1924, par. 43, par. 48 (Sec. 3872 and 3873; *Code of Va.*, 1887, par. 1408; *Acts of Assembly*, Mar. 22, 1916, 830; see p. 416, for distinction between the church and its agencies.

363 *Va. Law Register*, I, N. S., 163.

CHAPTER XIV

ACTIVITIES AND TENDENCIES OF NON-DENOMINA-
TIONAL AND PUBLIC EDUCATION

Religious Instruction In Private Non-Denominational Schools

In view of the stress placed by the leaders of the religious forces of the state upon the importance of maintaining denominational educational institutions as the best means of furnishing education under a proper religious environment,[1] it is of some interest to see in what respects, if any, the character of the religious life of various private non-denominational and public educational institutions differs.

Of the non-state and non-denominational institutions, Washington and Lee University because of its history, traditions, and present status is undoubtedly the most important. Having renounced its connection with the Presbyterian Church before the Civil War,[2] it has since been regarded as a non-sectarian, privately controlled institution.[3] The Civil War closed the college until 1865, when General Robert E. Lee was installed as president. At the close of the War, the college found itself with buildings and property damaged, and income seriously impaired. Through the management of its trustees and new president, whose fame and popularity were important factors, the work of restoration proceeded quickly. The year before the War, 95 students were registered, all but one from Virginia. In 1867–68, the enrollment was 410, representing twenty states and one foreign country, 68 per cent coming from outside of Virginia.[4]

---

[1] *Cf.* for recent expression, *Minutes, 15th Annual Meeting, Presbyt. Educ. Assoc. South*, 13, ''Also urged on the other side that the Church must endeavor . . . to educate all her children through all their education'' and *Christian Educ. Magazine*, Aug., 1927, XVII, No. 3, 24, ''. . . to emphasize the need of the religious element in all education; to inform our people of the work and character of our own schools, the contribution they are making to the life of the Church and nation, as well as the need of patronizing them and supporting them adequately.''

[2] See p. 310.

[3] Robertson: *Amer. Univ. and Colleges*, 790.

[4] *Wash. & Lee Catalog*, 1926, 23–25.

After the War, though most of the trustees and faculty were Presbyterian, the rector, president, and several of the professors were members of the Episcopal Church, and an apparent effort was made to keep and have the public regard the institution as non-sectarian.[5]   An important change in the charter was effected, in 1871, when the college was transformed into a University and the name changed to Washington and Lee University.[6]

During the régime of General Lee, who has been ranked along with Stonewall Jackson as one of the two "outstanding pietists" that America produced in the nineteenth century, the college was naturally permeated by a strong Christian influence.[7] The religious statistics at the beginning of 1870 revealed, however, that far from all the teachers and students were professed Christians.   Of seventeen instructors, seven only were church members, and, of three hundred and ten students, only one hundred professed religion.   There were, however, seventeen candidates for the ministry, two of whom expected to be foreign missionaries.   There had been sixteen professions of conversion within the past year.[8]   Through the influence of General Lee, a Y. M. C. A. had been established in 1868.   There were daily chapel services and two weekly prayer meetings.[9]   Though General Lee's short rule was marked by the expansion of the college in various directions, it was declared that the development of the "moral and religious character of the students was more precious in his eyes than even their intellectual progress."[10]   He was quoted as saying that the leading object which had made him assume the presidency was to make "these young men all become consistent Christians."[11]   A non-sectarian institution was clearly not intended, in this case, to be synonymous with an unchristian institution.   In 1886, Dr. Moses D. Hoge, in characterizing the University as loyal to its traditions, said:

---

[5] Lee, R. E.: *Recoll. & Letters General Lee*, 334–35.

[6] *Acts of Assembly*, Feb. 27, 1866, 433; Feb. 4, 1871, 60.

[7] Beard: *Rise Amer. Civilization*, I, 139; General Lee died on October 12, 1870.

[8] *Va. Educ. Jour.*, Jan., 1870, I, 93.

[9] *Ibid.; Wash. & Lee Catalog*, 1926, 199.

[10] *Old Dominion Magazine*, V, 213.

[11] *Ibid.*

The fact that the trustees and professors of Washington and Lee have almost uniformly been Christian men, and that so large a proportion of its graduates have been ministers of the Gospel—and this is notably true during the last decade—shows that the trend of the institution has been in the direction intended at its organization, and that the University, both in its origin and history, has borne a noble testimony to the character and value of Christian education.[12]

The traditional exemption of candidates for the ministry from tuition fees was continued in the post Civil War period. The catalogues of the eighties and nineties stated this exemption was given candidates unable to pay the regular charges, and who were recommended by competent ecclesiastical authority as suitable persons to be educated for the ministry. Students subsequently declining to enter the ministry were to regard their remitted fees as debts due the University. Upon satisfactory testimonials, sons of ministers in service unable to pay regular fees, or of deceased ministers, might also be admitted without charge.[13] In more recent years, the exemption has been for the major part, usually about two-thirds, of the fees.[14]

In the eighties and nineties, morning chapel services were conducted by the clergymen of Lexington in rotation, and students were expected to attend these exercises and their preferred church on Sunday. Students also had the opportunity of attending Sunday Bible classes.[15] In 1898, President Wilson, in his annual report, declared that the absence of the class system and the voluntary feature of the daily chapel service had tended "to produce an individualism, not sufficiently promotive of a genuine college spirit," and consequently he had introduced an obligatory weekly meeting of the full University body—faculty and students. This meeting was opened with brief religious exercises.[16]

The activities of the Y. M. C. A. included weekly religious meetings, Bible and mission study classes. The faculty urged parents and guardians to encourage the students to join the As-

---

[12] Hoge, M. D.: *Memories, Hopes and Duties*, 19.
[13] *Wash. & Lee Catalog*, 1883, 36.
[14] *Ibid.*, 1921, 47; 1926, 55.
[15] *Ibid.*, 1883, 36; and subsequent catalogs.
[16] *Annual report for 1897–98 of Pres. Wm. L. Wilson*, 5–6.

sociation.[17]   By 1926, students, upon matriculation, automatically became members entitled to its service privileges.   Active
membership was available to members of evangelical churches
who adhered to a certain statement of purpose.[18]

Religious affiliation of the students as reported, in 1922,
showed the Presbyterian denomination in the lead—apparently
the institution has not lost its hold on Presbyterian affection, in
spite of its separation.   The other denominations in descending
rank were the Methodist, Baptist, and Episcopalian.[19]

In view of the general interest in the religious welfare of the
student, it is interesting to note that there is no separate Bible
department at the University, but a three-hour course in Christian Ethics is given in the Philosophy Department.   The first
semester is devoted to a systematic study of the Life of Christ;
the second, to the social ethics of Jesus "with a view to the Kingdom of God and the social ideal."   The course is especially recommended to freshmen.[20]   A single course limited to a study of
the life of Christ is a surprising development in the history of a
college, which once attempted to have associated with it a theological seminary, and contrasts most strikingly with the development of departments of religious instruction at the University
of Virginia, William and Mary College, and other state controlled
institutions.[21]

Among private institutions for colored students in Virginia,
the Hampton Normal and Agricultural Institute holds a preëminent place.   It will be recalled[22] that soon after its establishment,
it came under partial state control through the appointment of
a board of curators, a situation brought about by its receiving a
certain share of the land grant funds.   Hampton Institute continued to benefit from these funds, and partial state control was
continued until 1920, the institution making annual reports to
the state during these years.   As the constitution of 1902 forbade state appropriations to non-state institutions, it appears

---

[17] *Cf. Wash. & Lee Catalog*, 1921, 168.
[18] *Ibid.*, 1926, 199.
[19] *Wash. & Lee Univers. Bull.*, May, 1922, XXI, No. 9, 21.
[20] *Wash. & Lee Catalog*, 1926, 132.
[21] See p. 607 *ff.*; the enrollment of students for the year ending June 30,
1926, was 903.   Robertson: *Amer. Univ. & Colleges*, 791.
[22] See p. 407.

that the dual form of control placed the institution in an anomalous position, and in 1920 the land grant funds were transferred to the Virginia Normal and Industrial Institute at Petersburg; and the curators, and with them, the state, ceased their official connection with the institution.[23]

Conceived as a missionary enterprise, it is not surprising that the religious phase of education has been strongly emphasized from the beginning.[24] In his first report, General Armstrong emphasized the importance of teaching the vital precepts of Christianity as a sustaining element in the lives of the young workers, who were to go out as examples to their race.[25] Evening prayer led by General Armstrong was a feature of the religious life in the early history of the school.[26] In 1871, a school pastor was appointed and an undenominational church organized.[27]

In 1881, a future principal of the school, Rev. Hollis B. Frissell, was appointed chaplain. Under Rev. Mr. Frissell there was a sustained religious interest in the school.[28] A committee, who had been appointed by the trustees to examine into the educational status of the school, reported, in 1882, that over 90 per cent of its graduates had entered upon teaching, and nearly all of these had reported Sunday Schools connected with their day schools.[29] The keen interest in religion may be gathered from the fact that, in 1883, the whole senior class dedicated themselves to the Christian life.[30] A Pastor's class was organized, in 1884, to aid colored pastors and those planning for the ministry; it consisted of a three years' course, taught by instructors of various denominations.[31]

The chaplain's report for 1884 emphasized the importance in the increasing growth of the school, "of building up the right sort of moral and religious character in the student."[32] The problem at Hampton, in his opinion, was not that of making

23 *From correspondence.*
24 See p. 407.
25 Peabody; *Hampton Institute,* 120–21.
26 *Ibid.,* 139.
27 *Ibid.,* 111–12.
28 *Ibid.,* 187; see p. 480.
29 *Jour. of Educ.,* 1882, XVI, 43.
30 Peabody: *Hampton Institute,* 188.
31 *U. S. Comm. Educ. Rep't,* 1884–85, 274.
32 *Va. Sch. Rep't,* 1884, 30.

scholars, but Christian men and women.[33]   He sought, therefore,
to impress upon the students "the insufficiency of a mere pre-
tence of piety."[34]   To ease the work for the teachers, the sched-
ule of Sabbath services had been changed so as to place the Sabbath School at 11 A. M., and the preaching service in the
afternon.   There were also evening services, morning prayers,
and weekly prayer meetings.   The religious work of the week
centered around the study of the International Series of Sunday
School lessons for that week.[35]   A Young People's Christian
Association had under its care the mission work in the neighborhood.[36]   Subsequent accounts and reports emphasize the importance of religious activities in the training of the students; apparently the fact that the state had a nominal control in the
institution because of state appropriations, in no way, deterred
the religious activities.[37]

In describing the religious life of the school in 1905, Principal
Frissell stated:

. . . An earnest effort is made to harness the emotional nature of the
Negro to the daily duties of life. A practical type of piety prevails at
Hampton. Public sentiment demands that the man who is prominent in
prayer meeting be earnest and straightforward in his daily life. An undenominational type of religious life, which lays more stress on doing than
on doctrine or feeling, sways the life.[38]

The emphasis was always upon translating Christian faith into
service, and the religious life was correlated with the thought of
"doing faithfully the day's duties."[39]   Since the early part of
the century, there has been carefully planned work in the Bible.[40]
This work was emphasized particularly for those preparing for
rural teaching.[41]   All teaching in history in the school, in 1914,
was centered in the Bible.

---

[33] *Ibid.*, 31.
[34] *Ibid.*
[35] *Ibid.*, 32.
[36] *Ibid.*, 33.
[37] *Cf. Ibid.*, 1886, 158 *ff.*; *N. E. A. Proc's*, 1900, XXXIX, 488; *U. S. Comm. Educ. Rep't*, 1900–01, I, 414; *World's Work*, July, 1901, II, 961.
[38] *Hampton Bull., 37th Rep't*, June, 1905, 27.
[39] *South Atlant. Quart.*, Jan., 1907, VI, 42.
[40] *Hampton Bull., 37th Rep't*, June, 1905, 27.
[41] *Ibid., 46th Rep't*, June, 1914, X, 24.

Having its origin in the ideal of service to students of the ministry, started with the Pastor's classes, in 1884, there has been organized, since 1915, a summer conference of negro ministers.[42] In 1926, 14 states and 14 denominations were represented at the conference which had an attendance of 320.[43]

The religious activities of the school, in 1916, consisted of daily evening prayers, Sunday School, and Sunday morning service. In the Sunday School, the Blakeslee Lessons on the Life of Christ were studied for two years, followed by a study of the Apostolic Church. In the senior year, the International lessons were used. A Y. M. C. A. and a Y. W. C. A. also contributed to the religious life.[44] The expense of conducting the religious work in 1915 was given as $7,509.63;[45] the appropriations by the state for the general use of the institution, at that time, amounted to $26,996.02.[46]

In 1921, it was reported that owing to a new rule permitting students to join the school church without giving up membership in their home churches, sixty-five students had been able to join on the new basis, and twenty-one had joined on confession of faith. Of the student body, only 11 per cent were unconnected with any Christian Church; and of the non-members, 54 per cent were new students.[47]

The present religious activities of the school continue along the lines already described. In the Sunday School, the student body is divided into 42 classes. In the secondary school, the first two years of Sunday School work are spent in a study of the Life of Christ, followed by a study of the Apostolic Church. The publications of the Chicago University Press are used. Special courses of study are followed by the college students. In the secondary school, five hours' work in the Bible is required in the second year.[48] In the college, a course in Religious Education

---

[42] *Ibid.*, *47th Rep't*, May, 1915, 20; *52nd Rep't*, May, 1920, 30.

[43] *Ibid.*, May, 1926, 17.

[44] *Hampton Bull.*, *48th Catalog*, 1916, 29–30; *cf.* also *50th Rep't*, May, 1918, 20–21.

[45] *Va. Sch. Rep't*, 1914–15, 603.

[46] *Ibid.*, 605; this did not include $800 for the Summer School, *Ibid.*, 606.

[47] *Hampton Bull.*, *53rd Rep't*, 1921, 24.

[48] *Ibid.*, *58th Catalog*, 1925–26, 20, 86–87.

is offered in the education department, but no systematic Bible study, except in the Sunday School.[49]

The spirit which animates the school life of Hampton may perhaps best be summed up in the statement of Ex-President Taft, President of the Board of Trustees, who declared, in 1923, that "in the use of the religious spirit and the discipline of labor" were to be found those features of Hampton education which contributed to making the students "real men and women," prepared to uplift their race.[50]

A school in many respects similar to Hampton Institute, though not so large, is the Miller Manual Labor School for white students. Few Virginia schools have a more interesting origin than this school which was the gift of an Albemarle County millionaire;[51] Samuel Miller died in 1869, and in his will left large gifts not only to the Lynchburg Orphan Asylum, and the University of Virginia, but also about two millions to establish and endow an industrial school for poor children in Albemarle County.[52]

The school was incorporated in 1874, with the members of the State Board of Education, the Second Auditor, and the judge of the County court of Albemarle County, and their successors in office, as the corporation of the school.[53] The Assembly reserved to itself, however, the privilege of any future changes in control. The privilege of designating pupils for the school was left to the district school trustees.[54] In 1877, the charter was amended to leave control in the Board and Second Auditor.[55] In 1884, certain powers and duties were conferred upon the county court of Albemarle,[56] and, in 1892, control was definitely vested in the court and Board of Education.[57] Present procedure leaves the selection of pupils to the County Trustees, and

---

[49] *Ibid.*, 66.
[50] *U. S. Bur. Educ. Bull.*, 1923, No. 27, 3.
[51] Rawlings, M.: *Albemarle of Other Days*, 116–18.
[52] *Ibid.*, Christian: *Lynchburg*, 267–69; *Va. Sch. Rep't*, 1894–95, 385, gives the "Miller Fund" as about $1,300,000.
[53] *Acts of Assembly*, Feb. 24, 1874, 52.
[54] *Ibid.*, 54.
[55] *Ibid.*, April 2, 1877, 292.
[56] *Ibid.*, Feb. 19, 1884, 167.
[57] *Ibid.*, Feb. 29, 1892, 793.

their appointment to the Judge of the Circuit Court, who also appoints the Board of Visitors and approves their recommendations and expenditures.[58]

Though classified as a private institution,[59] the fact that its control emanates from officials, acting in a public capacity makes the history of the religious life of the school, from that point of view, of some interest. A rather complete account of the religious life in 1889, appears in the report by the superintendent of the school for that year. It was customary for the whole school to attend the morning and evening chapel services, which were about ten minutes in length, consisting of Scripture reading, singing and prayer. The whole school likewise attended Sunday School, the International Series of lessons being taught. This instruction was followed by a preaching service. In the primary department, there was, in addition, daily Scripture reading, sometimes followed by questions and brief instruction to impress the lesson on the children's minds. The boys had two Y. M. C. A.'s and the girls a similar organization in their Christian Band.[60]

In 1895, the Superintendent reported that he found every officer and teacher, with probably two exceptions, a member of some evangelical church, and that about two-thirds of the pupils were church members. In addition to the religious features reported, in 1889, there were now a large number of voluntary "Group Bible Classes" held on Sunday evenings, in which an hour was spent in studying selected portions of the Scriptures under a leader chosen by the students. The teachers in the Primary department held exercises consisting of Bible stories and other religious instruction, for the children on Sunday evening. There had also been recently organized a "Mission Band" to

[58] *From correspondence:* the school is classified as a private school—the control of the state having been limited to a supervision of the handling of the funds, the Second Auditor at first, and the appropriate comptroller since acting as treasurer of the fund; the school has not received any appropriation from the state; *Ibid.; Va. Sch. Rep't*, 1914–15, 194, represents an adjustment on the part of the state to offset loss caused when the state refunded certain securities; *from correspondence.*

[59] *Bull. State B'd Educ.*, Nov., 1927, X, No. 2, 108; *cf. Va. Sch. Rep't*, 1904–05, lxxv, for classification as state institution.

[60] *Ibid.*, 1889, 143–44.

study various aspects of the mission problem.[61]   The present religious life of the school follows much along similar lines, with Sunday School, Sunday preaching services, and Y. M. C. A. meetings.[62]

Virginia has five colleges for girls which now rank as undenominational, private colleges.   They are Hollins College, Southern College, Sullins College, Virginia College, and Sweet Briar College.   Of these institutions, Hollins College may be regarded as the most interesting. and important because of its long continued history and because of its influence upon the education of women in the South.[63]   In 1882, the trustees leased the institution to Prof. Cocke, and it thus came under private management, though the trustees continued to function in sanctioning all improvements.[64]   In 1900, the trustees turned the institution over to Professor Cocke, and their connection with Hollins ceased.[65]   It then became a private institution, under the control of a Board of Governors chosen from members of President Cocke's own family,[66] and at his death, in 1901, the Presidency of the college went to his daughter, Matty L. Cocke.   It had in 1926–27 an enrollment of 361 students.[67]

---

[61] *Ibid.*, 1894–95, 392–93.

[62] *From correspondence.*

[63] See p. 316; this influence was exerted not only by the high standards set in this institution, but also by the inspirational addresses and work of its principal, Charles L. Cocke, in advancing the cause of higher education for women.   In the eighties, the Institute was distinguished for its successful work in English, *cf. Jour. of Educ.*, XVI, 121; XVIII, 89, 56; for Prof. Cocke's address on ''Discipline and Training of Girls,'' see *Va. Educ. Jour.*, Sept., 1879, X, 385; also, Smith: *C. L. Cocke*, 107.

[64] *Ibid.*, 78; this arrangement became necessary as the arrangement with Prof. Cocke, upon his coming to the school was that he was to receive the income from tuition fees, the trustees that from the boarding dpartment— the trustees consequently found themselves with the necessary expansion of facilities for the school, in debt to Professor Cocke;—*Ibid.*, 72, 78; in 1900, the trustees were indebted to Professor Cocke to the amount of ''$101,253, in addition to the $50,000 in bonds already executed.'' *Ibid.*, 85.

[65] *Ibid.*, 85.

[66] *Ibid.*, 160.

[67] *Bull. State B'd Educ.*, Nov., 1927, X, No. 2, 109; recently an effort has been made to raise an endowment fund of $650,000 in order to enable the owners to transfer the institution to public ownership with title vested in a self-perpetuating board of trustees.   One object in doing this is to make possible the accrediting of the institution by various associations, such as the Southern Association of Colleges and Secondary Schools; *Hollins Yesterday, to-day and to-morrow*, leaflet.

Though Hollins in its origin was under Baptist influence, and Prof. Cocke, in 1862, acknowledged the fact that it was to a certain extent denominational,[68] it has been regarded by those connected with its history as non-sectarian.[69] That the Baptists, on the whole, showed little substantial interest in the institution may be inferred from the fact, that an appeal for $100,000 made in the early seventies, when Baptists were "aroused on the subject of education, and made large plans for strengthening Richmond College" was received with such indifference as to make necessary the withdrawal of the financial agent.[70] Since 1900, its responsibility to the Baptist denomination, of course, ceased altogether. The college has always emphasized the fact that it is Christian in influence and atmosphere, and, according to Prof. Cocke's biographer, the memories of religious service at Hollins have been precious to her alumnae.[71] In the present religious life of the college, the resident chaplain, a Baptist, holds a prominent place, though other ministers from leading denominations are assigned as regular ministers to the college.[72] Sunday evening services are conducted by visiting ministers from the various denominations, but daily evening prayer service is led by the resident chaplain. Attendance is required at all services of all resident students. The college has a Y. W. C. A. with its usual program.[73]

The resident chaplain with the aid of student assistants conducts two two-hour, and two one-hour courses in the Bible. Two hours of work, to be taken in either the freshman or sophomore year, is prescribed.[74] The courses include one on Sunday School pedagogy, successful completion of which entitles the student to the Normal Teacher's diploma conferred by the various

---

[68] See p. 317.

[69] *From correspondence.* It was classified as a Baptist institution down to the close of the century, cf. *U. S. Comm. Educ. Rep't*, 1896–97, II, 1740; impression was probably strengthened by data given in American Baptist Year-Book, though school authorities in answering questionnaires specifically stated "that the college was not officially connected with the Baptist denomination." *From correspondence.*

[70] Smith: *C. L. Cocke*, 70.

[71] *Ibid.*, 92, 94–95; *Hollins Catalog*, 1926, 67.

[72] *Ibid.*, 6, 12.

[73] *Ibid.*, 67.

[74] *Ibid.*, 21, 26.

denominations.[75]　The work in the Bible is presented for its cultural, moral, and spiritual values.[76]　It was an early custom of Hollins to educate daughters of ministers free of tuition fees; more recently the practise is to allow a deduction in part.[77]

Southern College, at Petersburg, was organized in 1862, and incorporated in 1863, as Southern Female College.[78]　It appears to have been non-sectarian from the beginning.[79]　It now offers high school, junior college, and finishing courses, and is an accredited standard junior college.[80]　Its aim is in the "development of earnest Christian womanhood."[81]　A one-hour course in the English Bible is given, and though listed as an elective, students are advised to take it unless definitely excused.　Attendance is required at daily college prayers, Bible class, and church services on Sunday.　Students attend Sunday morning church service at their own church in company with a teacher of their own denomination.[82]　Religious training is also furthered by the Y. W. C. A.[83]

In 1869, Rev. David Sullins, D. D., of the Methodist Church, organized a college for women under the name of Sullins Female College, at Goodson, Washington County.[84]　A charter was obtained from the Assembly in 1873.[85]　The college remained under the control of the Methodist Episcopal Church, South, until 1917, when the destruction of the property by fire in 1915, having led to a complete reorganization and the removal of the college to new buildings at Virginia Park, Bristol, Washington County,[86] transfer of control was made to a corporation having no affiliation whatever with any church.[87]　Attendance at daily chapel services,

[75] *Ibid.*, 27.
[76] *Ibid.*, 26.
[77] Smith: *C. L. Cocke*, 110; *Hollins Catalog*, 1926, 61.
[78] *Acts of Assembly*, Jan. 27, 1863, 108; *U. S. Comm. Educ. Rep't*, 1876, 689.
[79] *Ibid.*
[80] *Southern College Catalog*, 1927; *Bull. State B'd Educ.*, Oct., 1923, VI, No. 2, 131.
[81] *Southern College Catalog*, 1927, 2.
[82] *Ibid.*, 13, 16.
[83] *Ibid.*, 13.
[84] *U. S. Comm. Educ. Rep't*, 1876, 603.
[85] *Ibid.*, gives the date of charter as 1870, probably referring to county charter; *Acts of Assembly*, April 1, 1873, 328.
[86] *Sullins College Catalog*, 1926, 13.
[87] *From correspondence.*

Sunday School and Sunday morning services at the church of one's choice is required.[88]   The Y. W. C. A. maintains its regular program.   Two courses in Bible study are offered in both the preparatory department and the college, and are elective.[89]   According to the authorities, the college while not sectarian, "strives always to maintain the high principles of Christian life and training."[90]

Virginia College was established at Roanoke, 1893, by Dr. William Anderson Harris,[91] who had had previous experience as an educator as President of La Grange Female College in Georgia, and Martha Washington College and Wesleyan Female Institute in Virginia.   His death, in 1895, resulted in the presidency of the institution going to his daughter, Miss Mattie P. Harris, who with her sister conducted the school until 1927, when it was sold to Mr. Christopher Markley and his son, who purchased it that the school might be retained in Roanoke.[92]

The college has always been ranked as non-sectarian, but it is declared to be "preëminently a Christian school."[93]   Attendance is required at the various religious exercises such as daily chapel and Sunday vesper services, as well as at the church of one's choice.   A Y. W. C. A. conducts its varied activities.   A three-hour course in the "Literature of the Old Testament" and a two-hour course in the "Life of Christ" are offered.[94]   The courses are given not only for their literary, but also for their spiritual value.[95]   The attitude of the school to the issue of religion in education may be gathered from the statement that "It proceeds on the assumption that all scholastic culture and refinement must rest on the solid basis of a Christian character."[96]   Virginia College has been an accredited junior college for a number of years.[97]

[88] *Ibid.; Sullins College Catalog*, 1926, 18.
[89] *Ibid.*, 31, 39, 40.
[90] *Ibid.*, 18.
[91] Dr. Harris, b. 1827, graduate Virginia Military Institute, 1851, received a D.D. degree from Randolph-Macon in 1875, first entered law, then transferred to education; Johnson, R.: *Biog. Dictionary of America*, V.
[92] *From correspondence;* The Virginia College Corporation was formed at this time to control the school and Mrs. George Collen was elected Principal.
[93] *Virginia College Catalog*, 1926, 14.
[94] *Ibid.*, 34–35.
[95] *From correspondence.*
[96] *Virginia College Catalog*, 1926, 14.
[97] *Bull. State B'd. Educ.*, Sept., 1921, IV, No. 2, 162.

Sweet Briar College, originally incorporated, in 1901, as Sweet Briar Institute, was established by a bequest left, in 1900, to certain trustees by Mrs. Indiana Fletcher Williams, as a memorial to her daughter Daisy Williams.[98]   Mrs. Williams in her will directed that the school or seminary should be for white girls and young women; the general scope and object to be to impart "such an education in sound learning, and such physical, moral, and religious training as shall in the judgment of the Directors best fit them to be useful members of society."[99]   At their first meeting, in 1901, the Board of Directors decided to keep the foundation free from denominational control, but at the same time "distinctly religious in character."[100]   Hence, the college, though non-sectarian, "emphasizes the fundamental principles of Christianity."[101]

Attendance is expected at the daily and Sunday religious services.[102]   The Sunday services are conducted by ministers of various denominations.   The Sweet Briar Christian Association, organized by the students, has charge of one of the chapel services, each week, and directs practical social service work among the employees and in the neighborhood of the college.[103]   Four hours' work in the Bible, sophomore year, is required for the B. A. or B. S. degree.   Electives, in the junior and senior years, are offered in "The Spread of Christianity From The First To The Sixteenth Century," and in "Modern Problems in Religion" respectively.   General electives are offered in "Biblical Hebrew" and "Readings from the Historical Books and Psalms."[104]   In addition to these systematic courses, there are voluntary Bible classes organized among the students.[105]

---

[98] *Sweet Briar College Catalog*, 1926–27, 7; *Acts of Assembly*, Feb. 9, 1901, 125.

[99] *Sweet Briar College Catalog*, 1926–27, 7–8; *Acts of Assembly*, Feb. 9, 1901, 127.

[100] *Sweet Briar College Catalog*, 1926–27, 7–8; since 1919, the preparatory department known as the Academy has been discontinued.   Robertson: *Amer. Univ. and Colleges*, 629.

[101] *Sweet Briar College Catalog*, 1926–27, 110.

[102] *Ibid.;* Robertson: *Amer. Univ. and Colleges*, 630, states chapel attendance is required.

[103] *Sweet Briar College Catalog*, 1926–27, 111.

[104] *Ibid.*, 48–49.

[105] *Ibid.*, 111.

Religious life in private non-denominational secondary schools in Virginia does not as a rule differ essentially from that characteristic in private denominational schools. It will be sufficient to gauge the nature of the religious program in schools for girls from accounts of such schools as the Fauquier Institute, Southern Seminary, and Fairfax Hall, representative of schools of this class.[106]

Fauquier Institute was established at Warrenton, Fauquier County, and incorporated in 1859.[107] It appears to have been non-sectarian from its beginning.[108] It is like other Virginia non-sectarian institutions decidedly Christian in its management and discipline, and the usual religious observances and requirements as to attendance are emphasized.[109] Pupils may attend any one of the various churches in town, accompanied by their teacher, but unless a special request is made by parents they accompany the Principal to the Episcopal Church.[110] Aside from a Bible class held at the school on Sunday afternoons, the only systematic Bible instruction appears as an elective in Christian Evidences given in the senior year of the Cultural Course; apparently the exigencies of the College Preparatory Course crowd it out from that course.[111]

Southern Seminary was established at Bowling Green, Caroline County, in 1868, by Rev. E. H. Rowe, and ranked as a Methodist institution until several years ago.[112] At the beginning of the century, the school was moved to Buena Vista, Rockbridge County.[113] It is now a privately owned institution without any church affiliation.[114] The school, however, continues to em-

---

[106] The schools for girls and boys in the secondary field, here commented upon by the writer, were selected after an exhaustive perusal of catalogues, school histories, or school literature, on the basis of their being representative of their class, in having the main features of their religious life in common with other schools; the final determination being based on such factors as long continued history, or unique features which the writer wished to present; practically all Virginia private secondary schools stress at least their general Christian character.

[107] *U. S. Comm. Educ. Rep't*, 1888–89, II, 1082–83.

[108] *Ibid.*

[109] *Fauquier Institute Catalog*, 1926, 6, 10.

[110] *Ibid.*, 8, 9.

[111] *Ibid.*, 13.

[112] *U. S. Comm. Educ. Rep't*, 1897–98, II, 2330; 1902, II, 1952.

[113] *Ibid.*

[114] *From correspondence.*

phasize the fact that it tries to lead all its students to a positive knowledge of Christ.[115]   Morning and evening devotional exercises, as well as all other religious exercises which may be held in the school, are compulsory.   Students are required to attend public worship Sunday morning in the churches of their denominations.[116]   A three years' course in the Bible is offered and required of all students whose religious faith does not forbid.[117]

A more recently established non-sectarian school which receives its enrollment from many states outside of Virginia is Fairfax Hall, established at Waynesboro, Augusta County, in 1920.[118] The atmosphere of the school is "consistently religious," and the faculty are chosen with a view to their exercising a Christian influence.[119]   Daily morning chapel exercises are held by the President, chaplain, or visiting ministers.   A Y. W. C. A. furthers the religious life of the school.   Sunday attendance at the church of one's choice is required.[120]   A course in the Bible, offered as an elective, aims to give the pupil a general familiarity with its contents.[121]   The school, according to its authorities, is dedicated to the ideal that "Education of the mind and the upbuilding of the body are a failure, unless there is also the education of the heart and spirit in the love and knowledge of our Saviour."[122]

The character of the religious life in secondary schools for boys may be gathered from accounts of religious instruction and activities at some representative schools.

Shenandoah Valley Academy, located at Winchester, Frederick County, regards itself as the successor of Winchester Academy, which according to local tradition was founded, in 1764, and which, except for interruptions during the Revolutionary and Civil Wars, has been in continuous session since.[123]   The name was changed to Shenadoah Valley Academy, in 1865.[124]   In 1907,

---

115 *Southern Seminary Catalog*, 1926, 18.
116 *Ibid.*, 63.
117 *Ibid.*, 47.
118 *From correspondence;* students from 25 to 30 states are represented.
119 *Fairfax Hall Catalog*, 1926–27, 4, 15.
120 *Ibid.*, 23.
121 *Ibid.*, 26.
122 *Ibid.*, 22.
123 *Shenandoah Valley Catalog*, 1926, 9; Winchester Academy was incorporated in 1786, see p. 168.
124 *Shenandoah Valley Catalog*, 1926, 9.

the character of the school was transformed into that of a military academy.[125] The school is strictly non-denominational, but it holds that "a knowledge of the essential facts of the history of Christianity is considered necessary for the complete education of every boy."[126] No systematic course in the Bible appears in the school curriculum, but the statement is made that "Religious instruction is provided either in the Sunday Schools of Winchester or in the Academy."[127] Attendance at the church of one's choice on Sunday is compulsory.[128]

Augusta Military Academy was established, under the name of Augusta Male Academy, as a non-sectarian institution about 1866, by Charles S. Roller, at Fort Defiance, Augusta County.[129] Attendance at religious exercises is required. The school has a Y. M. C. A. A school pastor "conducts classes in Biblical history and gives such religious instruction as may be deemed proper in a school that is strictly non-sectarian."[130] A "reverence for sacred things" is one of the ideals of the school.[131]

Fishburne Military School was established, in 1879, by Prof. Jas. A. Fishburne at Waynesboro, Augusta County. It has been a non-sectarian school from the beginning, but like other schools of this type it emphasizes the fact that its teaching and training are distinctly Christian, stating definitely, that "no boy is desired whose parents do not sympathize with the Christian work in the school." Attendance at chapel, Bible classes, and Sunday church services at the various churches is required, Catholic students being permitted to attend their own church.[132] Five courses are given in the Bible, beginning with the Books of Genesis and Exodus in the Fifth Class, and ending with the Life of Christ in the Second Class.[133] The school hopes to be able to

---

[125] Cartmell: *Shenandoah Valley Pioneers*, 158; *cf. Ibid.*, 288; *cf.* Morrison: *Beginnings Pub. Educ., Va.*, 119.
[126] *Shenandoah Valley Catalog*, 1926, 11.
[127] *Ibid.*
[128] *Ibid.*
[129] *Augusta Military Academy Catalog*, 1926, 7; *Richmond Enquirer*, Mar. 28, 1876.
[130] *Augusta Military Academy Catalog*, 1926, 16–17.
[131] *Ibid.*
[132] *Fishburne Military School Catalog*, 1926, 34.
[133] *Ibid.*, 44.

have the student "feel that it is his duty and privilege to unite with the church of his parents."[134]

Staunton Military Academy was transferred to Virginia in 1884, by Captain Wm. H. Kable, from Charlestown, West Virginia, where it had been established in 1872.[135] It was located at Staunton under the name of Staunton Male Academy, and seems to have received its present name with the charter in 1890.[136] The school appears always to have been non-sectarian. The present religious life of the school is supervised by a chaplain, who conducts special services on Sunday and Bible classes during the week, and acts as adviser to the students. The day's work is begun with Scripture reading and prayer. Attendance at all religious services, including church attendance, is required; students of the Catholic faith, as do others, attend their own church, under charge of a cadet officer. The school also has a Y. M. C. A.[137] A Bible course, devoted to the Old Testament in the first semester, and to the "Life and Works of Jesus and Paul," the second semester, is given as an elective.[138] The school stresses emphatically its Christian influence, declaring,

> There is nothing in education if *character* is not considered, and it is *not* enough for any institution to turn out educationally trained minds, but its pupils should go forth with high principles; with a set purpose to do the right for right's sake, and with the fear and love of God in their hearts.[139]

Woodberry Forest School at Woodberry Forest, Madison County, was established in 1889, by Captain Robert S. Walker. It stresses as its object thorough preparation for higher institutions, under conditions favorable to the "development of manly Christian character."[140] Its teaching and training are distinctly Christian, and boys whose parents are not in sympathy with and are unwilling to give their hearty support to the religious work of the school are not desired. Work in the classes in Sacred Study,

---

134 *Ibid.*, 34.

135 *W. Va. Hist. Mag.*, Jan., 1905, 18–33; *from correspondence.*

136 *U. S. Comm. Educ. Rep't*, 1888–89, II, 997; 1902, II, 1954; *Acts of Assembly*, Feb. 16, 1886, 131; Mar. 4, 1890, 853.

137 *Staunton Military Academy Catalog*, 1927, 41, 37.

138 *Ibid.*, 116.

139 *Ibid.*, 39.

140 *Woodberry Forest Catalog*, 1926, 8; *World's Work*, Nov., 1911, XXIII, 41 *ff.;* Yowell, *Hist. Madison Co.*, 111.

on Sunday, each form meeting separately, is required. The school chaplain conducts services on Sunday. Attendance is compulsory at all religious services of whatever nature, except the Thursday evening voluntary services conducted during a part of the year.[141]

It is evident from the nature and extent of religious instruction offered in the various privately controlled educational institutions here described that the general principles which form the basis of this instruction resemble largely those that are fundamental in denominational schools. Associations like the Y. M. and Y. W. C. A.; attendance at Sunday School and Sunday church services, daily or stated chapel services; and a certain amount of systematic Bible instruction characterize nearly all of them. They resemble many denominational institutions in their emphasis upon non-sectarian, but Christian atmosphere. It will now be of interest to see how institutions under public control have, since the Civil War, treated the problem of religious instruction—how the Ruffner policy of co-operation without alliance has affected their procedeure.

Effect Of The Ruffner Policy Upon State Controlled Institutions
1. *University of Virginia*

The University of Virginia had succeeded during the Civil War in keeping up its form of organization and though its enrollment had dropped from approximately 600 or more annually, which had been common in the decade before the War, to 217 for the entire four-year war period, its doors were not closed.[142] In the fall of 1865, it opened with an enrollment of 220 students.[143] At the earnest solicitation of the faculty and friends of the University, appropriations were resumed.[144] However, by 1874, the indebtedness of the University had accumulated to over

---

141 *Woodberry Forest Catalog*, 1926, 15; two other schools which are characterized by a similar attitude to the problem of religion in education, in the emphasis upon a non-sectarian but Christian tone, are the Swaveley School, established at Manassas, Prince William County, in 1901, and the Blackstone Military Academy, established at Blackstone, Nottoway County, in 1912.

142 Bruce: *Hist. U. of Va.*, III, 3, 322.

143 *Ibid.*, 348.

144 *Acts of Assembly*, Feb. 23, 1866, 214; Bruce: *Hist. U. of Va.*, III, 349; IV, 241.

$90,000, and in 1875 the Assembly passed an act consolidating the debt, and authorized a loan permitting its refunding.[145]

It became evident that more adequate financial assistance must be given the University, if it was to meet the demands made upon it, consequently a bill was proposed to increase the annuity to the University in lieu of tuition fees by students of the state. The news of this proposed bill threw denominational and smaller colleges of the state into a panic. The extension of the public free school system into the University seemed to them to threaten their student supply, and thus their very existence. Dr. Dabney, whose great controversy with Dr. Ruffner, a few months later, on the issue of free schools[146] was probably a partial consequence of the feeling stirred up by this issue, wrote an open letter to the Speaker of the House of Delegates opposing the bill. Dr. Dabney, an alumnus of the Unversity, but then associated with the theological seminary at Hampden-Sidney, based his objection on the ground that great injury would result to the moral character of youth in Virginia, from the assembling of so large a number of students in one place. He affirmed that he had gone to the University from a small college, and had found that "Even then, with two hundred and fifty students, . . . the degree of vice was frightfully larger, relatively to the numbers," and was confident that students going there now from the smaller colleges would testify to the same comparison.[147] Attracting to the University several hundred crude undergraduates would work a curse upon the state by corrupting the morals of youth. It was to the corruptions festering in the crowded northern colleges that he attributed the moral state of northern society. He would give the University the $30,000 annuity on the one condition that she stop taking into her academic schools anybody but graduates who had received their B.A. degree.[148]

Dr. Dabney's contention that the expansion of the University would be detrimental to the morals of youth was denied by Rev. J. Wm. Jones, also an alumnus, a distinguished Baptist minister, and subsequently chaplain of the University. Rev. Mr.

---

[145] *Acts of Assembly,* Mar. 25, 1875, 275; Bruce: *Hist. U. of Va.,* IV, 245.
[146] See p. 436 *ff.*
[147] *Richmond Enquirer,* Jan. 30, 1876.
[148] *Ibid.*

Jones declared he had been a student of the University immediately before the War, when the enrollment was over 600, and
that for more than twenty years he had made one or more visits
each year to the institution. His observation and experience
had made him conclude that "it would result in rich spiritual
blessing to crowd the halls of the University with students
(whether graduates or undergraduates), and allow them to
breathe the pure and religious atmosphere which hangs around
the institution."[149] He referred to the statement of Dr. Gessner
Harrison, which attributed the disorders and riots of the early
days of the University to the system of rules and penalties and
espionage which existed in those days, and Dr. Harrison's opinion that since placing the young men on their honor to behave
as gentlemen should, no set of college men on the continent were
more orderly, studious, and moral than the body of 600 men in
the university.

Rev. Mr. Jones attributed this improvement to the greater interest in things religious with the coming of the Y. M. C. A. in
1858. Besides the regular morning and Sabbath services, there
were in his day fourteen weekly prayer meetings, which were
largely attended. They had five mission Sunday Schools under
the charge of students. There had also been some "very precious
revivals," at which a number of the best students had made professions of religion. The present condition was even better,
nearly every member of the faculty was an active Christian.
The Y. M. C. A. in 1870–71 had a regular attendance of 33 per
cent of the student body at its ten weekly meetings, and during
that session there had been thirty professions of conversion.
During the present session there had been only a single disciplinary case. Rev. Mr. Jones was confident that a student coming
from any community or college "would find as few temptations
to vice, and as many inducements to well-doing, as he had been
accustomed to in previous surroundings." The University was
no exception to the moral and religious tone which pervaded
other higher schools and colleges in the state.[150]

---

[149] *Ibid.*, Feb. 9, 1876.
[150] *Ibid.*

The position taken on this issue by Rev. Mr. Jones was not unanimously echoed by other leaders in the Baptist denomination. The trustees of Richmond College, the leading Baptist institution in Virginia, at a meeting on February 7, 1876, adopted a formal protest to the General Assembly. They declared, that while in favor of such an appropriation by the state as would ensure the efficiency and success of the University, the provision of the bill for the gratuitous education of all the students of the state in the academic department of the University to be unsound in principle, unwise in policy, dangerous to the University, and detrimental to all the colleges of the state depending in whole, or in part, on tuition fees. It was unjust and oppressive to tax the supporters and patrons of private colleges to enable the University to offer instruction on terms that must prove injurious to those colleges. They therefore hoped that the Legislature would not "inflict on the most active and liberal friends of education in the State so unreasonable and heavy a burden."[151]

This attitude of the officers of Richmond College was dissented from by one of the most distinguished of Virginia's Baptists, Rev. John A. Broadus, an alumnus and former chaplain of the University.[152]   Dr. Broadus felt satisfied that prosperity of the University meant prosperity for all the colleges. The high degree at which the sentiment in favor of higher education stood in Virginia was largely associated with, and had been produced by the University. If this educational sentiment failed as a result of the depression of the University, all institutions would feel the consequences. By fostering the University, qualified teachers for the common schools of the next generation would be obtained. Only by having a multitude of highly educated persons could first class teaching be obtained in these schools.[153]

Rev. J. B. Jeter, who had presided at the meeting of the trustees of Richmond College, replied immediately. He did not see how the welfare of other colleges would be promoted by permitting the University to receive with fee students under 18, and without fee, above that age.   The University

---

151 *Ibid.*, Feb. 8, 1876.
152 See p. 386.
153 *Richmod Enquirer*, Feb. 23, 1876.

. . . would be brought into competition with the colleges for at least two-thirds of the students seeking higher education, with the decisive advantage on the part of the University of offering free instruction at the cost of a tax imposed on the friends and supporters of colleges, whose resources do not enable them to proffer gratuitous instruction.

This was contrary to justice and sound policy. By offering free tuition in the highest branches of academic learning, of which only the rich, or thrifty and enterprising can avail themselves, the great middle class, laboring, tax paying, state supporting part of the community, dependent on academies and colleges must be taxed for the gratuitous education of other classes of society.[154]

Richmond College was not alone in protesting against the University bill. The trustees of Randolph-Macon College, Methodist, held a meeting on February 11, and while agreeing that the prosperity of the University demanded the increased annuity, declared that, in justice to the other institutions of higher education, admission to the University should depend upon a rigid preliminary examination, and that no instruction be permitted free of tuition fees, as the procedure would operate injuriously and disadvantageously to other colleges, and be likely to prove disastrous to the University.[155]

Roanoke College, Lutheran, protested on a similar basis, and declared that the passage of the bill would be very discouraging; it would take the educational work out of her hands and give it with the profits to one favored institution, "making us pay, without our consent, our proportional tax for the sustentation of such favored institutions."[156]

The trustees of Washington and Lee University, no longer a sectarian institution, likewise protested.[157]

The first vote on the bill found it lacking six votes to pass. At a later reconsideration, it was pointed out the debt of the University had risen from $38,000 at the close of the War to the then $94,000, and that the appropriation was needed to make necessary repairs and pay the interest on the debt; not a dollar

---

154 *Ibid.*, Feb. 25, 1876.
155 *Ibid.*, Feb. 12, 1876.
156 *Ibid.*, Feb. 15, 1876.
157 *Ibid.*, Feb. 25, 1876.

was to go to increase salaries of professors. Resolutions in favor of the bill by the faculty of William and Mary were presented. The bill was passed with a large majority. It provided that a $30,000 annuity should be made the University on condition that it educate in the academic department all students of the state, over 18 years, who should matriculate under rules and regulations prescribed by the board of trustees.[158]

The action of the Legislature found an echo in the meeting of the General Association of the Baptists in June, and resulted in the proposal to seek a larger endowment fund for Richmond College, the opinion being that the action of the Legislature made it necessary for all the colleges to bestir themselves and to get into "such condition as to compete, if need be, with the University."[159] The echo of this grant by the Legislature continued to reverberate in even stronger force as the excitement regarding the readjuster issue[160] increased in the next few years. "Civis" writing in the *Religious Herald* in February, 1878, would remind the University of her danger. The continuation of her annuity, despite the protest of the great mass of the voting population, made it likely that opposition would at length successfully demand the withdrawal of the entire appropriation. He declared:

. . . Having abandoned tuition fees, and losing her annuity, she will hasten to her doom. Nor will it soothe her in the pangs of dissolution to remember that, in the supreme crisis of the Commonwealth, she did not set the heroic example of self-abnegation; that, oblivious of the public distress and impending dishonour, she demanded and obtained from the exhausted treasury of the State just double the amount that was considered abundant for her wants in the palmiest days of her pride and power.[161]

To this, Rev. J. Wm. Jones replied, refuting particularly the point that free tuition would destroy the self-respect, independence, and manhood of the student. He questioned whether the thousands of preachers scattered over the land, or toiling as missionaries in other lands, were "any the less *men* because they received 'free tuition' at college?" He wished to know whether

---

158 *Ibid.,* Feb. 18 and 25, 1876; *Acts of Assembly,* Feb. 26, 1876, 110.
159 *Richmond Enquirer,* June 3, 1876; see p. 547.
160 See p. 432 *ff.*
161 *Religious Herald,* Feb. 7, 1878.

the hundreds of "State students" who had gone out from the University in past years had shown less "self-respect and self-reliance" than those who had paid their way, or whether the generals and soldiers who had been graduated from West Point had been "less *true men*" because not only their tuition fees, but also their board and clothes had been paid for? Furthermore, about one-fourth of the students at Richmond College were exempt from tuition fees.[162]

The reply to Rev. Mr. Jones declared that the exemption at Richmond College represented a different situation. These students were exempted for a consideration more valuable than tuition fees. Donations, *"of their own free will,"* by good men had been given on condition that pious and promising young men, intending to devote their lives to the ministry, should be educated free. The "comparatively rich" students of the University were "put in the enjoyment of money wrung by taxation from the people at large, comparatively poor." The University students were educated to advance their own aims in life, for selfish ends; the others, in the abnegation of self, to devote themselves to the highest interests of humanity. "In the former case, self-reliance, manhood and personal independence are assaulted; in the latter case, in no sense and to no extent, whatever." The West Point graduate, by rendering and being ready to render service, returns the equivalent of his education, and there was no benefaction, no charity in the matter at all.[163]

In 1884, the Assembly seems to have been able, probably because the readjuster issue had shortly before been settled,[164] to raise the annuity of the University to $40,000 without creating any particular stir. The age of the students now to be admitted to the University, in view of the increased grant, was lowered to 16 years.[165] In the same year, the Assembly granted the Board of Visitors authority to "prescribe the duties of each professor and the course and mode of instruction."[166]

[162] *Ibid.*, Feb. 28, 1878.
[163] *Ibid.*, Mar. 7, 1878; see p. 587.
[164] See p. 434.
[165] *Acts of Assembly*, Mar. 15, 1884, 543.
[166] *Ibid.*, Nov. 22, 1884, 79.

On the subject of morality and religion, the University catalogues after the Civil War made the following statement:

These are recognized as the foundation and indispensable concomitants of education.   The discipline is sedulously administered with a view to confirm integrity, and to maintain a sacred regard for truth.   Great efforts are made to surround the students with religious influences; but experience has proved that the best way to effect this result is, to forbear the employment of coercion to enforce attendance on religious exercises, which is entirely voluntary.   Prayers are held every morning in the Chapel, and divine service is performed on Sunday by a Chaplain, selected, in turn, from the principal religious denominations.   By means of a Young Men's Christian Association, new comers are shielded, as much as possible, from vicious connections, and the energies of those willing to engage in the Christian enterprises of the neighborhood are called into active exercise.[167]

The chaplain system, which had been a prominent feature of the religious life of the University in the decades bofore the Civil War, continued until 1896.[168]   The practise of alternate two-year service by the four principal denominations had continued until that date, when the sudden death of the new chaplain left that office vacant.[169]   In view of the difficulty in filling that position at short notice, it was decided to call instead a General Secretary for the Y. M. C. A., and the office of chaplain came to an end.[170]

The Civil War had interrupted the plans for the building of a Chapel.[171]   In 1872, the project was renewed,[172] but it was not until 1883 that a concentrated effort was made to raise funds.[173] The chapel was finished and turned over to the University, in 1890.[174]   The Board of Visitors had carefully avoided giving any contribution from the public funds, though they had designated and given the site for the building.   The hesitation of the Board, in spending money on the building, but none in accepting it, has been characterized by Bruce, the historian of

---

[167] *Catalog, U. of Va.*, 1867–68, 38; *cf.* various catalogues of the seventies and eighties.

[168] Metcalf: *Cent. U. of Va.*, 10.

[169] *U. of Va. Alum. Bull.*, Feb., 1897, III, No. 4, 94–95.

[170] Metcalf: *Cent. U. of Va.*, 11; Bruce: *Hist. U. of Va.*, IV, 359.

[171] See p. 390.

[172] Bruce: *Hist. U. of Va.*, IV, 177.

[173] Horner: *Autographs*, 13–15.

[174] *Ibid.:* Bruce: *Hist. U. of Va.*, IV, 179.

the University, as being "an inconsistency slightly Gilbertian in character."[175]

The Y. M. C. A. continued in the decades after the Civil War to support Sunday schools, both in and out of the University precincts, to hold sectional prayer meetings on Wednesdays, and a combined prayer meeting on Sundays.[176] With the co-operation of members of the faculty, Bible classes were also held.[177] At this time, distinguished ministers were invited, once a month, to give public lectures.[178] Students were not required to join the Association, but membership was solicited by a friend or some especially appointed person. If already a member of an established church, the student usually joined the Association.[179] Membership cost was usually $2.[180] The Association held itself responsible for raising by subscription the salary of the chaplain.[181] Reference to the activities of the Y. M. C. A. was common in the catalogues of the University.[182]

The activities of the Y. M. C. A. had since its organization been hampered to a certain extent, because of the lack of adequate and suitable quarters. By 1886, definite suggestions looking to a suitable building were made;[183] but it was not until after 1902, when Dr. H. M. McIlhany, who had been travelling Secretary for the International Committee of the Y. M. C. A., came to the University as the local secretary, that the building was finally obtained as a gift from Mrs. Wm. E. Dodge, of New York, whose husband had contemplated the gift before his death.[184] An endowment fund was raised in part by the faculty and students, and the building opened in October, 1905.[185]

The abandonment of the chaplain plan of religious work, in 1896, opened the way for a new religious activity at the Univer-

---

175 *Ibid.*, 180.
176 *Ibid.*, 183.
177 *Ibid.;* Culbreth: *U. of Va.*, 311, 313.
178 *Ibid.*, 274–75.
179 *Lippincott's Magazine*, July, 1887, XL, 102.
180 Horner: *Autographs*, 19.
181 *Lippincott's Magazine*, July, 1887, 102.
182 *Cf. Catalog, U. of Va.*, 1888–89, 71.
183 Bruce: *Hist. U. of Va.*, IV, 182.
184 *Ibid.*, 362; Metcalf: *Cent. U. of Va.*, 11.
185 *Ibid.;* Bruce: *Hist. U. of Va.*, IV, 362; *cf. U. of Va. Alum. Bull.*, Oct., 1903, N. S., III, No. 4, 182–83; April, 1904, N. S., IV, No. 2, 22–24.

sity. The Christian Woman's Board of Missions, affiliated with the Disciples of Christ, undertook, in 1892, to establish Bible chairs at state universities.[186] By 1896, arrangements had been made for this work at six state universities, of which the University of Virginia was one.[187] Rev. Charles A. Young, who had been instrumental in introducing the work in other places, took charge of the work at the University in 1896–97. The work was arranged in co-operation with the Y. M. C. A. and the announcement appeared under its name.[188] The character of the work as then given may be described as a Bible lecture course. The object was stated as being to furnish opportunity for study of the Bible from historical and literary standpoints. In 1898, four courses of study were offered; over twenty students enrolled, devoting two hours to classroom work, and three hours to outside study.[189] Fees for the courses ranged from one to three dollars, with a reduction to members of the Y. M. C. A. and ministers.

The experiment, however, did not prove altogether satisfactory; voluntary study, not counting toward a degree, with difficulty competed for the time and attention of students.[190] Through the family of Colonel John B. Cary, of Richmond, who died before his plans for endowing a permanent lectureship for regular and systematic Bible instruction could be matured, an endowment was received for that purpose.[191] In 1902, the endowment amounted to more than $25,000.[192] The John B. Cary Bible Lectureship, which was thus created, was "not organically connected with the University," but was described as existing "with its approval and sympathy." Its object was declared to be to furnish non-sectarian instruction, and care was promised in the selection of lecturers on the basis, not of their denominational affiliation, but of their evangelical relations.[193] In the

---

[186] *Cf. N. E. A. Proc's*, 1907, XLV, 732; Metcalf: *Cent. U. of Va.*, 148; *U. S. Comm. Educ. Rep't*, 1897–98, II, 1572.
[187] *Ibid.*
[188] *Ibid.*, 1573.
[189] *Ibid.*
[190] Metcalf: *Cent. U. of Va.*, 12.
[191] Bruce: *Hist. U. of Va.*, IV, 358.
[192] *U. of Va. Catalog*, 1901–02, 160.
[193] *Ibid.*

sessions of 1901–02, various special lecturers were engaged; and
for the winter and spring sessions, two regular Bible teachers.[194]
The following year, no regular incumbent was obtained, but a
number of distinguished ministers were invited to give lectures.[195] In the fall of 1903, Rev. W. M. Forrest was engaged
as a permanent lecturer, and he is still connected with this foundation.[196] Rev. Mr. Forrest planned to give for that session
courses on ''The Orations of Moses, The Life of Jesus, Old Testament Prophecy, the Teaching of Jesus, The Wisdom Literature
of the Old Testament, Miracles and Parables of Jesus.''[197] In
1905–06, co-incident with the coming of President Alderman,[198]
the courses offered by Rev. Mr. Forrest were placed on a par
with other studies prescribed for the B.A. degree.[199] The catalogue of 1906–07 announced ''The John B. Cary Memorial
School of Biblical History and Literature,'' and stated that its
courses would be accepted as electives at large for the B.A. degree.[200] The new chair was supported by the fund created by
the Christian Woman's Board of Missions, which had started the
work, and the John B. Cary fund.[201]

The department, which originally had been placed on a trial
period of three years, prospered and gradually extended its
courses in both the undergraduate and graduate schools, and with
credit toward the various degrees, including the Ph.D.[202] As a
rule, four courses are offered in any one year. The nature of the
work is thus described in an official bulletin:

Primarily the courses are for general culture, but are of especial worth
to prospective ministerial students and Christian workers. While scholastic
rather than devotional, and conducted in harmony with modern scientific

---

194 *Ibid.*
195 *U. of Va. Alum. Bull.*, April, 1903, N. S., III, No. 2, 22; Oct., 1903,
N. S., III, No. 4, 183.
196 *Ibid.*
197 *U. of Va. Catalog*, 1903–04, 160–61; *cf. U. of Va. Alum. Bull.*, Oct.,
1903, N. S., III, No. 4, 184.
198 See p. 627.
199 Bruce: *Hist. U. of Va.*, V, 134; *U. of Va.,—A Statement of Accomplishment*, 11.
200 *U. of Va. Catalog*, 1906–7, 159; *U. of Va. Alum. Bull.*, 1907, N. S.,
VII, 80.
201 Bruce: *Hist. U. of Va.*, V, 135.
202 *Ibid.*, V, 135; *U. of Va. Catalog*, 1914–15, 137; 1919–20, 107; *U. of
Va. Rec., Ext. Ser.*, Dec., 1915, I, No. 4, 136.

principles of teaching and investigation such as characterize all true university work, the Bible instruction is reverent, and constantly mindful of the needs of growing intellects meeting for the first time the problems raised by a critical examination of faith in the light of history, philosophy and science.[203]

The work of this department, in 1915, was recognized as being of the highest standard by the Religious Education Association.[204]   In 1924–25, two three-hour courses in the under-graduate school were given in "The history of the Hebrew people throughout the Old Testament, the Apocrypha, and the New Testament," and "The literature of the Old and New Testaments, with attention to the literary features and the contents of the various books."   A course for graduate and undergraduate students was given in "The Origin and history of the English Bible," and one for graduates in "The religious idea of the Bible, or the theology of the Old and New Testaments."[205]

This by no means represented all the work of this department; for, from the beginning of the undertaking to introduce a Bible course of study into the high school curriculum, Rev. Mr. Forrest had taken an active part in that work.[206]   Upon the organization of the Extension Division of the University in 1913, Rev. Mr. Forrest extended his activities by offering courses and lectures in his subject in various parts of the state.[207]   In 1926, four courses were offered, practically identical with the regular courses in the University;[208] for 1927–28, six courses were announced.[209]

While it was thought, when the chaplaincy was given up in 1896, that the procuring of a General Secretary for the Y. M. C. A. would obviate the need for a regular pastor at the University, as the secretary was to arrange for Sunday chapel services by invited clergymen, it was decided after a few years to try the experiment of keeping the visiting clergyman in residence for a month.   This procedure was begun in the fall of 1900.   It made

203 *Ibid.*
204 *Ibid.*, 136–37; Bruce: *Hist. U. of Va.*, V, 135.
205 *U. of Va. Catalog*, 1924–25, 141.
206 See p. 500.
207 Bruce: *Hist. U. of Va.*, V, 218; *U. of Va. Rec.*, *Ext. Ser.*, Nov., 1921, VI, No. 3, 5, 6; *cf.* also III, No. 3, 12, 17.
208 *Ibid.*, July, 1926, XI, No. 1, 8.
209 *Ibid.*, Aug., 1927, XII, No. 2, 9.

possible a daily afternoon prayer service. The difficulty of finding men able to give their services for so limited a time, resulted in abandoning the scheme, and returning to the scheme of invited clergymen.[210] In 1902–03, over thirty clerical addresses were made.[211] The regular pastoral work among the students, including the conducting of chapel services, was then taken care of by the General Secretary of the Y. M. C. A.[212]

In 1902, the Y. M. C. A. was encouraging individual study of the Bible by small classes under student leaders, and by various Bible lecture courses. It maintained also a Wednesday night prayer service. Its members assisted in the work of Sunday Schools in the University and vicinity.[213] The courses offered by the Y. M. C. A. comprised a four years' cycle of Bible study, outlined by the Association's International Committee. The work was arranged to cover a period of thirty weeks of work, and was outlined for daily study. It was "primarily devotional in character," and intended for application to daily living.[214] The following endorsement of the work appeared in the catalogue for 1902:

> The Visitors and the Faculty of the University heartily commend the work of the Association, and it is earnestly desired that every parent or guardian see to it that the student under his care be encouraged to join the Association as soon as he reaches the University.[215]

In 1903, there were over eighty students in ten groups studying these courses.[216] By 1907, the enrollment had increased to more than two hundred men in twenty-five classes.[217] Associated with the Y. M. C. A., was a missionary committee, whose responsibility was the supervision of missionary addresses, a mission study class, and the solicitation of contributions for foreign missions.[218]

Chapel services, in the early years of the twentieth century, consisted of daily prayer service of fifteen minutes before the

---

210 Metcalf: *Cent. U. of Va.*, 11.
211 Bruce: *Hist. U. of Va.*, IV, 359.
212 *U. of Va. Alum. Bull.*, 1907, N. S., VII, 100–01.
213 *U. of Va. Catalog*, 1901–02, 159.
214 *U. of Va. Alum. Bull.*, April, 1903, N. S., III, No. 2, 22.
215 *U. of Va. Catalog*, 1901–02, 160.
216 *U. of Va. Alum. Bull.*, April, 1903, N. S., III, No. 2, 22.
217 *Ibid.*, 1907, N. S., VII, 41.
218 *Ibid.*, Oct., 1903, N. S., III, No. 4, 181.

supper hour, and regular preaching services twice on Sunday. It was at the Sunday services that representative ministers of the various evangelical denominations were invited.[219] The daily prayer services were conducted by the Association Secretary, faculty members, or invited ministers.[220]

By 1915, the University was deducting $2 from the contingent deposit fee of $10, to support "the chapel services and general religious work of the University." It was stated that since support of the religious work of the University was entirely optional, students, who objected to contributing, should, within one month after registration, request the Bursar not to deduct this amount.[221]

The Y. M. C. A., throughout this period, continued along the lines previously described. In 1915, in addition to the usual Bible work, courses were given in "Student Standards of Action," and student problems.[222] Chapel services were now no longer conducted on the first Sunday in each month, so that students might be free to attend communion services of their respective churches. Evangelistic campaigns were held frequently.[223]

In 1920, the work of the Y. M. C. A. included Home and Foreign Missions, a weekly meeting on Thursday evening, assistance through its membership to the work of churches and Sunday Schools, speakers to various preparatory schools in the state, the conducting of evangelistic campaigns throughout the state, the maintenance of medical clinics and night schools in the University neighborhood, the invitation of eminent speakers to address the students, and the promotion of social intercourse.[224] By 1922, the Association was attempting through denominational clubs "to relate the students to the churches of their particular affiliation."[225]

The impetus to the last activity had apparently been given by the feeling which had become general in 1917, "that the chapel

219 See p. 616.
220 *U. of Va. Catalog*, 1901–02, 161.
221 *Ibid.*, 1914–15, 104–05.
222 *Ibid.*, 285.
223 *U. of Va. Rec., Ext. Ser.*, Dec., 1915, I, No. 4, 135.
224 *U. of Va. Catalog*, 1919–20, 230; 1920–21, 248; 1921–22, 256.
225 *Ibid.*, 1921–22, 256; 1922–23, 268; 1924–25, 299.

system had served its day, and had become a burden to be borne rather than a stimulus to the religious life of the University."[226] Access to churches in Charlottesville had become easier; besides, there was an opinion that it was preferable for students to keep up or acquire denominational affiliation during their University life.[227] In 1917, owing to the upheaval caused by war conditions, it was decided to make an appeal to the various denominations to assume a more definite oversight of their adherents at the University. A step in this direction had been taken, in 1910, by the Episcopal Church. For many years, that denomination had led in the number of students at the University.[228] The difficulty of adding supervision of a large number of students to the parochial duties of the rector of the local church caused the diocese to organize a parish with its own rector in the University community. A building site was purchased and a temporary chapel erected.[229]

With the creation of an Extension Division, in 1913, the University proceeded to further its religious work through co-operation with various agencies, and to give publicity through bulletins to the numerous religious activities of the University, and its co-operating agencies throughout the state. The first bulletin was a Rural Life Bulletin entitled "The Country Church." In December, 1915, a bulletin was published describing the "Religious Activities and Advantages at the University of Virginia;[230] the following spring, "A Program for the Use of Sunday Schools and Churches in the Observance of Country Church Day."[231] In connection with the latter bulletin, it may be pointed out that Governor H. C. Stuart had declared in a proclamation, setting aside Sunday, May 7, 1916, as Country Church Day,

. . . The country church is a necessity of civilization, and not only must it be perpetuated and encouraged, but its sphere of usefulness must be constantly widened, so that it may reach its proper position as the community center. . . . There are thousands of city dwellers who might well turn their

[226] Metcalf: *Cent. U. of Va.*, 141.
[227] *Ibid.; U. of Va. Catalog*, 1919–20, 230.
[228] Bruce: *Hist. U. of Va.*, V, 250.
[229] Metcalf: *Cent. U. of Va.*, 142.
[230] *U. of Va. Rec., Ext. Ser.*, Dec., 1915, I, No. 4.
[231] *Ibid.*, April, 1916, I, No. 5; *Relig. Educ.*, XI, 292.

thoughts and prayers on that day to the mission and the services of the churches in the country where once centered their spiritual lives.[232]

This proclamation may well be contrasted with the reluctance of Governor Wise, before the Civil War, to issue a Thanksgiving proclamation.[233] In issuing this bulletin, the University made the explanation that it was doing so, in that the University of Virginia was "an instrument of the State for the service of the people."[234] The bulletin outlined the program for the day's observance in the Sunday School and church, and gave copies of prayers, recitations, and hymns to be used for the occasion. Ministers were invited to write to the Extension Bureau "for advice or information on all questions of rural church, home and farm life." A bibliography on the country church was also appended.

The University had shown, however, an interest in the religious aspects of rural life, before the inauguration of its Extension Division. There had been, since 1906, a Rural Life Conference in connection with the University.[235] The programs of these conferences devoted considerable space to consideration of religious phases of rural life. In 1916, Country Church Day, Country Y. M. C. A. Day, Country Sunday School Day, and Country School Day were part of the program. Features of the Conference were a daily Bible lecture, and "Fellowship with workers from many churches." Speakers included various ministers.[236] The program in 1919 included an address by Rev. Mr. Forrest on "Bible courses for High School Pupils," and an address by Dr. Harry Clark, of the University of Tennessee, on "The Country Church-Organization of a Coöperative Community."[237] In 1921, the Extension Division published the Proceedings of the Rural Life Conference called by the Governor, in May, of that year. Reports and addresses were read on rural schools, rural churches, and other religious problems. The Committee on the Rural Church declared that the church had not maintained its former

---

232 *U. of Va. Rec., Ext. Ser.*, April, 1916, I, No. 5, 155.
233 See p. 361.
234 *U. of Va. Rec., Ext. Ser.*, April, 1916, I, No. 5, 157.
235 *Ibid.*, Nov., 1919, V, No. 2, 3.
236 *Ibid.*, April, 1916, I, No. 5, 191.
237 *Ibid.*, Nov., 1919, V, No. 2, 5.

influence over the whole life of the people.[238]   A general survey had revealed the fact that more than 800,000 boys and girls in the state, under 25, had no connection with the church, and the majority of these were in the rural districts.[239]   The report declared:

. . . As our state encourages the reading of the Bible in the public schools and as the great majority of our school teachers are men and women of fine Christian character, we feel confident that our rural schools would welcome co-operation on the part of the pastors of the community.[240]

It was suggested, that where it was agreeable to public school authorities, rural pastors work out a program of co-operation with the schools for "conducting worship services and in speaking to the pupils on the fundamentals of the Christian life."[241]   Attention was also called to the Bible courses for high school pupils. Better equipment for Sunday School work was urged, and it was suggested that where there was no equipment that the public school building be used until a Sunday School building was erected.[242]   It was advised that state and conference training schools for church and Sunday School workers extend their terms and broaden their curriculum.[243]   Students in state schools should be prepared for lay leadership in the church by being given training courses for church work, even though on an elective basis, and without credit.[244]

Another bulletin published by the Extension Division was in connection with American Education Week, in November, 1924. Ministers were asked to make education the theme of their service for the Sunday designated as "For God and Country Day." The following slogans were given:

Religion, morality, and education are necessary for good government.
A godly nation cannot fail.
The educational triangle: The home, the school, the church.[245]

Suggestive texts and topics for sermons were also given.[246]

---

238 *Ibid.*, Oct., 1921, VI, No. 2, 79.
239 *Ibid.*, 80.
240 *Ibid.*, 81.
241 *Ibid.*
242 *Ibid.*, 82.
243 *Ibid.*, 83.
244 *Ibid.*, see p. 636 *ff.*
245 *U. of Va. Rec., Ext. Ser.*, Nov., 1924, IX, No. 3, 62.
246 *Ibid.*

In various other ways, the Bulletins of the Extension Division urged the introduction of the religious element into community activities.[247] It gave publicity to the work of the Co-operative Education Association and the Citizenship Creed of the town of Whitmell, which sets up the following criteria for good citizenship:

A good citizen is *Trustworthy.* . . .
A good citizen is *Christlike.* He takes as his example the perfect Citizen, Christ Jesus, and walks in His steps.[248]

The reaction to the religious situation at the University after the Civil War is in striking contrast with that before the War. The inauguration of the Y. M. C. A. and the gradual extension of its various activities tended to silence criticism. In 1873, the United States Commissioner of Education referred to the statement concerning the religious life at the University made by Prof. C. S. Venable, chairman of the faculty. Prof. Venable was said to have declared that the recognition of religious freedom as a right belonging to university students had resulted in "commendable liberality" on the part of the students in supporting the chaplain, and that there had been a "remarkably earnest, Christian activity" among the students for years.[249] An article on the University, in Barnard's *American Journal of Education,* referring to this statement, declared that the homage paid to religion at the University was unique among colleges.[250]

The *Richmond Enquirer,* in August, 1874, saw fit to bestow the following encomium upon the University: "We have made scholars at this institution, and at the same time made them Christians and gentlemen."[251] While it was not sectarian, and while it left the conscience free to select its own creed and faith, yet the University did not "by its teachings, encourage skepticism, disgrace the age, bring godliness into discredit, or make

---

[247] *Ibid.,* May, 1927, XI, No. 11, 82, "The Christmas Pageant of the Holy Grail," May, 1926, X, No. 9, 17.
[248] *Ibid.,* XI, No. 11, 10.
[249] *U. S. Comm. Educ. Rep't,* 1873, 398.
[250] Barnard: *Amer. Jour. Educ.,* XXVII, 543.
[251] *Richmond Enquirer,* Aug. 11, 1874.

a mockery of religion.'' The editorial was occasioned by Prof. Venable's address at a meeting of the National Education Association on ''The Plan of the University of Virginia.'' Prof. Venable in stating the criteria of a successful university had enumerated among these, ''the inculcation through its authorized religious exercises a spirit of earnest worship and reverence for religion; . . . keeping a high standard of Christian morality; and . . . the encouragement of Christian union and activity in benevolent enterprises.'' By this criterion, as well as others, the University was a success. Its influence was not confined to the state: ''It has made Virginia the great school of the South and South-West.''[252] The spirit of freedom from compulsory attendance at religious exercises and a system of free electives were distinguishing characteristics in comparison with other institutions of the seventies.[253]

The strong religious tone given to the University by its various religious activities reacted upon the Board of Visitors in their choice of members of the faculty.[254] Rev. J. Wm. Jones,[255] in an article in the *Alumni Bulletin,* in 1897, declared:

. . . It is a matter of very great gratification to all friends of evangelical religion that for many years the public sentiment in Virginia, and among the friends of the University, has been so strong in favor of evangelical influences there that no Board of Visitors would have ventured to elect a known infidel as professor in the University, and the result has been that nearly all of the Faculty have been members of some evangelical church, and there have been among them as noble specimens of the Christian scholar as ever graced any institution.[256]

The freedom which characterized the religious system at the University found a staunch advocate in Rev. Dr. R. H. McKim. In an address entitled ''The Relations of the State to the University,'' before the Society of the Alumni, in 1898, Dr. McKim declared:

. . . Compulsory Chapel, compulsory Bible Study, compulsory religious observance of any kind, for young men at a University,—these are parts of a system which, in my humble judgment, is nicely adapted to stifle faith and

---

[252] *N. E. A. Proc's,* 1874, XIV, 169.
[253] *Cf.* Richardson, C. F., & Clark, H. A.: *College Book,* 277.
[254] See p. 372, 382.
[255] See p. 612.
[256] *U. of Va. Alum. Bull.,* Feb., 1897, III, No. 4, 96–97.

to beget hypocrisy. The only genuine religion is the homage which the free soul offers freely to its God. Stifle freedom, and you strangle faith. Only in an atmosphere of liberty can the best fruits of religion be ripened. As soon as constraint is introduced, religion ceases to be religion and becomes superstition. For liberty and reason are the friends and allies, not the foes of religion.[257]

Dr. McKim stated that experience had vindicated Jefferson's wisdom in planting the institution upon the base of absolute religious freedom. After seventy-three years of trial, the verdict was "without doubt or question" that the system had been "eminently favorable to both morality and religion."[258]

A statement of the "Distinctive Features of the University of Virginia" in the *Alumni Bulletin,* in 1902, declared that the University might "fairly claim entire exemption from political and sectarian bias." Scientific attainment and teaching power, not creed, either in politics or religion, had been the basis for faculty ·selection. Students of all beliefs were treated impartially. Teaching and investigation were unhampered by prejudice, being "dominated by the single purpose of reaching sound results." The characters of the young men who had been submitted to her influences were "the best answer to the still lingering prejudice which confounds non-sectarian with irreligious training."[259]

An expression of praise and congratulation to the University was voiced in an address on "Harvard University and the University of Virginia," by Dr. Francis G. Peabody, of Harvard University, before the Southern Education Conference in 1906. Referring to the fact that Harvard had not given up her compulsory system of religious worship until 1886, Dr. Peabody said:

. . . Here all these years, without ostentation, without advertisement, you have assumed the religious life to be a thing of privilege, and have looked to the initiative of your students in religion as the secret of your spiritual vitality and health. I congratulate you upon your undisputed primacy in leading the way to the faith that religion asks no favors, that it asks only a fair chance among the competing influences of human life, and that given a free land and a free college, freedom and religion bring forth their natural fruit of righteousness, fidelity, and academic peace.[260]

---

[257] McKim, R. H.: *Relations of the State to the University,* 21.
[258] *Ibid.,* 24.
[259] *U. of Va. Alum. Bull.,* April, 1902, N. S., II, No. 2, 11–13.
[260] *U. of Va. Alum. Bull.,* Oct., 1903, N. S., III, No. 4, 161; *Procs. 6th Conf. Educ. South,* 1903, 239; *cf. Ibid.,* 242.

With the inauguration, in 1905, of Dr. Edwin A. Alderman as first President of the University, the University was destined to enter upon a new era. The Presidency replaced the unsatisfactory Chairmanship of the Faculty, which had been responsible for the administration of the University from its beginning. Dr. Alderman's inaugural address pointed out as one of the important distinguishing characteristics of the University character—"An absolute religious freedom, combined with wide and vital religious opportunities." He pledged himself to do what he could to cherish and magnify the essential features of the University character.[261] He stated further, that five hundred of the alumni, over three per cent of the total enrollment, had preached the Gospel throughout the world; of these, eleven had been made bishops of the Protestant Episcopal Church, one of the Methodist Episcopal, and one of the Reformed Episcopal.[262] Speaking of the relation of education to state and church, Dr. Alderman said: "I know of no more fruitful field of inquiry than that which has to do with the relation of part to part in our system of education, and of the intrinsic relation of the whole to State and Church."[263] On the subject of the relations between the state and the private and denominational colleges, he said:

. . . Nor should the reciprocal obligations be forgotten that exist between the State and the private and denominational colleges, chartered by the State, protected by its laws, educating one third of its youth. We should welcome the establishment here of halls and dormitories controlled by them, availing themselves of the opportunities of the University, and if this be impracticable, we should at least strive without ceasing to banish from our life any semblance of intercollegiate hostility. Let co-operation supplant rivalry in the service of men. This problem of unification is as difficult as it is inviting. The university that solves the problem holds the future.[264]

In an address at the Centennial celebration of the University, in 1921, Rev. B. A. Abbott, editor of the *Christian Evangelist*, a publication of the Disciples of Christ, discussed the topic of "Religious Culture in State Universities." He declared that while a strong case might be made out for the position that students

---

[261] *U. of Va. in Life of Nation*, 77–79.
[262] *Ibid.*, 118–19.
[263] *Ibid.*, 101.
[264] *Ibid.*, 103.

should not be admitted to the state university unless they had had training in a church school of worthy educational standards, it was admittedly impracticable, as more rather than less children would attend directly from the public schools.   It was, therefore, necessary for the church to follow the student to the classroom, the campus, and the dormitory of the University, as far as possible.   Through the Christian Woman's Board of Missions, the Disciples of Christ, almost three decades before, had determined to institute Bible chairs at such universities as would receive them.[265]   Chairs were now being supported at the state universities of Michigan, Texas, Kansas, and Virginia, the last referring to the John B. Cary Memorial School of Biblical History and Literature.   According to Rev. Mr. Abbott, these chairs were absolutely non-sectarian, and while the courses of study did not presume to be "sufficient in themselves to equip students for the pulpit or the mission field," they did make a moral and spiritual appeal.[266]

It is not without interest to note that the first public meeting of the Centennial was held "in commemoration of the religious contribution of the University."[267]   Rev. Dr. Samuel Mitchell, of the University of Richmond, in an address before the Clerical Alumni at the Centennial, in referring to the various plans for strengthening the religious influences of the University suggested that the various denominations co-operate with the Young Men's Christian Association in the maintenance of a University preacher on permanent tenure.   The advantage of this over the old two-year chaplaincy plan, and that of having different visiting ministers from Sunday to Sunday, would be the development of a really great personality, whose voice would command attention, whose interpretation of the spiritual life would be cumulative in effect.   Whatever would be lost to specifically denominational interests would "be more than made up by the emphasis upon the essentials of Christianity which such a preacher would

---

[265] See p. 616.

[266] Metcalf: *Cent. U. of Va.*, 147–48; Hinsdale, B. A., & Demmon, I. N.: *Hist. of U. of Michigan*, 161–62; *U. of Texas Catalog*, 1926–27, 46; *U. of Kansas Catalog*, 1927–28, 35.

[267] Metcalf: *Cent. U. of Va.*, 3.

give, thus enriching religious life and truth for all through the University.''[268]

Upon the same occasion, Rev. Thomas Cary Johnson, of the Union Theological Seminary, Richmond, declared that in as much as the state had neither adequate religious creed, nor holy character, it had neither the fitness nor the commission to give religious culture. If the state must not attempt to give an adequate religious culture, the state university, an organ of the state, should not attempt it. It therefore remained for the various denominations to bring religious culture to the state universities. This they should do by erecting a suitable building, employing proper personnel to have supervision of their communicants, and to give courses in the study of religion of a character that should receive credit of any equivalent elective in the university course. This adequate denominational care would have a desirable reaction upon the life of the whole community.[269]

In a consideration of the various devices employed to reach the students from a religious standpoint, it is not without interest to consider the actual status of the student body as to membership and affiliation with religious denominations. In 1907, statistics revealed that of 785 students, 460 were professed Christians and of this number 430 were members of the Y. M. C. A.[270] In 1913, of the 831 students, 595 were actual members of various religious denominations, and 223 were affiliated with religious organizations, and only 13 had indicated no preference.[271] The actual religious membership percentage of the enrollment, slightly over 71 per cent, had not changed for the past three years.[272] In 1917, the percentage of membership and affiliation was 98 per cent, practically the same as in 1913.[273] In denominational leadership, Episcopalians led, with Presbyterians and Methodists holding second or third place at various periods, and the Baptists, fourth.[274] It would appear from the high percentage of

[268] *Ibid.*, 143.
[269] *Ibid.*, 143–46.
[270] Bruce: *Hist. U. of Va.*, V, 249.
[271] *Va. Sch. Rep't*, 1912–13, 407.
[272] *Ibid.*
[273] *Ibid.*, 1916–17, 468.
[274] Bruce: *Hist. U. of Va.*, V, 250 *ff.*

religious connection of the student personnel, that the problem of religious instruction would lie merely in offering such opportunities for study and activity as would keep up and strengthen that phase of the student's life.

In view of the large number of alumni who were ministers, whose work ranged over every phase of ministerial activity, religious editorships, missionary work, work as bishops,[275] it is hardly likely that it will any longer be contended that a state university does not give adequate results in promoting the interests of the church, granted that this is a proper function of a state university. As far as the attitude of the University itself to the problem of religion in education is concerned, the statement in its catalogues, in the early part of the century, may be taken as its general attitude throughout this period:

> Morality and religion are recognized as the foundation and indispensable concomitants of education. The discipline of the University is sedulously administered with a view to confirm integrity, and to maintain a sacred regard for truth. Great efforts are made to surround the students with religious influences; but experience having proved that it is best to forbear the employment of coercion, the attendance on religious exercises is entirely voluntary.[276]

This attitude is essentially that which characterized the University in the period immediately after the Civil War.[277]

While the religious influences surrounding the University have been predominantly Protestant, the University in 1915 and 1916 extended the Jewish Chautauqa Society the privilege of delivering its courses of lectures on Jewish education and Jewish history before students of the summer sessions.[278] The number of Catholic students has generally been very small; in 1916–17, there were 39 Catholics in an enrollment of 1075 students.[279]

Important as was the introduction of the Y. M. C. A. for the religious life of the University in the period from the Civil War to the beginning of the century—the establishment of the John B. Cary Bible Lectureship, in 1902, and the creation of the Ex-

---

275 *Ibid.*, V, 356.
276 *U. of Va. Catalog*, 1907–08, 67.
277 See p. 614.
278 *Relig. Educ.*, Feb., 1917, XII, 37–39.
279 Bruce: *Hist. U. of Va.*, V, 251.

tension Division, in 1913, have been most significant for the first quarter of this century. Of the two developments, the more striking is that of the Extension Division with its increasing re-action upon the religious life of the state. Through its activities, the University has not only co-operated with the church and civic organizations interested in extending the church life of the people, but has brought specific religious instruction to commu-nities throughout the state. No denominational institution in the state has reached out in this way to the daily lives of the people.

In both the Bible chair and the Extension Division are to be found reflections of the Ruffner policy; whether their conduct involves, or has involved, a stepping beyond the proper limits of that policy, depends, of course, upon the interpretation of the limits properly placed upon the principle of separation of church and state in Virginia.

2. *Other Higher Institutions*

The second important higher educational institution created by the state before the Civil War, the Virginia Military Institute, was closed at the beginning of the War by the departure of its cadets to join the Confederate forces. In 1862, the school served as an officers' training school. The close of the War found the larger part of the property destroyed.[280] The Institute was re-opened, in 1865.

As has been indicated previously,[281] the Institute, since its foundation, had been strongly inclined to exert every possible religious influence upon the lives of its students. In January, 1870, it was reported that eighty-four cadets had professed con-version, and that there was then such a special religious interest among the students, that they were having daily meetings for prayer and exhortation, the average attendance of which was one hundred and fifty, almost one-half of the student body.[282] The annual report for 1873 stated: ''Attendance at church and Bible instruction is prescribed for each Sabbath.''[283]

---

[280] *Va. Military Instit. Catalog*, 1926, 8–9.
[281] See p. 366.
[282] *Va. Educ. Jour.*, Jan., 1870, I, 93.
[283] *Va. Sch. Rep't*, 1873, 134.

A more intimate picture of the religious life of the Institute may be gleaned from an address, by Colonel John M. Patton, before the Society of Alumni, in 1871. After indicating his view as heartily in sympathy with impressing upon students the dignity and worth of religion, and that its spirit should be made to pervade and elevate all other studies, Colonel Patton described the religious life at the Institute as follows:

> On Sunday mornings, the corps is assembled in holiday attire, with ''side arms'' only. . . . They are then marched in a body to the House of God, attending, in turn, the services of each of the denominations of Christians in town. Decorum and reverent attention are expected of them, and discipline is rarely needed on such occasions, as this attendance in a body seems to exert a conservative influence on the least devout. After the services, they are marched back to the Institute in the same order. No absence is permitted on this occasion, or indeed from any duty, except for urgent reasons, and by express permission.[284]

Besides, on Sunday, each class was required to attend instruction in the Bible, or in the evidences of Christianity. Exemptions were allowed only to Jews and Roman Catholics at the special application of parents or guardians. A daily prayer meeting, immediately after supper, and an early morning prayer service from April 1 to July 1, were left open to voluntary attendance.[285] With these exceptions, Colonel Patton went on to emphasize the fact that in every aspect of the school work nothing was done ''on the voluntary principle.''[286] It was yielding too much to the ''voluntary principle'' in education that had resulted in the evidences of depravity apparent everywhere. It was this principle which had resulted in the disastrous effects of the French Revolution of 1789.[287] It had contributed, too, to the spreading in the North of that blasphemous sentiment ''which parades Almighty God, if He conforms to its crude opinion, and repudiates Him if he differs from them,'' and had driven the Bible from public schools in the North. From the ''voluntary principle''

---

[284] Patton, J. M.: *Address*, 15.
[285] *Ibid.*
[286] *Ibid.*
[287] *Ibid.*, 18.

were derived "Women's rights, free-love, communism, and all the rest."[288]

The religious life of the institution followed the pattern of the seventies in subsequent decades,[289] and special evangelistic meetings continued to feature it, one being reported as late as the 1925 report of the Institute.[290] The rule with regard to church attendance on Sunday, was relaxed, in later years, to the extent of permitting students the privilege of attending morning services of the churches to which they belong; other cadets being marched to the different churches of the town in rotation, unless exempted upon application by parents.[291] As at practically all Virginia schools, the Y. M. C. A. contributes to the religious life.[292]

The Virginia Agricultural and Mechanical College was created by the state, in 1872;[293] its name was changed in 1896 to "Virginia Agricultural and Mechanical College and Polytechnic Institute."[294] By 1921, all departments except Military Science and Tactics had been opened to women.

A strong impetus to the advancement of the school's religious life came with the incorporation of a Y. M. C. A. in 1898.[295] At present, it conducts an elaborate program.[296] In 1921, President J. A. Burruss made a statement that more than 75 per cent of the students were members of the Y. M. C. A. and about 65 per cent of the student body were enrolled voluntarily in the Bible study classes under the auspices of the Association, the attendance for the year being 79 per cent of this enrollment.[297] In

---

[288] *Ibid.*, 19–20; Colonel Patton, however, a little further on, qualified his strictures, reflecting on the North, with the statement that "In every land, God has reserved 'seven thousand knees that have not bowed unto Baal.'"

[289] *U. S. Bur. Educ., Circ. Inf.*, 1888, No. I, 287, 290.

[290] *Va. Sch. Rep't*, 1894 & 1895, 140; *Annual Rep't Va. Military Instit.* for Session of 1924–25, under caption, "Mid-Year Mission."

[291] *Va. Military Instit. Catalog*, 1914–15, 24; 1926, 37.

[292] *Ibid.*

[293] See p. 405.

[294] *Acts of Assembly*, Mar. 5, 1896, 914; for a reference to the internal history which brought this change about, *cf.* Harris, W. H.: *School Days*, 34.

[295] *Jour. Senate*, 1899, Doc. No. VIII, 20; *cf.* also *Acts of Assembly*, Feb. 3, 1900, 292.

[296] *V. P. I. Catalog*, 1926, 163–64.

[297] *High School Quart.*, Jan., 1921, IX, 72.

addition, President Burruss stated that a careful poll of the faculty indicated no atheists, but more than 95 per cent as church members. These facts were made known in answer to certain statements signed by ministers, and published in Atlanta papers, that ''over fifty per cent of the professors in American universities did not believe in God and that only a small per cent of the graduates came from such institutions with their faith in God unshaken; . . . that Christian education means education in church schools.''[298] Investigation, according to President Burruss, proved this statement false in regard to his school.

A more recent statement declares that while a state institution, and hence strictly undenominational, the environment of the student is not any the less spiritual.[299] All cadets are required to attend daily morning chapel services and church services on Sunday morning. Students, whose parents request it, are excused from any religious exercise ''seriously at variance with the practise of their own religious affiliation.'' It is stated as an indication that religious ideals are not lacking, that more than 95 per cent of the faculty are church members, that about 80 per cent of the students are likewise, that about 30 per cent of the students voluntarily attend Sunday School, that 84 of the 85 per cent of the student enrollment in the Y. M. C. A. are enrolled in Bible and mission classes, the attendance being 75 per cent of the enrollment. A number of students regularly conduct Sunday School and prayer meeting in nearby rural districts.[300] In view of this general interest, it is surprising to find that this is one state institution in which systematic work in the Bible is not given, except in connection with the Y. M. C. A.[301]

The Virginia Normal and Industrial Institute, near Petersburg, may be regarded as the state institution for colored students parallel to the Virginia Polytechnic Institute for white students. As indicated previously, this institution, one of the outcomes of the ''readjuster issue'' was intended to give the

---

[298] *Ibid.*, 68.
[299] *V. P. I. Catalog*, 1926, 161.
[300] *Ibid.*, 161–62.
[301] The enrollment in 1925–26 was 1,347 men, 84 women, total, 1,431; Robertson: *Amer. Univ. and Colleges*, 781.

negro an education equivalent to that of the white man.[302] With the setting aside of the Underwood Constitution, in 1902, its college department was dropped, and it was not restored until 1922.[303]

As a state controlled institution, parallel to the private Hampton Institute, it is of interest to discover what has been the place of religion in the educational life of the school. A report on the school by its principal, in 1887, declared that "in every way, the moral and religious, as well as the mental, welfare and progress of the students have been carefully and assidulously cultivated."[304] Each student was permitted, at the beginning of the quarter, to choose which church he or she would attend, and regular attendance, except in case of illness, was expected thereafter on Sunday mornings. On Sunday afternoon attendance was required of all at the lecture, by the President, upon some Scriptural topic having to do with their moral and religious improvement.[305]

In 1916, the authorities of the school declared that in sending out "symmetrically trained men and women," it was necessary to develop the moral and spiritual natures, as well as the physical and intellectual. Very much attention was being given to the religious life. The faculty conducted a Sunday School, and preaching services were held on Sunday afternoons. The first year normal class was organized into a Sunday School training class. Systematic instruction was given in the Bible for a year and a half, and in the second half of the last year "they write outlines of lessons and give instruction under the direction of the Professor of Pedagogy." Students were required to attend the monthly prayer service led by some member of the faculty. In addition, there were voluntary services held by the students themselves. There was also an annual week of prayer "conducted with a view to stimulating the spiritual life of those students who are members of the church and to influencing those not Christians to make profession of religion." The school has a Y. M. C. A. and a Y. W. C. A.[306]

302 See p. 404.
303 *From correspondence.*
304 *Va. Sch. Rep't,* 1887, 137.
305 *Ibid.,* 140.
306 *Va. Normal & Industrial Institute Gazette, Catalog,* 1915–16, 21–22.

In 1921, Sunday School Teacher Training Classes were open to students of the third and fourth years of the high school and the Normal school. The work consisted not only of a study of the content of the Bible, but also methods of presenting the content to pupils. Upon successful completion of the course, students were awarded the diploma of the International Sunday School Association.[307]

These various activities have continued to the present. Students of the college department, opened since 1922, may also take the Sunday School Teacher Training classes.[308] In addition, one-hour courses, carrying credit, are offered in the Bible for both high school and college students.[309] In the English department, a five-hour course in the Bible is offered, as an elective to juniors and seniors, the object being "not religious, but to give a clearer knowledge of the Bible as a classic"[310]

From the point of view of historical interest, no educational institution which the state might add to its list of state controlled institutions could compare with the College of William and Mary. The assumption of state control of that institution, in 1906, marked the inauguration of a new era of usefulness.[311] This new arrangement made possible increased appropriations from the state, and liaison with the Federal government for Smith-Hughes funds.[312] In 1918, the Assembly authorized the college to admit properly prepared women to its collegiate and normal school course, conferring degrees on them upon the same terms as on men.[313] President Tyler referring to this change said:

. . . The faculty believes that the coming of women to the institution means a cleaner and more moral life, a keener and more active comprehension of the labors on hand, and a broader, deeper and higher college spirit, which will make for the expansion of social and educational ideas and principles.[314]

---

[307] *Ibid.*, May 15, 1921, 26; *cf.* also *Ibid.*, May 15, 1924.
[308] *Ibid.*, 1926, 21.
[309] *Ibid.*
[310] *Ibid.*, 60.
[311] See p. 531.
[312] Tyler: *Williamsburg*, 194; Robertson: *Amer. Univ. and Colleges*, 373; *Wm. & Mary Catalog*, 1926, 30; *Bull. State B'd Educ.*, Nov., 1927, X, No. 2, 118–19.
[313] *Acts of Assembly*, Mar. 15, 1918, 424; *Va. Jour. Educ.*, April, 1919, XII, 320–21.
[314] *Ibid.*

As a result of the admission of women, the college is rapidly taking its place as one of the very important factors in the educational life of the state. Its enrollment for 1926 was 640 men, 457 women, a total of 1097 students.[315]

With regard to the religious attitude and activities of the college, since its coming under state control, the college still exempts students for the ministry from payment of tuition fees; the present basis of admission being upon the same terms as Virginia students holding state scholarships.[316] The laws of the college, as published in 1874, admitted not only candidates for the ministry, but "indigent young men, of good moral character and respectable abilities," without fees.[317]

The regulations of the college after the Civil War required the attendance of students upon daily prayers, absence being permitted only upon good excuse. Students were also expected to attend the church of their preference every Sunday.[318] No regulations with regard to Sunday church attendance appear under its present régime; students are, however, required to attend at least one student assembly, that of their respective class, each week. These assemblies "are opened with song, Bible reading, and prayer."[319]

The college has had a Y. M. C. A. since 1889, and a Y. W. C. A. since 1920. According to recent statements, the visitors and faculty are in sympathy with these organizations, and students are urged to join them.[320] These associations are characterized by their usual activities, including classes for Bible study.[321]

A most interesting development of the college since it has come under state control was the establishment, in 1923, of a department of Biblical Literature and Religious Education.[322] Though the laws of the college after the Civil War provided that a course of Biblical study, including the evidences of Natural and Revealed Religion, might be given by the President or one of the

---

[315] Robertson: *Amer. Univ. and Colleges,* 373.
[316] *Wm. & Mary Catalog,* 1926, 55.
[317] Randolph & English: *Hist. Wm. & Mary College,* 175.
[318] *Ibid.,* 178.
[319] *Wm. & Mary Catalog,* 1926, 41.
[320] *Ibid.,* 224–25.
[321] *Ibid.*
[322] *From correspondence.*

faculty, no courses of this kind appear in the course of instruction for 1874.[323]   In 1926, in its department of Biblical Literature and Religious Education, twenty-one courses were listed, treating the Bible and religion from historical, literary, philosophical, and sociological standpoints, and offering a far broader field of study than is common in many denominational colleges. From the standpoint of the number and variety of courses, this is probably the most comprehensive department of its kind in the state.   To give these courses, three professors are employed; their salaries are paid in part by state, and in part by private funds.[324]

As to the emphasis and aims in these courses, they are described variously, depending on the course, as "The moral and spiritual significance" of the Old or the New Testament; or as showing "the fundamental and essential relationship of all education to the moral and spiritual forces and factors of life;" or as "an appreciation of the wealth of the Bible as a work of literary art;" or as an attempt "to train the student in the ability to see and understand the great message of the books." As these courses are given in a state institution, it is presumed that proper care is exercised to eliminate denominational bias. Good churchmen will undoubtedly hope that they are presented from a sufficiently Fundamentalist viewpoint, and that the pre-revolutionary traditions of heresy have not survived to taint this twentieth century venture.   The courses are elective and according to report are popular with the students.

An important phase of the state's development of higher educational opportunity has been that in connection with the training of teachers, begun first in connection with the Virginia Military Institute for men, and at Farmville for women.[325]   In 1894, the Assembly, to supplement the work given at these institutions, decided to make an appropriation for the establishment of summer normal schools under the control of the Board

---

[323] Randolph & English: *Hist. Wm. & Mary College,* 170 *ff.*

[324] *From correspondence.*

[325] See p. 366; while alumni of the University went frequently into the teaching profession, the University can not be regarded as having been at that time a specific teacher training institution.

of Education.[326] A further step was taken, in 1904, by the
Legislature in a number of acts looking forward to the creation
of normal schools.[327] It was not until March 14, 1908, that
additional normal schools for white women were provided for at
Harrisonburg, Rockingham County, and Fredericksburg, Spotsylvania County.[328] A fourth normal school for white women
was established by an act of the Legislature, in March, 1910, at
Radford, Montgomery County.[329] These schools were at first
known as Normal and Industrial Schools, but their names were
changed to State Normal Schools in 1914.[330] In 1916, the
Legislature authorized the transformation of these schools into
State Teachers Colleges, with the right to conduct four-year
courses leading to a collegiate degree,[331] but the names were not
changed to conform with the character of the new work until
1924.[332]

To balance this opportunity for teacher training for women,
the Legislature, in 1918, decided to offer a further opportunity
for teacher training for men, by authorizing the rector and visitors of the University of Virginia to offer one hundred and
nineteen state scholarships to students from Virginia. These
scholarships entitled the holder to have his "tuition in the college, room rent, light, heat, and attendance free," upon condition that such student shall within four years after leaving college serve two years in the school system.[333]

In 1920, the Assembly decided to place the University, the
College of William and Mary, the Virginia Agricultural and
Mechanical College and Polytechnic Institute, the Virginia Nor-
mal and Industrial Institute, and the four teachers' colleges for

---

[326] *Acts of Assembly*, Mar. 3, 1894, 655.

[327] *Ibid.*, Jan. 11, 1904, 920; Mar. 2, 1904, 80; Mar. 12, 1904, 235.

[328] *Harrisonburg Catalog*, 1926, 15; *Fredericksburg Catalog*, 1917, 17.

[329] *Acts of Assembly*, Mar. 10, 1910, 176. The Harrisonburg school was
opened in 1909, *Harrisonburg Catalog*, 1926, 16; the Fredericksburg school
in 1911, *Fredericksburg Catalog*, 1928, 22; and that at Radford, in 1913,
Radford Catalog, 1918, 11.

[330] *Cf. Ibid.*, 1926, 17; *Acts of Assembly*, Mar. 27, 1914, 567.

[331] *Radford Catalog*, 1926, 17; *cf. Acts of Assembly*, Mar. 21, 1916, 749.

[332] *Ibid.; Ibid.*, Feb. 13, 1924, 14. This heightening of standards has
been made possible, of course, only with the gradual development of the
high school system. Thus the school at Farmville, as late as 1911 had to
contend with the poor preparation of the students and conduct a preparatory department. Magruder: *Recent Admin. Va.*, 70.

[333] *Acts of Assembly*, Mar. 16, 1918, 538.

women on a year-round basis of instruction, in order to provide added facilities for the training of teachers.[334]

In view of the fact that the four teachers' colleges for women are state institutions, the nature of the religious life developed in them, and the attitude of the authorities towards it is of real significance. The catalogues usually contain a statement indicating that while the schools are state institutions and hence non-denominational, yet religious instruction, non-sectarian in character is fostered. As stated by the authorities at Farmville, "the importance of a life higher than the intellectual" is realized, and the religious interests of the students are made "a matter of constant concern."[335]

Daily chapel exercises seem to be the rule in all these schools, and are presumably required.[336] With regard to church attendance, students are expected to join the Sunday School and church of their choice and to attend regularly.[337] At Radford, in 1918, students were "required to attend once each Sunday the church to which they belong or with which they are affiliated."[338] More recently at Harrisonburg, the authorities state that the student at the beginning of her connection with the college is "asked to state the church which she is in the habit of attending at home, and she will be expected to attend regularly the services of the same denomination in Harrisonburg while a student at the college."[339] Apparently a survey of this kind is made at all the schools, in order to make possible effective cooperation with the pastors of the town and the Y. W. C. A.[340]

All of these schools have a Y. W. C. A. The statement of purpose of the Association at Farmville follows:

1. To lead students to faith in God through Jesus Christ.
2. To lead them into membership and service in the Christain Church.

---

[334] *Ibid.*, Feb. 25, 1920, 73.

[335] *Farmville Catalog*, 1926, 23.

[336] The statement is not always very definite, *cf. Farmville Catalog*, 1926, 23, "There is daily chapel exercise, with the reading of the Scriptures, a hymn and prayer"; the *Fredericksburg Catalog*, 1928, 37, indicates that daily chapel has given place to weekly chapel; *Radford Catalog*, 1918, 18, states "all the students are expected to attend."

[337] *Farmville Catalog*, 1926, 23.

[338] *Radford Catalog*, 1918, 24.

[339] *Harrisonburg Catalog*, 1926, 89.

[340] *Cf. Grapurchat*, Radford school publication, July 23, 1926.

3. To promote their growth in Christian faith and character especially through the study of the Bible.

4. To influence them to devote themselves in united efforts with all Christians, to making the will of Christ effective in human society, and to extending the Kingdom of God throughout the world.[341]

"Morning Watch" services appear as an activity of the Association.[342] Those at Fredericksburg, in 1917, were thus described:

. . . Fifteen minutes before breakfast each day Morning Watch is held in the Y. W. C. A. room. This is a simple service consisting of a hymn, Bible study, and prayer, and it has proved helpful to the girls.[343]

Over 75 per cent of the students at Fredericksburg were enrolled at that time in the Association.[344] As an example of a typical Y. W. C. A. program, the following program as given in a Radford publication is not without interest:

Thursday evening, August 20 came, and with it the weekly Y. W. C. A. vesper service.

The girls all assembled on the senior promenade for the meeting. The topic for the week was "Promises," and Miss ———— was the leader for the evening. After the hymn, "Jesus Calls Us," Miss ———— read the Fourteenth Chapter of St. John for the Scripture lesson. They all then united in praying the Lord's Prayer.

The hymn "Stand Up for Jesus" was then sung, after which Miss ———— gave a very interesting talk. The subject of her talk was "What Promises Mean To Me." She enumerated the promises of God and told how they inspired and helped one.

Following this talk a very interesting reading was given by Miss ————.

Miss ———— then gave a talk on "Some of God's Promises." She made a list of some of the special promises which had been of special benefit to her.

The vesper song, "Follow The Gleam," was sung and the meeting was dismissed by the Y. W. C. A. motto.[345]

Neither the school at Fredericksburg nor that at Farmville has a systematic course of Bible study except in connection with the Y. W. C. A. At Farmville, however, the Bible study classes are

---

[341] *Farmville Catalog*, 1926, 24.
[342] *Ibid.*
[343] *Fredericksburg Catalog*, 1917, 33.
[344] *Ibid.*
[345] *Grapurchat*, Aug. 27, 1926.

organized in the churches, through the Association; they "are taught by members of the faculty, who, together with the ministers and the Sunday School Superintendents, plan and outline courses of study suitable for the different groups of girls."[346] As these classes are organized in each church, presumably they have a denominational leaning.

At Harrisonburg, as early as 1918, courses in "Bible Study and Sunday School Methods," two hours a week, were available during the first three quarters of the year.[347] The work had been arranged in co-operation with the community Sunday Schools, and credit was allowed. It had resulted according to the authorities in greatly increased interest in Bible study.[348] As the title would indicate, the courses aimed to prepare students to teach in Sunday Schools. One period was devoted to a careful study of the Bible from the literary and historical standpoints, and the other to a discussion of the methods of presenting Bible lessons to children of various ages in Sunday Schools, with some attention given to the organization and management of these schools. For the most part, students were divided according to their denominational affiliation, and used their denominational course and literature.[349]

In addition to this Sunday School teacher training work, there has been established a department of Biblical literature, which is "planned to give a background training for the study of the Bible and to give assistance to prospective Bible school teachers."[350] The courses comprise Hebrew History and Literature, New Testament History and Literature, and Sociology of Religion.[351]

Not only at Harrisonburg, but also at Radford, work in Sunday School teacher training was begun in 1918.[352] The course was planned by the Professor of Education and Director of Training Schools, J. E. Avent. Professor Avent took the courses recommended by the five leading denominations of the student per-

---

[346] *Farmville Catalog*, 1926, 23.
[347] *Harrisonburg Catalog*, 1918, 65.
[348] *Ibid.*, 106.
[349] *Ibid.*, 65.
[350] *Harrisonburg Catalog*, 1926, 90, 58.
[351] *Ibid.*
[352] *Va. Jour. Educ.*, Dec., 1919, XIII, 141.

sonnel, effected a harmonization of these courses, submitted it for approval to the Sunday School Boards of these denominations, and obtained their agreement to award students of their denominations their complete diplomas upon completion of the course. The course was offered as an elective with credit to those needing the credit. Students used their denominational literature in studying the various assigned topics. The course was a three-hour-a-week course for 48 weeks. Thirty-two students received diplomas of their respective denominations at the end of the first year. Its success was such that the work has been continued as a regular course in the school. The aim of the course as described in 1919, was to train public school teachers to be good Sunday School teachers; the statement being made: "There is no proper divorcement of religious education from other education; and the public school teacher who leaves off the religious side of education has committed an unpardonable folly."[353]

The course as given in 1926 consisted of study of the Old Testament in the first quarter; the Life of Christ and the early history of the Church, the second quarter; and Sunday School Teachers' Interpretation and Adaptation of the Bible to the Departments of Sunday Schools, the third quarter. Study of memory passages was required the first two quarters. The courses continued to lead to the "Diploma in Sunday School Teacher Training" of the respective denominations, and carried credit.[354] As the courses are given by members of the regular faculty, whose salaries are paid by the state,[355] the boast of Virginians that the state has not, since 1776, paid a penny for the support of religion, in view of this and other cases cited, is clearly not valid.[356]

It is clear from the history of the development of religious instruction in the higher state-controlled educational institutions that the tendency has been not only towards incorporation of systematic religious instruction, but also toward co-operation with denominational religious instruction. By liaison with the

---

[353] *Ibid.*
[354] *Radford Catalog,* 1926, 92–94.
[355] *From correspondence.*
[356] See p. 94.

churches of the various communities in which these institutions are located, and by formation of denominational groups for study, students are being guided into and held to specific denominational affiliation.　The trend is now seemingly to provide two kinds of religious training; one, a kind of unsectarian Christianity for assemblies of all kinds of religious belief, including the various shades of evangelistic faith, the Catholic, and the Jewish faith;—and the other, specifically denominational training.

The amount and kind of religious training in most of these institutions, it has been found, measures as high as in the general run of denominational institutions; and, in some cases, as notably at William and Mary College, exceeds it.　The most captious critic of the public school system, on the score of inadequate Christian training, would seemingly be silenced before this record which so frequently exceeds what is being done either in private or denominational schools.　Whether the tendency in the policy of co-operation without alliance, which has resulted in this development, is in the direction of too large a civil control and responsibility to be compatible with a strict construction of the principle of separation of church and state; whether the rights of conscience are or will be violated by tendencies in this policy; whether expenditures necessary in the execution of this policy infringe upon Virginia constitutional law—are questions that may be raised, but answered in too many ways to be answered here categorically.　It will be sufficient at this time to consider the *Declaration of Rights* in relation to the present position of the church in Virginia—to consider the present status of the principle of separation of church and state.

The Present Status Of The Principle Of Separation Of Church And State

It will be recalled, that it was the dissenting religious groups in the colonial period of union of church and state which served as the external force resulting in the disintegration of that union. With the *Declaration of Rights* and the establishment of the principle of separation of church and state, and the consequent collapse of Anglicanism, a new era of expansion arose for the minority groups. Since the second and third decades of the nineteenth century, that expansion has been particularly marked for the Methodist and Baptist groups. To what degree all the former minority groups and the civil arm of the government have clung to the principle of separation of church and state in their attitudes to religious instruction in education has been indicated. It has also been seen that while, since the inauguration of the public school system, in the seventies, there has been a tendency away from a sharply defined cleavage between church and state, there has been, on the whole, a decided effort, in a measure from a sense of historic pride, to keep the principle of separation of church and state free from legal encroachment, tending toward its violation.

The question as to the tendency in the present development of the status of the church in Virginia with respect to keeping inviolate the principle of separation of church and state was the theme of a striking address by Edward P. Buford, before the annual meeting of the Virginia State Bar Association in 1926. Mr. Buford after referring to the fact that the *Bill of Rights* was designed to afford protection chiefly against the "evils inflicted on mankind in the name of ecclesiastical organizations," expressed the opinion that the Protestant churches, "under the influence of bad leadership," were developing a priestcraft and practises inimical to the separation of church and state.[357] This tendency was developing in those churches, in Mr. Buford's opinion, in which there was an attempt to exercise both political and spiritual control, such "political potentiality" being "an incident of numerical strength."[358] The advancement of scientific knowledge, in particular, had much to fear in the priestcraft of to-day, which "under the name of Fundamentalism, is inaugurating a new era of persecution for imparting scientific knowledge of man's origin and evolution."[359] It was against "such fanaticism, by restraining it from imposing punishments" that the *Bill of Rights* was designed.[360] Society must ever be on its guard not to be deceived by the delusion that it has "reached

---

[357] *Proc's, 37th Annual Meeting, Va. State Bar Assoc.,* 1926, 384–85.
[358] *Ibid.,* 385, 390.
[359] *Ibid.,* 395.
[360] *Ibid.,* 396.

a state of intellectual development which will prevent the re-currence of evils, against which the *Bill of Rights* was intended to guard.''[361]

While the Baptists may point with pride to their defeat of the Bible reading bill as a denial of the justice of his contentions, the pressure from all the denominations which resulted in the inauguration of the co-operation policy with its gradually broad-ening extension of religious instruction in publc education may be regarded by some strict constructionists of the principle of separation of church and state as furnishing a basis for Mr. Buford's contention that there may be danger with the increas-ing power of church organization of a tendency away from, rather than toward, the historic principle of separation of church and state.

---

[361] *Ibid.*, 389.

CHAPTER XV

IN CONCLUSION

The present attitude of Virginia toward the problem of religion in education, which seeks to pervade education with a strong religious tone, while barring any recognition of that fact in law, is comprehensible enough in light of the review of certain factors in her more than three centuries of history. The interacting relationships of church, state, and education during this period have been controlled by three political philosophies—that of union, that of separation, and that of co-operation without legal alliance between church and state. The conception of integration under which Virginia was founded, because it was the one which gave impetus to her establishment, because it has had a longer history, has had, in spite of the enthusiasm which the separation principle has inspired, a seemingly greater importance in the final determination of Virginia's attitude toward, and treatment of, the problem of religion in education.

The important weight which must be assigned to the integration philosophy in determining Virginian attitudes is realized when it is recalled that it was the dominating political philosophy of the country which created it, and under whose control it was for a longer period than it has yet been under the separation principle. The integration philosophy was responsible for the prominence given to the Indian conversion motive, to the carrying over of English traditions in education, to the positing collegiate education on a religious foundation, to placing the licensing of teachers under the control of both church and state, and finally to the preëminent place given the clergy in the control of education.

It was seen that the very attempt to draw the lines of church and state too close was responsible for developing weaknesses in its operation, which, together with the political and economic necessity of opening up the frontiers, paved the way for dissent both from within and from without. The precedent set by the

Quakers against passivity resulted in an accumulating encouragement being given to dissenting opinion, which, reënforced by the modernistic attitude at the College of William and Mary, and the publicity given in the *Virginia Gazette* to opinion subversive of the integration philosophy, resulted in a new outlook as to the proper political philosophy for society. The reaction against the old could be satisfied for the moment only by a complete separation of church and state.

While education under the Anglican theocracy had tended to place a supreme emphasis upon the religious concept in education, education under the dissenters had not tended to minimize religious influences, but merely to change its character somewhat. The most significant differentiation was that inspired by the Presbyterian church in its initiation of a movement toward denominational education divorced from purely state control, and, at the same time, free from a purely denominational color. The tendency toward private and denominational effort in education, of such consequence to later Virginian educational development, was reënforced by the conception of separate or guarded education, free from state control, into which the various dissenting groups had been forced under the establishment.

With the enactment into law of the separation principle, Virginia society was faced by the problem of making a new adjustment. It was in the attempt to make this adjustment, that the hold, which the concept of religion as necessary to education had upon the Virginia mind, became apparent. There arose a struggle between those who like Jefferson wished the separation principle interpreted from a strict constructionist standpoint and those who would restrict that principle merely to a purely political separation, and refused to see that it had any implications for educational philosophy which needed to be regarded.

The problem of religion in education now assumed, if anything, a greater importance, because there were now two separate forces, church and state, each imbued with the notion that it was the mainspring of the betterment of society. In this position, the church had been strengthened because the dissenter movement was, after all, an expression of the desire to get back to an unadulterated Christology. Was there anything germane to education which would determine where its proper sphere of control rested? Was education the base of a triangle which had its apex in the meeting of the lines of church and state? The answer depended, in part, upon the meaning of separation of church and state. It soon became apparent that it was not animosity to religion, but hostility to the idea of union of church and state, that had inspired the separation principle. If religion was permitted to function, should it function in education, if so, how?

The Jeffersonian philosophy of education was based essentially on a strict constructionist point of view. It held that a government which could not concern itself legally with religion, could not concern itself with religion in education, that it was necessary to parallel the elimination of ecclesiasticism from the government with its elimination from education. As a matter of fact, formal legislation in the period prior to the Civil War had to follow that principle largely, even when it looked for a time as if denominational education was receiving an unwarranted support in light of the separation principle, by liberality in dispensing charters, or by a certain measure of financial support which was given. This tendency to yield in one direction was counterbalanced by the tendency of the state to assert its right to control chartered educational institutions, particularly its right to modify or repeal charters, and for a time to place limitations on theological professorships and property.

While the state had to blaze a new path, the church was greatly aided by the fact that education had been its historic function, that tradition was back of its ascendancy in education, that the people had been imbued with the notion that education must be posited on a basic Christian conception of life. The church was now greatly strengthened by the penchant which sprang up for supporting organizations, by the revivalistic and missionary movements which animated it, and by fostering propaganda designed to impress public opinion with the necessity of permeating education with religious influences. Particularly effective was the inauguration of the Sunday School movement at a time when the state was interested in getting educa-

tion under civil control. In spite of a tendency by school officials
to encourage this movement, experience by 1840 showed its inadequacy as a real ameliorating force, and revealed the necessity, as reflected in the educational conventions of that decade,
of a public school system for the masses. As for the propaganda,
it fell on fertile soil because it was difficult for people to comprehend how education without religion could operate to produce a
virtuous and moral society, how it was consonant with the safety
of the state. However, the most important means taken by the
church to strengthen its position was the attempt to create theological seminaries and an educational system of its own. By
1860, in spite of the weakened position of Presbyterianism, in its
failure to convince the public of the genuineness of its declared
educational philosophy in practise, which had finally resulted in
the severance of its connection with Washington College, and the
evident difficulties, in practise, of reconciling education under
denominational affiliation with its implication of care for religious instruction of youth with a philosophy of state based on
the separation principle, other denominations coincident with
their increasing numerical strength began to reflect an increasing concern for education under denominational auspices.

The experience of the state during the period prior to
the Civil War revealed that its attempt to create a civil school
system was hampered largely because of the distrust felt by the
people of a system which they feared was not on a sufficient religious foundation. It was only by its emphasis on the fact that
it wished regard paid to the moral character of teachers and that
means had been taken to insure this, as well as the fact, that in
practise, a certain amount of attention was being paid to the
moral and religious instruction of the children, that the idea of
public schools became effective at all. The significance of the
increasing religious sentiment in Virginia for public education
was reflected particularly in the history of the University of
Virginia. The unfavorable reaction of the public to its founder,
to the Cooper, Kraitser, and Sylvester episodes, to the poor discipline attributed to its lack of spiritual tone, could be modified
only by an increasing support to religious activities.

By the Civil War, it was apparent that considerations for liberty of conscience and all the implications involved in the principle of separation of church and state were receiving important modifications, as far as practise in education was concerned, in consequence of the fact that society was dominated by a theistic conception of the universe and man's responsibility to that conception. Virginia society, in having promulgated a new philosophy at the Revolution, did not apparently feel that it was necessary to discard all that had been inherent in the old.

It was, therefore, an inevitable consequence, that with the creation of a new public school system after the Civil War, that an attempt at harmonization should be made, and that this should take its form in the shape of a policy of co-operation without legal alliance, protecting thus the principle of separation, in its legal aspects, while satisfying the insistence that a certain degree of religious tone should be given to public education. While this policy was opposed at first by those denominational interests, which either thought they saw their ascendancy in education threatened, or refused to trust the state in this matter, experience gradually gave a grudging assent to the wisdom of this policy. In view of the desire of the people to have education permeated by a religious atmosphere, and the reluctance of the state to legislate religion into education, it came to be regarded as a most satisfactory solution.

After 1902, the tendency toward co-operation received important support by the pressure brought to bear in that direction by the creation of various organizations. It has resulted in the introduction of the Bible Study courses into the public high schools, and departments of religious instruction into the state's higher institutions, and very important encouragement by representatives of the state to the religious forces of the state. This has all been done without express recognition of these activities in law, with constitutional retention as instruments of protection, if necessary, of the *Declaration of Rights* and the *Bill For Religious Freedom*. This has been done also while the various denominations have been left entirely free to create such educational systems as they chose and for which they could obtain support from the people. While as an outcome of the co-operation policy, the state secured a heartier support for the public educational system, with the result that there has been a depressing effect upon the ability of the denominational educational systems to reach their membership in any proportionate fashion, it cannot be said that this policy has been unfavorable to the real growth or influence of the churches.

Most illuminating has been the revelation, that though the state is interested in the prevention of crime, because of the financial loss involved in the cost of maintaining judicial and prison systems, and in the failure to receive that economic and constructive social contribution which it expects from every citizen, and that though the church is interested in the prevention of crime, because of the loss of souls represented, that perhaps, after all, the determining factors in the prevention of crime may not lie wholly in what is commonly called education, nor in more religion in education, but rather to a certain extent in counterbalancing factors in physical, emotional, and mental limitations, in crime-encouraging legislation, and in political, economic, and social wrongs.

In view of the historic pride of Virginia, in the principle of separation of church and state, the insistence on keeping that principle free from legal encroachment which has characterized the attitude of the state is comprehensible, as is also its assent to the co-operation policy in light of the forces which have tended to impress the people with the necessity of placing education upon a religious foundation. For the present, it is the answer of Virginia to the problem of the relation of church and state to education that church and state influences may work together upon education, provided the basis of co-operation is not a legal bond, but one of mutual understanding.

SUMMARY OF REPLIES TO COMMISSARY BLAIR'S QUESTIONNAIRE TO THE CLERGY*

Parish	No. of Families	Negroes	Indians	White children catechising	Public Schools
Westminster	100	Preaching and catechising.		Every Sunday and Lent.	No.
St. Paul's, Hanover Co.	1200	Baptism on ability to say catechism.		Spring and fall.	"several"—none endowed.
James City	78	Follows directions of S. P. G.		Lent.	No.
Bristol (upper part of James River)	430	Masters refuse to send to church. Some instruct at home for baptism.	Few Indian servants.	No catechism last two years.	No public, but several private hired by fathers.
St. Peter's	204	Some masters permit baptism, others not.		No.	No, but some private.
Westover	233	Masters urged to send during April to June period.		First Sunday in April till last in June.	No public; 2 private.
Hungar's, Northampton Co.	365	Ordinary preaching.		Several Sundays in summer.	No.
Newport, Isle of Wight Co.	400	Baptism after instruction.		Lent.	Four; none endowed.
Stratton Major	200	Generally unbaptised; church open to all.		Lent.	No.
Wilmington	180	Generally unbaptised.		During Lent until Whitsuntide.	No public; several private.
Blissland, New Kent Co.	136	Capable are instructed and baptised.		Lent.	No.

Parish	No. of Families	Negroes	Indians	White children catechising	Public Schools
Yorkhampton	200	Catechism every Saturday at Glebe House.		Sunday afternoons in Lent; 10 other Sunday afternoons.	No public; several small schools.
Christ Church South Farnham, Essex Co.	300	Church open to them.		Lent.	No.
	200	Regular Sunday service; few attend.		Spring; distance prevents attendance.	No.
Petsworth	146	Sent to read and instructed; many baptised.		Lent.	No; several private.
Lawn's Creek	About 300 (700 tithe-ables)	Some masters permit; others refuse baptism.		Parents and masters refuse to send.	No.
Washington	200	Some instructed and baptised.		Sundays during summer.	Glebe left for minister and schoolmaster. Minister provides schoolmaster.
Elizabeth City	350	Younger generally instructed and baptised.		Lent.	Two endowed; one very good private school.
Upper Parish, Isle of Wight Co.	400	Some taught and baptised; many neglected.	70 male; some sent to Boyle's School. Wicked Christian example.	On Sabbath, when permitted to come.	No.
Christ Church, Middlesex Co.	260	Natives when teachable, taught and baptised.		Lent.	No.

			Boyle Indian School.	Every Sunday in	Public
Bruton	110	Instructed and baptised.		Lent.	grammar school; 4 little schools.
Accomako	500	Instructed at masters' homes; 200 baptised. "As in other places."		March 11 to Sept. 11.	Mr. Sanford's endowed school.
St. Stephen's, King & Queen Co.	300			Lent.	Two or three little schools.
Henrico	400 (1100 tithables)	Some occasionally permitted to attend church.		Catechising done by schoolmaster.	No.
Southwark, Surry Co.	394	Some taught and baptised; not many.	1 settlement. Former school master, Chas. Griffin, now at Wm. & Mary.	Lent.	No.
Abingdon, Gloucester Co.	300	Public preaching at church.		Lent.	One free endowed school.
St. Mary's, Essex Co.	150	Particular means discouraged.		Lent.	No.
Overworton, Stafford Co. (?)	650	Instruction and baptism if permitted by masters.		Lent and a great part of summer.	No.
St. Ann's	130	Very few baptised; owners disapproving.		No mention.	No, but several private.

* [Based on Perry: *Amer. Col. Church*, I, 257–348; see Ch. II, p. 27; IV, p. 101; a question with regard to parochial libraries, indicated only two, one of which contained three books.]

APPENDIX II

GIFTS AND BEQUESTS FOR FREE SCHOOLS OR FOR EDUCATION OF POOR CHILDREN AND ORPHANS*

Source of Fund or Bequest	Date	Control	Remarks	Sources
Benjamin Symms	(Will) Feb. 12, 1634–35.	Justices of peace, ministers, and churchwardens.	Free School, 1753—Licensing, minister and governor. Elizabeth City County.	Hening: *Stat. at Large*, I, 252; VI, 389–92; *Perfect Desc. of Va.*, in Force's Tracts, II, 15; Stanard: *Colonial Va.*, 266; Bruce: *Inst. Hist.*, I, 350 ff; Wells: *Parish Educ. Va.*, 32–35; Tyler: *Williamsburg*, 112; *Wm. & Mary Coll. Quart.*, VI, 72–76.
Hugh Lee	Jan. 20, 1652.	County Court.	Free School. Northumberland County.	Bruce: *Inst. Hist.*, I, 357; *Va. Mag. Hist.*, X, 318; Stanard: *Col. Va.*, 268.
John Moon	(Will) Aug. 12, 1655.	Overseers of poor, (churchwardens), and testator's children.	Free School. Isle of Wight County.	Bruce: *Inst. Hist.*, I, 26; 357; *Wm. & Mary Coll. Quart.*, V, 113; VI, 77; Stanard: *Colonial Va.*, 268; Tyler: *Williamsburg*, 112.
Wm. Whittington	(Will) Mar. 4, 1659.	(To parish presumably).	Free School. Northampton County. (If it should go forward).	*Va. Mag. Hist.*, V, 41; Wise: *Eastern Shore*, 318; Stanard: *Colonial Va.*, 268.
Thomas Eaton	(Will) 1659.	Commissioners, minister, and churchwardens. Commissioners gave way to justice of peace, 1759.	Free School. 1759—Licensing. Elizabeth City County.	*Wm. & Mary Coll. Quart.*, XI, 19–20; VI, 73–76; Hening: *Stat. at Large*, VII, 317–20; Wells: *Parish Educ. Va.*, 35–39; Stanard: *Colonial Va.*, 267; Bruce: *Inst. Hist.*, I, 353 ff; Brock: *Col. Virginian*, 16; Tyler: *Williamsburg*, 112.

Richard Russell	(Will) July 24, 1667.	(To parish presumably).	Lower Norfolk County.	*Va. Mag. Hist.*, I, 326; Stanard: *Colonial Va.*, 268; Bruce: *Inst. Hist.*, I, 357; *Wm. & Mary Coll. Quart.*, VI, 80.
Henry King	(Will) Mar. 2, 1668.	To the parish.	Free School. Isle of Wight County.	*Wm. & Mary Coll. Quart.*, VI, 77; V, 112–13; Bruce: *Inst. Hist.*, I, 358; Wells: *Parish Educ. Va.*, 44–45; Tyler: *Williamsburg*, 112.
Henry Peasley	(Will) Mar. 17, 1675.	Minister, churchwardens, vestry.	Free Schools. 1756—Licensing. Gloucester County, Abingdon parish, Ware parish.	Hening: *Stat. at Large*, VII, 41–43; Stanard: *Colonial Va.*, 268; Wells: *Parish Educ. Va.*, 39–41; Brock: *Col. Virginian*, 16; *Wm. & Mary Coll. Quart.*, VI, 82; Tyler: *Williamsburg*, 114.
Frances Pritchard	(Will) Oct., 1679.	(To court presumably).	Free School. Lancaster County. (On failure of heirs).	Bruce: *Inst. Hist.*, I, 358; *Va. Mag. Hist.*, II, 97–99; Stanard: *Colonial Va.*, 268–69.
William Gordon	(Will) 1685.	Churchwardens, vestry.	Free School. Middlesex County, Christ Church parish.	Stanard: *Colonial Va.*, 269; *Va. Mag. Hist.*, XII, 286; Bruce: *Inst. Hist.*, I, 358; Chamberlayne: *Christ Church Parish*, see index; Wells: *Parish Educ. Va.*, 43–44; *Wm. & Mary Coll. Quart.*, VI, 82.
Hugh Campbell	(Gift) 1691.	(Unknown).	Norfolk County, Isle of Wight County, Namsemond County.	Tyler: *Williamsburg*, 126–27; *Wm. & Mary Coll. Quart.*, VI, 80.

Source of Fund or Bequest	Date	Control	Remarks	Sources
James Jouslin	(Will) Jan. 8, 1695.	Vestry.	Princess Anne County, Lynnhaven parish.	Hening: *Stat. at Large,* VII, 145–46.
Gov. Francis Nicholson	(Gift) 1695.	To court.	Free School. York County.	*Wm. & Mary Coll. Quart.,* II, 17; VI, 78; Brock: *Col. Virginian,* 16; Tyler: *Williamsburg,* 21.
Wm. Horton	(Will) 1700.	Vestry.	Free School. Westmoreland County.	Wells: *Parish Educ. Va.,* 42; Brock: *Col. Virginian,* 16; Tyler: *Williamsburg,* 127; *Wm. & Mary Coll. Quart.,* VI, 82.
Rev. John Farnefold	(Will) July 3, 1702.	(Parish presumably).	Free School. (Winchester School) Northumberland County, St. Stephen's parish.	*Wm. & Mary Coll. Quart.,* XVII, 244–46; Wells: *Parish Educ. Va.,* 42–43.
Wm. Rawlings	(Will) 1704.	(Unknown).	King William County.	Stanard: *Colonial Va.,* 269.
Mary Whaley	(Gift) 1706. (Will) Feb. 16, 1741.	Minister and churchwardens.	Free School. York County. (Mattey School).	Barton: *Col. Va. Decisions,* II, B 363 ff.; *Wm. & Mary Coll. Quart.,* III, 174; IV, 3–14; VI, 79; XXVII, 209; Stanard: *Colonial Va.,* 269; Wells: *Parish Educ. Va.,* 46–47; Tyler: *Williamsburg,* 127.
Wm. Broadrib	Cir. 1706.	(Unknown).	Free School. James City County.	Tyler: *Williamsburg,* 126.
Samuel Sandford (Sanford)	(Will) Mar. 27, 1710.	Justice of peace, churchwardens, vestry.	Free School. Accomac County.	Meade: *Old Churches, Ministers and Families,* I, 265–66; Brock: *Col. Virginian,* 16; *Wm. & Mary Coll. Quart.,* VI, 82; *Va. Mag. Hist.,* XVIII, 180–81; Wells: *Parish Educ. Va.,* 41.

Name	Date	Trustees	School	References
Wm. Starke	(Will) June 18, 1711.	Friends as trustees.	Free School. York County, Yorktown.	Stanard: *Colonial Va.*, 269; *Wm. & Mary Coll. Quart.*, VI, 79.
Edward Moseley	(Gift) 1721.	(Unknown).	Free School. Princess Anne County.	*Va. Mag. Hist.*, I, 326; Fiske: *Old Va.*, II, 246.
John Mayo	(Will) 1723.	(Unknown).	Middlesex County.	Stanard: *Colonial Va.*, 269.
Jonathan Druitt	(Will) 1726.	Vestry.	Free School. York County.	*Wm. & Mary Coll. Quart.*, III, 174.
John Yeates	(Will) Sept. 18, 1731.	Vestry.	Free Schools. Nansemond County.	*Va. Sch. Rep't*, 1885, 229 ff.; *Wm. & Mary Coll. Quart.*, VI, 82; N. S., V, 30–38; Wells: *Parish Educ. Va.*, 47–48.
Anthony Walke	(On motion to vestry). 1736.	Vestry.	Free School. Princess Anne County (Old church for public school).	James: *Lower Norfolk Co., Va. Antiquary*, I, 106; *Va. Mag. Hist.*, I, 326; Wells: *Parish Educ. Va.*, 28.
Daniel Hornby	(Will) Apr. 2, 1750.	(? Executors as trustees).	Richmond County. (Latin master for Travers Colston—5 yrs.—obliged to teach 10 children).	*Wm. & Mary Coll. Quart.*, XVII, 246–47; 188.
Elizabeth Smith (Stith)	(Gift) 1753. (Will) 1754.	Trustees.	Free School. Isle of Wight County, Smithfield.	Stanard: *Colonial Va.*, 269–70; *Wm. & Mary Coll. Quart.*, V, 113–17; VI, 77–78; VII, 266–67; Wells: *Parish Educ. Va.*, 48.
Thomas Walke	(Will) Nov. 28, 1760.	Vestry.	Free School. Princess Anne County.	*Wm. & Mary Coll. Quart.*, II, 16.
James Reed (Reid)	(Will) (?1763) 1764.	Vestry.	Free School. Middlesex County, Urbanna.	Stanard: *Colonial Va.*, 269; *Wm. & Mary Coll. Quart.*, VI, 82–83.
Joseph Royle	(Will) 1766.	Minister and church-wardens.	Free School. York County, Bruton parish.	Stanard: *Colonial Va.*, 270; *Wm. & Mary Coll. Quart.*, VII, 14.

Source of Fund or Bequest	Date	Control	Remarks	Sources
Alexander Frasier	(Will) 1768.	(Unknown).	Free School. Middlesex County.	Stanard: *Colonial Va.*, 269.
William Monroe	(Will) 1769.	Trustees.	Orange County.	Morrison: *Beginnings Pub. Educ.*, 90.
Landon Carter	(Gift) 1770.	Personal direction.	Free School. Richmond County.	Stanard: *Colonial Va.*, 270; *Wm. & Mary Coll. Quart.*, XIII, 51; XVII, 247.
Mordecai Cooke, Jr.	(Will) 1770.	(Unknown).	Free School. Gloucester County, Ware parish.	*Wm. & Mary Coll. Quart.*, VI, 82.
Wm. Robinson	(Will) 1774.	(Unknown).	Halifax County.	Stanard: *Colonial Va.*, 270.
Humphrey Hill	(Will) 1774.	Minister, wardens and vestry.	King and Queen County, St. Stephen's parish.	Stanard: *Colonial Va.*, 270; *Wm. & Mary Coll. Quart.*, XVI, 97–99; XVII, 247; Wells: *Parish Educ. Va.*, 48.
Robert Dixon	(Will) 1774.	Vestry.	Free School. Princess Anne County, Lynnhaven parish.	*U. of Va. Rec., Ext. Ser.* VIII, No. 9, 8; see p. 124. n. 155.
James Allen	(Will) Cir. 1774.	(Unknown).	Surry County. (After failure of certain devises).	*Wm. & Mary Coll. Quart.*, VI, 82.
A. Curtis		(Unknown).	Free School. York County, Williamsburg.	*Wm. & Mary Coll. Quart.*, VI, 80; XVI, 37; III, 174; Tyler: *Williamsburg*, 57.
(? By town)	(Gift)	Justices.	Free School.	Meade: *Old Churches, Ministers and Families*, I, 201; *Wm. & Mary Coll. Quart.*, III, 174.

* [See Ch. IV, p. 122; *cf.* also *Wm. & Mary Coll. Quart.*, VI, 80, re William Hunter, for negroes; 80–81, re town controlled Norfolk school.]

BIBLIOGRAPHY

1. *Primary Sources*

A Brief Narrative of The Revival of Religion in Virginia. In a Letter to a Friend. London, 1778.

The Acadians In Virginia. (From a copy of the Proceedings in Council—Virginia Archives.) [*Va. Mag. Hist.*, (April, 1899) VI, 386–89.]

Acts of Assembly. [For a check-list of the Session Laws, see *Bull.*, *Va. State Library*, (1917) Vol. 10, Nos. 1–4, Appendix AA, 1079–80.] Williamsburg, Richmond, 1776–1924.

A Collection of all such Acts of the General Assembly of Virginia . . . Published Pursuant to an Act of the General Assembly, . . . the twenty-sixth day of January, one thousand eight hundred and two. 2 vols. [Code, 1803.] Richmond, 1803.

A Collection of all such Acts of the General Assembly of Virginia . . . Since the Session of 1801 . . . Pursuant to an Act . . . the seventh Day of January One Thousand Eight Hundred and Seven. 2 vols. [Code, 1808.] Richmond, 1808.

The Revised Code of the Laws of Virginia . . . 2 vols. Richmond, 1819.

Supplement to the Revised Code of the Laws of Virginia . . . since the year 1819. Richmond, 1833.

Tate, Joseph. *Digest of the laws of Virginia . . . illustrated by judicial decisions.* Richmond, 1841.

The Code of Virginia: . . . Pursuant to an Act . . . the fifteenth day of August, 1849. Richmond, 1849.

Matthews, James M. *Digest of the laws of Virginia . . . Illustrated by Judicial Decisions.* 2 vols. Richmond, 1856, 1857.

The Code of Virginia. Second Edition. Including Legislation to the Year 1860. Richmond, 1860.

Third Edition of the Code of Virginia: Including Legislation to January 1, 1874. Richmond, 1873.

The Code of Virginia: . . . Pursuant to an Act . . . May Twenty-one, Eighteen Hundred and Eighty-seven. Richmond, 1887.

Acts, Orders And Resolutions Of The General Assembly Of Virginia At Sessions Of March 1643–1646. [*Va. Mag. Hist.*, (July, 1915) XXIII, 225–55.]

Address Of The Memorial Committee Of The Baptist General Association Of Virginia. [1872.]

The Addresses And Journal Of Proceedings Of The National Educational Association. 1871–1927.

Alderman, Edwin A. The Achievements Of A Generation. [*Proc's Ninth Conf. Educ. South*, (1906) 145–61.]

Alderman, Edwin A. Commencement Address. (June 12, 1923) [*Alumni Bull., U. of Va.*, (Oct., 1923) XVI, No. 4, 343 *ff.*]

Alexander, Archibald. *Address Delivered Before The Alumni Association Of Washington College, Virginia, on Commencement Day, June 29th, 1843.* Lexington, 1843. [Also, *Wash. & Lee Hist. Papers*, (1890) No. 2, 113–39.]

Alexandria Academy. [*Wm. & Mary Coll. Quart.*, (Jan., 1921) N. S., I, 58–60.]

Allan, William. Address . . . before the Educational Association of Virginia, Hampton, June 10, 1878. [*Va. Educ. Jour.*, (Sept., 1878) IX, 483–98.]

The Alumni Bulletin of the University of Virginia. [Vol. II, No. 3, Nov., 1895; III, No. 4, Feb., 1897; N. S., I, No. 2, April, 1901; No. 3, July, 1901; No. 4, Oct., 1901; II, No. 2, April, 1902; No. 3, July, 1902; No. 4, Oct., 1902; III, No. 2, April, 1903; No. 3, July, 1903; No. 4, Oct., 1903; IV, No. 2, April, 1904; No. 3, July, 1904; No. 4, Oct., 1904; V, No. 2, April, 1905; No. 3, July, 1905; VII, No. 1–4, 1907. Third Series, XII, No. 1, Jan., 1919; No. 2, April, 1919; XIII, No. 1, Jan., 1920; No. 4, Aug., 1920; No. 5, Oct., 1920; XIV, No. 1, Jan., 1921; No. 3, July–Aug., 1921; No. 4, Oct., 1921; XV, No. 2, April, 1922; No. 3, July–Aug., 1922; XVI, No. 2, April, 1923; No. 4, Oct., 1923; XVII, No. 1–4, 1924.] Charlottesville, 1895, . . .

Alvord, Clarence W. & Bidgood, Lee. *First Explorations of the Trans-Allegheny Region by the Virginians, 1650–1674.* Clark: Cleveland, 1912.

Ambler, Charles H., editor. *Correspondence of Robert M. T. Hunter 1826–1876.* [*Amer. Hist. Assoc., Annual Rep't*, 1916, II.]

Ambler, Charles H. *The Life And Diary Of John Floyd.* Richmond, 1918.

A Memorial Of The Case Of The German Emigrants Settled In The British Colonies of Pensilvania, and the back Parts of Maryland, Virginia, &c. London, 1754.

Animadversions on a Paper Entituled Virginia Addresses, Printed in Philadelphia. [*Va. Mag. Hist.*, (Oct., 1914) XXIII, 410–16.]

Annual Reports of the Superintendent of the Public Schools of the City of Richmond. Richmond, 1898–1920, 1924–26.

Annual Reports, Virginia Military Institute. Lexington, 1915–16, 1917–18, 1919–20, 1924–25.

Annual Reports of the Virginia State Library. 22 vols. [Biennial Reports for years ending 1923, 1925.] Richmond, 1904–27.

Annual Report For Year 1897–98 Of President William L. Wilson of Washington and Lee University. Lexington, 1898.

A Perfect Description of Virginia. [Force's *Tracts*, II, No. VIII, Washington, 1838; also *Va. Hist. Register*, (April, 1849) II, No. 2, 61–78.] London, 1649.

Application Of The Literary Fund. [(A Friend To The Poor) *Va. Evang. & Lit. Mag.*, (June, 1823) VI, 281–86.]

Arber, Edward. *Travels and Works of Captain John Smith.* 2 vols. Grant: Edinburgh, 1910.

[Archer, Gabriel.] Captain Newport's Discoveries In Virginia. (A Relatyon of The Discovery Of Our River) 1607. [*Archaeologia Americana,* (1860) IV, 34–65.]

A Report Of The Addresses In Commemoration Of The Life And Public Services Of J. L. M. Curry, D. C. L., LL. D., Supervising Director Of The Southern Education Board, Member Of The General Education Board, Agent Of The Peabody And Slater Funds. [*Proc's 6th Conf. Educ. South,* (1903) 251–69.]

A Short Account of The First Settlement of The Provinces of Virginia, . . . Pennsylvania . . . Anno. 1630. [Reprint: Amer. Geog. Society, June, 1922.] *London, 1735.*

A Treaty Between Virginia and the Catawbas and Cherokees, 1756. [*Va. Mag. Hist.,* (Jan., 1906) XIII, 225–64.]

A York County Petition Of The Latter Part Of The Eighteenth Century. [*Wm. & Mary Coll. Quart.,* (April, 1923) Ser. II, III, 113–14.]

Baker, Andrew. *The Poor Orphans Legacy: Being A Short Collection of Godly Counsels and Exhortations . . . By a Minister of the Gospel.* [Preface to 2nd edition signed by Andrew Baker, Spring Creek, Prince Edward County.] Richmond, 1792.

Ballagh, James Curtis, editor. *The Letters of Richard Henry Lee.* 2 vols. Macmillan: New York, 1911.

Baptists in Middlesex, 1771. [*Wm. & Mary Coll. Quart.,* (July, 1925) Ser. II, V, 208–13.]

Barbour, B. J. *An Address Delivered Before The Literary Societies Of The Virginia Military Institute, At Lexington, On The 4th of July, 1854.* Richmond, 1854.

Barringer, Paul B. The Relation of the University to the Public Schools. [(An address . . . educational conference at the University.) *Va. Sch. Jour.,* (Oct., 1902) 245–47.]

Barton, R. T., editor. *The Reports By Sir John Randolph and By Edward Barradall Of Decisions Of The General Court Of Virginia 1728–1741.* 2 vols. Boston Book Co.: Boston, 1909.

Bassett, John Spencer, editor. *The Writings Of ''Colonel William Byrd Of Westover In Virginia Esq'r.''* Doubleday, Page & Co.: New York, 1901.

Bayard, Ferdinand M. *Voyage Dans L' Intérieur Des États-Unis.* [*Cf. Sewanee Review,* (Jan., 1904) XII, 52–72.] Paris, An. VI. (1798).

Bennion, Milton. Report of Progress Committee On Character Education— The Sanctions of Morality. [*N. E. A. Proc's,* (1922) LX, 457–59.]

Bernard, John. *Retrospections of America.* 1797–1811. New York, 1887.

Bouchier, Jonathan. *Reminiscences of an American Loyalist 1738–1789.* Houghton Mifflin: Boston, 1925.

Brinsley, John. *A Consolation For Ovr Grammar Schooles.* [Hist. Soc. of Penn'a] London, 1622.

Brissot De Warville, J. P. *New Travels In The United States Of America Performed in 1788.* Dublin, 1792.

Brock, R. A. *The Colonial Virginian. An Address Delivered before the Geographical and Historical Society of Richmond College.* Richmond, 1891.

Brock, R. A. *Documents, Chiefly Unpublished, Relating To The Huguenot Emigration To Virginia.* [*Collections of Va. Hist. Society*, N. S., V.] Richmond, 1886.

Brock, R. A., editor. *Miscellaneous Papers, 1672–1865 . . . comprising . . . Report on the Huguenot Settlement 1700. Papers of George Gilmer, . . . 1775–1778 . . .* [*Collections of Va. Hist. Society*, N. S., VI.] Richmond, 1887.

Brock, R. A. *The Vestry Book of Henrico Parish, 1730–'73.* Richmond, 1874.

Brooke, Francis T. *Some Contemporary Accounts Of Eminent Characters. From "A Narrative Of My Life For My Family."* [*Wm. & Mary Coll. Quart.*, (July, 1908) XVII, 1–8.]

Brown, Alexander. *The Genesis of the United States.* 2 vols. Boston, 1891.

Brown, B. Warren. *Report of the Survey of the Educational Work and Responsibility of the Presbyterian Church in the United States.* Louisville, August, 1928.

Bruce, James C. *Popular Knowledge the Necessity of Popular Government. A Lecture Delivered Before The Danville Virginia Lyceum, March 18th, 1853.* [*So. Lit. Messenger*, (May, 1853) XIX, 292–302.]

Bruce, Philip Alexander. *Recollections of My Plantation Teachers.* [*South Atlant. Quart.*, (Jan., 1917) XVI, 1–13.]

Bryan, Daniel. *Thoughts on Education In Its Connection With Morals. A Poem Recited . . . Hampden Sidney College, . . . September, 1828.* Richmond, 1830.

Buchanan Baptist Mission School. [Pamphlet—descriptive] Council, [1926].

Buford, Edward P. *The Virginia Bill of Rights.* [*Proc's 37th Annual Meeting The Va. State Bar Assoc.*, (Aug. 4th, 5th, and 6th, 1926) 378.]

Bulletins State Board of Education. Richmond, 1918–1927.

Bulletin Virginia State Library. Quarterly. Richmond, 1908, . . .

Burgesses In 1692–'93. [*Wm. & Mary Coll. Quart.*, (Oct., 1896) V, 137–38.]

Burnaby, Andrew. *Travels Through The Middle Settlements In North America, In The Years 1759 and 1760. London, 1798.* Wessels: New York, 1904.

Burwell, William M. *Address Delivered Before The Society of Alumni Of The University of Virginia.* [Bound in *Va. Misc. Addresses,* Vol. II, Va. State Library] Richmond, 1847.

Buttrick, Wallace. The Beginning And Aims Of The General Education Board. [*N. E. A. Proc's,* (1903) XLII, 116–23.]

[Byrd, Wm.] *Neu-gefundenes Eden. Oder: Ausführlicher Bericht Von Sud-und Nord-Carolina, Pensilphania, Mary-Land & Virginia.* Helvetischen Societat 1737. [Library of U. of Pa.]

[Cabell, Margaret.] *Sketches And Recollections of Lynchburg. By The Oldest Inhabitant.* Richmond, 1858.

Calendar and Announcements Blue Ridge Industrial School. Dyke, Greene County, 1928–29.

Call, Daniel. *Reports of Cases Argued and Adjudged in the Court of Appeals of Virginia.* Vol. III. Richmond, 1805.

Campbell, Alexander. An address to the convention on the subject of primary or common schools, Sept. 8, 1841 [*Jour., H. Del.,* 1841–42, Doc. No. 7, Education Convention of Northwestern Virginia.] [Clarksburg, 1841.]

Campbell, David. Governor Campbell on Public Free Schools Message of January, 1839. [*Circulars,* 1870–76 Collection, Va. State Library; *cf. Jour., H. Del.,* 1839, Doc. No. 1.]

The Carnegie Foundation for Advancement of Teaching. Annual Reports, Third to Seventh inclusive. New York, 1908–12.

The Carnegie Foundation For the Advancement of Teaching. *Act of Incorporation By-Laws Rules For The Admission of Institutions And For The Granting of Retiring Allowances.* New York, 1922.

Carroll, D. L. *An Address Delivered Before The Franklin Literary Society Of Randolph Macon College, Virginia, June 19th, 1838, by . . . President Of Hampden Sidney College, Va.* Richmond, 1838.

Carroll, D. L. *Inaugural Address Of The Rev. D. L. Carroll, D.D., President Of Hamden Sydney College, Delivered On His Induction Into That Office.* Richmond, 1835.

Carter, James C. *The University of Virginia: Jefferson its Father, and his Political Philosophy. An Address . . . June 14, 1898.* University of Virginia, 1898.

C. [astell], W. [illiam]. *A Petition of W. C. Exhibited To The High Covrt Of Parliament. 1641.* [Force's *Tracts,* I, No. XIII, Washington, 1836.]

Catalogues.
Alexandria Boarding School, Alexandria, 1853.
Augusta Military Academy. Fort Defiance, 1925–26, 1926–27.
Averett College For Young Women. Danville, 1926–27.
Benedictine College. Richmond, 1924.
Bethany College. Bethany, 1855.

Bishop Payne Divinity School. Petersburg, 1926.
Blackstone College for Girls. Blackstone, 1928–29.
Blackstone Military Academy. Blackstone, 1926–27.
Bloomfield Academy. Charlottesville, 1855–56.
The Blue Ridge Industrial School. Dyke, Greene County. [No date –?
      1927.]
Bluestone-Harmony Academic and Industrial School. Keysville, 1925–26.
Bridgewater College Of The Bridgewater-Daleville System. Bridgewater,
      1925–26, 1928.
Buchanan Mission School. Council, 1928–29. [Folder].
Central Academy. Stuart, 1926–27. [Announcements].
Chatham Episcopal Institute. Chatham, 1926.
Christiansburg Industrial Institute. Cambria, 1925–26.
Culpeper Military Institute. Culpeper C. H., 1857–58.
Daleville Academy of Bridgewater-Daleville College. Daleville, 1926.
Danville Military Institute. Danville, 1926–27, 1927–28.
*David Turner's Select Classical and English School . . . For The Aca-
      demical Year 1852–53.* [*Virginia Education,* Vol. I, Va. State
      Library] Richmond, 1853.
Eastern Mennonite School. Harrisonburg, 1926–27.
Emory and Henry College. Emory, 1854–55, 1855–56, 1925–26, 1926–27.
The Episcopal High School in Virginia. Alexandria, 1859–60, 1925–26.
Fairfax Hall. Waynesboro, 1926–27.
Bulletin of the State Normal School for Women. Farmville, Vol. II,
      No. 4, 1916–17; V, No. 1, 1918–19; No. 3, April, 1919; No. 4, 1919–20;
      VI, No. 1, 1919–20; VII, No. 4, 1921–22; VIII, No. 4, 1922–23; X,
      No. 4, 1924–25; XII, No. 4, 1926–27.
Fauquier Institute. Warrenton, [1926].
Ferrum Training School. Ferrum, 1926–27.
Fishburne Military School. Waynesboro, 1925–26, 1926–27.
Fork Union Military Academy. Fork Union, 1926–27.
Bulletin State Teachers College. Fredericksburg, June, 1916–17, 1927–28.
Grundy Presbyterian School. Grundy, 1927–28.
Hampden-Sidney College. Hampden-Sidney, 1853, 1855, 1867, 1925–26.
The Hampton Bulletin. Hampton, 48th—Vol. III, No. 2, Mar., 1916;
      50th—XIV, No. 3, April, 1917, to 59th—XXIII, No. 1, Mar., 1927,
      inclusive.
Hargrave Military Academy. Chatham, 1926.
State Teachers College. Harrisonburg, 1918, 1920, 1926–27.
Hartshorn Memorial College. Richmond, 1925–26.
Hollins College. Hollins, 1925–26.
Kleinberg School. Schuyler, 1926–27.
Mr. Lefebvre's School. Richmond, [1856–57].
Linton Hall. Bristow, [1928].
Lynchburg College. Lynchburg, 1925–26.
McGuire's University School. Richmond, 1926–27.

Marion Junior College. Marion, 1924–25.

Martha Washington College. Abingdon, 1925–26, 1926–27.

Mary Baldwin College. Staunton, 1925–26.

Mary Baldwin Seminary. Staunton, 1925–26.

Massanutten Academy. Woodstock, 1925–26.

Medical College of Virginia. Richmond, 1927.

Monte Maria Academy. Richmond, 1921–22.

Norfolk Academy. Norfolk, 1926–27.

Old Point Comfort College. Old Point Comfort, 1920–21.

Petersburg Classical Institute. Petersburg, 1855–56, 1856–57.

Piedmont Baptist Mission School. Alhambra. [No date –? 1923; leaflet].

Piedmont Institute. Charlottesville, 1859–60. [Philadelphia, 1860].

The Radford State Teachers College Bulletin. East Radford, 1918, 1926–27.

Randolph-Macon Academy. Bedford, 1925–26, 1926–27.

Randolph-Macon Academy. Front Royal, 1925–26, 1926–27.

Randolph-Macon College. Ashland, 1853–54, 1925–26.

Randolph-Macon Woman's College. Lynchburg, 1925–26.

Randolph-Macon School for Girls. Danville, 1925–26, 1926–27.

Roanoke College. Salem, 1925–26.

St. Catherine's School. Richmond, 1925–26.

St. Christopher's School. Richmond, 1925–26.

St. Emma Industrial and Agricultural School. Rock Castle. [1928].

St. Mary's Academy. Alexandria, 1926–27.

Saint Paul Normal and Industrial School. Lawrenceville, 1924–25.

Shenandoah College. Dayton, 1925–26.

Shenandoah Valley Academy. Winchester, 1925–26.

Southern College. Petersburg, 1926–27.

Southern Seminary. Buena Vista, 1925–26.

South-Side Institute. Farmville, 1858–59. [Petersburg, 1859].

Staunton Military Academy. Staunton, 1926–27.

Stonewall Jackson College. Abingdon, 1926–27.

Stuart Hall. Staunton, 1925–26.

Stuyvesant School. Warrenton, 1925–26.

Sullins College. Bristol, 1926–27.

The Swavely School. Manassas, 1926–27.

Sweet Briar College. Sweet Briar, 1926–27.

The Theological Seminary, Of the Protestant Episcopal Church, in the Diocese of Virginia. Alexandria, Va., 1842–43, 1843–44, 1845–46, 1851–52, 1925–26.

Union Theological Seminary. Richmond, 1924–25, 1925–26.

University of Kansas Annual Catalog Section I General Information. Lawrence, 1927–28.

University of Richmond Bulletin—Catalogue of Richmond College. Richmond, 1925–26.

University of Texas Bulletin No. 2717: May 1, 1927. Austin, 1926–27.

University of Virginia. Charlottesville, 1839–40, 1841–42, 1847–48, 1850–51, 1851–52, 1852–53, 1855–56, 1857–58, 1867–68, 1868–69, 1872–73, 1874–75, 1878–79, 1882–83, 1883–84, 1884–85, 1889–90, 1890–91, 1897–98, 1898–99, 1903–13, inclusive, 1919–1927, inclusive.

Virginia College. Roanoke, 1925–26.

Virginia Female Institute. Staunton, 1859. [Baltimore, 1859].

Virginia Intermont College. Bristol, 1925–26, 1926–27.

Virginia Mechanics' Institute. Richmond, 1925–26.

Virginia Military Institute. Lexington, 1876–77, 1914–15, 1917–18, 1925–26.

The Virginia Normal and Industrial Institute Gazette. Ettrick, 1916, 1921, 1924, 1926.

Virginia Polytechnic Institute. Blacksburg, 1919, 1926.

Virginia Union University. Richmond, 1920–21, 1921–22, 1925–26.

Warrenton Country School. Warrenton. [1925–26].

Catalogue of the Officers and Alumni of Washington and Lee University. Lexington, Virginia, 1749–1888. Baltimore, 1888.

Washington and Lee University. Lexington, 1855, 1883, 1884, 1885, 1888, 1889, 1891, 1892, 1893, 1894, 1895, 1921, 1922, 1923, 1924, 1925, 1926.

Westhampton College. Richmond, 1926–27.

Catalogue of the Officers and Students of William and Mary College Session of 1843–44, 1844–45. Richmond, 1844, 1845. [Bound in one volume].

William and Mary College. Williamsburg, 1838–39, 1894–95, 1895–96, 1925–26.

Woodberry Forest School. Woodberry Forest, 1925–26.

Causes of Discontent in Virginia, 1676. [*Va. Mag. Hist.*, (Oct., 1894) II, 166–73; (Jan., 1895) II, 289–92; (April, 1895) II, 380–92.]

Chalkley, Lyman. *Chronicles Of The Scotch-Irish Settlement In Virginia.* 3 vols. Rosslyn, 1912.

Chamberlayne, Churchill Gibson. *The Vestry-book and Register of Bristol Parish, Virginia. 1720–1789.* Richmond, 1898.

Chamberlayne, Churchill Gibson. *The Vestry Book of Christ Church Parish, Middlesex County, Va. 1663–1767.* Old Dominion Press: Richmond, 1927.

Chapin, E. H. Anniversary Address, Delivered before the Richmond Lyceum, April 3rd, 1839. [*So. Lit. Messenger*, (Nov., 1839) V, 725–33.]

Character Education In The Public Schools. *A Report of a Conference led by Superintendent F. E. Clerk of the Winchester Schools.* [*Va. Teacher*, (June, 1923) IV, 147–57.]

Chastellux, Francois Jean. *Travels In North-America, In the Years 1780, 1781, 1782.* 2 vols. [Translated From the French By An English Gentleman.] Dublin, 1787.

Chesterman, E. R., editor. *Illiteracy In Virginia.* Dep't Public Instruction: Richmond, 1914.

Christian, Bolivar. The Scotch-Irish Settlers In The Valley of Virginia: Alumni Address At Washington College, July 1, 1859. [*Wash. & Lee Hist. Papers* (1892) No. 3, 1–43.]

Circulars. [1870–76 Collection of Documents, Circulars, in Va. State Library.]

Circulars, Doc. No. 6, Report State Superintendent Public Instruction, Mar. 28, 1870. [1870–76 Collection of Documents, Circulars, in Va. State Library.]

Circulars—Extract From Annual Report of Superintendent of Public Instruction, 1874, State Uniformity of Text Books: Tending to Despotism, Corruption, and Intellectual Death. [1870–76 Collection of Documents, Circulars, in Va. State Library.]

Circular No. 132, Department of Public Instruction, March 20, 1875. [1870–76 Collection of Documents, Circulars, in Va. State Library.]

Circulars—Review Of The School Law, 1871. [1870–76 Collection of Documents, Circulars, in Va. State Library.]

Claiborne, John Herbert. *Seventy-Five Years In Old Virginia.* Neale: New York, 1904.

Claiborne, J. Herbert. William Claiborne of Kent Island. Address delivered . . . before the Maryland Society of New York, April 14, 1919. [*Wm. & Mary Coll. Quart.*, (April, 1921) N. S., I, 73–99.]

Cocke, Charles L. *Address, Fiftieth Anniversary, June, 1893.* [Excerpt received through the courtesy of President Matty L. Cocke.]

Cocke, Charles L. Discipline and Training Of Girls. [*Va. Educ. Jour.*, (Sept., 1879) X, 385–92.]

Cocke, Charles L. Annual Address . . . Educational Association of Virginia, July 5th, 1881. [*Va. Educ. Jour.*, (Jan., 1882) XIII, 9.]

Cohen, S. M. *An Inquiry Into The Tendencies Of The Week Day Religious Education Movement In Its Relations To The Public Schools.* [Received through courtesy of author.]

Collections Of The Virginia Historical and Philosophical Society. Vol. I. Richmond, 1833.

Collections Of The Virginia Historical Society. New Series, 11 vols. Richmond, 1882, . . .

The College In The Years 1861–1865. [*Wm. & Mary Coll. Quart.*, (Oct., 1923) N. S., III, 221–30.]

College Papers. [*Wm. & Mary Coll. Quart.*, (April, 1917) XXV, 236–42.]

Collier, J. Payne. *Illustrations of Early English Popular Literature.* Vol. II. [A Good Speed To Virginia. London, 1609. (? Raleigh, Walter) (Gray, Robert—according to Torrence: *Trial Bibliography*, 19.)] London, 1864.

Colonel Scarborough's Report. Being An Account Of His Efforts To Suppress The Quakers In What Is Now Part Of Maryland, Then Claimed

By Virginia. (From the records of Accomac County.) [(Contributed by Thos. B. Robertson) *Va. Mag. Hist.,* (April, 1911) XIX, 173–80.]

Colonial Records of Virginia. (Senate Document—Extra.) Richmond, 1874.

Community League Bulletin Giving Plan of Organization, Constitution And By-Laws, Suggestions For The Work Of Each Committee. By The Co-operative Education Association of Virginia. Richmond, 1916.

Complaint by Germans Against Governor Spotswood. (From Virginia State Archives.) [*Va. Mag. Hist.,* (April, 1899) VI, 385–86.]

The Constitution of the State of Virginia, Adopted By The Convention Of 1901–2. Published By Authority. Richmond, 1902.

Cooper, Oscar H. Contributions of Religious Organizations To The Cause of Education. 1. By the Baptist Church. [*N. E. A. Proc's,* (1900) XXXIX, 87–94.]

Copy Of An Original Letter From The Rev. S. Davies. [*Va. Evang. & Lit. Mag.,* (Nov., 1823) VI, 567–69.]

Corey, Charles H. *A History Of The Richmond Theological Seminary.* Richmond, 1895.

Correspondence of Ezra Stiles, President Of Yale College, And James Madison, President Of William And Mary College, 1780. [*Wm. & Mary Coll. Quart.,* (Oct., 1927) N. S., VII, 292–96.]

Cotton, An. *An Account Of Our Late Troubles In Virginia.* 1676. [*Richmond Enquirer,* Sept. 12, 1804; Force's *Tracts,* I, No. IX; *Va. Evang. & Lit. Mag.,* (Mar., 1820) III, 128–40.]

Council Papers 1698–1701. (From the Original in the Virginia State Library.) [*Va. Mag. Hist.,* (July, 1914) XXII, 244–56; (April, 1915) XXIII, 139–45.]

Course of Study for the Public Schools of Virginia. [*Va. Jour. Educ.,* (Nov., 1907) I, 10–11.]

The Course of Studies at Hampden Sidney College. [*Va. Evang. & Lit. Mag.,* (May, 1819) II, 237.]

Crozier, William A. *Virginia County Records.* 10 vols. Fox, Duffield: New York, 1905.

Crozier, William A. *Spotsylvania County 1721–1800.* Fox, Duffield: New York, 1905. [*Virginia County Records,* I.]

Crozier, William A. *Williamsburg Wills.* Genealogical Assoc.: New York, 1906. [*Virginia County Records,* III.]

Curley, Michael J. *The Church And Education.* [Pamphlet: Address National Convention of the N. C. W. C., Washington, D. C., October, 1923.] National Catholic Welfare Conference: Washington [1923].

Cushing, Jonathan Peter. President Cushing's Address . . . February 4th, 1833. [*Va. Hist. Soc. Collections,* (1833) I, 9 *ff.*]

Dabney, R. Heath. Thomas Jefferson As An Educator. [*Proc's 6th Conf. Educ. South,* (1903) 240–43.]

Davies, Samuel. *The Curse of Cowardice: A Sermon Preached To The Militia Of Hanover County, In Virginia, At A General Muster, May 8, 1758.* New York, 1759.

Davies, Samuel. *The Duty of Christians to propagate their Religion among Heathens, Earnestly recommended to the Masters of Negro Slaves In Virginia. A Sermon Preached in Hanover, January 8, 1757.* London, 1758.

Davies, Samuel. *Letters From The Rev. Samuel Davies, &c. Shewing The State of Religion in Virginia, particularly among the Negroes.* London, 1757.

Davis, John. *Travels Of Four Years And A Half In The United States Of America. London, 1803.* [Morrison, A. J., editor.] Holt: New York, 1909.

Decisions Of The General Court. [*Va. Mag. Hist.,* (Jan., 1898) V, 233–41; (April, 1898) V, 361–68.]

De Saint-Méry, Moreau. *Voyage Aux États-Unis De L' Amérique, 1793— 1798.* [Mims, Stewart L., editor.] Yale University Press: New Haven, 1913.

De Toqueville, Alexis. *The Republic of the United States of America.* 2 vols. in one. New York, 1851.

Dew, Thomas R. An Address Delivered before the Students of William and Mary, at the Opening of the College, on Monday, October 10th, 1836. [*So. Lit. Messenger.* (Nov., 1836) II, 760–69.]

Dew, Thomas R. Baccalaureate Address Delivered to the Graduates of William and Mary College, on the Fourth day of July, 1837. [*So. Lit. Messenger,* (July, 1837) III, 401–06.]

Dilhet, Jean. *État De L' Église Catholique Ou Diocése Des États-Unis L' Amérique Septentrionale.* [*Cath. U. of America Studies in Amer. Church Hist.,* I, Browne, P. W. translator.] Salve Regina Press: Washington, 1922.

[Dinwiddie, Robert.] *The Official Records of Robert Dinwiddie, Lieutenant Governor of the Colony of Virginia, 1751–1758.* 2 vols. [*Collections of Va. Hist. Society,* N. S. III & IV, Brock, R. A., editor.] Richmond, 1883, 1884.

Documents of the Literary Fund. 1816 to 1851. Vol. III. [Second Auditor's Reports—1st 2 vols missing—Vol. III for 1847 (Sept. 30, 1846) to 1851 (Sept. 30, 1850.)]

Doc. No. XIII. Report Of The Superintendent Of Public Instruction. March 28th, 1870. [*Va. Educ. Jour.,* (1870) I.]

Documents—Virginia House of Delegates and Senate. 1776–1924. [*Cf. Bull., Va. State Library,* Vol. 10, Nos. 1–4, (1917); Documents appended to the *Journals* or appearing as separate volumes, in the Va. State Library.]

Doddridge, Jos. *Notes, On The Settlement And Indian Wars, Of The Western Parts Of Virginia And Pennsylvania, From The Year 1763 Until The Year 1783 Inclusive.* Wellsburgh, 1824.

Dreher, J. D.   The Benevolent Spirit And The Higher Education.   [*Va. Educ. Jour.*, (Jan., 1882) XIII, 51–55.]

Du Pont De Nemours, Pierre Samuel.   *National Education In The United States of America.*   [Du Pont, Bessie Gardner, editor.]   University of Delaware Press: Newark, 1923.

The Eaton Free School.   [*Wm. & Mary Coll. Quart.*, (July, 1902) XI, 19–20.]

Educational Council.   *Iowa State Teachers' Association Report of Committee On School Credit For Bible Study, Religious Instruction And Moral Training.*   Des Moines, 1916.

Edwards, Richard.   *Statistical Gazetteer Of The States Of Virginia And North Carolina.*   Richmond, 1856.

Eggleston, J. D., & Munford, B. B.   *School Clubs For Virginia Boys and Girls.*   [Pub. by Dep't Pub. Inst. & Co-operative Educ. Assoc.]   1916.

Emory and Henry College.   [(By Authority.)   *U. S. Bur. Educ., Circ. Inf.*, (1888) No. 1, 252–62.]

Enactment By The Rector And Visitors Of The University Of Virginia, For Constituting, Governing And Conducting That Institution.   For The Use Of The University.   Charlottesville, 1825.

Enactments Relating To The Constitution And Government Of The University of Virginia.   For The Use Of The University.   Charlottesville, 1831.

Enactments Relating To The Constitution And Government Of The University Of Virginia.   For The Use Of The University.   Philadelphia, 1847.

Essex County.   [(Contributed by Clayton Torrence.)   *Wm. & Mary Coll. Quart.*, (April, 1921) N. S., I, 142.]

Exiles In Virginia: With Observtaions On The Conduct Of The Society of Friends During The Revolutionary War.   Philadelphia, 1848.

Extracts From Diary Of Col. Landon Carter.   [*Wm. & Mary Coll. Quart.*, (July, 1904) XIII, 45–53.]

Extracts From Virginia County Records.   [*Va. Mag. Hist.*, (Jan., 1905) XII, 284–96.]

The Ferrar Papers At Magdalene College, Cambridge.   [(Communicated by M. L. Ferrar)   *Va. Mag. Hist.*, (Oct., 1902) 130–38.]

First Annual Report Of The Virginia Home And Industrial School For Girls, Chesterfield County, Va. . . . 1914–1915.   Richmond, 1915. [Also for 1916–17, 1922–23.]

Fithian, Philip Vickers.   *Journal and Letters, 1767–1774.*   [Williams, John R., editor.]   Princeton, 1900.

Fitzpatrick, John C.   *The Diaries of George Washington 1748–1799.*   4 vols.   Houghton Mifflin: Boston, 1925.

Fleming, Walter L.   *Documentary History of Reconstruction.*   2 vols.   Clark: Cleveland, 1906.

Fontaine, James.   *A Tale of the Huguenots, or Memoirs of a French Refugee Family.*   New York, 1838.

Force, Peter. *American Archives: Consisting of A Collection of Authentick Records, State Papers, Debates, and Letters and Other Notices of Publick Affairs. In Six Series.* [Six Series never published in full. Series 4, vols. 1, 2, 4, 5, 6; Series 5, vols. 1, 2, 3.] Washington, 1837–53.

Force, Peter. *Tracts and Other Papers.* 4 vols. Washington, 1836–1846.

Ford, Paul Leicester. *The Writings of Thomas Jefferson.* 10 vols. New York, 1892–99.

Ford, Worthington Chauncy, editor. *Letters of Jonathan Boucher to Geo. Washington.* Brooklyn, 1899.

Fordham, Elias Pym. *Personal narrative of travels in Virginia, . . . 1817–1818.* Clark: Cleveland, 1906.

Form X—No. 91, (Revised Aug. 1, 1911) *High School Text Books Selected By The State Board Of Education, 1910.* Richmond, October, 1910.

Form X—No. 46—Text Books And Educational Appliances For the Public Schools. Richmond, October, 1910.

Forrest, W. M. Bible Classes for High School Pupils. [*Va. Jour. Educ.,* (Dec., 1917) XI, 161–62.]

Forrest, W. M. Bible classes for high school pupils with credit towards graduation. [*U. of Va. Rec., Ext. Ser.,* (Oct., 1921) VII, No. 2.]

Forrest, W. M. High-School Bible Study in Virginia. [*Relig. Educ.,* (April, 1918) XIII, 136–37.]

Forrest, W. M. School Credit for Bible Study. [*Va. Jour. Educ.,* (Oct., 1916) X, 75–76.]

Frazer, Robert. Virginia's Educational Outlook. [*Proc's 5th Conf. Educ. South,* (1902) 35–37.]

Free Schools In Isle Of Wight County. [*Wm. & Mary Coll. Quart.,* (Oct., 1896, V, 112–17.]

Freeman, James E. Address At Vesper Service. [*N. E. A. Proc's,* (1926) LXIV, 667–75.]

Frissel, H. B. Address. [*Proc's 7th Conf. Educ. South,* (1904) 67–74.]

Frissel, H. B. Report From The Field. [*Proc's 6th Conf. Educ. South,* (1903) 47–56.]

Frissel, H. B. The Training of Negro Teachers. [*N. E. A. Proc's,* (1900) XXXIX, 482–89.]

Gaines, Richard Heyward. Richmond's First Academy, Projected By M. Quesnay De Beaurepaire, In 1786. A Paper Read Before The Virginia Historical Society Friday, December 22, 1891. [*Coll. Va. Hist. Society,* (1892) N. S., XI, 165–75.]

Gardner, Wm. F. Religious Education of Virginia Schools. [*Va. Educ. Jour.,* (Aug., 1871) II, 364–67.]

Garnett, James M. An Address On The Subject Of Literary Associations To Promote Education; Delivered before the Institute of Education of Hampden-Sidney College, . . . (Sept. 25th, 1834.). [Morrison: *Six Addresses,* 34–39; *Annals of Educ.,* (July, 1835) V, 317–18.]

Garnett, James M. Introductory Lecture To a Course on "The Obstacles to Education arising from the peculiar faults of Parents, Teachers, Scholars, and those who direct and control our Schools and Colleges," delivered before the Fredericksburg Lyceum, by James M. Garnett. [*So. Lit. Messenger*, (Sept., 1835) I, 725–34; (June, 1836) II, 436–45; (July, 1836) II, 477–86; (Aug., 1836) II, 561–68; (Sept., 1836) II, 613–22.]

Garnett, James M. *Lectures On Female Education.* Richmond, 1825.

Garnett, James M. Popular Education. An address before the Education Convention, Dec. 9, 1841. [*So. Lit. Messenger*, (Feb., 1842) VIII, 114–21.]

Garnett, James M. *Token Of Regard, Presented To The Pupils Of The Elm-Wood School, By Their Friend.* . . . Richmond, 1830.

Garnett, M. R. H. *An Address Delivered Before the Society of Alumni of the University of Virginia . . . 29th of June, 1850.* Charlottesville, 1850.

Gee, Henry, and Hardy, William John. *Documents Illustrative Of English Church History.* London, 1896.

Gilbert, D. M. *The Lutheran Church in Virginia. A Historical Discourse. . . . August 3rd–8th, 1876.* New Market, 1876.

Gilmer, Thomas W. *An Address, Delivered Before The Two Literary Societies Of Randolph Macon College, Va.* Richmond, 1843.

Gilmer, Thomas W. An Address, Delivered before the Virginia Historical and Philosophical Society, at its late Annual Meeting, . . . of the 14th instant. [*So. Lit. Messenger*, (Feb., 1837) III, 97–102.]

Glimpses Of Old College Life. [*Wm. & Mary Coll. Quart.*, (July, 1900) IX, 18–23.]

Grantham, Thomas. *An Historical Account of Some Memorable Actions, Particularly in Virginia. London, 1716.* [Brock, R. A., editor. Reprint by Carlton McCarthy & Co.: Richmond, 1882.]

Grattan, Peachy R. *Reports Of Cases Decided In The Supreme Court Of Appeals, And In The General Court, of Virginia.* Vol. III. Richmond, 1847.

Greater Richmond College An Appeal and a Prospect. Richmond, 1908.

G. [reene], R. [obert]. *Virginia's Cure: Or An Advisive Narrative Concerning Virginia. London, 1662.* [Force's *Tracts*, III, No. XV, Washington, 1844.]

Greenvile, Sir Richard. Voyages for Sir Walter Raleigh to Virginia in 1585–90. [In Pinkerton, John: *General Collection of voyages and travels*, London, 1808–14, XII, 571.]

Grigsby, Hugh Blair. The Founders Of Washington College: An Address . . . Delivered June 22, 1870. [*Wash. & Lee Hist. Papers* (1890) No. 2, 1–111.]

Grigsby, Hugh Blair. *The Virginia Convention Of 1776. A Discourse Delivered Before The Virginia Alpha of The Phi Beta Kappa Society,*

. . . *William and Mary College*, . . . *July the 3rd, 1855.* Richmond, 1855.

Guy, George W. Community Leagues Of Virginia And Their Contribution To Rural Education. [*N. E. A. Proc's*, (1922) LX, 1203–07.]

Hakluyt, Richard. *A Discourse on Western Planting.* [*Maine Hist. Soc. Coll.* II.] Cambridge, 1877.

Hakluyt, Richard. *The Principal Navigations Voyages Traffiques & Discoveries of the English Nation.* 12 vols. MacLehose: Glasgow, 1904.

Hall, W. L., editor. *Quesnay de Beaurepaire. Memoir Concerning the Academy of the Arts and Sciences for the United States of America.* [*18th Ann. Rep't, Lib. B'd, Va. State Library,* 1920–21.] Richmond, 1922.

Hammond, John. *Leah and Rachel, Or, the Two Fruitfull Sisters Virginia, And Maryland. London, 1656.* [Force's *Tracts*, III, No. XIV, Washington, 1844.]

The Hampton Bulletin. Report of the Hampton Negro Conference, [(Sept., 1905) I, No. 3; (Oct., 1912) VIII, No. 7.] *Principal's Reports,* [(June, 1905) 37th Rep't, I, No. 2; (June, 1914) 46th Rep't, X, No. 3; (May, 1915) 47th Rep't, XI, No. 4; (May, 1916) 48th Rep't, XII, No. 3; (May, 1918) 50th Rep't, XIV, No. 4; (May, 1919) 51st Rep't, XV, No. 4; (May, 1920) 52nd Rep't, XVI, No. 4; (Oct., 1921) 53rd Rep't, XVII, No. 5; (May, 1922) 54th Rep't, XVIII, No. 4; (May, 1926) 58th Rep't, XXII, No. 3.] Hampton Institute, Hampton, Va.

The Hampton Normal and Agricultural Institute Act of Incorporation By-Laws Extracts from the Code of Virginia, Etc. For The Use Of The Trustees. [Pamphlet] Hampton, 1916.

Handbook for Speakers Campaign for Catholic Education. [Pamphlet: *Education Bulletins,* (Feb., 1923) No. 8.] National Catholic Welfare Council: Washington, 1923.

Hansbrough, G. W. *Reports Supreme Court of Appeals.* Vol. LXXVII. Richmond, 1884.

Hariot, Thomas. *Narrative of the First English Plantation of Virginia. London, 1588.* [Reprint: Quaritch: London, 1893.]

Harman, John Newton. *Annals Of Tazewell County, Virginia From 1800 to 1922.* 2 vols. Richmond, 1922.

Harris, William T. The Relation Of School Discipline To Moral Education. [*Va. Sch. Jour.,* (Dec., 1897) VI, 324–30.]

Harris, William T. School Statistics And Morals. [*N. E. A. Proc's,* (1894) XXXIII, 342–49; *Va. Sch. Jour.,* (May, 1901) X, 134–37.]

Harrison, Corinne. What Makes—What Mars, The Teacher? [*N. E. A. Proc's,* (1894) XXXIII, 136–42.]

Harrower, John. Documents of John Harrower, 1773–1776. [*Amer. Hist. Review,* (Oct., 1900) VI, 65–107.]

[Hartlib, Samuel]. *The Reformed Virginian Silk-Worm.* London, *1655.* [Force's *Tracts,* III, No. 13.]   Washington, 1844.

Hartwell, [Henry], Blair, [James] & Chilton, [Edward]. *The Present State of Virginia, and the College: . . . To which is added, The Charter for Erecting the said College, . . .* London, 1727. [*Cf.* also *Coll. Mass. Hist. Soc.,* Ser. I, V, 124, [Harrison, Carter B.].   An Account of the Present State and Government of Virginia.]

Hawks, Francis L. *Contributions To The Ecclesiastical History Of The United States Of America.* Vol. I.   New York, 1836.

Hawks, Francis L. & Perry, W. S. *Journals of the General Convention of the Protestant Episcopal Church in the United States of America, from A. D. 1785 to A. D. 1853, inclusive.* Vol. I, Philadelphia, 1861.

Hazard, Ebenezer. *Historical Collections.* 2 vols.   Philadelphia, 1792.

Heath, James E.   A Lecture Delivered before the Richmond Lyceum, . . . July 13, 1838. [*So. Lit Messenger,* (Nov., 1838) IV, 705–11.]

Hening, William Waller. *The Statutes at Large,* 13 vols.   Richmond, 1809–23.

Henley, S. *The Distinct Claims of Government and Religion Considered In A Sermon Preached Before The Honourable House Of Burgesses, At Williamsburg, in Virginia, March 1, 1772.* Cambridge, 1772.

Henneman, John Bell.   Historic Elements In Virginia Education and Literary Effort.   A paper read before the Virginia Historical Society, Monday, December 21st, 1891. [*Coll. Va. Hist. Society,* (1892) N. S., XI, 25–46.]

Henry, William Wirt.   The Part Taken by Virginia, under the Leadership of Patrick Henry, in Establishing Religious Liberty as a Foundation of American Government.   New York, 1888. [Address, April 27, 1886; *Amer. Hist. Assoc. Papers,* II, No. 1, 29.]

Higher Female Education. [*Va. Educ. Jour.,* (May, 1879) X, 212–14.]

Hillman, J. N.   Directions For Securing High School Credit For Bible Study. [*Va. Jour. Educ.,* (Nov., 1921) XV, 102–03.]

Hinke, Wm. J.   (Trans. & Annotated by)   The Germans In Madison County, Va.   Documents Bearing on Their History. [*Va. Mag. Hist.,* (Oct., 1906) XIV, 136–69.]

Hinke, Wm. J., & Kemper, Charles E., editors.   Moravian Diaries Of Travels Through Virginia. [*Va. Mag. Hist.,* (Jan., 1904) XI, 225–42; (April, 1904) XI, 370–93; (July, 1904) XII, 55–82.]

Hinke, Wm. J., & Kemper, Charles E., editors.   Record Of The Peaked Mountain Church, Rockingham County, Va. [*Wm. & Mary Coll. Quart.,* (April, 1905) XIII, 247–56; (Jan., 1906) XIV, 186–93.]

Hinsdale, B. A.   President Elliot on Public School Problems.   Address before . . . the Michigan State Teachers' Association. [*Va. Educ. Jour.,* (May, 1886) XVII, 193–98.]

Hinsdale, Burke A., & Demmon, Isaac N. *History Of The University Of Michigan.   With Biographical Sketches.* Ann Arbor, 1906.

Historical and Genealogical Notes. [A State University.] [*Wm. & Mary Coll. Quart.*, (July, 1902, 74–78.]

Historical Notes and Queries. Free Schools and the Church in the Seventeenth Century. [*Va. Mag. Hist.*, (Jan., 1894) I, 326–27.]

Historical Notes And Queries. Free Schools In Virginia In The Seventeenth Century. [*Va. Mag. Hist.*, (July, 1894) II, 97–99.]

Hodgson, Joseph, Jr. *Science the Handmaid of Republicanism A Valedictory Oration: Delivered Before the Jefferson Society of the University of Virginia, July 28th, 1858.* Richmond, 1858.

Hoge, Moses D. *The Memories, Hopes And Duties Of The Hour: A Historic Discourse, Delivered At Washington And Lee University, Lexington, Virginia, June 15, 1886.* Richmond, 1886.

Holcombe, James P. *An Address . . . Before the Society of Alumni, of the University of Virginia, . . . June 29th, 1853.* Richmond, 1853.

Holland, R. A. *Integrity of Character: The Proper Aim of Education. An Address . . . Before The Literary Societies of Washington College, . . . June 24th, 1869.* Baltimore, 1869.

Holliday, Fred W. M. *The Higher Education The Hope of American Republicanism, Annual Address . . . Before the Society of the Alumni of the University of Virginia, June 29th, 1876.* Winchester, 1876.

Hornbeck, M. D. The Relation Of The College To The Morals Of The Student. [*N. E. A. Proc's*, (1890) XXIX, 690–96.]

Horner, Frederick. *Autographs Of The University Of Virginia.* 1892–93. New York, 1892.

House Bill, No. 353, 1924. Richmond.

Howard, John. *An Address On Popular Education In Virginia . . . July 13, 1850, . . . Richmond College.* [*Virginia Education Pamphlets,* Vol. II, Va. State Library.] Richmond, 1850.

Hunt, Gaillard. *The Writings of James Madison.* 9 vols. Putnam: New York, 1910.

The Inauguration Of William Lyne Wilson, LL. D. As President Of Washington and Lee University, Lexington, Va., September 15, 1897. Lynchburg [? 1897]

Instructions to Berkeley, 1642. [MacDonald Papers, Va. State Library, Pages 376–88.] [*Va. Mag. Hist.*, (Jan., 1895) II, 281–88.]

Instructions To Berkeley, 1662. [*Va. Mag. Hist.*, (July, 1895) III, 15–20.]

Instructions to Governor Yeardley, 1618. [*Va. Mag. Hist.*, (Oct., 1894) II, 154–65.]

Instructions to Yeardley, 1626. [McDonald Papers, I, Virginia State Library] [*Va. Mag. Hist.*, (April, 1895) II, 393–96.]

Ireland, John. State Schools And Parish Schools—Is Union Between Them Impossible? [*N. E. A. Proc's*, (1890) XXIX, 179–85.]

Isle of Wight County Wills. [(Contributed by R. S. Thomas) *Va. Mag. Hist.*, (Oct., 1898) VI, 111–23.]

Jacobitism In Virginia. Charges Against Captain Jacob Lumpkin. (From Virginia Archives.) [*Va. Mag. Hist.*, (April, 1899) VI, 389–96.]

Jackson, Luther P. The History of V. N. I. I. [Address delivered at the State College on President's Day, 1927; *Va. Normal and Industrial Institute Gazette*, (Sept., 1928) XXXII, No. 5, 18.]

James, Edward W. The Norfolk Academy. [*Wm. & Mary Coll. Quart.*, (July, 1894) III, 3–8.]

Jefferson, Thomas. *Notes On The State Of Virginia.* Boston, 1801.

[Johnson, Robert]: *The New Life of Virginea. London, 1612.* [Force's *Tracts*, I, No. VII, Washington, 1836.]

[Johnson, Robert]: *Nova Britannia. London, 1609.* [Force's *Tracts*, I, No. VI, Washington, 1836.]

Jones, Hugh. *The Present State Of Virginia. London, 1724.* [Sabin's Reprints, No. V, New York, 1865.]

[Jourdain or Jourdan, Silvester]: *A Plaine Description Of The Barmvdas. London, 1613.* [Force's *Tracts*, III, No. III, Washington, 1844.]

Journal Of The Acts and Proceedings of A General Convention Of The State of Virginia, Assembled At Richmond, . . . 1861. Richmond, 1861.

Journal Of Col. James Gordon, Of Lancaster County, Va. [*Wm. & Mary Coll. Quart.*, (Oct., 1902) XI, 98–112.]

Journal Of The Constitutional Convention Of The State of Virginia, Convened In The City of Richmond December 3, 1867. Richmond, 1867.

Journal Of The Constitutional Convention Of Virginia. Held In The City Of Richmond, Beginning June 12th, 1901. Richmond, 1901.

Journals Of The Council Of Virginia In Executive Sessions, 1737–1763. (From the Originals in the Virginia State Archives. [*Va. Mag. Hist.*, (July, 1906) XIV, 1–35.]

Journals of the House of Burgesses, 1619–1755. 13 vols. [Kennedy, J. P.; McIlwaine, H. R., editors.] Richmond, 1905–15.

Journals of the House of Delegates. [For check-list of volumes in Va. State Library, see *Bull., Va. State Library*, Vol. 10, Nos. 1–4, (1917), Appendix Y, 1076–77.] Richmond, 1776–1924.

Journal of the Meetings of the President and Masters of William and Mary College. [*Wm. & Mary Coll. Quart.*, (Oct., 1893) II, 122–27; (April, 1894) III, 256–59; (Oct., 1895) IV, 130–32.]

Journal of the Senate of the Commonwealth of Virginia. [For check-list of volumes, in Va. State Library, see *Bull., Va. State Library*, Vol. 10, Nos. 1–4, (1917) Appendix Z, 1077–78.] Richmond, 1776–1924.

Joynes, Edward Southey. *Education After The War. A Letter addressed to a member of the Southern Educational Convention, Columbia, S. C., 28th April, 1863.* Richmond, 1863. [Also, *So. Lit. Messenger*, (Aug., 1863) XXXVII, 485–92.]

Judge St. George Tucker's Pamphlet In Relation To Williamsburg. [*Wm. & Mary Coll. Quart.*, (Jan., 1894) II, 181–203.]

Junkin, George. *The Baccalaureate Address, Delivered On Commencement Day of Washington College, Lexington, Va., July 3rd, 1852.* Richmond, 1852.

Kemper, James L. *Address Of Gov. James L. Kemper Of Virginia, On The First Award Of The Jackson-Hope Medals, Virginia Military Institute, July 3, 1877.*

Kingsbury, Susan Myra. *The Records of The Virginia Company of London.* 2 vols. Washington, 1906.

Knox, Samuel. *An Essay On The Best System Of Liberal Education.* Baltimore, 1799.

La Rochefoucauld-Liancourt. *Voyage Dans Les États-Unis D' Amérique. Fait En 1795, 1796 Et 1797.* 8 vols. Paris, L' An VII De La Republique.

Lang, John Dunmore. *Religion And Education In America.* London, 1840.

Laying the Corner Stone of Quesnay's Academy. (From The Virginia Gazette or The American Advertiser, Richmond, June 28, 1786.) [*Va. Mag. Hist.,* (Jan., 1904) XI, 253–55.]

Lederer, John. *Discoveries in Three Marches from Virginia.* London, *1672.* [Reprint for G. P. Humphrey; Rochester, N. Y., 1902, No. 205; Reprint of Walker, Evans & Cogswell; Charleston, S. C., 1891.]

Lee, Robert E. *Recollections And Letters Of General Robert E. Lee.* Doubleday, Page: New York, 1904.

Legislative Journals of the Council of Colonial Virginia. 3 vols. [McIlwaine, H. R., editor] Richmond, 1918.

Leland, John. *The History of Hornworm and Pismire. Or, The Pismire's Plea, Don't Tread On Me.* Philadelphia, 1845. [In Hist. Soc. of Penn'a.]

Letters. [*Wm. & Mary Coll. Quart.,* (Jan., 1897) V, 149–59.]

Letters From Civis—No. 5. [*Relig. Herald,* (Feb. 14, 1878) XIII; *cf.* (Jan. 31, 1878) for No. 3, (Feb. 7, 1878) for No. 4, and (Mar. 14, 1878) ''A Response to the Rejoinder of 'Civis' '' by J. Wm. Jones, and (Mar. 21, 1878) ''Civis Reply to Dr. Jones''; (Feb. 28, 1878) ''The University of Virginia. Reply To Civis by J. Wm. Jones''; (Mar. 7, 1878) ''Rejoinder to Dr. Jones.'']

Letters From Samuel Davies. [*Va. Evang. & Lit. Mag.,* (Dec., 1819) II, 535–43.]

Letters From Thomas Jefferson To William B. Giles In Regard To Central College. [*Va. Mag. Hist.,* (Oct., 1921) XXIX, 445–57.]

Letters From Virginia Quakers. [(Contributed by M. Ethel Crawshaw) *Wm. & Mary Coll. Quart.,* (Jan., 1926) VI, 88–93.]

Letters From William and Mary, 1795–1799. From Originals in the Collection of Mr. Thomas S. Watson. [*Va. Mag. Hist.,* (July, 1922) XXX, 223–49.]

Letters From William and Mary College, 1798–1801. [*Va. Mag. Hist.,* (April, 1921) XXIX, 129–79.]

Letter of Judge John Tyler, [To Judge St. George Tucker,] Greenway, July 10th, 1795. [*Wm. & Mary Coll. Quart.,* (Jan., 1894) II, 200–03.]

Letter Of Sir Francis Wyatt, Governor of Virginia, 1621–1626. [*Wm. & Mary Coll. Quart.,* (April, 1926) N. S., VI, 114–21.]

Letters Of Patrick Henry, Sr., Samuel Davies, James Maury, Edwin Conway And George Trask. [*Wm. & Mary Coll. Quart.,* (Oct., 1921) N. S., I, 261–81.]

Letters of Prof. Robert Andrews To Major Everard Meade Of Amelia. [*Wm. & Mary Coll. Quart.,* (July, 1924) N. S., IV, 162–67.]

Letters Of Rev. James Madison, President Of The College Of William And Mary, To Thomas Jefferson. [*Wm. & Mary Coll. Quart.,* (April, 1925) N. S., V, 77–95; (July, 1925) V, 145–58.]

Letters of Wm. Fitzhugh. [*Va. Mag. Hist.,* (April, 1894) I, 391–410; (Jan., 1895) II, 259–75; (April, 1895) II, 370–79; (July, 1895) III, 1–15; (July, 1898) VI, 60–72.]

Letters On Education. [(A Country Correspondent) *Va. Evang. & Lit. Mag.,* (April, 1823) VI, 173–79; (May, 1823) VI, 249–56; (June, 1823) VI, 300–06.]

Letters To David Watson. [*Va. Mag. Hist.,* (July, 1921) XXIX, 257–86.]

Letter (I–VII) To The President and Directors of the Literary Fund. [(Philodemus) *Va. Evang. & Lit. Mag.,* (Feb., 1826) IX, 83–86; (Mar., 1826) IX, 133–37; (April, 1826) IX, 196–201; 201–04; 205–10; (June, 1826) 315–18; (July, 1826) 350–54.]

Lipscomb, Andrew A. *The Writings Of Thomas Jefferson.* 20 vols. Thomas Jefferson Memorial Association; Washington, 1904.

Lischka, Charles N., editor. *Private Schools and State Laws 1925.* [Pamphlet: *Education Bulletins,* (Jan., 1926) No. 3.] National Catholic Welfare Conference; Washington, 1926.

Lord Culpeper's Surrender Of The Arlington-Culpeper Grant Of All Virginia. [*Va. Mag. Hist.,* (April, 1924) XXXII, 192–95.]

McBryde, John M., Jr. Womanly Education For Women. [(Address . . . Richmond Education Association, . . . March 1, 1907.) *Sewanee Review* (Oct., 1907) XV, 467–84.]

McCabe, W. Gordon. The First University In America 1619–22. An Address . . . May 31, 1911. [*Va. Mag. Hist.,* (April, 1922) XXX, 133–56.]

M'Calla, Daniel. *The Works Of The Rev. Daniel M'Calla, D. D.* 2 vols. Charleston, 1810.

McIlwaine, Henry R., editor. *Executive Journals Of The Council of Colonial Virginia.* 3 vols. Richmond, 1925–28.

McIlwaine, H. R., editor. *Official Letters Of The Governors of the State of Virginia.* 2 vols. Richmond, 1926, 1928.

McIlwaine, Richard. *Addresses & Papers Bearing Chiefly On Education.* Richmond, 1908.

McKim, Randolph H. *The Relations Of The State To The University. An Address Delivered Before The Society of the Alumni of the University of Virginia, June 15, 1898.* Washington, 1898.

Madison, James. A Memorial and Remonstrance, Against the general assessment, presented to the general assembly of Virginia, at the session for the year of our Lord one thousand seven hundred and eighty-five. [Niles: *Register,* (July 5, 1817) XII, 295–97.]

Mahone, William. *Attitude Of The Readjusters Of Virginia Concerning The State Debt, Free Schools, A Free Ballot, And A Fair Count. Speech . . . March 28, 1881.* Washington, 1881.

Makemie, Francis. *A Plain And Friendly Perswasive To The Inhabitants Of Virginia And Maryland, For Promoting Towns And Cohabitation.* London, 1705. [*Va. Mag. Hist.,* (Jan., 1897) IV, 252–71.]

Markland, J.[ohn]. *Typographia. An Ode, On Printing.* Williamsburg, 1730.

Marryat, C. B. *A Diary In America, With Remarks on Its Institutions.* New York, 1839.

Martin, Joseph. *A New And Comprehensive Gazetteer Of Virginia.* Charlottesville, 1836.

May, Robert. *A voice from Richmond, and other addresses to children and youth.* Philadelphia, [1842.]

Meade, Wm. *A Brief Review of the Episcopal Church in Virginia, . . . Being Part of an Address . . . May 22d, 1845.* Richmond, 1845.

Meade, Wm. *Pastoral Letter On Schools And Teachers To The Ministers And Members Of The Dioceses of Virginia.* Washington, 1858.

Meade, Wm. *Sermon, By . . . Preached On Sunday, February 16, 1840, In The Chapel Of The Theological Seminary Of Virginia, To The Students Of The High School And The Fairfax Institute, And Published By Their Request.* Washington, 1840.

Meade, Wm. *Sermon, Delivered in the Rotunda of the University of Virginia, On Sunday, May 24, 1829.* Charlottesville, 1829.

Memorial of the Convention of Colleges, Recently Assembled in the City of Richmond, asking an appropriation From the Literary Fund. Richmond, 1844.

Memorial Number To Dr. L. A. Fox. [*Roanoke College Bulletin,* (Aug., 1925) XV, No. 1.] Salem, 1925.

Memorials To The General Assembly Of Virginia. [*Va. Evang. & Lit. Mag.,* (Jan., 1826) IX, 30–49.]

Mereness, Newton D., editor. *Travels In The American Colonies.* Macmillan: New York, 1916.

Metcalf, John Calvin, editor. *The Centennial Of The University of Virginia 1819–1921.* Putnam: New York, 1922.

Miller, J. I.   Courses and Standards in High Schools for Girls.   [*Va. Educ. Jour.*, (Nov., 1880) XI, 360–66.]

Minor, John B.   Social Life At The University Of Virginia.   [*Lippincott's Magazine*, (July, 1887) XL, 98–109.]

Minor, Lucian.   An Address On Education, As Connected With The Permanence Of Our Republican Institutions.   Delivered before the Institute of Education of Hampden Sidney College, . . . September the 24th, 1835, . . . by Lucian Minor, Esq. of Louisa.   [*So. Lit. Messenger*, (Dec., 1835) II, 17–24; Morrison: *Six Addresses*, 41–47.]

Minor, Lucian.   *Discourse On The Life And Character Of The Late John A. G. Davis, Professor Of Law In The University of Virginia, Delivered Before The Society Of Alumni, June 29th, 1847.*   Richmond, 1847.

Minutes Of The Council And General Court, 1622–1624.   From The Originals In The Library of Congress.   [*Va. Mag. Hist.*, (Oct., 1911) XIX, 374–89.]

Minutes Of The Council And General Court, 1622–1629.   (From the Originals in the Library of Congress.)   [*Va. Mag. Hist.*, (Jan., 1913) XXI, 45–61; (April, 1915) XXIII, 124–38; (July, 1915) XXIII, 269–79; (July, 1917) XXV, 225–38; (Jan., 1918) XXVI, 1–16; (Oct., 1922) XXX, 348–61; (April, 1923) XXXI, 146–52; (July, 1923) XXI, 207–14.]

Minutes Of The Council And General Court 1624–1629.   From the Originals in the Library of Congress.   [*Va. Mag. Hist.*, (Oct., 1917) XXV, 337–51.]

Minutes of the Educational Association of Virginia . . . July 17th, 1866.   Richmond, 1866.

Minutes of the Educational Association of Virginia . . . July 16, 17, 18, 19, 1867.   Lynchburg, 1867.

Minutes and Reports of the Educational Association of Virginia.   Third Annual Session . . . July 21–24, 1868.   Lynchburg, 1868.

Minutes of the Educational Association of Virginia.   Fourth Annual Session . . . July 13–16, 1869.   Lynchburg, 1870.

Minutes of the Educational Association of Virginia.   Fifth Annual Session . . . July 12–15, 1870.   Richmond, 1870.

Minutes of the Educational Association of Virginia.   Sixth Annual Session . . . July 11–14, 1871.   Richmond, 1871.

Minutes of the Educational Association of Virginia.   Seventh Annual Session . . . July 9–12, 1872.   Richmond, 1873.

Minutes of the Educational Association of Virginia.   Eighth Annual Session . . . July 8th, 9th, 10th, and 11th, 1873.   Richmond, 1874.

Minutes of the Evangelical Society of Philadelphia, 1808–17.   [Ms. in Hist. Soc. of Penn'a.]

Minutes of the Fifteenth Annual Meeting Of the Presbyterian Educational Association of the South.   Montreat, N. C. July 3–8, 1928.   Louisville, 1928.

Minutes Of The One Hundred And Forty-Second Annual Session of the Dover Baptist Association. Richmond, 1925.

Minutes of the Teachers' Convention, Assembled at Petersburg, Va., Dec. 29th, 1863; and of the Educational Association of Virginia, organized thereby. Petersburg, 1866.

Miscellaneous Colonial Documents. From The Originals In The Virginia State Archives. [*Va. Mag. Hist.*, (July, 1908) XVI, 72–84.]

Mitchell, S. C. The Part Of The Citizen In Aiding The Cause Of Public Education. [*Proc's 6th Conf. Educ. South*, (1903) 190–93.]

Mitchell, S. C. Present Situation in the South. [*Proc's 7th Conf. Educ. South*, (1904) 161–67.]

Montagu, Basil. *The Works of Francis Bacon.* 3 vols. Philadelphia, 1841.

Monteiro, Walter. *Address Delivered Before The Neotrophian Society Of The Hampton Academy, On The Twenty-Eighth Of July, 1857.* By . . . of Goochland, . . . Richmond, 1857.

Montgomery, Robert. *A Discourse Concerning the design'd Establishment Of a New Colony To The South of Carolina.* London, 1717. [Force's *Tracts*, I, No. I, Washington, 1836.]

Monuments In Living Leaders. [Pamphlet; no date] Presbyterian Church in the United States: Louisville.

Moore, T. V. *The Reformation The Source of American Liberty. An Address, Delivered Before the Union Society Of Hampden Sydney College, June 9th, 1852.* Richmond, 1852.

Moore, Walter W., Miller, William R., and Lacy, John A., editors. *General Catalogue Of The Trustees, Officers, Professors And Alumni Of Union Theological Seminary In Virginia 1807–1924.* Whittet & Shepperson: Richmond, 1924.

[Mordecai, Samuel]. *Richmond In By-Gone Days.* Richmond, 1856.

Morrison, Alfred J., editor. *Six Addresses On The State Of Letters And Science In Virginia Delivered Chiefly Before The Literary And Philosophical Society At Hampden-Sidney College And The Institute of Education of Hampden-Sidney College 1824–1835.* Roanoke, 1917.

Morrison, Alfred J., editor. *Travels in the Confederation (1783–1784) From the German of Johann David Schoepf.* 2 vols. Campbell: Philadelphia, 1911.

Morrison, Alfred J., editor. *Travels In Virginia In Revolutionary Times.* Bell: Lynchburg, 1922.

Morse, Jedidiah. *American Gazetteer.* Boston, 1804.

Morse, Jedidiah. *An Abridgment of the American Gazetteer.* Boston, 1798.

Neill, Edward D. *Early Settlement of Virginia and Virginiola.* Minneapolis, 1878.

Neill, Edward D. *History of the Virginia Company of London.* Albany, 1869.

Neill, Edward D. *Virginia Vetusta, During the Reign of James the First.* Albany, 1885.

Nelson County School Regulations. [*Va. Educ. Jour.*, (Nov., 1877) IX, 41–42.]

Nelson Letter Book. [*Wm. & Mary Coll. Quart.*, (July, 1898) VII, 25–30.]

Nelson, R. B. The Winchester School Situation. [*Va. Teacher*, (June, 1923) IV, 165–68.]

Nelson, Wm. H. Dr. Dabney and the Free Schools. [*Va. Educ. Jour.*, Feb., 1879) X, 68–72.]

News And Notes (Resolution at Rural Life Conference, U. of Va.) [*Relig. Educ.*, (Feb., 1916) XI, 76.]

The Norfolk Academy. [*Lower Norfolk Co., Va. Antiquary*, (1897) I, Part 1, 21–36.]

Norfolk Academy, 1848. [*Lower Norfolk Co., Va. Antiquary*, (1904) IV, Part 1, 26–32.]

Norfolk Public School. [*Lower Norfolk Co., Va. Antiquary*, (1897) I, Part 3, 78–81.]

Norfolk Schools 1795. [*Lower Norfolk Co., Va. Antiquary*, (1904) IV, Part 3, 106–08.]

The Normal Bulletin State Normal School. [S. S., V, No. 2, Mar., 1918; Announcements for 1918–19, No. 4, May, 1918] East Radford, Va.

Notes And Queries. Abraham Sallé to George I. [*Va. Mag. Hist.*, (April, 1926) XXXIV, 159–60.]

Notes And Queries. Early Presbyterians in Virginia. [*Va. Mag. Hist.*, (Oct., 1902) 208–17.]

Notes And Queries. Naturalization of Jacob Holtzclaw. [*Va. Mag. Hist.*, (Jan., 1921) 98–100.]

Notes And Queries. Society of the Cincinnati in Virginia. [*Va. Mag. Hist.*, (July, 1893) I, 95–97.]

Notes And Queries. Wills of Robert And John Page. [*Va. Mag. Hist.*, (July, 1926) XXXIV, 275–77.]

Official Attitude Of The Catholic Church On Education. [Pamphlet: *Education Bulletins* (Feb., 1923) No. 1.] National Catholic Welfare Council: Washington, 1923.

Official Department. The Hope of Society. [*Va. Educ. Jour.*, (Dec., 1881) XII, 369–70.]

Organization Of The Virginia Historical Society; Officers and Members: With A List Of Its Publications. Richmond, 1881.

Original Letters. [*Wm. & Mary Coll. Quart.*, (Oct., 1895) IV, 103–11.]

Papers From The Virginia State Auditor's Office, Now In The State Library. [*Va. Mag. Hist.*, (Oct., 1917) XXV, 376–88.]

Papers Relating to the Administration of Governor Nicholson and to the Founding of William and Mary College. [*Va. Mag. Hist.*, (Oct.,

1899) VII, 153–72; (April, 1900) VII, 386–401; (Oct., 1900) VIII, 126–46; (April, 1901) VIII, 366–85; (July, 1901) VIII, 18–29; (Jan., 1902) IX, 251–62.]

Papers Relating To The College. [*Wm. & Mary Coll. Quart.*, (Jan., 1908) XVI, 162–80.]

Papers Relating To The Founding Of The College. [*Wm. & Mary Coll. Quart.*, (Jan., 1899) VII, 158–74.]

Parks, William, printer. *The Charter, and Statutes of the College of William and Mary in Virginia. In Latin and English.* 1736. [In Hist. Soc. of Penn'a.]

Part of Sir John Randolph's Will. [*Wm. & Mary Coll. Quart.*, (Oct., 1924) N. S., IV, 286–88.]

Patton, James T. Letter On The Location Of Robert Alexander's School, John Brown's Residence, And Mount Pleasant. [*Wash. & Lee Hist. Papers*, (1890) No. 1, 125–29.]*

Patton, John M. *Address Delivered Before the Society of Alumni of the Virginia Military Institute* July 4th, 1871. Richmond, 1873. [*Va. Education*, II, Va. State Library.]

Payne, Bruce. Report From Virginia. [*Proc's Ninth Conf. Educ. South*, (1906) 34–36.]

Peabody, Francis G. Address. [*Proc's 6th Conf. Educ. South*, (1903) 237–40.]

Peabody, F. G. Harvard University And The University Of Virginia. Address at the Meeting of Conference for Education in the South, April 25, 1903. [*U. of Va., Alum. Bull.*, (Oct., 1903) N. S., III, No. 4, 159–62.]

Perry, William Stevens. *Historical Collections Relating to the American Colonial Church.* Vol. I—*Virginia.* Hartford, 1870.

Pitt, R. H. *Soul Liberty Some of Its Implications. An Address delivered at the Baptist General Association of Virginia, November 12, 1925.* Sunday School Board Southern Baptist Convention: Nashville.

[Pollard, John Garland]: *A Memorial Addressed by the Baptist General Association of Virginia to the General Assembly of Virginia 1926, Against the Compulsory Reading of the Bible in the Public Schools.* [No date]

Pollock, James K. *Readings in American Government.* Holt: New York, 1927.

Popular Education. [*So. Lit. Messenger*, (Feb., 1842), VIII, 114–21.]

Preliminary Report of Committee On Moral Training In Public Schools. [*N. E. A. Proc's*, (1908) XLVI, 44–57.]

Proceedings Of The Capon Springs Conference For Education in the South. 2 vols. Raleigh, 1899, 1900. [Second and Third Conferences.]

Proceedings Of The . . . Conference For Education In The South. 11 vols. [Fourth to Fourteenth Conference 1901–1911; continuation of Capon Springs Conference.]

Proceedings of The National Teachers Association. 1858–1870.

Proceedings of the Presbytery of Hanover, May 6, 1826. [Excerpt obtained through courtesy of officers of Union Theological Seminary.]

Proceedings Sixty-Second Annual Session of the Iowa State Teachers Association. Des Moines, 1916.

Proceedings Of The Vistors Of William And Mary College, 1716. [*Va. Mag. Hist.,* (Oct., 1896) IV, 161–75.]

Proceedings In York County Court. [*Wm. & Mary Coll. Quart.,* (July, 1902) XI, 28–38.]

Progress Of Education In The United States And Europe. [*De Bow's Review,* (Jan., 1855) XVIII, 132–39.]

Proposed Amendments To The Constitution of Virginia Agreed to by the General Assembly of Virginia at the Regular Session of 1926 and the Extra Session of 1927. Richmond, 1927.

Prosecution Of Baptist Ministers, Chesterfield County, Va., 1771–'73. [*Va. Mag. Hist.,* (April, 1904) XI, 415–17.]

Public Opinion And The Need Of Religious Education. [Pamphlet: *Education Bulletins,* (Feb., 1923) No. 7.] National Catholic Welfare Council: Washington, 1923.

Purchas, Samuel. *Hakluytus Posthumus or Purchas His Pilgrimes.* 20 vols. MacLehose: Glasgow, 1906.

[Puryear, B.]: *The Public School In Its Relations To The Negro. By Civis. Published By Request, From The Southern Planter and Farmer.* Richmond, 1877.

Quakers' Petition. [*Va. Gazette,* Williamsburg, Nov. 10–17, 1738; *Wm. & Mary Coll. Quart.,* (July, 1905) XIV, 23–25.]

Quesnay, Chevalier Alexander Maria de Beaurepaire. *Mémoire Statuts Et Prospectus Concernant L' Académie Des Sciences Et Beaux Arts Des États-Unis De L' Amérique Établie A Richmond, Capitale De La Virginie.* Paris, 1788.

[Randolph, J. W., edition]. *Early History Of The University of Virginia, As Contained In The Letters Of Thomas Jefferson And Joseph C. Cabell.* Richmond, 1856.

Randolph-Macon College. [(By Authority) *U. S. Bur. Educ., Circ. Inf.,* (1888) No. 1, 240–51] Washington, 1889.

The Randolph Manuscript. [Commission To Sir William Jones, &c., To Examine Into The State Of Virginia, May 9, 1624.] [*Va. Mag. Hist.,* (Oct., 1908) XVI, 113–31.]

The Randolph Manuscript. Memoranda From Virginia Records, 1688–90. [*Va. Mag. Hist.,* (Jan., 1912) XX, 1–13.]

The Randolph Manuscript. Virginia Seventeenth Century Records. From the Original in the Collection of the Virginia Historical Society. [*Va. Mag. Hist.,* (Jan., 1911) XIX, 1–12; (July, 1911) XIX, 240–47; (Oct., 1911) XIX, 337–47; (April, 1912) XX, 113–26; (July, 1912) XX,

225–34; (Oct., 1912) XX, 337–46; (July, 1913) XXI, 225–33; (Oct., 1913) XXI, 347–58.]

Mr. Randolph's Will. [Niles: *Register*, (July 30, 1836) L, 366–67.]

Records of John Casper Stoever. Harrisburg, 1896.

The Religious Education Association Proceedings. Vols. I–V. Chicago, 1903–08.

Religious Intelligence. [(Letter by Jesse S. Armstead) *Va. Evang. & Lit. Mag.*, (Feb., 1820) III, 95–97.]

Religious Intelligence. Domestic. A Plan for the organization, government and general arrangement of the Theological Seminary, adopted by the Synod of Virginia, Oct. 25, 1819. [*Va. Evang. & Lit. Mag.*, (Dec., 1819) II, 576–77.]

Religious Intelligence. Domestic. Constitution of the Board of Education of the Synod of Virginia. [*Va. Evang. & Lit. Mag.*, (Dec., 1819) II, 577.]

Religious Intelligence. Domestic. Seventh Anniversary Of The Bible Society Of Virginia. [*Va. Evang. & Lit. Mag.*, (April, 1820) III, 188–91.]

Remarks On A School Commissioner. [(A Friend To Learning.) *Va. Evang. & Lit. Mag.*, (Oct., 1825) VIII, 541–48.]

Report Of The Department Of Religious Education For The Year 1924. [Pamphlet.] The National Council [Prot. Episc. Church]: New York, 1925.

Report Of The Proceedings And Debates Of The Constitutional Convention State Of Virginia Held In The City Of Richmond June 12, 1901 to June 26, 1902. 2 vols. Richmond, 1906.

Report of the Virginia Education Commission To The General Assembly of the Commonwealth of Virginia 1912. Senate Doc. No. III. Richmond, 1912.

Rice, John H. A Discourse before the Literary and Philosophical Society of Hampden Sydney College, . . . 24th of September, 1824. [*Va. Evang. & Lit. Mag.*, (Jan., 1825) VIII, 1–9; (Feb., 1825) VIII, 57–65; Morrison: *Six Addresses, 7 ff.*]

Rice, J. H. *An Illustration of the Character and Conduct of the Presbyterian Church in Virginia.* Richmond, 1816.

Rives, Wm. C. *An Address Delivered Before The Society Of Alumni Of The University Of Virginia*, July 1, 1869. Richmond, 1869.

Robertson, John. *Introductory Address Delivered On Opening The Richmond Athenaeum January 31, 1852.* Richmond, 1852.

Robin, M. L' Abbé. *Nouveau Voyage Dans L' Amérique Septentrionale, En L' Année 1781; Et Campagne De L' Armée De M. Le Comte De Rochambeau.* A Philadelphie et se trouve a Paris . . . 1782.

Rowland, Kate Mason. *The Life of George Mason 1725–1792 Including His Speeches, Public Papers, and Correspondence.* 2 vols. New York, 1892.

Royall, Anne. *The Black Book; Or, A Continuation Of Travels, In The United States.* 2 vols. Washington, 1828.

Ruffner, Wm. H. Dr. Bittle and Roanoke College. [*Va. Educ. Jour.,* (Nov., 1876) VIII, 29–32.]

Ruffner, Wm. H. The Moral Element in Primary Education. [*N. E. A. Proc's,* 1876) XVI, 39–46.]

Ruffner, Wm. H. Moral Instruction in Schools. [*Va. Educ. Jour.,* (Nov., 1874) VI, 6–10.]

Ruffner, Wm. H. *The Public Free School System.* [1870–76 Collection of Circulars, Documents, in Va. State Library.]

Ruffner, Wm. H. *Public Schools—Difficulties Removed. Poverty VS. Education.* [1870–76 Collection of Circulars, Documents, in Va. State Library.]

Ruffner, Wm. H. Religion in the Public Schools. [*Va. Educ. Jour.,* (April, 1874) V, 258–62.]

Ruffner, Wm. H. Religious Worship In The Public Schools. [*Va. Educ. Jour.,* (Mar., 1871) II, 197.]

Ryan, James H. *A Catechism of Catholic Education.* National Catholic Welfare Council: Washington, 1922.

Salisbury, Albert. The Supplementing Of The War. [*N. E. A. Proc's,* (1884) XXIII, 96–105.]

Salley, Alexander S., editor. *Narratives of Early Carolina, 1650–1708.* [*Original Narratives of Early American History,* Vol. 12.] Scribner: New York, 1911.

Salyards, Joseph. *Shenandoah Valley, Extra Historical Review, of Shenandoah County, Virginia: Delivered . . . at Woodstock, Virginia, July 4th, 1876.* New Market.

Samuel, W. H. *The Debates and Proceedings of the Constitutional Convention of the State of Virginia, Assembled at the City of Richmond, Tuesday, December 3, 1867.* Vol. I. Richmond, 1868.

Sands, Alexander H. Intellectual Culture Of Women. An Address . . . before the Hollins Female Institute, at the Commencement, on the 6th April, 1859. [*So. Lit. Messenger,* (May, 1859) 321–32.]

Schermerhorn, John F., and Mills, Samuel J. *A Correct View of That Part of the United States Which Lies West of the Allegany Mountains With Regard to Religion and Morals.* Hartford, 1814.

Schools. [*Lower Norfolk Co., Va. Antiquary* (1904) IV, Part 1, 36–39.]

Schultz, Christian, Junior. *Travels on an Inland Voyage Through . . . Virginia . . .* 2 vols. New York, 1810.

Scott, Joseph. *A Geographical Dictionary: Of The United States Of North America.* Philadelphia, 1805.

Scott, Joseph. *The United States Gazetteer.* Philadelphia, 1795.

Sears, Barnas. *Education: An Address Delivered To The Constitutional Convention State of Virginia January 23, 1868.* Richmond, 1868.

Sears, Barnas. *Objections To Public Schools Considered: Remarks At The Annual Meeting Of The Trustees Of The Peabody Education Fund. New York, Oct. 7, 1875.* Boston, 1875.

Second Auditor's Report On The State Of The Literary Fund, And Proceedings Of The School Commissioners, In The Different Counties For The Year Ending . . . 1830, 1833, 1834, 1837, 1840, 1842–56 inc., 1858–61. [*Jour., H. Del., Doc.'s.*]

Semi-Centennial Celebration of the Theological Seminary of the Protestant Episcopal Church in the Diocese of Virginia. Baltimore, 1873.

Semple, Robert B. *A History Of The Rise And Progress Of The Baptists In Virginia.* Richmond, 1810.

Shields, Thos. Edward. Some Relations Between the Catholic School System and the Public School System. [*Cath. Educ. Assoc. Bull.*, (Nov., 1916) XIII, 51–62.]

Simon, Abram. Religion At A State University From The Jewish Point Of View. [*Relig. Educ.*, (Feb., 1917) XII, 37–39.]

Smith, Benj. M. Merits And Defects Of Common School Education In The United States. [In volume, *Circulars Common School Education*, Va. State Library; also in *Va. Educ. Jour.*, (Aug., 1870, I, 318–29.]

Smith, Benj. M. Report on the Prussian Primary School System. [*Jour., H. Del.*, 1839–40, Doc. No. 26.]

Smith, Charles Jeffery. Plan For An Academy At Providence, in New Kent. [*Wm. & Mary Coll. Quart.*, (Jan., 1923) N. S. III, 52–57.]

Smith, Francis H. *The Inner Life of the V. M. I. Cadet: Its Responsibilities And Its Privileges. Introductory Address . . . Sept. 10, 1866.* Lexington, 1873.

Smith, Francis H. *The Schools and Schoolmasters of Virginia in The Olden Time. An Address Read Before The Educational Association of Virginia . . . July, 1873.* Richmond, 1874.

Smith, John. [Gray, Wm. W. edition.] *True Travels Adventures and Observations.* 2 vols. Richmond, 1819.

Smith, John Augustine. *A Syllabus Of The Lectures Delivered To The Senior Students In The College Of William And Mary, On Government; . . . To which is added, A Discourse . . . On The Manner In Which Peculiarities In The Anatomical Structure Affect The Moral Character.* Printed For The University. Philadelphia; 1817.

Smith, Logan P. *Donne's Sermons.* Clarendon: Oxford, 1919.

Smythe, John F. D. *A Tour in the United States of America.* 1769–76. 2 vols. London, 1784. [Also, *Va. Hist. Register*, (Jan., 1853) VI, No. 1, 11–20; (April, 1853) VI, No. 2, 77–90; (July, 1853) VI, No. 3, 131–48; Morrison: *Travels in Virginia in Revolutionary Times*, Ch. I.]

Some Letters Of John Preston. [*Wm. & Mary Coll. Quart.*, (Jan., 1921) N. S., I, 42–51.]

Southall, James C. *An Address on the Subject of Democracy . . . Before the Society of Alumni of the University of Virginia, . . . July 3rd, 1860.* Baltimore, 1860.

Sparks, Jared. *The Writings of George Washington.* 12 Vols. Vol. IX, Boston, 1835.

[Spotswood, Alexander]. *The Official Letters of Alexander Spotswood, Lieutenant-Governor of the Colony of Virginia, 1710–1722.* 2 vols. [*Coll. Va. Hist. Society,* N. S., I & II, Brock, R. A., editor.] Richmond, 1882.

Squires, W. H. T. *The Turret's Twirl.* [Hampden-Sidney College, leaflet.]

Stanton, E. F. Manual Labor Schools. An Address Before the "Literary Institute" of Hampden Sidney College, at its annual Commencement, September, 1835. [*So. Lit. Messenger,* (Mar., 1836) II, 244–52.]

Statutes of the College of William and Mary in Virginia 1736. [*Bulletin of the College of William and Mary,* Williamsburg, Va. (Jan., 1914) Vol. VII, No. 3.]

Statutes of the Realm of England. Vol. VII. London, 1810.

Stearns, Wallace N. Religious Education In The State Universities. [*N. E. A. Proc's,* (1907) XLV, 729–35.]

Stephenson, L. B. *Why I believe in Hampden-Sidney.* [Hampden-Sidney College, leaflet.]

Stevenson, Jno. W. *An Address Delivered Before The Society of Alumni Of The University Of Virginia, June 30, 1870.* Charlottesville, 1870.

Strachey, William, editor. *For The Colony in Virginea Britannia. Lavves Diuine, Morall and Martiall, &c.* London, 1612. [Force's *Tracts,* III, No. II, Washington, 1844.]

Strachey, William. *The History Of Travaile Into Virginia Britannia.* [*Hakluyt Society Publications,* VI; Major, R. H., editor.] London, 1849.

Students of the University of Virginia A Semi-Centennial Catalogue with Brief Biographical Sketches. Baltimore, 1878.

Summers, Lewis Preston. *History of Southwest Virginia, 1746–1786, Washington County, 1777–1870.* Richmond, 1903.

Sundry Documents On The Subject Of A System Of Public Education, For The State Of Virginia. Richmond, 1817.

Sutherlin, William T. *Address Delivered Before The Mechanics' Association Of Danville, Va. March 11, 1867.* Richmond, 1867.

Sydnor, T. W. Education in Virginia—Its Excellence, its Defects, its Future. [*Va. Educ. Jour.,* (Nov., 1880) XI, 344–49.]

Swem, Earl Gregg, editor. *Considerations on the Present State of Virginia.* Attributed to John Randolph and *Considerations on the Present State of Virginia Examined* by Robert Carter Nicholas. [Printed for C. F. Heartman.] New York, 1919.

Text-books for public high schools of Virginia, adopted March 23, 1905. [Circular No. 268, (Va. State Library).]

Theme: Current Criticism Of Public Schools, And What Answer? [*N. E. A. Proc's,* (1888) XXVII, 127–65.]

Theme: Denominational Schools. [*N. E. A. Proc's,* (1889) XXVIII, 111–79.]

Theological Seminary Under The Care Of The Presbytery Of Hanover. [*Va. Evang. & Lit. Mag.*, (June, 1826) 330–32.]

Thom, William T. Secondary Education: The Proper Relation of Secondary Schools to the State System of Public Schools and to Denominational Control. [*Va. Educ. Jour.*, (Jan., 1882) XIII, 20–31.]

Thomas, R. S. The *Religious Element in the Settlement at Jamestown, Historical Address*, . . . *June 10th, 1898.* Petersburg, 1898.

Thomas, W. D. A Liberal Education. Address before the Albemarle Association. [*Va. Educ. Jour.*, (Sept., 1883) XIV, 269–70.]

Thompson, Jno. R. *Education and Literature in Virginia. An Address . . . Before The Literary Societies of Washington College, 18 June, 1850.* Richmond, 1850.

Thornton, Wm. M. The Honour System At The University of Virginia In Origin And Use. [(Read before Assoc. of Prep. Sch'ls & Colleges in the Southern States, Nov., 1906) *Sewanee Review*, (Jan., 1907) XV, 41–57.]

Treasurer's Report to the Board of Trustees of Union Theological Seminary, 1883. [Excerpt obtained through courtesy of officers of Union Theological Seminary.]

The Treaty of Logg's Town, 1752. [*Va. Mag. Hist.*, (Oct., 1905) XIII, 143–74.]

Tucker, Beverley. A Lecture, Delivered to the Law Class of William and Mary College, June 17, 1839, . . . on the Philosophy of Government and Constitutional Law. [*So. Lit. Messenger*, (Sept., 1839) V, 587–92.]

Tucker, George. A Discourse On The Progress of Philosophy, and its Influence on the Intellectual and Moral Character of Man; delivered before the Virginia Historical and Philosophical Society, February 5, 1835. By . . . Professor of Moral Philosophy in the University of Virginia. [*So. Lit. Messenger*, (April, 1835) I, 405–21.]

Two Early Philanthropists. [*Lower Norfolk Co., Va. Antiquary*, (1897) I, Part 2, 65–66.]

Tyler, John. An Address, Delivered before the two Literary Societies of Randolph-Macon College, June 19, 1838. [*So. Lit. Messenger*, (Jan., 1839) V, 20–25.]

Tyler, John. Early Times Of Virginia—William And Mary College. [*De Bow's Review*, (Aug., 1859) XXVII, 136–49.]

Tyler, Lyon G. Early Courses And Professors At William And Mary College. [Extract from an address, Dec. 5, 1904, before the Alpha Chapter, Phi Beta Kappa; *Wm. & Mary Coll. Quart.*, (Oct., 1905) XIV, 71–83.]

Tyler, Lyon G. *The Letters And Times Of The Tylers.* 2 vols. Richmond, 1884.

Tyler, Lyon G. The Medical Men Of Virginia. [From an address to the graduating class, Medical College of Virginia, May 18, 1910; *Wm. & Mary Coll. Quart.*, (Jan., 1911) XIX, 145–62.]

Tyler, Lyon G. *Narratives of Early Virginia,* 1606–1625. Scribner: New York, 1907.

Tyler, Lyon G. Original Records Of The Phi Beta Kappa Society. [*Wm. & Mary Coll. Quart.,* (April, 1896) IV, 213–59.]

Tyler, Lyon G. Virginia's Contribution To Science. [An Address before the American Antiquarian Society, Worcester, Mass., Oct. 20, 1915; *Wm. & Mary Coll. Quart.,* (April, 1916) XXIV, 217–31.]

United States Bureau of the Census. [Fourth-Fourteenth Decennial Census, including census of Religious Bodies, 1926.] Washington, 1820–1928.

United States Bureau of Census. *Census of Prisoners: 1923 (Preliminary Report.)* [Pamphlet; no date.]

United States Bureau of the Census. *Friends.* [Census of Religious Bodies, (1926) Booklet $\frac{No. 11}{086–089}$.] Washington, 1928.

United States Bureau of the Census. *German Baptist Brethren (Dunkers).* [Census of Religious Bodies, (1926) Booklet $\frac{No. 10}{026–030}$.] Washington, 1928.

United States Bureau of the Census. *Press Summaries Census of Religious Bodies: 1926.* [Released for use of press at various dates, fall of 1927 on; available from the Bureau.] Washington, 1927–28.

United States Bureau of the Census. *Reformed Church In America.* [Census of Religious Bodies, (1926) Booklet $\frac{No. 6}{173}$.] Washington, 1928.

United States Bureau of the Census. *Reformed Church In The United States.* [Census of Religious Bodies, (1926) Booklet $\frac{No. 5}{174}$.] Washington, 1928.

United States Bureau of Education *Bulletins.* 1906–26. Washington.

United States Bureau of Education. *Circulars of Information.* Washington, 1871–1903.

United States Bureau of Education. *Reports of the Commissioner of Education.* Washington, 1868–1926.

University of Richmond. A Brief Sketch of Organization History And Present Resources. Richmond, 1927. [Booklet.]

University of Virginia. [*Amer. Jour. of Educ.,* (May, 1827) II, 313–14; (Jan., & Feb., 1929) IV, 79.]

University of Virginia. A Statement of Accomplishment and of Recent Growth. June, 1907.

The University of Virginia in the Life of the Nation. Academic Addresses Delivered on the Occasion of the Installation of Edwin Anderson Alderman as President of the University of Virginia. [No date.]

University of Virginia Record Extension Series. Charlottesville, University. 1915–1928. [Vol. I–XII, miscellaneous numbers.]

Unpublished Letters of Fullham, In The Library Of The Bishop Of London. [*Wm. & Mary Coll. Quart.,* (April, 1901) IX, 218–26.]

Valedictory In July 1829. *At the final breaking up of the — School, in consequence of the ill health of Mrs. xxxx, the Principal, after it had continued for eight years.* [*So. Lit. Mess.*, (Dec., 1834) I, 172–76.]

Van Zandt, A. B. *The Claims of Virginia upon her Educated Sons. An Address Delivered Before The Union Society Of Hampden Sidney College, June 13th, 1854.* Petersburg, 1854.

Vawter, C. E. The Educational and Social Advantages of Virginia. Address delivered before the Immigration Convention of Virginia. [*Va. Sch. Jour.*, (Dec., 1894) III, 331–32.]

Venable, C. S. The Plan Of The University Of Virginia. [*N. E. A. Proc's*, (1874) XIV, 163–72.]

The Vestry Book of King William Parish, Va., 1707–1750. (Translated from the French and annotated by Prof. R. H. Fife, Wesleyan University, and with an introduction by Col. R. L. Maury, Richmond, Virginia.) [*Va. Mag. Hist.*, (Jan., 1904) XI, 289–304; (April, 1904) XI, 425–40.]

Vethake, Henry. *An Address, Delivered At His Inauguration, As President Of Washington College, Lexington, Virginia, February 21st, 1835.* Lexington, 1835.

Virginia And Maryland, Or, The Lord Baltamore's printed Case, uncased and answered. London, 1655. [Force's *Tracts*, II, No. IX, Washington, 1838.]

The Virginia Assembly of 1641. A List of Members and Some of the Acts. [*Va. Mag. Hist.*, (July, 1901) IX, 50–59.]

The Virginia Clergy. Governor Gooch's Letters to the Bishop of London 1727–1749 From the Fulham Manuscripts. [*Va. Mag. Hist.*, (July, 1924) 209–36; (Oct., 1924) 321–37.]

Virginia Company of London. *A Declaration Of The State Of the Colonie and Affaires in Virginia.* London, 1620, [Force's *Tracts*, III, No. V, Washington, 1844.]

Virginia Company of London. *A True Declaration Of The estate of the Colonie in Virginia.* London, 1610. [Force's *Tracts*, III, No. I, Washington, 1844.]

Virginia Council And General Court Records, 1640–1641. (From ''Robinson's Notes,'' Va. Hist. Soc. Collection.) [*Va. Mag. Hist.*, (Jan., 1904) XI, 277–84.]

Virginia Council Journals, 1726–1753. [*Va. Mag. Hist.*, (July, 1924) XXXII, 237–59; (April, 1926) XXXIV, 97–112.]

Virginia Education Pamphlets. 2 vols. [Va. State Library.]

''Virginia Gazette,'' Extracts. [*Wm. & Mary Coll. Quart.*, (April, 1904) XII, 207–20.]

Virginia Gleanings In England. [(Communicated by L. Withington) *Va. Mag. Hist.*, (April, 1905) XII, 396–406; (Jan., 1906) XIII, 303–12.]

Virginia In 1616. (John Rolf's Relation of the State of Virginia, 17th Century.) [*Va. Hist. Register*, (July, 1848) I, No. III, 101–13;

So. Lit. Messenger, (June, 1839) V, 401–06, under title "Interesting Account of Virginia, In 1617."]

Virginia Home And Industrial School For Girls. [1st Annual Report, 1914–15; 3rd, 1916–17; 9th, 1922–23.] Chesterfield County, Va.

The Virginia Law Register. [Vol. I, N. S., (May 1915–April 1916).] Michie: Charlottesville, 1916.

Virginia Legislative Papers. From the Originals In The Virginia State Archives. [*Va. Mag. Hist.*, (Jan., 1910) XVIII, 24–44; (April, 1910) XVIII, 140–50; (July, 1910) XVIII, 255–71.]

Virginia Military Institute Annual Reports. 1915–16; 1917–18; 1919–20; 1924–25. Lexington.

The Virginia Normal and Industrial Institute Gazette. Ettrick. [Vol. XXXII, No. 5, Sept., 1928.]

Virginia School Reports. [Annual and Biennial Reports of the Superintendent of Public Instruction—appearing as Bulletins of the State Board of Education after 1918.] Richmond, 1871–1927.

Washington and Lee University Bulletin. President's Report. [May, 1922) XXI, No. 9; (May, 1924) XXIII, No. 14; (May, 1927) XXVI, No. 9.] Lexington.

Week Day Religious Instruction. The Why and How of Co-operation with the Public Schools. [Pamphlet.] The National Council of the Protestant Episcopal Church: New York, 1925.

Wells, S. C. The Strong Points in Southern Society—How can they be Conserved? [*Va. Educ. Jour.*, (Nov., 1880) XI, 354–59.]

West, Thomas. 3rd Lord Delaware. *The Relation of the Right Honourable the Lord De-La-Warre, Lord Gouernour and Captaine Generall of the Colonie, planted in Virginiea.* London, 1611. [Hist. Soc. of Penn'a.]

Westmoreland County, Virginia 1653–1912 . . . *Addresses Delivered At Montross, Va., May 3, 1910.* Richmond, 1912. [Addresses by: Washington, Lawrence; McKim, R. H.; Beale, G. W.]

Wickersham, James P. (Chairman.) Education And Crime. [*N. E. A. Proc's*, (1881) XX, 45–55.]

Will of Josias Mackie, Presbyterian Minister, Norfolk and Princess Anne Counties, 1716. [(Communicated and annotated by Edward W. James.) *Va. Mag. Hist.*, (April, 1900) VII, 358–63.]

W. [illiams] E. *Virginia: More especially the South part thereof, Richly and truly valued.* London, 1650. [Force's *Tracts*, III, No. XI, Washington, 1844.]

Wingfield, Edward Maria. *A Discourse of Virginia.* [Amer. Antiquarian Soc., *Archealogia Americana*, (Dean, C., editor) (1860) IV, 67–103; Wingfield, M.: *A History of Carline County, Virginia*, Appendix.]

Wyatt Manuscripts. [*Wm. & Mary Coll. Quart.*, (Oct., 1927) N. S., VII, 246–54.]

Wynne, Thomas H., editor. *The History of the Dividing Line and Other Tracts. From The Papers of William Byrd, of Westover, In Virginia, Esquire.* 2 vols. Richmond, 1866.

Yeates' Free Schools. [(Contributed by W. E. MacClenny.) *Wm. & Mary Coll. Quart.*, (Jan., 1925) (N. S., V, 30–38.]

2. *Newspapers*

The Daily Compiler. Richmond, April, May, 1814.

Enquirer. Richmond. 1810, 1818 in part, 1821, 1822, 1845, 1846, 1854, 1870, 1874, 1876.

The Evening Bulletin. Philadelphia, Feb. 10, 1928.

Examiner. Richmond. 1801—incomplete file, 1811.

Kentucky Gazette. Frankfort, Ky. July 11, 1798 (Extraordinary).

The Philadelphia Inquirer. Philadelphia, Aug. 13, 1925.

Richmond News Leader. Richmond, 1925, 1926.

Richmond Times-Dispatch. Richmond, 1925, 1926.

The Times. Richmond, 1902.

The Virginia Gazette. Williamsburg, Va. [Est., 1736; files as available for years 1736–81, in Va. State Library, for finding list, cf. *Bull., Va. State Library,* (1912) Vol. V, 357–58; *cf.* also Mass. Hist. Soc. Photostat copy.]

The Virginia Gazette 1736–1780 Printed at Williamsburg, Virginia. Reproduced by Photostat in the Massachusetts Historical Society. Boston, 1925.

Virginia Gazette & General Advertiser. Richmond, 1791, 1802.

Virginia Gazette and Petersburg Intelligencer. Richmond, 1800.

Virginia Gazette and Richmond and Manchester Advertiser. Richmond, 1793.

Virginia Gazette & Weekly Advertiser. Richmond, Va. 1787–1791, 1802. [Files incomplete—Va. State Library.]

3. *Secondary Sources*

Abstract of Chancery Suit, President And Masters Of The College of William and Mary vs. Frewen. [(Contributed by Leo Culleton) *Va. Mag. Hist.*, (Oct., 1916) XXIV, 374–78.]

Abstract of the Report of the President and Directors of the Literary Fund, to the General Assembly of the State of Virginia, in Dec. 1816. [*The Academician*, (Mar. 25, 1818) I, 39–42; 52–54.]

Abstracts From Records Of Richmond County, Virginia. [*Wm. & Mary Coll. Quart.*, (Jan., 1909) XVII, 176–95.]

Adams, Herbert B. *The Church and Popular Education.* [*Johns Hopkins U. Studies in Hist. and Polit. Science*, Ser., XVIII, Nos. 8–9.] Baltimore, 1900.

Adams, Herbert B. *The College of William and Mary.* [*U. S. Bur. Educ., Circ. Inf.*, (1887) No. 1.] Washington, 1889.

Adams, Herbert B., editor. *Contributions to American Educational History.* [*U. S. Bur. Educ., Circ. Inf.,* 1887, 1888.] Washington, 1889.

Adams, Herbert B. Roanoke College. [*U. S. Bur. Educ., Circ. Inf.,* (1888) No. 1, 263–70.] Washington, 1889.

Adams, Herbert B. *Thomas Jefferson and the University of Virginia.* [*U. S. Bur. Educ., Circ. Inf.,* (1888) No. 1] Washington, 1889.

Addington, Robert M. *The Old Time School in Scott County.* [*The Radford Normal Bulletin,* (Aug., 1914) II, No. II.] East Radford, 1914.

Address On Associations To Promote Education. *An Address on the subject of Literary Associations to promote Education; delivered before the Institute of Education of Hampden Sidney College, (Va.,) at their last Commencement.* By James M. Garnett. [Review: *Amer. Annals of Educ.,* (July, 1835) V, 317]

Advice from a Father to his Only Daughter. [*So. Lit. Messenger,* (Dec., 1834) I, 187–88.]

A Few Abstracts From The Will Books At Annapolis, Maryland. [*Wm. & Mary Coll. Quart.,* (July, 1904) XIII, 27–36.]

A Historical Sketch of Norwood High School and College, Nelson County, Virginia. Richmond, 1881.

Ambler, Charles Henry. *Sectionalism in Virginia From 1776 to 1861.* University of Chicago Press. Chicago, 1910.

Ambler, Charles Henry. *Thomas Ritchie A Study In Virginia Politics.* Bell: Richmond, 1913.

A Memoir Of The Late Rev. William Graham, A. M. [*Va. Evang. & Lit. Mag.,* (Feb., 1821) IV, 75–79; (March, 1821) IV, 150–52; (May, 1821) IV, 253–63; (Aug., 1821) 397–412.]

Ames, E. S. *The Psychology of Religious Experience.* Houghton Mifflin: Boston, 1910.

An Address Delivered At The First Meeting Of The Society of Inquiry On Missions. [*Va. Evang. & Lit. Mag.,* (April, 1818) I, 171–76.]

An Address Delivered before the Franklin Literary Society of Randolph-Macon College, Virginia, June 19th, 1838, by D. L. Carroll, D. D., President of Hampden Sidney College. [Review: *So. Lit. Messenger,* (Nov., 1838) IV, 693–94.]

An Address on Popular Education in Virginia, . . . by John Howard, Esq. [Review: *So. Quart. Review,* (Jan., 1851) III, 302.]

Anderson, Dice Robins. *William Branch Giles: A Study In The Politics of Virginia.* Banta: Menasha, 1914.

Anderson, James S. M. *The History of the Church of England in the Colonies.* 2 vols. London, 1845.

Andrews, Charles M., & Davenport, Frances G. *Guide to the Manuscript Materials for the History of the United States to 1783.* Carnegie Foundation: Washington, 1908.

An Economic and Social Survey of Albemarle County. [*U. of Va. Rec., Ext. Ser.,* (Oct., 1922) VII, No. 2] Charlottesville, 1922.

An Excursion Into The Country. [*Va. Evang. & Lit. Mag.*, (Dec., 1818) I, 537–51.]

A Note of the Shipping, Men, &c., Sent to Virginia, 1619. [(Abstract from Eng. Pub. Rec. Office, by W. N. Sainsbury) *Va. Mag. Hist.*, (Jan., 1899) VI, 231–32.]

Archer, Adair P. The Quaker's Attitude Towards The Revolution. [*Wm. & Mary Coll. Quart.*, (July, 1921) N. S., I, 167–82.]

A Record of Virginia Copyright Entries (1790–1844) [*Seventh Annual Report of The Library Board of the Va. State Library, 1909–10.*] Richmond, 1911.

[Armstrong, Mrs. F. M.] *The Syms-Eaton Free School.* [Compiled for the D. A. R. and Assoc. for the Preservation of Va. Antiquities. Booklet.]

Armstrong, M. F., & Ludlow, Helen W. *Hampton And Its Students.* New York, 1874.

Arrowood, W. W. Teaching the Bible in the Tazewell High School. [*Va. Jour. Educ.*, (Mar., 1923) XVI, 294–95.]

Arthur, T. S., & Carpenter, W. H. *The History Of Virginia From Its Earliest Settlement To The Present Time.* Philadelphia, 1852.

A Short Life Of Samuel Chapman Armstrong Founder Of Hampton Institute. [Booklet] Hampton, 1914.

A Talk With My Class. [By A Teacher At The Old Market Hall Sunday School.] Richmond, 1885.

Athearn, W. S. *The Indiana Survey of Religious Education.* 3 vols. Doran: New York, 1923.

Athearn, W. S. *A National System of Education.* Doran: New York, 1920.

Athearn, W. S. *Religious Education And American Democracy.* Pilgrim Press: Boston, 1917.

Avary, Myrta L. *Dixie After The War.* Doubleday, Page: New York, 1906.

Bagby, Alfred. *King and Queen County, Virginia.* Neale: New York, 1908.

Bagley, Wm. C. *Determinism in Education.* Warwick & York: Baltimore, 1925.

Baird, Charles Washington. *History Of The Huguenot Emigration To America.* 2 vols. New York, 1885.

Baird, Robert. *Religion In The United States of America.* Glasgow, 1844.

Baker, Harry T. Work Of The Y. M. C. A. Among High School Boys. [*Va. Jour. Educ.*, (May, 1914) VII, 419–20.]

Ballagh, James Curtis. *A History of Slavery in Virginia.* [*Johns Hopkins U. Studies in Hist. and Polit. Science*, Ex. Vol. XXIV] Baltimore, 1902.

Ballagh, James Curtis. *White Servitude In The Colony Of Virginia.* [*Johns Hopkins U. Studies In Hist. and Polit. Science*, Thirteenth Ser., VI–VII.] Baltimore, 1895.

Ballou, Emma Louisa. *Guide Right: Ethics For Young People.* Simmons: New York, 1902.

Bancroft, George. *History Of The United States From The Discovery Of The American Continent.* 10 vols. Boston, 1872.

Bangs, Nathan. *A History Of The Methodist Episcopal Church.* 2 vols. New York, 1833.

Barclay, Anne H. R. William Henry Ruffner, LL. D. [*W. Va. Hist. Mag.*, (Oct., 1902) 33–43.]

Barnes, Albert, editor. *Sermons On Important Subjects, By The Reverend Samuel Davies, A. M.* 3 vols. New York, 1811.

Barringer, Paul Brandon, editor. *University of Virginia.* 2 vols. Lewis: New York, 1904.

Bass, Gertrude B. Opportunities For Moral Training In The School Room. [*Va. Jour. Educ.*, (Mar., 1915) VIII, 358–59.]

Bassett, John Spencer. The Relation Between the Virginia Planter and the London Merchant. [*Annual Report Amer. Hist. Assoc.*, (1901) I, 551–75.]

Baxter, Charles N., & Dearborn, James M. *A List of Books, and Newspapers, Maps, Music and Miscellaneous Matter Printed in the South.* Boston Athenaeum: Boston, 1917.

Baxter, Sidney S. Notes on Washington Academy And Washington College. [*Wash. & Lee Hist. Papers*, (1892) No. 3, 45–63.]

Beard, Charles A. & Mary B. *The Rise Of American Civilization.* 2 vols. Macmillan: New York, 1927.

Beer, George Lewis. *The Origins of the British Colonial System 1578–1660.* Macmillan: New York, 1908.

Bell, James P. P. *Our Quaker Friends Of Ye Olden Time.* Bell Co.: Lynchburg, 1905.

Bell, Landon C. *The Old Free State. A Contribution to the History of Lunenburg County and Southside Virginia.* 2 vols. Richmond, 1927.

Beman, Lamar T. *Religious Teaching in the Public Schools.* Wilson: New York, 1927.

Benefits Of The Reformation On The Happiness Of Man. By a Native of Goochland, Va. [*So. Lit. Messenger*, (Aug., 1838) IV, 524–28; under title "Benefits of Knowledge On Morals," (Dec., 1838) IV, 771–79.]

Bennett, H. E. Suggestions on Moral Education. [*Va. Jour. Educ.*, (Mar., 1908) I, 1.]

Bennett, William W. *Memorials Of Methodism In Virginia.* Richmond, 1870.

Better Church and Sunday School Day. [*Va. Jour. Educ.*, (April, 1917) X, 359–60.]

Betts, C. H. *The New Program Of Religious Education.* Abingdon: New York, 1921.

Beverley, Robert. *The History of Virginia. London, 1722.* Richmond, 1855.

Beyer, Edward. *Album of Virginia.* (Ill.) [Richmond] 1858.

The Bible, A Book for the World. An Address delivered before the Cadet's Bible Society of the Virginia Military Institute May 1st, 1849. By B. M. Smith, Pastor of the Presbyterian Church, Staunton, Va., New York, 1849. [Review: *Va. Hist. Register,* (1849) II, 227.]

The Bible And The Public Schools. [*Relig. Herald,* (May 2, 1878) XIII.]

Bible Classes. [*Va. Evang. & Lit. Mag.,* (June, 1824) VII, 302–06.]

Bible-Education—Suggestions. [*Va. Educ. Jour.,* (May, 1872) III, 253–58.]

The Bible In Education. [*Amer. Annals of Educ.,* (July, 1835) 301–04.]

The Bible in Public Schools. [*Va. Educ. Jour.,* (Jan., 1870) I, 88–91.]

Bible-Teaching In Colleges Standardization Of Biblical Departments In Colleges. [*Relig. Educ.,* (Aug., 1918) XIII, 281–86.]

Birch, Thomas. *Court and Times of James The First.* 2 vols. London, 1849.

Bittinger, Lucy Forney. *German Religious Life In Colonial Times.* Lippincott: Philadelphia, 1906.

Blackhurst, J. Herbert. A Plea against the Bible in the Schools. [*Education,* (Feb., 1923) XLIII, 381–85.]

Blandin, I. M. E. *History of Higher Education of Women in the South Prior to 1860.* Neale: New York, 1909.

Blankenhorn, Heber. The Grandma Of The Muckrakers. [*Amer. Mercury,* (Sept., 1927) XII, 87–93.]

Bond, Beverly W. Jr. A Colonial Sidelight. [*The Sewanee Review,* (April, 1912) XX, 213–34.]

Boogher, William Fletcher. *Gleanings of Virginia History.* Washington, 1903.

Boone, Richard G. *Education in the United States.* Appleton: New York, 1914.

Bowers, Claude E. *Jefferson and Hamilton The Struggle for Democracy in America.* Houghton Mifflin: Boston, 1925.

Boys. [*Va. Jour. Educ.,* (April, 1914) VII, 314–15.]

Brayshaw, A. Neave. *The Quakers, Their Story and Message.* Swarthmore Press: London, 1927.

The Brent Family. [(Compiled by W. B. Chilton) *Va. Mag. Hist.,* (July, 1909) XVII, 308–11.]

Brewer, Clifton Hartwell. *A History of Religious Education in the Episcopal Church to 1835. [Yale Studies In The History And Theory of Religious Education,* III.] Yale University Press: New Haven, 1924.

Brickhead, Anne L. C. Teachers As Public Conservators of Morality. [*Va. Sch. Jour.,* (June, 1892) I, 186.]

Brief Memoir Of The Rev. James Blair, Commonly Called Commissary Blair. [*Va. Evang. & Lit. Mag.*, (Aug., 1819) II, 341–45.]

Broadus, John A. *College Education for Men of Business: A Familiar Essay, written at the request of the Trustees of Richmond College.* Richmond, 1875.

Brock, R. A. *Abstract of the Proceedings of the Virginia Company of London, 1619–1624.* 2 vols. [*Coll. Va. Hist. Society*, N. S., VII– VIII.] Richmond, 1888, 1889.

Brock, R. A. *Richmond As A Manufacturing and Trading Centre: Including a Historical Sketch of the City.* Richmond, 1880.

Brook, Andrew T. *American State Universities: Their Origin and Progress.* Cincinnati, 1875.

Brooke, Lucy M. Literature As A Means Of Moral Training. [*Va. Jour. Educ.*, (Mar., 1908) I, 4.]

Brooks, Edward. Moral Education an Essential Feature in Public School Education. [*Va. Educ. Jour.*, (July, 1886) XVII, 289–92.]

Brown, Alexander. *English Politics in Early Virginia History.* Houghton Mifflin: Boston, 1901.

Brown, Alexander. *The First Republic in America.* Boston, 1898.

Brown, Arlo Ayres. *History of Religious Education in Recent Times.* Abingdon: New York, 1923.

Brown, Elmer Ellsworth. *The Making Of Our Middle Schools.* Longmans: New York, 1914.

Brown, Kirk. Early Settlement of Friends in the Valley of Virginia. [*W. Va. Hist. Mag.*, (Jan., 1903), III, 55–59.]

Brown, Marianna C. *Sunday-School Movements in America.* Revell: New York, 1901.

Brown, Samuel W. *The Secularization of American Education as Shown by State Legislation.* [*Teachers College, Columbia University Contributions to Education*, No. 49.] New York, 1912.

Brown, W. H. *The Education and Economic Development of the Negro in Virginia.* [*U. of Va. Phelps-Stokes Fellowship Papers*, No. VI.] Surber: Charlottesville, 1923.

Brubacher, John S. The Public School And Religious Instruction. [*School and Society*, (Nov. 20, 1926) XXIV, 621–25.]

Bruce, Philip Alexander. *Economic History Of Virginia In The Seventeenth Century.* 2 vols. New York, 1896.

Bruce, Philip Alexander. *History of the University of Virginia.* 5 vols. Macmillan: New York, 1920.

Bruce, Philip Alexander. *Institutional History of Virginia in the 17th Century.* 2 vols. Putnam: New York, 1910.

Bruce, Philip Alexander. *The Rise Of The New South.* [*The History Of North America*, Vol. XVII.] Barrie: Philadelphia, 1905.

Bruce, Philip Alexander. *Social Life of Virginia In The Seventeenth Century.* Richmond, 1907.

Bruce, Thomas. *Southwest Virginia and Shenandoah Valley.* Richmond, 1891.

Bruce, William Cabell. *John Randolph of Roanoke 1773–1833.* 2 vols. Putnam: New York, 1922.

Brumbaugh, Gaius Marcus. *Genealogy Of The Brumbach Families.* Hitchcock: New York, 1913.

Brumbaugh, Martin Grove. *A History Of The German Baptist Brethren In Europe And America.* Mount Morris, 1899.

Bryan, William Jennings. The Statute For Establishing Religious Freedom. [Lipscomb: *Writings T. Jefferson,* VIII, i–xi.]

Buckley, J. M. *A History of Methodists In The United States.* [*The American Church History Series,* V.] New York, 1896.

Bunker, Frank Forest. *Reorganization of the Public School System.* [*U. S. Bur. Educ. Bull.,* 1916, No. 8] Washington, 1916.

Burk, John Daly. *The History of Virginia.* 4 vols. Petersburg, 1804–16.

Burns, J. A. *The Catholic School System In The United States.* Benzinger: New York, 1908.

Burns, James A. Catholic Secondary Education in the United States. [*The Catholic Educ. Assoc. Bull.,* (Aug., 1915), XI, No. 4.]

Burns, James A. *The Growth And Development of the Catholic School System in the United States.* Benzinger: New York, 1912.

Bury, J. B. *A History of Freedom of Thought.* Holt: New York, 1913.

Butcher, Bernard L., & Callahan, James M. *Genealogical And Personal History Of The Upper Monangahela Valley West Virginia.* 3 vols. Lewis Hist. Pub. Co.: New York, 1912.

Butler, Nicholas Murray. Religious Instruction And Its Relation To Education. [*Principles of Religious Education,* I, in *Christian Knowledge Lectures.*] Longmans: London, 1901.

Cabot, E. L. *Ethics for Children.* Houghton Mifflin: Boston, 1910.

Calamity at Richmond, Being A Narrative Of the affecting circumstances attending the Awful Conflagration Of The Theatre, In The City Of Richmond, On the Night of Thursday, the 26th of December, 1811. Philadelphia, 1812.

Caldwell, H. W. *Studies in Early American History.* [*Amer. Hist. Studies,* No. 1.] Lincoln, 1897.

Calisch, Edward N. The Democracy of the Public Schools. [*Va. Sch. Jour.,* (May, 1897) VI, 152–53.

Campbell, Charles. *History of the Colony and Ancient Dominion of Virginia.* Philadelphia, 1860.

Campbell, Douglas. *The Puritan in Holland, England and America.* 2 vols. New York, 1892.

[Campbell, Samuel S.]. Washington College, Lexington, Virginia. [(Senex) *So. Lit. Messenger,* (June, 1838) IV, 361–67; *Wash. & Lee Hist. Papers,* (1890) No. 1, 107–23.]

Carrington, (Mrs.) Wirt J. *A History of Halifax County.* Appeals Press; Richmond, 1924.

Cartmell, Thomas Kemp. *Shenandoah Valley Pioneers And Their Descendants.* Winchester, 1909.

Cassidy, Francis Patrick. *Catholic College Foundations And Development In The United States.* Washington, 1924.

Catalogue Of The Books, Belonging to the Norfolk Athenaeum; With a Brief Compend of the Laws of the Institution. Norfolk, 1828.

The Catholic University Of America Studies In American Church History. 4 vols. Washington, 1922.

Catlett, C., & Fishburne, E. G. *An Economic and Social Survey of Augusta County.* [*U. of Va. Rec., Ext. Ser.,* (Jan., 1928) XII, No. 7.]

Centennial Organization For The Better Endowment of Washington and Lee University. Report Of The Meetings Held In Independence Hall, Phladelphia, October 10th, 1876, and June 8th, 1881. New York, 1882.

Chafee, Zechariah. *Freedom of Speech.* Harcourt, Brace & Howe: New York, 1920.

Chalmers, George. *An Introduction To The History Of The Revolt Of The American Colonies.* 2 vols. Boston, 1845.

C. [halmers] G. [eorge]. *Political Annals Of The Present United Colonies, From Their Settlement To The Peace Of 1763.* [*Coll. N. Y. Hist. Soc.,* (1868) I] New York, 1868.

Chandler, J. A. C. *History of Suffrage In Virginia.* [*Johns Hopkins U. Studies in Hist. and Polit. Science,* XIX, Nos. 6–7] Baltimore, 1901.

Chandler, J. A. C. & Thames, T. B. *Colonial Virginia.* Times-Dispatch: Richmond, 1907.

Charles Lewis Cocke, Founder of Hollins College. By W. R. L. Smith, Boston: Richard G. Badger, 1921. [Review by John M. McBryde, Jr.: *The Sewanee Review,* (Oct., 1921) XXIX, 504–06.]

Cheyney, Edward P. *A Short History of England.* Ginn: Boston, 1904.

Cheyney, Edward P. *European Background of American History 1300–1600.* [*The American Nation* Vol. I] Harper: New York, 1904.

Childs, Benjamin Guy. *The Negroes of Lynchburg, Virginia.* [*U. of Va. Phelps-Stokes Fellowship Papers,* No. V] Surber-Arundale: Charlottesville, 1923.

The Chiles Family In Virginia. [(Compiled by R. B. Cridlin) *Va. Mag. Hist.,* (Oct., 1911) XIX, 437–38.]

Chitwood, Oliver Perry. *Justice in Colonial Virginia.* [*Johns Hopkins U. Studies in Hist. and Polit. Science,* Ser., XXIII, Nos. 7–8.] Baltimore, 1905.

Christian Education. [*So. Lit. Messenger,* (April, 1835) I, 432–35.]

Christian, W. Asbury. *Lynchburg And Its People.* Bell: Lynchburg, 1900.

Christian, W. Asbury. *Richmond Her Past And Present.* Richmond, 1912.

Christianity in Public Schools. [*Va. Educ. Jour.,* (Oct., 1879) X, 449–52.]

Christmas. [*Va. Jour. Educ.,* (Dec., 1909) III, 145–46.]

Christmas. [*Va. Jour. Educ.*, (Dec., 1911) V, 98.]

Christmas. [*Va. Jour. Educ.*, (Nov., 1912) VI, 72–77.]

Christmas. [*Va. Jour. Educ.*, (Dec., 1917) XI, 167–73.]

Christmas. [*Va. Sch. Jour.*, (Dec., 1894) III, 330.]

The Christmas Holidays. [*Va. Jour. Educ.*, (Dec., 1907) I, 14–15.]

Christmas Traditions. [*Va. Jour. Educ.*, (Dec., 1910) IV, 136.]

Churchill Family. [*Wm. & Mary Coll. Quart.*, (Jan., 1899) VII, 186–88; (July, 1899) VIII, 47–50.]

Civil And Religious Toleration. [(J. L. R.) *So. Lit. Jour.*, (Sept., 1838) IV, 216–22.]

Claiborne, John Herbert. *William Claiborne of Virginia.* Putnam: New York & London, 1917.

Clark, Allen C. *Life and Letters of Dolly Madison.* Roberts: Washington, 1914.

Clark, Rufus W. *Romanism in America.* Boston, 1859.

Clarke, Peyton Neale. *Old King William Homes and Families.* Louisville, 1897.

Cleveland, Catherine C. *The Great Revival In The West—1797–1805.* University of Chicago Press: Chicago, 1916.

Cobb, Sanford H. *The Rise of Religious Liberty in America.* Macmillan: New York, 1902.

Coe, George Albert. *A Social Theory of Religious Education.* Scribner: New York, 1924.

Coleman, Lucy S. The Story of the Nativity. [*Va. Jour. Educ.*, (Dec., 1911) V, 98.]

College Convention of Virginia. [*So. Lit. Messenger*, (Feb., 1844) X, 121–22.]

Comegys, Benjamin Bartis. *A Primer of Ethics.* Boston, 1891.

Common Schools And Public Instruction. Virginia. [Barnard: *Jour. of Educ.*, (1873) XXIV, 324–26.]

Common Schools In Virginia. [*Jour. of Educ.*, (April 1, 1880) XI, 217.]

The Confessions Of A Pedagogue. [(Pedagogue) *So. Lit. Messenger*, (Jan., 1860) XXX, 46–50.]

Considerations On An Act Of The Legislature Of Virginia, Entitled, An Act For The Establishment Of Religious Freedom. (By A Citizen Of Philadelphia.) Philadelphia, 1786.

The Convention. [*Va. Lit. Museum*, (Nov. 11, 1829) I, 337–39.]

Converse, Henry A. A Workable Plan For Religious Education In Our Schools. [*Va. Teacher*, (Aug., 1922) III, 205–09.]

Conway, James. The Rights And Duties Of Family And State In Regard To Education. [*The Amer. Cath. Quart. Rev.*, (Jan., 1884) 105–26.]

Conway, Moncure Daniel. *Barons Of The Potomack And The Rappahannock.* New York, 1892.

Conway, Moncure Daniel. *Free-Schools In Virginia: A Plea Of Education, Virtue And Thrift, VS. Ignorance, Vice And Poverty.* Fredericksburg, 1850.

Cook, Elizabeth Christine. *Literary Influences In Colonial Newspapers 1704–1750.* Columbia University Press: New York, 1912.

Cook, Joseph. The High School. [*Va. Educ. Jour.*, (April, 1886) XVII, 166.]

Cooke, John Esten. Thomas Jefferson. [*So. Lit. Messenger*, (May, 1860) XXX, 321–41.]

Cooke, John Esten. *Virginia A History Of The People.* [*Amer. Commonwealths*, XI.] Houghton Mifflin: Boston, 1903.

Cooke, John Esten. William And Mary College. [*Scribner's Monthly*, (Nov., 1875) XI, 1–15.]

Course of Study in Washington College, and in the Grammar School connected with the College. [*Va. Evang. & Lit. Mag.*, (June, 1821) IV, 319–20.]

Crafts, Wilbur F. *Bible In School Plans Of Many Lands.* Illustrated Bible Selections Commission: Washington, 1914.

Craighill, Wm. P. The Old Academy In Charles Town. [*W. Va. Hist. Mag.*, (Jan., 1905) 18–33.]

Crooker, J. H. *Religious Freedom in America.* Amer. Unitarian Assoc'n: Boston, 1903.

Crosby, Howard. Religion and the Schools. [*Va. Educ. Jour.*, (Oct., 1890) XXI, 451–52.]

Cross, Arthur Lyon. *The Anglican Episcopate And The American Colonies.* [*Harvard Hist. Studies*, Vol. IX.] Longmans, Green & Co.: New York, 1902.

Cubberley, Ellwood P. *Public Education In The United States.* Houghton Mifflin: Boston, 1919.

Culbreth, D. M. R. *University of Virginia Memories of Her Student Life and Professors.* Neale: New York, 1908.

Cummings, A. W. *The Early Schools Of Methodism.* New York, 1886.

Current Events. [*Va. Sch. Jour.*, (Jan., 1892) I, 24.]

Curry, J. L. M. Pauperism—Sectarian Appropriations—Public Schools. [*Relig. Herald*, (June 27, 1878) XIII.]

Curtis, William E. *The True Thomas Jefferson.* Lippincott: Philadelphia, 1901.

Cutten, George B. *The Psychological Phenomena of Christianity.* Scribner: New York, 1909.

D. [abney], G. [eorge] E. Education In Virginia. [*So. Lit. Messenger*, (Sept., 1841) VII, 631–37.]

Dabney, Virginius. Virginia. [*Amer. Mercury*, (Nov., 1926) IX, No. 35, 349.]

Davidson, Robert. *History Of The Presbyterian Church In The State Of Kentucky; With A Preliminary Sketch Of The Churches In The Valley Of Virginia.* New York, 1847.

Davis, Arthur Kyle. *Education in Virginia.* Petersburg, 1912.

Davis, John. *The First Settlers of Virginia, A Historical Novel.* New York, 1806.

De Bow, J. D. B. *Industrial Resources of the Southern and Western States.* 3 vols. New Orleans, 1852–55.

Deck, Patrick A., & Heaton, Henry. *An Economic and Social Survey of Loudoun County.* [*U. of Va. Rec., Ext. Ser.,* (June, 1926) X, No. 10] University, 1926.

De La Rochefoucauld Liancourt. *Reisen in den Jahren 1795, 1796, und 1797.* 3 vols. Hamburg, 1799.

Denominational Education. Its Necessity and Practicability, . . . An Address delivered before the Thalion and Phi Delta Societies of the Oglethorpe University. By Rev. Thomas Smyth, D.D. . . . Charleston: B. Jenkins. 1846. [Review: *So. Quart Review,* (Jan., 1846) IX, 278–79.]

Dexter, Edwin G. *History of Education in the United States.* Macmillan: New York, 1916.

Dieffenbach, Albert C. *Religious Liberty. The Great American Illusion.* Morrow: New York, 1927.

Dillard, James H. A School of the Past. [*Sewanee Review,* (Oct., 1921) XXIX, 410–16.]

Dircks, H. *A Biographical Memoir of Samuel Hartlib, Milton's Familiar Friend.* London, [1865].

Dr. Cooper. [Niles: *Register,* (Dec. 31, 1831) XLI, 326.]

Dodd, William E. Another View Of Our Educational Progress. [*South Atlant. Quart.,* (Oct., 1903) II, 325–33.]

Douglass, Hazel B. A Moral Code for Girls and Boys. [*Va. Jour. Educ.,* (Feb., 1923) XVI, 256–57.]

Doyle, J. A. *English Colonies In America.* 5 vols. Holt: New York, 1889–1907.

Drake, Samuel A. *The Making of Virginia and the Middle Colonies.* Scribner: New York, 1902.

Duvall, Sylvanus Milne. *The Methodist Episcopal Church and Education Up To 1869.* [*Teachers College Contributions To Education, No. 284.*] Teachers College, Columbia University: New York, 1928.

Earle, Alice Morse. *Home Life In Colonial Days.* New York, 1898.

Earle, Swepson. *The Chesapeake Bay Country.* Thomsen-Ellis: Baltimore, 1924.

Early Episcopacy In Accomack. [*Va. Mag. Hist.,* (Oct., 1897) V, 128–32.]

Early Recollections Of John Randolph. [(From the Central Presbyterian) *So. Lit. Messenger,* (June, 1859) XXVIII, 461–66.]

Earnest, J. B. *The Religious Development of the Negro in Virginia.* Charlottesville, 1914.

Eckenrode, Hamilton J. *A Calendar of legislative petitions arranged by counties—Accomac-Bedford.* [*Rep't of Va. State Library,* 1908.] Richmond, 1908.

Eckenrode, Hamilton J. *The Political History of Virginia During The Reconstruction.* [*Johns Hopkins U. Studies in Hist. and Polit. Science,* Ser., XXII, Nos. 6–8.] Baltimore, 1904.

Eckenrode, Hamilton J. *The Revolution In Virginia.* Houghton Mifflin: Boston, 1916.

Eckenrode, Hamilton J. *Separation of Church and State In Virginia.* [*Sixth Annual Report Of The Library Board of the Va. State Library,* 1908–09.] Richmond, 1910.

Edgeworth, Maria. *Parent's Assistant; or Stories for children.* 2 vols. New York, 1827.

Edgeworth, Maria. *Popular Tales.* London, 1895.

Edgeworth, Maria and R. L. *Practical Education.* 2 vols. London, 1801.

Editorial. [*Va. Jour. Educ.,* (Dec., 1908) II, 18–19.]

Editorial. [*Va. Jour. Educ.,* (Oct., 1909) III, 2–3.]

Editorial. [*Va. Jour. Educ.,* (Nov., 1910) IV, 65.]

Editorial. [*Va. Jour. Educ.,* (Nov., 1910) IV, 66.]

Editorial. [*Va. Sch. Jour.,* (Jan., 1894) III, 6.]

Editorial. [*Va. Sch. Jour.,* (Jan., 1899) VIII, 4.]

Editorial. Are the Churches Negligent? [*Va. Jour. Educ.,* (May, 1914) VII, 392.]

Editorial. Presidency of the State Female Normal School. [*Va. Sch. Jour.,* (Dec., 1901) 284.]

Education. [By A Native Virginian.) *So. Lit. Messenger,* (July, 1839) V, 441–48.]

Education And Crime At The North And The South. [*De Bow's Review,* June, 1854) XVI, 578–81.]

Education and Literature in Virginia. An Address delivered before the Literary Societies of Washington College, Lexington, Virginia, 18th June, 1850. By John R. Thompson, of Richmond. Richmond: H. K. Ellyson, 1850. [Review: *So. Quart. Review,* (Jan., 1851) III, 290.]

Education At The South. [*De Bow's Review,* (April, 1851) X, 476–77.]

Educational Association Of Virginia. [Barnard: *Amer. Jour. Educ.,* (1871) XXII, 551–53.]

Educational Association Of Virginia. [*Va. Educ. Jour.,* (Dec., 1891) XXII, 529–30.]

The Educational Interest Of The United States. [Barnard: *Amer. Jour. Educ.,* (1856) I, 364–70.]

Educational News and Comments. [*Va. Jour. Educ.,* (Oct., 1923) XVII, 70–71.]

Educational Notes. The Commencement Exercises. [*Va. Educ. Jour.,* (July, 1879) X, 319.]

Educational Notes and News. [*School and Society* (Aug. 29, 1925) XXII, 269–73.]

Education In Colonial Virginia. Part III. Free Schools. [*Wm. & Mary Coll. Quart.,* (Oct., 1897) VI, 71–85.]

Education In Elizabeth City County. [*Wm. & Mary Coll. Quart.,* (July, 1915) XXIV, 35–43.]

Education in the Southern and Western States. [*So. Lit. Messenger,* (Oct., 1845) XI, 603–07.]

Education—Public Free Schools. [*Va. Educ. Jour.*, (May, 1870) I, 207–16.]

Education Societies And Theological Seminaries. [*Va. Evang. & Lit. Mag.*, (Jan., 1824) VII, 48–50.]

Education Statistics. [Niles: *Register*, (Feb. 26, 1848) LXXIII, 416.]

The Edward Pleasants Valentine Papers. 4 vols. Valentine Museum: Richmond. [No date].

Eggleston, Edward. *The Beginners of a Nation.* New York, 1899.

Eggleston, Edward. *The Transit of Civilization from England to America in the Seventeenth Century.* Appleton: New York, 1901.

Eliot, Charles W. The Teacher's Conscience. [*Va. Educ. Jour.*, (Mar., 1883) XIV, 71–73.]

Ellis, H. M. Thomas Cooper—A Survey of his Life. [*South. Atlant. Quart.*, (Jan., 1920) XIX, 24–42.]

[Ellyson, James T.]: *London Company of Virginia.* New York, 1908.

The Encyclopedia Americana. Vols. III, XXII. American Corporation: New York, 1927.

Ensign, Forest C. *Compulsory School Attendance and Child Labor.* Athens Press: Iowa City, 1921.

Everest, Robert. Pauperism and Crime—White And Colored—Native and Foreign. [*De Bow's Review*, (Sept., 1855) XIX, 268–85.]

Evidences Of Christianity. Lectures on the Evidences of Christianity, delivered at the University of Virginia, during the session of 1850–'51 . . . New York, 1852. [*Va. Hist. Register*, (Oct., 1852) V, No. VI, 231–32.]

Exercises For Opening School. [*Va. Sch. Jour.*, (Jan., 1892) I, 9.]

Extracts From The Records of Caroline County. [*Va. Mag. Hist.*, (July, 1912) XX, 318–20.]

Ezekiel, Jacob. The Jews Of Richmond. [*Publications Of The Amer. Jewish Hist. Society*, (1894) 22–27.]

Faunce, William H. P. *The New Horizon of State and Church.* Macmillan: New York, 1918.

Female Academy at Sturgeonville, Virginia. [*Amer. Jour. Educ.*, (Oct., 1828) III, 618–20.]

Female Education. Young Ladies Seminary, at Prince Edward Court House. [*So. Lit. Messenger*, (May, 1835) I, 519–20, & advertisement on back cover.]

Ferebee, E. E., & Wilson, J. P., Jr. *Economic and Social Survey of Princess Anne County.* [*U. of Va. Rec.*, *Ext. Ser.*, (May, 1924) VIII, No. 9.] University, 1924.

Ferguson, George Oscar. *Defectives Among Delinquents.* [*U. of Va. Rec.*, *Ext. Ser.*, (June, 1924) VIII, No. 10.] Charlottesville, 1924.

The Ferrar Family. [*Va. Mag. Hist.*, (Jan., 1900) VII, 319–22.]

Few, William P. The Standardizing Of Southern Colleges. [*South. Atlant. Quart.*, (Jan., 1908) VII, 1 *ff.*]

Fiske, John. *Old Virginia And Her Neighbors.* 2 vols. Boston, 1897.

Fitzgerald, Virginia. A Southern College Boy Eighty Years Ago. [*South Atlant. Quart.*, (July, 1921) XX, 236–46.]

Fitz-Hugh, Thomas. *The University of Virginia in Texas and the Southwest.* Lynchburg, 1897.

F. [itzpatrick], F. B. Our Task In Religious Education. [*Va. School Messages*, (Sept., 1925) VI, No. 9, 1.]

Flanders, Jesse Knowlton. *Legislative Control of the Elementary Curriculum.* [*Teachers College Contributions To Education*, No. 195.] Teachers College, Columbia University: New York, 1925.

Flippin, Percy Scott. *The Financial Administration Of The Colony Of Virginia.* Baltimore, 1915.

Flippin, Percy Scott. *The Royal Government in Virginia 1624–1775.* [*Columbia University Studies In History, Economics, and Public Law*, Vol. 84, No. 1.] Columbia University: New York, 1919.

Flippin, Percy Scott. William Gooch: Successful Royal Governor of Virginia. [*Wm. & Mary Coll. Quart.*, (Oct., 1925) N. S., V, 225–58; (Jan., 1926) VI, 1–38.]

Foote, Henry William. *Sketches of Virginia Historical and Biographical.* Philadelphia, 1850.

Fork Union Military Academy. [Leaflet.]

Forrest, William S. *Historical And Descriptive Sketches Of Norfolk And Vicinity.* Philadelphia, 1853.

A Forty Thousand Dollar Y. M. C. A. Building For The University. [*U. of Va. Alum. Bull.*, (April, 1904) N. S., IV, No. 2, 22–24.]

Fox, E. L. William Henry Ruffner And The Rise Of The Public Free School System Of Virginia. [*Branch Historical Papers*, (June, 1910) III, 124–44.]

Fox, James Wallace. Fox Family. [*Wm. & Mary Coll. Quart.*, (Oct., 1917, XXVI, 129–38.]

Fox, Wm. F. *Civil Government Of Virginia.* Richardson, Smith & Co.: New York, 1904.

Francis Fauquier's Will. [*Wm. & Mary Coll. Quart.*, (Jan., 1900), VIII, 171–77.]

The Free Schools And University Of Virginia. [*So. Lit. Messenger*, (Feb., 1854) XX, 65–75.]

Friedman, Lee M. The Parental Right To Control The Religious Education Of A Child. [*Harvard Law Review*, (Mar., 1916) XXIX, 485–500.]

Foster, Mary L. *Colonial Capitals of the Dominion of Virginia.* Bell: Lynchburg, 1906.

Frissel, H. B. Educational Progress in Virginia. [*South Atlant. Quart.*, July, 1903) II, 199.]

Frissel, H. B. The Progress of Negro Education. [*South Atlant. Quart.*, (Jan., 1907) V, 37–44.]

Fuller, Thomas. *The History of the Worthies of England.* 4 vols. London, 1840.

Garland, Hugh A. *The Life of John Randolph of Roanoke.* 2 vols. [in one.] New York, 1859.

Garnett, James Mercer. [*Wm. & Mary Coll. Quart.*, (Oct., 1908) XVII, 85–99; (Jan., 1909) XVII, 204–23.]

Garnett, James Mercer. Biographical Sketch of Hon. Muscoe Russell Hunter Garnett, of Essex County, Virginia. (1821–1864) [*Wm. & Mary Coll. Quart.*, (July, 1909) XVIII, 17–37.]

Gay, Constance M. The Campaign Of 1855 In Virginia And The Fall Of The Know-Nothing Party. [*Richmond Coll. Hist. Papers*, I, No. 2, (June, 1916) 309–35.]

Gayley, Charles Mills. *Shakespeare And The Founders Of Liberty In America.* Macmillan: New York, 1917.

Geiger, Joseph Roy. Evolution As ''Hypothesis'' And As ''Fact.'' [*School & Society*, (Aug. 22, 1925) XXII, 244–45.]

The General Education Board, An Account Of Its Activities 1902–1914. General Education Board: New York, 1916.

A Generous Heart. [*Va. Jour. Educ.*, (Dec., 1914) VIII, 161–62.]

Genesis Of The German Lutheran Church. [*The Lutheran Church Review*, (Oct., 1897) XVII, 522–32.]

Gilmour, R. What Shall The Public Schools Teach? [*The Forum*, (June, 1888) V, 454–60.]

Gilpin, H. D. [National Portraits.] *Thomas Jefferson.* 1836.

Gold, Thos. D. *History of Clarke County, Virginia.* Hughes: Berryville, 1914.

Goode, John. *Recollections Of A Lifetime.* Neale Pub. Co.: New York, 1906.

Goodwin, Edward Lewis. *The Colonial Church In Virginia.* Milwaukee Pub. Co.: Milwaukee, 1927.

Goodwin, Wm. A. R. *Bruton Church, Williamsburg, Virginia Brief Historical Notes.* 1903.

Goodwin, Wm. A. R. *Bruton Parish Church Restored and its Historic Environment.* Williamsburg, 1907.

Goodwin, Wm. A. R. *Historical Sketch of Bruton Church, Williamsburg, Virginia.* Petersburg, 1903.

Gordon, Armstead Churchill. *William Fitzhugh Gordon A Virginian Of The Old School; His Life, Times And Contemporaries. (1787–1858).* Neale: New York, 1909.

Graves, Frank P. *History of Education During the Middle Ages.* Macmillan: New York, 1920.

Graves, Frank P. *A History of Education in Modern Times.* Macmillan: New York, 1920.

Green, Claude B. Opening Exercises For Schools. [*Va. Jour. Educ.*, (Oct., 1915) IX, 71–72.]

Green, B. W. Personal Notes. [*Wm. & Mary Coll. Quart.*, (April, 1900) VIII, 271–72.]

Griggs, E. H. *Moral Education.* Huebsch: New York, 1904.

Grigsby, Hugh Blair. *The History of the Virginia Federal Convention of 1788.* 2 vols. [*Coll. Va. Hist. Society*, N. S., IX–X, Brock, R. A., editor.] Richmond, 1890, 1891.

Grinnan, A. G. The Last Indians In Orange County, Virginia. [*Va. Mag. Hist.*, (Oct., 1895) III, 189–91.]

Grinnan, Andrew G. Two Spotswood Boys at Eton in 1760, &c. [*Wm. & Mary Coll. Quart.*, (Oct., 1893) II, 113–20.]

Groome, H. C. *Fauquier During The Proprietorship.* Old Dominion Press: Richmond, 1927.

Guilday, Peter. *Life and Times of John Carroll.* Encyclopedia Press: New York, 1922.

Haas, John A. W. *The Problem of the Christian State.* Stratford: Boston, 1928.

Hale, John P. *Trans-Allegheny Pioneers.* Cincinnati, 1886.

Hale, Louise Closser. *We Discover The Old Dominion.* Dodd, Mead: New York, 1916.

Hall, Arthur Jackson. *Religious Education in the Public Schools of The State and City of New York.* University of Chicago Press: Chicago, 1914.

Hall, Granville Davisson. *Rending of Virginia: A History.* Mayer & Miller: Chicago, 1902.

Hall, J. Leslie. The Religious Opinions of Thomas Jefferson. [*Sewanee Review*, (April, 1913) XXI, 164–76.]

Halsey, Rosalie V. *Forgotten Books of the American Nursery.* Goodspeed: Boston, 1911.

Hamilton, J. G. De R. Jefferson And Adams At Ease. [*South Atlant. Quart.*, (Oct., 1927,) 359–72.]

Hampden Sydney College. [*Va. Evang. & Lit. Mag.*, (Oct., 1825) VIII, 553–54]

Hampton Normal and Agricultural Institute. Educational Status Of The Institution. [*Jour. of Educ.*, (July 6, 1882) XVI, 43.]

Hansen, Allen Oscar. *Liberalism and American Education In The Eighteenth Century.* Macmillan: New York, 1926.

Harris, H. H. Richmond College. [*U. S. Bur. Educ., Circ. Inf.*, (1888) No. 1, 271–85.] Washington, 1889.

Harris, Wade H. *My School Days, Reconstruction Experience in the South.* Neale: New York, 1914.

Harris, William T. The Division of School Funds for Religious Purposes. [*Atlantic Monthly*, (Aug., 1876) 171–84.]

Harris, William T. Moral Training in the Common Schools. [*U. S. Bur. Educ., Circ. Inf.*, (1888) No. 6, 81–100.] Washington, 1888.

Harris, William T. Report Of The Fifteen. Correlation of Studies in Elementary Schools. [*Va. Sch. Jour.*, (April, 1895) IV, 114–27; *cf. N. E. A. Proc's*, (1895) XXXIV, 287–333.]

Harrison, Constance (Cary). Col. William Byrd of Westover, Va. [*Century Magazine*, (June, 1891) 163–78, 638, 798.]

Harrison, Fairfax. Brent Town, Ravensworth and The Huguenots In Stafford. [(A Chapter from "Landmarks of Old Prince William.") *Tyler's Quart.*, (Jan., 1924) V, 164–85.]

Harrison, Fairfax. Parson Waugh's Tumult A Chapter From "Landmarks of Old Prince William." [*Va. Mag. Hist.*, (Jan., 1922) XXX, 31–37.]

Hartzler, John Ellsworth. *Education Among The Mennonites Of America.* Central Mennonite Publishing Board: Danvers, 1925.

Hartzler, J. S., & Kauffman, Daniel. *Mennonite Church History.* Mennonite Book and Tract Society: Scottdale, 1905.

Hauser, Conrad A. *Latent Religious Resources in Public School Education.* Philadelphia, 1924.

[Hawks, Francis Lister]. *The Early History of the Southern States: Virginia.* [By Lambert Lilly, schoolmaster (Pseud.)] Philadelphia, 1832.

Heartman, Chas. Fred. *Checklist Of Printers In The United States.* New York, 1915.

Heatwole, Cornelius J. *A History of Education in Virginia.* Macmillan: New York, 1916.

Henderson, John C. *Thomas Jefferson's Views on Public Education.* New York, 1890.

Henry, William Wirt. Causes which produced the Virginia of the Revolutionary Period. [*Amer. Hist. Assoc. Annual Report*, (1891) 17 *ff.*] Washington, 1892.

Henry, William Wirt. First Legislative Assembly in America. [*Amer. Hist. Assoc. Annual Report*, (1893) 300–316.] Washington, 1894.

Henry, William Wirt. Reply to Dr. Stillé upon Religious Liberty in Virginia. [*Amer. Hist. Assoc. Papers*, (1889) III, No. 2, 455.]

Hints For the Establishment Of A Tract Society. [(By Philopsuchos) *Va. Evang. & Lit. Mag.*, (Feb., 1819) II, 86–88.]

Historical and Genealogical Notes and Queries. Plan For Free School, Northumberland, 1652. [*Va. Mag. Hist.*, (Jan., 1902) X, 312–25.]

Historical and Genealogical Notes. [(Religious Freedom) *Wm. & Mary Coll. Quart.*, (Oct., 1916) XXV, 144–45.]

Historical And Genealogical Notes And Queries. Memoranda From the Fredericksburg, Va., Gazette, 1787–1803. [*Va. Mag. Hist.*, (April, 1906) XIII, 425–34.]

Historical Sketch of Bedford County, Virginia. Lynchburg, 1907.

Historical Sketches of Virginia. University of Virginia. [*Old Dominion & Va. Hist. Reg.* (1871) V, 120, 203, 265, 324.]

Historical Sketch of the College Of William And Mary, In Virginia. [Gary & Clemmitt, Printers] Richmond, 1866.

History of Christianity in the Southern States. (A Review of: 1. Sketches of North Carolina, . . . By Rev. Wm. H. Foote; 2. The Early Baptists in Virginia . . . By R. B. Howell, 3. Memorials of Methodism in Virginia . . . By Wm. W. Bennett.) [*Southern Review*, (July, 1873) XIII, 124–52.]

A History of the Mennonite Conference of Virginia and Its Work. Mennonite Publishing House: Scottdale, 1910.

History Of The Presbytery of Hanover. [*Va. Evang. & Lit. Mag.*, (Oct., 1828) XI, 531–38; (Dec., 1828) XI, 657–58.]

Hodge, Charles. *The Constitutional History Of The Presbyterian Church In The United States Of America. Part II. 1741 to 1788.* Philadelphia, 1840.

Hodges, George. *The Apprenticeship of Washington And Other Sketches of Significant Colonial Personages.* Moffat, Yard: New York, 1909.

The Hollins Female Institute in Roanoke county, Va. [*Jour. of Educ.*, (Aug., 24, 1882) XVI, 121.]

Hollins Institute. [*Jour. of Educ.*, (July 12, 1883) XVIII, 56.]

Hollins Yesterday, to-day and to-morrow. [Leaflet, 1928.]

Holmes, Abiel. *American Annals; or a chronological History of America from its Discovery in MCCCCXCII to MDCCCVI.* 2 vols. Cambridge, 1805

Holtz, Adrian A. *A Study of the Moral and Religious Elements in American Secondary Education up to 1800.* Banta: Menasha, Wisc., 1917.

Home Education. [*Va. Educ. Jour.*, (April, 1886) XVII, 165.]

Hood, William R. *The Bible In The Public Schools Legal Status And Current Practice.* [*U. S. Bur. Educ. Bull.*, (1923) No. 15.]

Hoops, Johannes. Virginien zur Kolonialzeit, Eine Kulturesgeschichtliche Studie. [In *Studien zur englischen philologie* (1913) v. 50, 473.]

Horne, Herman H. Moral and Religious Instruction in the Public Schools. [*Va. Jour. Educ.*, (Mar., 1924) XVII, 269–71.]

Hotchkiss, Jed. *The City of Staunton, Augusta County, Virginia.* Staunton, 1878.

[Hotchkiss, Jedediah]. *Virginia: A Geographical and Political Summary.* Richmond, 1876.

Howe, Henry. *Historical Collections of Virginia.* District of Columbia, 1849.

Howell, Robert B. *Early Baptists Of Virginia.* Philadelphia, (1857).

Howison, Robert R. *A History of Virginia.* Vol. I [2 vols.] Philadelphia, 1846.

Howland, George. Moral Training. [*Va. Educ. Jour.*, (Aug., 1888) XIX, 356.]

Humphrey, Edward Frank. *Nationalism And Religion In America 1774– 1789.* Law: Boston, 1924.

Hunt, Gaillard. James Madison and Religious Liberty. [*Annual Report Amer. Hist. Assoc.*, (1901) I, 163–71.] Washington, 1902.

Hunt, Gaillard. *The Life of James Madison.* Doubleday, Page: New York, 1902.

Hutchins, Wm. J. The Children's Morality Code. [*Va. Teacher*, (Mar., 1824) V, 79–81.]

Inaugural Address delivered by the Rev. Stephen Olin, President of Randolph-Macon College, on the occasion of his introduction into office. [Review: *Amer. Annals of Educ.*, (Dec., 1834) IV, 545–47.]

Inaugural Address delivered by the Rev. Stephen Olin, President of Randolph-Macon College, on the occasion of his induction into office, 5th March, 1834. Richmond: Nesbitt & Walker. [Review: *So. Lit Messenger*, (Aug., 1834) I, 15–16.]

The Indians Of Southern Virginia, 1650–1711. [*Va. Mag. Hist.*, (April, 1900) VII, 337–58.]

The Influence Of Morals On The Happiness Of Man, And The Stability Of Social Institutions. By a native (but not now a resident) of Petersburg, Va. [*So. Lit. Messenger*, (Mar., 1838) IV, 145–51; (May, 1838) IV, 273–80.]

Ingle, Edward. *Local Institutions of Virginia.* [*Johns Hopkins U. Studies in Hist. and Polit. Science*, Third Ser., II–III.] Baltimore, 1885.

Institute Of Virginia. [*Annals of Educ.*, (Dec., 1833) III, 596.]

Isle Of Wight County Records. [*Wm. & Mary Coll. Quart.*, (April, 1899) VII, 205–315.]

Jackson, M. W. *Wealth and Health Or A Guide To Parents In The Education Of Children.* Richmond, 1854.

James, Charles F. *A Documentary History of The Struggle for Religious Liberty in Virginia.* Bell: Lynchburg, 1900.

James Mercer. [*Wm. & Mary Coll. Quart.*, (Jan., 1909) XVII, 204–21.]

Jamestown and Plymouth. [*Wm. & Mary Coll. Quart.*, (April, 1909) 305–11.]

Jenkins, Willis A. Religious Instruction In The Public Schools. [*Va. Jour. Educ.*, (July, 1911) IV, 633–34.]

The John B. Cary Bible Lectureship. Rev. W. M. Forrest, Lecturer. [(C. W. K.) *U. of Va. Alum. Bull.*, (Oct., 1903) N. S., III, No. 4, 183–84.]

John, Walton C., editor. Hampton Normal And Agricultural Institute. [*U. S. Bur. Educ., Bull.*, (1923) No. 27.]

Johnson, Rossiter, editor. *The Bibliographical Dictionary of America.* Vol. V. American Biographical Society: Boston, 1906.

Jones, Arthur J. *Education And The Individual.* Century Co.: New York, 1926.

Jones, Charles C. *The Religious Instruction of the Negroes In the United States.* Savannah, 1842.

Jones, Howard Mumford. *America And French Culture 1750–1848.* University of North Carolina Press: Chapel Hill, 1927.

Jones, J. Wm. The Religious History and Present Status And Prospectus Of Religion In The University Of Virginia. [*U. of Va. Alum. Bull.*, (Feb., 1897) III, No. 4, 93–97.]

Joynes, E. S. General Lee As A College President. [*Old Dominion Magazine*, (1871) V, 209–13.]

Keach, O. A.   The Hack Family. [*Tyler's Quart.*, (April, 1926) VII, 253–62.]

Keen, William Williams.   *The Bi-Centennial Celebration Of The Founding Of The First Baptist Church Of The City Of Philadelphia.* Philadelphia, 1899.

Keith, William.   *The History of the British Plantations in America.* London, 1738.

Kemper, Charles E., editor.   The Early Westward Movement of Virginia, 1722–1734. [*Va. Mag. Hist.*, (April, 1905) XII, 337–52; (Oct., 1905) XIII, 113–38; (Jan., 1906) XIII, 281–97; (April, 1906) XIII, 351–74.]

Kemper, Charles E.   The Settlement Of The Valley. [*Va. Mag. Hist.*, (April, 1922) 169–82.]

Kemper, Charles E.   The Spotswood Mileage Accounts. [*Wm. & Mary Coll. Quart.*, (July, 1923) N. S., III, 171–72.]

Kennedy, John P.   *Virginia State Library Calendar of Transcripts.* Richmond, 1905.

Kile, J. H.   Desired Qualities and Qualifications of a Teacher For The Moral and Religious Welfare of Children. [*Va. Jour. Educ.*, (April, 1912) V, 312–19.]

Kinsolving, Arthur Barksdale.   *The Story Of A Southern High School, The Episcopal High School Of Virginia.* Norman, Remington Co.: Baltimore, 1922.

Kirkpatrick, John E.   The Constitutional Development Of The College Of William And Mary. [*Wm. & Mary Coll. Quart.*, (April, 1926) N. S., VI, 95–108.]

Klain, Zora.   *Educational Activities of New England Quakers.* Westbrook: Philadelphia, 1928.

Klain, Zora.   *Quaker Contributions To Education in North Carolina.* Philadelphia, 1924.

Knight, Edgar W.   *The Academy Movement in the South.* [*High School Jour.*, (Nov., Dec., 1919, & June, 1920) II, 199–204, 235–40, III.] [Reprint]   Chapel Hill, 1920.

Knight, Edgar W.   *The Evolution of Public Education in Virginia.* [Reprint from *Sewanee Review*, (Jan., 1916) XXIV, 24–41.] Sewanee, 1916.

Knight, Edgar W.   *The Influence of Reconstruction On Education In The South.* [*Teachers College Contributions To Education*, No. 60.] Teachers College, Columbia University: New York, 1913.

Knight, Edgar W.   *Public Education in the South.* Ginn: Boston, 1922.

Knight, Edgar W.   Reconstruction and Education in Virginia [Reprint from *South Atlant. Quart.*, XV, Nos. 1 & 2, (Jan. & April, 1916), 25–40, 157–174.]

Koontz, Louis K.   *The Virginia Frontier, 1754–1763.* [*Johns Hopkins U. Studies in Hist. and Polit. Science*, Ser., XLIII.]   Baltimore, 1925.

Latané, John H. *The Early Relations Between Maryland And Virginia.*
[*Johns Hopkins U. Studies in Hist. and Polit. Science,* Thirteenth Ser.,
III–IV.] Baltimore, 1895.

The Late Dr. Cooper. [Niles: *Register,* (June 22, 1839) LVI, 261–62.]

Leake, J. M. *Virginia Committee System & the American Revolution.*
[*Johns Hopkins U. Studies in Hist. & Polit. Science,* Ser., Thirty-five,
No. 1.] Baltimore, 1917.

Leuba, James H. *The Psychology of Religious Mysticism.* Harcourt,
Brace: New York, 1926.

Levinthal, Louis E. Is Christianity Part Of Our Law? [*Jewish Exponent,*
(Aug. 5, 1927.)]

Lewis, A. H. *A Critical History Of Sunday Legislation From 321 To 1888
A. D.* New York, 1888.

Lewis, Thomas Dean. Religious Education: The Need And The Remedy.
[*Va. Jour. Educ.,* (May, 1915) VIII, 466–72.]

Liberal Education. [Niles: *Register,* (Aug. 28, 1829) XXXVII, 2.]

Lingley, Charles R. *The Transition in Virginia From Colony To Commonwealth.* Longmans, Green: New York, 1910.

Literary Fund Of The State Of Virginia. [(Iota.) *Va. Evang. & Lit.
Mag.,* (Feb., 1822) V, 88–97; (Mar., 1822) V, 132–38; (April, 1822)
V, 184–89; (May, 1822) V, 235–42.]

Literary Institutions. The Course Of Studies At Hampden Sidney College.
[*Va. Evang. & Lit. Mag.,* (May, 1819) II, 257–58.]

Literature And Science. [*Va. Evang. & Lit. Mag.,* (Jan., 1819) II, 46–47.]

Lodge, Henry Cabot. *A Short History of the English Colonies in America.*
New York, 1881.

Lotz, Philip Henry. *Current Week-Day Religious Education.* [Abingdon
Religious Education Texts.] Abingdon: New York, 1925.

McCabe, W. Gordon. *Virginia Schools Before and After the Revolution.*
Charlottesville, 1890.

McClung, Calvin M. *Historical Collection of Books.* Knoxville, 1921.

McConaughy, James. The Young Man's Ignorance Of The Bible. [*Pa.
Sch. Jour.,* (Oct., 1908) LVII, 153–56.]

McCullock, D. A. Liberty Hall—Washington College. [*W. Va. Hist. Mag.,*
(Jan., 1905) 9–15.]

McCullock, Delia A. The Virginia Society of the Cincinnati. [*W. Va.
Hist. Mag.,* (Jan., 1905) 1–9.]

McDanel, Ralph Clipman. *The Virginia Constitutional Convention Of
1901–1902.* [*Johns Hopkins U. Studies in Hist. and Polit. Science,*
Ser., XLVI, No. 3.] Baltimore, 1928.

McDaniel, George W. The Bible In Its Place. [*Plain Talk,* (Dec., 1927)
95–98.]

MacDonald, Arthur. *Abnormal Man, Being Essays On Education And
Crime And Related Subjects.* [*U. S. Bur. Educ., Circ. Inf.,* (1893)
No. 3.] Washington, 1893.

McDonald, James J. *Life In Old Virginia.* Old Virginia Pub.: Norfolk, 1907.

McGregor, James Clyde. *The Disruption of Virginia.* Macmillan: New York, 1922.

McI. [lhany], H. M. Bible Study At The University. [*U. of Va. Alum. Bull.*, (April, 1903) N. S., III, No. 2, 21–23.]

McI. [lhany], H. M. Religious Work Of The Session. [*U. of Va. Alum. Bull.*, (Oct., 1903) N. S., III, No. 4, 181–83.]

McIlhany, Jr., H. M. Recent Development In The Religious Work Of The University. [*U. of Va. Alum. Bull.*, (Jan., 1907) N. S., VII, No. 1, 41–43.]

McIlwaine, C. R. Hampden-Sidney College. [*U. S. Bur. Educ., Circ. Inf.*, (1888) No. 1, 227–39.] Washington, 1889.

McIlwaine, Henry R. *The Struggle Of Protestant Dissenters For Religious Toleration In Virginia.* [*Johns Hopkins U. Studies in Hist. and Polit. Science*, Twelfth Ser., IV.] Baltimore, 1894.

McIlwaine, Richard. *Memories of Three Score Years and Ten.* Neale Pub. Co.: New York, 1908.

MacLeod, William Christie. *The American Indian Frontier.* Knopf: New York, 1928.

McMaster, John Stevenson. The Head, Hand and Heart Method. [*Va. Jour. Educ.*, (May, 1912) V, 389–91.]

McPherson, G. W. *The Crisis in Church and College.* Yonkers, 1919.

McPherson, G. W. *The Modern Conflict Over The Bible.* Yonkers, 1919.

Mackay, Constance D'Arcy. Christmas Celebrations And Where To Find Material. [*Va. Jour. Educ.*, (Dec., 1914) VIII, 199–201.]

Maddox, William Arthur. *The Free School Idea In Virginia Before The Civil War.* [*Teachers College Contributions To Education*, No. 93.] Teachers College, Columbia University: New York, 1918.

Magill, Mary Tucker. *Stories from Virginia History For The Young.* Lynchburg, 1897.

[Magri, F. Joseph]. *The Catholic Church In The City And Diocese Of Richmond.* (By A Priest Of The Diocese.) Richmond, 1906.

Magruder, F. A. *Recent Administration in Virginia.* Baltimore, 1912.

Malone, Dumas. *An Outline Of The Life Of Thomas Jefferson 1743–1826.* [*U. of Va. Rec., Ext. Ser.*, (Mar., 1924) VIII, No. 7.] Charlottesville, 1924.

Malone, Dumas. The First Years of Thomas Cooper In America, 1794–1801. [*South Atlant. Quart.*, (April, 1923) XXII, 139–56.]

Marshall, Charles C. *The Roman Catholic Church In The Modern State.* Dodd, Mead: New York, 1928.

Massey, John E. Public Free School Education. [*Va. Educ. Jour.*, (April, 1890) XXI, 177–79.]

Mattfield, Henry W. Can Any Good Come Out Of The Private School? [*School & Society*, (Aug. 22, 1925) XXII, 229–34.]

Matthews, E. G.   Do Our Schools Meet the Necessary Wants of the Country in Regard to Moral Training?   [*Va. Sch. Jour.*, (April, 1897) VI, 123–24.]

Maury, Dabney Herndon.   *A Young People's History of Virginia and Virginians.*   Richmond, 1896.

Maxwell, H.   The Use And Abuse Of Forests By The Virginia Indians.   [*Wm. & Mary Coll. Quart.*, (Oct., 1910) XIX, 73–103.]

Mayo, A. D.   The Charge of Godlessness and Shiftlessness Against the Public Schools.   [*Va. Educ. Jour.*, (Jan., 1879) X, 1–13.]

Mayo, A. D.   Common And Uncommon Religious Teaching In Common Schools.   [*Jour. of Educ.*, (Sept. 28, 1882) XVI, 197–98.]

Mayo, A. D.   *Southern Women In The Recent Educational Movement In The South.*   [*U. S. Bur. Educ., Circ. Inf.*, (1892) No. 1.]   Washington, 1892.

Meade, William.   *Old Churches, Ministers and Families of Virginia.*   2 vols.   Philadelphia, 1861.

Medical College, at Richmond, Va.   [*So. Lit. Messenger*, (Dec., 1839) V, 827–28.]

Meeting To Vindicate The Character Of Jefferson.   [Niles: *Register*, (Aug. 22, 1840) LVIII, 392.]

Memoir Of The Rev. Samuel Davies.   [*Va. Evang. & Lit. Mag.*, (Mar., 1819) II, 112–19; (April, 1819) II, 186–89; (May, 1819) II, 201–17; (June, 1819) II, 329–35; (Aug., 1819) II, 353–63; (Sept., 1819) 474–79; (Dec., 1819) 560–67.]

Mercer, Margaret.   *Popular Lectures on Ethics or Moral Obligations: For the use of schools.*   Petersburg, 1841.

The Methodists.   [Niles: *Register*, (Nov. 3, 1821) XXI, 148.]

Michael, O. S.   *The Sunday School In The Development Of The American Church.*   The Young Churchman Co.: Milwaukee, 1904.

Micou, Paul.   The Services of Commissary James Blair to the Colony of Virginia.   [*South Atlant. Quart.*, (April, 1909) VIII, 164–73.]

Miller, Elmer I.   *The Legislature Of The Province of Virginia. Its Internal Development.*   [*Columbia University Studies in History, Economics and Public Law*, Vol. 28, No. 2.]   Columbia University: New York, 1907.

Miller, H. Augustus.   The Bible and the School.   [*Va. Jour. Educ.*, (Nov., 1925) XIX, 94–96.]

[Miller, Thos. C.].   *The History of Education in West Virginia.*   Charleston, 1907.

Mims, Edwin.   *The Advancing South.*   Doubleday, Page: New York, 1926.

Mims, Edwin.   The South Realizing Itself.   [*World's Work*, (Nov., 1911) XXIII, 41–54.]

Minor, B. B.   The Chapel At The University.   [*U. of Va. Alum. Bull.*, (Feb., 1897) III, No. 4, 101–05.]

[Minor, B. B.].   University of Virginia.   [*So. Lit. Messenger*, (Jan., 1842) VIII, 50–54.]

[Minor, J. B.] [(Paragraph concerning his address "Bible Instruction in the Private Schools" cf. *Minutes Va. Educ. Assoc.*, July 13, 1871, 8, where title is given "Bible Teaching in Schools.") *Va. Educ. Jour.*, (Aug., 1871) II, 362.]

Mitchell, Samuel C.   Character And Culture.   [*Relig. Educ.*, (April, 1914) IX, 131–36.]

Mitchell, S. C.   The Task of the College in the South.   [*South Atlant. Quart.*, (April, 1907) V, 259 *ff.*]

[Moore, Clement Clarke].   *Observations Upon Certain Passages In Mr. Jefferson's Notes On Virginia, Which Appear To Have A Tendency To Subvert Religion, And Establish A False Philosophy.*   New York, 1804.

Moral Education.   [*Va. Educ. Jour.*, (Oct., 1891) XXII, 443–44.]

Morgan, Alexander.   *Rise And Progress of Scottish Education.*   Oliver & Boyd: Edinburgh, 1927.

Morgan, B. S., & Cork, J. F.   *Columbian History of Education in West Virginia.*   Charleston, 1893.

Morris, B. F.   *Christian Life and Character Of The Civil Institutions Of The United States.*   Philadelphia, 1864.

Morris, Caspar.   *Memoir of Miss Margaret Mercer.*   Philadelphia, 1848.

Morrison, A. J.   *The Beginnings of Public Education in Virginia, 1776–1860.*   Richmond, 1917.

Morrison, A. J.   *Four Revolutions and Virginia Education.*   [Reprint—paged 120 to 140—appeared first in the Texas Review—no date.]

Morrison, A. J.   Virginia Works and Days, 1814–1819.   [*South Atlant. Quart.*, (Jan., 1919) XVIII, 24–35.]

Morton, Oren F.   *Annals of Bath County, Virginia.*   McClure: Staunton, 1917.

Motley, Daniel Esten.   *Life of Commissary James Blair.*   [*Johns Hopkins U. Studies in Hist. and Polit. Science*, XIII, No. 10.]   Baltimore, 1901.

Mundie, Joseph R.   *An Economic And Social Survey of King and Queen County.*   [*U. of Va. Rec., Ext. Ser.*, (July, 1925) IX, No. 10.]   Charlottesville, 1925.

National Education.   [*Niles: Register*, (Nov. 1, 1817) XIII, 145–47.]

Necessity Of A Better System Of Instruction.   No. III, No. IV.   [(By A Provincial Protestant.)   *Va. Evang. & Lit. Mag.*, (June, 1818) I, 255–61; (July, 1818) I, 315–18.]

Negro Education, a Study of the Private and Higher Schools for Colored People in the United States.   2 vols.   [*U. S. Bur. Educ., Bull.*, 1916, No. 38, No. 39.]   Washington, 1917.

Neill, Edward D.   *The English Colonization of America.*   London, 1871.

Neill, Edward D.   *The History of Education in Virginia During the Seventeenth Century.*   Washington, 1867.

Neill, Edward D.   *Memoir of Rev. Patrick Copland.*   New York, 1871.

Neill, Edward D.   *Virginia Carolorum.*   Albany, 1886.

Neill, Edward D. *Virginia Company of London Extracts From Their Manuscript Transactions. With Notes.* Washington, 1868.

Neill, Edward D. *Notes on the Virginia Colonial Clergy.* Philadelphia, 1877.

Neuman, Henry. *Moral Values In Secondary Education.* [*U. S. Bur. Educ., Bull.,* 1917, No. 51.] Washington, 1918.

Nevins, Allan. *American Social History As Reported By British Travellers.* Holt: New York, 1923.

Nevins, Allan. *The American States During And After The Revolution 1775–1789.* Macmillan: New York, 1924.

New Foundations And Reorganizations. [*Alum. Bull., U. of Va.,* (Jan., 1907) 76–80.]

News and Notes. Randolph Macon College. [*Va. Educ. Jour.,* (Sept., 1884) XV, 396.]

Nickell, Lehman & Randolph, Cary J. *Economic And Social Survey Of Fairfax County.* [*U. of Va. Rec., Ext. Ser.,* (Aug., 1924) VIII, No. 12.] Charlottesville, 1924.

Nock, Albert Jay. *Jefferson.* Harcourt, Brace: New York, 1926.

The Norfolk Academy, 1840. [*Lower Norfolk Co., Va. Antiquary,* (1904) IV, Part 4, 150–63.]

The Normal Bulletin, State Normal School. [Magazine No., Jan., 1918; S. S., 1918, Vol. X, No. 2, Feb., 1918.] Harrisonburg, Va.

Norris, J. E. *History of the Lower Shenandoah Valley Counties of Frederick, Berkeley, Jefferson and Clarke.* Chicago, 1890.

Northampton County Records in 17th Century. [*Va. Mag. Hist.,* (July, 1897) V, 33–41.]

The North And The South. [*De Bow's Review* (Oct., 1849) VII, 304–16.]

Northern Colleges. [*De Bow's Review* (May, 1854) XVI, 551.]

The Northern Neck of Virginia. [*De Bow's Review,* (Sept., 1859) XXVII, 279–95.]

Norwood, John Nelson. *The Schism in the Methodist Episcopal Church 1844.* Alfred Press: Alfred, 1923.

Notes And Queries. A Religious Feud In The Valley. [*Va. Mag. Hist.,* (Oct., 1920) XXVIII, 361–69.]

Notes And Queries. "Sketches [&c.] by a Traveller." [*Va. Mag. Hist.,* (Jan., 1901) VIII, 330–31.]

Notes On Books. [*Wm. & Mary Coll. Quart.,* (Oct., 1896) V, 144–45.]

Objections To The Present Plan Of Education, And Some Suggestions Of A Better—To The Parents And Teachers Of Virginia. [(By Cleanthes) *Va. Evang. & Lit. Mag.,* (April, 1819) II, 177–86.]

O'Connell, William. The Reasonable Limits of State Activity. [*The Catholic Educational Association Bulletin,* (Nov., 1919) XVI, 62–76.]

O'Donnell, John Hugh. *The Catholic Hierarchy of the U. S. 1790–1922.* [*The Catholic U. of Amer. Studies in Amer. Church History,* Vol. IV.] Washington, 1922.

O'Donnell, William Charles, Jr. *Creed and Curriculum. A Discussion of the Question, Can the Essentials of Religious Faith and Practice be Taught in the Public Schools of the United States?* Eaton & Mains: New York, 1914.

Old Documents. Attempts to evangelize the Negro-slaves in Virginia and Carolina, from 1747 to 1755. [*Va. Evang. & Lit. Mag.*, (Oct., 1821) IV, 538–52.]

The Oldfield School. [(Buckskin) *So. Lit. Messenger*, (April, 1837) III, 217–21.]

Old Kecoughtan. [*Wm. & Mary Coll. Quart.*, (Oct., 1900) IX, 83–131.]

Oldmixon, John. *The British Empire In America.* 2 vols. London, 1741.

Old Virginia Editors. [*Wm. & Mary Coll. Quart.*, (July, 1898) VII, 9–17.]

Old William And Mary. [*So. Lit. Messenger*, (Mar., 1859) XXVIII, 172–76.]

On Public Education In Virginia. [*So. & West. Lit. Messenger & Rev.*, (Nov., 1847)' 685–89.]

Origin Of Presbyterianism In Virginia. [*Va. Evang. & Lit. Mag.*, (Aug., 1819) II, 345–53.]

Osgood, Herbert L. *The American Colonies In The Seventeenth Century.* 3 vols. Macmillan: New York, 1904.

Osgood, Herbert L. *The American Colonies In The Eighteenth Century.* 4 vols. Columbia University Press: New York, 1924.

O'Shea, M. V. *Public Education In Virginia.* Richmond, 1928.

Our Sunday And Anti-Sunday Laws. [*Literary Digest*, (Sept. 12, 1925) 32–33.]

Page, F. W. Our Library. [*U. of Va. Alum. Bull.*, (Nov., 1895) II, No. 3, 78–85.]

Page, Thomas Nelson. *The Old Dominion Her Making And Her Manners.* Scribner: New York, 1908.

Page, Thomas Nelson. *The Old South Essays Social And Political.* New York, 1894.

Painter, F. V. N. *A History of Education.* New York, 1886.

Palmer, William Scott & Du Bose, W. P. *Liberal and mystical writings of William Law.* Longmans, Green: London, 1908.

Parrington, Vernon Louis. *The Colonial Mind.* [Vol. I in series, *"Main Currents in American Thought."*] Harcourt, Brace: New York, 1927.

Parrington, Vernon Louis. *The Romantic Revolution in America 1800–1860.* [Vol. II in series, *"Main Currents in American Thought."*] Harcourt, Brace: New York, 1927.

Particular Account Of The Dreadful Fire At Richmond, Virginia, December 26, 1811. Baltimore, 1812.

Parton, James. *Life of Thomas Jefferson.* Boston, 1874.

Parton, James. Thomas Jefferson a Reformer of Old Virginia. [*Atlantic Monthly*, (July, 1872) 32, cf. also 174, 273, 405, 547, 704.]

Patton, Jacob Harris. *The Triumph of the Presbytery of Hanover; or Separation of Church and State in Virginia. With a Concise History of the Presbyterian Church in the United States from 1705 to 1888.* New York, 1887.

Patton, John S. *Jefferson, Cabell And The University Of Virginia.* Neale: New York, 1906.

Patton, John S., & Doswell, Sallie J. *The University Of Virginia. Glimpses Of Its Past And Present.* Bell Co.: Lynchburg, 1900.

Payne, Bruce R. The Rural Community. How To Provide For The Spread Of Religious And Ethical Teaching In The Local Community. [*Relig. Educ.*, (June, 1910) V, 131–35.]

Payne, Bruce R. Virginia Moral Education and Training. [*Relig. Educ.*, (April, 1911), VI, 99–101.]

Peabody, Francis Greenwood. *Education For Life The Story of Hampton Institute.* Doubleday, Page: Garden City, 1919.

Peabody, F. G., & Ludlow, H. W. *Armstrong's Ideas On Education for Life.* Hampton, 1926.

Pearson, Charles Chilton. *The Readjuster Movement In Virginia.* Yale University Press: New Haven, 1917.

Pearson, Charles Chilton. William Henry Ruffner: Reconstruction Statesman of Virginia. [*South Atlant. Quart.*, (Jan., 1921) XX, 25–32; (April, 1921) 137–51.]

A Perfect Christmas Day. [*Va. Jour. Educ.*, (Dec., 1914) 162.]

Peter, Robert, & Peter, Johanna. *Transylvania University, Its Origin, Rise, Decline, And Fall.* [Filson Club Publications No. 11.] Louisville, 1896.

Peyton, J. Lewis. *History of Augusta County, Virginia.* Staunton, 1882.

Pickell, John. *A New Chapter In The Early Life Of Washington In Connection With The Narrative History Of The Potomac Company.* New York, 1856.

Pleasants, J. Hall. The English Descent Of John Pleasants, (1645–1668) Of Henrico County, Virginia. [*Va. Mag. Hist.*, (Oct., 1908) XVI, 218–20.]

Pleasants, J. Hall. The Lovelace Family And Its Connections. [*Va. Mag. Hist.*, (Oct., 1920) XXVIII, 375–92; (April, 1921) XXIX, 227–43.]

Prayer. [*Va. Jour. Educ.*, (Dec., 1911) V, 122.]

The Present State of The County of Frederick, With Respect To Religion. [*Va. Evang. & Lit. Mag.*, (April, 1822) V, 220–22.]

Primary Schools. [(A School Commissioner) *Va. Evang. & Lit. Mag.*, (July, 1825) VIII, 367–74.]

Prince, Walter F. The First Criminal Code of Virginia. [*Annual Report Amer. Hist. Assoc'n*, (1899) I, No. IX.]

Pritts, J. *Mirror of Olden Time Border Life.* Abingdon, 1849.

Proceedings and Report of the Commissioners for the University of Virginia, Presented 8th of December, 1818. Richmond, . . . 1818. [Review: (Everett, Edward): *The North American Review*, (Jan., 1820) X, 115–37.]

Progress of Education In Virginia. The University And The Colleges.
[*So. Lit. Messenger*, (Mar., 1857) XXIV, 161–69; (April, 1857) 241–
47; (June, 1857) 401–09; (July, 1857) XXV, 55–62; (Aug., 1857)
131–33.]

Progress Of The United States, 1783–1855. [*De Bow's Review*, (Feb.,
1855) XVIII, 217–23.]

Pryor, Sara Agnes (Rice). *The Birth of the Nation, Jamestown, 1607*.
Macmillan: New York, 1907.

The Public Schools of Rockingham County, Virginia. Harrisonburg.

Randall, Daniel R. *A Puritan Colony In Maryland.* [*Johns Hopkins U.
Studies In Hist. and Polit. Science*, Fourth Ser., VI.]   Baltimore, 1886.

Randall, Henry S. *Life of Thomas Jefferson.* 3 vols. New York, 1858.

[Randolph, J. W., & English, edition]. *The History of the College of William and Mary From Its Foundation, 1660 to 1874.* Richmond, 1874.

Randolph, Thomas Jefferson. *Memoir, Correspondence, etc., from the
Papers of Thomas Jefferson.* 4 vols. Charlottesville, 1829.

The Randolph Manuscript. Extracts From Virginia Records, 1627–29.
[*Va. Mag. Hist.*, (Jan., 1909) XVII, 1–14.]

Randolph, Sarah N. *Domestic Life of Thomas Jefferson.* New York, 1871.

Rawlings, Mary. *The Albemarle of Other Days.* Michie: Charlottesville,
1925.

Reisner, E. H. *Nationalism And Education Since 1789.* Macmillan: New
York, 1922.

Relation Of Education To The Prevention Of Crime. [*De Bow's Review*,
(Mar., 1855), XVIII, 409–21.]

Religion and Civil Government. [*Southern Review*, (Oct., 1872) XI, 371–
93.]

Religion In Colleges. [(Olim] *Va. Evang. & Lit. Mag.*, (June, 1828) XI,
303–08.]

Religious Intelligence. [*Va. Evang. & Lit. Mag.*, (Mar., 1819) II, 139–43.]

Religious Intelligence. Domestic. [*Va. Evang. & Lit. Mag.*, (Feb., 1818)
I, 94–96.]

Religious Intelligence. Domestic. [*Va. Evang. & Lit. Mag.*, (April, 1818)
I, 188–90.]

Religious Intelligence. Domestic. [*Va. Evang. & Lit. Mag.*, (April, 1819)
II, 189–93.]

Religious Intelligence. Domestic. Account of a Sunday School upper end
of Essex County. [*Va. Evang. & Lit. Mag.*, (May, 1820) III, 238–42.]

Religious Intelligence. Domestic. Sunday School In Fincastle. [*Va.
Evang. & Lit. Mag.*, (Oct., 1820) III, 477–79.]

Religious Intelligence. Domestic. Sunday Schools, In Jefferson County,
Virginia. [(A Friend to Sunday Schools.) *Va. Evang. & Lit. Mag.*,
(Nov., 1819) II, 529–32.]

Religious Intelligence. Domestic. Theological Seminary of the General
Assembly. [*Va. Evang. & Lit. Mag.*, (Sept., 1818) I, 431–32.]

Religious Intelligence. Hampden Sidney College. [*Va. Evang. & Lit. Mag.*, (Aug., 1819) II, 389.]

Religious Intelligence. Revivals In Virginia. [*Va. Evang. & Lit. Mag.*, (Sept., 1828) XI, 500–01.]

Religious Intelligence. Sunday Schools. [*Va. Evang. & Lit. Mag.*, (Sept., 1819) II, 431–36.]

Religious Statistics. [*Va. Educ. Jour.*, (Jan., 1870) I, 93.]

Reminiscences Of An Old Student. [(A. L. N.) *U. of Va. Alum. Bull.*, (Feb., 1897) III, No. 4, 97–98.]

Reminiscences of Lutheran Ministers Article VIII. [Pamphlet, Hist. Soc. of Pennsylvania.]

Reply To "A Friend Of The Poor." [(Iota) *Va. Evang. & Lit. Mag.*, (Aug., 1823) VI, 425–32.]

[Resolution—Meeting of State Board of Education November 23, 1911.] [*Va. Jour. Educ.*, (Feb., 1912) V, 201–02.]

Resolutions Of The State Teachers Association. [*Va. Jour. Educ.*, (Jan., 1922) XV, 191–92.]

Rev. Samuel Henley. [*Wm. & Mary Coll. Quart.*, (Jan., 1899) VII, 153–54.]

Review Of Religious Intelligence Richmond Tract Society. [*Va. Evang. & Lit. Mag.*, (June, 1824) VII, 323.]

Review. Memoirs of Dr. Joseph Priestley . . . by Thomas Cooper, . . . London, 1806. [*Va. Evang. & Lit. Mag.*, (Feb., 1820) III, 63–74.]

Revival Of Religion in Lewis County, Va. [*Va. Evang. & Lit. Mag.*, (Jan., 1825) VIII, 45–47.]

Richards, John William. *Penn's Lutheran Forerunners and Friends.* Book Concern: Columbus, 1926.

Richardson, C. F., & Clark, H. A. *The College Book.* Boston, 1878.

Richardson, David. *Richardson's Virginia and North Carolina Almanac.* Richmond, Va. 1828, 1849, 1857, 1861, 1864, 1865.

(Richmond Enquirer, February 1, 1805) Sketch Of A Plan For The Endowment And Establishment Of A State University In Virginia. [*Wm. & Mary Coll. Quart.*, (Oct., 1924) N. S., IV, 266–76.]

Richmond Female Institute. [Barnard: *Jour. of Educ.*, (1856) I, 231–33.]

Richmond Female Institute And The Richmond Churches. [*Relig. Herald*, (Aug., 29, 1878.)]

Richmond Female Institute. [*So. Lit. Mess.*, (Oct., 1860) XXI, (320) Supplementary section.]

The Richmond Sunday School Union. [*Va. Evang. & Lit. Mag.*, (June, 1819) II, 290–92.]

Ripley, William Z. *The Financial History Of Virginia 1609–1776.* New York, 1893.

Rives, William C. *History Of The Life And Times Of James Madison.* 3 vols. Boston, 1866.

[Roane]. Common Schools And Universities, North and South. [*De Bow's Review*, (April, 1855) XVIII, 545–55.]

Roanoke College. [*Jour. of Educ.*, (June 28, 1883) XVIII, 11.]

Robertson, Archibald Thomas. *Life and Letters of John Albert Broadus.* Amer. Baptist Pub. Soc.: Philadelphia, 1901.

Robertson, David Allan, editor. *American Universities And Colleges.* Scribner: New York, 1928.

Robertson, William. *The History of America . . . Containing The History of Virginia to the Year 1688.* 2 vols. Philadelphia, 1822.

Robertson, William J. *The Changing South.* Boni & Liveright: New York, 1927.

Robinson, Conway. Notes From Council And General Court Records. [*Va. Mag. Hist.*, (April, 1906) XIII, 389–401.]

Robinson, Conway. Notes From Council and General Court Records, 1641–1659. [*Va. Mag. Hist.*, (July, 1900) VIII, 64–73.]

Robinson, Conway. Notes from the Council and General Court Records 1641–1644. [*Va. Mag. Hist.*, (Oct., 1900) VIII, 162–70.]

Robinson, Conway. Notes from the Council and General Court Records 1641–1672. [*Va. Mag. Hist.*, (Jan., 1901) VIII, 236–44.]

Rosengarten, J. G. *French Colonists And Exiles In The United States.* Lippincott: Philadelphia, 1907.

Ruffin, Kirkland. Christmas In The Kindergarten. [*Va. Jour. Educ.*, (Dec., 1914) 193–95.]

Ruffner, Henry. Early History of Washington College, Now Washington And Lee University. [*Wash. & Lee Hist. Papers*, (1890) No. 1, 1–105.]

R. [uffner], W. H. The Colleges and Col. Allan. [*Va. Educ. Jour.*, (Oct., 1878) IX, 550.]

Ruffner, William Henry. History Of Washington College During The First Half Of The Nineteenth Century: A Continuation Of The "Early History Of Washington College, By Henry Ruffner, D.D., LL.D." [*Wash. & Lee Hist. Papers*, (1893) No. 4; continued, (1895) No. 5.]

R. [uffner], W. H. Remarks on Col. Allan's Hampton Address. [*Va. Educ. Jour.* (Sept., 1878) IX, 499–500.]

Ruffner, W. H. What Are Normal Schools In Fact? [*Va. Educ. Jour.*, (June, 1884) XV, 225–36.]

Mr. Ruffner's Report. [*Va. Educ. Jour.*, (May, 1870) I, 223–25.]

Ruggles, Henry Stoddard. The Lineage of George Ruggle. [*Wm. & Mary Coll. Quart.*, (Jan., 1897) V, 203–04.]

Rugh, C. E. [et al.]. *Moral Training in the Public Schools.* Ginn: Boston, 1907.

Russell, John H. *The Free Negro In Virginia 1619–1865.* [*Johns Hopkins U. Studies in Hist. and Polit. Science*, Ser., XXXI, No. 3.] Baltimore, 1913.

Ryan, J. A., & Millar, M. F. X. *The State And The Church.* Macmillan: New York, 1924.

Sainsbury, William Noel. *Calendar of State Papers, Colonial Series, America and West Indies, 1661–1668.* London, 1880.

Sams, Conway Whittle. *The Conquest of Virginia. The Forest Primeval.* Putnam: New York, 1916.

Sandy, T. O. Mr. Sandy Appeals To Ministers. [*Va. Jour. Educ.*, (June, 1914) VII, 469–70.]

Savage, M. Notes [*Va. Educ. Jour.*, (Feb., 1890) XXI, 70.]

Savage, M. J. What Shall The Public Schools Teach? [*The Forum*, (Jan., 1888) IV, 460–71.]

Scale Of Education In The United States. [Niles: *Register*, (Nov. 19, 1842) LXIII, 184.]

Scarborough, Henry W. Quaker Pioneers Of Shenandoah And Rockingham Counties, Virginia. [*Wm. & Mary Coll. Quart.*, (Jan., 1926) N. S., VI, 39–46.]

Schaff, Philip. *America. A Sketch of the Political, Social and Religious Character of the United States.* New York, 1855.

Schaff, Philip. *Church And State In The United States.* [*Papers of the Amer. Hist. Assoc'n*, II, No. 4.] New York, 1888.

School Credit For Bible Study. [*Va. Jour. Educ.*, (Nov., 1921) XV, 107–08.]

Schools In Virginia. [*Wm. & Mary Coll. Quart.*, (April, 1909) XVII, 244–47.]

Schuricht, Hermann. *History Of The German Element In Virginia.* 2 vols. Baltimore, 1898.

Schurz, Carl, editor. *Geschichtsblätter: Bilder und Mittheilungen aus dem Leben der Deutschen in Amerika.* New York, 1885.

Scott, W. W. "The Knights Of The Horseshoe." [*Wm. & Mary Coll. Quart.*, (July, 1923) N. S., III, 145–53.]

Scull, G. D. *The Evelyns in America.* Oxford, 1881.

Seagle, William. The Moral Law. [*Amer. Mercury*, (Dec., 1926) IX, 451–57.]

Seagle, William. A Christian Country. [*Amer. Mercury*, (Oct., 1925) VI, 226–33.]

Seaver, Edwin P. Education in Morals. [*Va. Educ. Jour.*, (July, 1883) XIV, 205–07.]

The Shakespeare Examinations At Hollins Institute. [*Jour. of Educ.*, (Aug. 9, 1883) XVIII, 89.]

Shea, John Gilmary. *The Catholic Church In Colonial Days.* [*History of the Catholic Church in the United States*, Vol. I.] New York, 1886.

Shea, John Gilmary. *Life And Times Of The Most Rev. John Carroll.* [*History of the Catholic Church in the United States*, Vol. II.] New York, 1888.

Shelly, Patrick Joseph. The Catholic School and Citizenship. [*The Forum*, (Dec., 1925) LXXIV, 834–36.]

Short Chapters: By Patrick Pedant, School Master. [*So. Lit. Messenger*, (Feb., 1839) V, 112–16.]

Sisson, Edward O. *The Essentials of Character.* Macmillan: New York, 1911.

Sketches of Trustees. [*Wash. & Lee Hist. Papers*, (1892) No. 3, 86–128, (1893) No. 4, 167–96; (1895) No. 5, 33–210.]

Slaughter, Philip. *The Colonial Church of Virginia.* Boston, 1885.

Slaughter, Philip. *Genealogical and Historical Notes on Culpeper County, Virginia.* [Green, Raleigh Travers, compiler.] Culpeper, 1900.

Slaughter, Philip. *History of Bristol Parish Virginia.* Richmond, 1879.

Slaughter, Philip. *A History of St. George's Parish in the County of Spottsylvania and Diocese of Virginia.* New York, 1847. [Also, Brock, R. A., editor, Richmond, 1890.]

Slaughter, Philip. *The History of Truro Parish in Virginia.* [Goodwin, E. L., editor.] Jacobs: Philadelphia, 1908.

Slaughter, Philip. *Memoir of Col. Joshua Fry, Sometime Professor in William and Mary College, Virginia.* Richmond, 1880.

Smith, Francis H. The Rotunda. [*U. of Va. Alum. Bull.*, (Nov., 1895) II, No. 3, 85–90.]

Smith, J. W. Devereux Jarratt And The Beginnings Of Methodism In Virginia. [*Branch Hist. Papers*, (June, 1901) No. 1, 3–21.]

Smith, Sherman M. *The Relation Of The State To Religious Education In Massachusetts.* Syracuse University Book Store: Syracuse, 1926.

Smith, W. R. L. *Charles Lewis Cocke Founder Of Hollins College.* Badger: Boston, 1921.

Sneath, Elias H. & Hodges, George. *Moral Training in the School and Home; A Manual for Teachers and Parents.* Macmillan: New York, 1913.

Sneath, Elias H., & Hodges, George. *Religious Training in the School and Home; A Manual for Teachers and Parents.* Macmillan: New York, 1917.

Snidow, F. A., & McComas, F. W., Jr. *An Economic and Social Survey of Giles County.* [*U. of Va. Rec., Ext. Ser.*, (Feb., 1927) XI, No. 8.] University, 1927.

Snyder, Henry Nelson. The Denominational College In Southern Education. [*South Atlant. Quart.*, (Jan., 1906) V, 8 *ff.*]

Society Of The Cincinnati. [*Wm. & Mary Coll. Quart.*, (Jan., 1901) IX, 192–94.]

The South. *Richmond College.* [*Jour. of Educ.*, (April 19, 1877) V, 190.]

Spiller, Gustav. *Report on Moral Instruction and on Moral Training in Eighteen Countries.* Watts: London, 1909.

Squires, Vernon P. The Bible and the Rising Generation. [*Va. Jour. Educ.*, (Feb., 1912) V, 202–04.]

Stanard, Mary N. *Colonial Virginia Its People And Customs.* Lippincott: Philadelphia, 1917.

Stanard, Mary N. *Richmond Its People And Its Story.* Lipppincott: Philadelphia, 1923.

Stanard, W. G., editor. Abstracts of Rappahannock Co. Wills. [*Va. Mag. Hist.*, (Jan., 1898) V, 282–88.]

Stanard, W. G. Abstracts Of Virginia Land Patents. [*Va. Mag. Hist.*, (July, 1897) V, 92–101.]

Stanard, Wm. G., & Mary Newton. *The Colonial Virginia Register.* Munstell: Albany, 1902.

Stanard, W. G. Major Robert Beverley and His Descendants. [*Va. Mag. Hist.*, (Jan., 1896) III, 261–71.]

Stanard, W. G. Virginians at Oxford. [*Wm. & Mary Coll. Quart.*, (July, 1893) II, 22–24.]

State of Religion and means of Religious Improvement, in the Borough of Norfolk, Va. [*Va. Evang. & Lit. Mag.*, (April, 1822) V, 222–23.]

State of Religion, and means of Religious improvement in Fredericksburg, Va. [*Va. Evang. & Lit. Mag.*, (Mar. 1822) V, 166.]

State of Religion, and means of Religious improvement in Lynchburg, Va. [*Va. Evang. & Lit. Mag.*, (Mar., 1822) V, 167.]

State of Religion, and means of Religious improvement in Petersburg, Virginia. [*Va. Evang. & Lit. Mag.*, (Feb., 1822) V, 111–12.]

Steiger, E. *Steiger's Educational Directory.* New York, 1878.

Steiner, Bernard C. A Frenchman's Impressions of Maryland and Virginia in 1791. [*Sewanee Review*, (Jan., 1904) XII, 52–72.]

Steiner, Bernard C. Two Eighteenth Century Missionary Plans. [*Sewanee Review*, (July, 1903) XI, 289–305.]

Stephenson, Gilbert T. Education and Crime Among Negroes. [*South Atlant. Quart.*, (Jan., 1917) XVI, 14–20.]

Stevens, J. A. *Yorktown Centennial Handbook Historical and Topographical Guide to The Yorktown Peninsula.* New York, 1881.

Stewart, George. *A History of Religious Education in Connecticut.* [*Yale Studies In The History and Theory of Religious Education*, Vol. I.] Yale University Press: New Haven, 1924.

Stewart, Joseph S. Religious Life In State Institutions of the South. [*High School Quart.*, (Jan., 1921 & April, 1921, IX, 68 *ff.* & 173 *ff.*]

Stewart, Robert. *The United States of America.* London, 1853.

Stewart, William H., editor. *History of Norfolk County, Virginia, And Representative Citizens.* Biographical Publishing Co: Chicago, 1902.

Stillé, Charles J. *The Life and Times of John Dickinson 1732–1808.* [*Hist. Soc. of Penn'a*, XIII.] Philadelphia, 1891.

Stith, William. *History of the First Discovery and Settlement of Virginia.* Williamsburg, 1747. [Sabin's Reprints, No. VI.] New York, 1865.

Stoever, M. L. *A Brief Sketch Of The Evangelical Lutheran Church.* Philadelphia. [Pamphlet, no date; Hist. Soc. of Penn'a.]

Stowe, Calvin E. The Religious Element In Education. [*American Institute of Instruction Lectures*, (1845) XV, 1–32.]

Stratemeier, George Boniface. *Thomas Cornwaleys, Commissioner and Counsellor of Maryland.* [*The Catholic U. of America Studies in Amer. Church History*, II.] Washington, 1922.

Strother, French. Youth Takes The Helm In Virginia. [*World's Work*, (Dec., 1926) LIII, 148.]

Stubbs, J. E.   Value of Literary Culture to the Teacher.   [*Va. Educ. Jour.*, (Dec., 1884) XV, 513–20.]

Sulfridge, H. S.   The Curriculum Of The Modern High School.   [*U. of Va. Rec., Ext. Ser.*, (Dec., 1925) X, No. 4, 31 *ff.*]

Sullivan, Mark.   *Our Times The United States 1900–1925 America Finding Herself.*   [Vol. II.]   Scribner: New York, 1927.

Sunday Schools.   [*Va. Evang. & Lit. Mag.*, (Aug., 1819) II, 382–84.]

Sunday Schools, A Cause of Alarm!   [(Viator) *Va. Evang. & Lit. Mag.*, (May, 1828) XI, 245–50.]

Sunday-Schools And The American Sunday-School Union.   [Barnard: *Amer. Jour. Educ.*, (1865) XV, 705–20.]

Sunday School Teacher Training in the State Normal School East Radford, Virginia.   [*Va. Jour. Educ.*, (Dec., 1919) XIII, 141.]

Sunday School Union.   [*Va. Evang. & Lit. Mag.*, (July, 1819) II, 340.]

The Sunday Shop; Or, The Fourth Commandment.   Richmond, 1867.

System Of Common Schools.   [*So. Quart. Review*, (Oct., 1844) VI, 453–82.]

Sweet, William Warren.   *The Methodist Episcopal Church and the Civil War.*   Methodist Book Concern: Cincinnati, 1912.

Taylor, Abrutheus Ambush.   *The Negro in the Reconstruction of Virginia.* [The Association For The Study of Negro Life and History.]   Washington, 1926.

Taylor, James B.   *Virginia Baptist Ministers.*   [Series I.]   Philadelphia, 1859.

Taylor, Yardley.   *Memoir of Loudoun County, Virginia.*   Leesburg, 1853.

Theological Seminary In Prince Edward.   [*Va. Evang. & Lit. Mag.*, (Nov., 1826) IX, 611–13.]

Theological Seminary In Virginia.   [*Va. Evang. & Lit. Mag.*, (Nov., 1822) V, 604.]

Thom, William Taylor.   *The Struggle For Religious Freedom In Virginia: The Baptists.*   [*Johns Hopkins U. Studies in Hist. and Polit. Science*, Ser., XVIII, Nos., 10–11–12.]   Baltimore, 1900.

Thomas Jefferson.   Memoir.   [Barnard: *Amer. Jour. of Educ.*, (1877) XXVII, 513–50.]

Thomas, R. S.   Book Reviews.   The Early Relations Between Maryland And Virginia.   By John H. Latané, A. B. Johns Hopkins Press, Baltimore, March and April, 1895.   [*Va. Mag. Hist.*, (Jan., 1897) IV, 342–48; (April, 1897) IV, 469–72; (July, 1897) V, 106–12; (Oct., 1897) V, 228–32.]

Thoughts On Sunday Schools, And Sunday School Books.   [(W.) *So. Lit. Messenger*, (April, 1838) IV, 224–27.]

To The Visitors Of William And Mary College.   [(Justice To All.) Pamphlet, 11 pages—no title page—Hist. Soc. of Penn'a.]

Torrence, William Clayton.   *A Trial Bibliography of Colonial Virginia.* [*Va. State Library, Special Rep't, Dep't of Bibliography.*]   Richmond, 1908.

Torrence, William Clayton. *A Trial Bibliography Of Colonial Virginia* *(1754–1776.)* [*Va. State Library, Special Report Dep't of Bibliography, 5th Annual Rep't, 1907–1908.*] Richmond, 1910.

Torrence, William Clayton. Henrico County: Virginia: Beginnings Of Its Families. [*Wm. & Mary Coll. Quart.*, (April, 1916) XXIV, 262–83.]

Tracts. 3 vols. [Collection of Sunday School Tracts—for the most part published by the Sunday and Adult School Union, Philadelphia, in second decade, 19th C. Library, U. of Pennsylvania.]

Trent, William F. *English Culture In Virginia.* [*Johns Hopkins U. Studies in Hist. and Polit. Science*, Seventh Ser., V–VI.] Baltimore, 1889.

Tyler, Lyon G. Bruton Church. [*Wm. & Mary Coll. Quart.*, (Jan., 1895) III, 169–80.]

Tyler, Lyon G. *The Cradle Of The Republic: Jamestown and James River.* Richmond, 1900.

Tyler, Lyon G. Grammar And Mattey Practice And Model School. [*Wm. & Mary Coll. Quart.*, (July, 1895) IV, 3–14.]

Tyler, Lyon G. Inscriptions on Old Tombs in Gloucester Co., Virginia. [*Wm. & Mary Coll. Quart.*, (July, 1894) III, 28–43.]

Tyler, Lyon G. Lightfoot Family. [*Wm. & Mary Coll. Quart.*, (Oct., 1894) III, 104–11.]

[Tyler, Lyon G.] *The Making Of the Union.* Richmond, 1899.

Tyler, Lyon G. London Company Records. [*Annual Rep't Amer. Hist. Assoc.* (1901) I, 543–50.]

Tyler, Lyon G. William and Mary College, the College of Epochs. [*Va. Jour. Educ.*, (April, 1919) XII, 320–21.]

Tyler, Lyon G. *Williamsburg, the Old Colonial Capital.* Whittet & Shepperson: Richmond, 1907.

U. S. Commissioner of Education. (Harris, Wm. T.) The University's Contributions To Higher Education. [*U. of Va. Alum. Bull.*, (April, 1902) N. S., II, 7–16.]

University of Virginia. [*Amer. Jour. Educ.*, (Nov., 1826) I, 697–98.]

University Of Virginia. [*De Bow's Review*, (August, 1855) XIX, 218]

University of Virginia. [Niles: *Register*, (July 10, 1841) LX, 304.]

The University Of Virginia. [*De Bow's Review*, (Jan., 1857) XXII, 62–73.]

The University of Virginia. [Niles: *Register*, (June 26, 1824) XXVI, 279.]

The University of Virginia. [*Va. Evang. & Lit. Mag.*, (Dec., 1820) III, 587–88.]

The University of Virginia. [*Va. Hist. Register*, (Jan., 1849) II, No. 1, 56–57.]

University Of Virginia. [(From Richmond Enquirer, Dec. 6, 1805) *Wm. & Mary Coll. Quart.*, (Jan., 1923) N. S. III, 58–62.]

University Of Virginia. [(From Richmond Enquirer, Jan. 16, 1806) *Wm. & Mary Coll. Quart.*, (Jan., 1923) N. S., III, 63–64.]

Use Of the Bible In The Virginia High Schools. [*Va. Jour. Educ.*, (Sept., 1924) XVIII, 16–17.]

View Of Religion In The Southern And Western States. [*Va. Evang. & Lit Mag.*, (Jan., 1822) 53.]

Virginia. [Barnard: *Amer. Jour. of Educ.*, (1856) I, 456–57.]

Virginia. [Barnard: *Amer. Jour. of Educ.*, (1856) II, 557–61.]

Virginia. [*De Bow's Review*, (May, 1851) X, 536–49.]

Virginia. [Niles: *Register*, (Mar. 26, 1825) XXVIII, 50.]

Virginia. [Niles: *Register*, (Nov. 26, 1825) XXIX, 195.]

Virginia. *Education.* [Niles: *Register*, (June 6, 1846) LXX, 214.]

Virginia Educational Conventions. [Barnard: *Amer. Jour. Educ.*, (1866) XVI, 173–76.]

Virginia In 1624–25. (Abstracts from British Public Record Office, by W. N. Sainsbury.) [*Va. Mag. Hist.*, (Oct., 1899) VII, 129–36.]

Virginia In 1629 And 1630. (Abstracts by W. N. Sainsbury and Copies in McDonald Papers, Virginia State Library, from the British Public Record Office.) [*Va. Mag. Hist.*, (April, 1900) VII, 368–86.]

Virginia In 1632–33–34. (Abstracts by W. N. Sainsbury, and Copies in the McDonald Papers, Virginia State Library.) [*Va. Mag. Hist.*, (Oct., 1900) VIII, 147–61.]

Virginia In 1652–1653. (Abstracts by W. N. Sainsbury, and copies in the McDonald and De Jarnette Papers, Virginia State Library.) [*Va. Mag. Hist.*, (Oct., 1909) XVII, 351–63.]

Virginia In 1658–1662. (Abstracts by W. N. Sainsbury, and copies in the McDonald and De Jarnette Papers, Virginia State Library.) [*Va. Mag. Hist.*, (July, 1910) XVIII, 290–303.]

Virginia In 1677. (Abstracts by W. N. Sainsbury, and copies in the McDonald and De Jarnette Papers, Virginia State Library.) [*Va. Mag. Hist.*, (April, 1914) XXII, 140–49.]

Virginia Military Institute. [*U. S. Bur. Educ., Circ. Inf.*, (1888) No. 1, 287–92.] Washington, 1889.

Virginia Military Institute At Lexington. [Barnard: *Jour. of Educ.*, (1872) XXIII, 825–28.]

Virginia Public Schools A Survey of a Southern State Public School System. 2 vols. [By The Virginia Education Commission And The Virginia Survey Staff.] World Book Co.: New York, 1920.

Virginia Schools Their Progress And Their Needs. Ancient and Accepted Scottish Rite of Freemasonry. Richmond, 1923.

Virginia, United States Resources and Advantages of Lynchburg, Virginia. Lynchburg, 1872.

Virginia University. [Niles: *Register*, (May 3, 1845) LXVIII, 144.]

Virginia. *University riot.* [Niles: *Register*, (April 26, 1845) LXVIII, 119.]

The Visitors of the University. [*Va. Evang. & Lit. Mag.*, (Jan., 1820) III, 49.]

Waddell, H. Dr. William Henry Ruffner. [*The Virginia Teacher*, (Oct.-Nov., 1925) V, 268–74.]

Waddell, Jos. A. *Annals of Augusta County, Virginia. From 1726 to 1871.* Richmond, 1866.

Walker, T. C. Sunday Schools In Virginia. [*Ninth Annual Rep't, Hampton Negro Conference*, (1905) 54–60.]

Waller, Flint. School Credit For Bible Study. [*Va. Jour. Educ.*, (April, 1916) IX, 405–07.]

Wannamaker, William H. The German Element In The Settlement Of The South. [*South Atlant. Quart.*, (April, 1910) IX, 144–53.]

Ward, A. W. *Shakespeare and the Makers of Virginia.* [The British Academy The Annual Shakespeare Lecture 1919.] Oxford Univ. Press: London.

Wardle, Addie Grace. *History of the Sunday School Movement in the Methodist Episcopal Church.* Methodist Book Concern: New York, 1918.

Washington, Booker T. The Salvation Of The Negro The Value Of The Work of Hampton Institute. [*World's Work*, (July, 1901) II, 961–70.]

Washington College—Lexington, Virginia. [*So. Lit. Messenger*, (Sept., 1858) XXVII, 222–24.]

Washington College, Virginia. [*Annals of Educ.*, (Sept., 1835) V, 425.]

Washington and Lee University Historical Papers. 5 vols. Baltimore, 1890–1895.

Watson, F. B. Moral Force. [*Va. Sch. Jour.*, (Jan., 1897) VI, 9–11.]

Wayland, John W. *The German Element Of The Shenandoah Valley Of Virginia.* Charlottesville, 1907.

Wayland, John W. *A History of Rockingham County, Virginia.* Ruebush-Elkins: Dayton, 1912.

Weeks, Stephen B. *Southern Quakers and Slavery.* [*Johns Hopkins U. Studies in Hist. and Political Science*, Extra Vol. XV.] Baltimore, 1896.

Wells, Guy Fred. *Parish Education In Colonial Virginia.* [*Teachers College Contributions To Education*, No. 138.] Teachers College, Columbia University: New York, 1923.

Wenner, George U. *Religious Education And The Public School.* Bonnell, Silver: New York, 1907. [Also new edition, rev. and enl., giving the action of the Federal Council of the Churches of Christ in America in 1912. New York, Amer. Tract Society (1913).]

Wertenbaker, Thomas J. The Attempt to Reform the Church of Colonial Virginia. [*Sewanee Review*, (July, 1917) XXV, 257–82.]

Wertenbaker, Thomas J. *The First Americans.* [*A History of American Life*, II.] Macmillan: New York, 1927.

Wertenbaker, Thomas J. *Patrician and Plebeian in Virginia.* Charlottesville, 1910.

Wertenbaker, Thomas J. *The Planters of Colonial Virginia.* Princeton University Press: Princeton, 1922.

Wertenbaker, Thomas J. *Virginia Under The Stuarts 1607–1688.* Princeton University Press: Princeton, 1914.

West, Gerald M. *The Status Of The Negro In Virginia During The Colonial Period.* New York. [No date.]

What Jefferson Stood For. [*Tyler's Quart.*, (Jan., 1926) VII, 154–63.]

What The Editors Say. *Religious Instruction.* [*Va. Sch. Jour.*, (Nov., 1893) II, 313.]

What The Editors Say. *Religious Training.* [*Va. Sch. Jour.*, (April, 1893) II, 132.]

What Shall The Public Schools Teach? [*Va. Educ. Jour.*, (May, 1899) XX, 226–27.]

White & Harris. Washington and Lee University. [*U. S. Bur. Educ.*, *Circ. Inf.*, (1888) No. 1, 293–308.] Washington, 1889.

White, Emerson E. *School Management and Moral Training.* New York, 1893.

White, E. E. Moral Instruction. [*Va. Sch. Jour.*, (Sept., 1893) II, 229–30.]

White, E. E. Moral Training in the Public School. [*Va. Educ. Jour.*, (Feb., 1887) XVIII, 49–58.]

White, E. E. The Two Practical Results of School Education. [*Va. Educ. Jour.*, (Oct., 1884) XV, 419–21.]

Whitehill, A. R. *History Of Education In West Virginia.* [*U. S. Bur. Educ.*, *Circ. Inf.*, No. 1, 1902.] Washington, 1902.

[Whittet & Shepperson, edition.] *A Sketch of the University of Virginia.* Richmond, 1885.

Wickersham, J. P. *Education And Crime.* [*U. S. Bur. Educ.*, *Pamphlets*, 1881.]

Wigmore, Francis M. *The Old Parish Churches Of Virginia.* U. S. Gov't Printing Office: Washington, 1929.

William and Mary College. [*So. Lit. Messenger*, (Mar., 1855) XXI, 15–52.]

William And Mary College. [(Article from Ducyckinck's Cyclopaedia of American Literature) *So. Lit. Messenger*, (Oct., 1856) XXIII, 276–81.]

William And Mary College In 1802. [*Wm. & Mary Coll. Quart.*, (Jan., 1925) N. S., V, 61–62.]

Wm. L. Wilson And Southern Education. [*World's Work*, (Dec., 1900) I, 130.]

Williamsburg—The Old Colonial Capital. [*Wm. & Mary Coll. Quart.*, (July, 1907) XVI, 1–65.]

Wills, Elbert Vaughan. The Case of Doctor Cooper. [*South Atlant. Quart.*, (Jan., 1919) XVIII, 6–14.]

Wingfield, Marshall. *A History of Caroline County, Virginia, From its Foundation in 1727 to 1924.* Trevvet Christian & Co.: Richmond, 1924.

Winsor, Justin, editor. *The Narrative and Critical History of America.* Boston, 1884–89. 8 vols. [Vol. III, Ch. IV, V; Vol. V, Ch. IV.]

Winterbotham, W. American Schools And Education. Virginia. [Barnard: *Amer. Jour. of Educ.,* (1873) XXIV, 137, 152—Extracts . . . Winterbotham's *View Of The United States Of America.* London, 1796.]

[Wirt, William.] *The Letters Of The British Spy.* Baltimore, 1817.

Wise, Jennings Cropper. *Ye Kingdome Of Accawmacke Or The Eastern Shore Of Virginia In The Seventeenth Century.* Bell: Richmond, 1911.

Withrow, Margaret M. Happy Easter-Tide. [*Va. Jour. Educ.,* (April, 1909) II, 24–25.]

Wolcott, John D. The Southern Educational Convention of 1863. [*South Atlant. Quart.,* (Oct., 1909) VIII, 354–60.]

Wood, Clarence Ashton. Week-Day Religious Instruction. [*Relig. Educ.,* (Aug., 1917) XII, 259–61.]

Woods, Edgar. *Albemarle County In Virginia.* Michie: Charlottesville, 1901.

Woody, Thomas. *Early Quaker Education In Pennsylvania.* [*Teachers College Contributions To Education,* No. 105.] Teachers College, Columbia University: New York, 1920.

Woody, Thomas. *Quaker Education In The Colony And State Of New Jersey.* Philadelphia, 1923.

The Works of Virginia. [Niles: *Register,* (April 6, 1816) X, 89–90.]

Wylie, David G. Our Public Schools—The Tale of the Books. [*Va. Educ. Jour.,* (Sept., 1889) XX, 396–400.]

Wynne, John Huddlestone. *A General History Of The British Empire In America.* 2 vols. London, 1770.

Yocum, A. Duncan. Standards for Judging the Material and Method of Religious Education. [Available in mimeograph form from author.]

Yocum, A. Duncan. What Democracy Should Compel Through Religion. [*Relig. Educ.,* (June, 1919) XIV, 80–89.]

Yocum, A. Duncan, Chairman. *The Teaching of Democracy. Report of the Committee of the National Council of Education on the Teaching of Democracy, which was presented . . . at Boston, . . . July 7, 1922.* [Reprint: *Cf. N. E. A. Proc's,* (1922) LX, 430–51; 505–25.]

York County Records. [*Tyler's Quart.,* (April, 1921) II, 270–73.]

Yowell, Claude Lindsay. *A History of Madison County, Virginia.* Strasburg, 1926.

4. *Periodical Literature*

The Academician. [Picket, A., & Picket, J.] Vol. I. New York, 1820.

American Annals of Education and Instruction. Vols. 1–7, 9. Boston, 1831–39.

The American Education Monthly. Vol. I–IV. New York, 1864–68.
The American Journal of Education. 32 vols. [Barnard, Henry, editor.] Hartford, 1856–82.
American Journal of Education. Vols. 1–4, I N. S. Boston, 1826–30.
The American Mercury. New York, 1926, 1927.
The Brackety-Ack. [Roanoke College, Salem, Vol. 10, No. 21, (April 30, 1926.)
(John P.) *Branch Historical Papers.* 3 vols. Richmond, 1901–04.
The Catholic Educational Association Bulletin. [(1916) XIII; (1919) XVI.] Columbus.
Christian Education Magazine. [Yearbook Number Board of Education M. E. Church, South, (August, 1927) XVII, No. 3.] Nashville.
The Collegian: Conducted by the Students of the University of Virginia. [Vol. II, No. I, II, III, V, VI, VII & VIII, IX.] Charlottesville, 1839, 1840.
De Bow, J. D. B. *The Commercial Review Of The South And West.* Vols. II–XXIII, XXV–XXIX. New Orleans, 1846–60.
The Educational Journal of Virginia. 22 vols. [Vol. I begins with Nov., 1869, continued to Dec., 1891; was used as the organ of the Educational Association of Virginia and State Department of Education at various times.] Richmond, 1869–91.
The Forum. Vol. IV–VI. New York, 1887–89.
Grapurchat. [Radford, State Teachers College, 1926.]
The High School Quarterly. Vol. I, II, IV–IX, inc. Athens, Ga., 1912–20.
Jewish Exponent. Philadelphia, 1924–28.
Journal of Education. [*New England Jour. of Educ.*]. Vols. I–XI, XVII–XX. Boston, 1875–84.
The Lower Norfolk County Virginia Antiquary. (James, Edward W., editor.) 4 vols. Baltimore, 1897–1904.
The Mountain Echo. [Blue Ridge Industrial School; VIII, No. 8.] Dyke, Jan., 1927.
Niles' Register. 75 vols. [Title varies; place of publishing varies; Niles, H., first editor.] Baltimore, 1811–49.
The Old Dominion And Virginia Historical Register. Vols. IV–VI. Richmond, 1870–72.
The Oyez. [Massanutten Academy, (June, 1926) VIII, No. 3.]
Pennsylvania School Journal. Vol. LVII. Lancaster, Pa., 1908.
Religious Education. Vol. I–XXII, except IV, XV. Chicago, 1906–27.
Religious Herald. Richmond, 1878, 1879.
Richmond College Historical Papers. [Vol. I, II) Richmond College: Richmond, 1915.
School And Society. Vol. I–XXV. New York, 1915–27.
The Sewanee Review Quarterly. Vol. XI–XXXV, inc. Sewanee, 1903–27.
South Atlantic Quarterly. 23 vols. (Except 1, 3, 4.) Durham, 1902–27.
Southern Bivouac. [Vol. I, Dec., 1885, Jan., Mar., April, 1836; Vol. II, June, 1886, to May, 1887.] Louisville.

Southern Educational Review. Vol. IV–V, Feb., 1907, to Jan., 1909. Chattanooga.

Southern and Western Literary Messenger and Review. [Changed title for *So. Lit. Messenger,* 1846–47.]

The Southern Literary Journal and Monthly Magazine. [Vol. II, Mar., to Aug., 1836; III, Feb., May, June to Aug., 1837, Feb., 1838, to June, 1838; IV, July, 1838, to Sept., Nov., 1838.] Charleston.

Southern Literary Messenger. 38 vols. Richmond, 1834–64.

The Southern Quarterly Review. [6 vols. Vol. I, 1842; III, 1843; VI, 1844; IX, 1846; XIII, 1848; XIV, 1848.] New Orleans, Charleston.

The Southern Quarterly Review. 8 vols. New Series. Charleston, 1850–53.

The Southern Review. Vol. I, & VI. Charleston, 1828–30.

The Southern Review. 23 vols. Baltimore, 1867–78.

Tyler's Quarterly Historical and Genealogical Magazine. 8 vols. [Tyler, L. G., editor.] Richmond, 1920–28.

The Virginia Evangelical and Literary Magazine. 11 vols. [Title varies; Virginia Literary and Evangelical Magazine; Rice, John H., editor.] Richmond, 1818–28.

The Virginia Historical Register, And Literary Advertiser. [Title—And Literary Note Book, 1850, And Literary Companion, 1852 . . . ; Maxwell, William, editor.] 6 vols. Richmond, 1848–53.

Virginia Journal of Education. 18 vols. Richmond, 1907–25.

Virginia Literary Museum And Journal Of Belles Lettres, Arts, &c. [University of Virginia] Vol. I, 1829–30. Charlottesville, 1830.

The Virginia Magazine of History and Biography. 35 vols. Richmond, 1893–1927.

The Virginia Quarterly Review. Vol. I–III. Charlottesville, 1925–27.

The Virginia School Journal. 14 vols. [Volumes for 1903–05 in office of State Board of Education, Richmond.] Richmond, 1892–1905.

Virginia School Messages. [Vol. 6, No. 9, Sept., 1925; No. 10, Oct., 1925; Vol. 7, 1926; Vol. 8, 1926–27.] East Radford.

Virginia State Teachers Association Proceedings. Quarterly. 2 vols. Richmond, 1915, 1916.

Virginia Teacher. [Vol. III–VI, VIII in part, (1926–27).] Harrisonburg, 1920.

The Virginia University Magazine. Vol. III. University of Virginia, Oct., 1858–June, 1859.

The West Virginia Historical Magazine Quarterly. 5 vols. Charleston, 1901–05.

William and Mary College Quarterly. 27 vols.—1st series; 7 vols.—2nd series. [Tyler, L. G., editor, 1st series; Chandler, J. A. C., & Swem, E. G., editors, 2nd series.] Williamsburg, 1892–1920; 1921–27.

World's Work. Vol. I–LI, except V, XIV, XVI. New York, 1900–27.

INDEX*

* NOTE: The writer has taken the liberty of telescoping figures with a hyphen to indicate recurrence of item, and not necessarily sole or continuous discussion, e.g., Academies, 321–26. The necessity is regretted for calling the reader's attention to the following errors in the text, the correct form appearing in the index: p. 16, l. 4, Pocahuntas, [sp.]; p. 50, l. 7, Culpeper, [sp.]; p. 53, l. 22, Rappahannock, [sp.]; p. 76, l. 26, Plebeian, [sp.]; p. 260, n. 76, *Ibid.,* I, 188, reference is to *So. Lit. Messenger;* p. 286, last line, *Richmond Enquirer,* [italics]; p. 327, l. 34. *Youth's book on Natural Theology,* [italics], reference, T. H. Gallaudet's book; p. 345, n. 74, signatures, [pl.]; p. 363, l. 26, Mont De Chantal, [sp.]; p. 424, n. 166, education, [sp.]; p. 468, l. 6, Newell, [sp.]; p. 498, l. 3, principle, [sp.]; p. 506, n. 150, See p. 487, not 484; p. 550, l. 13, Richmond College, [sp.]; p. 640, last line, Christian, [sp.]; p. 653, 1st column, l. 2, Hanover, [sp.]; p. 657, 4th column, l. 15, Nansemond, [sp.]

Mental, culture, 463, cultivation, 276, darkness, 269, discipline, 484, 577, faculties, 320, 583, limitations, 652, philosophy, 315, powers, 269, reconstruction, 447, science, 197, training, 331, 538, welfare, 635

Mercer, Margaret, 246, 325–27

''Merits and Defects of Prevailing Schemes of Common School Education . . . '' [address], 421

Merritt's meeting house, 219

Metaphysical speculation, 184

Metaphysicks, 127, 172, 184

Methodism, 70–71, 151, 214–15, 220, 321

''Methodist,'' [poem], 71

Methodist, affiliation, 215, 363, auspices, 217, 245, clergyman, 526, Conference, 558, denomination, 380, 419, disapprobation, 217, educational activity, 571, activities, 318–22, 558–72, educational interest, 558, groups, 645, institutions, 558, 569, 571, 603, 611, leaders, 572, ministers, 364, organization, 215, petition, 71, position, 521, rank, 240, 274, n. 127, 312, 419, n. 139, 592, research, 216, school, 219, statistics, 571, n. 275, Sunday Schools, 246, Methodists, 70–71, 152, 214–20, 240–41, 274, n. 127, 312, 321–22, 476, n. 26, 558, 571–72

Methodist Church, 215, 300, 338, 396, 419, n. 139, 421, 425, 477, 520, 559, 561, 564, 572, 600

Methodist Episcopal Church, 396–97, 572, n. 277, 627

Methodist Episcopal Church, South, 396–97, n. 7, 559–60, 562, 565–66, 568, 570–72, n. 277, 600

Methodist Episcopal Church of Virginia and North Carolina, 412

Methodist Monument Church, 520

Michie, Rob, 182

Michigan, 155, n. 10, state university, 628

Midas, 436

Middle, class, 611, strata, 377

Middlesex County, 100, 533, 657, 660

Military, academy, 605–06, arm, 38, defence, 432, laws, 64, school, 308, 583, 605, Science and Tactics, 633

Military Institute, [see Virginia . . .]

Milk for Babes, 205

''Miller Fund,'' 596, n. 52

Miller, H. Augustus, 508

Miller Manual Labor School, 596–98

Miller, Samuel, 596

Millfield Academy, 168, n. 70

Milton, 24

Miltonic argument, 266

Mind, 189–90, 196, 271, 284, 313, 328, 342, 376, 382–83, 419, 525, 604, minds, 188, 248, 269, 318, 339, 408, 435, 456, 606

Mines, 193

Minis, 143

Minister, 38–39, 41–43, 53, 76–77, 99, 102–03, 109–10, 122, 126, 128, 142–43, 212, 214–15, 236, 238, 290, 327, 379, 384, 386, 390, 422, ministers, 9, 12, 16, 23, 27–28, 39–40, 42, 44, 54, 57, 63–64, 67, 69, 76, 78–79, 81, 100, 102, 107, 112, 117–18, 123–25, 143, 156, 181, 209–11, 216, 221–22, 227–28, 239, 255, 258, 273, 300, 312–14, 317, 334, 364, 380, 383, 396, 415, 417, 423–24, 430, 434, 478, 480, 483, 489, 493, 518–19, 540, 555–56, 559, 563–64, 566–67, 577, n. 272, 585, 587, 591, 599, 602, 604, 615–17, 620, 622–23, 628, 630, 634, 642, 656–60

Ministerial, activity, 630, duties, 142, function, 38, profession, 446, students, 617, study, 257, supply, 112, 115

''Ministerial Association,'' 540

Ministry, 67, 98, 102–03, 111, 115–16, 181, 211, 214, 225–26, 238, 245, 273, 286–87, 292, 300, 303–04, 314, 317, 385, 390, 457, 540, 547–48, 556, 559, 564, 570, 575, 587, 590–91, 593, 595, 613, 637

Minor, B. B., 281, 381, n. 270

Minor, John B., 385, 411, 427

Minor, Lucian, 263, 337, n. 34

Minority, 524, group, 461, groups, 645, religious denomination, 358, religious groups, 272, minorities, 497, 509

Minutes, [Council for Foreign Plantations], 114

Mission, 53, activity, 538, classes, 634, field, 628, problem, 598, school, 544, 546, Sunday schools, 609, study classes, 539, 563, 591, 619, work, 594, missions, 619–20